Hotel Operations Management

Second Edition

David K. Hayes, Ph.D.

Jack D. Ninemeier, Ph.D.

PEARSON
Prentice
Hall

Upper Saddle River, New Jersey 07458

Library of Congress Cataloging-in-Publication Data

Hayes, David K.
   Hotel operations management / David K. Hayes and Jack Ninemeier.—2nd ed.
     p. cm.
   Includes index.
   ISBN 0-13-171149-0
1. Hotel management.   I. Ninemeier, Jack D.   II. Title.
TX911.3.M27H39 2005
647. 94068—dc22

2005030860

Director of Development: Vernon R. Anthony
Senior Editor: Eileen McClay
Assistant Editor: Ann Brunner
Editorial Assistant: Yvette Schlarman
Executive Marketing Manager: Ryan DeGrote
Senior Marketing Coordinator: Elizabeth Farrell
Marketing Assistant: Les Roberts
Director of Manufacturing and Production: Bruce Johnson
Managing Editor: Mary Carnis
Production Liaison: Jane Bonnell

Production Editor: Donna Leik, *TechBooks/GTS*, York, PA
Manufacturing Manager: Ilene Sanford
Manufacturing Buyer: Cathleen Petersen
Senior Design Coordinator: Miguel Ortiz
Cover Designer: frutiDesign
Cover Image: © Gari Wyn Williams/Imagestate
Composition: *TechBooks*/GTS, York, PA
Manager of Media Production: Amy Peltier
Media Production Project Manager: Lisa Rinaldi
Printer/Binder: Courier Westford

Text photo credits appear on page 557, which constitutes a continuation of this copyright page.

Pearson Education LTD.
Pearson Education Singapore, Pte. Ltd.
Pearson Education Canada, Ltd.
Pearson Education—Japan
Pearson Education Australia PTY, Limited
Pearson Education North Asia Ltd.
Pearson Educación de Mexico, S.A. de C.V.
Pearson Education Malaysia, Pte. Ltd.

10 9 8 7 6 5
ISBN 0-13-171149-0

The second edition of this book, like the first edition, is dedicated to E. Ray Swan, former Executive Director of the Educational Institute of the American Hotel and Lodging Association, and his recognition of the importance of the individual entrepreneur ("the Little Guy") to the hotel industry.

Mr. Swan's conviction that lifelong training and education are the keys to individual and organizational success continues to inspire the authors.

* * * * *

The authors also wish to recognize and thank, in this edition, Peggy and Lani, our partners in all we do.

Contents

Companion website available at: www.prenhall.com/hayes

Foreword

I have been fortunate during the nearly thirty years of my career to have managed activities at some of the finest luxury hotels in the world. I know that a hotel general manager (GM) has one of the most challenging, exciting, and rewarding positions in the entire hospitality industry. As a result, I was pleased, in 2003, when Dr. Hayes and Dr. Ninemeier asked me to supply a foreword to the first edition of their excellent text *Hotel Operations Management*. I am equally pleased to participate in this expanded and enhanced edition.

I believe it is important for students and others in the hospitality industry to know that GMs become outstanding as a result of a combination of real-world experience and careful study. I also know that neither ever ends. The world of hotel administration is interdisciplinary. It draws upon economics, management theory, mathematics, food science, chemistry, microbiology, physics, engineering, accounting, marketing, law, psychology, sociology, and increasingly, technology. As Sinclair Lewis wrote in his 1934 book (*World of Art*) about hotel managers, "If you can do all of this, . . . you'll have a good time."

The truth is that, while hotel GMs truly can (and do!) "have a good time," they cannot ever truly know or "do" it all. Fortunately, they do not need to know everything to be successful. Rather, successful GMs rely on a talented group of other managers and team members to provide superlative service to guests, superior financial returns for owners, and fulfilling careers for their staff members.

If you want to become a hotel GM or want to better understand what GMs must do to be successful, you'll get a great start on your journey by studying the book you now hold in your hands. It is, in fact, a primer, which describes the role and responsibilities of GMs in today's lodging properties. I encourage our interns at the Four Seasons Resort Costa Rica at Peninsula Papagayo to study it carefully.

I recommend the book because experienced GMs understand that they are unlikely to know more about heating and cooling systems than their chief engineer. It is also the rare GM who can produce a crème brûlée with a better flavor and texture than that of their property's best chef. Likewise, the skills and "tricks of the trade" that are required of today's professional executive housekeeper may not be fully known (or even understood!) by the GM. Interestingly, however, it is the GM's job to supervise all of these highly skilled managers as well as their peers. The GM must know how to evaluate and even assist in the professional development of these specialized and highly skilled professionals. This book will show you how to do just that.

The second edition of *Hotel Operations Management* takes its readers on a by-department tour of a full-service hotel. Along the way, it consistently answers two questions: *what* do GMs need to know about each department, and *why* do they need to know it? These questions are addressed by information that emphasizes generalizations rather than details. In each chapter, a "Managers at Work" section outlines a "challenge" (some would call it a problem!), and allows readers to think and act like a GM to address the issue by applying what they learned from the chapter. Extensive and up-to-date glossaries provide insight on the language of hotel management, and the Web sites referenced by the authors point readers to valuable resources literally at the effective GM's fingertips. As well, another section ("Issues at Work") provides additional opportunities for readers to practice the art and science of a GM's work by applying real-world information to real-world problems.

The first edition of *Hotel Operations Management* met with great success because it was a unique and long overdue text. The current edition, with its especially strong treatment of e-distribution channels and their management, will ensure the book's continued success. I believe that is so because the value of any book, whether it consists of poetry, a biography, or management principles, can be assessed, in part, by the number of people who could benefit from reading it. In the case of *Hotel Operations Management*, there are many types of potential readers. Hotel owners and investors who read it will better understand the many tasks and responsibilities of the GMs they employ. Practicing GMs will be able to compare their own activities with those of their colleagues. Hotel department managers including those in the front office, food and beverage, and sales and marketing, will learn what their own GMs should expect from them and, in turn, what they should expect from their GM.

Most importantly, tomorrow's GMs, whether they are currently "working their way up" in the industry and/or participating in a formal education program before they begin their careers, will learn much and benefit from reading *Hotel Operations Management*. They will discover information that will help them to someday be a successful member of one of the most exclusive groups within the vast hospitality management industry.

I am proud to be a member of a cadre of GMs worldwide who cares deeply about their own properties, their guests, their on-site team of professionals, and the entire hospitality industry. As a GM, I thank the authors for their continued hard work, and I welcome you, the reader, into the fascinating study of what I believe to be the world's greatest profession. "Have a good time!"

Luis Argote
General Manager
Four Seasons Resort Costa Rica at Peninsula Papagayo
Guanacaste, Costa Rica

Robb Report—Best of the Best Resorts 2004
Conde Nast Traveler—2004 Hot List
Architectural Digest—Featured Resort, April 2004

Preface

As was true with the publication of the first edition, hotel managers in today's rapidly changing technological world hold some of the most complex yet rewarding jobs in the hospitality industry. The hotel general manager, as the on-site leader of the entire hotel's other managers, has the most challenging job. Ultimately, it is the responsibility of the general manager to ensure that each area within the hotel is running smoothly, profitably, and in a manner consistent with the guest service goals of the hotel. This book was originally written and has now been expanded and revised to help present and future general managers do just that.

Historically, hotel general managers have risen in the ranks from a variety of hotel departments. Thus, for example, an excellent director of hotel sales and marketing might become a hotel general manager. Such an individual will likely have an excellent grasp of hotel sales yet lack experience or expertise in food and beverage, housekeeping, accounting, and other areas. Similarly, a general manager who has been promoted from a prior job as director of food and beverage may find his or her knowledge of hotel sales, as well as other hotel departments, lacking. *Hotel Operations Management* has been written to fill a void for individuals such as these.

Just as the conductor in an orchestra need not be an expert player of each musical instrument to ensure the orchestra's outstanding sound, the hotel general manager need not have the most technical expertise in, for example, the food and beverage department, to guarantee the production of quality food. In this book, the reader will learn what general managers need to know and do to properly supervise and monitor the activities of the food and beverage, housekeeping, revenue management, sales and marketing, and engineering areas, to name but a few of the spheres of general manager responsibility.

To further clarify the stated purpose of the book, consider the simple case of carpet stains in a guest room corridor. It is not the intent of this book to detail the best procedures for removing the stains. That is the responsibility of the housekeeping department and the specialists within that area who are charged with the task of keeping the hotel clean. It is the general manager's job, however, to monitor the effectiveness of the housekeeping department and to ensure that the department has the funding, supervisory personnel, and equipment required to keep the carpets clean. Thus, readers seeking a book that explains "how to" operate individual hotel departments will be better served selecting books on those specific departments. For the general manager, however, this book is a compilation of the skills and knowledge required to effectively supervise all of the activities in a midsize full-service hotel. As a result, the book is comprehensive and detailed.

Hotel general managers are often perceived as the "best of the best" within the hospitality industry. The authors believe this perception is most often accurate. Outstanding hotel managers ensure that their hotels prosper by their attention to detail, support of the managerial and hourly staff within the hotel, and the vision they exhibit for the hotel's goals and achievements. In this book, current and future hotel general managers will learn about the procedures effective managers use to ensure their hotels', and thus their own, ultimate success.

NEW IN THE SECOND EDITION

In the three years since the first edition of *Hotel Operations Management* was published, the hotel industry has continued to experience monumental change. The challenges for general managers have never been greater, and this edition has been revised and expanded to address many of those challenges. Despite the success of the first edition, the authors acknowledge that "more" needed to be written about what general managers must know and do to be successful. With the constant encouragement of Prentice Hall as well as our editors Vernon Anthony, Eileen McClay, and Ann Brunner, this expanded version was rewritten with an emphasis on seriously adding "more." We believe we have been successful in that endeavor. Certainly, the authors of a single textbook on a subject as vast as hotel management must judiciously select content areas. Although this can be difficult, it is also challenging. In addition to the requisite updating of industry statistics, data, and Web sites that should be expected in any new text edition, in this edition the authors have:

- Added a completely new chapter on the increasingly important areas of revenue and distribution channel management (Chapter 6: Revenue Management) with special emphasis on e-distribution strategies.
- Added, in recognition of the continued globalization of the hotel industry, an entirely new chapter that addresses the special issues and challenges faced by general managers who are managing hotels in foreign countries for independent hotel owners or for multinational hotel companies (Chapter 15: Managing in the Global Hotel Industry).
- Included detailed job descriptions for general managers of various sized hotels.
- Expanded the chapter on management (Chapter 3: Management, Supervision, and Service Skills for the GM) to add emphasis on the general manager's role in planning and managing guest service procedures.

- Addressed in a newly designed chapter on financial control (Chapter 5: Accounting) the implications to general managers of Sarbanes-Oxley as well as a review of accounting fundamentals.
- Substantially expanded, or included for the first time, important information about:
  - The scope and expansion of the global hotel market
  - Hotel rating systems
  - Effective e-mail marketing techniques and the most recent legislation regarding their use
  - The general manager's role as a property's human resource specialist
  - The importance of an in-house marketing program for food and beverage services
  - Hepatitis B and blood-borne pathogens
  - "Green" hotel strategies
  - Computerized preventive maintenance (PM) programs
  - Factors to assess when outsourcing food and beverage (F&B) operations
  - Smith Travel Research (STR) report analysis
  - Franchise agreement negotiations
  - Planning and implementing procedures to manage hotel emergencies
  - Global terrorism threats and their implications for the general manager
  - Hotels and the Department of Homeland Security's terrorism alert levels

Although the above list is not intended to include every change made to this text during the revision process, it does serve to illustrate the breadth of review undertaken. In addition to adding two new chapters, the authors have expanded the content of every chapter by a minimum of 10 percent, with some chapters expanded by as much as 30 percent. As a result, readers of the second edition of *Hotel Operations Management* will find a completely up-to-date treatment of the issues critical to the success of general managers, their hotels, their employees, and most importantly, the experience of their guests.

INTENDED AUDIENCES

Instructors

With this edition, instructors again will find a comprehensive text that addresses all of the operating departments of a full-service hotel. The key word is *comprehensive* because *Hotel Operations Management* is detailed in its coverage of the general manager's responsibilities. It is intended to be so. It is not, however, redundantly laden with information on "how-to" perform tasks that are addressed in other hospitality courses or in hotel departmental-specific textbooks. It is unique in that it addresses hotel management from the viewpoint of the general manager, a position to which many hospitality students aspire.

Students

Serious hospitality students quickly learn that few individuals can be experts in every area of hotel management. It is simply unrealistic, for example, to assume that a hotel front-office manager will have the same technical knowledge as the hotel's chief maintenance engineer. Front-office managers are experts in their own functional areas, which may include managing Internet reservation sites, guests services, and sophisticated computerized property management systems, whereas the chief maintenance engineer stays current on topics such as the availability of improved building materials and energy conservation techniques. Either of these two individuals, however, may be promoted to the job of hotel general manager. At that time, they each need to understand what they must do to properly manage the new areas they will administer.

It is also unrealistic to assume that one's first hotel job will be that of general manager. In most cases, students will start in a functional area of the hotel, and as their careers progress, they will gain added expertise. This book will be of critical assistance when the student actually reaches the position of general manager. Thus, it should be an important addition to any hotel management student's professional library.

Industry Professionals

There are many entities interested in how effective general managers do their work. Hotel investors need to understand what general managers should be doing to help ensure the quality and growth of the hotel investment. Those lenders to the hotel industry can also make better lending decisions if they analyze the activities of a general manager. This book presents, in copious detail, the systems a general manager should have in place to monitor departmental effectiveness. Lenders who are aware of such systems and can verify their presence are in a better position to make quality lending loan decisions.

Those individuals in the franchise community, such as franchise sales representatives, quality assurance inspectors, franchise services directors, and others in corporate franchisor positions may not always have a strong background in hotel operations. This book will help those individuals better understand the challenges facing the modern hotel general manager.

Within a hotel, department heads, assistant managers, and supervisors all benefit if they understand how the segment of the hotel they manage meshes with all other areas within the hotel. The general manager has that perspective, and it is presented in this book. In addition, department heads and those who aspire to become department heads need to know what a general manager will expect from them. In this way, they can better develop their own skills and thus improve the quality of their work and their career advancement potential.

Chapter Order and Content

An important decision to be made in the production of a book such as *Hotel Operations Management* relates to the proper sequencing of information. There is no uniform agreement on this sequence. Thus, for example, some would state that a thorough knowledge of front-office management should precede learning about the sales and marketing department, whereas others would maintain that the reverse order best ensures understanding. The authors realize that there is honest disagreement on how best to "learn" the hotel business and celebrate the differences of opinion as healthy and quite beneficial to the field of study. In the final analysis, however, sequencing decisions do have to be made, and in this book the authors elected to begin with an overview of the industry (Chapter 1), followed by specific information about the role of the general manager (Chapters 2–3), information related to the actual management of the functional areas of the hotel (Chapters 4–12), a chapter related to the unique situations of hotel franchising and operating under a management contract

(Chapter 13), a review of the processes encountered when buying a hotel (Chapter 14), a long-term personal goal of many individual hotel general managers, and finally an examination of the factors that affect those general managers working internationally (Chapter 15).

Chapter Fundamentals

When we created the first edition, there was not, the authors believed, another book that took the unique approach to hotel management presented in *Hotel Operations Management*. This was (and is) still true as we created this edition. Thus the authors continue to be free to create a new, and first of its kind, user-friendly book. We were also challenged to produce the book in a way that could serve as a model for the efforts of future authors. As a result, this second edition includes the following fundamental components.

"This Chapter at Work"

Each chapter begins with a narrative summary that describes what will be presented in the chapter, as well as why the information is important to the success of a general manager.

Tiered Content Outline

Each chapter's outline has been carefully developed to provide the maximum ease in finding important information. The outline also provides a detailed preview of the chapter's content.

"Hotel Terminology at Work"

As is true in many professional fields, hotel managers often speak their own unique language. Thus, for example, guests may be "walked," "par levels" will be established for laundry items, "STAR" reports will be analyzed, and the "GDS" will ensure reservation connectivity. When hotel specific terms are used in the book (and they are used extensively), they are defined at first mention, often with direct usage examples that help to further clarify their meaning. The special language of hoteliers is both creative and extensive. In this book, the reader is thoroughly exposed to that language without being burdened by definitions of common words that are not unique to the hotel industry. The glossary of industry-specific terms included with this edition consists of over 400 definitions.

"Managers at Work"

Hotel general managers routinely face unique problems and situations that require outstanding decision-making skills. The "Managers at Work" component of this text places the reader in the position of general manager through vignettes that require decisions to be made to solve realistic problems of the type that must be faced now or in the future. The situations presented are often complex, reflecting the fact that in many cases, the problems presented to the general manager are not easily addressed, or require an analytical solution that can best be provided only by a manager with thorough knowledge of the goals of the entire hotel.

Instructors will find that the assignment of these problems as homework, in-class essays, or in-class discussion items will allow student knowledge and understanding of concepts to be readily assessed. This important text element is contained in every chapter.

"The Internet at Work"

In many cases, the amount of additional information a specific Web site could provide to a general manager was so significant that the site was presented at the point in the chapter where the information would be most useful. Thus, for example, in a description of the tasks and qualifications of a competent concierge, a reference to the organizational Web site of Les Clefs d'Or (the International Order of Concierges) at www.lesclefsdor.com provides additional information to the interested reader, as well as content that can be regularly reviewed as long as the Web site remains active. In many cases, the addition of Web resources enhanced the book's own content. The Web references in this book are purposefully extensive, have been verified for accuracy, and exist in every chapter.

Managerial Tools

Where it was deemed helpful, checklists, forms, and step-by-step procedures that help general managers better do their jobs were included. For example, inspection sheets that general managers would use to evaluate the effectiveness of a housekeeping department were included, as well as sample Pace reports used for monitoring the quality of the hotel sales effort. These examples are only a few of the dozens included in the book. As a result, readers will be saved the trouble of "reinventing the wheel" in the many situations where a common form or procedure is the industry standard, or where such information can be easily modified to meet the needs of a specific hotel.

"Hotel Terminology at Work Glossary"

At each chapter's end, a complete listing of the industry-specific terms defined in the chapter is presented. As a result, readers can quickly review these terms to ensure they are understood and can be used in their proper context.

"Issues at Work"

This chapter-concluding feature encourages students to think about the material they have mastered in that chapter. The questions and issues presented allow the readers the opportunity to reflect on and develop their own views of hospitality management, as well as challenge them to express themselves clearly to others.

The production of a book such as this is truly the culmination of the efforts of many. The authors' thanks go to Vernon Anthony, our Director of Development, for his belief in the project; Ann Brunner, our Assistant Editor, for her outstanding assistance in text development; and the entire production staff at Prentice Hall for its tireless efforts. In addition, our text reviewers, Kevin Anthony, College of the Canyons, Studio City, CA; Chris Roberts, University of Massachusetts; William A. Sullivan, University of Delaware; and Allen Powell, University of Arkansas, added much to improve both the structure and content of the text. For their efforts we are truly grateful.

The authors believe this second edition of *Hotel Operations Management* describes, in great detail, exactly what the general manager of a midsize full-service hotel must know and do to be successful. Its up-to-date and comprehensive coverage of all areas of hotel operations make it an essential addition to the professional library of the serious hospitality student. It is our hope that students, instructors, and industry professionals will find it to be a significant contribution to the field of hospitality management. If they do, its continued success is assured.

David K. Hayes, Ph.D.
Jack D. Ninemeier, Ph.D.

The Hotel Industry:
Overview and Professional
Career Opportunities

This Chapter at Work

The hotel industry has evolved from the very modest beginnings of families and landowners who opened their homes to travelers to the high-rise properties of today that contain thousands of guest rooms. This chapter will help you understand the environment within which hotel managers operate modern hotels. Managers of lodging facilities work in the tourism industry. It is exciting to be part of tourism, one of the largest industries in the world, and to gain the knowledge and skills that can be transferred to hotels of many types and sizes and to locations almost everywhere.

Lodging facilities can be classified by location, by room rate (the amount charged for a guest room), and by the number of rooms they contain. They can also be classified by the type of guests they serve (for example, business or leisure travelers) or by who owns and manages them. Fortunately, there are many common management principles that can be used regardless of the type of hotel being managed and the type of guests being served.

The purpose of this book is to help you understand what a general manager (GM) in today's hotel environment must know, and do, to be successful. As your career in the lodging industry progresses, you will be able to build on the base of information found here. As your personal experiences add to this foundation, you will find yourself able to manage more effectively in a wider range of positions with ever-increasing responsibilities.

The hotel industry is, first, a service industry. To succeed in this industry, a certain attitude or philosophy about serving guests is critical. As a hotel GM, you cannot "fake" your concern about your guests. You must have a genuine enthusiasm to please people who are visiting your property. This concern must be held both by you and by the hotel staff working with you because your employees will likely interact with guests far more than you will.

This chapter will help you begin your journey of emphasizing quality guest service as you learn how effective GMs manage their properties, using advanced technology and excellent human resource management skills to do so. It concludes with a brief discussion about career opportunities in the lodging industry because there are numerous kinds of management positions available. One advantage of working within the lodging industry already noted—useful knowledge and skills can be transferred from one type of hotel organization to another—will make it easier for you to have a diverse and exciting career in this vibrant industry.

Chapter 1 Outline

PROFESSIONAL LODGING CAREER
OPPORTUNITIES
    Alternative Management Positions
    Get Started with Career Planning

HOTEL TERMINOLOGY AT WORK
GLOSSARY
ISSUES AT WORK

LODGING IS PART OF THE TOURISM INDUSTRY

We are beginning our journey to explore the world of tourism and hospitality with a focus on one segment: lodging operations. Our journey will be long (there is a lot of information to cover because hotel management is complex). It will also be fun and exciting because these terms are typical ways that professional **hoteliers** describe their work.

HOTEL TERMINOLOGY AT WORK

Hoteliers: Those who work in the hotel business.
■

We will discuss hotel management by telling you, the reader, what a general manager of a 350-room property must know, do, and be concerned about. By focusing on a property of this size, we can present *practical* information applicable to many of the lodging businesses in the United States. Each of the policies and practices discussed are, in many ways, relevant to a property of any size. Therefore, as you study this information, you will be learning how to be an effective manager regardless of the size of hotel(s) you will manage.

The Tourism Industry

Lodging properties are a segment within the **tourism industry**. Figure 1.1 provides an overview of the different types of organizations that make up the tourism industry.

HOTEL TERMINOLOGY AT WORK

Tourism Industry: All businesses that cater to the needs of the traveling public.
▮▮

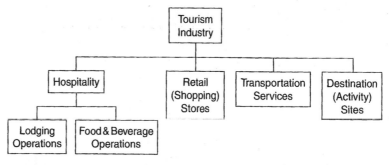

FIGURE 1.1 Segments in the Tourism Industry

When reviewing Figure 1.1, note that there are four major tourism industry segments. One (hospitality) is comprised of both lodging and food and beverage operations. This book is about the "lodging operations" sector. The other component of the hospitality segment, food and beverage operations, are organizations that include such businesses as follows: numerous types of restaurants that desire a profit; feeding operations in institutions such as schools, hospitals, and the military; and a wide range of other places where persons can eat when they are not at their homes.

Retail (shopping) stores include a wide variety of gift/souvenir shops, retail shopping malls, markets, and other businesses offering products for sale to those who reside within a specific location and to those who travel to that area. Transportation services include airplanes, rental cars, trains, ships, and alternative ways that people travel between destinations. Finally, destination (activity) sites include the many places that the traveling public visits, such as locations offering sporting, ethnic, entertainment, cultural, and other events. In addition to travel for personal reasons, people also travel for business including to professional meetings and conventions. Facilities that host these meetings are part of the lodging operations sector and include convention centers and private retreats as well as hotels.

In the United States, the tourism industry is the third largest retail industry following automotive and food stores. It is the nation's largest service industry and one of the country's largest employers. It is also the first, second, or third largest employer in thirty states.[1]

Lodging (Hotel) Sector

When most people think about "hotels," they think about a building containing guest rooms for sleeping. In its narrowest sense, this definition may be correct. However, today's traveling public has a wide variety of lodging alternatives, and the definition just cited is of limited use. For example, at one extreme, a person may choose a lavish destination resort in an exotic location that, in addition to sleeping rooms, offers many recreational alternatives, food and beverage outlets, and numerous other amenities. Other travelers prefer a **full-service hotel** that offers, in addition to sleeping rooms, a variety of food and beverage services. These may include **ala carte** dining rooms, coffee shops, or lounges, and **room service** and banquet facilities. Still other travelers desire a **limited-service hotel** that simply provides sleeping rooms with no food and beverage outlets except, perhaps, a limited breakfast. On the farthest end of our lodging alternative continuum are lodging organizations with sleeping spaces, some without even private restroom facilities such as **hostels**, and others rented on a short-term (ranging up to six or more hours) basis at airports and other locations (see Figure 1.2).

HOTEL TERMINOLOGY AT WORK

Full-Service Hotel: A lodging property that offers complete food and beverage products and services.

---

[1]American Hotel & Lodging Association. *Lodging Industry Profile.* 2004 (www.ahla.com; statistics are for 2003).

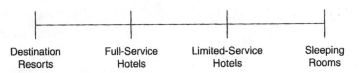

FIGURE 1.2   Range of Lodging Property Alternatives

Ala Carte: A food service operation in which the menu items offered are individually priced.

Room Service: Food and beverage products served to guests in their sleeping rooms.

Limited-Service Hotel: A lodging property that offers no or very limited food services; sometimes a complimentary breakfast is served, but there is no table service restaurant.

Hostels: Inexpensive accommodations, typically dormitory style with shared bathroom facilities, that are popular with young travelers.
■

This range of lodging options is still not inclusive. For example, facilities other than those commonly referred to as hotels may offer sleeping accommodations. These include private clubs, casinos, cruise ships, time-share condominiums, and campground lodges. In addition, there are unique hotels such as those that consist only of **suites** (known as all-suites hotels), those designed to attract guests who tend to stay for a long time (extended-stay hotels), and very small hotels usually operated out of converted homes (bed and breakfast properties).

HOTEL TERMINOLOGY AT WORK

Suites: This term generally refers to a guest room consisting of at least two physically separated rooms or, at least, a hotel room that is extra large when compared with that hotel's standard guest room.
■

To this point we have been discussing lodging operations open to all of the traveling public. Some other types of facilities offer sleeping accommodations for other groups of people away from their homes. These include schools, colleges, and universities offering residential services, health care (hospital and nursing homes) facilities, correctional institutions (prisons), and military bases.

A Brief History of Hotels

Travelers have always required places where they could rest at the end of the day. For the earliest travelers, this place was a campsite with, good fortune permitting, a campfire. Over time, places of rest became available at the crossroads of travel; in between these centers, persons living along travel routes frequently made a room (lodging) and board (meals) available in their own homes. Hotels in the United

Modern hotels have evolved a great deal since their earliest counterparts.

States have a tradition of innovation and orientation to guest service that is worth noting. Highlights of the growth of the hotel industry in the United States since 1900 are shown in Figure 1.3.

CLOSE LOOK AT LODGING ORGANIZATIONS

Figure 1.4 classifies lodging properties in the United States by location, by the price they charge for rooms, and by size. Note that, when analyzed by location, the vast majority of all lodging properties are in suburban and highway locations. The center city (urban), airport, and destination (resort) properties comprise a relatively small number of lodging properties and room inventory in the United States.

When reviewing lodging industry rate structures, you will see that the majority of guest rooms are sold at a per night rate ranging from $30 to $85 per room. Some hotel operators classify hotels by the rates they charge for rooms. However, this is difficult because the terms *upscale*, *midprice*, *economy*, and *budget* vary by geographic regions. For example, a very nice room in a small rural community may be less than $60 per night. In New York City, it may be difficult to find a nice room for even five times this rate!

The hotel industry can also be segmented by size. Figure 1.4 indicates that most properties are relatively small (less than 150 rooms).

Figure 1.4 also indicates that, in 2003, there were 47,584 properties containing 4,415,696 rooms; the average lodging property size was, then, 92.8 rooms (4,415,696 rooms ÷ 47,584 properties). This information should be of interest to those aspiring

1900 Fewer than 10,000 hotels 750,000–850,000 rooms	**1900**—A typical first-class hotel offers steam heat, gas burners, electric call bells, baths and closets on all floors, billiard and sample rooms, barbershops and liveries. **1904**—New York City's St. Regis Hotel provides individually controlled heating and cooling units in each guest room. **1908**—The Hotel Statler chain begins in Buffalo. All guest rooms have private baths, full-length mirrors, telephones and built-in radios, serving as the model for hotel construction for the next forty years.
1910 10,000 U.S. hotels 1 million rooms 300,000 employees Average size: 60–75 rooms	**1910**—Electricity is beginning to be installed in new hotels for cooking purposes, as well as for lighting. However, most hotels place candle sticks, new candles, and matches in every room—electric lightbulb or not.
1920 Occupancy: 85% Hotel construction reaches an all-time peak as thousands of rooms are added along the new state and federal highways	**1920**—Prohibition begins. **1922**—The Treadway Company has some of the first management contracts on small college inns. **1925**—The first roadside "motel" opens in San Luis Obispo, California, for $2.50 a night. **1927**—The Hotel Statler in Boston becomes the first hotel with radio reception; rooms are equipped with individual headsets to receive broadcasts from a central control room. **1929**—The Oakland Airport Hotel becomes the first of its kind in the country.
1930 Occupancy: 65% AHA's Hotel Red Book lists 20,000 hotels Typical hotel: 46 rooms Average room rate: $5.60	**1930**—Four out of five hotels in the United States go into receivership. **1933**—Due to the Great Depression, hotels post the lowest average occupancy rate on record (51%). Construction grinds to a halt. **1934**—The Hotel Statler in Detroit is the first to have a central system to "air condition" every public room.
1940 Occupancy: 64% Average room rate: $3.21	**1940**—Air conditioning and "air cooling" become prevalent. **1945**—Sheraton is the first hotel corporation to be listed on the New York Stock Exchange. **1946**—Westin debuts first guest credit card. The first casino hotel, the Flamingo, debuts in Las Vegas. **1947**—Westin establishes Hoteltype, the first hotel reservation system. New York City's Roosevelt Hotel installs television sets in all guest rooms. **1949**—Hilton becomes the first international hotel chain with the opening of the Caribe Hilton in San Juan, Puerto Rico.
1950 Occupancy: 80%	**1951**—Hilton is the first chain to install television sets in all guest rooms. **1952**—Kemmons Wilson opens his first Holiday Inn in Memphis, Tennessee. *(continued)*

FIGURE 1.3   Highlights in the Modern History of the United States Hotel Industry

Typical hotel: 17 rooms Average room rate: $5.91	**1954**—Howard Dearing Johnson initiates the first lodging franchise, a motor lodge in Savannah, Georgia. Conrad Hilton's purchase of the Statler Hotel Company for $111 million is the largest real-estate transaction in history. **Mid-1950s**—Atlas Hotels develops the first in-room coffee concept. **1957**—J. W. Marriott opens his first hotel, the Twin Bridge Marriott Motor Hotel in Arlington, Virginia, and Jay Pritzker buys his first hotel, The Hyatt House, located outside the Los Angeles Airport. Hilton offers direct-dial telephone service. **1958**—Sheraton introduces Reservation, the industry's first automated electronic reservation system, and the first toll-free reservation number.
1960 Occupancy: 67% $3 billion in sales Total hotel rooms: 2,400,450 Typical hotel: 39 rooms, independent and locally owned Average room rate: $9.99	**Early 1960s**—Siegas introduces the first true minibar (a small refrigerator displaying products). **1964**—Travelodge debuts wheelchair-accessible rooms. **1966**—Inter-Continental introduces retractable drying lines in guest showers, business lounges, ice and vending machines in guest corridors, and street entrances to hotel restaurants. **1967**—The Atlanta Hyatt Regency opens, featuring a twenty-one-story atrium and changing the course of upscale hotel design. **1969**—Westin is the first hotel chain to implement twenty-four-hour room service.
1970 Occupancy: 65% $8 billion in sales Total hotel rooms: 1,627,473 Average room rate: $19.83	**1970**—Hilton becomes the first billion-dollar lodging and food-service company and the first to enter the Las Vegas market. **1973**—The Sheraton-Anaheim is the first to offer free in-room movies. **1974**—The energy crisis hits the industry. Hotels dim exterior signs, cut heat to unoccupied rooms, and ask guests to conserve electricity. **1975**—Four Seasons is the first hotel company to offer in-room amenities such as name-brand shampoo. Hyatt introduces an industry first when it opens a concierge club level that provides the ultimate in very important person (VIP) service. Cecil B. Day establishes the first seniors program.
1980 Occupancy: 70% $25.9 billion in sales Total hotel rooms: 2,068,377 Average room rate: $45.44	**1983**—Westin is the first major hotel company to offer reservations and checkout using major credit cards. VingCard invents the optical electronic key card. **1984**—Holiday Inn is the first to offer a centralized travel and commission plan. Choice Hotels introduces the concept of market segmentation. Choice Hotels offers no-smoking rooms. Hampton Inns is the first to offer a set of amenities. **1986**—Teledex Corporation introduces the first telephone designed specifically for hotel guest rooms. Days Inn provides an interactive reservations capability connecting all hotels. **1988**—Extended stay segment introduced with Marriott's Residence Inns and Holiday Corporations Homewood Suites. **1989**—Hyatt introduces a chainwide kids program for ages three to twelve and a business center at the Hyatt Regency Chicago. Hampton Inns is the first hotel chain to introduce the 100% satisfaction guarantee.

FIGURE 1.3 *(Continued)*

1990	1990—Loews Hotels' Good Neighbor Policy becomes the industry's first and most comprehensive community outreach program.
Occupancy: 64%	
$60.7 billion in sales	1991—Westin is the first hotel chain to provide in-room voice mail. Industry sees record losses (61.8%).
Total hotel rooms: 3,065,685	1992—Industry breaks even financially after six consecutive years of losses.
45,020 properties	1993—Radisson Hotels Worldwide is the first to introduce business-class rooms.
Average room rate: $58.70	1994—First on-line hotel catalog debuts—TravelWeb.com. Promus and Hyatt Hotels are the first chains to establish a site on the Internet.
	1995—Choice Hotels International and Promus become the first companies to offer guests "real-time" access to its central reservations system. Choice and Holiday Inn are the first to introduce on-line booking capability.
	1999—Choice Hotels International is the first chain to test making in-room PCs a standard amenity for guests.
2000	2000—Hilton unveils plans for the first luxury hotel in space.
Occupancy: 63%	2001—September 11 destruction of the World Trade Center in New York causes occupancy rates to plummet.
$97 billion in sales	2002—Travel industry recovers from terrorist attacks amid heightened airport security.

Reproduced with permission from the American Hotel & Lodging Association, 1201 New York Avenue, NW, Suite 600, Washington, DC 20005.

FIGURE 1.3   *(Continued)*

By Location	Property[1]	Rooms[2]
Airport	3,239	444,860
Suburban	18,476	1,490,970
Urban	5,408	716,485
Highway	18,312	1,296,279
Resort	2,149	467,102
By Rate		
Under $30	853	50,642
$30–$44.99	7,862	499,350
$45–$59.99	16,680	1,102,845
$60–$85	14,334	1,393,633
Over $85	7,855	1,369,196
By Size		
Under 75 rooms	27,379	1,144,753
75–149 rooms	14,297	1,523,999
150–299 rooms	4,305	860,983
300–500 rooms	1,094	407,038
Over 500 rooms	509	478,923

[1]Total of 47,584 properties.
[2]Total of 4,415.696 rooms.

Note: To see current information, go to www.ahla.com. Click on "News & Information Center" and then click on "Information Center." Review the most recent "Lodging Industry Profile."

Reproduced with permission from the American Hotel & Lodging Association, 1201 New York Avenue, NW, Suite 600, Washington, DC 20005.

FIGURE 1.4   2003 U.S. Property/Room Breakdown

Hotels often occupy significant amounts of land in locations tourists want to visit.

to careers as hotel GMs. Many young persons see themselves as the GM of a very large, luxurious property in a large city. There are, of course, many properties of this type and managing one is an excellent goal. However, the "average" property is smaller, is in a nonurban location, and sells its rooms for a modest price. Realistic expectations of employment opportunities, especially early in one's career, are important. The good news is that excellent opportunities exist in all types of properties of all sizes in all locations, and the principles required to operate a smaller hotel are the same ones used to operate large properties.

Typical Lodging Guests

In 2003, 52% of lodging **guests** traveled for business; the remaining 48% of guests were traveling for pleasure.[2]

HOTEL TERMINOLOGY AT WORK

Guest: A hotel visitor. Most guests rent rooms and/or purchase food or beverages in a hotel outlet or a banquet function.

■

Throughout this book we refer to the person renting the hotel room as a *guest*—not a *customer*. In everyday use, these terms are often used interchangeably. However, in the language of the hospitality industry—including lodging—the terms have different meanings. For example, to the extent practical, hoteliers treat persons visiting the property the same as they would treat friends visiting in their own homes. In

[2]Statistics in this section are from: American Hotel & Motel Association. *Lodging Industry Profile*. 2004. (This can be viewed at: www.ahla.com.)

contrast, the term *customer* implies someone whose relationship with the property is based only upon the exchange of money for products and services provided. Yes, "guests" must pay for the products and services they receive; however, the tactic of treating visitors as "guests" rather than "customers" helps establish the service philosophy that is very important to a hotel's success.

People travel for one or more of four reasons: business, conference/group meetings, vacation, or other. Some hotels may cater to one category of guests all the time. However, it is just as likely that a hotel may generate much business from two or more types of guests. This occurs, for example, when business travelers visit the property during the workweek and other people visit the hotel on the weekend when they are in the area for personal reasons. Increasingly, travelers combine conference/group meeting attendance with vacations. They may, for example, bring their families, attend meetings during part of their stay, and enjoy a family vacation for the remainder of the visit.

Who travels for business and pleasure? The "typical" business guest is a male (71%), is thirty-five to fifty-four years of age (53%), is employed in a professional/managerial position (50%), and earns an average yearly household income of $82,800. Usually, these guests make reservations before arriving at the hotel (90%) and pay $91 per room night. Approximately 64% of business travelers spend one or two nights at a property. Business guests value hotel features such as oversized work areas, high-speed Internet access, and two line telephones. Wireless Internet access in public areas of the property is increasingly a desired amenity as is the availability of kiosks for checking in and out.

The typical leisure room night is generated by two adults (52%), ages thirty-five to fifty-four years (45%), earning an average yearly household income of $74,000. The typical leisure traveler travels by auto (73%), makes reservations prior to arriving at the hotel (84%), and pays $87 per room night. Most (73%) leisure travelers spend one or two nights at the property. Leisure travelers, more so than business travelers, look for facilities such as swimming pools, saunas, tennis courts, and game rooms.

THE INTERNET AT WORK

Want to see current statistics about the United States hotel industry? Check out the Web site of the American Hotel & Lodging Association (AH&LA) at

www.ahla.com

When you reach the site, click on "Information Center."

Lodging Industry Characteristics

As mentioned earlier, hotels can be classified by location, rate, size, or the type of guest served. However, there are several common characteristics that all good properties share:

- *Emphasis on Safety, Cleanliness, and Service.* Few, if any, guests consider only the room and other physical attributes of the property when making a will-stay or will not-stay decision. For example, safety and cleanliness are very important considerations. Friendliness (hospitality) of property staff is also an important issue that, along with the physical aspects (size, quality of maintenance, furnishings, and other factors), is part of the guests' evaluation. These become intangible (difficult to quantify) aspects of the purchase decision that potential hotel guests consider.

- *Inseparability of Manufacture and Sales.* It is not possible to separate the "manufacture" (production) of a guest room with its "sale." A room exists and is sold at the same site. Contrast this with, for example, the manufacture/sale of an automobile, a shirt, or a television set. Cars, shirts, and TVs are typically manufactured at one site and are sold at another. The hotel's GM and his/her staff, then, must be an "expert" at both manufacture and sales. Their counterparts in the auto/clothing/electronic industries must normally be an "expert" in only one aspect of either manufacturing products or selling them to the consumer in the marketplace.

- *Perishability.* If a guest room is not rented on a specific date, the **revenue** is lost forever. By contrast, an automobile/shirt/television can remain in inventory and be sold later. In this regard, empty sleeping rooms are similar in nature to empty airline seats on a flight that has just taken off.

HOTEL TERMINOLOGY AT WORK

Revenue: Money the hotel collects from guests for the use of rooms or from the purchase of hotel goods and services.

- *Repetitiveness.* The steps involved in making a guest room ready for sale or for preparing a specific meal or drink are basically the same every time these items are sold. These routines (operating procedures) allow for some standardization. At the same time, however, they create challenges because it is always important to focus on the individual needs of guests and because standardization provides less opportunity for creativity in the decision-making processes used to perform required work.

- *Labor Intensive.* In many industries, for example, automotive and electronics, technology and sophisticated equipment have replaced people in many work activities. By contrast, in the lodging industry, less of this has occurred. That is because much of a hotel's daily work requires employees to provide services. Beds are made, rooms are cleaned, and food is prepared. The traveling public increasingly wants and is willing to pay for services "delivered" by employees. As is discussed in Chapter 4 (Human Resources), a hotel's ability to attract and retain qualified staff who can consistently deliver excellent service is a key to the success or failure of a hotel.

Lodging Industry Overview

Three ways to consider the vast lodging industry are to learn about the largest hotel organizations, the world's best hotels, and the ownership and management structure of hotels. We will do so in this section of the chapter.

Largest Hotel Affiliations

What are the largest hotel organizations in the world? We will answer this question by considering the largest international and domestic (United States) **hotel groups**. We will also look at the largest **hotel brands** in the world and in the United States.

There are hotels throughout the world to serve the needs of world travelers. (Chris Stowers © Dorling Kindersley)

Note: it is a common industry practice to define the term, *largest* as the number of rooms not the number of hotels. For example, a hotel group with more rooms but fewer hotels than other organizations would still be considered the largest of the two organizations.

HOTEL TERMINOLOGY AT WORK

Hotel Group: An organization that owns or franchises groups of hotels that are of different brands. For example, Cendant Corporation in the United States owns Days Inn, Ramada Franchise Systems, Travel-odge hotels, and numerous other hotel brands (chains).

Hotel Brand: The name of a hotel chain. Sometimes referred to as a "flag."

Figure 1.5 lists the largest hotel groups in the world as of 2004. Note that, in fact, these organizations are very large. The InterContinental Hotels Group (Great Britain) operates approximately 535,000 rooms in more than 3,500 hotel properties. Cendant, headquartered in the United States, was a close second with approximately 520,000 rooms in about 6,400 properties. Recall, as noted above, that the ranking is by the number of rooms, not by number of hotels. Hotel groups typically grow larger by franchising, especially in geographical regions where they themselves operate few, if any, properties.

Figure 1.5 also indicates the hotel brands operated by each group. Note, for example, that the first two groups ranked (InterContinental Hotels and Cendant) may

Rank	Group	Country	Hotels	Rooms	Brands
1	InterContinental Hotel Group	United Kingdom	3,540	534,202	Candlewood, Crowne Plaza, Forum Hotel, Grand Chalet, Hampton Inn & Suites, Holiday Inn, Holiday Inn Express, Holiday Inn Garden Court, Holiday Inn Select, Holiday Inn Sun Spree, InterContinental, Royal Inns, Staybridge Suites by Holiday Inn
2	Cendant	United States	6,396	520,860	Amerihost Inn, Days Inn & Hotel, Daystop, Hearthside by Villager, Howard Johnson Express Inn, Howard Johnson Hotel, Howard Johnson Inn, Howard Johnson Plaza Hotel, Knights Inns, Ramada Inn, Ramada Limited, Ramada Plaza Hotel, Super 8 Motel, Thriftlodge, Travelodge, Villager Lodges, Villager Premier, Wingate Inns
3	Marriott International	United States	2,600	478,00	Courtyard by Marriott, Fairfield Inn & Suites by Marriott, Fairfield Inn by Marriott, Marriott, Marriott Executive Apartments, New World Hotel, Ramada Hotel, Renaissance, Residence Inn by Marriott, Ritz-Carlton, SpringHill Suites by Marriott, TownePlace Suites by Marriott
4	Accor	France	3,973	463,427	Hotel Sofitel, Novotel, Mercure, Dorint Resorts and Spa, Coralia, Suite Hotel, Ibis, Parthenon, Etap Hotels, Formule1, Pannonia, Motel 6, Studio 6, Jordin, Red Roof Inns, Accor Libertel, Vacances, Thalassa
5	Choice	United States	4,977	403,806	Clarion, Comfort Inn Hotel & Suites, Econo Lodge, Cambria Suites, MainStay Suites, Quality Inn Hotel & Suites, Rodeway Inn, Sleep Inn, Suburban Extended Stay
6	Hilton Corporation	United States	2,259	358,408	Club Hotel by Doubletree, Conrad International Hotel, Doubletree Guest Suites, Doubletree Hotel, Embassy Suites, Embassy Vacation Resort, Hampton Inn, Hampton Inn & Suites, Hilton, Hilton Garden Inn, Homewood Suites by Hilton, Red Lion Hotel
7	Best Western	United States	4,114	309,236	Best Western
8	Starwood	United States	733	230,667	Four Points Hotel by Sheraton, Sheraton, St. Regis/Luxury Collection, W Hotels, and Westin
9	Carlson Hospitality Worldwide	United States	890	147,093	Country Inns & Suites by Carlson, Park Inns & Suites, Park Inns International, Park Plaza Suites, Radisson, Regent International Hotels
10	Global Hyatt Corporation	United States	356	111,474	Hyatt, Hyatt Regency, Grand Hyatt, Park Hyatt

Source of data: MKG Consulting as published in *HTR* (*Hotel, Tourism and Restaurant*) magazine; www.mkg-group.com.

FIGURE 1.5   World's Largest Hotel Groups

Rank 2005	Chain	Group	Hotels 2005	Rooms 2005
1	Best Western	Best Western	4,114	309,236
2	Holiday Inn	InterContinental	1,484	278,787
3	Comfort Inn & Suites	Choice	2,415	182,038
4	Marriott Hotels Resort	Marriott International	490	179,519
5	Days Inn of America, Inc.	Cendant	1,872	153,701
6	Sheraton Hotels & Resorts	Starwood	391	134,866
7	Hampton Inn	Hilton Corporation	1,290	130,398
8	Express by Holiday Inn	InterContinental HG	1,512	126,035
9	Super 8 Motels	Cendant	2,076	125,844
10	Ramada Franchise Systems	Cendant	1,005	119,991
11	Radisson Hotels Worldwide	Carlson Hospitality	434	100,733
12	Quality Inns, Hotels, Suites	Choice	966	98,431
13	Courtyard	Marriott International	656	94,003
14	Hyatt Hotels	Hyatt Hotels & Resorts	213	93,474
15	Motel 6	Accor	893	92,948
16	Hilton Hotels USA	Hilton Corporation	230	89,256
17	Mercure	Accor	720	85,352
18	Hilton International	Hilton International	261	78,782
19	Ibis	Accor	692	75,602
20	Novotel	Accor	396	68,340

Source of data: MKG Consulting as published in *HTR* (*Hotel, Tourism and Restaurant*) magazine; www. mkg-group.com.

FIGURE 1.6   World's Largest Hotel Brands

not be familiar names to those who do not keep abreast of the hotel industry. Many of the brands they operate are, however, well known to the traveling public.

Figure 1.6 displays the worldwide ranking of hotel brands. Note the significant presence of the U.S. organizations that control 17 of the 20 largest hotel brands. Best Western, the largest hotel brand, does not, as an organization, own or franchise properties. Instead, it is considered an affiliation organization; properties meeting the organization's standards become part of (affiliate with) the Best Western organization to enjoy advertising, central reservation system, and reputational advantages.

Figure 1.7 shows the largest hotel organizations in the United States. Refer to Figure 1.5 to see the brands operated by these groups. (Note: HVM, L.L.C., ranking number 10 in Figure 1.7, operates Extended Stay America, Homestead Studio Suites, Studio Plus Deluxe Studios, and Crossland Economy Studio brands.) Note that some of the most famous and popular names in the U.S. lodging industry including Hyatt Hotel Corporations, Quinta Inns, The Ritz-Carlton Hotel Company, and Four Seasons Hotels and Resorts are smaller organizations compared to those shown in Figure 1.7.

World's Best Hotels

Which hotels are among the best in the world and what makes them so? In the United States, one organization (American Automobile Association) classifies hotels into five rating categories. (This system is discussed further in Chapter 7: Sales and Marketing). Unfortunately, there are no international standards for hotel excellence.

Rank	Name	Number of Domestic	
		Properties	Rooms
1	Cendant Corporation	5,622	439,279
2	Marriott International, Inc.	2,238	380,218
3	Hilton Hotels Corporation	2,184	357,332
4	InterContinental Hotel Group	2,523	337,643
5	Choice Hotels International, Inc.	3,891	313,982
6	Best Western International	2,181	186,422
7	Accor North America	1,252	134,803
8	Starwood Hotels & Resorts	355	123,747
9	Carlson Hospitality Worldwide	566	82,739
10	HVM, L.L.C.	654	72,961

Source: Top 50 Hotel Companies. American Hotel & Lodging Association. www.ahla.com.

FIGURE 1.7   Largest Hotel Organizations in the United States

Properties that receive a specific rating by the travel/tourism, professional association, environmental agency, or other entity within different countries may be evaluated according to very different standards. This, in turn, makes it difficult for travelers who wish to consider rating scores in their hotel selection to make a proper lodging choice.

Zagats survey is the world's leading provider of consumer opinion in the leisure market. Figure 1.8 lists property winners for several categories for 2005.

Top Hotel Chains and Groups (10 or more international properties)
1. Amanresorts
2. Four Seasons
3. Ritz-Carlton
4. Mandarin Oriental
5. Luxury Collection (Starwood)

Top Hotels (100 or more rooms)
1. Four Seasons George V, Paris
2. Peninsula, Hong Kong
3. Oriental, Bangkok
4. Peninsula, Bangkok
5. Ciragan Palace Kempinski, Istanbul

Top Resorts (100 or more rooms)
1. Four Seasons Jimbaran Bay, Bali, Indonesia
2. Four Seasons, Punta Mita, Mexico
3. Amarvilas Oberoi, Agra, India
4. Four Seasons, Nevis, West Indies
5. Burj Al Arab, Dubai, United Arab Emirates

Top Small Resorts, Inns and Lodges (less than 100 rooms)
1. Singita, Kruger Area, South Africa
2. Amankila, Bali, Indonesia
3. Four Seasons Sayan, Bali, Indonesia
4. Rajvilas Oberoi, Rajasthan, India
5. Four Seasons, Chiang Mai, Thailand

Source: www.hotel-online.com/News/PR2004_2nd/Apr04_Zagat.html.

FIGURE 1.8   Best Lodging Properties in the World: 2005

Top Hotels (100 or more rooms)
1. Peninsula, Chicago
2. Peninsula Beverly Hills, Los Angeles
3. Four Seasons, Chicago
4. Mandarin Oriental, Miami
5. Four Seasons, New York City
6. Windsor Court, New Orleans
7. Ritz-Carlton (Four Seasons), Chicago
8. Four Seasons, Philadelphia
9. Four Seasons, Las Vegas
10. Mansion on Turtle Creek, Dallas

Top Resorts (100 or more rooms)
1. Four Seasons Hualalai, Big Island, HI
2. Four Seasons at Wailea, Maui, HI
3. Ritz-Carlton, Naples, FL
4. Four Seasons Aviara, Carlsbad, CA
5. Ritz-Carlton, Orlando, FL
6. Lodge at Koele, Lanai, HI
7. Inn at Spanish Bay, Pebble Beach, CA
8. Stein Eriksen Lodge, Park City, UT
9. Greenbrier, White Sulphur Springs, WV
10. Royal Palms, Phoenix, AZ

Top Small Hotels, Resorts, and Inns (less than 100 rooms)
1. Lodge at Sea Island, Sea Island, GA
2. Blackberry Farm, Walland, TN
3. Canoe Bay, Chetek, WI
4. Twin Farms, Barnard, VT
5. Woodlands Resort, Summerville, SC
6. Chateau du Sureau, Oakhurst, CA
7. Fearrington House Country Inn, Pittsboro, NC
8. The Point, Saranac Lake, NY
9. Post Ranch Inn, Big Sur, CA
10. Bernsley Garden, Adairsville, GA

Source: www.hotel-online.com/News/PR2004_2nd/Apr04_Zagat.html

FIGURE 1.9   2005 Top U.S. Hotels

What properties are among the very best in the United States? The Zagat survey noted in Figure 1.8 provides one answer to this question. See also Figure 1.9.

THE INTERNET AT WORK

Want to learn more about Zagat Survey? You can do so at

www.Zagat.com

Hotel Ownership and Management

The dominance of large hotel organizations and lodging chains is obvious as you review the applicable figures in the previous section. What may be less obvious, however, is that in the great majority of cases, the brands do not "own" hotels. Instead, owners of hotels elect to affiliate, for a fee, with the brand. This arrangement is discussed in great detail later in this text (see Chapter 13) because the relationship between those who manage the brands (**franchisors**) and those who actually own and operate the hotels within the brand (**franchisees**) is unique.

HOTEL TERMINOLOGY AT WORK

Franchisors: Those who manage the brand and sell the right to use the brand name.

Franchisees: Those who own the hotel and purchase the right to use the brand name for a fixed period of time and at an agreed-upon price.

■

Let's consider a motorist who is driving along the highway and notices the sign for a popular hotel chain. The name is easily recognizable due, in part, to an extensive nationwide advertising campaign. One typical thought of this driver is likely to be, "I guess that the hotel company purchased some land and built another hotel to operate in this location." In fact, that is not likely to be the case. It is more likely that an independent investor or company has built the property on owned (or leased) land and signed an agreement with those who own the brand to operate the hotel in a manner consistent with that brand's standards. In many cases, the investor also hires a third party to manage the hotel.

There are numerous ways that hotels are owned and managed (see Figure 1.10), including:

- *Single-Unit Property Not Affiliated with Any Brand.* Some single-unit properties have been in business for many years, are extremely successful, and may be the preeminent hotel in a community or area. This, however, is the exception. These properties capture an ever-smaller **market share** in the lodging industry nationwide.

HOTEL TERMINOLOGY AT WORK

Market Share: The percentage of the total market (typically in dollars spent) captured by a property.

For example, a hotel generating $200,000 in business traveler guest room rental annually in a community where business travelers spend $1,000,000 per year will have a 20 percent market share.

■

- *Single-Unit Properties Affiliated with a Brand.* Properties that are part of a **hotel chain** are most prevalent. This brand affiliation, whether international, nationwide, regional, or local, is successful because of name recognition and because it is often easier to receive financing for businesses affiliated with a brand.

HOTEL TERMINOLOGY AT WORK

Hotel Chain: A group of hotels with the same brand name.

■

Of course, some owners have multiple hotels; when they do, they have a variety of options available to them:

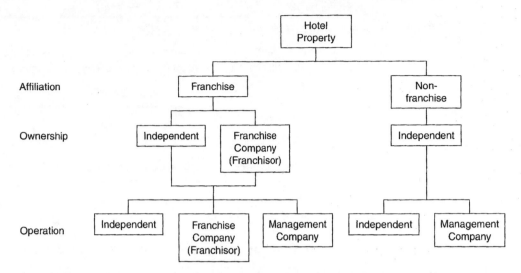

FIGURE 1.10 Summary of the ownership/management arrangements possible today. It confirms that the ownership/management of a hotel can be complex because of the many possible ownership/management alternatives.

- *Multiunit Properties Affiliated with the Same Brand.* Some owners own several hotels and affiliate all of them with the same brand. This often makes managing them easier because the expectations of the brand's owners are well known.

- *Multiunit Properties Affiliated with Different Brands.* Some owners elect to choose several brands. Sometimes this is done because they own more than one hotel in a market area and feel that two hotels with the same brand would compete with each other. In other cases, the owners may have some limited-service and some full-service hotels, and the same brand name would not represent both these types of properties.

- *Multiunit Properties Operated by the Brand or Others.* Some brands will, for a fee, offer management services to hotel owners. Also, some companies neither own the brands nor the hotels, but simply provide, for a fee, management services to the hotel's owners. These companies are known as **management companies**. There are many management companies that operate hotels of numerous brands owned by many separate owners. This special arrangement will also be examined more fully later in this text (see Chapter 13).

HOTEL TERMINOLOGY AT WORK

Management Company: An organization that operates a hotel(s) for a fee; sometimes called "contract company."

- *Multiunit Properties Owned by the Brand.* Some brands do own some of their own hotels. Independent (not controlled by the brand) ownership, however, is the most common in the United States.

THE INTERNET AT WORK

Want to learn more about many of the franchise lodging organizations and management companies in the United States? If so, check out the AH&LA Web site for daily news features

www.ahla.com

Hotel Organizational Structures

From the guest's perspective, the primary functions of hotel personnel remain the same regardless of property size. Guests, many of whom make advance reservations, want to be checked into a safe and clean room and expect to make payment upon departure. They may expect the food and beverage services offered in a full-service property as well. As the number of rooms in a hotel increase, the number of staff it employs grows, and the staff perform tasks in increasingly more specialized positions.

MANAGERS AT WORK

J.D. Ojisama is the assistant general manager of an independent (privately owned) full-service hotel with 250 rooms. The present GM, the son of the hotel's founder, has expressed an interest in early retirement; he has two children, one of whom is a department head in the property.

J.D. has been approached by a management company to assume the position of GM in a 350-room property in another city. The recruiter has noted the company's track record in quickly promoting its managers to larger properties with in-creasingly higher salaries. J.D. believes this to be true because of the increasing number of hotel management contracts the company is acquiring.

J.D. discusses the situation with his present GM who, in addition to being the boss, is also a friend. "You should do what is best for you," said the GM. "However, you have a secure position here. Your salary increases are fair, and I promise they will keep coming. Besides, you grew up around here, and all your friends and relatives are here. If you move on with the management company, you will have to move from the area. Then, what will happen later if they lose some properties or are acquired by another company? You have a good job with almost guaranteed employment here. Why jeopardize it?"

If you were J.D., what issues would affect your decision? Why might J.D. want to move on to employment with the contract management company? Why might J.D. want to stay with his present employer? What would you do?

To understand the differences in hotels of varying sizes, let's consider how small hotels (less than 75 rooms), large hotels (350 rooms), and mega properties (3,000 rooms and larger) might be organized.

Small Hotel

Figure 1.11, an organization chart for a smaller, limited-service hotel, shows the possible organizational structure for a ±75-room property. The property owner may even be the GM. Such a hotel is likely to have an individual in charge of maintenance, as well as some maintenance support staff, an executive housekeeper who supervises hourly paid employees who clean the hotel's rooms and public space, and a front-office Manager who supervises the staff working at the hotel's **front desk**. There may or may not be a designated individual responsible for hotel sales. A bookkeeper/accountant (typically part time) may be retained for completion of financial reports and tax returns.

HOTEL TERMINOLOGY AT WORK

Front Desk: The area within the hotel used for guest registration and payment.

■

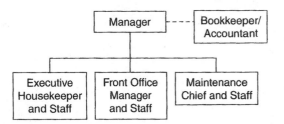

FIGURE 1.11 Organization Chart for Small (75-Room), Limited-Service Hotel

Large Hotel

Figure 1.12, an organization chart for a larger, full-service hotel, illustrates the departments and functions discussed in detail in the chapters that follow. With increased size, specialists (department heads) are hired by the GM to perform front office, housekeeping, food and beverage, safety/security, engineering/maintenance, marketing, accounting, and perhaps other functions. These top-level officials require assistance from managers and supervisors who, in turn, manage the day-to-day work of entry-level staff members.

Mega Hotel

Figure 1.13, an organization chart for a mega hotel, shows many of the positions required to operate a very large hotel. Note, for example, the food and beverage department and its many specialized positions. Specialized positions for the other departments are also necessary to handle the increased work required to effectively operate a hotel property with this many (or more) rooms.

Note that very large hotels require the service of a **resident manager** to assist the GM with the direct supervision and coordination of several operating departments: food and beverage, purchasing, engineering and maintenance, front office, and security.

HOTEL TERMINOLOGY AT WORK

Resident Manager: The manager in a large hotel who is directly responsible to the GM for the property's operating departments that often include food and beverage, purchasing, engineering and maintenance, rooms (front office and housekeeping), and security.

The MGM Grand Hotel is one of the largest in the world with more than 5,000 rooms.

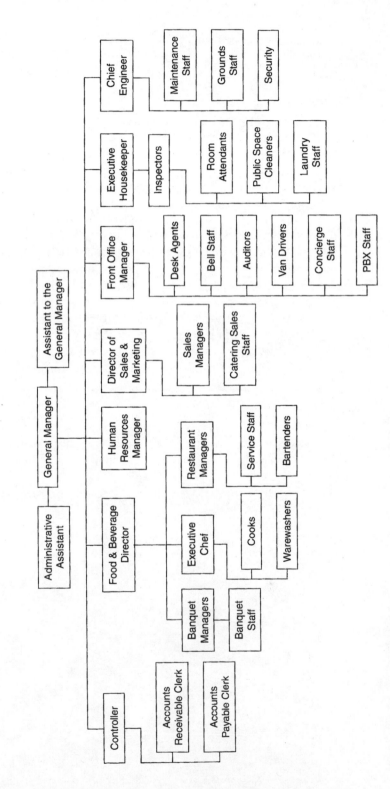

FIGURE 1.12 Organization Chart for Large (350-Room), Full-Service Hotel

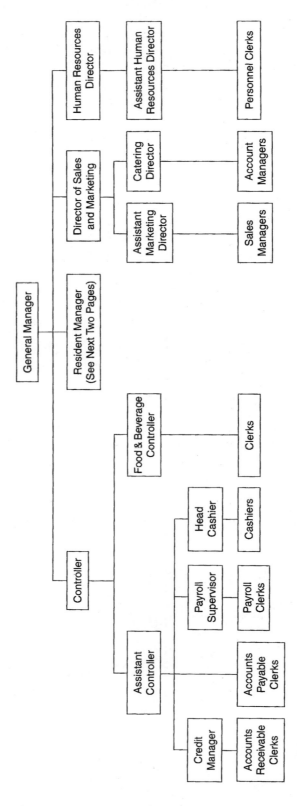

FIGURE 1.13 Organization Chart for Mega (3,000-Room) Hotel

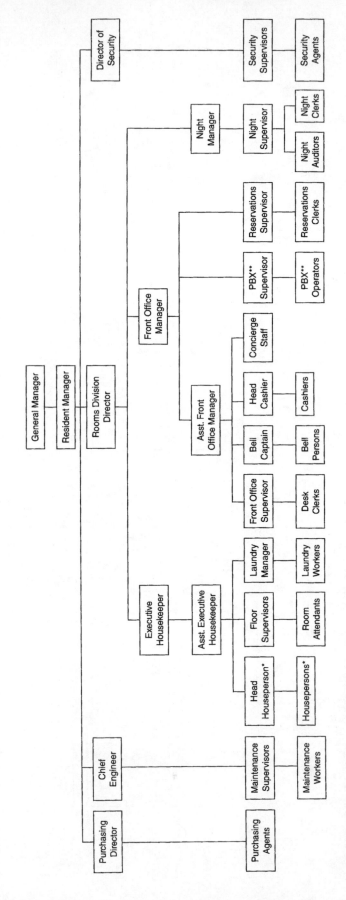

*Housepersons are responsible for cleanliness of public/group function spaces.
**Public Broadcast Exchange—a technology relating to the within-hotel communications (telephone) system.

FIGURE 1.13 *(Continued)*

24

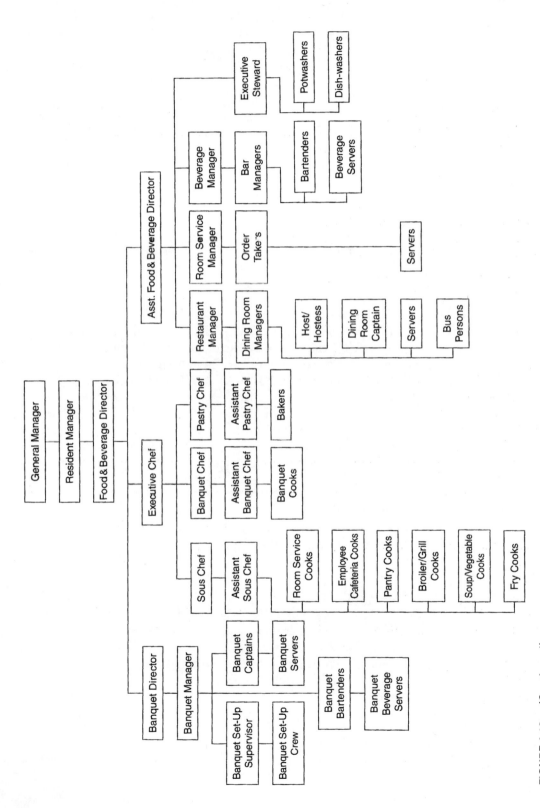

FIGURE 1.13 *(Continued)*

Hotel Departments

Later chapters in this book discuss hotel departments in detail with an emphasis on how a GM can best manage them. However, the concepts of line and staff departments and revenue and cost centers can be examined now.

Line and Staff Departments

Hotel departments can be classified according to line and staff functions. **Line departments** are those directly involved in the "chain of command." Managers in these departments are responsible for making the direct operating decisions that impact the success of the property. Examples of line departments are the front office, food and beverage, housekeeping, and the engineering/maintenance departments.

HOTEL TERMINOLOGY AT WORK

Line Departments: Hotel divisions that are in the "chain of command" and are directly responsible for revenues (such as front office and food and beverage) or for property operations (such as housekeeping and the engineering and maintenance departments).

■

Managers in line departments need the specialized and technical assistance of persons in **staff departments**. These specialists provide information to support the line decision makers. Typical staff departments in a hotel include purchasing, human relations, and accounting. For example, the purchasing staff buys only those items needed by line menu planners. Human relations personnel do not "hire and fire employees"; their role is to provide personnel needed by line departments and to provide technical advice about labor laws, training, and related specialized activities. Accounting personnel are responsible for developing accounting systems, collecting financial information, recording data in financial statements, and making recommendations to (but not decisions for) decision makers in line departments.

HOTEL TERMINOLOGY AT WORK

Staff Departments: Hotel divisions that provide technical, supportive assistance to line departments. Examples include the purchasing, human resources, and accounting departments.

■

Revenue and Cost Centers

Another way to think about hotel departments is to consider whether they generate revenue or, alternatively, whether they incur costs to support the departments that do generate revenue. The two most obvious examples of **revenue centers** are the front-office department, which generates revenue from the sale of guest rooms, and the food and beverage department, which sells products in dining rooms, lounges, room service, and banquets.

HOTEL TERMINOLOGY AT WORK

Revenue Center: A hotel department that generates revenue. Two examples are the front-office and food and beverage departments.

■

Contemporary hotels offer first-class services, amenities, and environments to their guests. (David McIntyre © Dorling Kindersley, Courtesy of the White Swan Hotel, Guangzhou, Hong Kong)

A hotel also may receive revenues from telephone services, space rental (such as leasing a gift shop or other space), and could include revenue sources such as fees from parking garages, vending machines, golf courses, business centers and other areas that vary by the hotel's product offerings.

A **cost center** exists to help revenue centers generate sales. Examples include the marketing, engineering and maintenance, accounting, human resources, and security departments. Today and in the future, cost centers will be increasingly required to quantify exactly how they provide value to the organization. Managers will challenge the cost-effectiveness of all money spent for salaries and wages and to purchase other resources required by all departments within the hotel.

HOTEL TERMINOLOGY AT WORK

Cost Center: A hotel department that incurs costs in support of a revenue center. Two examples are the housekeeping and engineering/maintenance departments.

■

LODGING IS A SERVICE BUSINESS

Earlier in this chapter we suggested that a hotel is more than just a building with guest rooms. Successful hotels are increasingly differentiated from their unsuccessful counterparts by an emphasis on serving their guests. Although the brand name a hotel uses is important, it is not the most critical factor in a hotel's success. Guests return to hotels they like for the same reasons they return to good restaurants. These reasons include personalized service, quality products, and fair prices. Today's hotel guests desire good service, and they are willing to pay for it. Effective GMs continually ask the question, "What's best for our guests?"

When hoteliers make decisions based on putting guests' needs first, their hotels are to likely do well. When decisions are made to put the hotel first by attempting to maximize revenue, minimize costs, and do "what's easiest" or what has always been done, invariably guest service will suffer, as will the long-term financial health of the hotel.

Successful hotels implement effective strategies to consistently deliver quality guest service. In today's marketplace, technological advancements can help this process, and we discuss many of them in this book. In addition, staff development will become increasingly important as GMs seek to effectively train their staff to deliver the quality guest service that will make their hotels excel.

As they seek to deliver quality service, the questions that must be addressed by hotel managers include:

- How will we demonstrate to our own staff members the need for high-quality guest service?
- How exactly will we evaluate the level of service quality being provided to our guests?
- What exactly are our service strategies and our service procedures?
- How will we train our staff about service concerns and the tactics to deliver service?
- How will we reinforce our service strategies?
- What can we do to emphasize service as a philosophy rather than as a program with a definite start and end time?
- What can we do to excel in the guests' **moments of truth**?

HOTEL TERMINOLOGY AT WORK

Moments of Truth: Any (and every) time that a guest has an opportunity to form an impression about the hotel. Moments of truth can be positive or negative.

■

CURRENT ISSUES CONFRONTING HOTELIERS

There are many issues and challenges confronting hoteliers in today's competitive hotel environment. This section contains a special focus on operating, marketing, technology, and economic issues.

MANAGERS AT WORK

J.D. Ojisama accepted a GM's position at a very nice hotel. The property was a good one: It had a great staff, a high occupancy rate, and consistently met budgeted revenue and profit goals. The previous GM had retired and had left J.D. with an excellent property with which to hone the skills he learned as the assistant GM at his previous property.

Within a week on the job, J.D. had an opportunity to make some decisions that would help set the pace for the staff's attitude toward guest service.

"Here's the situation," said the front-office Manager. "The couple in our bridal suite was due to check out at noon today. Their wedding generated about twenty sold guest rooms for their relatives, and the bride's father spent several thousand dollars on their wedding reception in our ballroom yesterday."

"Well," said J.D., "Sounds like the event was a big success. I hope they feel the same way."

"Yes, they do," replied the front-office Manager. "The problem isn't them—it's the weather. All outbound flights are delayed—they'll probably be canceled—because of the snowstorm we're having. I don't think they really care; they're enjoying our hotel, and the groom just called to inform me that they were planning to stay the second night—tonight—and he was looking for a good deal on the room rate."

"No problem. Let's give him a good rate," said J.D.

"That's where the problem lies," said the front-office Manager. "Another couple living here in town is scheduled to hold their reception at our property tonight and have booked the bridal suite for this evening. It's the only bridal suite with all the appropriate amenities that we have. It looks like we're going to have tonight's couple very mad at us. I hope they don't have lots of friends in the community . . . so they can't tell them we didn't give them the room they reserved on their wedding night!"

"Well," said J.D., "Let's think about this. I wonder if there's a way to please both couples rather than to disappoint one of them. Let's put our heads together and see if we can come up with a solution."

What are some alternatives that J.D., working with the front-office Manager, might consider? What might the hotel offer to the couple currently occupying the bridal suite to encourage them to move to another room? What might the hotel offer the incoming couple as an incentive to select another room? What other issues might be addressed by J.D. and the front-office Manager?

Operating Issues

Concerns confronting hoteliers as they consider the day-to-day operation of their properties are many, such as:

- *Labor Shortages.* Hoteliers almost everywhere are faced with the ongoing problem of finding enough good employees. This is especially true for some hourly paid and even management-level positions. GMs can address this concern by implementing procedures (a) to reduce turnover levels to minimize the number of new staff members that must be recruited, (b) to increase productivity levels so that fewer employees are needed to effectively operate the hotel, and (c) to recruit from nontraditional employee labor markets, including younger, inexperienced workers, the elderly, and physically challenged individuals.

- *Cost Containment.* Good hoteliers are continually examining all possible ways to reduce costs without impacting quality. Interestingly, **downsizing**, which involves reducing the number of staff members employed, has been met with only limited, if any, success in many hotels.

HOTEL TERMINOLOGY AT WORK

Downsizing: Reducing the number of employees and/or labor hours for cost-containment purposes.
■

This may speak to the effectiveness of past hotel management practices. Despite the observation that "all hotel rooms look alike when the guest is sleeping," it is a fact that the traveling public pays for both a product (the room) and services provided with the room. An excessive emphasis on reducing the quality of the product and/or the service to reduce costs will ultimately result in reduced hotel revenue.

- *Increased Competition.* Hoteliers in almost every geographic area in the United States indicate that their community is **overbuilt**. That is, that there are too many hotel rooms for the number of guests wanting to rent them. This has led to intense competition between properties in an effort to provide greater value to their guests and also lower profit levels for the hotel's owners.

HOTEL TERMINOLOGY AT WORK

Overbuilt: The condition that exists when there are too many hotel guest rooms available for the number of travelers wanting to rent them.
■

The traveling public has numerous lodging alternatives available.

Marketing Issues

Properly managed hotels capture their fair share of the market. This becomes increasingly difficult to do, however, as competition increases. Effective GMs need to be aware of the marketing issues that will affect them and respond properly. Current issues include an increase in **market segmentation**. Some lodging chains are attempting to focus on a very specific niche of travelers (business, long term, vacation travelers, etc.). In addition, limited service properties are increasing in popularity in many markets. These are frequently of interest to senior citizens, travelers on "mini-vacations," and others who are budget conscious.

HOTEL TERMINOLOGY AT WORK

Market Segmentation: Efforts to focus on a highly defined (smaller) group of travelers, for example, "executives desiring long-term stays" rather than "business travelers" (some of whom might only desire long-stay accommodations).

These are several niches within the lodging marketplace that hoteliers have recently determined to be significant enough to warrant focused advertising in efforts to solicit the business of persons in these groups.

For example, many travelers enjoy bringing their pets with them and are looking for pet-friendly properties for lodging locations. Amenities range from a simple acknowledgment that pets are welcome to an array of services including pet sitting, special meals, protected dog-walking areas, and listings of nearby veterinary services.

THE INTERNET AT WORK

Want to learn more about pet-friendly hotels? If so, go to

www.bringyourpet.com

Hoteliers are increasingly recognizing that many travelers are concerned about the environment and offer environmentally friendly facilities to accommodate them. Some lodging properties are affiliated with "Green Globe 21," an international system of certification for hotels. Hotels that comply with specific environmental standards receive a certificate that affirms their positive and proactive environmental actions.

THE INTERNET AT WORK

Want to learn more about Green Globe 21? If so, go to

www.greenglobe21.com

Many hotels by choice and/or by local ordinance offer smoke-free facilities in public areas of their properties. Some hotels are also offering smoke-free facilities throughout the property, including guest rooms. Concerns about the environmental effects of secondhand smoke are shared by enough persons that some hoteliers believe this niche market will increase their **occupancy rates**.

HOTEL TERMINOLOGY AT WORK

Occupancy Rate: The ratio of guest rooms sold (including comps) to guest rooms available for sale in a given time period. Always expressed as a percentage, the formula for occupancy rate is

Total Rooms Sold ÷ Total Rooms Available = Occupancy Percent (%)

THE INTERNET AT WORK

To view the Web site of a smoke-free property, go to the Web site of Ohana Hotels of Hawaii

www.ohanahotels.com

Review information about one property: the Ohana Reef Lanai Hotel in Honolulu (Waikiki), Hawaii.

At least one hotel organization (the Hotel Monaco Collection) offers "Tall Guest Rooms" that have extra-high ceilings, beds that are 96 inches (243 cm) long, and raised shower heads in the bathrooms. Higher door frames, raised vanities and toilets, and longer bath robes are featured as is in-room information about local tall-clothing stores.

THE INTERNET AT WORK

Information about the Hotel Monaco Collection can be seen at

www.kimptonhotels.com

When you reach the site, click on "Hotel Monaco Collection" and then "unique amenities."

Other marketing issues that confront today's hoteliers include:

- *Overlapping Brands.* There is great concern, especially among those in the limited-service markets, that some franchisors are expanding their number of brands to a point that franchisees purchasing franchises from the same franchisor are in direct competition with each other. In addition, as the number of brands increase, it becomes harder for consumers to differentiate between them.

- *Increased Sophistication of Consumers.* The use of the Internet for reserving hotel rooms has increased dramatically, resulting in a better-informed consumer but a more competitive selling environment for hoteliers.

- *Increased Number of Amenities.* Hotels are offering numerous new types of amenities, including business centers, exercise/recreational facilities, and creative innovations within guest rooms. These amenities increase costs for hotel owners, yet sometimes appeal to only a small segment of the hotel's market.

HOTEL TERMINOLOGY AT WORK

Amenities: Hotel products and services designed to attract guests.

Popular amenities include items such as complimentary continental breakfasts, in-room coffee makers, exercise rooms, and business centers.

Technological Issues

Recent technological innovations include:

- Interactive reservation systems that allow potential guests to quickly make reservations at preferred room rates in reduced time (fewer "clicks" on their computer keyboards).

- Guest room innovations that include two (or more) telephone lines enabling Internet access, interactive menu ordering for room service, electronic games, and guest room checkout.

- **Data mining** technology that allows hotel marketing/sales personnel to utilize guest-related data in new and creative ways. This allows hoteliers to learn more about guest needs and to then use this information for marketing and advertising purposes as well as to better serve current guests.

HOTEL TERMINOLOGY AT WORK

Data Mining: Using technology to analyze guest (and other) related data to make better marketing decisions.

- *Rate Management.* Hotels, like airlines, are increasingly matching guest demand with room rates. When demand for rooms is high, discounts for room purchases can be eliminated. When demand is low, discounts can be implemented. Advances in technology make room rate management practices more common than ever before.

Economic Issues

"As goes the economy, so goes the lodging industry" is an observation that is generally true. During "good" times business travel is up, and business travelers tend to utilize higher-priced guest rooms. The reverse is also true: weakened economies equate to lessened business travel with a negative impact on hotel revenues. Also, like many areas of business, there are fewer franchise companies, and they own more and more hotels. As noted earlier in this chapter, today's hotel organizations frequently grow larger by buying other hotel organizations. There are fewer independent properties, fewer franchisors, and fewer management companies as this consolidation trend continues. The result is not always good for consumers or the industry.

Today, with the impact of **globalization**, the economies of the United States (indeed, all nations) and the communities within them are increasingly interrelated to the economic status of every other country throughout the world. As stated at the beginning of this chapter, the lodging industry is an integral part of the tourism industry. As such, it is affected by the extent to which persons travel both within the country and around the world. Although this is obvious, it is also important to recognize the significant influence that the economies of the world, the country, the state, and the community play on the financial success of a lodging organization and the individual properties that comprise it.

HOTEL TERMINOLOGY AT WORK

Globalization: The condition in which countries throughout the world and communities within them are becoming increasingly interrelated.

■

PROFESSIONAL LODGING CAREER OPPORTUNITIES

If you are serious about the hospitality industry, this book will confirm your interest because it demonstrates how hotel management is both exciting and rewarding. What's next? How can you plan for and implement a professional development program leading to a career in the lodging industry?

Alternative Management Positions

The lodging industry is vast and so are the alternative management positions available within it. Figure 1.14 illustrates some of these positions. Those listed under multi-unit exist when a hotel company owns or manages multiple properties. Regardless of your vocational/professional preferences, there are likely to be rewarding positions available in the fast-paced and exciting lodging industry. As you read this book, you will become familiar with many of them. It is important to realize, however, that this book examines hotel management from the unique perspective of one professional: the hotel's GM.

Get Started with Career Planning

How does one start to plan for a career in the lodging industry? Here are some suggestions:

Typical Single Property Positions
- General manager
- Rooms division manager
- Front-office manager
- Controller
- Executive housekeeper
- Catering manager
- Executive steward
- Food and beverage manager
- Banquet manager
- Chef
- Executive chef
- Food production manager
- Pastry chef
- Sous chef
- Room service manager
- Food and beverage controller
- Restaurant manager
- Beverage manager
- Purchasing director
- Human resources manager
- Credit manager
- Executive assistant manager
- Convention manager
- Marketing/sales manager
- Auditor
- Director of security
- Convention services director
- Resident manager
- Chief engineer

Typical Multiunit Positions
- Area general manager
- Regional general manager
- Director of training
- Vice president, finance
- Vice president, real estate
- Director of franchising

FIGURE 1.14 Alternative Management Positions in the Lodging Industry

- Many secondary and postsecondary schools offer hospitality-related programs of study. Although enrollment in and graduation from these programs is not absolutely critical to a successful career in the lodging industry, formal education programs can help greatly by providing job-related knowledge and by allowing you to express your early interest in the lodging/hospitality industry.

- Working in a variety of lodging positions (including educational internships) provides additional job-related knowledge. This will help you to develop important skills and get to know people in the lodging industry who can help you advance your career.

- Developing a **career ladder** for professional development within the lodging industry can also be helpful. This is a graphic "road map" that indicates possible career progression through a lodging organization. Career ladders can help you to rationally plan career advancement strategies. Working with a **mentor**, you can develop a long-range career plan that will enable you to advance between desired positions within planned time frames.

HOTEL TERMINOLOGY AT WORK

Career Ladder: A plan that projects successively more responsible professional positions within an organization or industry. Career ladders also allow one to schedule developmental activities judged necessary to assume these more responsible positions.

Mentor: A senior employee of a hotel who provides advice and counsel to less experienced staff members about matters relating to the job, organization, and profession.

■

- If you seek a management career within the lodging industry, it will be helpful to talk with GMs at hotels near you, industry leaders, and educators to obtain suggestions from those currently employed within the lodging properties within your own community.

THE INTERNET AT WORK

Want to learn more about careers in the lodging industry? Check out the Council of Hotel, Restaurant and Institutional Educators Internet home page at

www.chrie.org

HOTEL TERMINOLOGY AT WORK GLOSSARY

The following terms were defined within this chapter. If you are not familiar with one of them, please review the segment of the chapter that contains the term.

Hoteliers	Hotel brand	Cost center
Tourism industry	Franchisors	Moments of truth
Full-service hotel	Franchisees	Downsizing
Ala carte	Market share	Overbuilt
Room service	Hotel chain	Market segmentation
Limited-service hotel	Management company	Occupancy rate
Hostel	Front desk	Amenities
Suites	Resident manager	Data mining
Guest	Line departments	Globalization
Revenue	Staff departments	Career ladder
Hotel group	Revenue center	Mentor

ISSUES AT WORK

1. You have learned about a wide variety of lodging properties, all of which must be managed. What type of hotel would you like to work in as you begin your career and as you gain more experience within it? Think about unique characteristics applicable to the management of a large urban property versus an isolated resort

facility. Consider preferences of guests renting rooms for $40 per night versus $400 per night. Think about management concerns in a property with 50 rooms and one with 5,000 rooms. Each of these and related examples illustrates unique opportunities and challenges that must be managed by those in charge. What are some of these unique management concerns? What are some guest-related concerns and management principles that apply regardless of the hotel's location, guest room charge, or size?

2. This chapter has emphasized the need to consistently deliver quality guest service. If you were a GM, what kind of guest relations training would you provide to your employees? What are principles that you would incorporate into the training? In addition to training, what other tactics could you use to emphasize quality guest service at your hotel? (Think about contests, role modeling in which you as GM "walk the talk," and coaching sessions in which you reinforce desired service tactics as you see employees perform them.)

3. Hotels exist in every city. Where would you like to work in your management career? Why? What types of hotels are operated there? Name three advantages to becoming a GM in the area you have selected. Are there disadvantages?

4. What would you do to address a labor shortage problem in your hotel? First, think about tactics you might use to retain current employees. (If they did not leave, there would be less need to recruit new staff members.) Then, think about tactics you could use to recruit new employees. How would you advertise employment opportunities in your hotel? What could you offer potential applicants that they might not receive from other employers that would help to make your hotel an "employer of choice" within the community?

5. The chapter briefly discusses career opportunities in the lodging industry. Think about what you would like to do in your career. What progressively responsible positions would you like to attain? What would you need to do, beginning now, to prepare yourself for these positions?

2

The Hotel General Manager

This Chapter at Work

Every hotel and lodging facility, regardless of size, has a leader on the property that makes the final day-to-day decisions about how that property will operate. From the largest mega hotel to the smallest bed and breakfast (B and B), this individual is critical to the hotel's image in the community, its reputation for guest service, and most important, its ultimate profitability.

Although this person's job title may vary depending on the hotel's size, the traditional term used is *general manager* (GM). In this chapter you will learn about the responsibilities of the GM and why the execution of these responsibilities is so important to the ultimate success of the property.

The GM's role as a hotel property manager is significant. Equally important, however, are other abilities, such as serving as a liaison with the property's owners (and in many cases, the property's franchise organization and/or operating company) and representing the property to the local commu-nity. Another important responsibility involves train-ing and facilitating the work of other managers.

In addition to understanding what a GM does, in this chapter you will discover alternative ways to de-velop the skills needed to become a GM. These include formal education offered by both two-year (associate's degree) and four-year (bachelor's degree) programs and advanced degrees. Another option—On-the job training offered by hotel companies—is also discussed.

Your development as a GM will continue long after you assume responsibility for your first prop-erty. Therefore, the chapter concludes with a dis-cussion of the opportunities and career paths for continued professional development offered by those organizations and trade associations dedi-cated to the advancement of the lodging profession.

If your goal is to become a GM, this chapter will help you better understand the types of daily activi-ties you will oversee and what you can do now to prepare yourself for the job.

Chapter 2 Outline

RESPONSIBILITIES

A **general manager** is, arguably, the single most important human variable affecting a hotel's short-term profitability. If you aspire to be a GM, you should know that the way you do your job will directly affect the owners of the hotel, your community, your employees, and of course, your guests.

HOTEL TERMINOLOGY AT WORK

General Manager (GM): The traditional title used to identify the individual at a hotel property who is responsible for final decision making regarding property-specific operating policies and procedures. Also the leader of the hotel's management team.

■

Property GMs "wear many hats" in the fulfillment of their duties. Although it may not be possible to identify any one role that is most important, the responsibilities involved in any GM position will vary based upon many factors, including ownership structure, location, and type of property. In some hotels, the GM may be very guest oriented and spend a great deal of time with the guests; in others, the GM may view his or her role to be one of staff development specialist who guides the growth of other managers in the hotel. Despite the demands of a particular hotel and the preferences of individual GMs, nearly all GM positions consist of some combination of the following significant tasks:

- Investor relations
- Brand affiliation management
- Community relations
- Executive committee development
- Property management

Investor Relations

The GM's role in investor relations is tremendously important. Investor relations include all communications between the GM and those who own the property. Property ownership can take many forms. A hotel may be owned and operated by the GM. More often, however, the GM is employed either directly by the hotel's owners or by a management company that has been selected to operate the hotel for the owner (in some cases, the management company may own all or part of the hotel).

Individuals or corporations who own or invest in the hotel property will rely on the GM to positively influence the hotel's standing in the market, its physical condition, and of course, its profitability. Note: A hotel consists of both an ongoing service business and a real estate asset. Some owners may view the hotel primarily in terms of its business success; others will focus on the real estate/physical asset worth of the hotel property. The GM must keep the ownership informed about the condition of both.

When the hotel requires additional investment in either the business (such as additional staff or more advertising) or the real estate asset (such as new **FF&E**, roof repair, or parking lot resurfacing), it is most often the GM who communicates that information to ownership.

HOTEL TERMINOLOGY AT WORK

FF&E: The term used to refer to the furniture, fixtures, and equipment used by a hotel to service its guests.

■

Owners/investors are usually willing to make additional investments in a property when doing so makes good economic sense. However, they generally must be presented with a persuasive case that additional investment is, in fact, a worthwhile course of action. It is an important part of the GM's job to help make that case. If this is not done, the hotel's infrastructure may deteriorate, resulting in a declining quality of service for guests and, ultimately, reduced business volume.

The talents required to successfully manage the owner/investor relations' portion of the GM's job include financial analysis, proficiency in written communication, and often effective public speaking/presentation skills. Owners want to know about the performance of their properties. No one will have a better idea of how the hotel is performing than its GM. The ability to effectively inform investors and owners about the current performance and future needs of their hotel will be critical to that property's long-term success.

Brand Affiliation Management

Clarion, Hampton, Comfort, Best Western, Hawthorn, Microtel, Holiday Inn, Ramada, Fairfield by Marriott, and Hilton are just a few examples of the many franchise brands in the market today. (Chapter 1 presents a more detailed overview of lodging brands.) Most hotels operating today are, in fact, affiliated with a franchise brand. The reason becomes very clear when you learn about front-office operations and guest room sales in Chapter 8, The Front Office. Sometime during your career you will likely manage a franchised property. You therefore should be aware that an important part of the GM's job is to manage the brand at the property level. This includes continually monitoring operational standards set by the brand to ensure property conformance, communicating effectively with franchise brand officials about marketing and sales programs, and using activities and programs offered by the brand that can improve the profitable operation of the hotel.

GMs who have worked with various franchise companies will verify that different brands have differing "personalities." Some brands attempt to exert extreme influence on day-to-day property operations; others take a more hands-off approach. In either case, it is up to you as a GM to manage the franchise relationship for the good of your investors, community, employees, and most important, your guests.

To illustrate just one aspect of brand affiliation management, consider the quality inspection scores (sometimes called quality assurance [QA] scores) regularly given to properties by the franchise brand.

Quality inspection scores are the result of annual (or more frequent) inspections conducted by a franchise company to ensure that its mandated standards are being met by the franchisee. In the typical case, a franchise brand inspector arrives at the hotel property (either with or without prior notification) and in the presence of the GM undertakes a complete property inspection. The property then receives a "score" based on its compliance with established brand standards that have previously been communicated to the hotel. If a property consistently scores too low on these inspections, it runs the risk of being dropped as a franchisee by the brand's managers.

HOTEL TERMINOLOGY AT WORK

Quality Inspection Scores: Sometimes called quality assurance scores, these scores are the result of annual (or more frequent) inspections conducted by a franchise company to ensure that franchisor-mandated standards are being met by the franchisee. In some cases, management companies or the property itself may establish internal inspection systems as well. In general, however, it is the franchise company's quality inspection score that is used as a measure of the effectiveness of the GM, the hotel's management team, and the owner's financial commitment to the property.

In some cases, management companies or the property itself may establish standards and inspection/rating systems in addition to, or in preparation for, the brand inspection. Often the resulting scores of brand inspections are used in property ratings, marketing efforts, and even by owners to partially determine the GM's and other hotel managers' compensation/bonuses. Therefore, quality inspection scores become an important example of how the GM interacts with franchisors and/or management companies.

The talents required to successfully handle the brand affiliation management portion of the GM's job include well-developed interpersonal skills, persuasive ability, listening skills, and effective writing.

THE INTERNET AT WORK

For an example of one company (United States Franchise System) that mandates the public reporting of the summary results of individual property Quality Inspection (Assurance) scores, go to

www.usfsi.com

Community Relations

In many communities, a hotel is more than merely another service business. In fact, the hotels in an area, collectively, dictate in large measure how those outside the community view the area. There is no doubt, for example, that the hotels located in the French Quarter of New Orleans lend ambiance to the entire area. This is just as true of hotels in nontourist areas. Local government and community leaders therefore

Many GMs work with their communities to enhance economic growth in their areas.

often look to local hotel GMs to become leaders in efforts to attract new businesses, expand tourism opportunities, and provide input as to the needs of the local business community. All these tasks are important because the health of any local hotel industry is partially dependent on the health of the overall local economy.

As a GM, the opportunities to assist your local community will be varied and significant. Consider, for example, the hotel GM who gets a call from the local mayor asking if the hotel can assist in hosting a gathering for the representatives of a manufacturing business that is considering building a new manufacturing facility in the community. The manufacturer's decision to do so would mean many jobs for the local community (as well as the opportunity for increased guest room sales by the hotel). Obviously, the GM would want to assist and, in fact, to be a very visible host and community representative.

Additional community efforts that often involve a GM include charity events and fund-raisers held at the hotel, as well as interactions with community organizations seeking activity sponsorships from area businesses.

The talents required to successfully perform the community relations segment of the GM's job include an outgoing personality, well-developed social skills, and very often effective public speaking and presentation skills.

Executive Committee Facilitation

Although GMs are leaders in the community, it is on the hotel property itself where their leadership skills should be most readily apparent. In today's rapidly advancing technological world, it is unlikely that a GM will be the most knowledgeable expert in each functional (departmental) area of the hotel. For example, in a large property, the GM's knowledge of the intricacies of the specific electronic lock system will probably be less than that of the chief maintenance engineer or the director of security. However, the GM is still the recognized leader of the managers who supervise the engineering and security departments. The GM is also partially responsible for their professional development. The GM in this example may not be able to provide technical assistance for a task as simple as the replacement of batteries in the actual locking device. However, the GM could instruct the managers responsible for this activity about the best way to train their staff members to replace the batteries with a minimum amount of guest disruption.

Larger properties may have more departments than smaller properties, but the hotel GM in both is generally responsible to provide direction to the departmental managers within the hotel. Each of the departments is examined in detail in the following chapters. The goal is to identify the key aspects of each area that should be monitored by an effective GM.

Functional Area	Responsible For
Human Resource Manager	Hotel staffing needs
Controller	Accounting for hotel assets and liabilities
Front-Office Manager	Guest services and sales
Executive Housekeeper	Property cleanliness
Food and Beverage Director	Food and beverage production and service
Director of Security	Guest, employee and property safety/security
Director of Sales and Marketing	Revenue production and hotel promotions
Chief Engineer	Upkeep of the hotel's physical facility

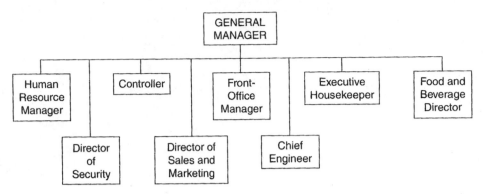

FIGURE 2.1   Typical Midsize, Full-Service Hotel Department Organizational Chart

Each of the department heads in these functional areas reports directly to the GM as seen in Figure 2.1.

To more effectively demonstrate the purpose of this book and the manner in which a GM interacts with departmental managers, let's look at housekeeping—a typical department within every hotel. There is a chapter relating to housekeeping in this text. However, it is not the purpose of this book to explain how to be an executive housekeeper or how to properly clean a room. In fact, to attempt to do so in a relatively few pages would trivialize the importance of the housekeeping department. Housekeeping is a tremendously complex area, and to do an excellent job as an executive housekeeper requires a unique individual with can-do attitude, detailed technical information, years of experience, and most important, a commitment to the profession of executive housekeeper. What, then, is the role of the GM in housekeeping? A GM without a strong housekeeping background should first learn the basics of the area, determine how best to monitor the effectiveness of the team performing housekeeping duties, and then develop his or her own role as a leader of and mentor to the executive housekeeper. This book, then, is written from the viewpoint of the general manager. It is not intended to be a quick overview of each hotel department, but rather an in-depth look at how a GM manages each area.

A football coach may lack the ability to play all the positions on the field as proficiently as the individual players who make up the coach's team. Similarly, the GM is not expected to be an expert in the specific day-to-day operation of each hotel department. The GM is expected, however, to work with the hotel managers who make up the **executive operating committee (EOC)** to improve their skills and the efficiency of the departments these individuals manage. Properly done, the GM, like the football coach, can create a winning team.

HOTEL TERMINOLOGY AT WORK

Executive Operating Committee (EOC): Those members of the hotel's management team (generally department heads) responsible for departmental leadership and overall property administration.

When you become a GM, you will need to become familiar with the tasks performed within each department. It is hoped that you would have gained some experience in many of the departments during earlier career training and experience. Also,

A GM's duties include supervising department heads. (© Dorling Kindersley)

effective GMs have a genuine interest in the professional development of the managers reporting to them. In fact, most successful managers can point to one or more individuals in their lives who took the time to "show them the ropes." As a GM, you have a responsibility to be that person for the managers who work with you.

The talents required to successfully handle this part of the GM's job include good listening skills, the ability to evaluate and implement managerial training and development programs, and a desire to assist in the professional improvement and growth of your EOC team. The EOC members will count on you to help them advance in their own careers. Your demonstrated interest in them will be immediately reflected in how they treat their own staff, and in turn, how their staff members treat your hotel guests.

Property Management

If you ask the average person on the street what hotel GMs do in their jobs, the property management function is most likely to be mentioned. Indeed, while this chapter points out that a GM performs multiple tasks, certainly one of the most important is that of "managing" the hotel.

As noted earlier, a GM is not likely to possess all of the highly technical skills required to directly manage each hotel department. However, as the title implies, the GM should be able to direct the overall **management** of the property. In this book, you will learn what a GM needs to know to effectively manage each of the functional areas of a hotel.

HOTEL TERMINOLOGY AT WORK

Management: The process of planning, organizing, staffing, directing, controlling, and evaluating human, financial, and physical resources for the purpose of achieving organizational goals.

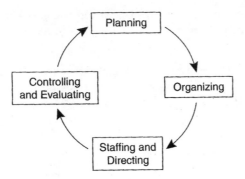

FIGURE 2.2 The Management Process

The property management goals of a hotel (as well as the goals of each department) will vary. However, it is the GM's job to help achieve those goals. Goals may be related to profitability, service levels, efficiency, or any other objective set by the GM and/or the property owners. Traditionally, those who study the management of hotels or any other enterprise have described the management process as consisting of the following distinct functions:

Functional Area	Purpose
Planning	To establish goals and objectives
Organizing	To maximize the deployment of resources
Staffing/Directing	To provide leadership
Controlling/Evaluating	To measure and evaluate results

These are presented in Figure 2.2. Let's look at each management function more specifically.

Planning

Planning is the process of creating goals and objectives and then designing action plans/strategies and tactics to achieve those goals and objectives. GMs engage in the planning function when they establish the philosophical and operational direction of the hotel. They also help departmental leaders plan for their respective departments. In most cases, the planning activities undertaken by the GM cut across hotel departmental areas and require an overall, integrated approach to planning.

Consider, for example, the process by which you as GM might evaluate the goal of improving your property's competitiveness in the marketplace by implementing a new guest service (improving your guests' ability to access the Internet from guest rooms). Also, assume the proposed service is the provision of unlimited, high-speed Internet access.

Sample questions you might consider in the planning (goal-setting) portion of your role include:

- Why does it appear that this service enhancement is desirable?
- What exactly is the service to be provided to the guests?
- What are the technological/physical facility requirements to add the service?
- Which operational department(s) will be responsible for implementing the new service?
- Which operational department(s) will be responsible for ensuring the continued quality of the new service?

- How will the hotel fund the cost of providing the service? (Will the service be **"free-to-guests"** or will there be a specific charge for use of the service?)
- What are the marketing implications of providing the service? What are the marketing implications of not providing the service?
- How will the hotel measure the sales volume or reputation value gained versus the cost of providing the service?

HOTEL TERMINOLOGY AT WORK

Free-to-Guests: A service provided at no additional charge (beyond normal room rental charges) to the hotel guest. Examples could include making local telephone calls, access to premium cable television channels such as HBO or Showtime, and use of the hotel's pool or work-out facilities. (Ultimately, the hotel must absorb the cost[s] of providing these services to guests, but guests are not charged on a per-usage basis. Therefore, the term does not mean that the services that are provided are free to the hotel.)

If, as you plan, you determine that the provision of in-room, high-speed Internet access is a goal you desire, you will have completed this phase of the planning process. It is then your responsibility to move to the next step of the management process: organizing resources that allow you to achieve your objective.

Organizing

The organizing function of management relates to arranging and deploying resources in a manner that most efficiently helps to achieve goals. When some managers think of the term *organizing*, they think of a business's organizational chart. Even though an organizational chart is an effective way of showing how "human" resources are organized, nonhuman resources such as financial capital and the hotel's property and equipment also must be organized.

Back to our example of providing high-speed Internet access to guest rooms. If the decision has been made to implement this goal, all the hotel's resources must be organized and deployed to best achieve the goal. Staff members may be given assignments to begin implementing the service; dollars will be required to fund the process; and the property itself may need physical reconfiguration to accommodate the service (for example, the recabling of guest rooms or the installation of wireless access points to provide for data transmission may be necessary).

Organizational skills are one of a GM's most important talents. For most hotel GMs, the reality is that they have approximately the same amount of resources available to them as did the property's prior GM and the GM who will follow. It is the skillful deployment of human, financial, and equipment resources that can markedly affect the profitability of the hotel. Some GMs can create great visions and plans for their property, but lack the organizational skills required to effectively implement those plans. Other GMs seem to have a great talent for organizing resources in a way that results in achieving (and often exceeding!) the goals set for the property.

Organizing always follows planning. That is, the hotel GM plans and develops the objective, then organizes resources to realize the objective. The next step in the managerial process involves directing those who will attain the objective.

Staffing/Directing

This concept relates, in its most comprehensive sense, to the GM's recruiting, motivational, and leadership characteristics. In fact, some management experts use the terms *coaching* or *leading* rather than *directing* when referring to this area of management. (They do so because *coaching* and *leading* implies the teaching and encouraging of skills, which will successfully impact the actions and attitudes of staff members.)

In most hotels, the GM is the "coach" or "leader" of the entire staff. From the clothes the GM wears, to picking up debris in the corridor, to the way the GM greets the hotel's guests, the entire staff looks to the GM to set the personal and service standards for the entire property.

THE INTERNET AT WORK

To read an account of how the "directing" actions of the GM profoundly affect the entire staff, read "Think Strawberries." This account, by James Levenson, past president and chief executive officer of the New York Plaza Hotel, describes his own hotel management experience. It was originally published in the October 1974 issue of the *Saturday Evening Post*. This timeless, insightful, and often humorous classic can be accessed at

www.easytraining.com/strawberry.htm

The attitudes of employees reflect the attitudes of management in the hotel business. Department heads and **line-level** staff including **guest service agents** look to their GM for leadership.

HOTEL TERMINOLOGY AT WORK

Line-Level: Those employees whose jobs are considered entry level or nonsupervisory. These are typically positions where the employee is paid an hourly (rather than salary) compensation. Examples include positions such as guest service agents, room attendants, and food and beverage servers.

Guest Service Agent: An employee working in the front desk area of the hotel. Also referred to by some in the industry as a "desk clerk."

In our high-speed Internet example, leadership occurs as the GM keeps individual staff members "on task" with project completion timelines, undertakes efforts to build team spirit, engages in coaching for maximum staff performance, and sets an example by indicating how important successful completion of the project is to the hotel's overall success.

Successful hotel managers know what needs to get done in their properties. They can identify needed improvements in operations. A few typical examples illustrate that GMs can identify when:

- Cleaning procedures used in the banquet kitchen must be improved
- The maintenance tool storage area should be reorganized
- Room attendants must be better trained in the proper disposal of hypodermic needles found in guest rooms
- Room-type preferences of top-client, frequent-stay guests should be tracked and reported weekly (not quarterly)

> • **"Comp"** room reports need to be submitted, with a justification for each comp, to the GM's office on a daily basis

---

HOTEL TERMINOLOGY AT WORK

Comp: Short for "complimentary" or "no charge" for products or services. Rooms, food, beverages, or other services are often given to guests by management if, in its opinion, the "comp" is in the best interests of the hotel. The term can be used as either an adjective (e.g., "I gave them a comp room") or a verb (as in "I told the assistant manager to comp the room").

Knowing what needs to be done is actually an easy part of the management process. Knowing how to get managers in each functional area to address the tasks in their respective departments is the hard part. It is here that the GM demonstrates real leadership, and often, through willpower, motivates a hotel staff to achieve things that were never before considered possible.

In review, managerial planning addresses what to do while organizing and directing how to do it. The next step in the management process involves control.

Controlling and Evaluating

When most managers think of controlling and evaluation, they think of finances and accounting. Earlier in this discussion, however, you learned that the purpose of the controlling and evaluating function is to measure and assess results. The complete controlling task for the GM, then, involves much more than journal entries, ledger balances, and changes in cash flow.

Again, consider our high-speed Internet service example. Perhaps none of the high-speed Internet service-related questions listed earlier are more important than this one: How will the hotel measure the sales volume or reputation value gained versus the cost of providing the service? This question is important because, generally, even the least effective GM can achieve increases in sales volume or service levels if unlimited resources are available. The reality, however, is that over the long-term resources are not unlimited. In fact, the excessive expenditure of resources is wasteful, inefficient, and reduces the assets of the hotel.

During the controlling process, the GM assesses the effectiveness of his or her own actions as well as that of the management team. Were room revenue budgets met? Did sales productivity in the food and beverage department meet expectations? Did quality inspection scores increase or decrease from the previous inspection? Were maintenance costs related to the swimming pool incurred as planned? Or, as in our high-speed Internet example, "Was the high-speed Internet service installed in the guest rooms at the proper cost to the hotel, marketed to guests within budget guidelines, and the final outcome a measurable improvement in room sales and/or guest satisfaction?" A GM controls the effectiveness of personal staff efforts. It is an important role that must be attended to on a continuous basis.

The actual management of the hotel property is one of the most visible and challenging aspects of a GM's job. It is also one of the most exciting. The talents required to successfully handle this part of the job include organizational and coaching skills, analytical and financial analysis skills, an ability to anticipate guest needs, competitive spirit, tremendous attention to detail, and even physical stamina. In addition, a truly effective GM has the near-magical ability to inspire the staff to make guests feel truly welcome when they stay at the property.

Many larger hotels require formal education for their GM positions.

It may seem somewhat odd to warn an aspiring GM about spending too much time "managing" the property, but this can happen. Remember, it is a well-trained staff, directed by highly motivated departmental leaders, that will best ensure guests receive reliably excellent service day after day. After all, no GM can (or should!) be on the property 24 hours per day, seven days a week.

Similarly, a GM who spends too much time in investor relations or any other job task may find that some other important job area(s) will suffer from neglect. GMs are challenged to define their own role while considering the best use of their time in the critical areas of investor relations, brand management, community activities, EOC development, and property operations to maximize the long-term value of the hotel, as well as their own career.

SKILLS DEVELOPMENT

The training and experience required to become a GM vary based on the size and complexity of the property to be managed: it takes more experience, preparation, and skill to effectively manage a 2,000-room resort than to operate an 80-room limited-service hotel. While the manager of the latter property certainly has a complex job, the manager of the resort property will be compensated to a higher degree and will find that the career path required to secure the position is longer. In both cases, however, the managers of these two types of properties, as well as all other properties, will find that the preparation required in their positions consists of some combination of formal education, on-the-job training, and continued professional development.

Formal Education

If you are interested in pursuing a formal educational degree that has traditionally helped prepare individuals for the role of GM, you are in good company. There are literally hundreds of such schools, and thousands of such students, in the United States. Formal hospitality education most often occurs at a two-year, four-year, or advanced degree program.

MANAGERS AT WORK

J.D. Ojisama is the GM of a full-service hotel owned by Partner's Equity Group (a collection of investors who have pooled their money to purchase the hotel). Because of the excellent way the property has been managed, J.D.'s hotel has achieved quality scores among the top 5 percent in the franchise chain each year J.D. has been the property's GM

At their annual convention, the franchise company announces a change in franchise standards that mandates all properties offer 27-inch televisions in their guest rooms within 12 months. This mandate represents a change from the current standard of simply providing each guest room with a traditional 25-inch TV. Any property that does not comply with the new policy within the 12-month time frame will face the certainty of reduced quality inspection scores. J.D.'s annual salary bonus is dependent, in part, on the quality scores achieved by the property.

Whose role is it to "sell" the owners on the expenditure required to implement the new standard? What would you advise J.D. do to help make the case for the improvement? What specific skills will J.D. likely need to achieve the goal of communicating the property's need for this mandated guest service enhancement? Where might J.D. have obtained these skills?

Two-Year Degree

Programs offering a two-year associate's degree in hotel (hospitality) management can be found in many local community colleges. Typically, these programs are designed for both traditional college students and more nontraditional working students. Required classes are often offered on the weekends or evenings. Program titles are not standard in hospitality education; it may be possible to find relevant programs under any of the following names (or variations of them):

- Hotel Administration
- Hotel and Restaurant Management
- Hospitality Administration
- Restaurant, Hotel, and Institutional Management
- Food Service Management
- Hospitality Business
- Tourism Administration
- Culinary Arts

A two-year associate's degree in hotel administration is a good choice for those individuals who wish to terminate their formal education after several years of study. In addition, the two-year degree may be a good choice for those individuals who already have a bachelor's degree in another subject and simply wish to gain knowledge of the hotel industry in an academic setting.

Classes required to complete the two-year degree generally consist of some general education courses (English, writing, math, history, and so on) and some courses specific to the hospitality industry. These are likely to include classes such as Introduction to the Hospitality Industry, Hospitality Operations Management, Cost Control, Hospitality Law, Marketing, Human Resource Management, and Food and Beverage Production/Management to teach students how to manage a hospitality operation. The largest two-year programs may allow students to select a concentration of courses specifically designed for hotel managers. Often courses will be applicable for both restaurant and hotel managers, so it is important to carefully select a program that has sufficient hotel emphasis.

Typically, hospitality-related courses at the two-year level are taught by a combination of full-time faculty and practicing professionals from the local hospitality community. This educational approach is usually very practical and current. An additional advantage of practicing professional instructors is that they may be well connected in the community and so will be able to assist you in seeking temporary or even permanent job placement in the local area.

Four-Year Degree

Four-year degree programs are less available than two-year programs; however, about every state has at least one or more quality institutions offering the bachelor's (four-year) degree in hotel, restaurant, or hospitality administration. Some programs are better known than others; the price students will pay to attend depends, in part, on the institution's status as a public or private school. The best of the four-year schools have a diverse faculty, quality facilities, and offer an excellent learning environment.

Most students today take longer than four years to complete a bachelor's degree, but the course of study is roughly twice as extensive as the typical two-year degree. As with the two-year degree, students pursuing a four-year degree will find about one-half of the coursework involves general education. The balance of the courses will be hospitality related, general business, or electives.

Although the time commitment is significant, the four-year degree is a good choice for students who wish to complete a bachelor's degree, who seek to learn from a larger number of qualified faculty, and who wish to obtain a degree that is generally considered "more advanced" than the two-year degree. In addition, some of those institutions offering undergraduate hospitality degrees for many years also have developed strong alumni groups that can assist recent graduates in job placement throughout their hospitality careers.

Advanced Degrees

For some people, an advanced (graduate) degree in hospitality management makes sense. The typical advanced degree completed by students is the masters in hospitality administration, and one or more colleges or universities in each state generally offers it.

Entrance to a master's degree in hospitality administration at most educational institutions is highly competitive. Admission typically requires that a student previously completed an undergraduate degree and achieved excellent grades while doing so.

In general, the requirements for completing the master's degree vary both by the educational institution offering the degree and the background of the student pursuing it. A typical master's degree program consists of one to two years of study beyond the bachelor's degree. In nearly all cases, faculty in charge of the degree program will require that students demonstrate that they have achieved mastery of the required subject matter and the ability to communicate effectively before the degree is granted.

Regardless of the degree you may wish to pursue, it is important to realize that formal education will not "make" you a qualified hotel GM. Formal education can provide, however, excellent tools with which to perform the job of GM when you attain this position.

THE INTERNET AT WORK

For current information on educational institutions in the United States offering two- and four-year degrees in your geographic area (as well as advanced degree programs), go to

www.hospitalitylawyer.com

and click on "Hospitality Schools."

On-the-Job Training

Most hotel management companies realize that, to be the very best, they must continually update and sharpen the skills of their GMs. Consider for a moment the challenge facing the president of a hotel company operating 100 properties when an advancement in data file server technology allows information on an individual guest's room preferences to be shared across the 100 properties. The opportunities to better serve the guest become significant but can only be achieved if each GM understands what must happen on his or her own property to fully utilize the benefit of a shared file environment. A situation such as this calls for **on-the-job training (OJT)**. That is, the company itself must provide the learning experiences needed for GMs to learn how to implement the property-level changes required to effectively share the guest information.

HOTEL TERMINOLOGY AT WORK

On-the-Job Training (OJT): Learning activities designed to enhance the skills of current employees. OJT programs are typically offered by management with the intent of improving guest service and employee performance at the hotel. There is generally no charge to the employee for the training.

◼

For hotel GMs, OJT in recent years has focused on two major industry trends:

- The impact of advancing technology
- The impacts of a changing workforce

This book addresses many of the results of these trends in each chapter because advancements in technology and the changing workforce affect every area of the hotel. As a future GM, you need to be aware of these changes and the role that OJT programs offered by your company can play in improving your skills. Just as important, when you lead a hotel, you will need to create and implement OJT programs for your own management staff to keep their skills up-to-date and your property running smoothly.

Professional Development

The hotel industry is dynamic; GMs must stay abreast of the business, societal, workforce, and increasingly, technological changes that affect how they do their jobs. In some companies, sufficient OJT programs to fully develop needed skills simply may not exist. If so, you must manage your own professional development. Fortunately, there are many resources available, including business and trade associations and industry publications.

It is important for GMs to understand how the Internet affects their business. (© Michael Newman/PhotoEdit)

"NEW" HOTEL TERMINOLOGY AT WORK?

The skills and knowledge required of GMs are constantly changing. The growing area of information technology (IT) as applied to the hotel industry is an excellent example. Today's GM must understand terms that, even 15 years ago, were virtually unknown to hoteliers. The following dozen terms are not specific to the hotel industry; however, GMs should understand them. These terms also serve as excellent examples of why today's GMs must continually seek to improve their skills, learn, and most importantly, transfer their new knowledge into practical ways to improve service to their guests.

- **Bandwidth:** The range or capacity of frequencies that a communications device can handle.
- **Converged Access Device:** Any electronic device that provides for the simultaneous transmission of voice and data.
- **Domain Name:** The unique name that identifies an Internet site.
- **Firewall:** Software program or hardware device that filters information coming into a private network or computer system through an Internet connection to help prevent attacks.
- **Hot Spot:** An area (within the hotel) that allows for wireless Internet reception.
- **IP Address:** Short for Internet Protocol Address, it is the unique identifying number assigned to each computer utilizing the Internet.
- **ISDN:** Integrated Services Digital Network. A digital connection that processes data, video, and voice traffic at speeds of 64 Kbps (thousand bits per second) to 1.5 Mbps (million bits per second).
- **Link:** An electronic connection between two Web sites. Also called a "hot link" or hyperlink.
- **Profiling:** The practice of tracking information about consumers' interests by monitoring their movements online. This can be done by analyzing the content, URLs, and other information about users' browsing path or click stream.
- **Search Engine:** A program that helps Web users find information or sites on the Internet. The method for finding this information is usually done by maintaining an index of Web resources that can be queried for the key words entered by the user.
- **T-1:** An electronic device that consolidates data, Internet, and telephone calls onto a single digital connection.
- **Voice Over IP:** The transmission of voice information (telephone calls) over the Internet.

Business Associations

In nearly every community large enough to support a hotel, you will be able to join local business associations. Local chambers of commerce and related business associations can be a critical part of your overall efforts to keep your skills "up to speed" without leaving your community. Chamber members benefit from business/skills enhancement programs, networking opportunities, timely publications, and seminars that include local economic data and best management practices.

Additional membership features include professional development opportunities to make you a better manager, and in some cases, provide low- or no-cost training for your entry-level workers. Other chamber activities include lobbying for business interests and facilitating public–private employment initiatives. Chambers of commerce and other professional service organizations often hold meetings and schedule speakers to update you on the newest business philosophies and practices. Although it is unlikely that these sessions will be hotel specific, many topics, especially those related to human resources and technology, will be applicable. Given all that they do and can help you accomplish, membership in local business associations is generally well worth the modest cost.

Trade Associations

As a GM, you will likely belong to one or more professional trade associations in addition to the American Hotel & Lodging Association (AH&LA). Trade associations typically serve the certification, educational, social, and legislative needs of their members. Associations usually hold monthly and annual gatherings, and in conjunction with these meetings, often offer educational seminars/workshops to improve the knowledge and skills of their members.

In addition, most trade associations, in conjunction with their annual meetings, invite companies who sell products and services of interest to the membership to participate in a trade show. These shows bring together a variety of vendors, all of whom are interested in exhibiting their latest product offerings. Trade shows are an extremely efficient way to see new products and service offerings of a large number of vendors in a very short time. Many trade associations also have both state- and local-level chapters, some of which host their own trade shows. Vendors can be an excellent source of information about new developments in the industry, and you should make an effort to attend association-sponsored meetings and trade shows when possible.

THE INTERNET AT WORK

For information on some of the professional associations you may wish to join, go to

American Hotel & Lodging Association: www.ahla.com
Asian American Hotel Owners Association: www.aahoa.com
International Hotel & Restaurant Association: www.ih-ra.com
National Restaurant Association: www.restaurant.org
American Culinary Federation: www.acfchefs.org
Hospitality Financial and Technology Professionals: www.hftp.org
Professional Convention Management Association: www.pcma.org

The hotel industry is fortunate to have an additional resource for professional development that exists in only a few other industries. It is called the Educational Institute of the American Hotel & Lodging Association, or **EI** for short.

HOTEL TERMINOLOGY AT WORK

EI: The shortened version of the name given to the Educational Institute of the American Hotel & Lodging Association (AH&LA). Located in Orlando, Florida, and Lansing, Michigan, EI is the professional development and certification subsidiary of the AH&LA.

■

The mission of EI is to help hotel owners and managers become better trained and to provide resources that allow these individuals to better train their own staffs. In addition, EI provides certification services for a variety of management, supervisory, and line-level industry positions including the CHA (certified hospitality administrator), the CFBE (certified food and beverage executive), the CLSS (certified lodging security supervisor), and the registered guest room attendant.

THE INTERNET AT WORK

For information on the professional development programs for GMs offered by the Educational Institute of the American Hotel & Lodging Association, go to

www.ei-ahla.org

Trade Publications

Trade publications take many forms. The book you are currently reading is a type of trade publication because it has been published specifically for those interested in the hotel industry. There are a variety of books and publishers in the hospitality field. Many of them, including this one, can be excellent additions to your own professional library.

THE INTERNET AT WORK

For a look at other hospitality books published by Prentice Hall, visit their Web site at

www.prenhall.com

Select the discipline "Hospitality & Travel/Tourism & Leisure."

Many industry publications are produced monthly or more frequently. Some are offered free of charge to industry professionals. Typically, these publications are produced in either newspaper or magazine formats; the best of them can be an excellent source of information on the latest hotel industry news, trends, and practices. Sometimes technology applications have become a large part of the editorial interest of these publications, and a technology editor is employed to monitor technological changes for the publication's readers. Developments in the area of Human Resources are also an important part of most trade publications.

While hotel GMs often find there are not enough hours in the day to complete all the tasks they wish to complete, those professionals who take the time to stay up-to-date by reading industry books and publications find the time is exceptionally well spent. These individuals are well informed, ahead of their competitors relative to current information, and ultimately are more successful with both their employees and guests.

THE INTERNET AT WORK

For a look at some of the important issues facing today's hotel GM, as well as other news you will find helpful in your career development, go to

http://www.ahma.com/news_ahla.asp

GENERAL MANAGER'S JOB DESCRIPTIONS

The actual job duties performed by GMs can be as varied as the hotels these individuals manage. Now that you have reviewed the major responsibilities of GMs, it should be easier to see why their daily tasks can vary based upon the size hotel they manage, the services offered by their hotels, and even the hotel's location. The following job descriptions, typical of the type used to advertise GM position vacancies, will help you even better understand how the GMs are viewed in their own hotels. Although some of the terms and concepts listed in these sample job descriptions may be unfamiliar to you, when you have successfully studied this entire text, you will understand all of them.

GM JOB DESCRIPTION: LIMITED-SERVICE HOTEL

SUMMARY: Responsible for generating profit to meet or exceed budget expectations, while maintaining operational and guest service standards.

SPECIFIC DUTIES

Develop, administer, and control the hotel revenue and expense budgets.

Analyze balance sheet, statement of cash flows, and income statement.

Submit P&L Variance Reports in a timely manner.

Review and approve the hotel payroll.

Authorize direct bill (credit) accounts and monitor the administration of accounts receivable.

Oversee tracking of leads and follow up with DOS to ensure leads are actively managed.

Maintain relationships with target accounts. Sustain pieces of business that are core business. Retain and service that business.

Take ownership of sales when the DOS is not available.

Coach and train all members of the hotel team on their role in the sales process.

Review room inventory management to ensure maximization of room revenue.

Ensure proper selection, training, counseling, and motivation of all team members.

Hire, train, counsel, and motivate management team members.

Review all hourly personnel performance appraisals.

Conduct all management performance appraisals. Review all hourly team member disciplinary procedures and documentation.

Ensure team member attitude of attentiveness and anticipation of guest needs.

Ensure proper delivery of guest special requests.

Meet with and solicit comments from guests on a regular basis to determine their level of satisfaction with guest services and facilities.

Respond and follow up on all written guest complaints. Ensure guest satisfaction with resolution of the complaint or problem.

Inspect rooms according to quality standards for cleanliness and proper preventative maintenance.

Develop and maintain hotel programs to assure that the quality program criteria are met.

Ensure all team members are trained to act according to procedure, in the event of an emergency or accident at the hotel.

Ensure a viable key control program is in place in all hotel departments, with documentation.

Ensure team members follow appropriate cash control procedures.

Ensure the security needs of the property and guests are met.

Maintain an active and visible position in the local community and industry.

Develop and maintain rapport with competitive hotels: City convention and visitors bureau, chamber of commerce, lead sources, clients, and so forth.

Participate in community activities, team member functions, and guest events.

Respond to requests from immediate supervisor.

QUALIFICATIONS

Must have at least three years of experience as GM of a limited-service hotel.

Must have had P&L, budgeting, and forecasting responsibilities.

Must be computer literate in Word and Excel.

Must have excellent leadership skills.

Must be neat and courteous with a pleasing personality.

Must enjoy people and be able to meet the public with poise.

Must be able to handle difficult situations with diplomacy.

Must be dependable and honest.

GM JOB DESCRIPTION: FULL-SERVICE HOTEL (300 ROOMS)

SUMMARY: The general manager is the key individual in the organization's chain of command with complete responsibility for all activities at the hotel. The general manager takes charge of all components of the property's business, serving as a positive role model for all subordinates while aggressively protecting the owner's financial interests.

SPECIFIC DUTIES

1. Generate maximum financial and operational performance within the framework of the corporation's guidelines, specific direction, and established policies and procedures.
2. Lead the revenue effort of the entire property with an emphasis on increasing driving market share and maximizing **RevPar**.
3. Champion the hotel's business plan and specific mission statement.
4. Develop and nurture a team of management and line staff members that are directed toward the achievement of the hotel's goals and priorities.
5. Lead the hotel in an entrepreneurial fashion.
6. Maintain and support the organization's professional image and high ethics. Represent the hotel in the local and professional communities.

MINIMUM QUALIFICATIONS

1. Strong interpersonal/leadership skills and caring behavior toward both guests and team members.
2. A positive reference from previous superiors, peers, and subordinates.
3. "Guest first" service approach. Demonstrated guest service success.
4. An entrepreneurial style that reflects a true sense of pride and ownership.
5. Self-starter who excels in time management.
6. Successful completion of an accredited college education—two-year degree.
7. A minimum of three years of experience as a general manager of a 250-room or larger, full-service hotel with a progressive track record.

DESIRABLE QUALIFICATIONS

1. Bachelor of science degree in hotel administration from an accredited college.
2. General manager of like-sized hotel for a minimum of five years.
3. Previous department head experience in two of the following:
   Rooms/front-office
   Food and beverage
   Sales and marketing
4. Specific technical expertise in common hotel technology systems and business software use.

HOTEL TERMINOLOGY AT WORK

RevPar: Short for "revenue per available room," the average sales revenue generated by each guest room during a given time period. The formula for RevPar is

$$\text{Occupancy \%} \times \text{Average Daily Rate (ADR)} = \text{RevPar}$$

THE INTERNET AT WORK

There are many career opportunities available in hotel management. You can search for some of these positions on a very popular industry Web site. To do so, go to

www.hcareers.com

HOTEL TERMINOLOGY AT WORK GLOSSARY

The following terms were defined within this chapter. If you are not familiar with one of them, please review the segment of the chapter that contains the term.

General manager (GM)
Furniture, fixtures, and
   equipment (FF&E)
Quality inspection scores
Executive operating committee
   (EOC)

Management
Free-to-guests
Line-level
Guest service agent
Comp (complimentary)

On-the-job training (OJT)
Educational Institute of the
   AH&LA (EI)
RevPar

ISSUES AT WORK

1. A GM has responsibilities to guests, employees, owners, and of course, themselves. What are some reasons these interests might come into conflict? If that were to happen, whose interests do you think you would consider to be the most important? Why?

2. Tremendous technological advancements continue each day in the hotel industry. Which two departmental areas in a hotel do you believe have been most affected by technological advancements during the past ten years? Why? Did you find that your lack of knowledge about a specific area resulted in your believing that few technological advances occurred in that area? How can effective GMs prevent these types of blind spots?

3. It has been said that 10 percent of managers' time should be spent on preparing themselves for the next higher level job, 80 percent of their time doing their current job, and 10 percent of their time helping those individuals who are at the level below them to prepare for advancement to the next level (their current) job. Do you think this is true for a GM? How would you modify the equation in your own situation?

4. Some practicing GMs elect to pursue four-year or higher degrees that they believe will assist in their career advancement. What are some of the advantages and potential disadvantages of such a career advancement strategy? What alternatives would you suggest to a GM whose geographic location prevents such an approach?

5. The EI offers the CHA designation for professionals who meet established standards and pass a competency exam appropriate for a hotel GM. Do you think that the CHA is a designation that would be valuable for you to seek? Why or why not?

3

Management, Supervision, and Service Skills for the GM

This Chapter at Work

In this chapter you will learn more about the management principles and procedures that GMs use to interact with their department heads and other staff. This is important because the way you manage others heavily influences how they, in turn, supervise their own staff. The GM is a significant influence on the organizational culture of the property. Good or bad, the GM serves as a key role model to the hotel.

Effective hoteliers manage staff members and other resources including money, equipment, energy, and time according to basic, proven management principles. These are reviewed in this chapter.

Historically, the GM was the ultimate authority and let everyone know it! Today there is an increasing focus on employee input, both as individuals and as members of the hotel team. Although it is true that successful GMs can practice a variety of management styles, good GMs know that creating a thriving hotel is a team effort and that every member of the team is important to the property's ultimate success.

Some GMs spend little time "planning" and much time "doing." This chapter emphasizes the need for up-front planning to precede the management of any asset including human resources. In addition, principles of decision making, organizing, and delegating are reviewed. A brief overview of the flow of communication up, down, and across the hotel organization then follows, as does essential information about the principles of motivation, leadership, and discipline.

GMs must know how to build and make the most effective use of employee teams. As well, they must use proven tactics for selecting, orienting, and training staff members. The basics of these activities are also presented in this chapter.

GMs must be concerned about guest service. They must direct the process used to determine the products and services desired by their guests and then encourage the development of systems and procedures to consistently attend to their guests' preferences. The "mechanics" behind these activities are relatively straightforward. However, the philosophy about their necessity must precede them. First, the hospitality spirit must be ingrained into "the way things are done" at the hotel. Then the GM becomes instrumental in creating and maintaining the guest focus culture. Information about important service planning basics is presented in this chapter.

Finally, although there is probably no such thing as an "average" day for a GM, this chapter provides examples of what GMs do in the course of their normal duties.

Chapter 3 Outline

THE GM SETS THE PACE

GMs MUST MANAGE
    GM Functions
    GM Skills
    GM Relationships
    GMs Manage in Times of Change

EVOLUTION OF TRADITIONAL HOTEL HUMAN RESOURCES PRACTICES

MANAGEMENT BASICS
    Planning
    Decision Making
    Organizing

    Delegation
    Flow of Communication
    Motivation
    Leadership
    Discipline

TEAM BUILDING TACTICS

EMPLOYEE SELECTION, ORIENTATION, AND TRAINING

THE GM AND QUALITY GUEST SERVICE
    Ingredients in a Quality Service Delivery System
    A Goal of Zero Defects

GM INTERACTIONS	HOTEL TERMINOLOGY AT WORK
GM's Monthly "Diary"	GLOSSARY
Employee and Guest Relationships	ISSUES AT WORK

THE GM SETS THE PACE

The old saying in the hospitality industry that "it all starts at the top" is true. How the GM feels about and acts toward issues such as safety and providing excellent guest service will impact the attitude of the hotel's staff when they address these same issues. So it is with a focus on **human relations** within the hotel.

HOTEL TERMINOLOGY AT WORK

Human Relations: Skills needed to understand and effectively interact with other people.

The hospitality industry is labor intense: It takes many staff members to produce services and products for guests. Typically, the GM only directs personally the work of department heads and perhaps a few other staff members. The importance of the GM's supervision style, however, cannot be overstated. By contrast, the department head in the housekeeping or food and beverage department directly supervises many more staff members. However, the manner in which the GM interacts with department heads will likely set the pace for the relationship between the department heads and their own staff members.

Consider a GM who genuinely respects the department heads, who values, solicits, when possible, uses their input, and who effectively communicates with them. Contrast this GM with one who does not respect or seek advice from the department heads and who "communicates" only one way: "Do it my way, or I'll replace you!" Department heads that, like the first GM, are effective "people persons" would not be able to work well with a GM of the second type. They would leave and eventually be replaced by others who, not surprisingly, treat their subordinates exactly as their own boss treats them.

The GM, then, has a direct impact upon how other hotel managers interact with their employees. This, in turn, influences the level of morale, the employee turnover rate, and the extent to which products and services of desired quality are consistently delivered to the guests.

GMs MUST MANAGE

The process of management involves using resources to attain organizational goals. One of the resources available to hospitality managers, people (human resources), is clearly the most complex and important for success. From the perspective of a specific hotel property, the GM is considered the top-level manager.[1] Figure 3.1 reviews four organizational levels within a hotel.

---

[1]In a multiunit hotel organization, the GM might more appropriately be considered a middle-level manager since he/she reports to someone at a higher organizational level outside of the property such as a district or regional manager.

FIGURE 3.1   Organizational Levels in a Hotel

As seen in Figure 3.1, GMs are at the highest management level at the property. They direct the work of department heads who are considered middle-level managers. These staff members, in turn, direct the work of supervisors and managers who oversee the work of entry-level employees.

GM Functions

GMs (and all other managers in any type of organization) must perform several management functions that were reviewed in the previous chapter. Figure 3.2 indicates each of the basic management functions and provides an example of applicable work activities. It illustrates that all of a GM's broad and complex management activities can be categorized into one or more basic management functions.

Hotel managers spend much of their day interacting with guests, employees, and others.

Management Function	Example of Activity; Working with Department Head (If Applicable) to:
Planning	Develop an operating budget or a marketing plan
Organizing	Assign responsibilities for an upcoming banquet or conference event
Staffing	Recruit, select, orient, and train a new department head
Directing	Supervise the work of department heads in each department
Controlling	Take corrective action(s) when budgeted financial plans are not attained

FIGURE 3.2   Basic Functions of a GM's Role

GM Skills

Hotel GMs, like managers in other organizations, must be able to apply four basic types of skills to be effective:

- *Conceptual Skills.* The ability to collect, interpret, and use information in a logical way. As a GM learns about a new, competing hotel opening nearby and makes future marketing decisions accordingly is one example of using this skill.
- *Interpersonal Skills.* The ability to understand and interact well with people, including guests, employees, and suppliers. Examples include "meeting and greeting" guests, resolving employee-related problems, and negotiating with suppliers.
- *Administrative Skills.* The ability to organize and direct required work efforts; an example would be the ability to develop policies and operating procedures needed for ensuring safety within the property.
- *Technical Skills.* The ability to perform hotel management-specific aspects of the job. Examples include forecasting guest demand for rooms, establishing room rates, and perhaps checking in a guest in the absence of a front-desk agent.

GM Relationships

GMs, like other hotel employees, must be able to effectively interact with many groups of persons including:

- *Staff Members Whom They Supervise.* Some GMs use a dictatorial style of leadership. By the power of their position, they are the "boss" and make that clear. Increasingly, however, managers tend to be facilitators. They assist their staff by providing necessary resources and by giving advice and help as necessary. Many managers practice the art of **empowerment**. They help employees to plan broad goals and then give them the discretion about how to achieve the goals while remaining in the background ready to provide assistance if needed.

HOTEL TERMINOLOGY AT WORK

Empowerment: The act of granting authority to employees to make key decisions within the employees' areas of responsibility.

- *Other Hotel Employees.* GMs have contact with many hotel employees, and good GMs make sure that they constantly do so. As they "manage by walking around," there are opportunities to interact with staff members in numerous ways.

- *Guests.* Outstanding hoteliers take every possible opportunity to interact with guests on a basis that extends far beyond the "How was everything?" comments often heard in hotel lobbies, in dining rooms, and at the front desk. They make a serious effort to learn what their guests want and how the hotel can best meet and exceed their expectations.

- *External Organizations.* GMs represent their hotels when they join professional business and community service organizations, interact with suppliers, and meet with representatives of community government.

- *Others in the Community.* Effective GMs are well recognized in their own communities. They are known as the manager of the "XYZ Hotel" as they participate in their community's social events, attend school and athletic events with their children, interact with their neighbors, and otherwise live their personal lives. Almost everything they do, in subtle or overt ways, impacts the reputation and therefore the success of their hotel.

GMs Manage in Times of Change

The world of hotel management is changing, and GMs must keep up with these changes. Throughout this book, many examples of change are addressed as technical aspects of the job are discussed. Others relate to changes in the world in general and to business more specifically. All these changes impact the way managers interact with people. For example, relative to their counterparts in years past, GMs must:

- Interact with a more diverse workforce.
- Emphasize teams rather than the performance of individual employees.
- Cope with the fast-paced change of technology.
- Adjust to workplace changes, sometimes including **reengineering** and/or downsizing.
- React to global challenges. The impact of one country's economy in another part of the world often has a direct impact on the economy of a local community and other areas from which the hotel attracts its business and pleasure travelers.
- Improve quality while increasing productivity. "Doing more and better with less" is no longer a slogan. Instead, it is a philosophy and a work objective in many hotels.
- Improve ethical/social behavior. Hoteliers must be fair to all and must ensure that the hotel is a good "citizen" within the community.

HOTEL TERMINOLOGY AT WORK

Reengineering: Reorganizing hotel departments or work sections within departments.

Approach/Viewpoint	
Traditional	**Contemporary**
Manager-focused work unit	Team-focused work unit
Manager is dominant	Manager is supportive
Emphasis on technical skills	Emphasis on employee facilitation skills
Manager seeks stability	Manager encourages change
Manager tells and sells their own views	Manager listens
Manager personally responsible for results	Manager shares responsibility for results
Manager personally solves problems	Team problem solving is employed
Fear and pressure are used to motivate staff	Pride, recognition, and growth are used to motivate staff
Autocratic (dictatorial) decision style	Participative decision style
Individual behavior	Team behavior
GM forces compliance	GM earns the team's support
What one says is inconsistent with what one does	What one says is consistent with what one does
Inconsistent "moments of truth"	Consistent "moments of truth"
Reactive management/supervision style	Proactive management/supervision style
Bureaucratic "rituals"	Flexible routine
Top down—one-way communication	Multidirectional communication
Hierarchy of control	Empowerment
Power	Consensus
Short-term human resources strategies	Long-term human resources strategies

FIGURE 3.3   Evolution of Hotel Human Resources Practices

EVOLUTION OF TRADITIONAL HOTEL HUMAN RESOURCES PRACTICES

Like managers in other organizations, hotel GMs have had to reconsider their interactions with employees. Figure 3.3 displays some changes applicable to managing hotel employees.

When reviewing Figure 3.3, consider that some changes are not fully used in all hotels by all GMs. Rather, it indicates an evolution from a traditional viewpoint to a more modern one.

MANAGEMENT BASICS

Hotel GMs must use many management skills that, at their most basic level, are part of a universal process of management. These basics represent a range of **strategies** and **tactics** that managers use to attain organizational goals.

HOTEL TERMINOLOGY AT WORK

Strategy: A method or a plan developed to achieve a long-range goal.

Tactic: An action or method used to attain a short-term objective.

Planning

Figure 3.2 indicated that planning is the first management function. Unfortunately, this activity is frequently overlooked or ignored by many GMs. In practice, there are many types of planning tools that GMs, with help from their staff, must develop and apply. Some are illustrated in Figure 3.4.

Let's look at Figure 3.4 to review how planning activities are interrelated. First, the hotel's owners will have established specific financial performance goals for the property. They invest in hotels with the expectation that the resulting **ROI** will be as good or better than alternative investments.

HOTEL TERMINOLOGY AT WORK

ROI: Short for "return on investment." The percentage rate of return achieved on the money invested in a hotel property, as in "We expect our hotel to produce an ROI of 12 percent this year."

Hotel managers must know how to effectively motivate, delegate, and communicate with their staff members.

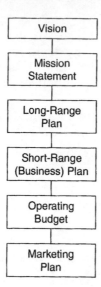

FIGURE 3.4   Flowchart of Management Planning Tools

To achieve ROI goals, owners, GMs, and EOC members, among others, will develop a broad, but generally less quantifiable, vision about what the hotel will strive to be. For example, one vision may be that the property be perceived as the "preferred" destination in the community for corporate business travelers. In all cases, the vision of management must support the goals of the hotel's owners.

Second, a mission statement is developed that is driven by the vision. It becomes more specific and indicates what the hotel must do to be successful and how this will be accomplished. For example, planners may want the hotel to be the destination of choice for business travelers by providing exemplary products and services at competitive prices.

Third, the mission statement drives a long-range plan. For example, within five years, the hotel may wish to have a 55 percent market share of all business traveler stays in the community.

Fourth, the short-range (business) plan indicates the hotel's goal within a one-year time span. For example, by the end of the year, the hotel will be judged successful if it has attained a specified percentage of the desired market share of business travelers.

Fifth, an operating budget is developed to indicate the amount of revenues and associated expenses that are anticipated as the short-range (business) plan is implemented.

Finally, a marketing plan indicates what must be done to generate the revenue anticipated by the operating budget.

Clearly, there are a wide range of interrelated planning tools required for successful hotel operation. The GM works with the EOC to develop, implement, and monitor progress toward goals using these planning tools. This is best accomplished by a team-oriented approach that allows input to be solicited from all affected personnel. Then, ideas judged best are selected and applied.

Decision Making

GMs use resources including money, people, and time to attain objectives. All resources are in limited supply. Therefore, GMs must constantly make decisions about how to best use these limited resources to maximize the chances of attaining planned objectives.

There are two basic types of decisions that GMs make: **programmed decisions** and **nonprogrammed decisions**.

HOTEL TERMINOLOGY AT WORK

Programmed Decisions: Routine or repetitive decisions that can be made after considering policies, procedures, or rules.

Nonprogrammed Decisions: Decisions that occur infrequently and require creative and unique decision-making abilities.

Programmed decisions are routine, are repetitive, and can typically be made by considering guidelines such as policies, rules, and other requirements. One example is to enforce a policy found in the employee handbook. By contrast, nonprogrammed decisions occur infrequently; there are few, if any, systems in place to deal with them. A scenario can relate to an issue, such as "Should we extend the hours of operation for the dining room?" Effective GMs make good nonprogrammed decisions and look forward to the challenges and opportunities for the creativity that these decision-making occasions present.

GMs must consider numerous factors before making decisions, including:

- Who is the correct person to make the decision? Usually, the person with authority or power closest to the point of action is the best person to make the decision.

- Will a decision about a specific issue bring the hotel closer to attaining its objectives and goals?

- How will the decision affect guests? Often decisions made to "improve" the hotel do so at the expense of guests. For example, assume guests currently make free local telephone calls and managers are considering whether to begin charging for them. If only the additional revenue is considered, this would exclude possible concerns about increased guest dissatisfaction and potentially reduced hotel room revenues from reduced occupancy rates. The net result could be a decline in overall hotel revenue because the decision negatively affected the guests. Management decisions that negatively affect guests will usually have a negative long-term impact on the hotel.

- Is there only one acceptable alternative? Typically, as alternatives for decision making are generated, there may be several possible responses. Frequently, the "best" decision is arrived at as a result of consolidating essential aspects of several different alternatives.

- Should the decision be based upon objective facts and analysis alone, or alternatively, can some subjective ("common sense") issues be addressed?

- How much time and effort can be spent on the decision? In the fast-paced hotel business, the issue creating the greatest problem at the moment typically receives the priority. Some decisions, such as what to do with a burst water pipe, must be made quickly. Others, such as which local radio station to use to advertise a Valentine's Day room special, can be made more slowly.

- How does my experience help with decision making? Through practice and experience, GMs become better decision makers. The impact of past decisions can be very helpful as you make decisions today.

- Must the decision please everyone? Often "good" decisions do not uniformly please all persons who are affected by them.
- What, if any, are the ethical aspects to the decisions being made? **Ethics** relates to the "rightness" or "wrongness" of one's behavior and frequently involves judgments about "fairness." Decisions should not be arbitrary or revengeful.

HOTEL TERMINOLOGY AT WORK

Ethics: Standards used to judge the "right" and "wrong" (or "fairness") of one's actions when dealing with others.

Decisions can be made by the GM alone or by using a team approach. This is illustrated in Figure 3.5. Note that managers have traditionally made unilateral decisions. That approach evolved into a modified team method in which the manager solicited input from others and then applied it to the extent desired. The manager using the contemporary approach realizes the worth of the team decision-making process and allows the team to make decisions.

There are advantages as well as disadvantages to the use of a group decision-making process. First, consider the advantages:

- The group will likely have a broader range of information that can be considered, because each group member brings unique information to the decision-making process. This is similar to the old problem-solving saying that "two (or more) heads are better than one."
- More creative alternatives can be generated.
- The entire team becomes aware of issues and problems that need to be addressed, and in the long run, this may make the team more supportive of the final decision.
- There can be higher morale issues because team members who are involved in decision-making appreciate that their ideas are considered to have merit.
- The decision will be easier to implement because the team helped to develop it.

There are, however, several potential disadvantages to a team decision-making approach:

- The manager will ultimately be accountable for the group's decisions and perhaps will even be held responsible for them even if they conflict with his/her own ideas about what should have been decided.
- Team members will spend time on decision making that otherwise could be used for other purposes.

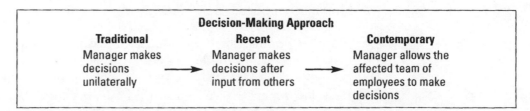

FIGURE 3.5   Continuum of Decision Making

- The manager may be forced to "choose sides" if alternative opinions are expressed.
- Staff members with the strongest personalities may dominate the decision-making process.
- The manager will need excellent leadership skills to facilitate the group's decision-making process.
- Group decision making is often time-consuming and may not be applicable when fast decisions must be made.

An effective GM often implements all three of the approaches to decision making presented here. The situation and the issue being addressed frequently determine the specific process used.

Organizing

GMs must know and practice several organizing principles. For example, they must recognize the concept of **unity of command**: every employee in the hotel should report to/be accountable to only one boss when performing a specific activity.

HOTEL TERMINOLOGY AT WORK

Unity of Command: Each employee should report to/be accountable to only one boss for a specific activity.
∎∎

MANAGERS AT WORK

"He's really mad!" said the sales manager.

"Who's mad?" asked J.D. Ojisama, the hotel's GM as he watched the man the sales manager had been talking to enter the hotel elevator.

"The couple in room 531," replied the sales manager. "They checked in at 3:30 this afternoon. They're here for tonight's New Year's Eve package. But the champagne and strawberries that were supposed to be in their room are not there."

"Why not?" asked J.D.

"Well, I guess, from what I can gather, the front desk reserved their room for them this morning, and then notified food and beverage that they would be in that room . . . so the wine and berries could be put in it . . . but when the couple checked in, he wanted to be on a higher floor, not the ground floor. . . . So, the desk agent moved them to an upper floor room."

"OK," said J.D. "That's the right thing to do."

"Well, I guess the food and beverage department was never notified about the change. And then, when the guests complained and the front-desk manager called the food and beverage department, the food and beverage director said he was too busy preparing for tonight's dinner event to fix some other department's screw up!"

"What's the current status on the guest?" asked J.D.

"Well," replied the sales manager, "it's been two hours and the items are still not in his room. He just said if they are not there in 15 minutes he's leaving. . . . The bad news is that he is head of the corporate travel department for Tech-Mar Industries, one of our largest corporate clients."

What are the decisions that J.D. must make unilaterally and immediately in this situation? What decisions would best be made after consulting with others in the hotel? Last, what decisions could best be made by the managers and employee team members involved? As a GM, how would you go about creating and managing such a decision-making group?

They should also know about the principle of **span of control**—that is, there is a limit to the number of staff members that one supervisor can effectively manage. Generally, top-level managers can supervise the work of fewer persons who perform diverse duties than can subordinates at lower levels who generally supervise staff members who perform similar duties.

HOTEL TERMINOLOGY AT WORK

Span of Control: The number of people one supervisor can effectively manage.

GMs also must know how to avoid conflict between line and staff personnel. They define levels of **authority,** and they assure that there is ongoing and effective communication between personnel in all departments.

HOTEL TERMINOLOGY AT WORK

Authority: The power to tell others to do or not to do something in efforts to attain the hotel's objectives.

Figure 3.6 provides benchmarks that GMs can use as they organize the distribution of authority within their property.

Delegation

GMs are too busy to do all the work for which they are responsible. Effective managers delegate some work assignments to others. **Delegation** is the process of assigning authority (power) to others to do required work.

HOTEL TERMINOLOGY AT WORK

Delegation: The process of assigning authority (power) to others to enable subordinates to do work that a manager at a higher organizational level would otherwise do.

GMs benefit in several ways as they delegate:

- It allows them to do the most important tasks first.
- It can train employees so they can grow in their jobs.
- It allows more work to be accomplished.
- It improves control because, when effective, delegation focuses on results confirmed through feedback. It does not focus on activities.

When managers delegate, responsibilities are assigned; in turn, those to whom work is delegated are held accountable for the work. **Accountability,** then, flows

Type of Authority	Used By	Example
Advisory	Staff (rather than line) managers	Development of an orientation program for use by all hotel employees
Line	Line managers (in their own departments)	Hiring and firing the employees needed to operate the department
Functional	Line managers (assisting other departments)	Executive housekeeper establishes the schedule for cleaning table linens used by the food and beverage department

FIGURE 3.6 Types of Authority in a Hotel

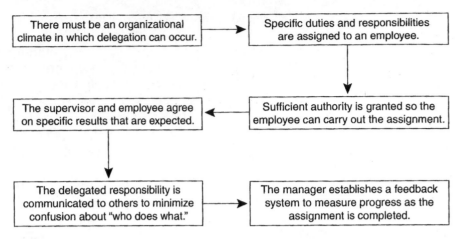

FIGURE 3.7   Steps in Effective Delegation

downward throughout the hotel organization. However, a person who delegates an assignment is still accountable to his or her own manager for performance of the work.

HOTEL TERMINOLOGY AT WORK

Accountability: An obligation created when a person is delegated duties/responsibilities from higher levels of management.

■

What work might be delegated by the GM? Examples include:

- Work that others can do as well as the GM
- Work that is less important than other higher priority tasks
- Work that should be learned by more than one person

Figure 3.7 demonstrates how delegation should be undertaken.

Flow of Communication

GMs must be effective communicators. They must speak and write professionally as they interact with staff members, guests, and others, and their ability to do so is critical. Figure 3.8 illustrates the multidirectional flow of communication required within the hotel itself.

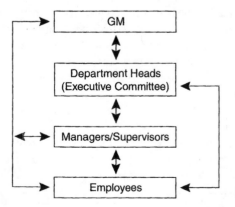

FIGURE 3.8   Multidirectional Communication

When reviewing Figure 3.8, notice that there is vertical communication to and between personnel at each organizational level. Policies, rules, and procedures applicable to all staff members flow through the hotel organization from the GM and department heads to all employees at all organizational levels. Also, staff members receive instructions, such as assignments and work schedules, from their immediate supervisors. Communication, however, also goes up the organization by use of formal communication channels. Examples include on-the-job feedback between staff members and their immediate supervisor and through other opportunities such as performance evaluation sessions, "suggestion boxes," and "open door policies."

In addition to **vertical communication** (up and down the organization) channels, there is also **horizontal communication**. This occurs, for example, when department heads, managers, or supervisors communicate with others at their same organizational level.

HOTEL TERMINOLOGY AT WORK

Vertical Communication: Communication between individuals that flows up and down throughout the organization.

Horizontal Communication: Communication between individuals at the same organizational level.

There is another informal type of communication commonly referred to as the "grapevine." Sometimes called the "rumor mill," informal communication can flow very quickly throughout the hotel and often can be very accurate. Employees may use the grapevine to communicate "politics" and personnel-related topics. Wise GMs "listen" to the grapevine and use it both to assess employee perceptions of the hotel's current events and to know when accurate information required to counter grapevine rumors is needed.

Effective GMs recognize barriers that can prevent or inhibit effective communication. Examples include the impact of distortion as communication flows between organizational levels and the impact of employees who may be anxious about "telling the truth" to supervisors. Jargon (specialized job-related terms) can also leave communication muddled. An example of jargon occurs when a food server says "86" to imply that a menu item is no longer available, and/or a front-desk agent says he is "short" to communicate that the contents of the cash drawer do not match its expected dollar value.

Cultural differences, language barriers, and the hotel environment itself can impact the effectiveness of communication. GMs should be aware of these and related factors and must emphasize the need for feedback from employees. Hotel employees are often very aware of guest perceptions and "challenges" in their work areas and can, if encouraged, share valuable information with their managers.

Information about the hotel's mission statement should be communicated to all staff members because it provides the foundation upon which other planning tools are developed and implemented. How can the mission statement be "communicated" throughout the hotel? Some GMs simply hang a copy on their office wall, place a statement in the preface to the employee handbook, or explain it during new employee orientation sessions. These tactics, however, are far different from "walking the talk" that occurs as managers make frequent reference to the mission and discuss ways to better attain it. Some GMs probably know and actually believe in the mission. However, department heads may have only a vague idea about its content, and its spirit and intent become even more abstract for employees at lower organizational levels. Another all-too-frequent situation arises when entry-level employees are unaware that the hotel even has a mission statement, much less know what it is! Communication in words and actions helps the mission statement's philosophy to be conveyed down and throughout the hotel's organization.

Motivation

The term "**motivation**" refers to an inner drive that a person has to attain a goal.

HOTEL TERMINOLOGY AT WORK

Motivation: An inner drive that a person has to attain a goal.

Poorly motivated staff members do not consistently perform work that meets required quality or quantity standards. Therefore, guest dissatisfaction is likely to result, operating costs are likely to increase, and at some point other, more motivated, employees leave the organization.

The GM is probably in the best position to influence, by words and deeds, how other managers and supervisors within the hotel will treat staff members because he/she most strongly influences the hotel's **corporate culture**. A "pro-employee" philosophy, along with supportive rules, policies, and procedures, helps to recognize the worth and dignity of employees and encourages their active participation as a productive member of the hotel's staff.

HOTEL TERMINOLOGY AT WORK

Corporate Culture: The generally accepted values and shared meanings that help determine how employees in an organization will act.

Figure 3.9 lists numerous no- and low-cost techniques that can be used by hotel managers as they interact with their employees. Use of these and related tactics helps to motivate staff and to retain them.

Strategy 1: Follow Sound Management Advice
Serve first and lead second
Learn your turnover costs
Eliminate workers who won't
Eliminate managers who can't
Manage your guests

Strategy 2: Effective Orientation
Understand the role of starting wages
Inform employees about their total compensation

(continued)

FIGURE 3.9   "Common Sense" Tactics to Motivate Employees

Explain the long-term benefits of staying
Share your vision
Motivate entry-level employees
Conduct an entrance interview
Create career ladders

Strategy 3: Train Correctly
Invest in training
Encourage employees to try your hotel
Train trainers to train
Reward your trainers
Relieve trainers of other job duties
Conduct preshift training

Strategy 4: Manage a Professional Hotel
Strictly enforce a zero-tolerance harassment policy
Create a culturally diverse workforce
Make employee safety a top priority
Ensure reasonable accommodations for disabled employees
Share financial numbers with employees

Strategy 5: Supervise Like You Want to Be Supervised
Enforce "on-time" policies fairly and consistently
Be careful not to overschedule
Give employees a personal copy of their work schedule
Seek out employee assistance programs
Invite "fast-track" employees to attend management meetings
Implement a "catch the employee doing something right" program
Conduct an exit interview with employees who leave

Strategy 6: Encourage Effective Communication
Hold employee-focused meetings for nonmanagement staff
Communicate the benefits of your hotel
Create an employee retention committee
Recognize employee birthdays
Make daily "howdy" rounds

Strategy 7: Manage a Friendly Hotel
Use employee recognition programs
Build a great team and praise it often
Write a personal letter to parents of teenage employees
Share scheduling responsibilities with employees
Reward employees who work on nonscheduled days
Invite family members of new employees to visit your hotel
Make the hotel a fun place to work

Strategy 8: Help Your Employees Succeed
Identify state-approved (licensed) child care options
Help employees learn about public transportation systems
Reward success in each employee
Recognize your employees' elder care responsibilities
Don't punish your best for being good
Stay in touch by going to lunch with hourly and supervisory employees

FIGURE 3.9   *(Continued)*

Leadership

The GM must be a leader. While entire books and whole bookshelves have been devoted to the topic, most successful leaders would agree that an effective leader will:

- Have a good understanding of the hotel's values and be able to translate these values into practice. In other words, the GM implements the mission statement.
- Have an objective and measurable "picture" of the desired future for the hotel.
- Help others develop the knowledge and skills needed to attain the hotel's vision. This is done, in part, through orientation, training, and follow-up **coaching** activities.
- Use the empowerment process to help others move toward the vision by enabling them to use discretion.
- Develop a team of staff members who are committed to the hotel's success.
- Achieve a reputation for consistent quality guest service.
- Cultivate a reputation for fairness and honesty.

HOTEL TERMINOLOGY AT WORK

Coaching: A process whose goal is helping staff members, and the hotel team, reach their highest possible levels of performance.

■

THE INTERNET AT WORK

One of the most popular books about leadership ever written is Stephen Covey's *The Seven Habits of Highly Effective People* published by Simon & Schuster. Amazon.com displays 40+ pages of this popular book at their Web site. To view these pages, go to www.amazon.com. Then, under the "Books" search field, enter the name "Stephen R. Covey."

Discipline

Discipline is one of a manager's most important, but sometimes most uncomfortable, tasks. It refers to specific management actions designed to reinforce desired performance (positive discipline) and to correct or eliminate undesired performance (negative discipline).

HOTEL TERMINOLOGY AT WORK

Discipline: Activities designed to reinforce desired performance (positive discipline) or to correct undesired performance (negative discipline).

■■

Some managers think of discipline only in its negative context: to punish a staff member for doing something wrong. A much better approach is to view discipline as one aspect of the coaching process to help staff members reach for their highest levels

Step 1:	Oral warning (no entry in employee's record).
Step 2:	Oral warning (with entry in employee's record).
Step 3:	Written reprimand (often from a manager at an organizational level above that of the employee's immediate supervisor).
Step 4:	Suspension for a specified number of days.
Step 5:	Discharge from the organization.

FIGURE 3.10   Steps in a Progressive Discipline Process

of performance. Highly motivated employees are much less likely to need negative discipline than are their less-motivated counterparts, and motivating staff is a much more rewarding task than using negative discipline to solve problems.

When negative discipline is required, enlightened GMs use a **progressive discipline** process in which a graduated scale of penalties is applied.

HOTEL TERMINOLOGY AT WORK

Progressive Discipline: A process of negative discipline in which repeated infractions result in an increasingly severe penalty.

Figure 3.10 details typical steps in a progressive discipline program. For discipline to be effective, GMs must:

- Assure that there is a clear communication of expectations. Staff members must truly know what is and is not expected of them.
- Begin the disciplinary process as soon as possible after the problem has occurred.
- Assure that the discipline is similar when the same offense is committed by two or more persons in the same situation.
- Assure that discipline addresses an employee's behavior and not the employee as a person.

TEAM BUILDING TACTICS

Figure 3.3 indicated that contemporary management focuses on teams rather than individual behavior. A **team** is a group of individuals who accomplish mutually agreed-upon goals through cooperation.

HOTEL TERMINOLOGY AT WORK

Team: A group of individuals who place the goals of the group above their own.

Teamwork will only be effective to the extent that it is part of the hotel's culture established in large measure by the GM.

The GM is the leader of the hotel's entire team of staff members. Excellent staff want to work for excellent GMs who care about their team members and do what is possible to help them advance in their careers.

Hotel managers must know and use team-building tactics.

To be a good team leader, the GM must:

- Have high standards and expectations.
- Support individual members of the teams and maintain relationships of trust and respect.
- Practice participative management and solicit input from team members as goals and objectives are established and as plans to achieve them are implemented.
- Demonstrate that their own personal goals, like those of the individual team members, should not be placed before the goals of the team.
- Share credit for the successes that the team achieves.

In the future, GMs may facilitate the work of self-directed teams that have significantly more control over their work responsibilities than do many present-day teams. For example, team members may, within the team, make work assignments, schedule themselves, evaluate each other's work, assign compensation increases, and identify priorities for studying ways to improve the work done by the team. Traditional GMs believe the hotel industry is far from attaining this level of team-led responsibilities. However, there has been, and may well continue to be, an evolution in hotel management toward interaction with teams and away from individual employees.

THE INTERNET AT WORK

Some organizations organize exotic trips, extensive activities and games to help build teamwork among their members. One company that specializes in developing such activities is "Team Builders." To view their Web site and examine their product offerings, go to

www.teambuilding.org

One-on-one interviews are part of the employee selection process.

EMPLOYEE SELECTION, ORIENTATION, AND TRAINING

In today's increasingly cost-conscious lodging environment, it is necessary to maximize the use of people. Staff at all organizational levels must be effectively recruited and selected, appropriately oriented, and properly trained to consistently produce results that meet established standards. Some of these duties may be within the responsibility of the human resources department in larger properties. However, the GM will still be influential and must assure that the methods used are effective. As well, GMs should personally employ these tactics as they interact with department heads and others who report directly to them.

Figure 3.11 reviews procedures that can be helpful as the GM ensures that new employees receive a favorable first impression of the hotel and get off to a good start in their jobs.

Recruitment/Selection Tactics
- Human resources officials, if applicable, interview applicants, before being referred to line department personnel for a second selection interview.
- The department head interviews all applicants for positions within the department.
- The applicant's potential supervisor conducts a preselection interview with the applicant.
- Background checks, including validation of references, are made.
- Tests for job knowledge/skills are administered to applicants for positions in which experience is required.
- Interview discussions about job-related topics including use of "open-ended" questions are used to reveal information relating to job applicants' attitudes.
- Human resources personnel conduct the initial interview of all applicants for supervisory/management positions.

FIGURE 3.11   Personnel Tactics Checklist

- The department head and other interviewers attend special training sessions to learn procedures helpful in questioning applicants during employment prescreening.
- Paperwork that must be signed by new employees is completed with the department head present to show his or her interest in and concern about the new staff member.

General Orientation Tactics

- All new employees participate in a general orientation program conducted, at least in part, by human resources officials.
- Content of the orientation program includes:
  - Overview of the department
  - Detailed explanation of employees' benefits
  - Applicable policies and procedures (including handbook)
  - General guest relations training
  - Safety and security issues
  - Emphasis on teamwork and cooperation
  - Property tour
- Teamwork is addressed through small-group training activities.
- The hotel's mission statement is discussed in detail and is referred to frequently as the orientation program is presented; a copy is provided to employees.
- The concept of a "career—not a job" begins during orientation; new employees can schedule vocational counseling sessions with department personnel at any time.

Departmental (Workstation) Orientation (Induction) Tactics

- New employees receive an introduction to department members (especially peers) and a tour of their workstation.
- New staff members receive a review of department-specific policies/procedures; written information is also provided.
- Employees are assigned to a mentor (who will not be their trainer).
- Employees work in, or observe at least briefly, other related positions that are affected by their work, in efforts to develop teamwork/cooperation.
- A detailed departmental induction checklist helps assure that all employees receive the same basic information about the department.

Train-the-Trainer Tactics

- The department has selected one or more departmental trainer(s).
- Personnel who train have received extensive train-the-trainer information.
- Human resources officials, if applicable, randomly/routinely monitor departmental on-the-job trainers/training.
- Trainers receive ongoing recognition (certificate, promotional priority, and so on) for their training efforts.
- Trainers are relieved of some job duties while training to reduce the pressure to get their own work done first.
- Trainers from each department meet together regularly to learn more about training techniques.
- Training projects (e.g., developing a job breakdown for or conducting a group training session within their department) must be completed before trainers are eligible to conduct on-the-job training.
- Experienced trainers belong to a trainers' club, which meets regularly; trainers receive a certificate of completion when they are certified eligible for training.
- An award (Trainer of the Year) is given for the best trainer.
- A competency test comprised of a videotaped training session evaluated by human resources staff and the GM, among others, is used for all trainers before they are certified to train.
- Employees formally evaluate their on-the-job training/trainer.
- Trainees attending group-training sessions formally evaluate their trainer/training; this information is used by human resources and/or other personnel to counsel trainers about possible improvements.

On-the-Job Training (OJT) Tactics

- A task list noting each task for which training is required is available for each position.
- A job breakdown explaining (a) how each task is to be done and (b) observable standards that must be consistently attained has been developed and is used by the trainer to help teach/evaluate each job task.

FIGURE 3.11   *(Continued)*

- Both the trainer and the trainee sign off after each/all tasks identified in the training task list is/are addressed.
- Employees are encouraged to participate in cross-training (job rotation) activities within and between departments.
- Initial on-the-job training involves observing—not physically performing—required tasks.
- Written materials are available for all identified tasks for which on-the-job training is necessary.
- When applicable, initial tasks for which on-the-job training is required do not involve contact with the guests being served.
- Training manuals based upon departmental operating manuals are used as part of the OJT process.
- A department official visits with each new staff member at least by the end of the first month of employment.
- Entry-level employees receive a certificate of completion when their initial training is successfully completed.
- A detailed training schedule is developed that indicates both the sequence of and completion dates for successful performance of job tasks.
- Employees being trained do not replace employees required for a specific shift; their presence is in addition to the required number of staff members so that standards are not reduced during training.

Supervisory/Other Training Tactics
- Employees nominated by the department head can begin supervisory training before they are promoted to supervisory positions.
- Employees are encouraged to obtain education/training external to the department; a full/partial reimbursement program is in effect.
- Group training about selected, modularized topics is continually available for employees nominated by department officials.
- Nominated employees are allowed to attend selected managers' meetings.
- Qualified employees participate in ad hoc (task force) activities that are an integral part of their planned professional development program.
- A monthly training schedule lists topics and times for generic training and is used by schedule planners to release trainees for required training.
- A promotion test is given after required supervisory training and must be successfully passed before promotion is granted.
- Before being appointed to a supervisory position, those being considered for promotion serve as acting supervisors and receive special guidance/evaluation from an experienced supervisor.

Training Budget
- A list of recommended training activities on a by-employee (position) basis is used to help build the department's annual training schedule and budget.
- A significant amount of the training budget is spent for management training.
- Funds for the annual training budget are driven by a specified percentage of payroll or another objective formula.
- *All* employees receive some training for which funds are budgeted each year.

Other Training Issues
- Employees formally evaluate their supervisors.
- Career development planning is available for staff at midlevel management positions and above.
- A promotion track has been developed that suggests advancement opportunities for personnel in specific positions.
- Some career planning is done during formal performance appraisal sessions.
- Extensive training about the department's goals and limits of employee discretion precede empowerment and/or delegation activities.
- Managers understand the importance of role modeling: they act the way they desire their employees to act!
- Performance appraisal addresses the extent to which career development goals made at the previous performance appraisal sessions have been attained.
- General staff meetings are held for all employees.
- Employee reward programs are in place to motivate employees.
- Exit interviews given to department staff address, in part, training activities.
- Group training (especially involving employees from more than one department) is scheduled during times of slow business volume and at slow shift times, when possible.
- The facility offers afterwork activities (special interest groups) to help facilitate socialization (teamwork).

FIGURE 3.11 *(Continued)*

- The department maintains a library of professional books, magazines, videotapes, and so forth, which are loaned to employees for professional development and personal enjoyment purposes.
- Before new employees are granted permanent employee status, they must be interviewed by the department head and department trainer and are given paper/pencil tests addressing training topics.
- Recognizing that training never ends, training opportunities are constantly available for all position-competent employees in the department.
- A formal empowerment training program is conducted for all employees.
- An internship program is available for selected entry-level employees to be trained for fast progression into supervisory (and higher) positions.
- Each department head is responsible for conducting some group training programs on a regular basis.
- An official from each department randomly/routinely attends training sessions conducted throughout the department.
- Information from employee performance appraisals relative to training needs is accumulated by each department and is used in planning generic training programs for the next year.
- The department's mission statement is translated into training objectives and is broken down into small parts, and each part is addressed each year in planned training programs.

From Jack Ninemeier, "Training Strategies in a World-Class Asian Hotel: Relevance to the United States Lodging Industry." *Hospitality and Tourism Educator 7*, no. 4 (Fall 1995).

FIGURE 3.11   *(Continued)*

THE GM AND QUALITY GUEST SERVICE

The concepts of **quality** and **service** are widely discussed in the world of hotel management today. Unfortunately, it is much easier to talk about the terms than it is to effectively implement the underlying philosophy and to maintain it within a lodging property. Concerns about quality and service should be integral to the hotel's corporate culture, and the emphasis must begin with the GM.

Hotel employees such as bell persons must ensure that they consistently please guests.

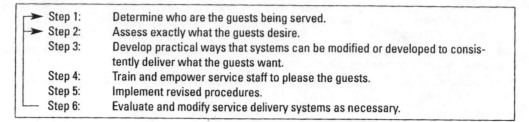

Step 1:	Determine who are the guests being served.	
Step 2:	Assess exactly what the guests desire.	
Step 3:	Develop practical ways that systems can be modified or developed to consistently deliver what the guests want.	
Step 4:	Train and empower service staff to please the guests.	
Step 5:	Implement revised procedures.	
Step 6:	Evaluate and modify service delivery systems as necessary.	

FIGURE 3.12   Steps in Developing Quality Service Delivery Systems

HOTEL TERMINOLOGY AT WORK

Quality: The consistent delivery of products and services according to expected standards.

Service: The process of helping guests by addressing their wants and needs with respect and dignity in a timely manner.

■

Guests who rent a room or purchase a meal or service want to receive an expected standard of service as part of what they are paying for. Increasingly, guests are willing to pay more as they visit hotels that offer products and services that meet or exceed their expectations. The perceived level of service quality is an important factor in the total experience that guests receive during their visit to the hotel.

Ingredients in a Quality Service Delivery System

The hotel industry's emphasis on quality is not just a fad that will go away. It requires a dramatic change in attitude about the need to focus on the guests and to use what is learned to reconsider how the operation should work. There are six ingredients in a process that can be used to develop and implement a quality service system, and these are reviewed in Figure 3.12.[2]

Let's look at each of these steps that can be used to develop quality service delivery.

Step 1:   Determine who are the guests being served. Some hotels serve a narrow range of guests. Consider, for example, a small rooms-only lodging property with a strategic location next to a busy interchange on an interstate highway. Most of its guests probably want the same thing: a relatively inexpensive, safe, and clean sleeping room at a price representing a value to the travelers. By contrast, a downtown hotel may serve business guests during the week and other guests visiting the downtown area for shopping and recreation during the weekend. It is important that the GM and his/her management team know as much as possible about the guests being served.

Step 2:   Assess exactly what the guests desire. Routine questioning can be used to determine guests' wants and needs. These and related questions can be posed to guests by managers as they interact with guests and/or by a simple questionnaire (comment card) left in the room.

---

[2]Except where noted, this section is adapted from: Jack Ninemeier and Joe Perdue. *Hospitality Operations: Careers in the World's Most Exciting Industry.* Upper Saddle River, NJ. Pearson Education, 2005 (see Chapter 2).

Every hospitality manager has another way to collect information about the guests: they can ask the employees. It is ironic but true that, many times, line-level employees know more about the likes and dislikes of guests than do their supervisors or perhaps even department heads and the GM. These staff members frequently have more of guest contact than do any other hotel employees. Consider, for example, guests complaining about long lines at time of check-in to a front-desk clerk or a food server receiving compliments (or complaints!) about food in the hotel's dining room. Want to know what the guests desire: ask the employees who provide the products and services to them.

Step 3:   Develop practical ways that systems can be modified or developed to consistently deliver what the guests want. Two of the best ways to make procedures more guest friendly are to **benchmark** and to use **cross-functional teams** of employees. Benchmarking is the process of understanding exactly how one's own organization does something and, additionally, determining how it is done by the competition. If, for example, guests desire fast check-in (and most guests do!), it is important to determine what the property currently does and what other properties do to minimize guest check-in times.

HOTEL TERMINOLOGY AT WORK

Benchmark: The search for best practices and an understanding about how they are achieved in efforts to determine how well the hotel is doing.

Cross-Functional Team: A group of employees from different departments within the hotel who works together to resolve operating problems.

■

Wise GMs know the benefit of asking employees for advice about ways to improve a work method. Cross-functional teams are comprised of staff members from several departments who meet, brainstorm, and consider ways to improve work methods. (Consider a more traditional alternative of using employees from the same department to address a problem: hotel dining room staff addressing a slow service problem may well conclude that the problem does not rest with them; it is caused by the cooks! Alternatively, if employees from the dining room, food production, and even housekeeping departments address the problem, creative ideas not limited to "how we have always done things" might be generated.)

Step 4:   Train and empower service staff to please the guests. New work methods require, at the least, changes in how work is done. New or additional tools or equipment may also be necessary. Staff members must be trained in revised work tasks, but they must also be empowered to make decisions about any unique needs of the guests being served. You have learned that empowerment is the act of granting authority to employees to make key decisions within the employees' areas of responsibility. For example, front-desk agents have a primary responsibility to please the guests with whom they interact. They should have some discretion about how this is to be done as they interact with guests with differing wants, needs, and expectations. Before staff members can be empowered, they must be trained and provided with the tools and other resources needed to do their jobs.

Step 5:   Implement revised procedures. Implementation does not always need to be on an "all or nothing" basis. Perhaps, for example, employees working on specific floors in a hotel could apply new work methods to test and further refine, if necessary, more guest-friendly processes before they are "rolled out" to the entire property.

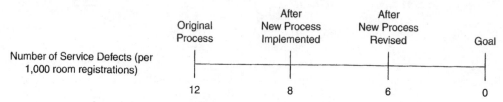

FIGURE 3.13   Counting Defects to Evaluate Service Processes

Step 6:   Evaluate and modify service delivery systems as necessary. Over time, guest preferences may (and are likely to) change. Technologies will evolve, as will, perhaps, new or improved work methods. These can affect what guests desire and/or how products or services can be most effectively delivered.

One method to keep up with changing guest perceptions about service is to measure defects against the goal of meeting service standards at all times. The next section will introduce this concept.

A Goal of Zero Defects

Every hotel GM would like to enjoy **zero defects** in every process used to deliver guest service.[3]

HOTEL TERMINOLOGY AT WORK

Zero Defects: A goal of no guest-related complaints that is established when guest service processes are implemented.

As explained above, guests' needs and concerns are addressed when processes are developed. Therefore, an ongoing measurement of guest responses to the process can provide information about how well the process satisfies guests.

Figure 3.13 provides an overview of how the measurement (count) of defects helps to evaluate a process.

This figure shows that input from guests during a recent period of analysis suggested there were approximately 12 service complaints about the guest registration process per 1,000 rooms rented.

Assume that this defect rate is judged excessive (after all, the GM desires a zero defect rate), and a new process is implemented. Ongoing assessment then determines that the problems were reduced to approximately 8 service defects per 1,000 rooms registered. Some GMs would likely believe this reduction in complaints was significant (and it is!) and would look elsewhere to determine how, if at all, guests could be better served. They might continue to evaluate the registration process because it was identified on the guest comment card or other survey system in use. However, they might discount registration service concerns noted with the thought that "the process has already been improved, and there is nothing more that can be done."

---

[3]The remainder of this section is adapted from: David Hayes and Jack Ninemeier. *Professional Front Office Management*. Upper Saddle River, NJ. Pearson Education, 2007.

By contrast, a GM with a zero defect goal will continue to pay serious attention to ways that the new registration process can be further revised, especially if analysis of other processes indicates more defects for registration than for other service delivery processes. Figure 3.13 notes that further revisions in the registration process were implemented and have reduced the defect rate still further (to 6 service defects per 1,000 rooms rented).

The process of analyzing defects with the goal of eliminating them should be ongoing and will help the GM and his/her management team to move further along the journey toward quality service (zero defects).

Some observers may question the use of a zero defect goal since it is not reasonably attainable. Isn't it likely that, if 200 guests are checked in on an "average" day, defects will sometimes occur even in the best-managed front-office department using the very best registration procedures? If a goal is not attainable, won't that lead to frustration and stress? In fact, improvement efforts should be judged successful; there has been a reduction in the number of defects from 12 to 6 per 1,000 rooms!

In this case, affected staff should be rewarded for their efforts to reduce the number of defects during guest registration. A challenge: How can the defect rate be lowered from less than the current 6 defects per 1,000 rooms? Ongoing efforts may yield still fewer defects and improved guest comment scores.

GM INTERACTIONS

Every day is different for hotel GMs. This is one attraction of the job because the work is never boring. On the other hand, it can also bring surprises—both pleasant and not-so-pleasant!

The responsibilities of a GM are diverse. No textbook or course (or even postsecondary school curriculum!) can completely prepare you for your career as a GM. Let's explore examples of what GMs do by looking at a monthly professional "diary" and by reviewing typical interactions with employees and guests.

GM's Monthly "Diary"

A GMs daily activities vary from day-to-day and month-to-month as well as from property-to-property. The tasks involved in managing a hotel are numerous. Some, such as daily involvement in guest relations, are visible. Others, such as emotionally supporting a key department head who is implementing an important, but potentially unpopular, hotel policy, are much less noticeable.

Much of the GM's job involves the day-to-day management of the hotel property. The following entries in a GM's diary suggest the range of activities that may be encountered in a typical month:

Day 1:   Conduct an all-employee meeting; explain changes in health insurance benefits. Submit a ninety-day room revenue reforecast to the hotel's owner.

Day 2:   Review previous month's income statement with the controller. Contact bank branch president to review hotel bank statement mailings schedule changes.

Day 3:   Lunch with director of sales and marketing and potential high-volume client in hotel's dining room after the director's sales presentation.

Day 4:   Prepare owner's month-end revenue and expense recap report for prior month.

Day 5:   Attend franchiser's co-op advertising meeting to discuss recommendations about the next fiscal quarter's advertisement placements.

Day 6:   Attend the mayor's gala fund-raising dinner at the convention center.

Day 7:   OFF (but makes one call to and takes two calls from hotel staff).

Day 8:   Review prior meeting's minutes and attend the property's safety committee meeting. Review all department heads' quarterly staff wage increase recommendations.

Day 9:   Conduct weekly room inspections with executive housekeeper and supervisors. Meet with food and beverage director to review bids from new linen supplier.

Day 10:   Accept award from city council for chairing community beautification committee (breakfast).

Day 11:   Meeting with front-office manager; telephone call to long-distance calls vendor to discuss new contract as well as interstate, intrastate, and international long-distance phone rates.

Day 12:   Work half-day (review month's trade journals); OFF half-day.

Day 13:   Serve as property manager on duty (MOD).

Day 14:   OFF (only one call from a department head!).

Day 15:   Begin work on developing long-range plans resulting in a capital improvement budget to be used in the next fiscal year.

Day 16:   Meet with the hotel's insurance company representative to review hotel swimming pool policies and safety procedures. Review disputed invoice from furniture vendor related to poor product quality.

Day 17:   Proof proposed new menu copy; taste test new menu items with director of food and beverage and chef.

Day 18:   Attend chamber of commerce member mixer (evening reception).

Day 19:   Review monthly employee turnover statistics with human resources director; evaluate annual community salary survey results.

Day 20:   OFF (golf vacation out of state; no telephone contact).

Day 21:   OFF (see day 20).

Day 22:   Meet with the city fire marshal and hotel's chief engineer to review the first draft of the safety/evacuation portion of the hotel's emergency plan.

Day 23:   Inspect boiler area as well as heating, cooling units with city building inspector.

Day 24:   Weekly executive committee staff meeting to choose employee of the month and review upcoming convention meetings schedule.

Day 25:   OFF (but come to office because of some forgotten "paperwork").

Day 26:   Review previous results and prepare documentation for next week's quality review (inspection) by franchisor.

Day 27:   Present employee of the month award to staff member.

Day 28:   Attend Hotel and Lodging Association luncheon.

Day 29: Attend sales and marketing client appreciation reception and dinner.

Day 30: OFF.

Day 31: Meet with the director of sales and marketing and sales team to review Smith Travel Research (Star) reports.

When reviewing these activities, you should note that the daily entries only record one or two unique activities for each date. In fact, the GM is on duty eight or more hours daily and is often on call even when not on the property.

The schedule above indicates that the GM is off work for six-and-a-half days during the thirty-one-day period. Many hold a stereotype of a hotel GM who works very long hours and with very few days off. Unfortunately, in the past, this has been true in many properties and hotel organizations. Increasingly, however, employers recognize that the position of GM must be competitive with other employment options. Although there are "peaks and valleys" of busy and slow times, and although there may be some work duties such as telephone calls on days off, today's GMs enjoy a shorter work week than did their counterparts in the past. Successful GMs enjoy their work, but they must have an appropriate amount of time away from the job for rest and relaxation. They cannot work themselves to exhaustion! Those who do so demonstrate a lack of managerial ability or reflect unrealistic expectations on the part of the hotel's ownership.

Employee and Guest Relationships

Effective GMs are good "people persons." They enjoy interacting with employees, guests, and others. These activities are a significant factor in their level of job satisfaction. The range of potential interactions is broad and results in very rewarding but sometimes discouraging or even unpleasant experiences. Even the most seasoned GMs will be confronted with an interpersonal experience unlike any they have ever encountered. Figures 3.14 and 3.15 illustrate examples of these positive and negative experiences that GMs may encounter.

Fortunately, there are many more positive than negative interactions with the hotel's employees and guests. The job of the GM is often not easy, but it is always challenging and rewarding.

Positive Examples	Negative Examples
Daily conversations with long-term staff members	Disciplining or terminating staff members
Learning suggestions about possible operating improvements from employees	Confronting staff members known to be stealing
Welcoming new staff members to the team	Learning about illegal acts committed off-property by staff members
Congratulating personnel about significant events in their/their families' lives	Assigning work responsibilities to cover "no-show" employees
Mentoring younger workers	Discovering employee "sabotage"
Following the careers of employees as they are promoted within the hotel organization and industry	Supervising employees who consistently violate the hotel's policies/rules and personnel requirements
Providing non-job-related advice when requested	Comforting an employee whose only child has passed away
Observing staff members who participate in community organizations/activities	Explaining to a staff member why they did not get a promotion they sought
Observing employees at a company picnic enjoying themselves	Observing an intoxicated employee attempting to come to work

FIGURE 3.14   Possible Interactions with Employees

Positive Examples	Negative Examples
Interacting with frequent guests	Interacting with police called to the hotel for disturbances and/or illegal guest activities
Receiving spontaneous "thank you notes" from happy guests	Guest deaths in sleeping rooms or in the hotel's public spaces
Observing guests celebrate significant family or professional occasions in the hotel	Dealing with obviously and visibly intoxicated guests
Providing assistance (service) to guests who require it	Preventing on-site prostitution activities
Receiving guest input about hospitable staff members	Discovering overt guest room damage
Receiving input from guests who genuinely want the hotel to be successful	Preventing guest theft of money, products, and/or services from the hotel
Interacting with guests as peers at community/professional meetings	Preventing property vandalism
Providing accommodations to grateful guests stranded by adverse travel conditions	Calming irate guests stranded by adverse travel conditions

FIGURE 3.15   Possible Interactions with Guests

MANAGERS AT WORK

"It's in his car," said the room attendant. "I saw him take the television set out of his room and put it in his car trunk. He didn't see me. I'm in a nearby guest room and immediately called you."

The call was placed to the front-desk clerk who transferred it to J.D. Ojisama, the hotel's GM.

By the time J.D. arrived in the wing of the hotel where the room with the stolen television set was located, the guest had already left. "What happened? What did you see?" asked J.D.

"Well, I saw Mr. Dolcifino just as he was going through the exit door carrying a television set. That's when I went back into the room I was cleaning and called the front desk."

"How do you know it was Mr. Dolcifino?" asked J.D.

"I've seen Mr. Dolcifino many times. He stays here at least a couple of times per month. Besides, he reminds me of a guy I know . . . . It was him for sure."

A review of front-desk records indicated that, in fact, Mr. Dolcifino had stayed at the hotel the previous evening.

However, he did not stay in the room from which the television was missing. In fact, his room was in another wing and on another floor.

What should J.D. do now? What, if any, difference does it make if Mr. Dolcifino is a frequent guest? Should the police be called in response to this (alleged) guest theft? How would J.D. ensure that the staff member reporting the theft was not involved? How would knowing as much as he could about the hotel's security policies and procedures help J.D. respond in the best manner possible?

HOTEL TERMINOLOGY AT WORK GLOSSARY

The following terms were defined within this chapter. If you are not familiar with each of them, please review the segment of the chapter that contains the term.

Human relations	Unity of command	Coaching
Empowerment	Span of control	Discipline
Reengineering	Authority	Progressive discipline
Strategy	Delegation	Team
Tactic	Accountability	Quality
ROI	Vertical communication	Service
Programmed decisions	Horizontal communication	Benchmark
Nonprogrammed decisions	Motivation	Cross-functional team
Ethics	Corporate culture	Zero defects

ISSUES AT WORK

1. This chapter has established that the GM needs conceptual, interpersonal administrative, and technical skills to be effective. It also provides an example of each type of skill. What are three additional examples of each type of skill? How can a GM increase his or her skills in each of these areas? Which type of skill do you believe is the most important? Why? Which type of skill, if any, is the least important? Why?

2. There has been an evolution of hotel human resources practices from the GM as "boss" to the GM as a facilitator and/or team leader. Why has this occurred? Will this trend continue? Explain why you believe it will or will not.

3. There are several types of authority in a hotel: advisory, line, and functional. What are some examples of advisory authority? What can you as a GM do to assure that line and staff personnel recognize their responsibilities and the limitations involved when this type of power is used? Functional authority was also defined. What are examples of functional authority between departments? How, if at all, does a GM help to assure that there are clear distinctions about duties and responsibilities as functional authority within the hotel is established?

4. GMs do not have enough time to do all the work required of them. Some tasks simply must be delegated. What are three specific things you could do when delegating work to subordinates to help ensure they do not think you are "dumping" additional work onto them? If employees are already busy with assigned tasks (and every staff member should be!), how can you explain to staff members that you expect them to do all of their current work and, in addition, take on the newly delegated work?

5. Motivation has been defined as "an inner drive that a person has to attain a goal." If this is the case, how can a GM "motivate" an employee? What motivates you? To what extent do you think a motivated employee will be more likely to remain with the property than an unmotivated counterpart? How could you discover what motivates an employee? Do you think the goals that motivate people change over time?

4

Human Resources

This Chapter at Work

Hotel organizations are very labor intensive. People, in addition to machines, are needed to perform many of the tasks yielding the delivery of quality products and services for the hotel's guests. Employees at all organizational levels must be recruited and trained to consistently perform their jobs well if guests are to come back and if the hotel is to gain a reputation for providing quality service. GMs must know about and assume numerous human resources responsibilities to ensure that the staff members employed by the hotel are truly the best they can be.

In this chapter, you will learn how human resources activities facilitate the work done by hotel employees. In addition to employee orientation, training and professional development, performance evaluations, safety and benefit issues, governmental regulation compliance, and many other concerns must be addressed. Large hotels typically employ one or more persons to administer these human resources–related responsibilities and to assist line-operating managers with employee-related issues. Smaller properties decentralize the process (e.g., department heads may "hire and fire"). However,

responsibilities for personnel record keeping and implementation of applicable laws and regulations must still rest with someone, and this person is typically the GM.

Employee-related legal issues can drastically impact the workplace. In this chapter you will learn about those that are most important. In addition, you will discover the process by which a hotel undertakes the recruitment, selection, orientation, training, and evaluation of staff.

Another important human resources function involves planning for future staff needs. This may involve either staff size increases or decreases. In addition, employees' safety and health concerns are critical. The GM and all managers and supervisors must be advocates dedicated to helping ensure safe and healthy working conditions for all employees.

Other important human resources functions include the development of programs that help improve the quality of the workforce and its work output. These efforts are vitally important to the success of the staff and to your performance as the hotel's GM.

Chapter 4 Outline

THE ROLE OF HUMAN RESOURCES

Good managers in every department in the hotel care about their own employees. In a well-run large hotel, specialists in the human resources department assist departmental managers with concerns relating to recruitment, selection, orientation, training, performance evaluation, compensation, labor relations, safety and health, legal, and a wide range of other specialized tasks.

In years past, the term *personnel* or *personnel management* was the name given to describe the human resources function. Regardless of the term used, however, there are many important activities required to support all staff members in the hotel's operating departments. Some, such as involvement in getting paychecks to workers, are very visible; others, such as filing required paperwork with governmental agencies, go on "behind the scenes" of the hotel's day-to-day operations.

Hotels of any size cannot be successful unless human resources activities are properly attended to. In most limited-service and smaller full-service hotels, the GM and perhaps one additional full- or part-time staff person is responsible for the administration of the **HR** functions. In properties larger than 300–350 rooms, many HR activities may be undertaken by a full-time director. As the number of rooms increase, additional staff members may be added to the HR department.

HOTEL TERMINOLOGY AT WORK

HR: Short for human resources; for example, "When is HR going to distribute the results of the turnover study?"

Regardless of the hotel's size, department heads and supervisors in some properties misunderstand the HR function. This can be seen by the type of manager's comments about HR that can commonly be heard, including:

"Our work would be much easier if only those HR people would send us better applicants."

"How in the world did this guy (or girl) pass the HR screening?"

"We're busy serving guests and putting out fires—it's the job of the HR department to train our employees!"

"Who do those HR people think they are, believing that they can train my employees? What do they know about our area?"

"I wish the HR department would do something to motivate my employees!"

"We just don't have enough staff members. Why doesn't the HR department send us more people?"

"We're doing all the work around here. What does the HR department do? All they can do is give us more paperwork."

These and related concerns suggest the unfortunate relationship that sometimes exists between HR and other operating departments in the hotel. The GM must work hard to prevent this from occurring. Throughout this book we have noted that a hotel is a very labor-intensive operation. Most of a hotel's work must be done by and through people. A successful hotel, like any other service organization, must treat all staff members like the important resource they can become, even if all members of the staff are not yet achieving all that they can.

HR activities in larger hotels are actually performed by two groups of staff members. The first group consists of the operating managers in line departments and the second consists of the specialist(s) in the HR department. GMs must understand these split responsibilities and assure that their staff does as well.

Activities of line managers include making the final employee selection decision, providing some departmental-specific orientation, and initiating ongoing training. They must also undertake numerous supervision activities, including performance appraisal, scheduling, and discipline. HR specialists help managers and supervisors with these and many other HR-related activities that otherwise would not get done, or possibly might not be performed properly or legally. You can begin to see, then, why managers in small hotels must be generalists and know much about many relatively specialized disciplines.

Because HR is both a line and staff function, conflict sometimes occurs between line managers and their HR counterparts. This can be caused by confusion about the boundaries of authority. For example, the question of who determines the content of new employee orientation programs may arise. Conflicts of this type, however, can be rather easily resolved if the GM clearly defines the role of the HR department. When that happens, the HR department becomes a true asset to line managers. Examples of ways that HR personnel assist in the overall operation of the hotel include:

- Implementing policies and tactics to effectively recruit, select, motivate, and retain the most qualified management and nonmanagement staff members.
- Developing and delivering orientation, safety, security, supervisory, and some departmental-specific training programs.
- Developing and communicating equitable and fair HR policies to all employees while protecting the rights of the hotel.
- Interpreting, implementing, and enforcing the ever-increasing body of laws and regulations that affect people at work.
- Helping to maintain appropriate standards of work-life quality and ethical business policies and practices.

Recall that each of these activities must be done in all properties of all sizes. Without an HR department, these and related responsibilities become part of the job of each department head, manager, and/or supervisor. Then it is the GM's responsibility to train these leaders and to provide the necessary resources to assure that HR activities are effective and legal.

The HR department does not unilaterally develop policies and mandate "how things should be done" relative to the management of employees. Rather, it has an important role to play in working closely with all employees of the hotel. This includes those who are managers and those who are not. When an HR department is successful, the chances the hotel will be successful increase greatly.

STAFFING THE HUMAN RESOURCES DEPARTMENT

In most cases, the HR director reports directly to the GM. In larger hotels, the director may have one or more professional assistants to do interviewing, personnel records management, and other tasks; the director may also have an associate to perform word

---

JOB TITLE: HR DIRECTOR

General Job Description:
Performs responsible administrative work managing the HR of the hotel. Responsibilities involve the planning and administration of an HR program that includes recruitment, selection, evaluation, promotion, and other change of status of all employees. Must also develop and implement a system of communication to provide necessary information to staff. Works under general supervision. Exercises initiative and independent judgment when performing assigned tasks.

Job Activities:
- Participates in overall planning and policy making to yield effective and consistent HR services.
- Communicates applicable policies through all organizational levels by use of bulletins, meetings, and personal contact
- Interviews applicants, evaluates qualifications, and classifies applications.
- Recruits and screens applicants to fill vacancies.
- Reviews applications of qualified persons.
- Meets with departmental managers and supervisors on personnel-related matters, including hiring, retention, or release of probationary employees, transfers, demotions, and dismissals of permanent employees.
- Develops and delivers orientation and training activities and coordinates these activities with managers in all departments.
- Establishes and maintains an effective performance appraisal system and assists departmental supervisors in making employee evaluations.
- Maintains employee personnel files.
- Supervises staff employees in the HR department directly and through subordinates.
- Performs related work and undertakes special HR projects as assigned.

General Qualifications (Job Specifications):
Should have considerable experience in area of HR management and administration.
Preferred Education:
Graduation from a four-year college or university with major work in human resources, business administration, hospitality management, or related field.
Knowledge and Skills:
Considerable knowledge of principles and practices of HR management.
Basic word processing and spreadsheet development skills highly desirable.
Responsibility:
Supervises HR professional and supportive staff.

FIGURE 4.1   Job Description of a Human Resource Director

processing, filing, and other clerical duties. Regardless of the specific staffing levels, however, the tasks related to HR must be completed. Typical tasks are identified in Figure 4.1.

When reviewing this figure, note that the terms **job description** and **job specification** are used.

HOTEL TERMINOLOGY AT WORK

Job Description: A list of tasks that an employee working in a specific position must be able to effectively perform.

Job Specification: A list of the personal qualities judged necessary for successful performance of the tasks required by the job description.

The job description in Figure 4.1 suggests the very broad range of tasks that must be performed by the HR director. Like all department heads, this individual is typically a member of the hotel's EOC.

The job specification noted in Figure 4.1 provides some general suggestions about the knowledge and skills necessary for a successful HR director. Some industry observers believe that a working background in HR leading to increasingly more responsible positions in larger hotels provides a good background. Still others think that the "best" HR directors have "come up through the ranks" by working in several operating departments. The manager with this experience is thought to have a better perspective about the work done in the departments and the type of employees most likely to succeed in them. In fact, there is probably no one best background for an HR director. Regardless of the person selected for the job, the GM must have trust in the director, value his or her opinions, and envision that person as a true partner in the hotel's success.

LEGAL ASPECTS OF HUMAN RESOURCES

There are numerous legal matters that impact hotel employees. These change rapidly. GMs and their management teams that do not pay attention to the law are likely to spend much of their time involved in employee-related disputes, grievances, and lawsuits that distract the hotel from its goal of serving guests. There are several legal areas of HR that must be understood by HR directors as well as GMs and line managers who must implement policies and procedures that are in compliance with the law.

Employee Selection

The importance of job descriptions was noted earlier. These tools are also important because they help to confirm that job requirements were established prior to making employee selection decisions. The job specification, then, is driven by tasks identified in the job description. It logically (not arbitrarily) identifies a candidate's job qualifications.

Job specifications must address **bonafied occupational qualifications (BOQs)**.

HOTEL TERMINOLOGY AT WORK

Bonafied Occupational Qualifications (BOQs): Qualifications to perform a job that are judged reasonably necessary to safely or adequately perform all tasks within the job.

Competent GMs carefully review all job descriptions to assure that they list only BOQs that are truly legitimate and that do not unfairly or illegally screen out qualified candidates. Legitimate BOQs include:

- Education or certification requirements
- Language skills
- Previous experience
- Minimum age requirements (for jobs such as waitress or bartender)
- Physical attributes needed for a job including amounts to be lifted and carried, or the need to stand for long periods or walk long distances
- Licensing

- Demographic information (such as name, address, dates available for work, and social security number)
- Employment history
- Educational background and skills
- Criminal history and pending criminal charges
- Employment status/authorization
- References
- Drug/background testing and authorizations

FIGURE 4.2   Information Permitted on Employment Applications

It is important to realize that a legitimate BOQ cannot be used inappropriately to illegally deny employment opportunities to a candidate. For example, a food and beverage manager who prefers to hire male servers cannot list as a BOQ "must be able to lift fifty pounds" to unfairly discriminate against females, because service staff typically do not have to lift items of that weight. On the other hand, a manager in the maintenance department may specify that lifting furniture weighing fifty pounds is a BOQ for a specific job in that department.

In addition to proper job specifications, there are laws that impact many of the tools used to screen employee applicants as part of the selection process including:

- *Applications.* Applicants should only be required to provide data about their name, address, work experience, and other information directly related to the job for which they are applying. (*Note:* Proposed application forms should be reviewed by a qualified attorney to assure that they are in compliance with applicable federal and/or state laws.) Figure 4.2 lists the type of data permitted on a hotel's employment application form.

THE INTERNET AT WORK

For a free, downloadable copy of a "legal" application form related to the hospitality industry, go to

www.hospitalitylawyer.com

This helpful site, operated by Stephen Barth, an attorney for hospitality companies, is an excellent source of legal information related to HR and employment issues.

- *Interviews.* It is important that questions asked of job applicants be written down to help assure that all applicants are asked the same issues. Questions should not be designed to screen out any class of applicants and should be directly related to judging the applicant's competence for the job. Questions about race, religion, and physical traits (height and weight) should not be asked. Questions of age can be asked only to the extent that they relate to the hotel's legal requirements. For example, it is certainly legal to ask, in a state where bar wait staff must be eighteen or older to serve alcohol, if an applicant for a cocktail server's job is "over eighteen."
- *Testing.* Some hotels use skill, psychological, and/or drug screening tests. While pre-employment drug testing is allowed in most states, there are typically strict guidelines that must be followed when it is implemented. These

must be known and consistently followed, and GMs should be familiar with their state's requirements if drug screening or testing is done.

- *Background Checks.* The only information to be sought should be that directly applicable to the position for which an applicant is applying. A consent form authorizing a background check should be signed by the applicant before background checks are made.

- *References.* As with background checks, the applicant's permission to check references should be obtained in writing. In addition, a GM's hotel should never provide information about a previous employee without having received a copy of that person's signed release. Even then, many hotels prefer not to divulge information about past employees other than their name and dates of employment.

There are numerous laws and regulations that affect a hotel's employee selection process. The Federal Civil Rights Act of 1964 did many things, one of which was to form the Equal Employment Opportunity Commission (EEOC) to administer and enforce laws relating to employment. Under federal law, hoteliers and other employers with fifteen or more staff members, who are engaged in **interstate commerce**, cannot discriminate against employees or others on the basis of race, color, religion, sex, or national origin.

HOTEL TERMINOLOGY AT WORK

Interstate Commerce: The commercial trading or transportation of people or property that occurs between and/or among states.

■

In addition, many states have specific civil rights laws that address or prohibit discrimination. As a result, GMs may encounter state antidiscrimination laws that include categories such as marital status, arrest records, or sexual orientation during their career.

Another example of a law affecting hotel staffing practices is the Americans with Disabilities Act (ADA). Enacted in 1990, it prohibits discrimination against persons with disabilities who are seeking employment. The ADA does not require the employment of an applicant who is not qualified to perform necessary work. It does, however, prohibit the elimination of applicants simply because they have disabilities covered by the act. In some situations, the hotel may be required to make a reasonable accommodation to enable a disabled staff member to perform the job. For example, perhaps modifications could be easily made to a front-desk area that would enable a front-desk clerk in a wheelchair to perform necessary guest check-in and check-out duties.

The Age Discrimination in Employment Act (ADEA) applies to employers with 20 or more staff members and protects individuals forty years of age or older from employment discrimination based on age. Of course, this law affects staffing decisions also.

Competent GMs and their management staff know that, before a qualified applicant can be selected, it is necessary to determine that the potential employee is legally allowed to accept the position. This involves verification of work eligibility and compliance with applicable child labor laws. The Immigration Reform and Control

Act (IRCA) of 1986 prohibits employers from knowingly hiring illegal persons to work in the United States. All employers, including hoteliers, must verify that staff members who are hired are legally authorized to work in the United States. A Form 1-I developed by the Department of Immigration and Naturalization Services (INS) must be completed. Applicants must present one or more of several approved documents to establish eligibility for employment:

- Social Security card
- Original/certified copy of birth certificate
- Unexpired INS employment authorization
- Unexpired reentry permit
- Unexpired refugee travel document
- Birth certificate issued by the Department of State
- Certificate of Birth abroad issued by the Department of State
- U.S. citizen identification
- Native American tribal document
- Identification used by resident citizen in United States

The Fair Labor Standards Act (FLSA) passed in 1938 protects young workers from employment that interferes with their education and/or that is potentially hazardous to their health or well-being. Persons ages sixteen and seventeen can work for unlimited hours at any time in jobs if the U.S. secretary of labor has declared that the jobs are not hazardous. Youths aged 14–15 may work in selected jobs during nonschool hours under specified conditions.

Hotel managers must comply with youth employment provisions of the FLSA. Figure 4.3 shows part of a self-assessment tool developed by the U.S. Department of Labor that identifies common problems that must be addressed as young employees work at hospitality properties including hotels.

THE INTERNET AT WORK

To review information about some of the laws that affect the employee selection process, you can use the Internet.:

Civil Rights Act of 1964 (Equal Employment Opportunity Commission [EEOC]): www.eeoc.gov
Americans with Disabilities Act (ADA): www.usdoj.gov/crt/ada/adahom1.htm
Age Discrimination in Employment Act (ADEA): www.eeoc.gov/types/age.html
Immigration Reform and Control Act (IRCA): www.usda.gov
(Then type "IRCA" in the search box for the Web site.)
Fair Labor Standards Act (FLSA): www.dol.gov/elaws/flsa.htm

As seen in the above discussion, there are many laws that impact employee staffing decisions made by hoteliers. There can also be other, perhaps more strict, state and/or local laws and regulations. Unfortunately, legal restraints do change, can be open to interpretation, and may have serious consequences for noncompliance. The GM must interact with the HR director and other knowledgeable professionals to help ensure those employee selection procedures, as well as all other HR practices, are legal and defensible. It is equally important to train and monitor the actions of managers and supervisors who direct the work of employees.

	Yes	No
Do Any Workers Under 18 Years of Age Do the Following:		
1. Operate or clean power-driven meat slicers or other meat processing machines?	☐	☐
2. Operate or clean any power-driven dough mixer or other bakery machines?	☐	☐
3. Operate, load, or unload scrap papers baler or paper box compactors?	☐	☐
4. Drive a motor vehicle on the job?	☐	☐
Do Any Workers Under 16 Years of Age Do the Following:		
5. Cook?	☐	☐
6. Bake?	☐	☐
7. Clean cooking equipment or handle hot oil or grease?	☐	☐
8. Load or unload goods from a truck or conveyor?	☐	☐
9. Work inside a freezer or meat cooler?	☐	☐
10. Operate power-driven bread slicers or bagel slicers?	☐	☐
11. Operate any power-driven equipment?	☐	☐
12. Work from ladders?	☐	☐
13. Work during school hours?	☐	☐
14. Work before 7:00 A.M. on any day?	☐	☐
15. Work past 7:00 P.M. between Labor Day and June 1?	☐	☐
16. Work past 9:00 P.M. between June 1 and Labor Day?	☐	☐
17. Work more than 3 hours on a school day, including Fridays?	☐	☐
18. Work more than 8 hours on any day?	☐	☐
19. Work more than 18 hours in any week when school was in session?	☐	☐
20. Work more than 40 hours in any week when school was not in session?	☐	☐
21. Do you employ any workers who are less than 14 years of age?	☐	☐
22. Do you fail to maintain in your records a date of birth for every employee under 19 years of age?	☐	☐

Note: If any of the above questions is answered "yes," the property is likely to be out of compliance.

Source: www.youthrules.dol.gov/selfassess_restaurant.htm.

FIGURE 4.3   Employer Self-Assessment Tool

Employment Relationships

As a GM, you and your managers likely have the right to hire/terminate staff members as you see fit because, in most states, the relationship with the employee is **"at-will" employment.**

HOTEL TERMINOLOGY AT WORK

At-Will Employment: The employment relationship that exists when employers can hire any employee as they choose and dismiss that employee with or without cause at any time. The employee can also elect to work for the employer or terminate the work relationship any time that he or she chooses.

■

Assuming that no antidiscrimination laws are violated, this allows an employer to hire and dismiss an employee at any time if it is in the best interests of the business to do so. In situations where an employee's union or other contractual agreement is in place, this relationship may, of course, be modified.

After an employee has been legally selected, an **employment agreement** can be drafted to specifically indicate the terms of the employment relationship.

Hoteliers must consistently comply with all applicable laws to help avoid the time, cost, and negative publicity of a legal matter being tried in a court of law. (Picture Quest/PNI)

HOTEL TERMINOLOGY AT WORK

Employment Agreement: A document specifying the terms of the work relationship between the employer and employee that indicates the rights and obligations of both parties. The employment agreement often takes the form of an official written offer letter.

The Law in the Workplace

There are numerous other laws that can have a significant impact upon the management of employees after they are hired. These laws and regulations change constantly. GMs and HR directors, if available, must stay abreast of these changes and inform the appropriate managers about them. Although there are far too many specific HR issues to include in this chapter, there are some legal issues that are so significant they must be addressed. For example, discrimination was noted in an earlier section. Additional important legal issues include those related to sexual harassment, family and medical leave, compensation, employee performance, unemployment, and required employment records.

THE INTERNET AT WORK

The Society for Human Resource Management (SHRM) is the professional association for HR directors and staff. To view its Web site, go to

www.shrm.org

Note that this group produces *HR Magazine*, a monthly information publication distributed to its membership.

Sexual Harassment

One cannot ask a subordinate for sexual favors in exchange for employment benefits; neither can one punish an employee if an offer is rejected. Environmental harassment including the use of improper language or conduct is an additional example of prohibited harassment. To protect against liability that can result from allegations of discrimination or harassment, it is important that **zero tolerance** policies and procedures be in place throughout the hotel and all of its departments.

HOTEL TERMINOLOGY AT WORK

Zero Tolerance: The total absence of behavior that is objectionable from the perspectives of discrimination or harassment. This is achieved by the issuance of appropriate policies; the conduct of applicable workshops; the development of procedures for employees alleging discrimination or harassment to obtain relief; and written protocols for reporting, investigating, and resolving incidences and grievances.

Today's professional GM strongly supports and aggressively follows a strict zero tolerance policy related to sexual and other forms of harassment.

Family and Medical Leave Act (FMLA)

Signed by President Clinton in 1993, this law states that hotels employing 50 or more staff members are required to provide up to 12 weeks of leave (unpaid) to an employee if the time is needed for the birth, adoption, or in some cases, the foster care of a child. The act also applies when the employee or one of his/her family members has a serious illness.

Compensation

FLSA was discussed earlier relative to child labor standards. It also established a **minimum wage** to be paid to employees covered by the act and rates that must be paid for **overtime** work.

HOTEL TERMINOLOGY AT WORK

Minimum Wage: The lowest amount of compensation that an employer may pay to an employee covered by the FLSA or applicable state law. Minimum wage provisions cover most hotel employees; however, exceptions can include youthful employees being paid a training wage for the first 90 days of employment and some tipped employees.

Overtime: The number of hours of work after which an employee must receive a premium pay rate. This premium rate is generally one and one-half times the basic hourly rate.

The FLSA requires that most employees in the United States be paid at least the federal minimum wage for all hours worked and overtime pay at time and one-half the regular rate of pay for all hours worked over 40 hours in a workweek. Details about FLSA requirements change and hoteliers, including those without access to an HR department, must keep current with the changes.

There is no limit on the number of hours employees aged 16 and older may work in any workweek, and the FLSA does not require overtime pay for work on Saturday, Sundays, holidays, or regular days of rest, as such.

The act applies on a workweek basis. A workweek is a fixed and regularly recurring period of 168 hours: seven consecutive 24-hour periods. It does not have to coincide with the calendar week, and may begin on any day and at any hour of the day. The averaging of hours over two or more weeks is not permitted. Normally, overtime pay earned in a particular workweek must be paid on the regular pay day for the pay period in which the wages were earned.

The FLSA provides an exception from minimum wage and overtime pay for staff employed as bona fide executive and administrative employees (among others). To qualify for exemption, employees must meet certain tests regarding their job duties and be paid on a salary basis at not less than (at the time of this writing) $455 per week. Job titles do not determine exempt status. In addition to receiving the above salary, several tests must be met for the FLSA exemptions:

Executive

- The employee's primary duty must be managing the enterprise or managing one of its department's subdivisions.

- The employee must direct the work of at least two or more other full-time employees or their equivalent.

- The employee must have the authority to hire or fire other employees. Alternately, the employee's suggestions and recommendations about hiring, firing, advancement, promotion, or other status change of employees must be given particular weight.

Administrative

- The employee's primary duty must involve office or nonmanual work directly related to the management or general business operations of the employer or the employer's customers.

- The employee's primary duty involves discretion and independent judgment on significant matters.

THE INTERNET AT WORK

To learn more about current requirements for overtime and/or exempt employees, go to

www.wagehour.dol.gov

Click on "Overtime Pay" and/or "Exempt Employees."

Another provision of the FLSA relates to equal pay. Regardless of their gender, employees who hold essentially the same job must be equitably compensated with both financial and nonfinancial rewards.

In the United States, there are laws related to compensation and others related to taxes because there are numerous taxes and credits that employers must pay based upon the compensation paid to employees. Employees must pay taxes as well, and the employer must withhold some of these taxes from the employee's paycheck. Tax credits are also sometimes granted to employers and employees. Examples of these taxes and tax credits include the following:

- *Income Tax.* State, federal, and sometimes local income taxes must be withheld from employees' paychecks.

- *Federal Insurance Contribution Act (FICA).* Taxes must be contributed by both employers and employees to fund the federal Social Security and Medicare programs.
- *Federal Unemployment Tax Act (FUTA).* This mandates that employers contribute a tax that is based on the employer's total payroll to help care for persons who are out of work through no fault of their own.
- *Earned Income Credit (EIC).* This is a refundable credit for employees whose incomes fall below preestablished levels.
- *Work Opportunity Tax Credit (WOTC).* This provides employers with tax credits for hiring disadvantaged workers.

Specific requirements related to the above tax and credit programs are complicated and change often. It is important for GMs to confirm that their HR directors, if applicable, interact closely with the hotel's accounting (payroll) employees to help ensure full compliance with all provisions of these tax-related laws.

Employee Performance

Hoteliers must comply with laws relating to the management of employee performance:

Employee Evaluation. Hoteliers violate the law if it can be demonstrated that a performance assessment system is biased against a class of employees protected by the law. It is important to assure that work performance (and nothing else!) forms the basis for employee evaluations.

Discipline. Workplace rules and policies must be established that do not violate the law. They must be effectively communicated and consistently enforced. Some hotels use a progressive discipline system to encourage employees to improve and to help ensure that managers and others who discipline employees do so fairly.

Termination. The at-will employment relationship discussed earlier does *not* allow a hotelier to terminate employees for any reason. Unacceptable reasons to terminate an employee include the following:
- Actions approved in the hotel's employee manual
- In an effort to deny benefits
- For allowed work absences
- Because of attempts to unionize staff members
- For reporting violations of the law
- For being a member of a protected class of worker(s) (for example, race, sex, or religion)
- When an oral promise of continued employment has been made
- In violation of a written employment agreement or contract

Unemployment Issues

Unemployment insurance is a large cost to hotels and can be difficult to administer. Federal and state governments operate this program. Each state requires employers to pay different costs to maintain the state's share of funds used to assist workers who have temporarily lost jobs.

HOTEL TERMINOLOGY AT WORK

Unemployment Insurance: Funds provided by employers to make available temporary financial benefits to employees who have lost their jobs.

Employees can file an **unemployment claim**, and as this is done, a series of steps mandated by states will be used to determine whether an applicant is eligible, and if so, (a) for how much, (b) the length of time payments will be made, and (c) the length of time an employee must work for an employer to qualify for assistance.

HOTEL TERMINOLOGY AT WORK

Unemployment Claim: A claim made by an unemployed worker to the appropriate state agency asserting that the worker is eligible for unemployment benefits.

Employment Records

Federal and state agencies require that selected employee records be maintained. Penalties for noncompliance can be severe. There are many requirements related to record keeping:

- For the Department of Labor, the FLSA requires that numerous records be maintained for each employee, including information about the employee's name, address, gender, job title, work schedule, hourly rate, regular and over-time earnings, wage deductions, and dates of pay days.
- Records must be kept of any deductions from wages for meals, uniforms, and/or lodging.
- Records for tipped employees must include the amount of tips reported.
- Records applicable to the FMLA require information about dates that FMLA-eligible employees take a covered leave, the amount of leave (in hours or days), as well as other documentation.
- The IRCA requires that an Employment Eligibility Verification (I-9) Form be completed and retained for each employee.
- The ADEA requires that employers retain certain records, including those related to personnel matters and benefit plans.

As can be seen, there are a wide variety of laws and regulations that impact how hoteliers can interact with applicants before employment and with employees after selection decisions are made. GMs with an HR department count on these specialists to ensure that the hotel stays in compliance with these requirements.

It is easy to see why extensive knowledge about employment laws and the need to spend significant amounts of time to keep up with legal aspects as they (seemingly) constantly change are integral requirements for an effective HR director. GMs, too, must understand the basics of these laws and know when to ask HR personnel questions about the hotel's policies and practices. Most important, perhaps, they must also know when external legal assistance is warranted.

HUMAN RESOURCES IN ACTION

The legal aspects of managing staff members just discussed provide some of the context for and, sometimes, many of the limitations within which GMs direct the work of their staff members. In this section we review some of the day-to-day activities that involve the "people" aspects of the GM and his/her management team.

Recruitment

In many hotels, the employee **turnover rate** is extremely high. This makes recruiting employees a seemingly never-ending and absolutely critical task.

HOTEL TERMINOLOGY AT WORK

Turnover Rate: A measure of the proportion of a workforce replaced during a designated time period (for example; month, quarter, year).

The turnover rate can be computed as

$$\frac{\text{Number of employees separated}}{\text{Number of employees in the workforce}} = \text{Employee turnover rate}$$

■

Recruitment can be especially tough in areas where the **unemployment rate** is low and because of common stereotypes suggesting that entry-level positions in hotels are undesirable.

Unfortunately, few, if any, hotels enjoy lines of applicants seeking a position.

HOTEL TERMINOLOGY AT WORK

Unemployment Rate: The number, usually expressed as a percentage, of employable persons who are out of work and looking for jobs.

■

An astute GM recognizes that the need to recruit for vacant positions is directly related to the hotel's turnover rate. If fewer employees leave, the need to recruit for vacant positions will be lessened. There are many things that the hotel's EOC, along with all other managers at the property, can do to influence turnover rates. However, they should realize that the HR department (if the property has one) does not control most of them. The point is that while an HR department may be responsible for recruitment, it is the management and operation of the individual hotel departments that will most influence turnover rates. (Note: Employee retention practices are discussed later in this chapter.)

Close interaction between the GM, department heads, and the HR director, if one is available, can lead to hotel policies, procedures, and standards that will help the hotel recruit effectively within its own community or market. As this occurs, the need for extensive recruitment activities is lowered.

Often, a good mix of **internal recruiting** and **external recruiting** techniques is best. As the names imply, internal recruiting focuses on currently employed employees (internal applicants) for vacant positions; by contrast, external recruiting focuses on searching for applicants not currently employed by the hotel.

HOTEL TERMINOLOGY AT WORK

Internal Recruiting: Tactics to identify and attract currently employed staff members for job vacancies that represent promotions or lateral transfers to similar positions.

External Recruiting: Tactics designed to attract persons not current hotel employees for vacant positions.

■

The concept of "promotion from within" is an example of an internal recruiting technique. Many hoteliers look first to high-performing current staff members when management positions become vacant. This is an excellent idea. Promotional opportunities are incentives for many employees to remain with the hotel and to make efforts to excel while they are employed. Other staff members may want to make transfers to other positions and to other departments; they should be allowed to do so whenever they are qualified, as it is in the best interest of the hotel.

Alerting friends and relatives of current employees about position vacancies is another example of internal recruiting. Often, bonuses are paid to staff members who nominate applicants who then are employed at the hotel for a specified time period.

There is a wide range of external tactics that may, or may not, be effective. Some of these are well known. They include newspaper and other media advertisements, job fairs, the use of employment or executive search firms for management positions, recruitment at community schools and colleges, and the all-too-frequently used "Help Wanted" signs placed outside or inside the hotel.

Only shortsighted GMs think that "recruitment is the job of the HR department" or "each department head is responsible to recruit for his/her department." In fact, all employees, by what they do and by what they fail to do, make an impression

Tactic 1: Use effective retention strategies to reduce the number of employee vacancies for which recruitment is necessary. Become an "Employer" of choice within the community and enjoy the advantage of the reputation as "a good place to work."

Tactic 2: Know the requirements of each position that are based upon a current job description identifying the tasks to be performed by an employee working in the position.

Tactic 3: Identify the best features of the hotel property. Communicate these to potential applicants.

Tactic 4: Identify the best features of the jobs that are available and communicate these to potential applicants.

Tactic 5: Use job titles that reflect the position ("Hotel Horticulture Specialist" versus "Hotel laborer").

Tactic 6: Assure that your total compensation package is competitive and indicate the economic value of benefits.

Tactic 7: Consider current employees first: promote from within.

Tactic 8: Reward current employees for referrals.

Tactic 9: Recruit former employees.

Tactic 10: Use creative employment ads ("Friendly people needed! Flexible hours; good pay. Come grow with our team!")

Tactic 11: Use current employee endorsements in employment ads.

Tactic 12: Recruit your guests.

Tactic 13: Contact your state employment commission.

Tactic 14: Add an employment section on the hotel's Web site.

Tactic 15: Participate in community events and programs.

Tactic 16: Sponsor work–study programs and invite classes for tours and discussions.

Tactic 17: Consider seniors and applicants in career transitions.

Adapted from: David Hayes and Jack Ninemeier. *Fifty One-Minute Tips for Recruiting Employees.* Menlo Park, CA. Crisp Learning, 2001.

FIGURE 4.4 Hotel Recruitment Tactics

on current staff members. This, in turn, impacts the hotel's turnover rate. In addition, they influence the perceptions of potential applicants because employees will certainly talk to candidates about how "great" or "terrible" it is to work for the hotel. As well, current staff will quickly share their positive and negative work experiences with newly recruited staff members.

Figure 4.4 reviews some relatively common and creative recruitment tactics that may increase the number of applicants for hotel positions.

Selection

Selection involves evaluating applicants to determine those most likely to be successful in vacant positions. Hoteliers are sometimes criticized for hiring any "warm body" that applies for work. Unfortunately, however, if the recruitment process is not effective, those selecting employees may not have many candidates from which to choose. It is from this situation that the **"warm body syndrome"** typically surfaces.

HOTEL TERMINOLOGY AT WORK

Selection: The process of evaluating job applicants to determine those more qualified (or potentially qualified) for vacant positions.

"Warm Body Syndrome" (Employee Selection): The concept that proper employee selection procedures are deemphasized and, instead, the first applicant ("warm body") who applies is hired.

An effective selection process helps to ensure that the best candidate for the job is chosen. Typically, the selection decision is made by the appropriate line-operating manager and not by HR staff even in hotels that have this department.

To make a proper selection decision, information about each candidate's eligibility for a position must be gathered. This may be done by using several selection devices:

- Preliminary screening, including reviewing the candidate's application.
- Employment interviews.
- Employment tests. Sometimes tests are given to applicants, especially when experience is required. For example, an applicant may be given a paper-and-pencil test that addresses the arithmetic involved in cashiering skills or the spelling and grammar skills required for word processing. Alternatively, a skills test could be given. For example, an "experienced" cook could be asked to prepare a sauce that one with appropriate food preparation skills should know how to prepare.
- Reference checks. These can be done to confirm employment dates and positions held.
- Drug screening. If used by the hotel.

Note: In hotels with an HR department, the above selection tasks may be done by HR specialists. Then, those applicants judged most qualified and potentially successful in vacant positions are referred to the department head or supervisor in the department where the vacancy is located. There, additional interviewing can be done, and the selection decision is made.

Orientation

After applicants are recruited and new staff members are selected, **orientation** becomes important. Orientation is the process of providing basic information about the hotel that should be known by all of its employees. Effective orientation is critical because it helps to establish the long-term relationship between the hotel and its employees.

HOTEL TERMINOLOGY AT WORK

Orientation: The process of providing basic information about the hotel that must be known by all of its employees.

Orientation programs must be well thought out. They cannot be done in an inconsistent, haphazard fashion, depending, in part, on how busy the hotel's staff is when a new employee begins work. The GM, in concern for the hotel's staff, must assure that the orientation program is organized, consistently comprehensive, and professionally well done.

Important goals of an effective orientation program are as follows:

- *To Reduce Anxiety.* New staff members are looking for reinforcement that their decision to work for the hotel is a good one. The new employees' evolving impressions of the hotel will be enhanced as they learn about the organization and as they observe the genuine respect and attention given to them by all of the hotel's staff and managers including the GM.
- *To Improve Morale and to Reduce Turnover.* An effective orientation program can reduce turnover rates.

- *To Provide Consistency.* An effective orientation process will yield a team of employees who are aware of and believe in the property's goals. They will know what to do, for example, in the case of a fire or other emergency, and they will understand the hotel's personnel policies about issues such as vacation, sick leave, and benefits.

- *To Develop Realistic Expectations.* New employees want to know what the hotel and its management staff expect of them. Orientation programs can help to provide this information.

If available, the HR department should conduct the general orientation program. This does not prevent, of course, individual departments from initiating their own departmental-specific **induction** programs. In most departments, in fact, there should be such a program. For example, while all employees in the hotel must know about guest security and safety, generally only food and beverage personnel must know about concerns in safe food preparation.

HOTEL TERMINOLOGY AT WORK

Induction: The process providing specific information about a department that must be known by all employees in the department.

■

Effective GMs have two critical orientation concerns. The first is that of content; the second involves attendance and participation. Topics that a GM should ensure are covered in an orientation program include:

- A hotel overview, including a presentation of its mission statement, the importance of effective guest service, and the emphasis on teamwork.
- A review of important policies and procedures (many programs specifically address harassment polices at this time).
- A detailed discussion about compensation, including fringe benefits and pay periods.
- Guest and employee safety and security concerns.
- A review of employee and union relations (if applicable).
- A facility tour of all hotel areas (sometimes a meal in the hotel's restaurant is included as part of the tour).
- Any special topics related to the specific hotel.

Attendance concerns relate to who should be present. Obviously, the new employees should be there. Just as obviously, it is necessary that the GM be involved in every orientation program. After all, the GM is the hotel's leader, and new employees want to meet the leader.

Many hotels have an **employee handbook**, or manual, that is provided to staff members during orientation.

HOTEL TERMINOLOGY AT WORK

Employee Handbook: Written policies and procedures related to employment at a hotel. Also sometimes called an employee "manual."

■

Employees in a cross-functional team meet with the hotel manager and human resources director to provide input on personnel-related issues.

The purpose of the employee handbook is to provide details of the basic subject matter covered during orientation. For example, handbooks often contain information about the hotel's mission statement and goals, as well as details about its policies and procedures relating to compensation, benefits, and work-related behavior.

In some hotels, a follow-up orientation is held several weeks or months after the initial orientation session. This allows employees to provide input about their initial job experiences. Feedback gained at this time can be used to revise and improve the initial orientation program.

Training

Training is designed to help improve the knowledge or skills of the hotel's staff. Some, but not all, observers also believe that training can be used to modify attitudes, such as those related to providing guest service or working closely with a team of fellow employees. Regardless of what the GM believes to be the limitations, if any, of training, all hotel employees will require training of some type throughout their careers. In fact, even GMs require training as new operational techniques and management approaches change in response to advances in technology, modifications of the hotel's goals, and/or guests' needs and desires.

It is obvious that new employees must be trained to perform their required job tasks. When these employees are trained well, reasonable quality and quantity standards can be consistently attained. However, even experienced staff members need training as, for example, new equipment is purchased or as revised operating procedures are implemented. As well, ongoing professional development opportunities can motivate individuals and help the hotel by preparing employees for advancement opportunities.

Employee training can be done in groups or on an individual basis. Group training is an effective method when several or more staff members must learn the same thing. For example, consider a front-office manager interested in providing **upselling** training for front-desk agents. In this example, the manager of the area may request assistance from HR personnel, if available, to assist with training efforts.

HOTEL TERMINOLOGY AT WORK

Upselling: Tactics used to increase the hotel's average daily rate **(ADR)** by encouraging guests to rent higher-priced rooms with better or more amenities (for example, view, complimentary breakfast and newspaper, and/or increased square footage) than those provided with lower-priced rooms.

■

Those responsible for training can request and preview potentially applicable generic training programs developed by professional associations or commercial training organizations. They could also provide some property-specific elements of the program, such as developing suggested upselling dialog that might be used in a **role-play** or other group training activity.

HOTEL TERMINOLOGY AT WORK

ADR: Short for "average daily rate," the average selling price for all guest rooms for a given time period. The formula for ADR is

Total Room Revenue ÷ Total Number of Rooms Sold = ADR

Role-play: A training activity that allows trainees to practice a skill by interacting with each other in simulated roles, such as pretending that one trainee is a guest and the other is an employee interacting with the guest.

■

Individualized on-the-job training is a one-on-one training method that involves, for example, teaching a new staff member how to make a bed or providing instructions to an experienced maintenance staff member about how to maintain a new piece of equipment. Individualized training is most frequently the responsibility of line department managers and their staff. In most individualized training situations, the individual departments prefer to be responsible for the development and delivery of the training.

HR personnel in large properties can play an additional training role by implementing "Train the Trainer" programs designed to teach individual department managers how to better implement training for their own staff.

THE INTERNET AT WORK

More than ever, the Internet is being utilized to train hotel employees. To view a Web site developed just for that purpose, go to

www.hoteltraining.com

Human resources staff and/or department managers desiring to review and purchase "off-the-bookshelf" training resources have access to excellent materials developed by two industry-related associations:

Educational Institute of the American Hotel & Lodging Association: www.ei-ahla.org
National Restaurant Association Educational Foundation: www.nraef.org

---

GMs should be sure that training responsibilities are properly delegated. Training is absolutely critical to a hotel's success. As the GM, you must ascertain that it is being done as effectively as possible.

Performance Evaluation

Most employees want to know how their boss views their performance. Staff members in the HR department may be responsible for ensuring the consistency of the hotel's employee performance evaluation process. In small properties, this responsibility generally rests with the GM. Essentially, there are two types of evaluation approaches that can be used. GMs must know about and support the approach used at their hotel.

The first type of approach requires managers to compare employees to a standard. In this case, managers evaluate employees individually without regard to other staff members. In the second approach, managers rank employees in comparison to other employees in their department. That is, the employee's performance is "good" or "bad" in comparison to that of other workers with similar responsibilities. The former method (comparison of an employee's performance against a standard such as completion of tasks required by the applicable job description) is best.

MANAGERS AT WORK

J.D. Ojisama, the hotel's GM, was having lunch with the HR director in the hotel's dining room.

"I've got some possible budget problems," the director said. "Remember our pep talk at last month's executive operating committee meeting? The one where we all agreed that we needed to do more staff training?"

"Yes," agreed J.D., "I recall the meeting."

"I've had the department heads from food and beverage, housekeeping, and the front office visit me since then to request help in finding some training materials for their entry-level staff, and they are asking my department to pay for it. You know there's not much in the budget for the purchase of materials from external suppliers."

"I do know that," J.D. responded, "but I also know that not training our staff will cost those departments more money than will training them."

J.D. and the director flinched a bit as they heard a drinking glass and several plates break with a loud, shattering sound.

"I hope no one got hurt," said J.D., quickly rising from the table and moving toward the sound of the broken dishes.

What can J.D. do to ensure that department-specific training occurs in the hotel?

How might inexpensive training materials be secured or developed?

What can be done with department heads who maintain that they have neither the time nor the funds needed to undertake training efforts? Where do the costs of "not training" in a business show up?

However, GMs in hotel chain operations must typically use whatever standard method is required by their organizations. Regardless of the evaluation approach used, a regular system of employee evaluation can:

- Help determine where, if at all, staff members can improve their performance.
- Help assess who will be eligible for raises in pay and promotions.
- Improve morale. Effective performance evaluation systems show employees that they are respected and that their supervisor wants to help them improve their job performance.
- Help assure legal compliance. A written record of information supporting promotions, rewards, disciplinary actions, and the like is available if employees make legal challenges.

1. Performance standards are established.
2. Policies relating to the frequency of and responsibilities for ratings are established.
3. Employees' performance data are gathered.
4. The raters (and sometimes the employee) must evaluate performance.
5. A performance evaluation discussion is held with the employee.
6. Performance approval agreements/decisions are made.
7. Evaluation information is filed.

FIGURE 4.5   Steps in Systematic Performance Approval System

A systematic performance appraisal system involves at least seven steps. These are illustrated in Figure 4.5.

Although the task of evaluating a staff member's performance is clearly the responsibility of his or her boss, the GM and/or HR department has an important role to play in:

- Developing policies and procedures for a propertywide system
- Communicating these policies and procedures to all managers and staff
- Addressing and resolving employee concerns as they arise
- Filing performance evaluation results in the employee's records

For some employees, performance evaluations are a difficult procedure. Few people like to be told that they are doing anything other than an excellent job, even when they are not! Also, many managers find it uncomfortable to periodically "rate" and then communicate results "face-to-face" with the employees with whom they must work every day. A good GM recognizes the importance of an effective evaluation system and the challenges faced by both employees and managers as they participate in the process. The value of an effective performance appraisal system is worth facing the challenges that operating such a system presents.

Compensation (Salaries and Wages)

Administration of a hotel's **compensation** program is very important and is a primary function of the HR department or the GM.

HOTEL TERMINOLOGY AT WORK

Compensation: All financial and nonfinancial rewards given to management and nonmanagement employees in return for the work they do for the hotel.

▮

When many staff members think of "compensation," they often think of the **salaries** and **wages** they are paid.

HOTEL TERMINOLOGY AT WORK

Salary: Pay calculated on a weekly, monthly, or annual basis rather than at an hourly rate.

Wage: Pay calculated on an hourly basis.

▮▮

Although these are the most significant forms of compensation paid to most staff, **benefits** can also be significant.

HOTEL TERMINOLOGY AT WORK

Benefits: Indirect financial compensation consisting of employer-provided rewards and services other than wages or salaries.

Examples include life and health insurance, paid vacations, and employer-provided meals.

■

Salaries and wages are examples of direct financial compensation that also includes bonuses and commissions if paid to hotel sales personnel. By contrast, benefits provide indirect financial compensation.

Compensation is a necessity of life and the primary reason the majority of people work. Pay is important because, of course, employees require money to purchase food, shelter, clothing, and other necessities. However, it is also important because it indicates an individual's worth to the organization. For this reason, it is important that employees consider the hotel's compensation program to be fair.

Well-conceived compensation programs are important to the hotel because, typically, an "average" property pays approximately 44 percent of its total revenue to employees in the form of payroll, benefits, and meals.[1] As well, the level of pay attracts or discourages qualified applicants and either motivates or alienates employees as managers attempt to attain work quality and quantity goals.

Compensation must be equitable from the perspectives of both the hotel and its employees. Effectively administered, its compensation program will be:

- *Legal:* It will meet any requirements imposed by governmental agencies.
- *Fair:* Each employee will be paid relative to the value of his/her input.
- *Balanced:* Financial and nonfinancial rewards will represent a reasonable part of the total compensation package.
- *Cost-Effective:* The hotel will receive reasonable productivity for the labor costs incurred.
- *Viewed as Reasonable by Staff:* Employees will perceive their compensation is equitable in relation to the work they do and relative to what they would be paid by competitive employers (some of whom are probably not hotels).

It is difficult to administer a compensation program that adequately addresses all these factors. Doing so provides an ongoing challenge for those hoteliers who must make compensation decisions. The GM must interact with the HR director, if applicable, and other managers to establish pay for specific positions based upon:

- What other employers attempting to attract the same applicants pay in their hotels. It is a good idea to use local salary/wage surveys for this purpose.
- What employees working in different jobs within the hotel are paid. For example, those doing cleaning work in the food and beverage department should be paid a reasonable amount relative to those with cleaning responsibilities in another department. Differences between pay must be reasonable, defensible, based upon the worth of the position to the hotel.
- What other employees working on the same job within the hotel are paid. This decision is often based upon the length of time the employee has worked for the hotel and each individual's performance appraisal.

[1]2002 data from: *Trends in the Hospitality Industry,* USA Edition. Hospitality Asset Advisors International, San Francisco, CA. 2003.

Line department managers will find information about the financial compensation practices of competitive hotels and other potential employers very useful. In addition, information about benefits programs offered by other employers in the community will be of interest to the GM and others as compensation decisions are made.

Other Compensation (Benefits)

Different employees receive different salaries and wages based upon factors such as the position they hold and their length of time with the hotel: the executive housekeeper with many years of experience will enjoy an annual salary much greater than a newly hired entry-level laundry worker. The benefits package of these two employees, however, may be very similar. Although full- and part-time employees may qualify for different types of benefits, most of these benefits are available to all employees as long as the hotel has employed them for a specified period of time.

The GM, the HR director, and/or others in the EOC typically make benefits decisions. Top-level management, however, must approve the benefits budget. As noted earlier in this chapter, the federal or state governments mandate some benefits programs including those relating to unemployment insurance and Social Security, Medicare, and workers' compensation programs. There are, in addition, a wide range of voluntary benefits that hotels can offer employees in an effort to attract and retain qualified employees. Figure 4.6 lists examples of these.

The GM and his/her management team have a variety of responsibilities as they manage a benefits program. They should:

- Determine the objectives for the benefits programs. Most hoteliers want to match the benefits they offer with those of competing hotels. However, hotels compete with other industries for potential employees. Therefore, what these competitive industries offer employees should also be considered.

- Facilitate discussions with employees about desired benefits. This can be done through employee surveys and advisory committees.

- Communicate the "benefit" of benefits. Many staff members think of their compensation as only their hourly pay or salary. However, benefits comprise a large and growing proportion of the total compensation provided by employers. Therefore, the types and especially the value of benefits provided by the hotel should be effectively and consistently communicated to staff members. These efforts should begin at the time of orientation, be explained in the employee handbook, and should continue, for example, with presentations at employee meetings.

- Monitor costs. An ongoing assessment of labor costs and how they might be reduced or more effectively managed should be an important activity of every GM and department head. Benefit costs related to medical insurance coverage are rising at an especially rapid rate. Programs designed to control costs such as these have a direct and positive impact on the hotel's bottom line.

Historically, hotels and other hospitality organizations have been very conservative in offering benefits programs. Other than granting some vacation, holiday time, and limited medical coverage, few additional benefits were made available. Increasingly, however, hospitality businesses including hotels are offering a wider range of benefits to their staff members. This trend will continue as hotels compete with other employers to fill staff positions.

Paid Leave Benefits
- Holidays
- Vacations
- Sick Leave
- Jury Duty
- Funerals
- Military Service
- Personal
- Breaks
- Maternity
- Paternity

Unpaid Leave Benefits
- Maternity
- Paternity

Life Insurance Benefits
- Wholly employer-financed
- Partly employer-financed

Medical Care Benefits
- Employee Coverage:
    Wholly employer-financed
    Partly employer-financed
- Family Coverage:
    Wholly employer-financed
    Partly employer-financed

Dental Care
- Employee Coverage:
    Wholly employer-financed
    Partly employer-financed
- Family Coverage:
    Wholly employer-financed
    Partly employer-financed

Other Insurance Benefits
- Sickness/Accident:
    Wholly employer-financed
    Partly employer-financed
- Long- and/or Short-Term Disability:
    Wholly employer-financed
    Partly employer-financed

Retirement Benefits
- Defined Benefit Pensions:
    Wholly employer-financed
    Partly employer-financed
- Defined Contributions:
    Savings and thrift
    Deferred profit sharing
    Employee stock ownership
    Money purchase pension

Other
- Reimbursement Accounts
- Flexible Benefit Plans

Services
- Tuition Reimbursement
- Child Care
- Elder Care
- Financial Services
- Relocation Services
- Social/Recreational Programs

FIGURE 4.6   Examples of Employee Benefits Programs

Employee Retention

We noted earlier in this chapter that a hotel's need to recruit new staff members was directly related to its turnover rate. In other words, if fewer people leave the organization, there would be less need for the ongoing recruitment necessary in many properties. All members of the hotel's management team must be concerned about employee **retention**.

HOTEL TERMINOLOGY AT WORK

Retention (Employee): The use of organizational and supervisory policies and procedures designed to encourage employees to remain with the property rather than to leave it.

Many employees working in the lodging industry are not looking for careers. They may be students, for example, desiring part-time employment during the school year or full-time employment for a few summer months. They may be "empty nesters" or senior citizens who work for "something to do" and/or to supplement other income. Still others "may be in between jobs" and, for other reasons, are not desirous of long-term employment.

Fortunately, other applicants, such as those with postsecondary degrees in hospitality management do find the work in the industry exciting and challenging. Still others enjoy their work because of their coworkers and desire careers in the property, organization (if multiunit), and/or lodging industry.

Strategies and tactics to retain employees can be useful in maximizing the time that both types of employees remain on the job.

Traditionally, many lodging industry supervisors have used a leadership style focusing on directing rather than on leading, and they used a "stern taskmaster approach" to do so. By contrast, contemporary leadership approaches involve facilitation and empowerment to create an environment in which many of today's employees' at all organizational levels feel most comfortable. Lodging managers are also benefiting from the positive results that come from treating their staff members with genuine respect and from thinking about how they (the managers) would like to be supervised if they were the subordinates.

Modern approaches to hotel leadership also address concerns such as the ongoing solicitation of input from affected employees, from managing teams who make team decisions, and for rewarding employees based upon performance rather than on tenure on the job. Still other practices that encourage employee retention include those relating to early-job mentoring, training that adequately prepares one for the initial position, and career-long professional development opportunities. Figure 4.7 lists other tactics that can help with employee retention efforts.

Tactic 1: Track retention on a by-department basis. Know where the lowest retention rates are and determine whether there is need for supervisory retraining in human resources skills for managers in those departments.

Tactic 2: Don't punish the "best" employees by giving them special assignments without reducing their work loads in other areas.

Tactic 3: Explain the long-term benefits of staying (compensation and, especially, fringe benefit packages often increase with job tenure).

Tactic 4: Make first impressions count. Share the hotel's mission with staff members.

Tactic 5: Create career ladders and provide professional development opportunities that help prepare staff members for promotions.

Tactic 6: Invest in training. Give it a priority and provide "train the trainer" programs to prepare managers and supervisors for this work responsibility.

Tactic 7: Implement and enforce an effective zero-tolerance harassment policy.

Tactic 8: Enforce "on-time" policies fairly and consistently.

Tactic 9: Invite "fast-track" employees to attend management meetings.

Tactic 10: Implement a "catch the employee doing something right" program.

Tactic 11: Conduct employee exit interviews and learn from them.

Tactic 12: Conduct regularly scheduled staff meetings.

Tactic 13: Regularly communicate the benefits of working at the hotel.

Tactic 14: Make the workplace fun; ask the staff how this might be done.

Tactic 15: Become an "employer of choice." Enjoy a reputation within the community of being a desirable place to work.

Note: This figure is adapted from David Hayes and Jack Ninemeier. *Fifty One-Minute Tips for Retaining Employees.* Menlo Park, CA. Crisp Publications, 2001.

FIGURE 4.7 Hotel Retention Tactics

MANAGERS AT WORK

J.D. Ojisama was holding the weekly EOC meeting. Almost before J.D. could finish saying, "Good morning," the questions began:

"What are we going to do about that new hotel opening across town? They're stealing all of our employees!" said the food and beverage director.

"One of my housekeepers said she was offered twenty-five cents more per hour to work there!" said the executive housekeeper.

"And ... they're offering transportation reimbursement for local employees and free bus tokens for the employees they recruit from the inner city," said the front-office manager. "We've got to raise our employee's pay, or we won't be able to keep anyone. I say forget any increases in our benefits package this year. We've got to raise our hourly rates."

Everyone in the room looked toward the HR director and J.D.

Their community, like many others, has a labor shortage problem. What are specific steps J.D. and his management team can take to ensure that the hotel retains its best staff and can effectively recruit for the employees it will need in the future? How important is employee compensation in this process? What do you believe makes employees decide to stay at current jobs or move to new ones? Are benefits more important than hourly wages? If so, why? To whom?

OTHER HUMAN RESOURCES ACTIVITIES

Our study of a hotel's HR function continues as we review its role in planning for future staffing needs, in protecting the health and safety of the hotel's employees, and in improving the quality of work.

Planning for Human Resources

The high rates of turnover experienced by many hotels and other hospitality organizations require many hoteliers to spend significant amounts of time in recruitment activities to fill vacant positions needed for day-to-day operations. Some jobs are filled from outside the hotel while others are filled by promoting from within. Most smaller and even medium-size hoteliers do not spend significant amounts of time in formalized HR planning. All, however, probably do informal planning as they anticipate how the future may impact upon the hotel's staff needs.

Traditionally, hotels have not needed to undertake long-term HR planning because most positions required only physical or entry-level technical skills that could be learned on the job. Historically, as well, there has been an abundant supply of these applicants. Today, however, with increasingly intense competition for staff members with entry-level skills, this approach does not work well. Also, with the advent of technology, many staff and nearly all supervisors in hotels need to have some, if not extensive, computer-related abilities. Given this situation, it is easy to see that the HR training function is very much related to its long-range planning function and will continue to be.

Employee Safety and Health

All hoteliers, including the GM and every manager and supervisor in line-operating as well as staff departments, must be concerned about their employees' safety and health. Many persons do not think of a hotel environment as unsafe or unhealthy. However, some jobs, if improperly performed, can be. Work-related accidents and illnesses in hotels can be related to:

- *The Work To Be Done.* For example, cooks may need to work with knives and meat slicers, housekeepers may need to use potentially hazardous chemicals when cleaning guest rooms, and maintenance staff operate power equipment in their daily jobs.

Regularly scheduled hotel building inspections are critical to ensure the safety of employees and guests.

- *Working Conditions.* Greasy floors and wet, slippery surfaces can cause accidents for those persons working in kitchens or employees cleaning floors anywhere in the hotel.

Managers in line-operating departments are responsible for maintaining their workplaces and conditions to minimize accidents. In addition, they should be responsible for safety and other training for staff members. HR personnel in larger properties also help by facilitating hotelwide safety efforts. In addition, employees need someone to report problems if a supervisor or manager asks them to perform an unsafe task. The GM and HR department must be vocal advocates for employee safety. Other aspects of employee safety and security are discussed in Chapter 12, Safety and Property Security.

There is also a variety of health-related activities that will likely be of concern to the GM and the HR director, if the hotel has one:

- Developing and selecting programs to help employees cope with stress.
- Developing procedures that address violence in the workplace.
- Communicating updated information about the human immunodeficiency virus (HIV—the virus that causes acquired immune deficiency syndrome [AIDS]) in the workplace.
- Providing information about and helping to address concerns relative to cumulative trauma disorders, including repetitive motion injuries such as carpal tunnel syndrome.

Workforce and Work Quality Improvement

As a hotel's workforce improves in quality, the quality of its work (and services delivered to the guests) will also improve. The GM and HR director, when available, will need to help make that improvement. Some techniques designed to do this include:

- *Professional Development Activities.* Working with line managers to implement ongoing programs that allow employees to gain additional job-related knowledge and skills leading to more responsible and higher-paying jobs within the hotel.
- *Cultural Diversity.* Educating managers and employees about the numerous professional, personal, and societal advantages inherent in recognizing the worth of all employees without regard to gender or race.
- *Quality Improvement.* Helping the hotel facilitate a total quality improvement effort, including **continuous quality improvement (CQI)** to meet organizational goals by becoming more competitive.

HOTEL TERMINOLOGY AT WORK

Continuous Quality Improvement (CQI): Ongoing efforts within the hotel to better meet (or exceed) guest expectations and to define ways to perform work better, less costly, and with faster methods.

Human resources-related activities are critical to a hotel's success. GMs in large properties that listen to the advice of a wise HR director will find that their legal problems related to employees and regulatory agencies are greatly reduced. GMs in smaller properties must, in effect, become their hotel's HR director for many issues and will likely need to obtain competent legal advice about other matters. As they do, numerous problems will be avoided that detract from the business of the hotel, consuming valuable time and resources that could be better used serving guests.

HOTEL TERMINOLOGY AT WORK GLOSSARY

The following terms were defined within this chapter. If you are not familiar with each of them, please review the segment of the chapter that contains the term.

HR	Unemployment insurance	Upselling
Job description	Unemployment claim	ADR
Job specification	Turnover rate	Role-play
Bonafied occupational qualifications (BOQs)	Unemployment rate	Compensation
Interstate commerce	Internal recruiting	Salary
At-will employment	External recruiting	Wage
Employment agreement	Selection	Benefits
Zero tolerance	"Warm body syndrome"	Retention
Minimum wage	Orientation	Continuous quality improvement (CQI)
Overtime	Induction	
	Employee handbook	

ISSUES AT WORK

1. A shortage of entry-level employees is a major concern of almost every GM today. To the extent that currently employed staff members can be retained, there will be less need to recruit new employees in today's very tight labor market. What are some specific activities that you, as a GM, can undertake to help reduce

the employee turnover rate? List at least three activities and discuss why these would positively impact turnover. Would these same activities reduce supervisory and management turnover? Why or why not?

2. Many jobs in one hotel are similar to those in another. Assume that the compensation including benefits in your hotel and that of a nearby competitor were identical. Identify three features you could ensure existed in your hotel that would help make your property competitive with other potential employers. Assuming you had an HR department, how would its staff be involved in your efforts?

3. Some GMs feel job descriptions are a waste of time. Others believe accurate job descriptions are critical to a hotel's staffing success. Think of two jobs you have held. Did you receive a job description for either of them? If not, would a description have been helpful? If so, how were they helpful? Prepare a job description and job specification, patterned after the one presented in this chapter, for the first job you ever held. Would the results of your efforts be helpful for the person currently holding that job? Why or why not?

4. Many hotels now test all employees who have accidents at work for the presence of illegal drugs. Assume that you are a GM, that this is the case in your hotel, and that all employees are made aware of this during orientation. Assume also that an excellent employee in your hotel slipped and fell at work. Upon receiving medical treatment, it was confirmed that the employee tested positively for marijuana use. Because you operate a drug-free hotel, your options are to terminate the employee or to suspend the employee and mandate a thirty-day, unpaid drug treatment program that the employee must complete. The treatment program would be followed by two years of mandatory, random drug testing that the employee must pass or be automatically terminated. Would you terminate or mandate treatment? Why?

5. Some hotels have very different employment policies in place for their salaried and hourly workers. In addition to the fact that pay is generally higher for salaried employees, what other benefits do you believe are appropriate for salaried staff, but not, perhaps, for hourly paid staff? What are three specifics a GM can do to encourage talented hourly employees to consider supervisory or management positions in the hotel industry?

5

Accounting

This Chapter at Work

As a GM, you are ultimately responsible for the financial performance of your property. This includes generating appropriate sales levels, a responsibility shared by all departments, as well as the appropriate management, or control, of all of your financial resources. In Chapter 2, we identified "control" as one of the four major functions of management. It is not surprising, then, that the job title of the person most responsible for assisting the GM in the financial management of a hotel is the "controller." The primary task of the controller is to help the GM "control" and analyze performance results.

In this chapter you will learn about the accounting function and the major responsibilities of the hotel's accounting department, as well as how an effective hotel controller will help you make appropriate financial management decisions by providing you with the timely and accurate accounting data you need to make those decisions.

In a large hotel, the accounting office may consist of several individuals, but in a smaller property, it may consist of only one person. In all cases, however, the tasks performed by the accounting office are critical to the success of the hotel. These tasks include forecasting hotel revenue, budgeting, preparing precise financial documents, compiling accurate operating statistics, assisting in the development and implementation of internal control systems, and serving, along with the GM, as a liaison with internal and external auditors.

You should know that, although it may be possible to operate an excellent hotel without an exceptional controller, experienced GM's will tell you that a strong accounting department is a critical component of any truly successful hotel. Information is indeed power, and it is the controller's office that will give you the information you need to make powerful and timely decisions. In fact, in many properties, it is the controller who will actually serve as the "acting GM" when the GM is away from the property. Even though that is not always the case, it certainly is an indication of the value of this office and the work it performs. If the hotels you are interested in managing are too small to have a full-time controller on property, you will still find this chapter to be extremely valuable because it may very well be you, the GM, who will perform many of the tasks traditionally assigned to the controller's office.

Chapter 5 Outline

THE ACCOUNTING FUNCTION
    Generally Accepted Accounting Principles (GAAPs)
    Uniform System of Accounts for Hotels
ACCOUNTING SYSTEMS
    Centralized Accounting Systems
    Decentralized Accounting Systems
REVENUE FORECASTING
BUDGETING
    Long-Range Budgets
    Annual Budgets
    Monthly Budgets
FINANCIAL STATEMENTS
    Income Statement
    Balance Sheet
    Statement of Cash Flows

DAILY OPERATING STATISTICS
    Manager's Daily Sales Report
    Detailed Room Revenue Statistics
    Adjustments and Allowances
INTERNAL CONTROLS
    Cash
    Accounts Receivable
    Accounts Payable
        Payment of Proper Amounts
        Payments Made in a Timely Manner
        Payment Records Properly Maintained
        Payment Totals Assigned to the Appropriate Department Head
    Purchasing and Receiving
    Inventories
    Payroll

AUDITS
    Internal Audits
    External Audits

HOTEL TERMINOLOGY AT WORK
GLOSSARY

ISSUES AT WORK

THE ACCOUNTING FUNCTION

Although GMs in most hotels will have one or more staff persons to help them, ultimately they must ensure that their hotel is using proper **accounting** procedures.

HOTEL TERMINOLOGY AT WORK

Accounting: The process of summarizing and reporting financial transactions.

In smaller hotels, nearly 100 percent of all accounting activity may be processed by front-office personnel. In very large hotels, accounting activities will take place in a variety of locations. In larger hotels there may be a significant number of food and beverage outlets as well as gift shops and other revenue-producing areas that sell products and collect money. At the front desk, guests will pay for:

- All guest room charges
- Taxes related to the sale of guest rooms
- Guest-initiated telephone charges

In most hotels, front-office managers will work closely with their accountants and/or controllers.

- Food and beverage purchases charged to the guest's room
- Charges for all goods and services directly interfaced with the property management system

In fact, in the hotel industry, the accounting processes performed at the front desk are so important that hoteliers actually make a distinction between **front-office accounting** and **back-office accounting**.

HOTEL TERMINOLOGY AT WORK

Front-Office Accounting: The process of summarizing and reporting financial transactions occurring at the front desk.

Back-Office Accounting: The process of summarizing and documenting the financial activity and standing of the entire hotel.

■

GMs certainly do not need to be **certified public accountants (CPAs)** to do their jobs well; it is important, however, that they understand the basic accounting principles that should be used by the hotel's **controller**.

HOTEL TERMINOLOGY AT WORK

Certified Public Accountant (CPA): A designation given to an individual who has passed a national qualifying examination related to accounting practices and principles. CPA designations are granted and administered by state boards of accountancy.

Controller: The individual (or department) responsible for maintaining the back office accounting system.

■

THE INTERNET AT WORK

The Hospitality Financial and Technology Professionals (HFTP) administer the Certified Hospitality Accountant Executive (CHAE) and the Certified Hospitality Technology Professional (CHTP), a program developed jointly by HFTP and the EIAH&LA. These programs recognize individuals who excel in the specialized fields of hospitality accounting and technology management. To see how to qualify for these certifications, go to

www.hftp.org

When you arrive, click on "Certification."

Generally Accepted Accounting Principles

If the readers of a hotel's financial information are to have faith in the collection and reporting systems used, the principles and practices used in these systems must be known and understood. If they are not known, or when those reporting information do so in a manner intended to intentionally, or even unintentionally mislead the reader, ineffective decision making is the sure result. Therefore, financial information reported by GMs as well as their hotel controllers should follow **generally accepted accounting principles** for hotels.

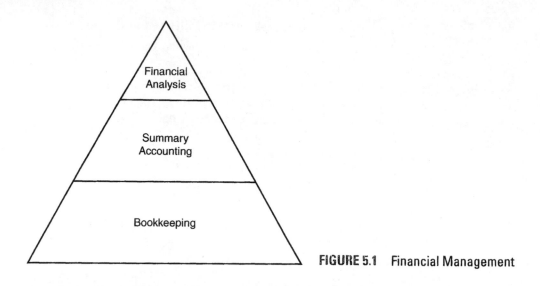

FIGURE 5.1   Financial Management

Although it is not the intent of this text to examine hotel accounting procedures in depth (most degree-granting educational institutions teaching hospitality management devote one or more entire classes to the topic), it is critical to master the basic fundamentals used in hotel bookkeeping and accounting.

The work of bookkeeping (recording transactions) yields the data analyzed by managers and accountants. Thus, for example, the recording of an individual financial transaction such as an in-room movie sale is a bookkeeping task. Bookkeeping would also be used to tally the hotel's total monthly movie sales. These revenue numbers would then be incorporated into the hotel's monthly financial statements to be analyzed by the hotel's controller, GM, and others. Clearly, if bookkeeping tasks are not properly performed, the resulting financial data provided by the hotel's accounting staff will not be accurate and decisions made based upon the numbers supplied are likely to be flawed as well.

As can be seen in Figure 5.1, bookkeeping forms the foundation of financial management. It is simply impossible to make a meaningful analysis of a hotel's financial standing if the data summarized by the hotel's accounting staff was erroneously or carelessly supplied by those performing the hotel's bookkeeping tasks.

In actuality, the distinctions between bookkeeping and accounting are not always clear-cut. As a result, the common hotel practice is to simply consider all of the bookkeeping and accounting tasks performed in the front office as front-office accounting, and all of the remaining bookkeeping and accounting tasks as back-office accounting.

Uniform System of Accounts for Hotels

In most cases, GMs are not legally required to follow any specific procedures when recording financial transactions. There are, however, laws requiring owners to properly report and pay taxes due, to file certain documents with the government, and to supply accurate business data. Therefore many hotel owners do require that their managers use a series of suggested accounting procedures created specifically for hotels. These have been developed by hospitality accountants in conjunction with the EI, and are called the **Uniform System of Accounts for the Lodging Industry**.

HOTEL TERMINOLOGY AT WORK

Uniform System of Accounts for the Lodging Industry (USALI): A standard set of accounting procedures used to record a hotel's financial transactions and condition.

◼

The USALI gives hoteliers and their accountants a consistent and easily understood "road map" to record revenues and expenses, as well as report the hotel's overall financial condition. GMs who wish to do so can purchase a copy of the USALI (now in its ninth edition) at www.ei-ahla.org.

Hoteliers seek accurate financial information to ensure good decision making, but they are not the only ones interested in consistently and accurately recording and reporting a hotel's financial activity. In addition to a hotel's owners, those who invest in hotels are very interested in how their hotels perform financially. The individuals and business entities that review the financial information of a hotel of course will count on it to be collected and reported in a way that yields information accurately reflecting the hotel's financial position. Accurate financial information is so important that, in 2002, the federal government passed a law making it a criminal activity for a hotel (or any other) company's executives to knowingly provide investors with false financial information.

The 2002 **Sarbanes-Oxley Act** came on to the statute books as an attempt to rebuild public confidence in the way corporate America governs its business activities. The act has far-reaching implications for the tourism, hospitality, and leisure industry, as well as for its corporate customers and supply chain.

HOTEL TERMINOLOGY AT WORK

Sarbanes-Oxley Act: Technically known as the Public Company Accounting Reform and Investor Protection Act, the law provides criminal penalties for those found to have committed accounting fraud. In addition, Sarbanes-Oxley covers a whole range of corporate governance issues including the regulation of auditors.

◼

Although Sarbanes-Oxley is long and complex, most of the attention of hotel GMs has focused on a few key areas. Section 302 of the act imposes much greater responsibility on top executives at public companies. This is because it states that if company executives misrepresent financial statements or the internal control environment of their companies, their personal assets are at risk, and they may face significant fines and/or imprisonment.

Section 404 requires companies to verify the work quality of those who inspect and report on their bookkeeping and accounting methods. Lastly, companies are required to disclose publicly all significant deficiencies and material weaknesses relating to their internal controls and accounting systems.

A centralized accounting system is often preferred by those owners who control more than one property.

ACCOUNTING SYSTEMS

The main responsibility of the controller is to oversee the accounting and bookkeeping functions in the hotel. Because this includes the development of the systems to collect and report financial information, analyzing this same information, and making finance-related recommendations to assist in management decision making, a good controller (one who has a thorough understanding of the hotel business) can truly help you interpret your hotel's financial information.

Regardless of your controller's skill level, in some cases the financial records of your hotel will still likely be examined by a CPA before owners, investors, creditors, governmental agencies, and other interested parties will accept them as accurate. In larger hotels, the controller is likely to be a CPA, whereas in smaller properties, it is more likely that an individual who is not a CPA will be responsible for the bookkeeping and accounting functions. It would be a mistake to discount the importance of a CPA to a hotel; however, it would be just as big a mistake to assume that only a person who has earned the CPA designation can be an effective controller. This is true because today's accounting systems can be classified as either centralized or decentralized.

Centralized Accounting Systems

In a **centralized accounting** system, the financial data from your property is transmitted via computer (e-mail, network, Web page, etc.) to a "central" location, where it may be recorded and then analyzed by management or combined with other hotel properties for analysis.

Understanding and implementing budgets is essential for the effective operation of a hotel. (© Jose Luis Pelaez, Inc./CORBIS)

HOTEL TERMINOLOGY AT WORK

Centralized Accounting: A financial management system that collects accounting data from an individual hotel(s), then combines and analyzes the data at a different (central) site.

To illustrate why some hotels operate under a centralized system, assume that you own five full-service hotels in the Southeastern United States. Assume also that your office is in the Midwest. If you wanted to know, on a daily basis, what the combined sales revenue for your five hotels was on the prior day, you would want those hotels to have reported their previous days sales to your office, where, for convenience, you would have the sales revenue of the five hotels added together to yield one number that represents your hotels' prior day's total sales. Centralized accounting is most prevalent in chain-operated or multiproperty hotel companies.

If the hotel you will manage is one of a number of hotels owned or managed by the same company, you are likely to operate under a centralized accounting system. If you do, it is also likely that the company, rather than your individual hotel, will employ a CPA for data analysis. This is true because it is generally more cost-effective to employ one CPA in a central location than multiple CPAs in multiple locations.

Decentralized Accounting Systems

In a **decentralized accounting** system, the GM and the controller must take a larger role in the preparation of financial documents.

HOTEL TERMINOLOGY AT WORK

Decentralized Accounting: A financial management system that collects accounting data from an individual hotel site and combines and analyzes that data at the same site.

If neither the GM nor the controller is a CPA, it is likely that the hotel's owners will, at least annually, employ the services of a CPA to review the work of the on-site controller and give a professional opinion about the reliability of the financial statements prepared by the controller's office. This review process is discussed later in this chapter in the section on **audits**.

HOTEL TERMINOLOGY AT WORK

Audit: An independent verification of financial records.

∎

In this text, we will assume a decentralized accounting system is in use to illustrate all of the variety of bookkeeping and accounting functions taking place in the modern controller's office. In a property you might manage, all, some, or none of these functions may be centralized. It is essential, however, for you to understand the importance of each function.

REVENUE FORECASTING

An estimate or forecast of all future hotel revenue is of great help to the GM, and it is the role of the controller to work with the hotel's revenue management team (see Chapter 6) and other department heads to keep it current and accurate. Revenue forecasting is an important part of the controller's job; thus an up-to-date revenue forecast, including rooms, food and beverage, and other income revenues, should always be available for the GM's inspection. It is important to understand why this information is so critical to the GM. To do so, let's examine five typical questions that might well be posed to a GM by members of the EOC.

1. *From Sales and Marketing:* "Would the budget segment devoted to winter marketing programs next year be better spent focusing on improving sales in January or February?

2. *From Maintenance:* "Would this July be a good time to replace carpets in one wing of the hotel (consisting of 20 percent of the guest rooms) or would the replacement be less disruptive if scheduled for August?"

3. *From F&B (food and beverage):* "Would September be a good time for the F&B director to take vacation?"

4. *From Housekeeping:* "Would Tuesday or Saturday be the better day for holding the monthly departmental staff meeting?"

5. *From Safety and Security:* "Should we add an additional security person to next Friday night's schedule, or is the current staffing level appropriate?"

Clearly, in each of these situations (as well as others) a GM's knowledge of current and future sales levels is critical to the decision-making process. Accurate revenue estimates are essential for excellent property management. In summary, an outstanding controller helps the GM make outstanding decisions by providing outstanding revenue forecast information.

BUDGETING

Budgeting for revenue, expenses, and profit is a process that consumes a significant portion of the GM's time. A good controller is the GM's essential partner in this budgeting process. In fact, it is the controller's office that will actually spearhead the assembly and submission of the budget to the GM. Some hotel managers simply view a budget as an onerous, self-imposed plan for spending money that will ensure hotel revenues always exceed hotel expenses. But a GM does not need a budget simply to ensure that expenses are less than revenues. If the GM fails to approve necessary expenditures (funds for needed repair and maintenance of equipment, the purchase of quality guest room supplies, staffing levels that provide proper guest service, and wage increases that ensure the best staff in the hotel are not lured away by competitors), the budget may be met, but the hotel will surely suffer.

A GM who simply sees his or her role in the budget process as one of "never exceed the budget" does not fully understand the importance or function of the budget. Together, the controller and GM must develop a budget that is a crucial tool for effective management.

In a business context, a budget is much more than a plan for spending cash resources. In fact, it is a plan for utilizing resources of all kinds, including cash, tools and materials, and labor, to operate the hotel in its most effective manner.

Budgeting is sometimes described as a financial expression of the GM's business strategy. This makes sense when you consider that a business strategy seeks to project where the hotel is going, how it will get there, what it will cost, and what the profit outcome will be if the strategy is implemented successfully. A well-developed budget, however, can do even more than project revenues and expenses. If used properly, the budget is an important means of developing internal controls, another function that is critical to the controller's role.

The effective controller/GM team builds their budget, monitors it closely, modifies it when necessary, and achieves their desired results. Yet some controller/GM teams do a poor job developing budgets because they feel the process is too time-consuming. Developing a helpful budget does take time; however, good budgets assist the hotel in many ways, including:

1. Allowing management to anticipate and prepare for future business conditions.

2. Providing a communication channel whereby the hotel's objectives are passed along to its various departments.

3. Encouraging department managers who have participated in the preparation of the budget to establish their own operating objectives and evaluation techniques and tools.

4. Providing the GM with reasonable estimates of future expense levels and serving as a tool for determining future room rates and other price structures.

5. Helping the controller and GM to periodically carry out a self-evaluation of the hotel and its progress toward its financial objectives.

In the hotel industry, operating budgets generally are one of three types:

- Long range
- Annual
- Monthly

Long-Range Budgets

A long-range budget is one that encompasses a relatively lengthy period of time, generally from two to five years, or in some cases even longer. The GM and controller prepare these budgets, with input from each of the hotel's operating departments. In conjunction with the marketing and sales department, the GM's role in the process would be to forecast changes in the number of guest rooms available to sell, predicted occupancy percentage, and ADR given future market conditions; the role of the controller (as well as the GM) would be to estimate expenses.

Obviously, with such a long-term outlook, these budgets are subject to changes due to unforeseen circumstances and market forces, yet they are useful for long-term planning, as well as for considering the wisdom of debt financing and refinancing and the scheduling of **capital expenditures**.

HOTEL TERMINOLOGY AT WORK

Capital Expenditure: The purchase of equipment, land, buildings, or other fixed assets necessary for the operation of the hotel.
■

Annual Budgets

Usually, preparation of the annual budget consumes a significant amount of the controller and GM's time. This is because, in large, multiunit hotel companies, annual budgets must be produced by the individual hotels, submitted to a central office for review, then sometimes revised to ensure they are in keeping with the overall financial objectives and goals of the hotel company. This process can begin as early as June or July for the following year.

As the name implies, these budgets are developed to coincide, in most cases, with the calendar year. As such, they provide more detail than a long-term budget and are subject to less fluctuation based on unforeseen events.

Monthly Budgets

The monthly budget is a natural outgrowth of the annual budget. In fact, truly outstanding controllers produce an annual budget as a result of previously producing 12 monthly budgets. With a well-developed annual budget, you might wonder why the controller should be concerned with an accurate monthly budget. The importance of the monthly budget, however, can be seen quite clearly in the example of the annual revenue and expenses of a hotel near a ski resort. In each of the winter months, revenues will likely greatly exceed one-twelfth of the annual revenue budget, as will expenditures. In a like manner, summer month revenues and expenditures will likely fall far short of one-twelfth the annual budget. In the case of this **seasonal hotel**, to effectively reach the annual targets, great care will need to be taken with each individual month's budget. During its busiest months, these hotels will sell all or nearly all of its rooms at **rack rate**.

HOTEL TERMINOLOGY AT WORK

Seasonal Hotel: A hotel whose revenue and expenditures vary greatly depending on the time (season) of the year the hotel is operating. Examples include hotels near ski resorts, beaches, theme parks, some tourist areas, sporting venues, and the like.

Rack Rate: The price at which a hotel sells its rooms when no rate discounts of any kind are offered to the guest. Often shortened to "rack."

■

In general, hotels will see some variation in annual sales based on the time of year. Because that is true, monthly budgets are an excellent managerial tool for helping to determine whether the hotel is maintaining progress toward the goals developed in the annual budget.

Typically, a hotel's operational budget would indicate specific sources of revenue as well as well-defined categories of anticipated expense. While the complete development of a hotel's operating budget is beyond the scope of this text, Figure 5.2 is an example of

Payroll & Related:	Actual This Year	Budgeted This Year	Actual Last Year
Chief Engineer	$ _____	$ 4,444	$ 4,100
Engineer Assistants	_____	9,000	8,752
Benefit Allocation	_____	3,700	3,611
Total Payroll		$ 17,144	$ 16,463
Expenses:			
Computer Equipment	_____	$ 500	$ 1,108
Equipment Rental	_____	0	400
Electrical & Mech. Equipment	_____	2,000	1,985
Elevators	_____	580	551
Elevator Repairs	_____	0	0
Engineering Supplies	_____	300	239
Floor Covering	_____	250	210
Furniture	_____	1,000	1,740
Grounds	_____	250	195
Heating, Ventilation, Air-Conditioning (HVAC)	_____	3,000	4,152
Kitchen Equipment	_____	500	481
Laundry Equipment	_____	400	310

(continued)

FIGURE 5.2   Waldo Hotel Property Operations and Maintenance Department Operating Budget for January

Payroll & Related:	Actual This Year	Budgeted This Year	Actual Last Year
Lightbulbs	_____	200	105
Maintenance Contracts	_____	2,500	2,500
Operating Supplies	_____	300	653
Painting & Decorating	_____	500	399
Parking Lot	_____	200	110
Pest Control	_____	500	431
Plants & Interior	_____	300	274
Plumbing & Heating	_____	500	453
Refrigeration & Air-Conditioning	_____	1,600	1,783
Signage Repair	_____	0	50
Snow Removal	_____	1,000	1,121
Swimming Pool	_____	3,000	3,524
Travel & Entertainment	_____	1,000	974
Telephone	_____	200	170
Trash Removal	_____	425	399
Uniforms	_____	300	271
Total Expenses	_____	$ 21,275	$ 24,588
Total Prop. Ops. & Maint.	$ _____	$ 38,419	$ 41,051

FIGURE 5.2   *(Continued)*

the detail commonly found on the expense segment of a monthly operating budget. Note how the budget is compared with the actual results of the prior year, with a space on the document for filling in the actual expenses of the month once those numbers are known.

FINANCIAL STATEMENTS

In addition to producing budgets, the controller's office is also responsible for preparing, or in a centralized accounting system, supplying the information to prepare, the financial statements that summarize the hotel's operating results. As we have seen, the budget looks to the future of the hotel's performance. There are three additional, key financial

By reviewing financial statements, hoteliers are able to view their past and present operating expenses. (© Benelux Press/Index Stock Imagery)

documents that look at the hotel's past accomplishments and its present financial condition. These statements, each of which should be prepared monthly for the GM, are

- Income statement
- Balance sheet
- Statement of cash flows

Income Statement

The income statement (more technically known as the income and expense statement) is sometimes better known as the profit and loss statement, or even more simply, the **P&L**.

HOTEL TERMINOLOGY AT WORK

P&L: Short for the profit and loss statement, also a synonym for the income and expense statement. The P&L records total hotel revenues and expenses for a specific time period.

The P&L is supplied by the controller's office, and is one of the two or three most critical monthly documents a GM will receive from any department head. Essentially, this document, when properly prepared, lists the hotel's revenues, expenses, **GOP**, and **fixed charges** for a specific time period. This specific time period is typically a month, fiscal quarter, or year.

This Period's Actual		
		Revenues
	Less	Direct operating expense
	Equals	Departmental operating income
	Less	Overhead (undistributed) expense
	Equals	Net income (GOP)
	Less	Fixed expense
	Equals	Income before taxes

FIGURE 5.3   Income Statement Information

HOTEL TERMINOLOGY AT WORK

GOP: Short for gross operating profit. This popular term is taken from a pre-1990 version of the Uniform System of Accounts for Hotels (USAH) published by the New York Hotel Association. It refers to hotel revenue less those expenses typically controlled at the property level. It is generally expressed on the income statement and in the industry as both a dollar figure and percent of total revenue.

Fixed Charges: Those expenses incurred in the purchase and occupation of the hotel itself. These include rent, property taxes, insurance, interest, and depreciation and amortization.

◼

Typically, a financial or managerial accounting text would include a full discussion regarding the preparation and analysis of the income statement. For the purposes of this text, it should simply be pointed out that a competent controller will produce an accurate income statement in a time frame that the GM finds helpful for the proper management of the hotel. In no case should this time period exceed the middle of the next reporting period. For example, if the income statement is to be produced monthly, the January statement should be available to the GM no later than February 15. Simply put, a controller who cannot achieve this time frame needs further assistance, training, or replacement. If as a GM you are to properly manage your hotel, a timely and accurate income statement is crucial to your success.

An income statement that details monthly, quarterly, and/or annual revenue and expense such as that in Figure 5.3 is helpful, but is actually the bare minimum when it comes to providing the GM with useful information. With the information in Figure 5.3, the GM can answer the question: *How did the hotel perform during this time period?*

A much more helpful format for the income statement (but one that requires more effort on the part of the controller), is the **tricolumned statement** shown in Figure 5.4.

		This Period's Actual	This Period's Budgeted	Last Year Same Period Actual
	Revenues			
Less	Direct operating expense			
Equals	Departmental operating income			
Less	Overhead expense			
Equals	Net income (GOP)			
Less	Fixed expense			
Equals	Income before taxes			

FIGURE 5.4   Tricolumned Income Statement

HOTEL TERMINOLOGY AT WORK

Tricolumned Statement: An income statement that lists (1) actual hotel operating results from a specific time period, as well as (2) budgeted operating estimates for the same time period, and finally (3) the actual operating results from the prior year's same time period.

With the income statement information shown in Figure 5.4, the GM can evaluate and formulate answers to the following types of questions:

1. How did the hotel perform during this time period?
2. How did the hotel perform compared with our performance estimate (budget)?
3. Where did our estimates vary significantly?
4. How did the hotel perform compared with the same period last year?
5. Where were significant changes from last year evident?

Clearly, the controller who can supply more information on the income statement does so to the benefit of the GM, and of course, his or her own career.

Balance Sheet

An income statement will tell the GM whether the month or other period in question has been a good one, but it is the balance sheet that provides a point-in-time statement of the overall financial position of the hotel. The balance sheet has often been described as a "snapshot" of the financial health of a hotel. This analogy is a good one because the balance sheet captures the financial condition of the hotel on the day produced. It does not tell how profitable the hotel was in a given accounting period, but this snapshot can be compared with previous or later snapshots to determine the financial movement of the hotel.

The format of the balance sheet is really rather simple, listing first the hotel's assets (what the hotel owns), then its liabilities (what it owes to non-owners of the business), and finally, the amount owed to owners (owners' equity).

Assets owned by the hotel will typically include such items as cash, monies owed to it by others, the value of items in inventory (food, beverages, cleaning supplies, and the like), and **prepaid expenses**.

HOTEL TERMINOLOGY AT WORK

Prepaid Expenses: Expenditures made for items prior to the accounting period in which the item's actual expense is incurred.

In addition, the asset portion of the balance sheet lists the value of the hotel's property and equipment (fixed assets), less any accumulated **depreciation**.

HOTEL TERMINOLOGY AT WORK

Depreciation: The process used to lower the value of a fixed asset during a specific accounting period because it is assumed to have been "used up" during that period.

Assets		
Cash	$ 75,000	
Accounts receivable	50,000	
Inventories on hand	25,000	
Prepaid expenses	10,000	
Total Assets		$ 160,000
Property and equipment	$ 7,000,000	
(Less accumulated depreciation)	500,000	
Net property and equipment		6,500,000
Total Assets		**$ 6,660,000**
Liabilities and Owners' Equity		
Current liabilities		
Accounts payable	$ 75,000	
Wages payable	25,000	
Total current liabilities	$ 100,000	
Long-term liabilities		
Mortgage payable	$ 6,300,000	
Total Liabilities		**$ 6,400,000**
Owners' equity		260,000
Total Liabilities and Owners' Equity		**$ 6,660,000**

FIGURE 5.5   Simplified Balance Sheet for the Waldo Hotel as of January 1, 20XX

The liabilities section of the balance sheet includes current and long-term liabilities. The current liabilities section is generally defined as those debts that will be paid within one year and long-term liabilities are those debts that will be paid in a time period longer than the next 12 months. Thus, for example, an invoice for fresh produce, to be used by the food and beverage department, which is due and payable on the day the balance sheet is produced, would be considered a current liability, while the amount remaining to be paid on the hotel's 20-year mortgage would, on the same date, be classified as a long-term liability.

The difference between what a hotel owns (assets) and what it owes (liabilities) represents the property owners' equity in the hotel. Figure 5.5 represents a sample balance sheet for the "Waldo Hotel."

The information presented by the balance sheet is important, and the controller should prepare it as often, and in as timely a manner, as the income statement is prepared. The balance sheet is especially useful when a specific time period (e.g., the end of the current year) is compared with a prior time period (e.g., the end of the prior year). The balance sheet's "point-in-time" perspective makes it a useful tool for the GM in the analysis of the overall financial health of the hotel.

Although little seems written about the limitations of the balance sheet, it is important to realize that in the hotel industry these limitations can be significant. A complete discussion of the balance sheet's limitations are best reviewed in a fundamental accounting text; however, of most significance is that of all the assets listed on the balance sheet, none take into account the relative value, or worth, of the staff, including the GM, who is actually operating the hotel.

Hotel companies are fond of saying that "people [our employees] are our *most important* asset," yet the value of experienced, well-trained staff members is not quantified on the balance sheet. To further clarify this important concept, assume you are the hotel GM and that you are considering a $1,000 expenditure for your marketing and sales department. Your alternatives are spending the $1,000 to replace an aging computer used by one of your sales managers, or using the same $1,000 to send the entire five-person marketing and sales team to a one-day training class on the advanced usage of Microsoft Excel, the spreadsheet software used in your property for producing sales contracts and guest invoices.

If you decide to purchase the computer, the value of assets (property and equipment) on the balance sheet will increase, whereas if you elect to "invest" in your staff via the training program, no such increase will occur. Yet, in this case, it is highly likely that the training class, rather than a single upgraded computer, will make a much greater difference in the effectiveness, efficiency, accuracy, and "worth" of the hotel's marketing and sales effort. Astute GMs recognize both the value and limitations of the balance sheet when reviewing it.

Statement of Cash Flows

Traditionally, a hotel's accounting support staff has regularly provided the GM with an income statement and balance sheet. As we have seen, the income statement details the financial performance of the hotel throughout a specified time period, whereas the balance sheet shows the hotel's financial position at a specific point in time (usually the end of an accounting period). These two documents are extremely useful to management, but an excellent controller provides the GM with a third important financial summary. That summary is the statement of cash flows. In this case, *cash* refers to any coins and currency on hand and in checking account balances. Because cash itself does not generate income for a hotel, keeping enough (but not too much) cash on hand is an important task typically undertaken by the hotel's controller or GM.

The statement of cash flows is essential because it provides answers to the following types of questions that cannot be answered by either the income statement or the balance sheet:

- How much cash was provided by the hotel's operation during the accounting period?
- What was the hotel's level of capital expenditure for the period?
- How much long-term debt did the hotel commit to during the period?
- Will cash be sufficient for the next few weeks or will short-term financing be required?
- At what time(s) of the year does the business generate (or spend) the most cash?

In the hotel business, as in many others, "Cash is King." Savvy GMs often make this statement because they know it is critical that a hotel not only is profitable, but also that it maintains its **solvency**. This is done by monitoring the cash that flows into a business (through its revenue-generating activities) as well as how the cash flows out of the business (through the expenditures incurred to support its revenue-generating efforts).

HOTEL TERMINOLOGY AT WORK

Solvency: The ability of a hotel to pay its bills as they become due.

The statement of cash flows shows the effects on cash of the hotel's operating, investing, and financing activities. A simplified illustration may help to clarify the importance of the statement of cash flows. Assume that a hotel's income statement shows sales revenue of $200,000 for a given month. Assume also that the hotel shows a "profit" (income before taxes) figure of $50,000 for that month. All may seem well until it is realized that $100,000 of the sales for the month were made to a guest to whom the hotel has extended credit. Thus, the income statement may show the hotel has "made" $50,000 for the month, but those funds are not yet on deposit in the hotel's bank accounts and are not available to assist in the payment of the hotel's debts. And in fact, the hotel has been required to use $50,000 of its own cash or credit to finance the operation of the property until the $100,000 due is collected from the guest. As you can see, then, it is important for a GM to know how much cash debt is outstanding, as well as the likelihood of collecting on that debt. This concept, called "accounts receivable aging," is discussed more fully in the "Internal Audit" section of this chapter.

In addition to credit sales, the GM must be aware of the hotel's own short- and long-term cash needs if the hotel is to remain solvent. The cash standing of a hotel is vital, and the controller should provide the statement of cash flows detailing that standing to the GM just as frequently as both the income statement and balance sheet. In fact, the Financial Accounting Standards Board (FASB), which is the current accounting rule-making body, has required since 1988, the statement of cash flows to be included with these two other financial statements when issued to external users.

MANAGERS AT WORK

J.D. Ojisama has recently been assigned to serve as the GM and oversee the renovation and expansion of a hotel just purchased by the real estate investment group J.D. is employed by.

Currently, the hotel consists of 300 rooms and 8,000 square feet of meeting and banquet space. The expansion calls for adding 150 guest rooms, as well as 8,000 additional feet of meeting space. Assume the expansion will take one year.

How is J.D. likely to begin the process of budgeting revenue for the hotel in its first year after expansion? What historical hotel data would be useful in helping J.D. complete this task? What additional information about the area in which the hotel is located would be helpful?

Where is J.D. likely to find such information? How important is the controller likely to be in this process? Why?

THE INTERNET AT WORK

To stay abreast of issues and changes in accounting procedures, periodically visit the Web site of the FASB.

You can access it by going to

www.accounting.rutgers.edu

DAILY OPERATING STATISTICS

To effectively manage your hotel, the controller must provide you with the information you will need to make sound decisions.

Manager's Daily Sales Report

As a GM, you will depend on the controller's office to give you a daily summary of the hotel's previous day's sales. That is, every day, in a timely manner, the controller's office should be able to provide you with an accurate recap of the prior days' rooms,

Some PMS reports identify the specific type of traveler using the hotel.

Food and Beverage, and other revenues. This report is referred to as the Manager's Daily Sales Report, or more simply, the "Daily."

The Daily is prepared from data supplied nightly by the **PMS**. In some cases, the PMS may actually produce the Daily. We will examine the PMS in greater detail in Chapter 8 (The Front Office), because it is the front office that is most responsible for its maintenance and accuracy. In fact, the PMS is the heart of the front office. The controller's office, however, uses the nightly data produced by the PMS for a variety of tasks, one of which is the preparation of the Daily.

HOTEL TERMINOLOGY AT WORK

PMS: Short for "property management system." This term refers to the computerized system used by the hotel to manage its rooms revenue, room rates, room assignments, and reservations, as well as other selected guest service functions.

Information that should be contained in the Daily includes the following:

For Rooms:

Number of rooms available for sale
Number of rooms sold
Occupancy rate
ADR
RevPar
Other rooms revenue information desired by the GM

For Food and Beverage:

>   Restaurant sales
>   Bar/lounge sales
>   Meeting room rentals
>   Banquet sales
>   Other Food and Beverage revenue information desired by the GM

For Other Income:

>   Telephone revenue
>   In-room movie revenue
>   **No-show** billings
>   Other income categories unique to the property

HOTEL TERMINOLOGY AT WORK

No-Show: A guest who makes a confirmed room reservation but fails to cancel the reservation or arrive at the hotel on the date of the confirmed reservation.

Although it is called the Daily, somewhat implying that it contains only one day's information, many controllers increase the value of the Daily by including, on the report, cumulative monthly data totals, as well as individual and cumulative data from the same day in the prior year. Thus, a sample one-page daily, produced via Excel spreadsheet, might be designed in a manner similar to that shown for the Waldo Hotel in Figure 5.6.

Obviously, the more detail a GM seeks, the longer and more complex will be the Daily. Some managers prefer great detail, including in their Daily information on room types sold, number of guaranteed reservations made, cash overage and shortages, or any of a variety of pieces of information the GM feels will be helpful in staying abreast of the hotel's business on a daily basis. It is the job of the controller to produce the Daily. That job is made substantially easier when the PMS system is used to generate either all or part of the report.

Detailed Room Revenue Statistics

One very important function of the controller's office is the documentation and verification of the night auditor's report. This report, generated by the PMS, will, depending on the PMS, give management a complete and detailed breakdown of the previous day's business. Often running ten or more pages in length, the night audit report is used by the controller to verify credit card charges, cash on hand, revenue sales totals, detailed room revenue statistics, and **allowances and adjustments**. These last two categories many GMs wish to have detailed on a regular basis.

HOTEL TERMINOLOGY AT WORK

Allowances and Adjustments: Reductions in sales revenue credited to guests because of errors in properly recording sales or to appease a guest for property shortcomings.

THE WALDO HOTEL

January 15, 20XX

	Today	To Date	Last Year Today	Last Year To Date
Rooms Available	285	4275	285	4275
Rooms Occupied	**191**	**3035**	**180**	**3011**
Occ. %	67%	71%	63%	70%
ADR	$ 105.20	$ 103.98	$ 98.99	$ 100.20
RevPar	$ 70.50	$ 73.82	$ 62.52	$ 70.57
Rooms Revenue	**$ 20,093.20**	**$ 315,579.30**	**$ 17,818.20**	**$ 301,702.20**
Food and Beverage				
Banquets	$ 4,550.00	$ 68,250.00	$ -0-	$ 71,250.00
Meeting Room Revenue	$ 1,250.00	$ 18,750.00	$ 150.00	$ 19,850.00
A/V Rental	$ 140.00	$ 2,240.00	$ 75.00	$ 2,500.00
Restaurant	$ 650.00	$ 8,450.00	$ 710.00	$ 10,650.00
Total F&B Income	**$ 6,590.00**	**$ 97,690.00**	**$ 935.00**	**$ 104,250.00**
Telephone Revenue				
Local Calls	$ 85.00	$ 1,105.00	$ 79.50	$ 1,033.50
Long Distance Calls	$ 210.00	$ 2,730.00	$ 185.00	$ 2,220.00
Other Income				
Gift Shop	$ 231.25	$ 2,312.50	$ 221.00	$ 2,210.00
In-Room Movie Sales	$ 185.00	$ 2,035.00	$ 78.00	$ 1,850.00
Guest Laundry	$ 71.50	$ 858.00	$ 61.50	$ 738.00
No-Show Revenue	$ 198.50	$ 2,580.50	$ 520.00	$ 3,200.00
Total Daily Revenue	**$ 27,664.45**	**$ 424,890.30**	**$ 19,898.20**	**$ 417,203.70**

FIGURE 5.6   Sample Manager's Daily Report

As a GM, the Manager's Daily Report gives you much of the information you need to assess the day's operation; however, the night audit report provides much greater detail on room revenue. This is because the GM must be aware both of how much room revenue has been produced, as well as from whom that revenue is being produced. The night audit report, taken from the nightly data generated by the PMS, provides a wealth of information on room sales if the controller properly uses it.

For example, the information (provided by the PMS) required to fully understand the daily sales revenue and RevPar picture on a given day includes information related to ADR, rooms sold, and market segment. Figure 5.7 details exactly why a GM needs comprehensive information on the type of guests staying in the hotel.

As can be seen, the "makeup" of the guests in the hotel would be very different under these two scenarios. In scenario one, the hotel is filled primarily with people on a tour (91 rooms) and those in a group of leisure travelers (40 rooms). In the second scenario, **transient** corporate travelers make up the largest portion of guests (75 rooms), followed by corporate travelers staying in a group (60 rooms).

HOTEL TERMINOLOGY AT WORK

Transient: Guests that are neither part of a group booking or tour group. Transient guests can be further subdivided by traveler demographic to gain more detailed information about the type of guest staying in the property.

MANAGER'S ROOM REVENUE DETAIL REPORT

THE WALDO HOTEL
January 15, 20XX

Rooms Available	285					
Rooms Sold	191					
Occupancy %	67.0%					

Market Mix	Scenario 1 (285 Rooms Available)			Scenario 2 (285 Rooms Available)		
	Rooms Sold	ADR	Total Revenue	Rooms Sold	ADR	Total Revenue
Transient Guests						
Corporate	25	119	$ 2,975.00	75	119	$ 8,925.00
Leisure	25	139	$ 3,475.00	5	139	$ 695.00
Government	0	0	$ 0.00	15	75	$ 1,125.00
Total Transient Guests	**50**		**$ 6,450.00**	**95**		**$ 10,745.00**
Group Guests						
Corporate	5	105	$ 525.00	60	105	$ 6,300.00
Leisure	40	118	$ 4,720.00	6	118	$ 708.00
Government	5	78	$ 390.00	30	78	$ 2,340.00
Total Group Guests	**50**		**$ 5,635.00**	**96**		**$ 9,348.00**
Tour Guests	91	88	**$ 8,008.00**	0		0
TOTAL GUESTS	**191**		**$ 20,093.00**	**191**		**$ 20,093.00**
ADR			**$ 105.20**			**$ 105.20**
RevPar			**$ 70.50**			**$ 70.50**

FIGURE 5.7   Two Alternative Guest Profiles/Same RevPar

Assume, for a moment, that the GM at the Waldo Hotel knows, from past records, that the average leisure or tour room sold by the hotel houses 2.2 individuals, whereas each corporate room sold is occupied, on average, by 1.1 persons. Obviously, then, the demands placed on the hotel's restaurants and any recreational facilities, as well as housekeeping services required by these two groups, will be very different. Taking all occupied rooms into consideration, the **house count** in the first scenario is likely to be nearly twice that of the second scenario. Because of this, it is important for the GM to know not only how many rooms have been sold in the hotel, as well as the day's RevPar, but also to what type of client those rooms have been sold. It is the role of the controller to provide this information on a daily basis.

HOTEL TERMINOLOGY AT WORK

House Count: An estimate of the number of guests staying in the hotel on a given day.

A detailed room revenue report, which can in some cases be produced directly from the PMS, should contain, at minimum, the following information:

• Rooms available
• Total rooms occupied

- Rooms occupied by guest type
- Occupancy percent
- Total ADR
- ADR by guest type
- Total RevPar

The GM may, if he or she chooses, add additional decision-making rooms statistics to the above data, which the controller should be prepared to supply.

Adjustments and Allowances

In addition to room revenue detail, the controller should, on a daily basis, provide the GM with a detailed listing of any adjustments or allowances made by the managers or employees of the hotel. From the perspective of the controller, these vouchers are important because they help to balance actual monies collected with monies that have been previously billed to guests. From the perspective of the GM, however, the vouchers are important because they point out shortcomings in the hotel's operation that must be addressed and continually monitored by the GM.

Figure 5.8 is an adjustment (and allowance) form used by a typical hotel. Note that the form has:

1. A sequence number for control purposes
2. A space for the date the voucher is used
3. A space for the name of the guest(s) for whom the adjustment was made

(1) ADJUSTMENT

Nº 348685

DATE (2) 20xx

NAME (3) ROOM OR ACCT. NO. (4)

EXPLANATION (5)

X (6)

SIGNATURE

11-09-0199 (7)

FIGURE 5.8 Adjustment Voucher

4. A space for the guest's identifying room number or account

5. A space for an explanation of the event or circumstances that justified the issuing of an adjustment

6. A space for the initials or signature of the employee issuing the adjustment

7. An identification number for reordering purposes

In a small property, each of these vouchers would be tabulated and reviewed for accuracy by the controller, and then the vouchers themselves would be given to the GM. In a larger property, their information might be combined and a summary of their contents passed on to the GM. An effective GM, however, insists on seeing the actual vouchers, whenever practical, and not merely the total of vouchers.

Why the GM should view these vouchers or other guest relations complaint monitoring devices on a daily basis becomes clear when you understand that there are three fundamental situations that could result in the completion of an allowance and adjustment voucher.

- *Employee Error in Charges.* Despite appropriate training, employees can sometimes make errors in the amount they charge guests. This problem can range from charging guests the wrong room rate for their stay, to charging guest A for services actually used by guest B.

   When an error is discovered, the guest's bill, if previously submitted as a sale to the controller's office, must be adjusted to reflect the correct charge. Assume, for example, that Mr. and Mrs. Bakal, staying in room 417 on a Saturday night, have two drinks in the hotel lounge. They sign the guest check charging their drinks to their room; however, the bartender mistakenly charges the drinks to the guest in room 471. The Bakal's check out on Sunday morning. On the following Monday, the guest in 471 approaches the front desk to check out. Obviously, the guest in room 471 will, upon reviewing the bill, refuse to pay the incorrect charge. At that point, an allowance and adjustment voucher, removing the drink charges, would be prepared for the guest in 471. In such a case, it may be impossible to collect on the charges originally incurred by the Bakals (remember that they left the hotel on the previous morning).

   The need for the GM to see this voucher is evident. Shortcomings in employee training programs, cash sales systems, or guest services techniques may become clear to the GM if a pattern in employee error allowance and adjustment vouchers is evident.

- *Hotel-Related Problems.* Despite the best efforts of the hotel's management and staff, some guests will still experience problems with the hotel's facilities or guest service. For example, an ice machine on a particular floor may have stopped working, and before it could be repaired by the hotel, inconvenienced a guest who had to walk to another section of the hotel for ice. Or unfortunately, a hotel employee may not have been courteous, thus offending the guest. In both cases, as well as others, a guest may, upon check-out, request or demand a reduction in the bill. In these situations, an allowance or adjustment in the bill may need to be made, and the voucher would be filled out. The importance of such vouchers being seen by the hotel GM on a daily basis is self-evident. Changes may be required in equipment inspection programs, guest service training, or a variety of other areas where the GM's intervention is critical to correct recurring problems.

- *Guest-Related Problems.* In some cases it is the presence of other guests, rather than the hotel, that causes a particular guest to have an unpleasant experience at the hotel. Complaints ranging from excessive noise in adjacent rooms to rowdy guest behavior in public spaces can cause a guest to feel they should be compensated for the unpleasantness of their experience. If, in the opinion of the proper hotel staff member, an allowance or adjustment to the guest's bill were warranted, the adjustment and allowance voucher would be completed. The hotel GM of course would want to be made aware of all such incidents on a daily basis. And certainly the GM would want to take corrective action; in many cases, these same guests may contact the GM, or the hotel's owners, or the franchise brand organization with the same complaint. If, as a GM, you are unaware of problems on your property, curative action cannot be taken. For that reason, you should require that the controller or other appropriate staff member give you, on a daily basis, the allowance and adjustment vouchers completed by the hotel staff.

The total dollar amount of allowances and adjustments compared with total overall rooms revenue can be tracked on a monthly basis using the following formula:

$$\frac{\text{Total Monthly Allowances and Adjustments}}{\text{Total Room Revenue}} = \text{Room Allowance and Adjustment \%}$$

This percentage will vary based on the age of the hotel, the quality of staff and training programs, and even the type of guest typically served. As the GM you should know your average monthly room allowance and adjustment percentage; more importantly, however, you should know the reason(s) for any increases in that average on a given month. Unless you know your problem areas, you will not be able to correct them. The controller's best efforts to supply you with the information from the actual allowance and adjustment vouchers will always be well worth that effort.

INTERNAL CONTROLS

The title of "controller" is derived from the word *control.* It is not surprising, then, that one of the very most important functions of the controller's office is the development and maintenance of internal control systems. Hotels, and the restaurants they often include, routinely contain large amounts of cash, products, and equipment that can, be the subject of fraudulent activities by guests or employees if not carefully controlled. A good controller helps the GM by carefully developing policies and procedures designed to ensure the safety of the hotel's assets.

Cash

Any business that routinely collects cash payments from guests must develop a system of safeguarding this important asset. Hotels are no exception. Of course, in today's hotel environment, cash assets, in addition to currency, include credit and debit card charges and personal and business checks. The potential to lose these assets to theft, fraud, or outright carelessness always exists. It is the role of the controller as well as the GM and the department head of each area that handles cash to develop and enforce a system of checks, balances, and controls designed to ensure the security of these important assets.

In most hotels, cash is collected in a variety of locations in addition to the front desk. Restaurants, bars, lounges, parking areas, vending areas, and gift shops are just a few locations within a typical hotel that routinely process cash sales. In all of these situations, at least one individual serves as a cashier/money handler. A bartender, for example, may serve as his or her own cashier during an evening shift. Likewise, the individual responsible for replenishing soft drink vending machines will serve as a cashier of sorts when cash is removed from the machines.

In hotels, cash assets are at greater risk from internal threats than from external ones. That is, while the potential for robbery by a nonemployee certainly exists in all hotels, the greater threat to the security of the hotel's cash assets is the internal threat of employee theft or fraud.

Any time a cashier is responsible for the collection of money, several instances of potential employee theft or fraud can exist. The cashier, for example, may make a sale, collect payment from a guest, not record the sale at all, but keep the cash.

The methods used by cashiers to defraud guests and/or the hotel are varied and depend to a great degree on the type of sales made. That is, the methods used by an unscrupulous bartender to defraud the hotel's food and beverage department will be different from those used by a dishonest front-desk agent. In either case, management must have systems in place to verify sales and the cash receipts those sales produce. An effective, experienced controller is invaluable in designing and establishing these systems.

Even though it is fairly straightforward to consider the theft of cash by a cashier, the hotel industry affords some cashiers the opportunity to defraud guests paying by credit card as well. These, too, must be guarded against. Some common credit card-related techniques used to defraud guests include:

- Charging guest's credit cards for items not purchased, then keeping the money from the erroneous charge.
- Changing the totals on credit card charges after the guest has left or imprinting additional credit card charges and pocketing the cash difference.
- Incorrectly adding legitimate charges to create a higher-than-appropriate total, with the intent of keeping the overcharge. This, of course, can also be done on a cash sale.
- Charging higher-than-authorized prices for products or services, recording the proper price, and keeping the overcharge.
- Giving, or selling, the credit card numbers of guests to unauthorized individuals outside the hotel.

The GM's role in asset management regarding cash is, quite simply, to monitor the quality of the cashier-related security programs designed by the controller. For example, a bartender working a shift from 5:00 P.M. to 2:00 A.M. and serving as his or her own cashier might have recorded $1,000 in beverage sales during that time period. If that were, in fact, the case, and if no errors in handling change occurred, the cash register should contain cash, checks, and bank charges equal to $1,000 (plus, of course, the amount of the beginning cash bank). If it contains less than $1,000, it is said to be **short**; if it contains more than $1,000, it is said to be **over**.

HOTEL TERMINOLOGY AT WORK

Short: A situation in which cashiers have less money in their cash drawer than the official sales records indicate. Thus, a cashier with $10 less in the cash drawer than the sales record indicates is said to be $10 "short."

Over: A situation in which cashiers have more money in their cash drawer than the official sales records indicate. Thus, a cashier with $10 more in the cash drawer than the sales record indicates is said to be $10 "over."

■

Overages and shortages should be monitored by the controller and, when excessive, brought to the immediate attention of the GM. Cashiers rarely steal large sums of money directly from the cash drawer because such theft is easily detected, but management should make it a policy to monitor cash overages and shortages on a daily basis.

Some GMs believe only cash shortages, but not overages, need to be investigated. This is not the case. Consistent cash overages may be an indication of employee theft or carelessness and should be investigated.

It is also possible for a dishonest cashier to avoid being short and still defraud the hotel. If, for example, the cash register or computerized cash control unit has a void key, a dishonest cashier could enter a sales amount, collect for it, and then void (erase) the sale after the guest has departed. In this way, total sales would equal the amount of the cash drawer. If the cashier then destroys records involved with this sale, the cash register total sales figure and cash drawer would all balance. To prevent this, management should insist that all cash register voids be performed by a supervisor or at least be authorized by management on an individual basis. In addition, because today's computerized cash registers record the number, individual, and time at which cashier voids are performed, these, too, should be monitored by the controller.

Yet another method of hotel cashier theft involves the manipulation of reduced price or complimentary rooms or products. Assume, for example, that, at the Waldo Hotel, your sales and marketing department has produced and distributed a large number of guest coupons good for 50 percent off a guest's night stay. If the front-desk cashier has access to these coupons, it is possible to collect the money from a guest without a coupon and then add the coupon to the cash drawer while simultaneously removing sales revenue equal to the value of the coupon. A variation on this theme is for the cashier to declare a room to be complimentary after the guest has paid the bill. In cases like this, the cashier would again remove sales revenue from the PMS in an amount equal to the "comped" room.

These kinds of fraud can be prevented by denying cashiers access to unredeemed cash value coupons issued by the hotel and by requiring special authorization from management to "comp" rooms. While the previous scenarios do not list all possible methods of revenue theft and fraud, it should be clear from this discussion that you must have a complete revenue security system if you are to ensure that all services and products sold generate sales revenue that finds its way into the hotel's bank account. It is a good idea for the controller and GM to regularly evaluate the cash control systems in place on the property. This includes a thorough evaluation of

- Cashier training programs
- Sales revenue recording systems
- Cash overage and shortage monitoring systems
- Enforcement of employee disciplinary procedures for noncompliance

For some cashiers, the theft of cash is very tempting. Today's sophisticated cash management systems make it easier than ever to detect cashier theft, but a diligent controller and GM is still critical to that process.

Accounts Receivable

When a hotel elects to extend credit to a guest, it creates a **direct bill**(ing) account for that guest and then, as the guest incurs charges, an invoice is periodically prepared and sent to the guest.

HOTEL TERMINOLOGY AT WORK

Direct Bill: An arrangement that allows a guest to purchase hotel services and products on credit terms.

This direct guest billing may take place on the same day the guest incurs the charge, at the end of each month, quarterly, or at any mutually agreed-upon point in time. When a hotel extends credit to guests, the dollar amount of outstanding charges owed to the hotel by these guests is called the hotel's **accounts receivable (AR)**.

HOTEL TERMINOLOGY AT WORK

Accounts Receivable: Money owed to the hotel because of sales made on credit. Sometimes referred to as "AR" for short.

There are many reasons, including guest preference, why a hotel might elect to extend credit to some of its guests. In all cases, however, it is the controller's job to establish:

1. Which guests will be allowed to purchase goods and services on credit
2. How promptly, and frequently, those guests will receive copies of their bills
3. The total amount owed to the hotel and the length of time those monies have been owed

The credit worthiness of guests is one frequently debated between the sales and marketing area and the controller's office. In many cases, the sales office will pressure the controller to extend credit (to complete the sale), whereas the controller, in many cases, takes a more conservative view and may suggest that the hotel deny credit to potential guests who should, in the view of the sales staff, be extended credit terms. A good controller will work with the GM to establish credit policies that maximizes the number of guests electing to do business with the hotel, yet minimizes the hotel's risk of creating uncollectible accounts receivable.

To assist the controller's office in determining which groups should be allowed to enjoy the advantages of buying on credit, a Direct Bill Application (for credit) will be completed by the guest, reviewed by the controller's office, and then passed to the GM for final approval or denial. Figure 5.9 is an example of a Direct Bill Application that a guest seeking credit terms would complete.

To appreciate the reasons for a hotel electing to extend credit to a guest organization, consider the case of Rae Dopson, president of Dopson Construction, a midsize road construction firm. In this scenario, Rae's company has been awarded the state contract to construct two miles of new highway near your hotel. The job is a big one and will last many months. It will also involve the use of dozens of workers, each of whom will require Monday through Thursday night lodging near the work site. Since the lodging of its

Waldo Hotel

Application for Direct Billing

Date: _____ **Federal ID #** _____

Company/Organization: _____

Division/Department: _____

Mailing Address: _____

Street Address   Suite #

_____

City   State   Zip Code

_____

(Area Code) Phone Number   (Area Code) Fax Number

Billing Address: _____
(if different from above)
(Name of Invoice Recipient–Attention To)

_____

Street (PO Box #)   Suite #

_____

City   State   Zip Code

List of those persons entitled to authorize (call in reservation):

1. _____   _____
   FULL NAME   TITLE

2. _____   _____
   FULL NAME   TITLE

3. _____   _____
   FULL NAME   TITLE

Please circle the charges employees are authorized to bill. Circle all that apply:

| Room & Tax only | Phone | Restaurant Bills |
| All Charges | Movies | Banquet/Meeting Charges |

Credit References:

1. _____
   Hotel Name

   _____
   Phone Number

(continued)

FIGURE 5.9   Direct Bill Application

2. _____
Hotel Name

_____
Phone Number

3. _____
Other

_____
Phone Number

Company Bank:

Bank Name: _____   Account Type: _____

Account Number: _____

At least three credit references and at least one company bank account are **required** to complete this application. At least two of the references must be hotel references, while the third may be a company with whom you have a billing history.

If for some reason the application cannot be completed with the requested information, please contact the Accounts Receivable Department of the Waldo Hotel.

Please allow at least 15 days for proper processing and approvals.
*Applications must be approved **before** any direct billing may take place. You will be contacted in writing mail about your approval status.*

By signing this document, I allow the creditors and bank listed above to release to the Waldo Hotel all necessary information for the proper processing and approval of this application. I understand that all accumulated charges are submitted to the accounting department upon the completion of each authorized function/stay. I also understand that payment is due within 30 days from the date of the invoice. I further understand that it is my company's responsibility to keep the list of authorized personnel updated and current to avoid improper or unauthorized usage of this direct bill account, and may do so by requesting an authorization/status change form from the Accounts Receivable Department of the Waldo Hotel.

Signature of Applicant: _____   Date: _____

For Company Use Only:

Recommendation of Controller _____

_____
_____
_____
_____
_____
_____
_____
_____
_____

Approved By
Signature: _____   *Date:* _____

FIGURE 5.9   (*Continued*)

workers will be an expense of Dopson Construction, its managers face the alternatives of either (1) allowing each worker to stay at a hotel of their own choosing and then reimbursing each individual worker for his or her night's lodging, or (2) negotiating with a single hotel to place all of the business at that property and then requesting that the hotel bill the company directly for all lodging expenses. Clearly, it is in the best interest of both the hotel and the guest to select the second alternative. The bookkeeping of the construction company will be simplified if it is awarded direct bill status, and the construction company will also likely be able to negotiate a better nightly rate from the hotel because it will be able to guarantee a predetermined number of room nights needed on a regular basis. The hotel benefits from simplified billing as well. Finally, it is highly likely that other hotels who desire the business from Dopson Construction will be competing for that business, in part, by granting Rae's company's direct bill status.

After the determination has been made that credit terms will be extended, it is the responsibility of the controller's office to bill guests promptly. Finally, it is the controller's important job to monitor accounts receivable and to keep the GM informed as to their status. This is done via the **accounts receivable aging** report.

HOTEL TERMINOLOGY AT WORK

Accounts Receivable Aging: A process used to determine the average length of time money is owed to the hotel because of sales made on credit.

Figure 5.10 shows an example of an accounts receivable aging report for a hotel with $100,000 in outstanding accounts receivable.

Figure 5.10 indicates that the total amount owed to the hotel is $100,000. This amount can be broken down into four distinct time periods. One-half of the total accounts receivable ($50,000) is owed to the hotel by guests who have received their bills 30 or fewer days ago, whereas 5 percent ($5,000) is due from guests who have had over 90 days to pay their bills. As a general rule, as the age of an accounts receivable increases, its likelihood of being collected decreases. Also, as the percentage of accounts receivable 90 days or older increases, the likelihood of collecting on these receivables decreases.

As a receivable account ages, an effective controller will contact the affected guest to determine if there is a problem in billing, documentation, or some other item that is delaying payment to the hotel. In severe cases of nonpayment, the guest could have their direct billing status revoked and the hotel would undertake collection efforts.

Waldo Hotel: Accounts Receivable Aging Report For January, 20XX

Total Amount Receivable $100,000.00

| | Less than 30 | **NUMBER OF DAYS PAST DUE** | | |
		30–60	60–90	90+
	$ 50,000			
		$ 30,000		
			$ 15,000	
				$ 5,000
	———	———	———	
	———	———	———	
Total	$ 50,000	$ 30,000	$ 15,000	$ 5,000
% of Total	50%	30%	15%	5%

FIGURE 5.10 Accounts Receivable Aging Report

The extension of credit and the collection of accounts receivable is one important function of the controller's office. As a GM, your role is to monitor credit policies, direct bill applications, and the aging of accounts receivable to ensure that this cash management activity is operating properly and with the attention that it is due.

Accounts Payable

Just as a hotel will sell to some of its guests on a credit basis, many suppliers and service companies will provide goods and services to the hotel on a credit basis, with the hotel being billed by these vendors according to credit terms previously established. For example, a dairy products vendor may deliver fresh milk daily to the hotel. Obviously, it makes little sense to pay that vendor thirty times per month for the milk products delivered. Typically, a vendor such as this would establish the credit worthiness of the hotel and then send the hotel an invoice on a weekly, biweekly, or monthly basis. The charges for goods and services used by the hotel, invoiced by the vendor, but not yet paid are called a hotel's **accounts payable**, or AP.

HOTEL TERMINOLOGY AT WORK

Accounts Payable: The sum total of all invoices owed by the hotel to its vendors for credit purchases made by the hotel. Also called AP.

■

As a GM interacting with the controller's office, there are four major areas of concern you will have in regard to your own accounts payable system:

- Payment of proper amounts
- Payments made in a timely manner
- Payment records properly maintained
- Payment totals assigned to the appropriate department area

Payment of Proper Amounts

Despite the skill of any individual, mistakes can be made in paying invoices. Data entry errors can be commonplace unless the controller has established solid procedures to ensure that legitimate invoices are paid only for the amount actually due. In a well-run controller's office, invoices and payments for those invoices are checked by at least two individuals. Software developed to match invoice numbers against hotel check numbers is invaluable in this process. The intent of this type of software is simply to help ensure that AP are processed only for the amount of the invoices due.

THE INTERNET AT WORK

To view the features of a Windows-based software program that includes modules on AP, go to

www.hallogram.com/ias/

Scroll down and select "Accounts Payable" to review this program's features.

Payments Made in a Timely Manner

In addition to paying the proper amount, an effective controller understands that there is a proper time to pay each invoice. Some hotels gain a reputation with their suppliers for paying invoices very promptly. This can be good, but it is important to know that cash maintained in the hotel's cash accounts is also valuable. Thus, an effective controller maintains good relations with vendors, many of which are likely to be such local businesses as plumbers, electricians, and food vendors that are important for the continued successful operation of the hotel. Remember that those customers who pay bills slowly are also likely to be serviced slowly by their vendors. In fact, prompt payment of invoices is so important to many smaller businesses providing goods and services to a hotel that better purchase prices and delivery terms can often be negotiated if the hotel simply has a reputation for paying its bills on time. In addition, some vendors will actually offer the hotel the choice of paying less than the full invoice (discounts for on-time payments) if invoices are paid promptly.

In general, an effective controller should take advantage, whenever possible, of discounts offered by vendors for prompt payment. Some vendors will give a discount of 1 to 5 percent of the invoice price if a bill is paid within a specific time period. The controller should take advantage of every opportunity to build positive vendor relations and help ensure lowest costs by managing the accounts payable process professionally.

Payment Records Properly Maintained

It may seem fairly simple to ensure that each accounts receivable invoice to be paid is paid only once, but in fact that is not the case. Careful attention to detail is needed to make sure that invoices are paid and recorded properly. An effective controller creates a system whereby total payments to vendors match vendor billings exactly, with no overpayments or underpayments.

Payment Totals Assigned to the Appropriate Department Area

It is not only important for the controller to pay the hotel's bills, but it is equally important to know which area within the hotel has incurred a given expense. For example, as the GM, you may want to know how much money is being spent on plumbing repairs for a given month or year. Obviously, then, the controller must keep a record of how much money is being spent by the maintenance department for plumbing parts and labor for the time period of interest. To do so, controllers use a system of **coding** to assign actual costs to predetermined cost centers.

HOTEL TERMINOLOGY AT WORK

Coding: The process of assigning incurred costs to predetermined cost centers or categories.

For example, the maintenance department in a hotel will certainly be interested in its total expenditures for a month, but the expenditure breakdown in Figure 5.11 does a much better job of helping the head of maintenance, as well as the GM, know where the money in the maintenance department is being spent and why it was somewhat over budget in the month of January. Note that each expense subcategory has been developed to help managers understand total property operations and maintenance expenditures.

An effective controller will work with those involved in the purchasing process to code the expenses incurred by the hotel to the correct departmental expense category so these expenses can be clearly analyzed by the GM. Departmental expense categories can be developed by an individual hotel or a hotel company operating multiple hotels. In all cases, however, it is the controller's role to implement a functioning expenses coding system.

	Actual	Budgeted
Payroll and Related		
Chief Engineer	$ 4,444	$ 4,444
Engineer Assistants	8,450	9,000
Benefit Allocation	3,520	3,700
Total Payroll	16,414	17,144
Expenses		
Computer Equipment	425	500
Equipment Rental	1,000	0
Electrical & Mech. Equipment	2,520	2,000
Elevators	600	580
Elevator Repairs	200	0
Engineering Supplies	250	300
Floor Covering	0	250
Furniture	0	1,000
Grounds	850	250
HVAC	2,800	3,000
Kitchen Equipment	150	500
Laundry Equipment	0	400
Lightbulbs	250	200
Maintenance Contracts	2,500	2,500
Operating Supplies	185	300
Painting & Decorating	270	500
Parking Lot	1,000	200
Pest Control	350	500
Plants & Interior	280	300
Plumbing & Heating	1,585	500
Refrigeration & Air-Conditioning	1,500	1,600
Signage Repair	0	0
Snow Removal	1,000	1,000
Swimming Pool	3,500	3,000
Travel & Entertainment	1,600	1,000
Telephone	150	200
Trash Removal	450	425
Uniforms	280	300
Total Expenses	$ 23,695	$ 21,275
Total Prop. Ops. & Maintenance	**$ 40,109**	**$ 38,419**

FIGURE 5.11   Waldo Hotel Property Operations and Maintenance Expenditures for January

Purchasing and Receiving

Perhaps the most important role the controller can play in the AP process is that of ensuring payment is made to vendors only for goods and services actually received. For example, a lawn service invoice may be received by the controller's office that includes charges for lawn mowing, edging, and chemical weed treatment. Obviously, the invoice should be paid if the services have been performed. However, payment should be withheld if all services have not been performed, or not completed at the agreed-upon quality level. Thus, the controller's office should pay only those vendors who have delivered the hotel's authorized goods and services at the preauthorized price and in the manner agreed upon by both the hotel and vendor.

In regard to purchasing products for the hotel, before an AP invoice is paid the controller should have in place a system that verifies the terms of the sale, the product prices quoted by the vendor, and a list of the products received by the hotel so these can be checked against actual vendor's invoices. In regard to services purchased by the hotel, it is the role of the controller to devise a payment system that ensures that some member(s) of the property management team has

- Preauthorized the work to be done
- Confirmed the cost of the work to be done
- Verified that the work has been satisfactorily completed

Inventories

To properly create the income statement on a monthly basis, the controller must have a system in place to secure an accurate inventory from each department where monthly inventories are taken. This is true because the value of an inventory at the beginning of a month must be reconciled with purchases made during the month, as well as the dollar value of inventories at the end of the month. For example, if the controller is to state the dollar value of towels expense for a given month, he or she would determine the cost of providing towels for the month by using the following formula:

Beginning period value of towel inventory
+ Towel purchases
= Cost of towels available
− Ending period value of towel inventory
Cost of towels used in the period

To illustrate, assume that the Waldo Hotel had $8,000 of towels in inventory at the beginning of the accounting period and that it purchased $1,000 worth of towels in the month. Assume also that at the end of the month, $8,300 worth of towels remained in inventory. Using the above formula, the hotel's actual cost of towels for the month would be:

$ 8,000.00	Beginning period value of towel inventory
+1,000.00	Towel purchases
9,000.00	Cost of towels available
−8,300.00	Ending period value of towel inventory
$ 700.00	Cost of towels used in the period

Accurate, timely inventories must be submitted to the controller on a monthly basis from those departments designated to do so by the GM. It is then up to the controller to use those inventory values and the relevant accounting formulas to properly document actual expenses.

Payroll

An important function of the controller's office is the proper payment of employees' salaries and wages. If the hotel is large enough, this function may be shared with the human resources department because accurately paying employees is of course a necessary part of good human resources management. From the point of view of the GM, another important aspect of the payroll process is that of knowing exactly how property payroll dollars are being spent. This includes knowing both the total dollar amount of payroll expended by the hotel, as well as the departmental allocation of those dollars.

If, for example, the controller informs the GM that total payroll dollars for the month are higher than that which was budgeted, the GM will want to know where and why these extra dollars were expended. The controller must be prepared to promptly provide this information. Doing so will require that the controller keep detailed, department-specific payroll information. That is, the payroll dollars expended by the hotel should be segmented to allow easy viewing of each hotel department's individual payroll. This is important due to the fluid nature of labor use in the hotel.

To illustrate, assume that you originally anticipated selling 3,000 room nights in a given month, and you planned to schedule the appropriate housekeeping staff required to clean those rooms. If you then find that your actual room sales for the month were 3,500 room nights sold, you would expect to have expended more dollars for cleaning rooms than you originally budgeted. The question for you as the GM, of course, is whether the extra dollars spent were the proper number of extra dollars. With too many extra dollars spent, payroll resources may have been wasted; however, if too few extra dollars were spent (or if the department head elected to stay within the originally budgeted schedule regardless of the extra 500 sold rooms), guest service may suffer because the housekeeping staff would be too small to properly clean all of the rooms used by guests. The controller should provide the data to answer questions of this type.

A competent controller plays a critical role in the evaluation of payroll dollars spent. By working with the GM and the appropriate department heads, the controller can provide advice to the GM about prevailing wage rates, worker productivity, variations from budget, and future labor needs, each of which are critical for the efficient operation of the hotel.

MANAGERS AT WORK

After learning that the controller's office paid an invoice for some office supplies that had never actually been delivered to the hotel, J.D. Ojisama, the GM of the Hotel Waldo, is convinced that the process of purchasing all hotel supplies, verifying their delivery, accounting for them in inventory, and paying the invoices for those supplies is in need of a thorough review.

Assume that you are J.D. What would be other clues that the process is in need of review? Which individuals within the hotel need to be involved in this review process? Who should head the review team? What would be the likely consequence(s) if you do not institute the review process on a regular basis? What factors would influence your view of how frequently such a review should be undertaken?

AUDITS

Earlier in this chapter, we defined an *audit* as an independent verification of financial records. Although an audit includes the examination of many financial records, it is important to remember that the **auditor** will not examine every financial record produced by the controller's office since the last audit. Instead, the auditor will thoroughly inspect a sampling of records from a variety of areas (e.g., cash deposits, paid invoices, payroll records, restaurant sales, and the like) to determine whether consistent bookkeeping practices and standard accounting procedures are used.

If, during the sampling of records, the use of standard accounting procedures is in clear evidence, the auditor will report that, in his or her professional opinion, the financial records produced by the controller's office fairly and accurately represent the financial picture of the hotel.

If proper bookkeeping and accounting procedures are not in evidence, it is the role of auditors to describe the areas of deficiency they have found and to suggest procedures to improve the financial reporting system. It is the role of the GM to see that these procedures are implemented.

Internal Audits

An audit of records performed by accountants employed by the organization operating the hotel is known as an **internal audit**. This is a common practice that is cost-effective and quite helpful, particularly in multiunit hotel companies seeking to standardize the reporting activity of all the individual company hotels.

External Audits

In many cases, an independent verification of financial accuracy performed by accountants not employed by the hotel's operating company is required. Such an impartial examination of financial records is known as an **external audit**.

An example of a situation that would require an external audit is that of a hotel owned or operated by companies who issue stock purchased by the general public. In this case, it is important (and as you learned earlier, required by law) that the shareholders of the company know that an independent source is verifying the accuracy of the financial records created by the hotels. In such circumstances, an audit by a CPA may be needed, and many privately-owned companies also retain an independent CPA for at least an annual audit. It is important to remember that, even in the external audit, the CPA does not perform a detailed examination of all recorded transactions, and the objective of the assessment is the expression of an opinion about the accuracy of the hotel's financial position, in conformity with generally accepted accounting principles.

Both the internal and external audit are of great value. Often, because the internal auditors employed by a hotel company are more knowledgeable about hotel operations than are external auditors, the internal audit can detect intentional errors and theft not easily detected by the external audit.

Many of the fraudulent actions in hotels are the result of **collusion**, often so carefully planned that problems exist for a long time before they are finally discovered.

HOTEL TERMINOLOGY AT WORK

Collusion: Secret cooperation between two or more hotel employees for the purpose of committing fraud.

Since the external audit is not primarily designed to uncover fraud (although it may!), the GM should truly value the work of the internal auditor, particularly as it relates to a review of the hotel's internal financial controls.

In some cases, both the GM and the controller view an audit, either internal or external, with some dread. That should not be the case. Remember that an audit is performed because hotel room nights, the principle saleable product of a hotel, are an extremely perishable commodity that cannot be held and controlled in a normal manner. This is because unsold room nights disappear at midnight on each sale day. In addition, normal service to hotel guests includes a wide variety of transactions in which fairly large amounts of cash are handled. Finally, in smaller hotel properties, there are frequently a limited number of employees among whom duties can be divided and rotated.

It is important to realize that, in nearly every case, an audit will uncover areas of financial reporting and control that can be improved. This is to be expected and should not be cause for you, as a GM, to be alarmed. If the controller is a professional committed to excellence in his or her department, the audit is a tremendous opportunity for growth and improvement. An honest controller experiencing an audit will look to the GM for guidance as well as support. As GM, it is your job, for the good of the hotel and the controller's office, to provide both. Frequent and detailed auditing of hotel records is vital because of the need to establish and maintain a sound system of internal control. As hotel GM, an audit is a chance for you to see where the controller's office can be improved and to work with the controller to implement those improvements.

The role of the controller and others performing bookkeeping and accounting tasks in the hotel are complex and critical. It is imperative that the GM maintains a positive and professional working relationship with this essential aspect of the lodging industry. Working as a team, a strong controller, trained staff, and an excellent GM can be a formidable competitor for any rival hotel in the market, as well as a critically valuable asset to the hotel's ownership.

THE INTERNET AT WORK

Most controllers and bookkeepers are honest, but some are not. To request a free newsletter that identifies possible areas of fraud in financial reporting and records, go to the Association of Certified Fraud Examiners' Web site at

www.cfenet.com

and view their free antifraud newsletter.

HOTEL TERMINOLOGY AT WORK GLOSSARY

The following terms were defined within this chapter. If you are not familiar with one of them, please review the segment of the chapter that contains the term.

Accounting
Front-office accounting
Back-office accounting
Certified Public Accountant
    (CPA)
Controller
Generally accepted accounting
    principles (GAAPs)
Uniform System of Accounts
    for the Lodging Industry
    (USALI)
Sarbanes-Oxley Act
Centralized accounting
Decentralized accounting

Audit
Capital expenditure
Seasonal hotel
Rack rate
P&L
GOP
Fixed charges
Tricolumned statement
Prepaid expenses
Depreciation
Solvency
PMS
No-show
Allowances and adjustments

Transient
House count
Short
Over
Direct bill
Accounts receivable (AR)
Accounts receivable aging
Accounts payable (AP)
Coding
Auditor
Internal audit
External audit
Collusion

ISSUES AT WORK

1. Some GMs measure their own effectiveness using primarily ADR, while others prefer to evaluate their effectiveness by the occupancy rate generated. More recently, RevPar has become the standard by which the effectiveness of a hotel's management team is evaluated. Describe at least one strength and one weakness of each of these approaches. Are all three measures still useful? Would you, as a GM, use RevPar as your exclusive measure of effectiveness? Why or why not?

2. The balance sheet, income statement, and statement of cash flows each yield important pieces of information. To truly understand these documents, however, it is helpful to know what they cannot tell you. Using this chapter and an introductory accounting text available from your library, list and consider some of the limitations of each of these three financial documents.

3. Many hotels experience difficulty when establishing credit policies. List five factors you believe would be important when determining whether to offer credit terms to a new client in your own hotel. Explain your reason for choosing each factor.

4. Improvements in technology have affected the controller's office more than most areas within a hotel. Assume you were the GM of a large full-service property. What specific steps could you take to ensure that your controller stays abreast of the advances that impact his or her area? How will you evaluate that individual's efforts to maintain and improve skills? How will you keep up with the changes that will continue to revolutionize this area?

5. Often it is difficult to determine whether errors made in the financial records of a hotel, and then uncovered in an audit, represent intentional fraud or simply mistakes resulting from poor training or lack of knowledge. As the GM, what specific criteria might you use to evaluate the honesty of the controller's office if an independent audit revealed multiple areas of consistent mistakes?

6

Revenue Management

This Chapter at Work

To maximize its profitability, a hotel must do an outstanding job pricing and then successfully selling its guest rooms. This is so in full-service hotels as well as those properties selling sleeping rooms only. It is true that every hotel employee has an impact on hotel sales, but in most properties those areas directly responsible for pricing and selling rooms are the sales and marketing department and the front office. Because both departments must be coordinated, a GM should thoroughly understand the revenue-enhancing processes they commonly use.

The determination of precisely what a hotel's rooms should sell for and the methods (called channels) used to sell them make up the increasingly complex process the hotel industry now calls "revenue management." Revenue management is the single focus of this chapter. Its purpose is to familiarize GMs with the concepts, principles, and administrative activities required to positively influence, and in the long run to maximize, the income generated by their hotels.

In some hotels, the GM may be solely responsible for revenue management decision making while in other hotels the duties may be assigned to staff who ultimately receive the GM's approval for their revenue management plans report to the GM. In all cases, however, hotel GMs should understand room rate economics and ensure that their properties carefully manage the relationships between supply, demand, and the hotel's established room rate. Professional GMs understand that demand for guestrooms, as indicated by revenue forecasts, provide the important information needed to establish appropriate room rates. Because the essential goal of a revenue manager is the maximization of RevPar, the role of the revenue manager in the management of occupancy levels and ADR are analyzed, as well as how these concepts have been affected by the increasingly popular use of the Internet for buying and selling rooms.

This chapter includes an overview of a revenue-enhancing methodology first used in the airline industry and then introduced to the hotel industry as "yield management." Although that is still a popular term and is used in this text, it actually has evolved from its original set of managerial techniques because of the many methods now applied by modern hotels to market their rooms. Finally, the most important channels used to sell rooms are presented in this chapter to help GMs evaluate the effectiveness of their own property's channel management efforts.

Chapter 6 Outline

THE ROLE OF THE REVENUE MANAGER

A hotel's revenue manager is responsible for making decisions to maximize RevPar. In larger hotels, this may consist of one or more full-time positions. In midsized to smaller hotels, the front office manager and/or the director of sales and marketing may serve in this role and make recommendations to the general manager. In very small hotels, it will likely be the GM who retains this responsibility. In this chapter, the term, *revenue manager*, refers to any individual(s) who assumes RevPar management responsibilities for their property.

Realistically, the task of maximizing RevPar is part of every employee's job. For example, housekeepers must clean rooms properly so these rooms can be sold at the highest possible rate. The restaurant server who addresses the needs of hotel dining guests encourages them to return. In both cases and in others, employees provide value to guests and encourage their return by delivering quality service. The revenue manager's specific task is to devise and implement pricing strategies that meet the revenue-generating goals of the hotel's owners and bring value to guests.

How important is the revenue manager to the success of a hotel? The Kimpton Hotel and Restaurant Group (www.Kimpton.com) operates outstanding hotels including the Allegro (Chicago) and the Monaco (Denver). Its chairman and CEO believes the most important person in a hotel is the revenue manager because of his/her role in managing the hotel's rooms **inventory**. He states that the revenue manager "should be the highest paid (person on a hotel's staff)."[1] Not every hotelier might agree, but there is no question that a skilled revenue manager is crucial to a hotel's success.

HOTEL TERMINOLOGY AT WORK

Inventory (Rooms): Rooms of all types that are available to be sold by the hotel.
∎

Revenue Management

Some hoteliers mistakenly believe the terms *room rate management* and *revenue management* are synonymous. They are not. Although in many cases revenue managers actually establish room rates, in many other hotels they do not. For example, the hotel's owners, the GM, the director of sales and marketing (DOSM), or front-office manager may dictate the room rate to be charged at a specific time or on a specific date. The revenue manager, however, must still "manage" that rate. In a properly managed hotel, even with an established pricing structure, there is typically not one single, inflexible "rate" for a guest room. For most revenue managers, the correct reply to the common question, "How much are your rooms?" is "Who are you, how many rooms do you want, and when do you want them?"

To illustrate, assume that the GM of a 300-room hotel desires a $100.00 per night ADR and sets the rack rate for the hotel's standard room type at $100.00 nightly. A guest wishes to purchase 50 rooms per night for each of the next three Sunday nights. Assume the hotel traditionally achieves a 20 to 25 percent occupancy level on Sunday nights, and the GM wants this particular business. The guest,

---

[1]Thomas La Tour. Quoted in *Hotel and Motel Management*. July 5, 2004. Page 29.

A basketball tournament is an example of a localized special event that can generate high revenue for hoteliers.

however, has a budget of only $80.00 per night. Should the hotel accept the business? In the overwhelming majority of cases, the GM's answer would be "Yes." Why? The hotel will have the rooms available and can generate an additional $4,000.00 each night ($12,000.00 for the three nights) with the only real increase in direct costs being those required for housekeeping staff to clean the rooms.

Alternatively, assume that for the last five years the same hotel has experienced a sellout during the weekend that the Girl's State High School Softball Championships are held in the city. For that weekend, a potential guest has requested five rooms for two days (10 room nights) but has a budget of only $80.00 per night. Normally, the GM would assume that the revenue manager would *not* recommend that the hotel extend a discount even though the potential guest will go elsewhere. Why? The hotel, based upon historical data, will sell these rooms to other guests who are willing to pay the $100.00 rack rate (or more) for them.

In addition to forecasting future room sales, another reason that a revenue manager's job can be complex is because hotels routinely offer discounts off rack rate to a variety of entities. For example, to attract more mature leisure travelers, discounts may be offered to guests who are members of the American Association of Retired Persons (AARP). Similarly, some hotels identify other large groups and offer their members specific discounts. One group offered discounts by many hotels is the American Automobile Association (AAA) whose members merely verify their membership at time of check-in to receive the discount. AAA uses these discounts to solicit new members. For example, consider the following information posted on the AAA Web site:

> *"At Choice Hotels (Comfort Inn, Comfort Inns & Suites, Quality, Sleep Inn, Clarion, MainStay Suites, Econo Lodge and Rodeway Inn), AAA members save 10 percent when you show your membership card."*[2]

In this example, Choice Hotels executives, as part of their overall marketing strategy, have determined that the advantages gained from offering the AAA discount will more than offset the resulting 10 percent decline in ADR that their hotels will experience by participating in the program. Other large groups that have traditionally received significant discounts off a hotel's rack rates include local, state, and federal government employees, members of the military and clergy, and in the case of franchised hotels, groups that make an agreement with the franchisor (who then may require all its franchisees to honor the rate).

In addition to larger groups and nonprofit entities, most hotels empower the revenue manager to approve exclusive rates for select hotel guests. These **negotiated rates** are usually established for a specific time period (one year or more), at which time the hotel and the client can renegotiate the rate.

HOTEL TERMINOLOGY AT WORK

Negotiated Rate: A special room rate offered for a fixed period of time to a specific hotel client.

Used as in "What is the negotiated rate we should offer to Wal-Mart employees next year?"

In some cases, the negotiated rate may be in effect on any date the guest wishes to use it. In other cases, **blackout dates** may be identified and become part of the **negotiated rate agreement**.

HOTEL TERMINOLOGY AT WORK

Blackout Date: Any day on which the hotel will not honor a negotiated rate. Blackout dates should be identified at the same time the hotel and the client agree on a negotiated rate. Common blackout dates include New Year's Eve and other times the hotel believes its best interests are served by disallowing acceptance of the negotiated rate.

Negotiated Rate Agreement: A document that details the specific contractual obligations of a hotel and client when the hotel has offered, and the client has agreed to, a negotiated rate. Typical agreement content includes start date, room rate to be charged, agreement duration, and blackout dates (if any). The agreement should be signed by a representative of the hotel and the client.

Although room rates are important to a hotel's revenue manager, they are not the only factor that influences RevPar. In many hotels, the revenue managers are just as concerned about **length of stay (LOS)** as they are about rate.

---

[2]Posted at http://www.autoclubgroup.com/michigan/savings/partner_results.asp?vendorID=2560&city=&zip=&distance=1.

HOTEL TERMINOLOGY AT WORK

Length of Stay (LOS): The number of nights a hotel's individual guests use their rooms. LOS is computed on a per stay basis. For example, in a hotel that sold 300 group room nights to 100 guests, the LOS would be computed as

$$\text{Room nights sold} \div \text{Rooms sold to guests} = \text{LOS}$$

$$300 \div 100 = 3$$

∎

Recall that RevPar is affected by both the rate at which rooms are sold and by the number of rooms sold. Revenue managers who devise strategies to encourage increased LOS will also positively impact their property's RevPar. Revenue managers can encourage meeting attendees to increase their LOS by offering special discounts for arriving one day prior to and/or staying one day after the meeting. This is especially true for properties located in leisure/resort areas where attendees may have a reason to extend their stay. Promotions such as "Stay Four Nights, Get the Fifth Night Free" or "Come Early, Stay Late" are examples of programs designed to increase LOS and the property's RevPar.

The average LOS is important to any leisure or business hotel. Operationally, as LOS increases, housekeeping costs decrease because the time and material costs required to clean a **stay-over** room is almost always lower than those required for a check-out room. At the front desk, it is obviously less labor intensive to reserve a room for and to check in and check out one guest for three nights than it is to complete these processes for three guests each staying one night.

HOTEL TERMINOLOGY AT WORK

Stay-Over: A guest not scheduled to check out of the hotel on the day his or her room status is assessed. That is, the guest will be staying at least one more day.

∎

Room Rate Management

Guests are becoming increasingly sophisticated about locating lodging alternatives and making price comparisons when selecting their hotels. In most consumer surveys (assuming the rooms are considered clean), the location of a hotel is the most important reason for its selection by a guest. The second most important consideration is price (room rate). Many guests will travel a significant distance from their desired location to secure a room with a lower room rate. Importantly, the decision to select a hotel based upon its location and rate is most often made without guests contacting the hotel directly. Instead, they receive their information from a variety of sources. These can include the hotel's franchisor-operated or independently affiliated **central reservation system (CRS)**, property-level reservations agents, the hotel's sales and marketing department, **e-distribution channels**, and the property's own Web site.

HOTEL TERMINOLOGY AT WORK

Central Reservation System (CRS): An entity, operated by a franchisor, that offers potential guests the opportunity to make reservations at its affiliated (branded) hotels by telephone, fax, and/or the Internet.

Used, for example, in "What percentage of our transient business last month was generated through the CRS?"

E-Distribution Channel: Technically, any source of reservation delivered to the hotel electronically. Most commonly, however, the term is used to identify those distribution channels that use the Internet when communicating with the hotel.

Each of these sources are typically promoted or managed by either the front-office manager (FOM) (in the case of property-level reservation agents) or by the DOSM (in the case of the sales and marketing department). In some circumstances, the management of one or more revenue-generating sources may be shared. When different departments or individuals within a hotel are responsible for revenue-generation management, difficulties can arise and sometimes the GM may need to become involved.

To understand the type of difficulty that can arise, assume the DOSM of a 300-room property won a group bid for 100 room nights during a slow period for the hotel. The DOSM offered the group a room rate of $100.00 per night—a rate $10.00 below the hotel's normal ADR—as well as two "comp" rooms for every 50 rooms picked up by the group.

Assume also that, two days before the group's arrival, the demand for the hotel's rooms was still light and the FOM instructs the on-site reservation agents to quote a rate of $75.00 per night to guests calling the hotel directly for the same arrival and departure dates as group members. Further instructions are to post this reduced rate on the hotel's Web site. When this strategy is implemented, group members (who could easily access the hotel's rates via the Web site) begin to cancel their room reservations within the group block and rebook the lower priced rooms on the Web site.

The result is likely to be reduced RevPar for the hotel as well as an unhappy group organizer (because the reduced pickup in the group block will yield a reduced number of comp rooms). In addition, you can imagine the difficulties at the front desk when arriving group members begin to "share" information about the two different rates they are paying. Finally, it is also *very* likely that conflict will result between the FOM and the DOSM because each, in attempting to meet their own goals, has created a difficult situation for themselves, the hotel, and its guests.

In a very large property the positions of revenue manager, FOM, and DOSM may be at the level of department head and may entail supervising staffs of a significant size. It is helpful, therefore, for GMs to understand how, as shown in Figure 6.1, room rate management tasks intermingle (because they do so in significant ways) and how they can be coordinated.

- *Revenue Manager and FOM.* Many guests locate a hotel through key word searches on Internet search engines. Others may locate the hotel on an Internet travel site such as Travelocity or Expedia and then access the hotel's proprietary Web site. Still others may call the hotel directly to book their reservation. Regardless of the source, it is critical that the rates encountered by the guest be identical or at least internally consistent. Rates on a Web site and all other e-based delivery systems should be monitored (reviewed) regularly by the hotel's revenue manager and, if adjusted, the information must be relayed to the hotel's in-house reservations staff. This is true of rates to be charged for dates far into the future as well as for **day of**.

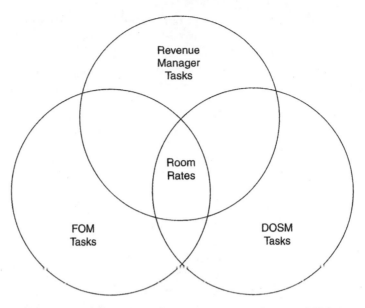

FIGURE 6.1   Shared Room Rate Management Responsibilities

HOTEL TERMINOLOGY AT WORK

Day Of: Short for "day of arrival." Used as, for example, in "Let's hold the rates at $100.00 per night for the 22nd, but reexamine that decision on the day of."

- *Revenue Manager and DOSM.* Ideally, the hotel's plan for rate positioning is developed as part of the overall business/marketing plan developed by the DOSM and approved by the hotel's GM. The marketing plan should consider the hotel's competitors, its group bookings history, **rate resistance** as reported by the property's reservation agents, and the demand forecasts that include the period of time covered by the marketing plan.

HOTEL TERMINOLOGY AT WORK

Rate Resistance: Refusal to make a reservation because the rate quoted is perceived, by the guest, to be too high.

Although the revenue manager and the DOSM do not need to attend an excessive number of revenue meetings, they must be able to make decisions, coordinate their efforts, and adjust rate strategies as conditions warrant. Additionally, the revenue manager's input about the number of rooms to be sold by group sales versus those to be held for transient travelers is always important.

For example, assume that a business-oriented hotel has 300 rooms. The hotel's sales department has a client that wants all 300 rooms on a Wednesday two months in the future. If the sales department makes the sale, no rooms will be available on that Wednesday night for any other guests. Assume also that the hotel has a core of approximately 50 transient business guests who check in every Monday and stay through Friday morning. In this case, the decision to make the group sale would mean that some revenue generated from the 300-room group would merely **displace** a significant amount of revenue that the hotel would have received from its 50 transient business travelers, each of whom would now be staying at an alternative property and may be sufficiently upset to continue staying there rather than return.

HOTEL TERMINOLOGY AT WORK

Displace (Revenue): To substitute one source of revenue for another.

■

- *Revenue Manager, FOM, and DOSM.* Every individual reservation made through the hotel's front office as well as every group room sale made by a hotel's sales department affects the property's revenue projections and, therefore, can affect rate management. The methods used by the revenue manager, FOM, and DOSM to share information and to coordinate their activities vary between properties. However, collaboration can be achieved through periodic updates involving all members of the revenue management team.

Coordination meetings involving all those who manage revenue sources should be attended, or chaired, by the GM. If those involved in the revenue management process do not follow a cohesive strategy, the consequence is likely to be the presentation of an inconsistent or even incoherent rate message. In some cases, consumers may correctly perceive that a hotel that cannot manage to get its pricing structure straight may well have the same problem when it comes to serving them as guests.

As you can see, for a variety of reasons, the management of room rates is a critical activity. Properly coordinated within the hotel, it serves to maximize RevPar. Improperly done, it can damage a hotel's reputation, alienate guests, create unnecessary rate resistance, and actually reduce occupancies and ADRs.

THE INTERNET AT WORK

Increasingly, software specific to the hotel industry that is designed to assist in the revenue-management process is becoming readily available for sophisticated hoteliers. To view the offerings of several such companies that have developed tools to assist lodging managers, go to

Maxim Revenue Management Solutions	www.maximrms.com
Optims	www.optims.com
IDeaS	www.ideas.com
Profit Optimization Strategies, Inc.	www.profitoptim.com

Room Rate Economics

Any serious exploration of hotel room rates and their management must include basic information about room rate economics. The study of **economics** related to room rates examines the social science associated with the making, marketing, and consumption of goods and services and involves considering how the forces of **supply** and **demand** allocate scarce resources (such as hotel rooms). Revenue managers must know and use **room rate economics** to price rooms and to understand how consumers react to the pricing strategies they employ.

HOTEL TERMINOLOGY AT WORK

Economics: The social science associated with the making, marketing, and consumption of goods and services and how the forces of supply and demand allocate scarce resources.

Supply: The total amount of a good or service available for sale.

Demand: The total amount of a good or service consumers want to buy at a specific price.

Room Rate Economics: The processes by which revenue managers price rooms while considering how consumers may react to pricing strategies used.

■

Interestingly, the fundamental rules of economics of most importance to hoteliers differ based upon the time frame examined. In the short-term, the **law of demand** is most important.

HOTEL TERMINOLOGY AT WORK

Law of Demand: The concept of economics that recognizes, when supply is held constant, an increase in demand results in an increase in selling price. Conversely, with supply held constant, a decrease in demand leads to a decreased selling price.

■

Understanding the law of demand is critical because, unlike managers in other industries, hoteliers cannot increase their inventory levels (supply) in response to known (or projected) increases in demand. The ability to comprehend the impact of this fundamental concept is a salient characteristic of outstanding GMs because they are ultimately responsible for revenue management.

To illustrate, assume a city will be the site of a major annual convention to be held 12 months from now. It will attract enough attendees to sell every hotel room in the city. Even though demand will increase greatly for the several days of the convention, the number of hotel rooms available to be sold (supply) will remain constant. This is because new hotels simply cannot be conceived, financed, designed, and constructed in 12 months. In this example, the city's hoteliers cannot add more rooms to their existing inventory, nor would it likely be advisable to do so even if they could because demand for these extra rooms will disappear when this convention ends.

Contrast that situation to managers of taxi cab businesses in the same city. These managers will likely increase the number of cabs available during the convention. They may extend the hours drivers are on duty, add more vehicles, secure additional drivers, or most likely, use a combination of all these strategies.

The impact of the law of demand on hotel inventory is immense and twofold. Outstanding revenue managers understand that the short-term supply of rooms cannot be increased, but they also understand that their own inventory of rooms is highly perishable. Consider, for example, the actions of a shoe store manager in the convention city. If, on Monday, the convention begins, a specific pair of shoes does not sell, the manager can attempt to sell the shoes on Tuesday. Contrast that situation with a hotel's revenue management team. If the hotel does not sell room 101 on Monday night, it will never again be able to sell that room, on that night, and the potential revenue that would be generated from the sale is lost forever.

Let's return to the shoe store manager for an analogous inventory situation. Assume that, at one minute prior to closing, a pair of shoes had not sold. Also assume that, at one minute after the store's closing, these shoes would disappear forever. How should that store manager price those shoes if a customer walked into the store at one minute prior to its closing? Understanding the shoe store manager's dilemma in this situation is the key to understanding the challenges of a hotel's revenue manager. In a hotel, unsold inventory vanishes forever!

It is important to understand the law of demand, but because of its long-term impact, all GMs must also understand the **law of supply**.

HOTEL TERMINOLOGY AT WORK

Law of Supply: The concept of economics that recognizes, when demand is held constant, an increase in supply leads to a decreased selling price. Conversely, with demand held constant, a decrease in supply leads to an increased selling price.

The price a hotel charges for its rooms is influenced by many factors. One of the most important is the number of rooms (supply) available relative to the degree of demand for these rooms. Consider, for example, a city in which the average demand from all sources for rooms during an entire week consists of 600 room nights. Assume also that the total number of rooms available to house these travelers is 1,000 with five hotels each offering 200 rooms for sale. The citywide occupancy rate is 60 percent (600 rooms ÷ 1,000 rooms = 60 percent). If one of the hotels closed, and the demand for rooms remained unchanged, the occupancy rate would increase to 75 percent (600 rooms ÷ [1,000 rooms − 200 rooms] = 75 percent). If this happened, the laws of supply and demand examined earlier will likely affect the pricing strategy implemented by each remaining hotel's revenue manager.

Similarly, assume that a new hotel with 200 rooms opened in the city. If there were no change in demand for rooms, the occupancy levels for the hotels would now be 50 percent (600 rooms ÷ [1,000 rooms + 200 rooms] = 50 percent). Again, prices for hotel rooms would likely be affected by the laws of supply and demand. In the long-term, new hotel openings (that create additions to supply) and hotel closings (that yield reductions in supply) affect the number of rooms available to sell. As a result, if total demand is unchanged, the pricing strategies best used to determine room rates will likely be affected in both scenarios.

The supply (number) of rooms in a market area is relatively easy for revenue managers to assess. When they have determined the amount of supply and have accurately estimated room demand, effective pricing decisions can be made. If, however, revenue managers significantly over- (or under-) estimate demand, critical errors can be made as a hotel's room rates are established and marketed. That is why a hotel's ability to accurately forecast demand (a concept examined next in this chapter) is so important to the hotel's financial success. Since information about supply is readily known and forecast data helps estimate demand, revenue managers can gauge the relationship between guestroom supply and demand. Using this information, they can determine the best rates to be assigned to each of their room types, because when revenue managers consider their hotel's room rates, they must generally consider multiple **rate types**.

HOTEL TERMINOLOGY AT WORK

Rate Type: A single (unique) rate for a specific type of room. Rate types are typically preprogrammed into a hotel's PMS.

Room Type	Rack Rate
Standard Double	$ 109.00
Standard King	$ 119.00
Executive Double	$ 149.00
Executive King	$ 164.00
Executive Double (Concierge level)	$ 199.00
Executive King (Concierge level)	$ 214.00
Double Parlor Suite	$ 269.00
King Parlor Suite	$ 289.00

FIGURE 6.2   Sample Hotel Rack Rates

HOTEL TERMINOLOGY AT WORK

Concierge Level: A section of a hotel (usually with restricted access) reserved for special guests paying higher room rates and receiving special amenities.

■

As defined in Chapter 5, rack rate is the price at which a hotel sells its rooms when no discounts of any kind are offered to the guests. Rack rates, however, will vary based upon the type of room sold. For example, the rack rate for a hotel's best, or most popular, room will be higher than for its least popular room. Larger rooms, suites, rooms with special amenities, views, or other features typically have their own unique rack rates. Figure 6.2 lists the rack rates that might be associated with a midsized convention hotel with a fairly limited number of different room types.

Note that, in this example, rack rates vary by bed type (kings at this hotel are more expensive than doubles), by amenities (executive rooms are likely to have features not found in standard rooms), by location (concierge-level rooms are more expensive than rooms not located on restricted floors), and by size (suites are more expensive than nonsuites). Some larger hotels may have dozens of different room types, each with its own unique rack rate. Even the smallest of hotels, however, will likely have several room types and therefore multiple rack rates.

Some hotels have very strong seasonal demand. For example, a hotel near a ski resort with a high occupancy during the ski season may experience a lower occupancy in the off season and will likely respond by varying its rack rates. These hotels, then, will have a **seasonal rate** that is higher (or lower) than the standard rack rate.

HOTEL TERMINOLOGY AT WORK

Rate (Seasonal): An increase (or decrease) in rack rate based upon the dates when the room is rented. For example, a beach-front hotel may have a seasonal rate offered in the summer with a lower "winter" rate offered in the off season.

■

In some cases, it makes sense for revenue managers to create **special event rates**. Sometimes referred to as "super" or "premium" rack, these rates are used when a hotel is assured of very high demand levels.

HOTEL TERMINOLOGY AT WORK

Rate (Special Event): A temporary increase in rack rate based upon a specific event such as a concert, sporting event, or holiday. Also sometimes known as "super" or "premium" rack. Examples include rates for rooms during Mardi Gras (New Orleans hoteliers) and on New Year's Eve (Manhattan hoteliers).

Hotels often negotiate special rates for selected guests. In most cases, these negotiated rates will vary by room type. In addition to rack and negotiated rates, hotels typically offer **corporate rates, government rates,** and **group rates**.

HOTEL TERMINOLOGY AT WORK

Rate (Corporate): A special rate offered to individual business travelers.

Rate (Government): A special rate offered to the employees of local, state, or federal governments.

Rate (Group): A special rate offered to a hotel's large volume guest room purchasers.

When a hotel creates a package, the **package rate** charged must be sufficient to ensure that all costs associated with the package have been considered.

HOTEL TERMINOLOGY AT WORK

Rate (Package): A special rate that allows a guest to pay one price for all of the features and amenities included in the package.

Special package rates used so frequently that they have become a standard in the industry include the **American plan (AP), modified American plan (MAP),** and **all-inclusive plan**.

HOTEL TERMINOLOGY AT WORK

American Plan (AP): A special rate that includes specifically identified guest meals (typically breakfast, lunch, and dinner).

Modified American Plan (MAP): A special rate that includes a specifically identified guest meal (usually one per day, often breakfast).

All-Inclusive Plan (Rate): A special rate that typically includes all guest meals and unlimited beverages as well as the use of other specifically identified hotel amenities and services.

Although the American or modified American plans are popular in many resort areas, the majority of full-service American hotels continue to operate under the **European plan (EP)** and provide no meals with the room charge. Increasingly, and in response to the complimentary breakfasts offered by most limited-service hotels, some full-service hotels have adopted a variation of the MAP and offer guests some type of partial or full complimentary breakfast.

HOTEL TERMINOLOGY AT WORK

European Plan (EP): A room rate that does not include guest meals.

■

Additional common rate types include the **day rate** and the **half-day rate**.

HOTEL TERMINOLOGY AT WORK

Day Rate: A special rate that typically includes 8–12 hours (but not overnight) use of a room.

Half-Day Rate: A special rate that typically includes 1–4 hours (but not overnight) use of a room.

■

These two rate types can result in hotel occupancy levels in excess of 100 percent. Especially in high demand areas such as near airports and train stations that generate significant need for short-term room use, the effective marketing of these rates can positively impact a hotel's RevPar.

Revenue managers can create discounts at various percentage or dollar levels for each rate type we have examined. The result is that a hotel, with multiple room types and multiple rate plans, may have literally hundreds of rates types programmed into its PMS. In addition, the use of one or more **fade rate** levels may create dozens more.

HOTEL TERMINOLOGY AT WORK

Fade (Rate): A reduced rate authorized for use when a guest seeking a reservation exhibits price (rate) resistance. Sometimes called "flex" rate.

▪▪

A fade rate is initiated when potential guests exhibit price resistance after being quoted a room rate. For example, a family traveling on vacation may enter a hotel lobby without a room reservation and inquire about prices. If, when quoted a price of $100.00 per night, the front-desk agent believes these potential guests will decline the rate to seek less costly accommodations elsewhere, the agent may be empowered to "fade" or "flex" the rate to a lower level. In this example, for instance, the agent may be authorized to "fade" (reduce) the original quote by $10.00 or more in an effort to sell the room.

The use of fade rates requires excellent front-desk agent training to justify the fade, or sophisticated travelers will wonder why they were not offered the more attractive rate originally. Fade rates can be very effective, however. In a hotel located at the entrance to or exit from a major Interstate highway, large numbers of travelers may arrive at the hotel without a reservation and inquire about rates. When rate resistance is encountered, some hotels authorize their front-desk agents to fade the rate *if* it is the guest's first time visiting the hotel. Since the overwhelming majority of travelers will likely be first-time visitors, this fade approach may be effective and will likely be perceived as a logical marketing strategy to many potential guests.

Given the number of room types found in a typical hotel and the number of rate types associated with each room, you can now appreciate the complexity of determining and managing a hotel's room rates. Add to that challenge the fact that each rate type can be discounted or increased by any number of percentages and at various times of the year or in response to specific special events. Now the true intricacies of the rate management process become apparent. GMs, as the ultimate leaders of their property's revenue-generation efforts, must have a thorough understanding of how these various rates are best established.

Despite some arguments to the contrary, the old saying *"There is nothing new under the sun"* applies to the development of a hotel's room rates. Professional hoteliers have been required for centuries to effectively price and market their rooms. It appears to be a uniquely modern (and many times unfortunate) belief of contemporary hoteliers that there are "new" ways to manage hotels (including the pricing of rooms) and that these new methods are much superior to the "old" ways. Some hoteliers appear much more interested in understanding "today's" methods than in reflecting upon the lessons learned from history. As a result, looking backward is not perceived to be of much value. However, contemporary hoteliers can definitely benefit from an understanding of the strengths and weaknesses of traditional room-pricing techniques. They can then incorporate the best historical tactics into modern pricing strategies that are increasingly dependent on and must be compatible with e-distribution.

Traditional Pricing Strategies

Historically, hoteliers wanted to maximize their profits and charge the highest rate possible for their rooms. They still do. However, the rate cannot be so high that it discourages guests from staying at the hotel. Similarly, the rate cannot be so low that it prevents the hotel from being profitable. Therefore, the room rate charge should not result from a mere "guess" about its appropriateness, but, ideally, would evolve from a rational examination of guest demand and a hotel's costs of operation. Mathematically, such a rate should be easy to compute with specific and accurate assumptions.

Well managed hotels offer a range of room rates to their various clients.

GMs reviewing older, or even the most current hotel accounting or front-office management texts will likely encounter a description of the "Hubbart" room rate formula. Known by hoteliers worldwide, this formula for determining room rates was developed in the mid-1950s by two national accounting firms (Horwath & Horwath and Harris Kerr Forster). The model was named in honor of Roy Hubbart, a Chicago hotelier and a major advocate of a "Hubbart" formula-style approach to room pricing.

Essentially, the formula is for determining what a hotel's ADR *should* be to reach the hotel owner's financial goals. To compute the Hubbart formula, specific financial and operational assumptions must be produced. These include dollar amounts for property construction (or purchase), the total cost of operations, the number of rooms to be sold, and the owner's desired ROI on the hotel's land, building, and FF&E.

The Hubbart formula continues to survive, probably less for its tangible usefulness in determining ADR than for its systematic evaluation of the factors important to those who buy and operate hotels. To illustrate the formula's use, assume an investor considers paying $8,000,000 for a 200-room hotel and desires a 12 percent return on the investment. Assume that the owner will incur mortgage repayments of $750,000 per year and additional fixed costs of $250,000 per year. Assume also that, at a 60 percent occupancy level, direct operating costs related to providing rooms and food and beverage services to the hotel's guests are $2,000,000, and indirect expenses related to operating the hotel are $1,000,000. Finally, assume that the investor wants to generate a profit of $125,000 per year from the food and beverage department and $25,000 from the telephone and all other nonrooms departments.

The steps required to compute the Hubbart formula in this example are as follows:

1. *Calculate the Hotel's Target Profits.* Multiply the required rate of return (ROI) by the owner's investment:

$$\$8,000,000.00 \times .12 = \$960,000.00$$

2. *Calculate All Fixed Expenses.* Include accurate estimates of all fixed costs including leases, depreciation, interest expense, property taxes, insurance, mortgages, and fixed management fees. In this example, the total cost of mortgage and other fixed costs is

$$\$750,000 + \$250,000 = \$1,000,000$$

3. *Calculate All Operational Costs.* Include expenses directly associated with selling and cleaning rooms and providing food services. All costs incurred to operate the front office would be included. Additional direct operating costs include housekeeping-related expenses for labor, guest room supplies, and laundry, as well as cleaning the hotel's public spaces. Interestingly, the expenses required to operate a food and beverage department are also considered a direct expense of selling rooms.

In addition to direct operating expenses, indirect operating expenses that cannot readily be assigned to the front office, housekeeping, or the food and beverage department must be computed. These will include a variety of costs such as those for administrative and general tasks, data processing, human resources, marketing, property operation and maintenance, franchise fees, and energy costs. In this example, operating costs are

$$\$2,000,000 + \$1,000,000 = \$3,000,000$$

4. *Calculate Nonrooms Profits.* Hotels can make profits from a food and beverage department or from telephone toll charges as well as from other minor sources unique to a specific hotel. If these sources generate a loss, the Hubbart formula requires the amount of the loss to be entered into the formula. In this example, the profit from nonrooms departments would be

$$\$125,000 + \$25,000 = \$150,000$$

5. *Determine the Total Room Revenue Required to Meet the Hotel's Goals and Obligations.* Sum the owner's desired ROI ($960,000), hotel's fixed expenses ($750,000 + $250,000), direct expenses ($2,000,000), and all indirect operating costs ($1,000,000). Then *subtract* the amount of nonrooms profit anticipated by the hotel ($125,000 + $25,000). Note: if there was a loss from the nonrooms departments, this loss would be *added* to the total room revenue required to meet all of the hotel's goals and obligations. In this example:

$$\$4,810,000 = \$960,000 \,(+)\, \$1,000,000 \,(+)\, \$2,000,000 \,(+)\, \$1,000,000 \,(-)\, \$150,000$$

$$\begin{array}{l}\text{Total Required}\\ \text{Room Revenue}\end{array} = \text{ROI} \,(+)\, \begin{array}{l}\text{Fixed}\\ \text{Expenses}\end{array} \,(+)\, \begin{array}{l}\text{Direct}\\ \text{Expenses}\end{array} \,(+)\, \begin{array}{l}\text{Indirect}\\ \text{Expenses}\end{array} \,(-)\, \begin{array}{l}\text{Nonrooms}\\ \text{Profit}\end{array}$$

6. *Determine the Forecast of Rooms to be Sold.* Multiply the number of rooms available by the projected occupancy rate. In this example:

$$(200 \text{ rooms} \times 365 \text{ days}) \times .60 = 43,800 \text{ rooms}$$

7. *Calculate the Hotel's Required ADR.* Divide the required room revenue (Step 5) by the number of rooms to be sold:

$$\$4,810,000 \div 43,800 = \$109.82$$

The seven steps required to compute the Hubbart formula are summarized in Figure 6.3.

The Hubbart formula is useful because it requires the user to consider the owner's investment goals and the costs of operating the hotel before determining the room rate. It has been criticized for relying on assumptions about the reasonableness of an owner's desired ROI (Step 1) and the need to know operating costs (Step 3) when these costs are affected by the quality of the hotel's management. Another criticism is also frequently voiced: the formula requires the room rate to compensate for operating losses incurred by other areas (such as from food and beverage operations).

The formula's primary shortcoming, however, relates to the number of rooms forecasted to be sold (Step 6). Based upon the room rate economics principles we have examined, the number of rooms sold is typically dependent on the rate charged for the rooms. However, the Hubbart formula requires that the number of rooms sold be estimated *prior* to knowing the rate at which they would sell.

Despite its limitations, for GMs the Hubbart formula remains an important way to view the necessity of developing a room rate that:

• Provides an adequate return to the hotel's owner(s)
• Recovers the hotel's fixed costs
• Considers the hotel's operating costs
• Accounts for all the hotel's nonroom net income (or loss)
• Results in a definite and justifiable rate goal

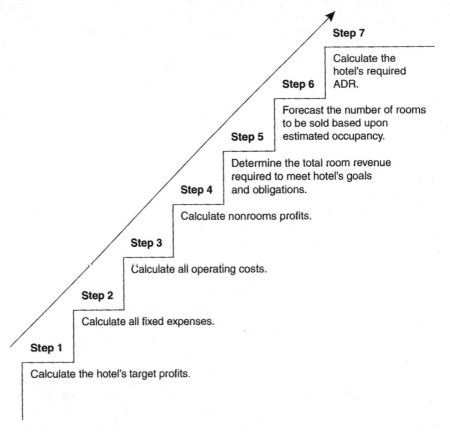

FIGURE 6.3   Computation of the Hubbart Room Rate Formula

There are alternative ways that hoteliers have historically determined rate. One of the most interesting applies the "$1.00 per $1,000 rule." Critics and proponents frequently argue the merits of the approach introduced in the 1940s; however, even with its limitations, it has remained helpful.

Essentially, the rule states that, for every $1,000 invested in a hotel, the property should support $1.00 in ADR. Some proponents feel the investment amount should include FF&E—most do not. Because the rate is so closely tied to occupancy level, most proponents also believe a 70 percent occupancy assumption (and appropriate management) is required for the formula to be useful. Also, the computed rate must be *increased* proportionately if occupancy is below 70 percent and decreased proportionately if it exceeds that level.

Few would argue that the "cost" of items such as the land and labor required to build a hotel in Manhattan is the same as that of rural Indiana. However, advocates defend this rule of thumb because areas in which building or purchase costs are higher tend to be the areas where ADRs can also be higher.

To illustrate the rule's use, assume that an investor is considering the purchase of a 117-room limited-service hotel for $6,000,000. The $1.00 per $1,000 rule would be computed as follows:

$6,000,000   (÷) 117   (÷) $1,000 (=) $51.28
Purchase price (÷) Number of rooms (÷) $1,000 (=) Rate to be achieved

Assume also that this buyer projects a 60% (not 70%) occupancy rate. Since the occupancy rate projected is 14.3% lower than the rule's standard ([70% − 60%] ÷ 70 = 14.3%), the rate to be achieved would be *increased* by that amount as follows:

$51.28   (×) .143   (+) $51.28   (=) $58.61
Rate to be achieved (×) Adjustment (+) Rate to be achieved (=) Adjusted rate to
                                                                                                be achieved

The rate computed using the $1.00 per $1,000 rule does not become the hotel's rack rate—it is its ADR. In this example, the hotel's GM may establish a rack rate of, for example, $89.00 per night. However, the GM would seek an ADR of $58.61 after all rate discounts. Few (if any) sophisticated investors would use the $1.00 per $1,000 rule exclusively to evaluate the feasibility of a hotel purchase. It does, however, promote the tendency for hotel buyers to discuss selling prices in terms of a hotel's **cost per key** (a mathematical variation of the $1.00 per $1,000 rule).

HOTEL TERMINOLOGY AT WORK

Cost Per Key: The average purchase price of a hotel's guest room expressed in thousands of dollars. For example, a 200-room hotel offered for $12,000,000 is selling at a cost of $60,000 per key ($12,000,000 ÷ 200 rooms = $60,000). Sometimes called "cost per room."

Additional historical methods of rate determination include those based upon the square footage of guest rooms (assuming that a hotel's larger rooms should sell for more than its smaller rooms) and rates determined by various "ideal" sales levels of the different hotel room types available to be sold. These include rates derived from **bottom-up selling** (selling the hotel's least expensive rooms first), **top-down selling** (selling the hotel's most expensive rooms first), and pricing schemes considering an equal sale of higher- and lower-priced rooms.

HOTEL TERMINOLOGY AT WORK

Bottom-Up Selling: A tactic to first sell the hotel's least expensive rooms.

Top-Down Selling: A tactic to first sell the hotel's most expensive rooms.

Web-Influenced Pricing Strategies

Modern GMs understand that properly pricing their rooms is critical to attracting first-time and repeat business. However, close examination of many tactics used by revenue managers would reveal that they often use one or more of the following nontraditional methods to establish rates:

- *Competitive Pricing.* Charge what the competition charges.
- *Follow-the-Leader Pricing.* Charge what the dominant hotel in the area charges.
- *Prestige Pricing.* Charge the highest rate in the area and justify it with better product and/or service levels.
- *Discount Pricing.* Reduce rates below that of the likely competitors without considering operating costs.

Travelers of all ages are now using the Internet to help them find the lowest rates possible.

All of these pricing systems appear to be "seat of the pants" approaches because they reflect supply, demand, and the psychological aspects of consumer behavior without considering a hotel's cost structure. Closer examination, however, reveals that they are also the logical responses to a simple but vitally important observation:

With the advent of the Internet, the world of rate determination as known by previous generations of hoteliers is gone forever.

The best GMs understand this. Hotel investors will continue to use traditional accounting formulas to determine whether they believe specific hotels are (or are not) a wise purchase. Determining the proper room rates to charge in a hotel, however, is more complex and more important than it has ever been. The reasons for the change in rate-setting "rules" are straightforward:

- The consumer's use of the Internet
- The competition's use of the Internet

Today, GMs must determine room rates based upon the realities of a challenging environment unknown to previous generations of hoteliers. To better understand today's rate-determination realities, consider a consumer-friendly Web site such as www.sidestep.com/hotel. Here users can compare alternative room rates for all of the hotels in their desired travel area within seconds. Any traveler with access to the Web can compare the room rate offered by one hotel to the rates offered by all of its competitors. The evaluation will contrast the prices of well-known hotel brands and franchises and independents. Guests can then book their rooms online as rapidly increasing numbers of travelers choose to do.

Consumers can easily compare prices, but so can a hotel's major competitors. Gone are the times when night auditors or others on the front-office staff conducted the nightly **"call-around"** and then used that information (often of questionable accuracy) to make decisions about what the hotel's rates should be.

HOTEL TERMINOLOGY AT WORK

Call-Around: A telephone "shopping" technique in which a hotel staff member calls competitive hotels to inquire about room rates and availability. The information is used by the calling hotel to help determine room rates.

While the call-around was standard practice as late as the early 2000s, consider the modern revenue manager utilizing one of the many Web sites similar to Travelaxe.com and others that allow him/her to easily:

- Select competitive hotels whose rates are to be monitored
- Obtain real-time room rates offered by these hotels on any number of travel Web sites advertising the rates
- Search the rates and sites as frequently as desired
- Perform rate comparisons by specific check-in and check-out dates
- Make rate comparisons based on LOS
- Assess rate comparisons based upon room type
- Analyze rate comparisons based upon **tracking codes**
- Group and print the data by competitive hotel, specific travel Web site(s), arrival date, and other factors important to the revenue manager

---

HOTEL TERMINOLOGY AT WORK

Tracking Codes: Guest types differentiated by traveler demographics. Typical tracking codes include those related to the travelers membership in a group (AAA or AARP), the purpose of the traveler's trip (such as business [Corporate] versus leisure) and those related to LOS (transient versus long-term). A tracking code can be created for any traveler demographic determined important enough to create and monitor a (reservation) field in the PMS.

For revenue managers who believe they are too busy to closely monitor their competitors' rate information, companies such as RateGain (www.rategain.com) will create daily, weekly, or on-demand competitor reports and e-mail the revenue manager whenever a competitor's rates rise or fall below preselected thresholds.

When guests and competitors can discover rates online, the dynamics of rate making change and rates are often set independent of traditional operating cost considerations. The hotel's rates are more heavily influenced instead by the laws of supply and demand. For example, assume that, on a given Saturday, all similar hotels in a market area offer guest rooms in the range of $100–$150 per night. In this situation, it would be difficult for a single hotel of the same type to command a rate of $250 per night even if its operating costs justify this rate. If the revenue manager of that hotel placed a $250 per night rate on the hotel's Web site, it is unlikely that any but perhaps the most brand-loyal consumers would select the property. This would be less important if the Web were not the major source of traveler information related to hotel room prices. In fact, however, it is. Even senior citizens, one of the last demographic groups to "log on," are now using the Web in ever-larger numbers. Future generations of travelers will grow up without knowing anything except the Web as a source of travel-pricing information and the impact of that is tremendously significant.

In the past, if a traveler called a hotel directly, was quoted the rack rate, and then booked the reservation, the hotel would have perceived this as a successful sale. Today, however, that same guest could make the hotel reservation and, every day until the day of arrival, go online to shop for an even lower price for the same room. If a lower rate was found, the guest could recontact the hotel, cancel the original reservation, and secure the new, lower rate. In addition, the consumer would likely feel frustrated that the hotel did not offer its lower rate initially!

Modern pricing techniques cannot involve purely subjective approaches. Instead, they must be highly sophisticated and logical reactions to the availability of real-world information and resulting supply and demand forces examined earlier in this chapter. Revenue managers must use PMS information along with specific pricing strategies that are adjusted (often daily) to meet the known realities of their own market areas. As they do so, revenue managers can have a tremendous influence on increasing their property's RevPar.

REVENUE MANAGEMENT ESSENTIALS

As you have seen, room rates fluctuate based upon room demand. It is therefore important that GMs who will lead the revenue management process have an accurate estimate of future room demand. When they do, they are able to respond to demand (occupancy) changes by adjusting price (ADR). In this way, GMs seek to maximize long-term RevPar. A hotel's effectiveness at estimating demand, maximizing the income yield of the hotel, and measuring the effectiveness of that process are revenue management essentials, and we will examine each of them.

Making Forecasts

Demand for a hotel's rooms affect more than just their selling price. In fact, one of the most critical managerial questions a GM can ask his or her staff is, "How many guests will be in the hotel today?" When the future number of guests, or stated another way, the future level of sales volume, is known, the proper number of staff and the supplies those staff need to do their jobs can best be predicted. At the front desk, knowing the number of guests arriving at the hotel on a given date ensures the proper number of guest service agents will be available to promptly check guests in and out of the hotel.

Similarly, in the food and beverage department, sufficient service staff, bartenders, bussers, and back-of-house staff must be available to serve the estimated number of guests. When a hotel provides other services such as parking, guest laundry, and recreational activities, knowing how many people will be on the property requesting such services is key to proper staffing. With too few staff, of course, guest service suffers. Even prior to their arrival, however, room demand forecasts help establish what guests will pay for the hotel's services.

A room revenue forecast is of great assistance to the GM because room revenues make up 50 to 75 percent of the monthly sales revenue in full-service hotels and an even greater percentage in limited-service hotels. The rooms revenue forecast will likely be assembled, using a variety of methods, by those employed in the sales and marketing department and/or in the front office (see Chapters 7 and 8). Although a rooms revenue forecast can be very detailed or quite simple, it should include, at minimum, the following data:

- Rooms available to sell for the forecasted period
- Estimated rooms to be sold for the period
- The estimated occupancy rate for the period
- The estimated ADR for the period
- The RevPar for the forecasted period

Reasons why these three measures are the best forecasters of rooms revenue and thus are useful for establishing room rates will become more clear in the chapters that follow, but the fact remains that the GM, as the hotel's lead revenue manager, should always know or have available accurate forecasted data on these statistics for the following periods:

- Daily
- Weekly
- Monthly
- Quarterly
- Annually

Obviously, the further into the future the forecast is made, the more uncertain are the estimates. It is reasonable to expect, however, that with allowances for adjustments due to uncontrollable events such as severe weather and canceled contracts, revenue forecasts within 5 to 10 percent of actual realized revenue are realistically achievable. With excellent forecasting methods in place, estimates can be even more accurate, especially in the short time frames of weekly, monthly, and quarterly forecasts. In fact, one characteristic of an outstanding revenue management team is its ability to generate, in a timely fashion, room revenue forecasts that prove highly accurate.

It is important to remember that full-service hotels must forecast nonroom revenues as well as room revenues. In addition to the restaurant and bar areas commonly associated with the food and beverage department, the demand for rooms can impact

- Room service
- Banquets
- Meeting room rental revenue
- Meeting room food and beverage revenue
- Audio and visual equipment rental
- Service charges

In addition to food and beverage income, heightened room demand will affect hotel revenues that are neither room sales nor food and beverage sales. On the income statement, these are classified as **other revenue** and include such items as:

- Pay-per-view movies
- Parking charges
- Internet access charges

- Gift shop sales of newspapers, candy, lotions, soft drinks, and other items
- Telephone (local and long distance calling charges)
- Guest laundry
- Coat check fees
- Golf fees
- Tennis fees
- Health club usage fees
- Pool fees

HOTEL TERMINOLOGY AT WORK

Other Revenue: Revenue derived from the sale of hotel products and services that are not classified as rooms, food, or beverages.

Of course, all of these revenue-producing areas will be affected by a hotel's skillful (or unskillful!) management of occupancy levels.

Managing Occupancy

When revenue managers understand how to use their room types and tracking codes to assist their efforts, they can address the important tasks of managing their hotels' occupancies and ADRs. A hotel's DOSM is most often held responsible for maximizing the hotel's sales effort, but the revenue manager is responsible for maximizing occupancy. The two tasks are related but not identical. Skillful revenue managers can make decisions that improve their hotels' occupancy rates based upon unique demand situations experienced by the property. A few examples will help to demonstrate this.

Assume that a hotel's sales team did an excellent job discovering and marketing to potential hotel customers for a specific weekend now one month away. Assume also that this 300-room hotel's revenue manager now faces the situation displayed in Figure 6.4.

In this case, demand for rooms is very strong on Saturday, but weaker on Friday and much weaker on Sunday. With a consistent goal of maximizing RevPar, to confront this situation an effective revenue manager will attempt to drive (increase) occupancy by identifying Saturday as a day that has a **minimum length of stay (MLOS)** attached to it, or alternatively, by designating Saturday as a day that is **closed to arrival (CTA)**.

HOTEL TERMINOLOGY AT WORK

MLOS: "Minimum length of stay." In this situation, a hotel requires guests who seek a room to stay for a designated minimum number of nights.

CTA: "Closed to arrival." In this situation, the hotel declines reservations for guests attempting to arrive on this specific date.

	Friday	Saturday	Sunday
Rooms Available	300	300	300
Rooms Left to Sell	120	25	250

FIGURE 6.4 Sample Forecasted Room Availability

FIGURE 6.5   Two-Day MLOS Strategy

In this situation, the hotel's revenue manager may identify Saturday as a day that has a MLOS of two days attached to it. As a result, only reservations from guests requesting arrival on Saturday with the intention of staying for two (or more) days are accepted. Those guests requesting a one-night stay with arrival on Saturday are declined. By managing the length of stay required for a Saturday arrival, the revenue manager seeks to maximize *total* weekend occupancy by selling potential guests a room on both Saturday and Sunday nights. This MLOS strategy is illustrated in Figure 6.5.

Recall that, in this example, the hotel has only 25 rooms remaining to be sold on Saturday night. The revenue manager is making the MLOS decision based upon a belief that the proportion of potential guests wanting to stay two nights is significantly smaller than those wanting to stay one night. The revenue manager also believes, however, that there is a sufficient number of potential guests who will accept the two-night MLOS and allow the hotel to sell, within the next 30 days, all 25 of its remaining Saturday night rooms and an additional 25 room nights on Friday, Sunday, or beyond.

If the hotel's revenue manager does not elect a MLOS strategy, a CTA strategy may be employed. Identifying Saturday as a day that is CTA is logical if, again, it is assumed that, based upon current booking patterns, the demand for Saturday night reservations is likely to far exceed the hotel's number of available rooms for that night. If so, it may be a good idea to deny a reservation for a guest requesting only a room for Saturday night in favor of guests who will arrive on Friday and request both a Friday and Saturday (or longer) stay. By denying guests the opportunity to arrive on Saturday (closing that day to arrival), the revenue manager seeks to maximize total weekend occupancy through increased Friday night sales.

Some revenue managers who frequently use a MLOS strategy, employ a CTA strategy only rarely because, as they point out, the hotel (as in this example) that implements a CTA approach runs the risk of denying a reservation to a guest who may have wished to stay 30 (or more!) days. Clearly, the hotel may want to accept such a reservation; however, a rigid CTA strategy would prevent it.

The question of when to use MLOS and CTA is subject to industry debate because, in many cases, the actual demand for a date or set of dates is not clearly known but, instead, must be estimated. This is especially true when one-time or first-time events held in an area strongly affect local room demand. Properly employed, the skillful use of MLOS and CTA strategies can make a significant impact on a hotel's overall occupancy rate. In fact, they are so important that many modern PMS systems will, based upon booking patterns, automatically identify any dates that should be considered for their use.

It is fairly evident that, in times of minimal demand, the management of occupancy is more closely tied to pricing and sales efforts than to the individual restriction decisions of revenue managers. In times of strong demand and potential sellouts, however, the decision making of revenue managers is extremely important. Many revenue managers believe that in times of strong demand, to maximize the chances of a sellout, they must actually oversell. This technique, perhaps the most well known but least understood method of managing occupancy, is also known as **overbooking** the hotel.

HOTEL TERMINOLOGY AT WORK

Overbook(ing): A situation in which the hotel has more guest reservations for rooms than it has rooms available to lodge those guests. Sometimes referred to as "oversold."

■

Any discussion on overbooking must begin with a simple truth. That truth is, "No experienced hotelier would ever want to knowingly take a reservation for a room that it is not going to be available for the guest upon arrival."

There are at least two reasons this is true. First, in an overbooked situation, a guest with a confirmed reservation who arrives to find that the hotel has no room available is inevitably angry, and rightly so. No revenue manager should seek to create angry guests! Second, from a financial point of view, the guest will be expensive to relocate. This is because, in most cases, the hotel that has **walked** a guest must pay for, at least:

- Transportation to/from the alternative property
- Telephone calls made by the guest to inform those who need to know about the alternative lodging accommodations
- The cost of the first night's room charges at the alternative hotel

---

HOTEL TERMINOLOGY AT WORK

Walk(ed): A situation in which a guest with a reservation is relocated from the reserved hotel to another hotel because no room was available at the reserved hotel.

Used in, for example, "We are three rooms oversold tonight; if we don't get some cancellations or no-shows we will need to decide where we want to walk those guests."

■

Why, then, do hotels overbook? Sometimes it is a mistake on the part of the hotel. This would be true, for example, if a guest reservation were made but mistakenly not recorded. Sometimes, however, experienced revenue managers, in seeking to maximize occupancy, intentionally accept more reservations than it at first appears they can accommodate because they want to fill the hotel and anticipate some of the reservations for rooms will no-show.

For example, in a 100-room hotel that experiences a typical 5 percent no-show rate, the sale of 101 rooms on a given night, while technically overbooking the hotel, is not likely to result in a guest being "walked." This is because the number of no-shows (5) will, on average, exceed the size of the reservation oversell (1).

No-shows are not unique to the hotel business. Restaurants, airlines, and rental car agencies are just a few of the businesses that must also manage their reservations while knowing that a certain percentage of those reserving will simply not show up to claim their product or service. If a hotel's total occupancy management plan is too conservative and does not factor in no-shows, rooms will likely go unsold even on sell-out nights. If it is too aggressive and factors in excessively large numbers of no-shows, too many guests will arrive at the hotel. These guests will, inevitably, need to be walked and will inevitably be upset!

THE INTERNET AT WORK

The issuers of credit and debit cards can be a hotel manager's best friend when it comes to reducing and controlling no-shows. To see one such card company's resources that are available for free, go to

usa.visa.com/download/business/accepting_visa/ops_risk_management/merchant_catalog.pdf

Scroll down to review (free) a copy of "The No-show Challenge," a 16-minute video designed to help hotel managers reduce no-shows.

The forecasting skills of the revenue manager allow a hotel to sell the "right" number of total rooms during high demand periods. As a result, revenue managers seek to identify periods of high demand and they do so utilizing three specific forecast types. These are detailed in Figure 6.6.

Managing ADR

Most revenue managers understand that, because of the room rate economics examined earlier in this chapter, the best way to maximize ADR is to manage room rates in conjunction with anticipated demand. That is, when total demand is forecasted to

Management Forecast	Purpose/Characteristics
Occupancy Forecast	1. Helps improve employee scheduling
	2. Shows guest arrival and departure patterns
	3. Forecasts at least 2/7/14/21/ and 30 days out
	4. Produced daily
	5. Never exceeds 100%
Demand Forecast	1. Identifies periods of 100% occupancy or more demand for rooms
	2. Identifies periods of very low demand
	3. Forecasts 30/60/90 days out
	4. Produced at least weekly
	5. Used to help establish room rate selling strategies
Revenue Forecast	1. Helps manage the hotel's cash flows
	2. Considers important tracking codes when evaluating estimated total revenues
	3. Matches revenue forecast to preestablished budgets (forecasts 30 days out or more as determined by management)
	4. Produced at least monthly
	5. Estimates RevPar (occupancy and rate)

FIGURE 6.6   Forecast Types

During high-demand periods such as graduations or home football games, hotels near colleges and universities may decide to set a higher rack rate for guests requesting a reservation at those specific times.

be strong, discounting room rates (and thus reducing ADR) is not typically necessary to ensure the sale of rooms. Similarly, when demand for a single room type is strong, discounting that specific room type is not generally advisable even if discounts will be offered on other, less popular, room types. Philosophically, the ADR management goal of all revenue managers is to achieve an ADR that is as close as possible to the hotel's rack (non-discounted) rate.

To illustrate: In a hotel that has established its rack rate at $125 and that now anticipates a sell-out date, the revenue manager would not typically want to sell any rooms, for that date, at a discounted rate. The goal would be to achieve an ADR for the high-demand date that is as close as possible to $125. The hotel may be required, of course, to honor rates previously agreed upon or negotiated with specific guests; however, the transient room rates and any group room rates offered would reflect the date's anticipated strong demand as well as the hotel's resulting "no discounting" selling strategy. In fact, when demand is predicted to be exceptionally strong, revenue managers may even establish a special event rate for all the hotel's unsold rooms.

Interestingly, although hotels can achieve success in driving ADR up during high-demand times, reducing ADR does not typically result in increased benefits to a hotel. Most experienced hoteliers agree that reducing room rates is a strategy to employ only in the most extraordinary of times. Hotels will have difficulty selling their rooms if rates are too high relative to their value as perceived by guests. Significantly lowering rates, however, typically will not result in the hotel attracting significantly higher numbers of guests to offset the revenue loss incurred by the rate reduction. This is because, when aggregate demand for rooms is slight, the reduction of room rates by a single hotel in a market is unlikely to significantly increase that aggregate demand. The concept of reducing rate to drive demand is based upon the assumption that room rate is a guest's most important consideration when selecting a hotel. It is not. Price is important, but location, brand quality, brand loyalty, and **frequent guest programs** all are equally or more important factors than rate alone. Note that these factors are not affected by rate reduction.

HOTEL TERMINOLOGY AT WORK

Frequent Guest Program: A promotional effort administered by a hotel brand which rewards travelers each time they choose to stay at that specific brand's affiliated hotels. Typical rewards include free night stays, room upgrades, and complimentary hotel services.

The tendency to try and "influence" a hotel's overall occupancy percentage by varying published room rates (and thus ADR), is one that experienced revenue managers must resist. Although revenue managers cannot significantly increase demand by reducing room rates, this does not imply room rate discounts should never be offered. For example, in all of the following situations room discounting may be an effective managerial strategy and should be seriously considered:

- When the guest's anticipated length of stay is long enough to offset a loss in room rate. For example, a corporate guest requesting a reservation for a seven-night stay may be offered a rate lower than another corporate guest requesting only a one-night stay.
- When the date(s) requested by the guest includes one or more days for which the hotel anticipates minimal demand. Thus, for example, in a hotel with minimal demand for Sunday night rooms, a guest seeking to arrive on a Sunday night (for a two-night stay) may be offered a lower rate than a guest arriving on a Tuesday (a high-demand day) for a two-night stay.
- When the number of room nights to be purchased is large. Thus, for example, a guest seeking to reserve 50 rooms for a three-night stay (150 total room nights) may be offered a lower rate than a guest seeking to reserve only one room for a three-night stay.
- When the number of unique stays per year is high. Thus, for example, a guest seeking to reserve 50 rooms every other month for 12 months (six stays) may be offered a lower rate than a guest seeking to reserve 50 rooms for a one-time stay.
- When the total revenue to be achieved by the hotel is high. Thus, for example, a guest seeking to reserve 100 rooms for three days and electing to purchase three banquet meals a day for the rooms' 100 occupants may be offered a lower rate than a guest seeking to reserve 100 rooms for the same three days but who is not making food and beverage purchases.

The examples above all illustrate that the manipulation of ADR in some cases does make good sense and can contribute to the achievement of a revenue manager's RevPar goals.

Yield Management

Hoteliers know that when demand for rooms is high, rates can also be high. Alternatively, when occupancy levels (demand for rooms) are relatively low, room rates may also be lower. RevPar is obtained by multiplying occupancy times ADR (RevPar = Occupancy % × ADR). Therefore, any change (decrease or increase) in one of the factors comprising RevPar that is offset by an equal change in the other factor will yield the same RevPar. **Yield management** is a set of techniques and procedures used to manipulate occupancy, ADR, or both for the purpose of maximizing the revenue *yield* achieved by a hotel. This term, first coined by the airline industry, is now used less commonly in the hotel industry than is the term *revenue management*, but its grounding philosophy and the actual techniques originally employed to implement it are all important concepts for revenue managers to grasp.

HOTEL TERMINOLOGY AT WORK

Yield Management: Demand forecasting systems designed to maximize revenue by holding rates high during times of high room demand and by discounting room rates during times of lower guest room demand. These systems may be applied manually or with programs built into a hotel's PMS.

■

Philosophy

Assume that, as a typical consumer, you went to your local grocery store one day to buy your favorite bread. It normally costs $3.00 per loaf. On this particular Saturday, however, when you arrive at the store you find that the same loaf of bread is priced at $6.00. When you ask why the price is changed, you are told that the store anticipates significant demand for that type of bread on this particular day, that the store is likely to sell all of that type of bread available, and that, as a result, its price has increased. Would you still buy the bread? Would you return to that store in the future?

Now assume that you want to attend a concert where your favorite musical group will appear. You want front row seats and are told that, because only a few are available, they will cost twice as much as tickets for a seat dozens of rows back. Would you buy the better seats?

Assume further that you would like to have a guest room near Times Square in Manhattan on New Year's Eve so you can easily join the crowds counting down the "Old Year" and ringing in the New Year. You are told that, because demand for rooms near Times Square on December 31 is so heavy, available rooms on that date have been assigned a special event rate and will cost twice as much as normal. Would you book the room?

In each of the cases presented previously, the interaction between consumer and business is affected by strong demand, supply shortage, or both. It is commonly accepted that the airline industry was one of the first to actively manage (vary) pricing in response to strong changes in consumer demand. They perfected techniques designed to increase ticket prices when demand was very heavy and sought to maximize revenue by lowering prices when they anticipated that fewer tickets were likely to be sold. As a result, most air travelers know that, historically, passengers on the same flight would often pay different fares. Some of the price fluctuation was due to variation in service levels (first class, business class, or coach), some was due to time of ticket purchase (21-day advance, same-day purchase, and so on), or the number of tickets purchased (wholesaler, travel agent, leisure traveler). Not surprisingly, rental car agencies also manage their yield via pricing. Additional industries using yield management include cruise ships, railroads, time shares, and live theaters. The common denominator in all of them is the daily perishability of inventory (such as unsold hotel rooms) that cannot be carried over to be sold the next day.

Because hotel rooms are perishable items (as are airline seats), it makes sense for hotels to study how their rooms are typically rented to understand the best time to discount a room or to increase its price. For example, if a hotel is usually booked solid in October of each year, there is little reason to offer a discount to a group wanting a block of rooms at that time, unless the group is willing to purchase enough additional hotel services to justify the discount.

In most cases, consumers intuitively understand that businesses will increase prices in the face of limited product inventories. Not all industries, however, can effectively implement yield management strategies. Ethically, for example, few consumers would condone an emergency medical supply company's significantly increased product prices immediately following a disaster that caused a surge in product demand. In a similar manner, consider the public's consistent response to the (seemingly) routine increases in gasoline prices prior to holidays in which automobile use is expected to significantly increase. The public's reaction to gasoline price increases typically ranges from one of cynicism to absolute outrage (and demand for federal investigations and price controls!) directed toward the "big oil companies." It is important for hoteliers to understand that, when improperly planned or instituted at a time that makes little sense to guests, the use of a yield management philosophy can generate the same negative consumer reactions. For this reason, it is important that revenue managers have a thorough understanding of the principles and techniques essential to effectively implement yield management.

Implementation

Yield management can be viewed as the application of specific tactics that predict (forecast) consumer behavior and effectively price highly perishable products to maximize RevPar. Retailers that can easily carry inventory to the next day such as carpet, lumber, and computer suppliers have difficulty employing yield management because customers do not readily accept price variation in their products. Interestingly, retailers perceived by customers to be easily able to increase inventory (think bread, milk, and restaurant meals) do not generally use yield management even though they may sell a perishable commodity.

Because hotel rooms are highly perishable, the goal of yield management is to consistently maintain the highest possible revenue from a given amount of inventory. Remember that yield management techniques are used during periods of high, as well as low, demand. Revenue managers should be implementing yield management procedures at their hotels if:

- Demand for their rooms varies by day of week, time of month, season, or in response to local special events.
- Their demand variance is predictable.
- They have ever turned away a customer willing to pay a higher price for a room because available inventory had been previously sold to another guest at a lower price.
- Their hotel serves guests who are value conscious as well as those who can afford to spend more for the sake of convenience, status, or another motivating factor.
- They have, or can create, clearly discernable differences in service or product levels that can easily be explained to guests.
- Their property is willing to commit the resources necessary to properly train staff prior to implementation of yield management.
- They seek to maximize RevPar.

Techniques

Although the actual yield management techniques used by a revenue manager will vary by property, in their simplest form, all these techniques are employed to:

- Forecast demand.
- Eliminate discounts in high-demand periods.
- Increase discounts during low-demand periods.
- Use MLOS and CTO to maximize revenue in high-demand periods.
- Implement "Special Event" rates during periods of extremely heavy demand.

Sophisticated mathematical programs that help hoteliers manage yield are built into most PMSs used in the industry today. In the final analysis, however, it is the revenue manager's skill and experience in maximizing yield that is most critical to the yield maximization process. To illustrate the validity of that statement, assume you are the revenue manager in a hotel that is hosting a regional tournament in the National Collegiate Athletic Association (NCAA) basketball finals. Your hotel has secured the business of the number twelve-seeded team within its bracket, and they are playing the number one-seeded team on this night. The team you are hosting has reserved rooms for the next three nights, but if your team loses tonight's game, it will go home in the morning. If it wins, it will stay another night or two. There is a 95 percent chance it will lose. You know that because you understand basketball rankings and the historical frequency with which a number twelve-seed beats a number one-seed (almost never); thus you predict the team at your hotel will be an early departure. Your PMS does not understand this. It simply knows that the team is now planning (perhaps hoping?) to stay until the final game. Computers and sophisticated software programs are yield management tools to be used by revenue managers, but they cannot replace common sense and human insight.

For a final example of the importance of human intervention, consider the case of the corporate traveler who stays at her favorite hotel nearly every Tuesday and Wednesday night. On a particular Tuesday she arrives and is told that her normal discounted corporate rate of $99 cannot be honored on that night because the hotel forecasts a sellout. The rate she must pay is $149. In this case, the hotel's new revenue manager is aggressively managing yield and, perhaps appropriately, has eliminated corporate rate discounts on this day. When, however, the guest complains that she is a loyal customer who has always been willing to pay their assigned rate (even when the hotel was not busy), she is told by the front-desk agent, "There's nothing I can do." Should the hotel be surprised when that guest leaves and never returns? It should not and she likely will not return. Recall that the goal of a talented revenue manager is to increase RevPar, not only on a daily basis, but long-term as well. In the long-term, offending loyal guests by incompetently managing yield benefits neither guests nor a hotel.

Measures of Effectiveness

How do revenue managers typically evaluate the effectiveness of their occupancy and ADR management decisions? Just as importantly, how are a revenue manager's decisions evaluated by GMs or others who are responsible for their supervision? Historically, the individuals at a hotel who are responsible for occupancy and rate management decisions have been evaluated based upon the hotel's occupancy rate (percentage) and the ADR it achieves. More recently, RevPar has been the major factor applied in the evaluation of revenue managers. Currently, some industry observers and professionals have suggested that **GoPar** is a more useful measure of selling effectiveness than is RevPar.

HOTEL TERMINOLOGY AT WORK

GoPar: Short for "gross operating profit per available room." Using a term from the Uniform System of Accounts for Hotels, it is computed as:

$$\frac{\text{Total Revenue} - (\text{Direct Operating Expense} + \text{Indirect Operating Expense})}{\text{Total Rooms Available to Be Sold}}$$

GoPar considers the "cost" of selling rooms (not simply the total revenue achieved) when evaluating sales effectiveness.

■

In most hotels, however, GMs seeking to measure revenue management effectiveness will evaluate their own property's ADR, occupancy, and RevPar performance.

Occupancy Index

One of the questions hoteliers are frequently asked by those whose knowledge of the industry is somewhat limited is, "How's your occupancy?" The question implies, of course, that a high level of occupancy is "good" and a lower level of occupancy is "bad." That may, in fact, be true at times, but it is a tremendously limiting manner in which to view occupancy management. In most hotels, if rooms were sold for $1.00 per night, the hotel would sell out each day and achieve a 100 percent occupancy. Of course, the hotel would not likely stay in business long, despite its good occupancy. It is difficult to separate a hotel's occupancy level from the rates it charges. However, assuming that a hotel's rates are in line with its **competitive set**, the **occupancy index** is the industry's standard for measuring the management of occupancy rates.

HOTEL TERMINOLOGY AT WORK

Competitive Set: The group of competing hotels against which an individual hotel's operating performance is compared.

Occupancy Index: A ratio measure computed as:

$$\frac{\text{Occupancy Rate of a Selected Hotel}}{\text{Occupancy Rate of That Hotel's Competitive Set}} = \text{Occupancy Index}$$

■

To truly understand the value of the occupancy index, assume that you are a hotel owner. Assume also that you are told by those responsible for revenue management at your hotel that last month the property achieved a 60 percent occupancy. You are interested, of course, in knowing whether your managers did a good job of managing the hotel's occupancy. To make such an evaluation, it is important to know how those hotels with which you directly compete (your competitive set) managed their own occupancy levels. If their occupancy levels were much higher than yours, you would be less pleased with your hotel's performance. Alternatively, if your competitors achieved occupancy levels much lower than yours, you would be more pleased with your property's performance. An occupancy index is the measurement tool used in the hotel industry to make this important comparison.

Occupancy Index	Assessment/ Recommended Action
Far Below 100%	Management is ineffective. ADR excessive for the market. Reduce rack rate.
Below 100%	Management is less than effective. Evaluate weekday/weekend ADR Index. Closely examine sales efforts.
At (Near) 100%	Management is effective. Consider eliminating discounts for most popular room types during high-demand periods to test the hotel's ability to maintain index.
Above 100%	Management is less effective. Immediately eliminate discounts for most popular room types during high-demand periods.
Far Above 100%	Management is ineffective. ADR too low. Increase rack rates on all room types at all times.

FIGURE 6.7   Occupancy Index Evaluation

The most widely utilized effectiveness indices (those collected for hotels and reported back to them by the Smith Travel Research Company) will be discussed in greater detail in the next chapter but understanding the concept of an index is not difficult. In the preceding example of the hotel achieving a 60 percent occupancy, the performance of its revenue managers would likely be considered good if the occupancy rate achieved by its competitive set were, for example, 45 percent and therefore the occupancy index was 133 percent (60 ÷ 45 = 133 percent). If, however, the competitive set's occupancy rate for the same period were 80 percent, then the hotel's occupancy index would be 75 percent (60 ÷ 80 = 75 percent), an indication that your managers were less effective in their decision making than were their direct competitors. Figure 6.7 details the evaluations GMs would routinely make when examining their hotels' occupancy indexes.

For some hotels, an evaluation of monthly or even weekly occupancy indices may be very misleading. This is because the hotel's volume may vary greatly within a week. For example, a hotel may run a very strong occupancy index through the week and a much lower index on the weekends. In other hotels, this trend is reversed. For this reason, many revenue managers monitor their weekday and weekend occupancy indices separately.

ADR Index

Mathematically, ADR is the equally weighted first component of RevPar (ADR × Occupancy rate = RevPar) and thus its control is just as important for revenue managers as is occupancy management. Many hoteliers believe that, while a hotel's occupancy rate is tied to the hotel's selling ability, ADR is more related to the guests' perception of "value." Guests who feel the room rates they have paid are reasonable are likely to return. Those who do not share this feeling are less likely to return. The job of revenue managers is to ensure a rate structure that maximizes their own guests' feelings of value.

Earlier in the chapter we examined a variety of methods used for determining initial room (rack) rates. Recall that the development of rack rates is a starting point, not an ending point, in room rate management. Revenue managers continually make decisions related to transient room discounting, the establishment of negotiated rates, and the granting of discounts for large group sales. In addition, the skillful use of special event rates and blackout dates will all significantly affect a hotel's ADR.

Assuming that a hotel's rack rates are essentially in line with its competitive set, the **ADR index** is the industry's standard for measuring the effective management of room rates.

ADR Index	Assessment/ Recommended Action
Far Below 100%	Management is ineffective. Evaluate appropriateness of the competitive set. Evaluate rack rate structure; increase rack rate.
Below 100%	Management is less than effective. Evaluate weekday/weekend ADR Index, increase rates for either period if the index for that portion of the week exceeds 100 percent.
At (Near) 100%	Management is effective. Monitor the competitive set's percent change in ADR (from prior month and prior year) for evidence of competitor increases in room rates and maintain rate parity.
Above 100%	Management is less effective. Evaluate room rates in conjunction with occupancy index. If occupancy index is above 100 percent, increase rates. If occupancy index is below 100 percent, consider increasing discounts during slower periods to maximize RevPar.
Far Above 100%	Management is ineffective. Evaluate competitive set for appropriate fit. ADR may be too high if occupancy index is significantly below 100 percent.

FIGURE 6.8   ADR Index Evaluation

HOTEL TERMINOLOGY AT WORK

ADR Index: A ratio measure computed as:

$$\frac{\text{ADR of a Selected Hotel}}{\text{ADR of That Hotel's Competitive Set}} = \text{ADR Index}$$

When evaluating an ADR index, it is especially important that a hotel's competitive set is truly competitive. If a hotel's competitive set is comprised of hotels that are inferior to the hotel being evaluated, the resulting ADR index will be artificially inflated. In a similar manner, a hotel whose competitive set consists of properties that are in a significantly higher market segment having a higher average selling rate, will find that achieving a 100 percent or higher ADR index may be difficult or even unrealistic. Figure 6.8 details the evaluations typically made when evaluating a hotel's occupancy index.

RevPar Index

A hotel's **RevPar index** is the ultimate measurement of a revenue manager's skill.

HOTEL TERMINOLOGY AT WORK

RevPar Index: A ratio measure computed as:

$$\frac{\text{RevPar of a Selected Hotel}}{\text{RevPar of That Hotel's Competitive Set}} = \text{RevPar Index}$$

In addition to the revenue manager's decision-making skills, there are, of course, a variety of other factors that can cause a hotel's RevPar index to be lower than that of its competitive set. These can include:

- Inferior management of room cleanliness and facility maintenance
- Poor franchise (brand) name

- Poor exterior signage or facility access
- Poor **room mix** for the market
- Substandard furnishings or décor
- Sales and marketing/advertising budget too small
- Sales and marketing staff too small
- Marketing staff ineffective

HOTEL TERMINOLOGY AT WORK

Room Mix: The ratio of room types contained in a hotel. For example, the number of double-bedded rooms compared to king-bedded rooms, the number of smoking-permitted rooms to no-smoking-permitted rooms, and the number of suites compared to standard rooms.

■

Some revenue managers dislike index reports because they view them as an objective measure (indices) of a subjective activity (management). Despite the objections of some, however, RevPar indices are still perceived by those in the industry as the best indicator of a hotel's operational quality and managerial proficiency.

Because a high occupancy index will compensate for a lower ADR index (and the reverse is also true), the interpretation of a RevPar index is more complex than that of either the occupancy or ADR index. A RevPar index above 100 percent, however, generally implies that a hotel leads its competitive set and is likely making good revenue management decisions. Figure 6.9 details the evaluations typically made when examining a hotel's RevPar index.

RevPar Index	Assessment/ Recommended Action
Far Below 100%	Management is ineffective. Evaluate room rates in conjunction with occupancy index. If occupancy index is near or above 100 percent, increase rates. If ADR index is near or above 100 percent, consider increasing discounts during slower periods to maximize RevPar. If both indices are substantially below 100 percent, reevaluate the competitive set.
Below 100%	Management is less than effective. Evaluate room rates in conjunction with occupancy index. If occupancy index is below 100 percent, reduce rates. If ADR index is below 100 percent, consider raising rates or eliminating discounts during high-demand periods.
At (Near) 100%	Management is effective. Monitor occupancy and ADR indices to maintain no more than a 10-point difference between these two measures.
Above 100%	Management may be effective. Evaluate room rates in conjunction with occupancy index. If occupancy index is above 100 percent, increase rates. If ADR index is above 100 percent, consider increasing discounts during slower periods to further maximize RevPar. If more than 10 percentage points separate the two indices, take the corrective actions required to improve the lower index.
Far Above 100%	Management (or ownership) is less effective. Evaluate competitive set for appropriateness of fit; increase rack rates, aggressively seek to increase ADR during high-demand periods; consider building additional room capacity.

FIGURE 6.9   RevPar Index Evaluation

Despite honest individual differences in philosophic approach, most revenue managers would agree that:

- *Revenue Management Is a Daily Activity.* Revenue managers should monitor room demand daily (or hourly!). To keep current with market demand, monitor the competitors' room rates daily. In addition, many revenue managers check their competitors every day (by doing a call-around) to determine these competitors' walk-in rates.

- *Occupancy and ADR Indices Should Be Close.* Ideally, the occupancy index and ADR index should be tight. That is, the percentages should be within a few percentage points of each other. If the occupancy index is well over 100 percent (110 percent or more), the hotel should drive rate but be prepared to lose some occupancy index points. If the occupancy index is well below 90 percent, the hotel should drive rate very conservatively.

- *It Is Necessary to Gamble at Times.* An aggressive revenue manager can make a significant difference in a hotel's RevPar. Overbook on high-demand nights but do so based on known no-show data for similar dates. Minimize costly walks.

MANAGERS AT WORK

"The occupancy index looks great!" said J.D. Ojisama. One of J.D.'s monthly activities involved meeting with the property's DOSM to review the hotel's STR report. They were in that meeting now.

"Yes," replied Michele, the DOSM. "But we really left money on the table with this ADR index."

J.D. had to agree. The hotel's Smith Travel Index report showed an occupancy index of 117 percent, but the ADR index for the month was only 82 percent. That brought the property's overall RevPar index to 95.9 percent, and represented the first time in two years that the

property had posted a RevPar index that trailed its competitive set.

What decision-making errors likely led to the results viewed by J.D. and Michele? What specific steps might they take to prevent such mistakes in the future?

DISTRIBUTION CHANNEL MANAGEMENT

Distribution channels are sources of potential room reservations, and understanding how they work is critical to understanding revenue management. For example, a hotel's telephone can be a distribution channel. That is, guests seeking a reservation could use the telephone to inquire about room rates, availability, hotel features, and amenities. It follows that GMs seeking to maximize their hotels' room sales would want their property's telephones answered promptly by friendly, knowledgeable, and well-trained reservation agents. In ensuring that they are, the GM would be actively managing this specific distribution channel. If it were managed well, it would likely result in larger numbers of reservations made, and at higher ADRs, than that of a hotel with poorly trained staff.

HOTEL TERMINOLOGY AT WORK

Distribution Channel: A distinct and definable source of hotel rooms or services sales. Some confusion about this term exists within the hotel industry. Some hoteliers use the term *distribution channel* only when referring to electronic sources of reservations. Thus, for example, these individuals would view

Using a travel agency is still popular with many hotel guests.

the GDS or a hotel's own Web site as two distinct distribution channels. These two reservation sources are distinct and are distribution channels, but are more properly considered *c distribution channels* (see page 172).

Individual hotel staff (e.g., staff members working in a hotel's sales department) or individual travel agencies are also unique sources of reservations and should be considered distribution channels (but certainly they would not be considered electronic!). E-distribution channels then, are best described as a distinct subset of distribution channels. For example, the Internet is one distribution channel and meeting planners are another.

■

In a similar manner, a hotel guest could send an e-mail to a hotel requesting either property information or a reservation. In this case, the hotel's ability to promptly and effectively reply to the guest using this unique distribution channel is also important. In fact, it is critical that hotels professionally manage *all* of the distribution channels that today's guests use when communicating directly with the hotel. This is especially important when you consider that different distribution channels cost hotels different amounts to operate effectively. As a result, reservations generated by a specific distribution channel may be much more profitable for a hotel than a reservation generated by a different distribution channel (even though the rate at which the room is sold is identical). To best understand hotel distribution channels, their emerging importance, and how they can better be managed, it is useful to begin an examination of them from a historical perspective.

Historical Distribution Channels

In the earliest days of the hotel industry, travelers contacted an inn or hotel for a room only after they had physically arrived in the hotel's reception area. With no dependable mail service, no telephone, and even no guarantee of the date when one would arrive, early travelers were truly on their own when seeking to secure overnight accommodations.

The advent of a governmentally operated mail service was an important milestone in the hospitality industry because, for the first time, guests could use this new distribution channel (mail service) to communicate directly with hotels. Equally importantly, it allowed intermediaries assisting individual travelers the ability to contact hotels on behalf of their clients, as well as to keep a written record of what the intermediary had requested for the traveler and what the hotel had promised to provide.

Intermediaries have a long history within the travel industry. The most common is the travel agent. Traditionally, travel agents either dealt directly with travelers, or were **travel wholesalers**.

HOTEL TERMINOLOGY AT WORK

Travel Wholesaler: An entity that purchases large numbers (blocks) of hotel rooms and, in turn, sells them to travel agents.

It is advantageous to examine this earliest of intermediary relationships in detail because it can help today's hoteliers better understand the current complex intermediary environment that will likely continue in the future. Figure 6.10 details the fairly simple process in which the following steps occur:

Step 1:   A hotel sells rooms to a travel wholesaler.

Step 2:   The wholesaler sells rooms to a travel agent.

Step 3:   The travel agent sells rooms to an individual guest (or group).

Step 4:   The guest stays at the hotel.

To understand the goals of each entity in the transaction, let's examine, in detail, the motivation of each party in each step of the transaction:

Step 1: A hotel sells rooms to a travel wholesaler.

Seller's Motivation: As we saw earlier a revenue manager may determine, when preparing forecasts, that there are periods of slack demand for the hotel's rooms. In such a case, it may be in the hotel's best interest to sell, even at a significant discount, those rooms it believes will be vacant on the dates of reduced demand. For example, a hotel in a ski area may sell rooms at a much reduced rate during periods when no snow is on the ground (summer) and thus no skiers will be seeking rooms.

During these periods, alternative activities may be available and the rooms at the ski resort will still be of good quality. However, they must be marketed to nonskiers. If a travel wholesaler approached the ski resort's managers and offered to purchase a substantial number of the rooms projected to be vacant during the no-snow period, the hotel would likely sell the rooms, even if those rooms were sold at a significant discount.

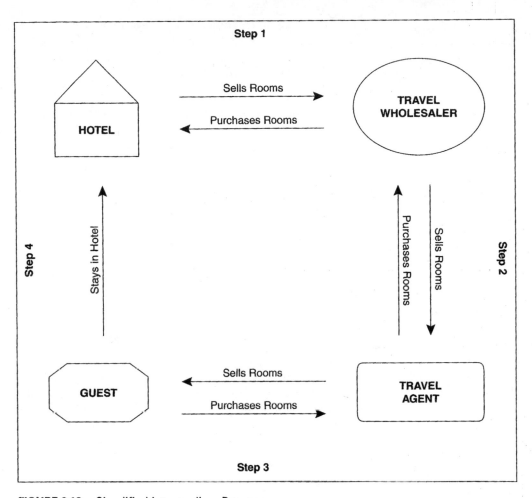

FIGURE 6.10 Simplified Intermediary Process

The hotel and travel wholesaler would sign a contractual agreement setting forth the terms of the sale. The agreement would contain details about:

- The selling price of the rooms
- The actual number of room nights sold by the hotel to the wholesaler
- The specific dates on which the rooms could be used
- Any hotel services and amenities, such as meals and activities, that would accompany the sale of the rooms
- Payment terms acceptable to both parties
- Penalty clauses for nonperformance on the part of either party

When a hotel, as a large-volume rooms seller, establishes a very positive relationship with a travel wholesaler, the hotel ultimately sells rooms it would not likely have otherwise sold and the wholesaler gains the potential to make a profit.

Buyer's Motivation: The buyer's motivation in this transaction is very straightforward. The travel wholesaler seeks to buy rooms at such a reduced rate that, when they are resold to individual guests (or as in this example, to travel agents representing guests), the wholesaler can make a profit by simply charging more for the rooms than he or she paid for them.

In this example, an individual guest may have been able to get a lowered rate on a hotel room during the no-snow period simply by contacting the hotel directly, but it is unlikely that the guest would be willing to purchase the very large number of rooms purchased by the travel wholesaler. As a result, the individual traveler would not likely receive a quoted rate as low as that of the travel wholesaler.

Step 2: Travel wholesaler sells rooms to a travel agent.

Seller's Motivation: A hotel room is an extremely perishable commodity. A travel wholesaler that purchases, even at a significant discount, a large number of hotel rooms, must now sell those rooms before the dates for which they have been reserved passes and the rooms generate no income. For the wholesaler, it follows that the best manner in which to sell what can now be considered the wholesaler's rooms, is to

- Price the rooms attractively
- Solicit as many individual travelers or travel agents as possible to maximize the prospects of selling all the rooms.

Buyer's Motivation: Unless extremely large, it is unlikely that a single travel agency can buy hotel rooms, in significant quantity, at as low a price as can a tour operator. Because a travel agency will market the room(s) it has purchased to its own clients, it is always in the travel agent's best interest to secure hotel rooms at the lowest possible price. In that way, the travel agency can deliver real value and cost savings to its clients while still making a reasonable profit.

Interestingly, in Europe, some of the largest national and multinational travel agents serve as their own successful tour wholesalers. In the United States, the AAA is an example of an organization that serves as both a travel agency and tour wholesaler.

Step 3: Travel agent sells (markets) rooms to a guest.

Seller's Motivation: Travel agents typically secure travel services on behalf of their clients. From a legal perspective, travel agents, unlike travel wholesalers, have a **fiduciary** responsibility to their clients.

HOTEL TERMINOLOGY AT WORK

Fiduciary: A relationship based upon trust and the responsibility to act in the best interest of another when performing tasks.

■

Travel agents are expected to be knowledgeable about the products they sell; if they are not, they risk assuming liability for their own actions as well as the service levels and behavior of the travel service providers (such as hotels) with which they do business. As a result, it has always been in the best interests of travel agents to recommend only those hotels that they were convinced would provide excellent travel products. Doing business only with dependable tour operators and wholesalers helps them achieve that goal.

Buyer's Motivation: Historically, travel agents have been of great value to their clients because they possessed specialized knowledge about the travel industry. The quality of hotels in faraway cities, which restaurants to choose, and the lowest cost means of travel were all areas in which travel agents could advise their clients and be paid for their services either by the clients or by those businesses they recommended. Today, the Internet brings the average traveler tremendous amounts of valuable information. However, many travelers, for a variety of reasons including convenience, potential cost savings, and specialized knowledge, still rely on travel agents to guide them in their travel purchases.

Step 4: Guest stays in hotel.

Hotel's Motivation: Note that this section is not titled "Seller's Motivation." This is because, in this situation, it is the travel wholesaler that is the hotel's client, *not* the guest staying at the property. Even though the guest is very important, and the treatment the guest receives may very well influence future hotel room purchases by the travel wholesaler, the hotel's first legal responsibility is fulfilling its contractual obligation to its own client (the travel wholesaler). Clearly, however, it is in the hotel's best interest to satisfy the guests actually staying in the hotel. If it does it may be able, in the future, to sell additional rooms to the travel wholesaler and thus increase the hotel's RevPar.

Guest's Motivation: When guests arrive at a hotel, they expect to receive a quality lodging experience regardless of how they have arranged to purchase their night's stay. In most cases, the guests arriving on a travel package anticipate the same level of service they would have expected had they called and made a reservation directly with the hotel.

A critical point to remember, however, is that, despite the fact that the guest is only indirectly the hotel's client, the individuals arriving at the front desk on a travel package remain the hotel's guests. As such, they must be treated in the same manner as any other guest arriving at the property. This can sometimes be a challenge when hotel staff are aware of, and may even resent, the steep room discounts sometimes given to travel wholesalers and as a result, to those guests buying and staying in the heavily discounted rooms.

Despite the very large number of complex distribution channels in use today, the fundamental motivations of travel supplier and intermediary in each portion of the distribution channel just examined have remained essentially unchanged. Prior to the 1970s, the primary distribution channels in use by hotels, travelers, and travel agents were the telegraph, the mail system, and the telephone. In the mid-1970s, travel wholesalers, travel agencies, and hotels found their relationship headed toward a major transformation. Interestingly, the change was initiated not on the part of hotels, but rather by the airlines.

As the commercial airline business in the United States developed, it created much the same traditional relationships with travel wholesalers and travel agencies as had hotels, cruise lines, and trains. In the early stages of the commercial airline industry, travel agents would refer to printed flight schedules distributed by the airlines and then contact an airline to inquire about availability on specific flights requested by their clients. By the end of the 1970s, however, travel agencies were provided, by each of the major airlines, a specific electronic method for verifying availability and making reservations. Dubbed the GDS (see Chapter 8), those companies in the emerging airline industry found that the electronic booking of tickets was more efficient and cost-effective than attempting to do so by the existing distribution channels of telephone, telegraph, or mail. The continued development of the GDS would soon allow travel agents to book car rentals and hotel room reservations on the same systems.

As travel agencies increasingly found electronic booking on the GDS less costly for their own businesses, they began to insist that all the products they reserved or purchased be available for booking through this emerging distribution channel. In the late 1970s, GDS bookings made up less than 5 percent of all hotel reservations made. It now exceeds 20 percent, despite fierce recent competition from the Internet, another distribution channel that would, when it emerged in the 1990s, radically change the way hotels sell their rooms.

Expansion and improvement of the GDS as well as the entire structure of the system revolved around the airlines, and because it was developed by them, evolved with that specific industry foremost in mind. In actuality, some leaders in the airline business found the fact that travel agencies wanted to book both air travel and hotel rooms on the same system as somewhat bothersome. As a result, it was left to the hotel companies to electronically connect (interface) their own independent or chain reservation systems with each of the various airline systems found in the GDS. Not surprisingly, the airlines were not inclined to allow hotels to have access to their GDS without paying for it. As a result, the use of the GDS significantly altered a savvy hotelier's traditional view of room rate. A hotel guest who walked into a hotel directly off the street and, for example, rented a room for a rate of $99.00, would result in the hotel receiving $99.00. If that same guest's travel agent booked a reservation through the GDS, the hotel's owners would be required to pay:

- A commission to the travel agent (usually 10 percent)
- A fee (set by the airlines) for the use of the GDS
- A reasonable amount to the hotel chain or brand's centralized reservations department to help offset the cost of developing the chain's reservation interface system

Clearly, the costs to the hotels of this new distribution channel were significantly higher than that of walk-ins. Traditional telephone reservation systems that were staffed around the clock seven days a week (24/7) by the hotel chains, however, were also expensive to operate while telegraph and mail were simply too slow to be effective.

All of those labor-intensive, time-consuming, and expensive tasks could be accomplished, in seconds, and at little cost to the travel agency when the GDS was used.

The mid-1990s would see the advent of the next major distribution channel. In 1994, Hyatt Hotels, working with TravelWeb, went online with an integrated reservation system. The hotel industry now had its own, non-GDS-managed reservation system. Of course, the individual hotels whose rooms were booked on the system paid the system managers an Internet booking fee for making any reservation as well as a fee simply to have their hotels listed on the site. Because the availability of rooms changes so rapidly, this new system needed to be interfaced with the GDS. Travel agents with access to the Internet could also use it and many agents (particularly those who were computer literate) found it easier to use than the traditional GDS terminals. Simultaneously, airline companies, who had once encouraged travel agents to book through the GDS, were cutting (or eliminating) travel agent commissions for airline bookings.

The introduction of Internet-based room reservations, the deteriorating relationship between airlines and travel agents, and the public's love of booking their own travel on the Internet has not spelled the end of the GDS. Instead, it has added another significant distribution channel for hoteliers to manage. In fact, all of the remaining GDS entities (now separated from their original airline parent companies) maintain their own Web sites to make access to the GDS easier for travelers and travel agents.

Current Distribution Channels

After virtually hundreds of years of relatively no change in the number of distribution channels used, hoteliers today must manage traditional channels, new channels, and the many variations each of these have developed. The rapidly evolving landscape of GDS modification, Internet and Web site development, and changing interface technology makes predicting the future of distribution management quite complex. In fact, new variations of existing distribution channels seem to develop monthly. For most hotels, however, the following distribution channels or sources of business and their variants will likely be of most importance:

- Walk-ins
- Telephone
- Fax
- E-mail (or in some cases, regular mail)
- GDS
- Chain or Brand Central Reservation System (CRS)
- Internet

Walk-Ins

In the past, hotels clearly preferred that guests arrive with a previously made reservation. In fact, those guests who arrived without one were often viewed with some amount of suspicion. Of course, if the hotel had vacant rooms, these guests would, somewhat reluctantly, be quoted a rate (often higher that that quoted to other guests). Today, walk-in guests are often taken for granted in the hotel industry. For a variety of reasons, that should simply never be the case. As can be seen in Figure 6.11, the hotel pays "zero" reservation fees on a walk-in reservation.

When compared to the same guest making a reservation via the Internet, no less than three reservation-related fees (Internet site, GDS, CRS) simply "disappear" when a walk-in guest arrives and requests a room. Because these systems were not used to generate the reservation, the individual hotel will not pay them. Because these fees may constitute anywhere from 5 to 30 percent of the guest's quoted room rate, the wisdom of making every effort to sell a room to every walk-in guest becomes apparent. To do so, GMs should ensure that the rates quoted to them maximize the chances that these guests will actually accept the quoted rate and elect to stay in the hotel. Some factors that GMs can evaluate to maximize the effectiveness of this channel include:

- Immediate welcome and friendly "acceptance" of potential walk-in guests
- Attractive and clean lobby area
- Special discounts off of rack rate for "last minute travelers"
- Upgraded room assignment from a standard to a higher-level room type to increase perceived value and help ensure the room's sale
- Use of a logical fade (rate) if rate resistance is encountered

Telephone

All hotels still receive reservations via telephone. Although individual circumstances vary, in most hotels with less than 200 or so rooms (and thus no full-time telephone reservations department), the hotel's front-desk staff may also serve as the hotel's

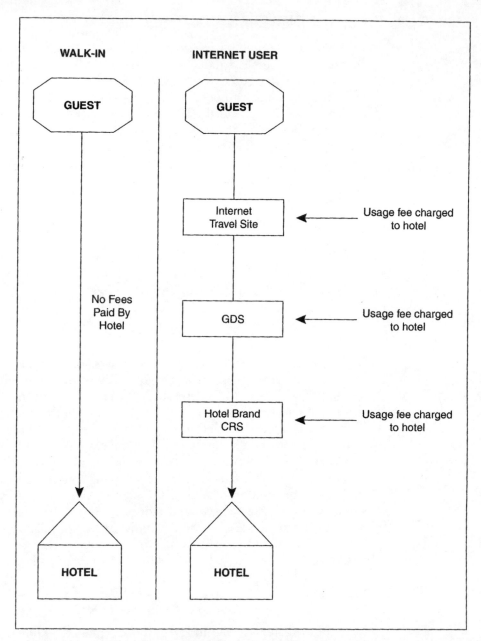

FIGURE 6.11   Walk-In Versus Internet User Fees Charged to Hotel

telephone reservations contact. In many cases, guests simply prefer to place a telephone call directly to the hotel when they want a reservation. The manner in which these calls are handled by the front-office staff can make a tremendous difference in the booking success of the hotel. Compare, for example, the two alternative telephone greetings that might be used by a front-office staff member responsible for answering the telephone at the "Grand Hotel":

Front-Desk Agent A: *"Hello, ... Grand Hotel."*

Front-Desk Agent B: *"It's a grand day at the Grand Hotel. This is Kimberly, how may I assist you today?"*

To check the effectiveness of the telephone sales effort, some GMs employ outside parties to "shop" their hotels. These shoppers call the hotel for the purpose of making a reservation. How the hotel staff handles the reservation request and later the cancellation process is critiqued in detail with a written summary provided to the hotel's management. These critiques can then be used to identify areas of improvement in the sales effort. Some chains also telephone shop their franchisees and offer assistance in telephone selling skills improvement. In addition, several training organizations have created tools to assist FOMs in making their telephone distribution channel an effective (and lower cost) option than many other alternatives. The art of selling rooms via telephone is highly developed and training aids are available to help.

THE INTERNET AT WORK

For an example of some excellent DVD format training aids related to telephone skills and sales for hotels, go to

www.ei-ahma.org

When you arrive, select "Product by Classification," and then select "Department/Position: Front Office."

Facsimile (Fax)

Despite tremendous advances in computer technology, the fax remains a much used reservation request method. This distribution channel is especially popular internationally, with noncomputer users, and where the guest wants confirmation (in writing) from the hotel that a reservation has been made. Because guests continue to request reservation information by fax (and because the costs associated with accepting a fax for an individual reservation are relatively low), FOMs and their hotels are well served by the careful management of this reservation source.

If the fax channel of distribution is to be significantly utilized, the following are specific steps that can be taken to help maximize its effectiveness:

- Provide guests with a designated toll-free number used for all incoming fax reservations.
- Train staff to respond to a fax reservation request immediately upon its receipt.
- If reservation personnel have access to the Internet, consider purchasing the software necessary to allow the use of the hotel's e-mail system to reply to fax reservation requests to enhance quality, speed, and record keeping.
- Keep adequate fax supplies including ink cartridges, paper, and cover sheets on hand to ensure no incoming fax (or reply to it) is unnecessarily delayed.
- Ensure that fax cover and content sheets used to respond to reservations are professionally prepared, consist of large, easily readable type, and are recognized as a selling tool that will reflect positively on the quality of the hotel.

E-Mail/Traditional Mail

Although they are very different, the distribution channels of e-mail and traditional mail can easily be considered together because of their similarities. In both cases, the sender has the opportunity to ask, in detail and directly to hotel personnel, reservations related questions. In addition, there is a written record of the reservation inquiry. Despite the similarities of the two channels, however, the users of these two channels often have different timing expectations. The e-mail user would reasonably expect a reply the same day or, at the very latest, the next day. The traditional mail user would, depending upon his/her own location and the location of the hotel contacted, expect a reply to take several days or even longer.

Mail channels, like some others, bypass the fees associated with other reservation methods. Franchise fees must still be paid on the value of the reservation if the guest stays, but the **net ADR yield** from mail sales is much higher than from many other distribution channels. This is especially true of e-mail, where reservation costs are limited to the maintenance of a computer terminal and an e-mail address plus the actual labor required to answer the e-mail.

HOTEL TERMINOLOGY AT WORK

Net ADR Yield: The rate (ADR) actually received by a hotel after subtracting the cost of the fees and assessments associated with a room sale. The formula for Net ADR Yield is

$$\frac{\text{Room Rate } - \text{ Reservation Generation Fees}}{\text{Room Rate Paid}} = \text{Net ADR Yield}$$

Typical reservation related fees include those charged by travel agents, the GDS, a hotel's CRS, and the operators of Internet booking sites.

Professional hoteliers understand that all revenue dollars are *not* created equally. A $100.00 room sold via a high net ADR yield channel is more profitable than the same rate sold on a channel with a significantly lower net ADR yield.

Because guests continue to request reservation information by e-mail and (to a lesser degree) traditional mail, the management of these two channels will continue to be important. If these channels of distribution are significantly used by an FOM, the following specific steps can be taken to help maximize their effectiveness:

- Reply to all mail inquires within 24 hours (sooner if possible).
- For e-mail, use the name of the hotel in the "response" message title line.
- For traditional mail, have stationary professionally printed; prohibit use of photocopied standard "fill-in-the-blank" letter replies that are not personalized for each guest.
- Use automated spell-check software on each mail reply before it is sent.
- "Sign" all mail clearly, including the typed name, position, address, and direct contact information (telephone or e-mail) of the person replying to the reservation inquiry.

Global Distribution System (GDS)

As we saw earlier in this chapter, the GDS is one of the older and more established hotel distribution channels. It began as a partnership between airlines and those travel agencies that sold their plane tickets, and has continued to evolve. Today there are some in the hospitality industry who believe the GDS, because it has been the traditional booking choice of travel agents, is in a state of severe decline. It is true that the Internet has emerged as a powerful challenger to the GDS. It is also true that many individual travelers no longer feel they need the assistance of a travel agent when booking their hotel rooms. Hoteliers who dismiss the GDS and its influence, however, fail to understand its actual position in the industry. Recall that reservations booked by a travel agency (and thus through the GDS) must be interfaced directly with a hotel's PMS to provide real-time room inventory, rates, and availability information.

Hotels have gone to significant expense to create the interfaces needed to connect their PMS systems to the GDS. They are unlikely to abandon these in favor of creating the hundreds of devices that would be required to directly connect the (currently) thousands of Internet booking sites to their individual hotels' PMSs. It is also important to remember that a travel agent using the GDS can book airfares, hotels, and car rentals at the same time. Most hotel-operated Web sites do not currently provide this option.

The GDSs and their operation are likely to be transformed but not replaced by the Internet. Interestingly, travel agents are increasingly checking the Internet to compare the prices hotels offer their clients through the GDS with the prices these hotels are posting elsewhere on the Web. GMs should remember this.

Far from disappearing, the services the GDS offers to travel agencies and hotels are likely to expand and improve. If this channel of distribution is to be used significantly, the following specific steps can be taken to help maximize its effectiveness:

- Monitor, on a regular basis, the number of hotel reservations received from the GDS.
- Ensure that the hotel's information on the GDS is accurate and up-to-date and that fees charged the hotel for GDS usage are fully understood.
- Establish a relationship with one or more travel agents who can evaluate on a regular basis the accuracy of the hotel's information on the GDS.

Central Reservation System (CRS)

For a franchised hotel, the chain or brand's CRS is an important source of reservations. In a strong brand, the reservations generated by the CRS may constitute 20% or more of a hotel's total monthly room revenue. Typically, a brand's CRS will consist of a

- Toll-free telephone-call center
- Chain-operated Web site
- E-mail/traditional mail reservations division
- Group-sales division

Of these, the call center and chain-operated Web site are generally the two components that generate the largest number of reservations. It is also important to remember that, because the hotel brand's CRS is interfaced with a switch to the GDS, in most hotels 70 percent or more of their travel agent and Internet bookings will actually be routed through the brand's CRS. In most cases, the brand will be able to provide a hotel with significant detail regarding the origination of the reservations that have been channeled through the CRS. This data should be monitored carefully.

While it is common for hoteliers to "complain" that their CRS does not generate "enough" volume, those desiring to maximize the revenue generating potential of this important distribution channel can follow some specific steps to improve its effectiveness:

- Ensure that all hotel-related information supplied to the brand's call center staff is accurate and up-to-date.
- Conduct periodic shopper calls to the call center to ensure that effective selling of the hotel's services and amenities is actually occurring.

- Consider an annual visit to the brand's call center to meet personally with call center staff and to further promote the hotel.
- Ensure that all information listed on the hotel's specifically assigned location on the brand's Web site is accurate and up-to-date.
- Supply attractive photos and creative site copy describing the hotel's features and amenities to maximize interest.
- Follow up promptly (or coordinate the follow up with the sales and marketing department) on any group business leads provided by the CRS.

Internet

It is interesting to note that, if this book had been written only five years ago, this section would have been of little or no interest to most GMs. Today, entire books are being written on the importance of managing a hotel's Internet presence. The reason for this is clear. Travel is the single most popular item sold on the Internet. Beginning in early 2001, hotel room sales growth on the Internet was nothing short of explosive. That growth continues each year, and it is now estimated that by 2008 over 50 percent of all room reservations will be made via the Internet.

The hotel industry's relationship with other travel-service entities operating on the Internet did not get off to a particularly good start. In 2001, just as travelers' use of the Internet began to rapidly accelerate, the hotel industry began a multiyear slump that some feel started with the tragic events of September 11, but others believe had begun months earlier. The result was hoteliers who faced, for several years, large numbers of unsold rooms at the same time many travel wholesalers were moving their businesses onto the Internet. The result was steep discounts (often 30% or more) given to those travel wholesalers selling on the Internet. What hoteliers simply failed (or refused) to understand was that, for the first time, *all* customers could view the discounted rates travel wholesalers posted on their Web sites. This was not the case in the pre-Internet hotel world. As a result, in the earliest days of hotel room sales on the Internet, hotels

- Excessively discounted rooms sold to **e-wholesalers.**
- Failed to appreciate the importance of rate consistency across channels.
- Gave up too much control over how their rooms were sold on the Internet.
- Were ultimately forced to take major steps to enhance their Internet presence quickly and regain control of their pricing and business structures.

HOTEL TERMINOLOGY AT WORK

E-Wholesaler: A room reseller that obtains reduced (wholesale) rooms prices and inventory commitments directly from a hotel or through an agreement with the hotel's corporate brand managers and then publishes "retail rates" on its Web sites, usually at a markup of 20 to 40 percent. Examples include Travelocity, Hotels.com, TravelWeb and Expedia.

■

As a channel, the Internet gives net ADR yields that can be 15 to 25 percent below those of other distribution channel alternatives. In fact, it is accurate to state that, one of today's most popular distribution channels (the Internet), if improperly managed, can also be one of the least desirable (profitable) for hotels.

For today's FOMs and revenue managers, Internet sales can be good or very bad. For example, if a hotel "sells", via a travel agent, a $100.00 per night room on the Internet, the actual amount received can be $60.00 per night or even less. Recall that when a hotel sells a room through an online intermediary, it will typically incur Internet usage fees, GDS, and CRS fees, and as in this illustration, will still pay a 10% commission to the travel agent who booked the room. In addition, franchised hotels will pay a franchise fee of 2 to 10 percent (to their franchisor) on the room revenue generated by this sale. When you consider that, in most cases, a room sold on the Internet will originally have been discounted heavily by the hotel, it is no wonder hoteliers must monitor their e-wholesaler internet "sales" very carefully. Managing this distribution channel is even more critical when, as is often the case, the e-wholesalers promise the hotels working with them better placement on their Web sites in exchange for even greater room discounts.

Clearly, those who allow their hotels to rely too heavily on some portions of this distribution channel for securing hotel revenue may be successful in building sales, but not hotel profits. A room properly sold through an Internet intermediary may be profitable and in the long-term best interest of a hotel. However, if it is inappropriately sold it may actually cost the hotel much more money than is at first apparent. This is because hotel rooms that are heavily discounted on a public distribution channel such as the Internet will unquestionably be more difficult to sell at higher rates on other higher net ADR yield distribution channels. To effectively administer the Internet distribution channel, revenue managers must:

- *Manage Search Engines.* If there was one "most important" Internet process FOMs must understand, it is that of **search engines** and their role in selling rooms. Simply put, search engines direct Internet users to hoteliers' sites.

HOTEL TERMINOLOGY AT WORK

Search Engine: A Web Site specifically designed for the purpose of directing its visitors to other Web sites.

- *Maintain Rate Integrity.* Rate integrity (parity) is a hot topic for hoteliers. In relation to Internet sales, however, rate integrity simply means making logical decisions regarding the prices listed on each site advertising the hotel's room rates. This is not to imply that rates should (or even could) be identical on all Web sites. In fact, hotel brand managers (franchisors) increasingly are insisting that their affiliated hotels not offer, on any Internet site, room rates lower than those offered on the hotel's own brand site. Although the legality of such a brand mandate has as yet gone untested, it makes little sense to have widely varying room rates posted, for all to observe, on various Internet sites unless there is a compelling rationale for doing so.
- *Monitor Results.* A surprisingly high number of otherwise sophisticated hoteliers fail to monitor the results achieved by those Internet sites with which they do business.

THE INTERNET AT WORK

For continuous updates on a variety of hotel-related topics including channel distribution management, subscribe to one or more e-delivered newsletters. You can find a good one without a subscription cost at

www.hotel-online.com

For many revenue managers, administering and monitoring Internet results actually entails monitoring a

- Property Web site
- Chain Web site
- Third-party Web site(s)

Property Web Site.   A hotel's individually developed and maintained Web site is one of the best ways to secure an Internet room sale. The reason for this is strictly a financial one. When an Internet user buys a room directly from a hotel (as is also the case with a walk-in or fax request), the fees paid by the hotel on that sale are reduced. In the past, franchised hotels may have resisted operating their own independent sites because they did not have the ability to interface these sites directly with their PMS. Independent hotels that also needed the ability to sell online, however, were able to carefully design procedures to work through this challenge. Despite this, even now surprisingly few chain-affiliated hotels (the vast majority of hotel types in the United States) have designed and operate their own Web sites.

Properly understood and managed, the Internet provides any hotel with an easily accessible location for it to meet and interact with its customers, thus lowering its dependence on third parties to increase bookings. It is imperative therefore that in the Internet age, meaningful and effective e-distribution channel management must start with the hotel's main (and independently operated) Web site. A hotel's own Web site should be one of its lowest-cost, highest net ADR yield distribution channels. This can happen when a hotel's site encourages visitors to book rooms in a quick, easy, and logical manner.

The complete development of a hotel's Web site is beyond the scope of this text, but from a distribution channel management perspective hoteliers should carefully consider the following when developing their own property Web sites:

- *Written Content.* A site's written content should seek to answer questions that site visitors might have regarding the hotel (what, where, how much) and to encourage these visitors to book rooms. Key information about a hotel will already exist. It can be found in the hotel's current brochures, sales letters, promotional kits, and other marketing pieces, and should of course be designed for and placed on the Web site. Other important content areas include nearby attractions, activities, and local areas of interest.

- *Visual and Audio Content.* This includes logos, graphics, digital photography, and all forms of streaming audio or video. As more and more Internet users in the United States acquire high-speed Internet access, hoteliers can expand in this area. It is important to remember, however, that not all users will be content to "waste time" with extensive streaming video or audio unless they expressly choose to do so. Long lead-ins and excessive delays caused by too much content download between the time a user clicks a content area and that content's actual display should be avoided.

- *Reservations Device.* Guests must have the ability to book a room directly from a hotel's proprietary Web site. Potential guests want to know immediately if their requested room is available. Thus a site must have a reservation device that displays real-time reservation availability. If it does not, many site visitors will browse to another hotel site in a matter of seconds.

- *Appropriate Links.* Effectively linking a Web site is a key strategy. Links from other Web sites means your Web site is connected to a larger portion of the Web and may improve your hotel's exposure on the Internet.

Chain Web Site.   Technically, a chain's own Web site is a part of its CRS. In the mid-1990s it was estimated that chain-operated Web sites accounted for more than half of all Internet hotel bookings. In the first decade of the 2000s, however, franchisors realized, to their dismay, that travelers were also booking large numbers of rooms on **third-party Web sites.**

HOTEL TERMINOLOGY AT WORK

Third-Party Web Sites: A Web site operated by an entity other than a hotel or a hotel's franchisor.

■

These third-party site room bookings most often consisted of rooms sold by hotels to wholesalers at a significant discount and meant reduced income for franchisees and reduced franchise fees to franchisors.

The reason for the popularity of the third-party sites was twofold. First, travelers could often purchase rooms at a lower rate on these sites, and second, users had the opportunity to compare the prices of different chain hotels on one site. Obviously, this was much faster than users having to surf multiple chain-operated sites, each of which listed only their own hotels, when comparing room prices. It was, and still is, the case that the vast majority of consumers want the capability to shop multiple hotel brands at a time; in addition, they may want to simultaneously book airfares and rental cars.

To respond to the challenges of third-party Web sites, most franchisors instituted **lowest rate guarantee** programs.

HOTEL TERMINOLOGY AT WORK

Lowest Rate Guarantee: A program that assures travelers the lowest available rate for a specific room type on a specific date will be found on the guarantor's Web site.

■

Lowest rate guarantees proved popular with travelers. An additional method used to drive consumers to their own sites are the chains' practice of denying frequent guest program points to consumers who do not make their Internet room purchase on the chain's Web site.

Chain-operated Web sites will continue to be a strong distribution channel. Many travelers are now conditioned to research one or more third-party-operated Web sites for area hotel availability and rates. Then they surf to the preferred chain-operated site to secure a hotel's guaranteed "lowest" rate available and other benefits provided by chain sites for their desired travel dates.

Third-Party Web Sites.   Third-party Internet Web sites work in a manner similar to the way the telephone company's Yellow Pages would work if travelers could easily have access to every single Yellow Pages hotel listing in the world. With the Yellow Pages, consumers can easily at one time see the names and addresses of competing hotels located in the same geographic area. Third-party Web sites provide consumers with the same benefit, and it is a powerful one. The comparison shopping tools available on third-party sites such as Expedia and Hotels.com are what the sites believe will ensure their long-term viability even though chain-operated sites guarantee that the lowest rates will be on the chains' own sites.

Although third-party Web site operators also continue to improve their sites, products, and services in the hope of attracting more consumers, hoteliers should remember that these site operators do not own or operate hotels and possess no rooms to sell that have not been provided by actual hoteliers. It is not surprising that the hotel industry has had mixed feelings about selling rooms to some of these third-party sites. In the past, hoteliers made the business decision that it was advantageous to sell rooms at a steep discount to travel wholesalers. The decision to sell rooms at deeply discounted prices to third-party sites, however, came back to haunt hoteliers when they found that these rates were advertised widely on the Internet. Effectively, hotels found it was difficult to promote a rate of $100.00 per night at the front desk or on their own Web site when alternative third-party Internet sites offered the same rooms that had been sold to those sites at up to 50 percent off for $75.00 per night. In this case, the third-party sites marked "their" room up by 50 percent (room purchased at $50.00 and sold at $75.00 = 50 percent markup). When the additional costs of travel agent, GDS, and CRS fees are factored in, some hotels found their net ADR yields to be less than 30 percent on rooms sold to third-party sites!

Not all third-party sites operate in the same manner. When examining third-party Internet sites, it is important to understand that there are actually two significant but very different models currently in operation:

- Merchant model
- Opaque model

GMs need to be aware of the fundamental differences in these two types of third-party sites and how they affect distribution channel management.

- *Merchant Model.* In the early first decade of the 2000s, lack of understanding among hoteliers on how the Internet and online distribution worked resulted in the proliferation of **merchant model** sites. In the merchant model, third-party Internet site operators bought, at great discount, hotels' excess room inventory and then advertised those rooms for sale online.

HOTEL TERMINOLOGY AT WORK

Merchant Model: An Internet sales method in which hotels sell rooms to Internet site operators. These sites, in turn, allow consumers to enter requested location and arrival dates and are presented with a choice of specific hotels and associated rates available for immediate purchase on the site.

The hospitality industry was, at that time, way behind other travel industry sectors in adopting the entire Internet as a significant distribution channel. A weak travel environment and the results of September 11 found many hoteliers unprepared (financially, technologically, and e-knowledgewise) to deal with the explosion in online bargain hunting and bookings. Online discounter merchants exploited the naivety and desperation in the hospitality industry after September 11. Hoteliers, looking for a quick fix for their eroding occupancies and RevPars, turned to these Internet discounters' "free" services.

What many revenue managers did not realize, or chose to ignore, was the long-term impact on hotel-brand image and the downward rate pressures that would result from publicly advertising heavily discounted rates. This had simply never happened before in the hospitality industry. The new breed "yield manager" of a 300-room hotel could make the decision to sell (or make available to), for example, a third-party site operator 100 rooms for a Sunday night when these rooms were certainly going to be vacant. As the logic went, if these rooms were sold to the site operator for $50.00, who then resold them on the Internet for $75.00, the hotel still achieved an additional $5,000 (100 rooms at $50.00 = $5,000) in revenue. Unfortunately, even in the best case scenarios, hotels achieved acceptable occupancy rates only at the expense of much lower ADRs and permanent damage to their rack rates. Because hotels felt they had little expectation of maintaining occupancy otherwise, they made their inventory available at extremely steep discounts. This allowed the third parties to virtually charge whatever they wanted. In fact, these third-party Web site operators routinely achieved net profit margins on their sales of 25 to 40 percent, which was much more than the 10 percent commission traditional travel agents received.

Most hotel owners and managers liked the sites because of the sales they generated. Consumers liked the sites because of the savings they achieved. The third-party site operators themselves enjoyed the much greater levels of profits they generated when compared to the traditional travel agent distribution channel. In fact, travel agents also liked the sites because they frequently offered room rates lower than those that could be found on the GDS; additionally, hotels would pay travel agents their 10 percent commission as always, regardless of the distribution channel (telephone, fax, GDS, Internet, and so forth) the agents used. Finally, however, the hotel chains (franchisors), and some savvy GMs began to realize the tremendous difficulties associated with overdependence on third-party merchant sites.

Clearly, the chains were not happy that their own franchisees who, in exchange for using the brand name, pay franchise fees based on total room revenue (sales), were offering big discounts to merchant model sites. When they did so, it left the chain-operated Web sites selling at significantly higher rates, or in some cases, unable to sell any rooms at all because the available rooms had been sold/committed to the merchant model site operators. Chain operators soon realized that their hotels were training customers to shop for their brands only when they were sold at a significant discount, thus diluting the value of the brands. Hotel franchise executives also realized that the extensive television marketing campaigns designed by third-party site operators were reinforcing the message that the chain-operated sites were a more expensive place to shop. Individually, the chains were usually too small to spend the money required to refute these claims on national television media.

To combat the rise of third-party merchant model sites, chains began investing more heavily in, and improving, their own Web sites. As we have seen, the chains also started guaranteeing and publicizing that their brands' sites would offer the same or lower prices available anywhere else, or customers would receive the lower price and sometimes an additional discount as well. The tactics worked and more consumers began using sites operated by hotel chains to book their travel. In the future, those who operate hotel chain sites will continue, in all likelihood, to seek additional ways to move consumers away from third-party merchant model sites and onto their own sites.

Merchant model Web sites, however, will continue to flourish because they allow for comparison shopping. Fundamentally, there is nothing wrong with a hotel using online discounters to unload excess or distressed inventory.

But it is very wrong to turn these online services into a hotel's primary and in many cases only Internet distribution channel. This is because, if a hotel appears on the Internet only through discounted rates offered by the online intermediaries and merchants, Internet users will always "bump" into the hotel's discounted rates and, because no other rates are listed on the Internet, these discount rates will become, in the consumer's mind, the hotel's "rack" rate.

- *Opaque Model.* On an **opaque model** site, the buyer (consumer) does not know the name of the hotel they have chosen until after they have committed to purchasing the room.

HOTEL TERMINOLOGY AT WORK

Opaque Model: An Internet sales method in which consumers "bid" an amount they are willing to pay for a room on a specific arrival date and the third party Web site operator matches that bid with a hotel willing to sell a room(s) at that rate.

Studies have shown that rooms sold by opaque sites that do not disclose the brand name or exact location of a hotel until after the room is booked are 30 to 40 percent less expensive than the same rooms sold through merchant model sites. They are used by a large number of travelers who are price conscious and are not loyal to a specific hotel brand.

Opaque models have been popular with hoteliers. To revenue managers, the advantage of such sites is that they do not publicly display heavily discounted rates that, as in the case of the merchant model, may make it more difficult for hoteliers to sell their rooms at higher ADRs through alternative distribution channels.

For travelers, opaque models are typically less expensive, but they do come with some of their own disadvantages. The nondisclosure of hotel names and specific locales may be annoying to shoppers who have a favorite chain and want to acquire or redeem frequent guest program points or who desire to stay in a specific location. The opaque model, however, does benefit hotels that can potentially sell more rooms, as well as consumers who get good deals. Opaque sites are hotel-friendly businesses because they help protect the integrity of a hotel's overall pricing structure.

The Internet continues to evolve as an effective distribution channel. Professional GMs should continue to monitor its progression for the purpose of positioning their hotels to maximize RevPar. All GMs ultimately must lead their property's revenue management process. Fully understanding room rate economics, the management of RevPar and the distribution channels important to their own hotels can help ensure that GMs are well positioned to lead their team in this important process.

THE INTERNET AT WORK

The management of e-distribution channels has become so important that a separate industry association has been developed for those who work in this area of revenue management. The Hotel Electronic Distribution Network Association (HEDNA) is growing. You can learn more about it at

www.hedna.org

MANAGERS AT WORK

J.D. Ojisama, the GM of the Hotel Waldo, has been contacted by an airline and asked to bid on a contract that would have the Waldo house that airline's pilots and flight attendants who stay overnight in the city.

The airline crews would occupy 20 rooms per night, 365 days per year. The airline has indicated, however, that the room rate it would pay the Waldo represents approximately 50% of the Waldo's current year-to-date ADR.

What are the important factors J.D. should consider prior to deciding if the airline contract would be a good one for the hotel? Under what conditions might J.D. decline to bid?

HOTEL TERMINOLOGY AT WORK GLOSSARY

The following terms were defined within this chapter. If you are not familiar with one of them, please review the segment of the chapter that contains the term.

Inventory (rooms)
Negotiated rate
Blackout date
Negotiated rate agreement
Length of stay (LOS)
Stay-over
Central reservation system (CRS)
E-distribution channel
Day of
Rate resistance
Displace (revenue)
Economics
Supply
Demand
Room rate economics
Law of demand
Law of supply
Rate type
Concierge level
Rate (seasonal)

Rate (special event)
Rate (corporate)
Rate (government)
Rate (group)
Rate (package)
American plan (AP)
Modified American plan (MAP)
All-inclusive plan (rate)
European plan (EP)
Day rate
Half-day rate
Fade (rate)
Cost per key
Bottom-up selling
Top-down selling
Call around
Tracking codes
Other revenue
MLOS
CTA
Overbook(ing)

Walk(ed)
Frequent guest programs
Yield management
GoPar
Competitive set
Occupancy index
ADR index
RevPar index
Room mix
Distribution channel
Travel wholesaler
Fiduciary
Net ADR yield
E-wholesaler
Search engine
Third-party Web sites
Lowest rate guarantee
Merchant model
Opaque model

ISSUES AT WORK

1. Ultimately, GMs are responsible for maximizing the revenue-generating potential of their hotels. The work of the revenue manager has a big impact on a hotel's capacity to increase revenues. In smaller properties, the GM may actually assume the role of revenue manager. In large properties, several individuals may be needed to accomplish all of the required revenue-management tasks. Explain two advantages enjoyed by GMs who complete all of their required revenue-management activities themselves. Describe two advantages that accrue to those GMs who have the benefit of multiple staff members participating in the revenue-management process.

2. Some individuals feel room rates should not be increased significantly when room demand is high. Why do you think they feel that way? What would you say to a regular guest who called you to complain that the room rate she was quoted for her next stay was 50 percent higher than the rate she paid on her last visit? Assume you have forecasted a guaranteed sellout for the dates requested by the guest.

3. Some GMs focus most of their revenue-management efforts on increasing occupancy, while others emphasize the maximizing ADR. Discuss one advantage and one disadvantage related to each of these approaches.

4. The amount of marketing dollars spent promoting a specific distribution channel will typically affect the capacity of that channel to generate revenues for a hotel. Consider the Internet and a group sales department as two distinct distribution channels. What factors might influence you as a GM to increase funding of the Internet channel? What factors might result in increased funding for the members of the sales department?

5. Consumers increasingly book their hotel rooms via the Internet. When you shop for a room on the Internet, what attracts you to a specific hotel? Do you feel most guests "shop" the Internet in the same manner? List at least three things that you feel impact a guest's decision to select a particular hotel when reserving rooms on the Internet.

Sales and Marketing

This Chapter at Work

The economic health of a hotel is dependent on it securing its proper share of the available market. If a hotel does not have an effective sales and marketing department, it will not capture the amount of the business it should. An excellent sales and marketing department ensures that the hotel gets its fair share of the business, and more!

As a GM, the interaction you will have with sales and marketing is extensive. In addition, your working relationship with the director of this department will play a large role in your own success. Ultimately, a well-run hotel must attract, maintain, and expand a strong customer base. This is the job of the sales and marketing department.

The sales and marketing department does its work both inside and outside the hotel. Within the hotel, the sales and marketing department initiates and manages the sales effort. Externally, the department effectively markets and promotes the products and services offered by the hotel.

In very small hotels, the GM may serve as the director of sales and marketing. In larger hotels, the department may be segmented among many departmental members based on the hotel service sold, the type of customer buying the service, or by the way the service is purchased. In this chapter you will learn about alternative ways hotels segment their sales and marketing efforts to improve effectiveness.

Good GMs are very aware of the relationship between effort and success in a sales and marketing department. This is a challenging task because a strong effort in a weak market may actually yield less business than a weak effort in a strong market. Because this is true, GMs must understand the tools available to properly and impartially evaluate the sales and marketing department's internal and external efforts. In this chapter, you will learn about those tools.

You will also learn how technology has changed and is changing the way sales and marketing departments operate. As a GM, you must stay abreast of technological advances affecting the way your hotel is marketed and sold so that you will grow and expand your business and so that you can fairly evaluate the quality of your sales and marketing department and help them improve.

Chapter 7 Outline

THE ROLE OF SALES AND MARKETING
   In the Hotel
   In the Community
SEGMENTATION OF THE SALES AND
MARKETING DEPARTMENT
   By Product Sold
   By Market
      Corporate
      Leisure
      Long–Term Stay
      SMERF and Others
   By Source
      Drop–Ins
      Meeting Planners
      Travel Agents
      Consortia
      Internet

SALES AND MARKETING ACTIVITIES
   Sales Efforts
      The Sales and Marketing Committee
      The Sales Cycle
      Trace Systems
      Sales Leads/Cold Calling
      Client Appreciation Activities
   Marketing Efforts
      Marketing Plan Development
      Advertising
      Promotions, Publicity, and Public Relations
   E-Marketing
      Internet Sales and Marketing
      Online Reservation Systems
      Property Web Sites
      E-Mail Systems

THE ROLE OF SALES AND MARKETING

Very few hotels operate in a noncompetitive environment. In most cases, a guest who elects to use a hotel does so after evaluating several alternative properties. Also, not all hotels will appeal equally to all guests. For example, a couple with children looking for a nearby weekend getaway may want to stay only at a hotel with a swimming pool their children can use. In a similar manner, a large business group that meets weekly for breakfast in a city will require that the hotel site it chooses for its meeting can accommodate its average of hundred attendees. Hotels that cannot accommodate this number will not meet their needs: In both cases, the guest has needs and the hotel has facilities that may, or may not, meet those needs. It is the job of the sales and marketing department to find and cultivate those potential guests whose needs match the product offerings of the hotel. This effort is led by the hotel's **DOSM**.

HOTEL TERMINOLOGY AT WORK

DOSM: Short for "director of sales and marketing." Variations include DOS (director of sales) and DOM (director of marketing).

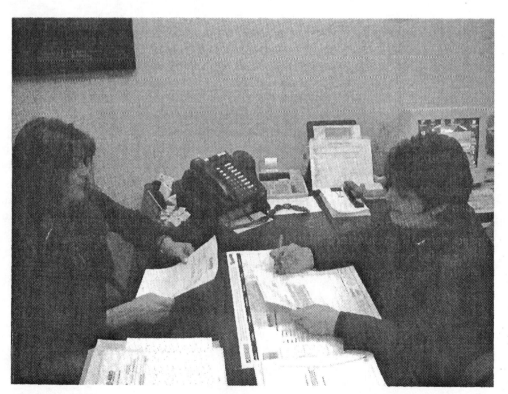

One responsibility of a hotel sales manager is the preparation of contracts in a timely manner.

The DOSM not only identifies and cultivates clients; he or she effectively manages the hotel's marketing efforts, sets rates to maximize RevPar, negotiates sales contracts on behalf of the hotel, and serves as a leader of the hotel's sales and marketing team.

Entire books and extensive magazine articles are devoted to the topic of hotel sales and marketing. In fact, because of its immediate impact on the hotel profits, in most cases no department within the hotel gets more attention from the GM than does sales and marketing. Nor is any area of hotel management subject to more debate regarding how it is best done. There are nearly as many unique approaches to the sales and marketing of hotels as there are hotel sales and marketing staffs. Even definitions of the terms *sales* and *marketing* are often debated within the hotel industry. In fact, there is no universally accepted definition for these terms as they relate to the hotel business. For the purposes of this text, we will consider marketing as all those activities designed to increase consumer awareness and demand by promoting and advertising the hotel and sales as those activities related directly to servicing consumer demand and **booking** clients.

HOTEL TERMINOLOGY AT WORK

Booking: Hotel jargon for making a confirmed sale. As in "What is the current booking volume for the month in the food and beverage department?" or "How many out-of-state tour buses were booked into the hotel last month?"

Most hospitality industry professionals understand that marketing includes the act of selling, but may also include:

- Product design
- Pricing
- Revenue management
- Media advertising development and placement
- Direct mail
- Packaging (such as holiday or other all-inclusive specials)
- Developing marketing plans
- Evaluating the marketing effort

The distinction between sales and marketing activities is sometimes clear-cut but more often is somewhat uncertain. For example, conceiving an advertisement and placing it in the local Yellow Pages telephone directory is clearly a marketing activity. Typing a final sales contract for a group reserving one hundred sleeping rooms is clearly a sales activity. If, however, the DOSM is representing the hotel at a trade show whose attendees are professional meeting planners, that activity could be considered marketing (an activity related to increasing demand), or sales (activities related to meeting demand), or both. For the GM, a distinct definition of sales or marketing is less important than knowing that those sales and marketing activities that must be implemented inside and outside of the hotel are implemented effectively.

THE INTERNET AT WORK

The professional association for those individuals interested in hotel, travel, and tourism sales and marketing is called the Hospitality Sales and Marketing Association International (HSMAI). To read this group's mission statement and to view a calendar of their activities, go to

www.hsmai.org

In the Hotel

In many hotels, the majority of a sales and marketing staff's time is spent inside the property. The type of hotel, its size, and the structure of the sales and marketing staff will determine the actual amount of the staff's on-property time. In all cases, however, the DOSM will be an important member of the EOC and thus will heavily influence the hotel's internal operational decisions. When new hotel policies, procedures, and product and service offerings are considered, they must always be evaluated for their potential positive or negative impact on sales.

The marketing efforts of the sales and marketing department affect the entire hotel. Although the front office is a major selling force for transient rooms and the sales and marketing department actively works to develop sales of this type, an additional effort of most sales departments involves **group sales**.

HOTEL TERMINOLOGY AT WORK

Group Sale: A large sale (in number of rooms or dollar volume) of the hotel's rooms or services. The sales and marketing department, not the front desk, books sales of this type.

■

With their group sales focus, the sales and marketing staff will be active in a large number of in-hotel tasks, including:

- Planning the hotel's sales and marketing strategy
- Preparing and issuing sales contracts in a timely manner
- Maintaining accurate sales records, forecasts, and histories
- Coordinating and communicating special client requests with the affected hotel departments
- Hosting clients during their stay
- Conducting **site tours**

HOTEL TERMINOLOGY AT WORK

Site Tour: A physical trip (tour) around the hotel, usually hosted by a sales and marketing staff member, for the purpose of introducing potential clients and other interested parties to the hotel's features.

■

MANAGERS AT WORK

"What's wrong with being first? We should be proactive, not reactive," said Jenna Walbert, executive housekeeper at the Waldo Hotel.

"I'm telling you, it's simply a bad idea . . . at this time . . . in this market," replied Michele Austin, the hotel's DOSM. "No one else is doing it."

"It" was the idea of converting all of the guest rooms that currently permitted smoking to a nonsmoking status. It was being proposed by the executive housekeeper and maintenance chief, both of whom pointed out the operational cost savings involved with prohibiting smoking in the guest rooms.

"We'll save thousands of dollars just in not having to replace burn holes in carpets!" said the maintenance chief.

"We have over eighty-five percent of the rooms as nonsmoking now," replied Michele. "I need some rooms to stay as smoking rooms or we will lose group sales to other hotels that are not as restrictive."

J.D. Ojisama, the hotel's GM, listened to the discussion carefully. Ultimately, it would be the GM's decision to change the number of nonsmoking rooms or to keep the current number.

If you were J.D., what nonsales-related factors would influence your decision? Would it be important to know how other hotels in your market area were thinking about this issue? How would you find out? What are the sales-related factors that would influence your final decision? How, if at all, should your own views on smoking influence your decision?

GMs seeking to evaluate the effectiveness of their sales and marketing staff will examine, as part of that evaluation, the staff's ability to successfully complete their important in-hotel duties, as well as those performed in the community.

In the Community

A hotel's perceived and actual presence in its own business community is critical to its success. In a smaller city, a major full-service hotel will be a focal point for important community events, gatherings, and celebrations. In larger cities a hotel plays all of these roles and should also play a significant role in representing the city as a business or tourism destination to its own state, the country, or even internationally. Regardless of the size of the business community the hotel impacts, its DOSM and the entire sales team should have a noticeable, positive impact on the lodging-related business community.

Opportunities to impact the business community are many and always yield two significant sales opportunities for the hotel. The first is that of informing those in the community about the hotel and the services it offers. Occasions that allow for disseminating information can be pursued if the DOSM and sales team (including the GM) are active members of the business community. This involves taking a leadership role in service organizations, business organizations, and the local **chamber of commerce**.

HOTEL TERMINOLOGY AT WORK

Chamber of Commerce: An organization whose goal is the advancement of business interests within a community or larger business region.

As a GM, the memberships, activities, and appointed or elected offices your sales team holds in appropriate community organizations is a good indicator of their stature, visibility, and promotion efforts in the business community.

THE INTERNET AT WORK

Chambers of commerce exist in nearly every community. There are also regional, state, and national chambers. Also called "The Chamber" for short. Go to

www.chamberofcommerce.com/

and utilize the site's search engine to find and explore the chamber nearest you.

In addition to promotion opportunities, sales efforts in the community include innumerable **networking** opportunities.

HOTEL TERMINOLOGY AT WORK

Networking: The development of personal relationships for a business-related purpose. For example, a chamber of commerce–sponsored breakfast open to all community business leaders interested in improving local traffic conditions would be an excellent example of a networking opportunity for a member of a hotel's sales team.

Perhaps no organization provides hotel sales staff with better promotion and networking opportunities than does the local **Convention and Visitors Bureau (CVB)**.

HOTEL TERMINOLOGY AT WORK

Convention and Visitors Bureau: An organization, generally funded by taxes levied on overnight hotel guests, that seeks to increase the number of visitors to the area it represents. Also called the "CVB" for short.
■

Good GMs are active members of their CVBs. In addition, these GMs encourage significant CVB participation at the DOSM and sales team level. DOSMs not considered by the CVB to be active leaders in their community will have fewer chances to influence the CVB in ways that increase business opportunities for their hotels.

The ability of a DOSM and individual sales team members to seek out and take advantage of the networking opportunities available to them is an excellent indicator of the effectiveness of the sales team. These opportunities will result in increased numbers of **sales calls**, and as experienced DOSMs will attest, as sales calls increase, hotel sales levels typically will increase.

HOTEL TERMINOLOGY AT WORK

Sales Call: A meeting arranged for the purpose of selling the hotel's products and services.
■

THE INTERNET AT WORK

Convention and Visitors Bureaus work hard to promote the areas they represent. One of the very best is the CVB of New York City. To view their Web site and explore the ways a CVB can help promote tourism-related and other visitors to a business community, go to

www.nycvisit.com

As a GM, you should be aware of and evaluate the impact your own sales team makes in your community. A sales team that is not active and visible will undoubtedly lose opportunities to improve the sales volume of the hotel because it will miss promotional and networking opportunities that could be capitalized upon by the team if it were aggressively seeking such opportunities.

A hotel sales staff that is performing well will do an excellent job inside the hotel and in the business community it impacts. Exactly how it will do that job is determined in large part by how the GM and DOSM decide to structure the department.

SEGMENTATION OF THE SALES AND MARKETING DEPARTMENT

The type of hotel, its clients, and the services it offers usually determine the structure and number of staff in the sales and marketing department. Traditionally, this department is organized or segmented based upon:

- The product(s) sold by the sales and marketing staff member
- The market (client) type served
- The source of the reservation

Some DOSMs will target a specific market segment, such as corporate travelers, when selling their hotel's services.

We will examine these three alternative approaches to departmental organization because you will likely encounter variations of each in your career.

By Product Sold

Some DOSMs organize their departments based on what their salespeople sell best. For example, the skills required to effectively sell a banquet require greater knowledge about food production and service than does the sale of a group of guest rooms. When hotels find that the variety of products they sell is great, segmentation of the sales and marketing staff by product sold can make good sense. Typical product designations that can become sales specialty areas include:

- Group guest rooms
- Conferences
- Catered events
- Meetings
- Conventions
- Weddings and special events

Thus, for example, a DOSM may assign a specific salesperson to sell one or more of the above products. In this way, that individual can become very skilled at selling the product (or service) involved.

By Market

In some cases, the DOSM will decide that the department is best organized by considering not the product sold, but rather the type of guest who buys the product.

Guests with a common characteristic are referred to as a market or market segment. The market segment approach to departmental organization is a traditional one in the hotel industry, and it is frequently used. Market segments commonly identified include the following.

Corporate

This segment consists of the business traveler. It is a very important segment because the room rates paid by business travelers are among the highest the hotel will be able to achieve. Business travelers have special needs, and those in the sales and marketing staff that sell to them must be keenly aware of both the source of these travelers and the hotel services they desire. As seen in Chapter 1, the business traveler makes up a large portion of the traveling public. Its makeup is increasingly changing from one dominated by male travelers to one divided almost evenly between male and female travelers. Also, it has moved from a group that heavily relied on the services of **travel agents** when reserving their rooms, to a group that now heavily relies on the Internet for the same purpose. Business travelers are a demanding group, but one that pays well for what it wants. It is for this reason that many hotels assign their very best salespeople to this market segment.

HOTEL TERMINOLOGY AT WORK

Travel Agent: A hospitality professional that assists clients in planning travel. Also known as a TA.

∎

Leisure

Leisure travelers come to the hotel for a variety of reasons. These include vacations, weddings, visiting friends and family, or any of a number of other nonwork-related reasons. Unlike the corporate traveler who may return to the same geographic area frequently, leisure travelers tend to visit a specific area or hotel less often. Because that is true, leisure travelers have traditionally relied heavily on the advice of travel agents (TAs) and other travel advisory groups to recommend hotels. When travel agents book their clients in a hotel, the hotel, in most cases, pays a commission to the TA for the booking.

One of the largest and most popular travel advisory groups is the AAA. AAA is a not-for-profit membership organization of over 80 motor clubs, with more than 1,000 agency offices serving over 44 million people in the United States and Canada. AAA publishes a tour book that rates hotels for leisure travelers. Without announcing that they are coming, but at the hotel's specific request, AAA evaluators visit a hotel and rate it on the following six characteristics:

- Exterior, grounds, and public areas
- Guest rooms and bathrooms
- Housekeeping and maintenance
- Room décor, ambiance, and amenities
- Management
- Guest services

One Diamond: Essential, no-frills accommodations. These hotels meet basic requirements related to comfort, cleanliness, and hospitality.

Two Diamonds: Modest enhancements to the one-diamond type property are required. Moderate prices prevail, and amenities and design elements are modest as well.

Three Diamonds: These properties appeal to the travelers with greater needs than those provided by Two Diamond hotels. Marked improvements in physical attributes, amenities, and level of service above the two diamond properties are evident in these hotels.

Four Diamonds: These hotels are upscale in all areas. Accommodations are refined and stylish. The hallmark of a Four Diamond hotel is its extensive array of amenities and a high degree of hospitality, service, and attention to detail.

Five Diamonds: This highest level reflects a hotel of the first class. The physical facilities are extraordinary in every manner. The fundamental hallmarks at this level are meticulous service and the ability to exceed all guest expectations while maintaining an impeccable standard of excellence and personalized service.

FIGURE 7.1 What the AAA Diamond Ratings Represent

Based on the evaluator's assessment, the hotel is assigned an overall property rating consisting of one to five diamonds, with five diamonds being the highest possible score. Figure 7.1 summarizes the criteria used by AAA for their ratings.

THE INTERNET AT WORK

AAA ratings are important to leisure travelers as well as to GMs. To learn more about this membership travel organization, go to their Web site at

www.aaa.com

In addition to AAA, there are several other organizations that publish hotel ratings for leisure travelers. These include Mobile, Fodor, Michelin, Zagat, and a variety of travel magazines. Whether the ratings are issued with stars, diamonds, pineapples, or other symbols, all are intended to give travelers a sense of a hotel's quality and amenities.

Figure 7.2 describes, in detail, examples of the specific criteria inspectors would use to rate hotels (using, in this case, "stars" as the measurement). Note especially the differences that will distinguish a four-star hotel from a five-star hotel.

Many franchise companies also rank their hotels based upon specific criteria. For example, in the Choice Hotels systems, properties that meet written specifications related to service and amenities may be awarded Platinum (the highest), Gold, or Silver status. In this case, as is true in all ranking systems, the intent is to let travelers know more about the quality of the property they are electing. Whether staying at the finest five-star properties or simply stopping overnight at a well-managed limited-service hotel, the leisure market relies, in good measure, on rating systems, is vast, and in some resort and tourist areas, represents an extremely large proportion of nearly all of the rooms that will be booked in the area's hotels.

Long-Term Stay

In some cases, when guests check in to a hotel they plan to stay for a very long time. These long-term or extended-stay guests are an emerging market segment. In fact, some entire hotel brands have been designed to appeal specifically to them. Not all

ONE STAR

A one-star property would be clean, comfortable, and maintained well. It is worth the room rate charged when compared to other hotels in its area. It offers limited services. Good housekeeping and maintenance, combined with courteous service, would be evident. One-star hotels will have:

- 24-hour front desk or direct-dial phones
- Clean, well maintained
- Serviceable furniture in good condition
- Comfortable beds; clean linens changed daily
- Quiet, lightproof rooms
- Good lighting
- Television or radio available in all rooms
- Plumbing in good working order
- Parking area well lit

TWO STAR

A two-star hotel offers guests more than a one-star including some, but not necessarily all, of the facilities and services listed below. A two-star hotel will include all of the features of a one-star hotel and:

- Medium to large rooms with adequate closet space
- Attractive, appealing room décor
- Color television in all rooms
- Good-quality furniture, comfortable chairs
- Swimming pool
- Room service
- Some oversized beds
- Attractive, functional baths
- Adequate closet space
- Good-quality towels

THREE STAR

A three-star establishment offers guests an excellent lodging experience. The range of facilities is extensive. In addition to the features found in lower-rated hotels, a three-star hotel will have:

- Excellent maintenance
- Excellent housekeeping
- Spacious, attractive lobby
- Well-designed check-in/check-out area with 24-hour desk service
- Large, comfortable rooms with sitting area, lightproof and soundproof
- Bright, attractive room décor; some attention to detail (i.e., prints on wall); writing table
- Some nonsmoking rooms available
- Central air-conditioning/heating plant
- A quality mattress in excellent condition
- Individual room thermostat
- Oversized color TV
- Luxury level accommodations
- Two direct-dial phones in guest rooms; one phone by the bed and another on the desk or in the bath
- Internet connection
- Some special services available, such as poolside service, concierge, valet services, doormen, meeting rooms, business services

FOUR STAR

A four-star hotel has every service of one- to three-star properties, but also has its own style and personality. It is luxurious, with a well-integrated, creative décor. Housekeeping and maintenance are superb. Guest rooms are large, with spacious, comfortable sitting areas. A variety of room types are usually available, lobbies are spacious and well decorated and a very good restaurant is on the premises. Room service is gracious and often 24-hour service is provided. In addition, four-star hotels regularly include:

(continued)

FIGURE 7.2   Specific Rating Criteria for Hotels

- Carefully landscaped grounds
- Distinctive building design
- Luxuriously appointed lobby, public space, art work, fine furnishings, superior carpet quality, fresh flowers, plants
- Well-groomed staff, uniformed bellmen, doorman, courteous, helpful staff, and articulate and knowledgeable staff
- Room service, extended hours, superior service, and a varied menu
- Excellent restaurant facilities, including at least one fine dining room
- Television in armoire or on attractive, decorative stand; remote control
- Well-integrated décor; fine artwork; superior drapery, spread, and furniture fabrics
- Closed, lighted closets, ample hangers, full-length mirrors
- Fine linen, double top sheet; large, fresh pillows, extra blankets, pillows provided
- Twice-daily maid service; turn-down service
- In-room computer/ office equipment
- Enhanced bedding
- Bathroom telephone
- Nearby; recreation facilities on premises; poolside services, beverage and food; complimentary limousine service to theater and shopping; complimentary shoeshine; complimentary newspaper

FIVE STAR

A five-star hotel is unique and will typically include no more than 1 or 2 percent of all hotels rated. There is no "typical" five-star establishment because most of these hotels are truly "one-of-a-kind;" however, some common characteristics exist.

Each one offers service levels that provide a memorable experience for each guest. Lobbies will be places of beauty, often displaying fine works. A superior restaurant must be present. Grounds should be meticulously groomed and landscaped. This type of hotel requires the presence of professional, articulate, knowledgeable staff members capable of identifying and meeting the needs of all guests.

A five-star hotel will offer guests all of the features of a four-star property as well as:

- Unique architectural building design
- Superior maintenance throughout
- Grounds meticulously groomed and landscaped
- Impeccable housekeeping
- Flooring or carpeting of exceptional quality
- Guests escorted to rooms by professionally trained personnel
- Rooms spacious, offering a comfortable sitting area, working area and chair
- Carefully integrated guest room decor, with emphasis on elegance or reflecting a design of distinctive quality
- Amenities, special soaps, linens designed to coordinate with bath décor
- Welcome gift from management
- Minibars, refrigerators in rooms
- Staff who are well groomed, uniformed, attractively dressed
- Management that is committed to guest satisfaction
- A continuous commitment to excellence

FIGURE 7.2   *(Continued)*

hotels appeal to the long-term stay guest, but most hotels have some clients who fit this category. At the less expensive end of the room charge scale, some properties that attract extended-stay guests do so by providing larger rooms (or suites), cooking facilities, and refrigerators. At the higher end of the room charge scale, hotels have always appealed to some wealthy clients who prefer to live in an environment that provides food, security, and cleaning services rather than in an apartment.

Long-term stay guests come to hotels for a wide variety of reasons and include individuals working on construction projects, those seeking permanent housing in the area, or those whose homes are temporarily uninhabitable. This is a highly desirable market segment for several reasons, including the guaranteed occupancy such guests bring to the hotel, the ease of cleaning their rooms, and their relatively uncomplicated billing. A disadvantage is that these rooms are often sold at very low daily rates. Despite that fact, some DOSMs assign specific sales managers to this segment and have great success with it.

THE INTERNET AT WORK

To view the features offered by one of the very best managed extended-stay brands, now owned by Hyatt Hotels, visit the Hawthorn Suites Web site at

www.hawthorn.com/

SMERF and Others

Groups consisting of social, military, educational, religious, or fraternal organizations are known by the acronym **SMERF**.

HOTEL TERMINOLOGY AT WORK

SMERF: Short for social, military, educational, religious, or fraternal organizations as in "We should assign Vernon to work the SMERF market next year because he has extensive contacts with these groups."

This market segment can also be of significant size. Group members hold organizational meetings, may travel as a group, and frequently hold conferences and conventions. Additional market groups that may require, depending on the hotel, a dedicated sales staff include sports teams, government workers, tour bus, or any other defined group large enough that, in the opinion of the DOSM, a designated salesperson should be assigned to it.

By Source

Increasingly, DOSMs structure their departments based on "how" the hotel's sales are made. The specific sources or distribution channels important to a hotel will vary based on the hotel's type and its market; however, the following are important distribution channels that should be addressed by the sales and marketing department regardless of whether they influence departmental structure.

Drop-Ins

Sometimes overlooked, the importance of the **drop-in** cannot be overstated.

HOTEL TERMINOLOGY AT WORK

Drop-In: A potential buyer (guest) who arrives at the hotel without an appointment.

This potential guest simply arrives on the property and requests a site tour that may include sleeping rooms, meeting rooms, or banquet facilities. If a member of the hotel's staff is not available to meet with this prospect upon arrival, the sales opportunity may be lost. Drop-ins are a reminder to management that some member of the hotel's sales staff should be available the maximum number of reasonable hours per day to conduct site tours.

Meeting Planners

Professional meeting planners annually buy large numbers of sleeping rooms, as well as reserve significant amounts of meeting and catering space. These individuals may represent a variety of corporations, groups, and organizations. They are sophisticated buyers of a hotel's products who often use comparison-shopping techniques and who can heavily influence a hotel's reputation based on their experience with it. It is not unusual for a DOSM to designate one (or more) experienced staff members to deal exclusively with this group of professionals.

THE INTERNET AT WORK

Meeting Professionals International (MPI) is the world's largest association of meeting planning professionals with more than 19,000 members in 64 countries. To visit their Web site, go to

www.mpiweb.org

Note the large number of member educational services they offer.

Travel Agents

Despite recent declines in their numbers, travel agents (TAs), are still a significant factor in the hotel industry. TAs may be retailers, wholesalers, or both. Retail travel agencies and their agents sell directly to the public. For example, if a couple wished to reserve a room at the Waldo Hotel described in this book, they could simply contact a local travel agency in their city (or anywhere in the world), and the agent, using the GDS, would make the reservation. In return, the hotel would pay the travel agency a commission for the sale. Depending on the agency and its arrangement with the hotel, this commission can range from 5 to 20 percent of the room rate paid by the guest.

Wholesale travel agencies purchase hotel, airline, and other services in bulk from hotels and other businesses, and then offer them for resale through retail TAs. In many cases, the wholesaler will **package** the hospitality services it has purchased before offering them for resale.

HOTEL TERMINOLOGY AT WORK

Package: A group of hospitality services (such as hotel rooms, meals, and airfare) sold for one price. For example, a Valentine's Day getaway package to Las Vegas offered by a TA might include airfare, lodging, meals, and show tickets for two people at one inclusive price.

In addition to individual packages, group tours are often packaged and sold. For example, individual travelers from many different geographic areas purchase a tour package developed by a wholesaler and marketed through retail TAs. When travel wholesalers work with travel retailers, the commission paid by the hotel is split, in a prearranged manner, between the wholesale and retail TA.

In some cases, larger retail TAs put together their own packages. In all cases, the TA market is an important one for the hotel, and many DOSMs feel it is deserving of a designated sales manager.

THE INTERNET AT WORK

While many people know them as a credit card company, American Express is also a large wholesale and retail travel agency. To view their travel site and investigate the types of services they offer go to

www.travel.americanexpress.com

THE INTERNET AT WORK

ASTA, short for the American Society of Travel Agents, is the world's largest association of travel professionals. Its 26,000 members include travel agents and the companies whose products they sell such as tours, cruises, hotels, and car rentals. As professionals, they are held to high ethical standards. To review their code of ethics, go to

www.astanet.com/about/codeofethics.asp

Consortia

Consortia are the largest customers of many hotels. Consortia are simply multiple large buyers of hotel (or other hospitality) services who affiliate for the purpose of obtaining lower prices for their members.

HOTEL TERMINOLOGY AT WORK

Consortia: Groups of hotel service buyers organized for the purpose of reducing their client's travel-related costs. A single such group is a consortium.

For example, a consortium representing dozens of large corporate travel departments may request that a hotel offer significant discounts if any of the corporate travelers represented by the consortium stay at the hotel. If the hotel agrees to work with the consortium, it is the job of the DOSM or other member of the sales team to evaluate the potential volume level of this client, establish a negotiated rate, identify any blackout dates, and then monitor the consortium's **pickup**.

HOTEL TERMINOLOGY AT WORK

Pickup: The actual number of rooms used by a client in a defined time period. As in "What was the Travelsavers Company total pickup last year?"

Internet

The Internet is a fairly recent but continuously growing distribution channel. In addition, it is a channel that many DOSMs who are not technologically up-to-date have not used to its fullest capacity. Technically, the Internet is both its own distribution channel and a way for other channels to communicate with the hotel. Consider, for example, that drop-ins, meeting planners, travel agents, and consortium members may all have learned about a specific hotel by surfing hotel Web sites on the Internet. In addition, individual buyers can purchase via the Internet, and meeting planners can view a hotel's rooms and meeting space through the hotel's online brochure or, more recently, streaming video tours. In addition, many travel wholesalers sell on the Internet, and technology-savvy hotel DOSMs can link their own hotel Web sites to those sites likely to draw potential customers from any distribution channel. The total percentage of room nights booked exclusively over the Internet makes it the fastest growing distribution channel in the hotel industry today. Accordingly, some DOSMs designate a qualified sales staff member exclusively to monitor and manage this growing area.

THE INTERNET AT. WORK

For an example of how a hotel can effectively link its own Internet site to that of a site that may bring it additional business, visit the site of the Atlanta Convention and Visitor's Bureau at

www.atlanta.net/atlantanet/meetingPlanners/accommodations/
accommodations.asp?section=ALL

When you arrive at the site, choose "Hyatt Regency Atlanta;" and note how easy it is for potential clients to both "see" and "book" a hotel using today's Internet technology.

SALES AND MARKETING ACTIVITIES

The pressure to increase sales placed upon the DOSM by the GM and the hotel's owners is often intense. But for a GM without a strong background in sales and marketing, the productivity and quality of work performed in this department can be difficult to evaluate.

As a good GM, you should strive to stay current with the most recent trends in hotel sales techniques. You should also know that all individuals responsible for the sales and marketing of the hotel must accomplish some tasks that can, indeed, be evaluated. These tasks include a variety of important activities in the areas of selling and marketing. By examining the presence and quality of key sales and marketing areas, the GM can more fairly and effectively evaluate the work of the DOSM and the sales and marketing department's staff.

Sales Efforts

When GMs are asked about who is responsible for the sales and marketing effort at their hotels, their answer should be "everyone." Every staff member in the hotel should be a salesperson. That is, every employee of the hotel, doing his or her job properly, helps the sales and marketing department to better "sell" the hotel. It falls to the DOSM and his or her staff, however, to perform the tasks required to identify potential clients, to maintain records of the department's interactions with them, and to undertake activities to ensure that clients know they are appreciated.

The Sales and Marketing Committee .
Well-managed hotels have a designated DOSM. Those properties that are best managed, however, will also have a **sales and marketing committee** chaired by the hotel's GM.

HOTEL TERMINOLOGY AT WORK

Sales and Marketing Committee: The group of individuals responsible for coordinating the hotel's sales and marketing effort.

Many areas within the hotel are affected by the sales effort. If, for example, the DOSM wishes to create and promote an all-inclusive weekend getaway package for couples that include a room at the hotel, a complimentary pay-per-view movie, dinner buffet, and late check out the next morning, the impact on the hotel's operations will be significant.

In this example, the staff required to service and the food production cost required to prepare the dinner buffet affect the food and beverage department. The FOM is affected because the front-office staff must be instructed that the package price includes the free movie and thus movie charges, as they occur, should not be posted (charged) to the guest's folio, because the guest has in fact already paid for the movie as part of the inclusive package. The controller must assign prorated portions of the inclusive revenue to the appropriate department, and the housekeeping staff must be informed that rooms reserved for this package will have to be cleaned later than usual (because of the late check out). In this example, a coordination of efforts is clearly required. It is the role of the sales and marketing committee to provide that coordination.

The sales and marketing committee will generally consist of the GM, the DOSM, all members of the sales and marketing staff, the controller, the food and beverage director, the FOM, and the executive housekeeper (or **rooms division manager**).

HOTEL TERMINOLOGY AT WORK

Rooms Division Manager: An individual in a hotel responsible for the management of both the front-office and the housekeeping departments. (This position does not exist in every hotel.)

Additional members may be added depending on the needs of the hotel and the talents of the management staff. This committee harmonizes efforts across departmental lines, engages in long-term planning, and ensures the cooperation of all involved in the sales and marketing process. The GM's participation is important in two ways. First, the mere presence of the GM demonstrates the significance of the group. Second, when departments must be encouraged (or instructed) to modify their current activities or procedures to assist in new sales or marketing initiatives, the GM is on hand to confirm that the modifications should be undertaken and that they have the GM's support.

The Sales Cycle

One beneficial way to examine the sales activities of the sales and marketing department is to consider the activities involved before, during, and after a hypothetical sale. Of course, not all sales involve each of the activities we will examine, but each does exist in the sales cycle. At each phase in the sales cycle, hotel employees must perform well or risk losing the sale to another property. As a GM, if you continually find client dissatisfaction at any one of these phases, immediate corrective action is required to help ensure that your sales and marketing department maintains its reputation for quality and competency. In addition, uncorrected problems in the sales and marketing department will ultimately be damaging to the long-term economic health of the hotel, so it is a good idea to regularly monitor and correct sales-related problems as they are identified.

The following events are typically encountered in the sales cycle.

Presale Phase

- Aleshia M., a Waldo Hotel sales manager, meets, for the first time, Mr. Jodi at a golf outing held to raise funds for the American Cancer Society. Mr. Jodi mentions that he is this year's president of the Society of Antique Furniture Appraisers.

- At dinner following the golf outing, Aleshia inquires about any meetings held in the city by the society. Mr. Jodi replies that they annually meet in the area, for three days, and that the society's board of directors votes each year on which hotel the group will select. In the past, states Mr. Jodi, the group has stayed exclusively at the Altoona Hotel (a competitor) and that they are relatively happy with that hotel.

- After dinner, Aleshia invites Mr. Jodi to the Waldo Hotel for lunch and a site tour. Based primarily on the friendship established on the golf course, Mr. Jodi agrees to the meeting.

- At the lunch, Aleshia determines that the Waldo has meeting space and sleeping rooms sufficient to meet the needs of the society and that the hotel could accommodate the dates of the society's next meeting. On the site tour, Aleshia points out the Waldo Hotel's best features, subtly contrasting them to the Altoona Hotel, but without disparaging that competitor. At the conclusion of the lunch, Aleshia asks Mr. Jodi if he could arrange to include the Waldo on the list of hotels allowed to submit a **bid** on the society's next meeting. Mr. Jodi agrees to do so.

HOTEL TERMINOLOGY AT WOR.K

Bid: An offer by the hotel to supply sleeping rooms, meeting space, food and beverages, or other services to a potential client at a stated price. If the bid is accepted, the hotel will issue the client a contract detailing the agreement made between the hotel and the client.

Sales Phase

- With the help of Mr. Jodi, Aleshia receives an **RFP** from the society.

HOTEL TERMINOLOGY AT WORK

RFP: Short for "request for proposal." An RFP is a request from a potential client for the hotel to submit its pricing offer (proposal) to the client in writing. An RFP may include questions about the hotel's features and services in addition to the prices it is offering.

- In conjunction with the DOSM, the RFP is completed and submitted on time. Room rates are established based on the hotel's estimate of the group's sleeping room pickup, as well as the food and beverage and meeting room revenue the group will generate.
- Based on the RFPs received, the society's board narrows its choice of hotels to two, one of which is the Waldo Hotel. The society, following a site tour by the entire board, a complimentary lunch served by the food and beverage department (and attended by the GM), and with the visible support of Mr. Jodi, selects the Waldo Hotel as the site for its next meeting.
- Aleshia, in conjunction with the DOSM, prepares a **group contract** for the society detailing the agreement with the hotel that specifically addresses any **attrition** and cancellation penalties.

HOTEL TERMINOLOGY AT WORK

Group Contract: A legal document used to summarize the agreement between a hotel and its group client.

Attrition: The difference between the original request and the actual purchases of a group. For example, a group might reserve 100 rooms, but actually use only 50. The hotel's standard group contract may stipulate in such a case that the group pay a penalty for "over reserving."

- Aleshia arranges with the controller's office to forward a direct bill application to the society. The society's bank references are reviewed by the controller's office, and a credit line is established.
- Aleshia establishes a group **block** for the society to ensure they have sleeping rooms reserved for their meeting.

HOTEL TERMINOLOGY AT WORK

Block: Rooms reserved exclusively for members of a specific group. As in "We need to create a block of 50 rooms for May 10 and 11 for the Society of Antique Furniture Appraisers."

- Aleshia, or another member of the sales and marketing team, details the client's contracted requirements, in writing, to those hotel departments (food and beverage, controller, front office, housekeeping, and so forth) needing this information.
- Aleshia, or some member of the sales and marketing team, monitors the client's block to ensure that the hotel meets contractual terms regarding the block. That is, it holds, for the group's purchase only, the required number of rooms for the length of time stipulated in the contract.
- Aleshia attends a preevent sales meeting of hotel staff. The staff reviews the needs and special requests of the groups that will be coming to the hotel in the next week. One such group is the society, and Aleshia reviews the contract terms with the staff.
- Aleshia is present on the first day of the society's meeting to welcome the client. Periodically throughout the meeting, she checks in on the group's main contact person to ensure the meeting is going well and to solve any problems that may arise.

○ Aleshia is on hand at the society's closing cocktail party/dinner event to personally thank Mr. Jodi and the board for selecting the Waldo.

Postsale Phase

○ Aleshia writes to each member of the society's board thanking them for choosing the Waldo Hotel. The letter is cosigned by the DOSM or GM. Aleshia hand delivers a special token of appreciation to Mr. Jodi and thanks him for his assistance with the society.

○ Aleshia reviews with the accounts receivable clerk in the controller's office the society's final bill to ensure that it is accurate.

○ The society is added to the preferred client list, ensuring that it will be contacted and recognized, in some manner, by the hotel on a regular basis.

○ An entry is made in the sales activity calendar ensuring that the hotel sales team will begin the bid process with the society next year in ample time to retain the business.

○ All written records related to the society's event are properly filed.

As you can see, there are many activities that must be performed flawlessly in the competitive hotel sales process. People skills, organizational skills, and conflict management abilities are essential characteristics of sales and marketing department staff members. Many of the sales activities identified earlier (and more) are complex and vitally important. Errors could be made in any of the processes required for a successful sale, and these errors could cause as much client dissatisfaction as would errors in any of the hotel's operating departments.

The marketing activities of a hotel typically draw a great deal of attention from the GM; however, it is a wise GM who recognizes that sales execution is equally as or more important than marketing activities. Although it is somewhat of an oversimplification, it can be said that sales is the process of servicing business currently identified while marketing seeks to generate new business. It makes little sense to expend tremendous effort attracting new clients if the sales processes involving the hotel's current clients are not properly managed. In fact, until the hotel's sales process is a smooth and efficient one, it is probably best not to risk permanently alienating new clients by serving them poorly as well.

Trace Systems

All sales and marketing departments must have a way to keep a record of the hotel's clients. This record includes those who have used the hotel in the past, those who are currently using the hotel, and those **prospects** who might use the hotel in the future. In addition, records of guest rooms and meeting spaces that (a) have been sold, (b) are currently reserved, and (c) that will be sold in the future, as well as the rates at which these are sold, must be accurately maintained.

HOTEL TERMINOLOGY AT WORK

Prospect: An individual or group who, while not currently using the hotel, are considered potential clients with a good likelihood of using the hotel in the future.

Note: *Prospecting* is the verb used to indicate the process of finding prospects.

When you consider that a sales and marketing department makes hundreds or thousands of client contacts and sales per year, it is not surprising that a system must be in place to keep track of all these contacts. A good DOSM has a **trace system** to help the department maintain its sales records, meet deadlines, and plan future activities.

HOTEL TERMINOLOGY AT WORK

Trace System: A methodical process used to record what has been done in the past and what must be done in the future to maximize sales effectiveness. An effective trace system includes a "contact management" component that allows records to be kept for each individual client (contact).

By examining a simple sales call, you can see the importance of an effective trace system. Assume that a member of the Waldo Hotel's sales team visits the office of the president of a local environmental group that holds quarterly meetings of its membership. The prospect states that they could be interested in moving their meeting business to the Waldo Hotel, but have a current contract with a competing hotel that will not expire for eight months. The following are activities that, at minimum, should happen following the sales call:

- A thank-you note or letter is written to the prospect thanking them for the meeting.
- A calendar notation is made of when to contact the client in the future so that a sales proposal can be submitted for the client's review.
- A site tour should be scheduled, if possible.
- The client's demographic data should be added to the hotel's group database.

Without an effective trace system, deadlines will be missed, follow-up calls will not be made, important client information will be misplaced, overbookings or underbookings will occur, and business will ultimately be lost. In today's competitive environment, it is imperative that the DOSM use an automated trace system. As a GM, you should review the features of the system in use at your hotel to ensure that it is being used to its fullest potential.

THE INTERNET AT WORK

One of the most popular computerized contact management systems available is the "ACT" program developed by the Interact Commerce Corp. You can view their Web site at

www.act.com

To see a demonstration of the system that will familiarize you with its many features, click on "Watch an ACT demo."

Sales Leads/Cold Calling

The majority of guests who visit a hotel are not return guests. Some guests do return week after week or year after year, but most guests do not. Because that is true, a hotel must continually seek new clients. Prospecting for new clients is, arguably, the single most important task of the DOSM's staff. A sales **lead** can come from many sources.

HOTEL TERMINOLOGY AT WORK

Lead: Information about a prospect who is likely to buy from the hotel.

Networking can create leads. Leads can come from a CVB, from a referral by a current guest, by employees, or simply by a prospect's telephone call to the hotel. A DOSM's ability to seek out and cultivate quality leads is critical to his or her own success as well as that of the hotel. In fact, one good way for a GM to evaluate the quality of a DOSM's skills is to meet and discuss on a regular basis:

- New leads that have been uncovered since the last meeting
- The realistic sales potential of these leads
- Who in the department is following up on the leads
- How the leads will be pursued
- What, if anything, the GM can do to help cultivate the prospect
- Any sales that have resulted from the leads discussed at previous meetings

An effective DOSM structures the sales and marketing department in a way that provides for plenty of time to adequately follow-up leads with a sales call, and even more important, reserves adequate time for **cold calling**.

HOTEL TERMINOLOGY AT WORK

Cold Calling: Making a sales visit/presentation to a potential client without having previously set an appointment to do so.

■

Good salespeople seek opportunities to cold call whenever they can. The objective of such sales calls is to qualify prospective clients by identifying those who have a high likelihood of using the hotel's rooms or services. Of course, those who are likely prospects are further cultivated until a sale is made. While an in-depth discussion of the techniques good hotel salespeople use to identify and qualify prospects is beyond the scope of this book, it is important for you, as a GM, to be able to identify an active prospective client solicitation program. That is, sales and marketing staff should not simply "answer the phone" and take an order for a sale. Rather, they should actively go out to seek and create sales opportunities by following up on sales leads and by making an appropriate number of cold calls each week.

Despite its industry importance, there is not a significant amount of regularly published, hotel-specific sales information available to DOSMs. Because of that, HSMAI memberships, as well as subscriptions to hotel magazines and journals that do publish articles and in-depth features related to hotel sales techniques, are a worthwhile investment for GMs to make in a sales and marketing staff.

THE INTERNET AT WORK

One of the best and most popular writers about hotel sales is Howard Feiertag. An experienced industry veteran and professor of hospitality, his work is published in *Hotel and Motel Management* magazine. You can review articles he has written by going to

www.findarticles.com

When you arrive, enter "Hotel and Motel Management" and "Howard Feiertag" in the search fields.

Client Appreciation Activities

Experienced DOSMs know that making a sale is the beginning, not the end, of the client/hotel relationship. Too many hotels lose clients simply because they did not let the client know how much their business was appreciated. Client appreciation activities are designed to allow the hotel to express its gratitude to clients for their current business. These activities can include anything from inviting a client or group of clients to join the DOSM or GM for dinner or drinks, to organizing an elaborate, yearly or twice yearly client appreciation gala. Golfing and other sporting events, concerts, and theater tickets are all common ways to express a genuine appreciation for business that has been received. Gift giving is another traditional way to express appreciation to a hotel's best clients. Gifts given to clients as tokens of appreciation can range from the simple to the elaborate. It is, of course, important to first determine whether his or her employer allows the client to accept such gifts. In all cases, the goal of a successful client appreciation event or activity is to both solidify the business relationship with current clients and to communicate to potential clients the seriousness with which the hotel views the hotel/client relationship.

As a GM, you should be able to objectively review and evaluate the quality of client appreciation activities designed and executed by your sales and marketing department. In addition, simply talking to current clients will give you a good idea of what, if any, client appreciation activities are actually being implemented and how well these are received.

Marketing Efforts

Earlier in this chapter we noted that the definitions of *sales* and *marketing* vary widely. Add to the confusion the terms *publicity*, *promotion*, *public relations*, and *advertising*, and you can readily see why so many involved in sales and marketing view these activities differently.

For the purposes of this book, marketing is considered to involve all the activities designed to improve the hotel's profitability by increasing ADR, occupancy percentage, or both. These activities include market research to discover, for example, what groups of potential clients exist, what their needs are, and which of those needs you can meet. It also includes communicating your abilities to meet needs to those potential clients you identify so that they can, in time, become clients to whom you sell regularly.

Marketing Plan Development

Effective marketing begins with the development of a **marketing plan**. The marketing plan is simply a compilation of activities designed to meet the goals of the sales and marketing department. Marketing plans are typically prepared on an annual basis. In a hotel, the DOSM, in conjunction with the GM, is responsible for developing the marketing plan. Activities often included in a marketing plan involve analysis of your competition, an analysis of your own hotel, establishing your prices, and publicizing your offerings through continued advertising, promotions, and public relations activities.

HOTEL TERMINOLOGY AT WORK

Marketing Plan: A calendar of specific activities designed to meet the hotel's sales goals.

■

DOSMs should work closely with their GMs when selecting the marketing efforts to be used in the coming year. (© David Pollack/CORBIS)

The format of marketing plans can vary greatly, but most include the following:

- A review of the market in which you compete, including historical
  - Occupancy trends
  - ADR trends
  - Performance of your hotel in the market
- Competitive analysis, including a review of your competitor's
  - Strengths
  - Weaknesses
  - Price structure
- Competitive analysis of your own hotel, including a review of your hotel's
  - Strengths
  - Weaknesses
  - Price structure
- Forecast of future market conditions, including
  - Estimates of market growth or contraction
  - Performance goals and objectives for your hotel
  - Timeline for achieving these goals and objectives
- The determination of specific marketing strategies and activities designed to meet your goals and objectives, including those related to
  - Advertising
  - Public relations
  - Promotions
- Preparation of a marketing budget

- The development of measurement and evaluation tools to help assess the marketing plan's effectiveness and allow for needed modifications

When completed, the marketing plan is submitted to the GM and often the hotel's owners for approval and funding. A marketing plan is essentially a blueprint for the sales and marketing effort. As a GM, you will want to carefully review marketing plans submitted to you for approval and monitor those currently in place to ensure that they are being implemented by the DOSM and the sales and marketing department staff.

Advertising

Although a thorough discussion of advertising principles and philosophies is beyond the scope of this book, hotel managers should become familiar enough with them to assist the DOSM in decision making. Essentially, hotel advertising involves bringing the hotel's products and services to the attention of potential and current customers. Hotel advertising is typically done using one or more of the following:

- Exterior signage
- In-hotel and in-room signage and materials
- Brochures
- Radio or television commercials
- Direct mailings
- Internet banners
- E-mail messages
- Yellow Pages
- Franchisor-supplied advertising vehicles (directories, co-ops, and so on)
- Billboards
- Personal contact

Effective advertising can be costly and thus its effectiveness must be constantly evaluated. There is a great deal of variability in successful advertising pieces and campaigns, but the best of these:

- Are eye- or ear-catching
- Are memorable
- Sell the hotel's features
- Are cost-effective
- Do not become quickly outdated
- Reflect positively on the hotel's image
- Can be easily directed to the hotel's core client groups

An effective marketing plan will include the advertising activities (and their costs) that are to be undertaken by the sales and marketing department in the period covered by the marketing plan, as well as a way in which to measure the advertising's value to the hotel.

Promotions, Publicity, and Public Relations

In addition to advertising, an effective sales and marketing department includes promotion, publicity, and public relations activities. These three terms are closely related, sometimes overlap, and are often confused; however, each plays a part in the successful sales and marketing of a hotel.

- *Promotions.* In the hotel industry, the term *promotion* most often refers to a "special" packaging of products or services. For example, a hotel in a cold climate may create a "Summer Getaway" promotion to be marketed in the winter. The inclusive package might include a sleeping room, the use of the hotel's pool, a special "Beach Theme" dinner party, and complimentary rum-based drinks reminiscent of those consumed on the beach. Specially priced, this promotion would be "promoted" through advertising and publicity. Similarly, a franchise company may offer, as a special promotion, triple airline (frequent flier) miles for all stays completed between two fixed dates. Again, information about this promotion would be disseminated through advertising and possibly through publicity.

- *Publicity.* Publicity refers to information about the hotel that is distributed, free of charge, by the media. The good news is that publicity costs the hotel nothing. The bad news is that the publicity may be either good or bad. The news media is, of necessity, an independent force in the shaping of public opinion. Cultivating good relationships with the media is an important job of the GM. When such a relationship exists, it may be easier for the hotel to achieve positive publicity. If, for example, the governor of the state is visiting your hotel and that fact is mentioned in the newspaper, the publicity value is good. However, even with good media relationships established, a highly publicized drug-related shooting in a nearby hotel carrying the same brand affiliation as your hotel will likely reflect poorly on your own property. In situations such as this, it is important that the hotel have an active public relations program in place.

- *Public Relations (PR).* PR includes those activities designed to ensure that the hotel has a positive public image. PR activities help the hotel let potential clients know that it is (as it should be) a good citizen of the community. PR efforts can include, among many other activities, hosting charity events, contributing cash or in-kind services, or the donation of the hotel's staff time for a worthy cause. It is important to remember that the hotel's community can, depending on the hotel, be viewed as affecting local, state, national, and even international inhabitants. In all cases, it is the intent of the hotel that its PR activities positively reflect the values of the hotel and those of its ownership and that, if necessary, the hotel can rely on positive PR to help counter any unwarranted negative publicity.

In the hotel business, the terms *marketing, advertising, promotion, publicity, public relations,* and *sales* are intertwined. They become more clear-cut, however, when evaluating a single event. For example, if the city in which your hotel is located is hosting the annual convention of Rodeo Cowboys, if you are the **headquarter hotel**, and if your hotel decides to offer an evening of free country western dance lessons on your outdoor patio during that same period, you could certainly create a sign saying you are offering the free lessons. If you do, that's "advertising."

HOTEL TERMINOLOGY AT WORK

Headquarter Hotel: The hotel that hosts the main group of attendees during an event in which there are multiple host hotels.

If you place a copy of that sign in 100 locations in town, that's "promotion." If, as part of the patio décor, you lease the use of a live bull for the night and the bull escapes, and tramples the head of the city council's flower bed, that's "publicity." If you can get the head of the city council to laugh about it because you are known as a big supporter of community beautification efforts, that's "public relations." If some of the people in your city who purchase significant numbers of hotel rooms and meeting spaces each year attend the free dance lessons, see the hotel's features, discuss the costs and benefits with your sales staff, and ultimately become clients who spend money at your hotel, that's "sales."

An effective DOSM and sales and marketing department must be adept at all aspects of marketing because marketing, properly executed, produces profitable sales. As a GM, it is sales volume, in addition to other important hotel goals, that will ultimately be used to gauge your own effectiveness.

E-Marketing

E-marketing is increasingly important to hoteliers. It can be viewed as consisting of the following components:

- Internet sales and marketing
- Online reservation systems
- Property Web sites
- E-mail systems

Internet Sales and Marketing

Although the Internet is, in many respects, simply another marketing tool used by a hotel, its significance, growth, and potential requires special attention. When properly used and managed, the Internet is an excellent vehicle for communicating with current and potential clients. The explosion of the Internet after September 11 caught the hospitality industry by surprise; in general, the industry did a poor job incorporating the Internet to improve itself. Since then, those in hotel management, sales and marketing have struggled with how to best apply it. Effective GMs and DOSMs must evaluate both the effectiveness and cost of using all segments of the Internet as a significant selling vehicle.

An important point for the GM to remember is that the Internet allows smaller hotels to compete, on an equal footing, with larger ones. The Internet, at this point in its development, delivers just three media components. These are audio, text, and images, all of which can be just as good as (or better) on your site(s) than on your competitor's site.

Effective use of the Web allows your hotel to take advantage of an inexpensive direct line to consumers. This is a situation that hotel sales and marketing departments have never before experienced and may not know how to manage properly. Prior to the widespread use of the Internet, if you wanted the individual consumer or TA to "see" and experience your hotel, you were required to do costly direct mail pieces or site visits. Both these strategies are expensive. On the Web, you can sell directly to your potential clients for a few hundred dollars a month.

While there are many sales and marketing uses of the Internet, three that are of growing importance to hotels are:

- Online reservation systems
- Web sites
- E-mail systems

The Internet has replaced the telephone as the guest-preferred method of making room reservations.

Online Reservation Systems

The teaming of the GDS with the Internet has been one of the most significant technological advancements in the hotel industry in the past 50 years. TAs have, for many years, been able to check availability, compare prices, and book a hotel online. Now, virtually any traveler can do the same. Simply typing the words "Discount Hotel Reservations" into the search bar of a typical Web browser produces hundreds of alternative sites to review. On many of these sites, consumers can book hotels online if the hotel has given the site authority to do so. Some online sites, such as Travelocity.com (American Airline's site), and Expedia.com (Microsoft's site) are very popular and well known because they service virtually all the hotels found on the GDS. Other, smaller sites, such as A1-discount-hotels.com, specialize in specific larger cities.

THE INTERNET AT WORK

One of the most popular international booking sites since its inception in 1971, as well as one of the best managed, is the German site HRS. To view this multilingual site, go to

www.hrs.com

Note that the site has been translated into 22 languages.

In all cases, placing your hotel's room inventory online and allowing consumers the ability to book rooms in real time is clearly a critical part of a hotel's overall marketing strategy. Those online reservation sites selected should be in keeping with the hotel's desired image, and the booking results of the sites should be measurable.

Like all consumer advertising and communication mediums, online booking sites vary in quality and popularity. They are, however, the fastest growing source of reservations in the hotel industry and deserve the special attention of the DOSM. As a GM, it is important that the sites you use accurately reflect the products and services you offer at the prices at which you wish to sell.

Property Web Sites

As the popularity of the Internet has grown, many large hotels have created their own Web sites. In addition, smaller hotels affiliated with a brand often share Web sites with other brand franchisees. In this way, even small hotels can achieve some level of visibility on their own Web page.

The appearance of a hotel's Web site has become increasingly important and will continue to become even more so. The placement of text, images, other media, and white space on a Web page makes a strong statement about the quality of a hotel's products and services. Despite that fact, most hoteliers simply do not have the ability to create an effective Web page, nor do they have the technical skill required to evaluate the site's effectiveness.

THE INTERNET AT WORK

Some companies specialize in providing Web site design and other technology application solutions to hotels. To view one such company's product offerings, go to

www.esitemarketing.com

Even evaluating the work of a Web site designer can be complex for a DOSM and GM. There are, however, some facts that are true about all effective hotel Web sites:

- The site is easy to navigate.
- The site has some level of interactivity.
- The site is connected (linked) to appropriate companion sites.
- The site allows for online booking.
- The site balances guest privacy needs with the hotel's desire to build a customer database.
- Updating and revising room rates on the site is easy.
- The site includes a virtual tour of the property (with at least enough pictures or streaming video to ensure that potential guests get an accurate image of the hotel).
- The site complements your other marketing efforts.
- The site is in the language(s) of your clients.
- The site address is easy to remember.

Too often, DOSMs evaluate the quality of their site based on the number of visits (hits) the site receives per day or week. It is important to remember that the end goal of a Web site is not simply hits. The goal is sales. Site traffic is important, but the quality of that traffic in terms of potential sales is much more important. Measures of Web site effectiveness must be tied to sales production, not to hits. This, of course, is no different than the normal procedure of evaluating a salesperson on their actual sales production (sales made) rather than sales calls (hits).

Some hotels fail to produce the results they seek from their Web sites because they do not **link** their sites properly nor do they take full advantage of Internet search engines to identify those sites.

HOTEL TERMINOLOGY AT WORK

Link: A relationship between two Web sites. When Web site users select a link at one site, they are taken to another Web site address. An external link leads to a Web page other than the current one; an internal link leads elsewhere on the current page.

Effective DOSMs ensure that their Web sites are linked in a manner designed to maximize the sales potential of the site. For example, assume your hotel is located near the stadium of a professional sports team. Those Internet users who enter the name of the sports team in an Internet search engine (e.g., Excite or Yahoo) are likely looking for information about the team, such as its roster, won/lost record, and schedule. These are not necessarily consumers seeking hotel rooms. Thus, linking with sites that appear on a search for the team "name" may not be effective, even though the number of hits to these sites may be high.

Alternatively, however, those consumers who search for "driving directions to the stadium" are likely to be:

- Attending one or more of the games
- Unfamiliar with the area
- Potentially seeking a place to dine or stay overnight

In this example, Web sites that appear when "stadium," "stadium driving directions," and similar entries are entered into search engines are likely to produce the consumers the hotel truly seeks, even though the number of hits from such related sites may be smaller. Of course, this is no different from the experience of retail stores who have long recognized that there is a big difference between those who are "just looking" and those who are "buying."

Which sites should you link with? The answer is easier when you put yourself in your guest's position. If your hotel is near a museum, search for "museum." The sites to which you will be sent are the same ones to which your clients will be sent, so those are where an effective DOSM will seek reciprocal links. As a GM, it is relatively easy to use the same search engines as your potential clients to see if your DOSM has linked you with the **demand generators** you have identified for your hotel.

HOTEL TERMINOLOGY AT WORK

Demand Generator: An organization, entity, or location that creates a significant need for hotel services. Examples in a community include large businesses, tourist sites, sports teams, educational facilities, and manufacturing plants.

Another misunderstood aspect of hotel Internet sites relates to offering discounts on packages or guest rooms when those items are purchased on the hotel's Web site.

One of the best ways to spend money promoting your Web site is to reduce the selling prices on the products you feature on it. Spending money on regular advertising means you must pay for everyone who sees (and does not see) the ad, whether or not they ever make a purchase. When, however, you spend advertising money by charging less for your products booked online, you only have to pay for the people who actually place orders. As a result, you only pay for this form of advertising when it works! Web shoppers are often looking for the best quality of hotel they can select at the lowest price available, and Web advertising makes it easy for them to identify which hotel offers it. Selling rooms on the Web for a reduced price makes economic sense in the long run. Because it is less expensive to sell on the Web, if you split your savings with your guests, you and your guests will both benefit.

There is little question that hotel Web sites will continue to play an increasingly large role in every hotel's sales and marketing efforts. Therefore, a good DOSM will always promote his or her Web site to current clients and contacts by including the hotel's Internet address on business cards, as well as in all promotional materials.

E-Mail Systems

Hotels have long communicated with guests through direct mailings, the telephone, and more recently, by fax. Today, e-mail systems are a newer method of mass communication that is increasingly used. All DOSMs and sales managers are expected to put e-mail addresses on their own business cards. The same is true of most hotel clients. Therefore an effective, up-to-date e-mail list is today's equivalent of traditional systems of manually filing business cards. Unlike direct mail, e-mails can be inexpensively sent to virtually hundreds of clients and potential clients in a matter of seconds.

E-mails must be carefully designed and used. Since 1991, the Telephone Consumer Protection Act (TCPA) has prohibited unsolicited (junk) fax advertisements. In December 2003, then President Bush signed the Controlling the Assault of Non-Solicited Pornography and Marketing Act (the CAN-SPAM Act). This law became effective January 1, 2004, and essentially placed the same restrictions on unsolicited e-mail as had been in place for unsolicited faxes. To avoid having its own e-marketing pieces confused with unwelcome spam, hotels using e-mail for marketing must ensure that:

1. The e-mail recipient they communicate with has an ongoing business relationship with the e-mail marketer, or should have had such a relationship during the past 8 months. A hotel guest definitely qualifies.
2. The e-mail clearly identifies the hotel sending it.
3. The subject line authentically represents the content of the e-mail message.
4. The sender's full name and address is included in the e-mail message.
5. The recipient can **opt out** by following the directions to be removed from the e-mail list, usually found at the bottom of the e-mail.

HOTEL TERMINOLOGY AT WORK

Opt out (e-mail): To make e-mails stop by expressing the desire to the sender that unsolicited e-mails are unwelcome e-mails.

Legally and properly managed, an aggressive hotel sales staff may communicate with clients via e-mail in a variety of ways. Consider, for example, Kathy Showers. Ms. Showers reserved a room at the Waldo Hotel via e-mail. In return, the hotel:

1. Sends a confirmation e-mail to her at the time of booking.

2. Sends a follow-up e-mail one week prior to her arrival.

3. Sends, following her stay, a poststay e-mail inquiring whether she was satisfied by her experience at the hotel and offering a list of new hotel specials or additional hotel-related information.

4. Keeps their database current and their awareness level high by sending at least once monthly info-mails to Ms. Showers.

Another sales-related use of e-mails relates to attachments. Contracts, hotel photos, and even traditional business correspondence can all easily be sent to clients using an e-mail system's document attachment feature. In addition to their usefulness in quickly moving documents, most e-mail systems also automatically update the user's database whenever an e-mail is received. Properly used, this database can be accessed whenever the hotel wishes to communicate a special rate, promotion, or new hotel feature to its client list in an innovative manner.

E-mail is a powerful direct-to-consumer distribution and marketing tool. It allows hoteliers to engage customers in strong, personalized, and mutually beneficial interactive relationships, increases bookings, and sells more efficiently. E-mail marketing is an important aspect of today's multichannel marketing efforts. E-mail systems will continue to play an increasingly important communications role in hotel sales and marketing and should be used to their fullest potential.

Evaluating the Sales and Marketing Effort

One of the most difficult tasks faced by the GM is that of evaluating the effort of the sales and marketing staff. Reduced sales and guest counts, for example, are not always the result of ineffective sales and marketing department efforts. Consider, for example, that a hotel facing stagnate or declining sales may not provide good service. This could be the case when the housekeeping, maintenance, or food and beverage staffs do not perform well. In other cases, the hotel may face lowered sales levels if the property is older or if newer competitors are capturing market share. If the total market size declines, it is reasonable to expect that sales levels, at least in the short run, will decline as well. Despite the difficulties of isolating the impact of the efforts of the sales and marketing staff, it is a task that must be done. Fortunately, there are a variety of tools available to make this job easier.

Certainly GMs can subjectively evaluate the professionalism and appearance of the staff, their diligence at work, and their creativity in presenting the hotel's best features. Further, in some cases, increasing occupancies may indicate good effort by the sales and marketing department, as may an increase in ADR. It is important to remember, however, that both of these increases could be the result of an increase in guest demand and thus could actually mask a decline in the quality of sales and marketing efforts. Fortunately, there are also quantitative reports designed to measure the actual end result of the DOSM's efforts. Two of the most widely used and most closely watched of these are the Pace and the STAR reports.

Reviewing reports such as the STAR report allows management members to compare the operating results of their hotel with those of their competitors.

The Pace Report

With the proper marketing plan in place and with the DOSM's staff trained in effective selling techniques, a hotel sales and marketing department will sell, at some volume level (pace), the hotel's group rooms and services. As a GM, it is important for you to know and monitor the group rooms sales pace set by the DOSM and the sales and marketing staff.

Confirmed group sales made by the sales and marketing department during the month should be recorded. Some of these sales may be made during the month, for that month, but most will be made for a future date that will likely be months or even years in the future. Of course, in a given month, the hotel may also experience some group cancellations. In addition, during the month some clients will have requested that a contract be sent to them for review before signing. These tentative pieces of business may represent significant work on the part of the sales and marketing staff and will likely yield sales in the future.

To determine the pace at which actual group sales take place, GMs should rely on a monthly (or more frequently prepared) group **Pace Report**. Figure 7.3 is an example of a monthly group rooms Pace Report.

HOTEL TERMINOLOGY AT WORK

Pace Report: A document summarizing confirmed (group) sales made by the sales and marketing department.
■

Note that the Pace Report details sales made in a given month (January, in this example) that will be realized in future months. A review of the data in Figure 7.3 reveals

Waldo Hotel Group Rooms Pace Report for JANUARY, 200X				
	Sold This Month	Total Sold YTD	Sold Same Month Last Year	Total Sold Last YTD
Jan	25		150	
Feb	450	750	250	550
Mar	550	1,550	330	1,250
Apr	650	1,550	550	1,350
May	875	1,175	650	1,050
June	1,100	1,400	800	1,700
July	1,350	2,250	1,100	2,150
Aug	1,700	2,900	1,500	1,900
Sept	500	700	750	1,750
Oct	300	800	550	1,050
Nov	850	1,150	300	600
Dec	200	550	125	225
Total	8,550	14,775	7,055	13,575

FIGURE 7.3 Sample Pace Report

that the selling pace of the hotel for January (8,550 rooms) is up a total of 21 percent over last year (7,055 rooms). This percentage change is computed as:

$$\frac{\text{Total Sales This January} - \text{Total Sales Last January}}{\text{Total Sales Last January}} = \text{Percentage Change}$$

In this example, using January sales data:

$$\frac{8,550 - 7,055}{7,055} = 21.1\%$$

Using the same formula, for year to date (**YTD**) data:

$$\frac{14,775 - 13,575}{13,575} = 8.1\%$$

HOTEL TERMINOLOGY AT WORK

YTD: Short for "year to date." Used when comparing performance from the beginning of the year up through, and including, the present period.

In this example, it appears that sales in the month of January were very good (up 21 percent) compared with January of last year, and that the YTD sales productivity of the DOSM's staff is good (up 8 percent) compared with the same period last year.

A Pace Report can be prepared based on the number of rooms sold, the sales value (in dollars) of the sales made, or both. It can also be produced to include any period of time in the future. In this example, the Pace Report was prepared based on the number of group rooms sold in January for a 12-month period that ends in December of the same year.

Traditionally, cancellations are tracked separately and reported in the month they are canceled, not when the group was slated to arrive. That is, if a group of one hundred rooms canceled, in January, their contract for rooms in the coming June, that value would be noted in the January cancellation total. Tentative contracts, which may also be monitored, are not counted as a sale until a signed contract has been returned.

Note that the Pace Report tells management where future occupancy problems may exist. For example, in Figure 7.3 it is possible that a potential problem exists in September because, compared with last year, much less business was booked (700 rooms this YTD versus 1,750 YTD at this same time last year). Corrective management action in this case may consist of increased sales efforts and attention devoted now to sales in September.

Of course, the number of rooms reserved by a guest is only an estimate of the rooms sold until those rooms are actually occupied. Therefore, it is important that the group contracts signed by the hotel and its group guests are realistic in regard to the number of rooms that will actually be sold. If the sales department overestimates the pickup on a contract, the Pace Report will be artificially inflated. Many GMs also request that the DOSM prepare a catering Pace Report detailing the monthly food or meeting room sales made by the sales and marketing staff. A Pace Report should be prepared for any identifiable segment of business that the GM would like to monitor.

A strong Pace Report would show that sales made by the sales and marketing department are increasing on a monthly and/or annual basis. A weaker report would show they are level or declining. By comparing the Pace Report in any given month with the Pace Report of the same month in the prior year, a GM can evaluate the bottom-line effectiveness of the sales and marketing department's efforts. Of course, unusual circumstances can cause a Pace Report to fluctuate. An exceptionally large sale or cancellation can materially affect the Pace Report in a given month. In addition, market conditions will affect sales results. In any of these situations, however, the joint evaluation of Pace Reports by the GM and the DOSM gives them the opportunity to discuss the hotel's selling environment and plan reactive strategies. Preparing accurate Pace Reports is the job of the DOSM. The DOSM and GM should review them at least once a month.

The STAR Report

The Pace Report tells the hotel's owner and management the actual sales volume generated by the sales and marketing department. It does not indicate, however, what the actual sales volume should be. That is, if the hotel is experiencing a 60 percent occupancy rate, it is difficult to know whether that level of occupancy is good or bad unless the occupancy level of competing hotels is also known. If, for example, your hotel is averaging a 60 percent occupancy and your competitors are averaging 50 percent, you may be pleased with the performance of your sales and marketing team. If, on the other hand, you are averaging a 60 percent occupancy and your direct competitors are averaging a 70 percent occupancy, it is clear that you are not achieving your fair share of the business available in your market.

In a similar manner, if your ADR is $100 and your competitors' ADR is $80, your sales team is showing success in selling at a good rate. If your competitors' ADR is $120, you are comparatively less successful. As a GM, you want to know the comparative strength of your hotel and its sales and marketing staff. One or more Smith Travel Accommodations Reports (**STAR Reports**) are the recognized measures of comparative performance in the hotel industry and GMs must learn to read and interpret them.

HOTEL TERMINOLOGY AT WORK

STAR Report: Short for a Smith Travel Accommodations Report. Produced by Smith Travel Research (STR), this report is used to compare a hotel's sales results with those of its selected competitors.

■

Unbiased occupancy rate, ADR, RevPar, and market share comparisons are important to a wide range of interest groups. These include:

- *Hotel Owners.* Hotel owners and investors want to know if the management team they have put in place is effective in competing in the marketplace. Managing the asset (hotel) to maximize its financial potential is an important goal, and the STAR report indicates how well this goal is being achieved.

- *Management Companies.* These companies know that their effectiveness as managing consultants will be based, to some degree, on how well they perform on the STAR Report. Good results are used to demonstrate the value of these companies to owners.

- *Property Managers.* GMs and DOSMs want to know the effectiveness of their marketing plans and sales abilities, as well as those of their competitors.

- *Franchisors.* Brand managers want a measure of how well their brands compete in the marketplace. Strong brand performance helps sell additional franchises. Weak performance by the brand helps indicate where brand managers can better assist current franchisees.

- *Appraisers.* These professionals interpret STAR Report results to assist in establishing the financial value of a hotel.

- *The Financial Community.* Those asked to invest or lend money to buy or renovate hotels want to know about the sales strength of the hotel seeking funding. Good relative performance (a strong STAR Report) helps persuade lenders to lend, whereas a weak STAR Report indicates potential problems and will make it more difficult to secure funding.

While a variety of groups may be interested in the STAR Report for a specific hotel or a specific geographic area, for many GMs and DOSMs, the STAR Report is the primary measure used to judge their own performance.

STAR Reports can provide a wealth of information to those sophisticated enough to read and analyze the data they contain. This is so because STAR Reports can be created for a variety of different time frames, geographic locations and hotel types. Fortunately, Smith Travel Research produces excellent materials that teach managers how to fully interpret their STAR Reports.

THE INTERNET AT WORK

STAR Report interpretation and analysis is an important, but not often recognized, part of a GM's job. To request instructional information on interpreting STAR Reports, and to see the wide variety of benchmarking products Smith Travel Research produces, go to

www.smithtravelresearch.com

Smith Travel Research (STR) produces its variety of comparative reports on a daily, weekly, monthly, and annual basis. Hotels voluntarily submit financial data to STR. In return, Smith maintains the confidentiality of all individual hotel data it receives. By combining the operating data submitted by selected competitors, an individual hotel's operating performance can be compared with that of its competitive set (see Chapter 6). Understanding the competitive set is a key component of understanding the STAR Report. Essentially, a competitive set is a group of hotels used to establish a performance benchmark. To illustrate, assume that you manage a 300-room full-service property in a large city. You compete for most of your customers with five other hotels in your area, each of which has approximately the same number of rooms, services, and quality as your own property. Assume also that you have identified these five properties to Smith

Travel as the group you wish to consider as your competitive set. In most cases, each of these hotels will, as will you, voluntarily submit monthly (or more frequent) actual sales data to Smith. These data are then tabulated and returned to your hotel in the form of a STAR Report. Smith will only report the aggregate results of the competitive set. They never release or divulge information on an individual property or brand.

Operating comparisons produced by Smith can be customized but popular comparisons include those related to:

- Occupancy
- ADR
- RevPar
- Market share
- Historical trends
- To-date performances
- State or region

The segment of a STAR Report related to hotel occupancy helps illustrate how the STAR performance Report is used to assess hotel performance. To interpret Figure 7.4, assume that your hotel (property) is the 300-room property referred to earlier. Your competitive set is the five similar hotels that you have identified as your competition.

In Figure 7.4, the Property column refers to the hotel under examination (your hotel). The Comp. Set column refers to the five hotels you have chosen as your competitive set (as well as your own hotel). The monthly occupancy percentages listed represent the occupancy rates, respectively, of your hotel and the combined (average) occupancy of your competitors. The Index column is computed as property performance

YEAR	Month	Property	% Change	Comp. Set	% Change	Index	Index % Change
Last	Jan	55.2		52.2		105.7	
Last	Feb	59.7		58.2		102.6	
Last	Mar	63.1		63.6		99.2	
Last	Apr	64.2		64.4		99.7	
Last	May	63.9		61.7		103.6	
Last	June	67.6		66.1		102.3	
Last	July	68.9		63.5		108.5	
Last	Aug	72.7		58.8		123.6	
Last	Sept	81.8		82.9		98.7	
Last	Oct	83.1		85.5		97.2	
Last	Nov	65.6		67.1		97.8	
Last	Dec	60.2		57.6		104.5	
This	Jan	57.5	4.2	51.3	−1.7	112.1	6.0
This	Feb	61.3	2.7	59.6	2.4	102.9	0.3
This	Mar	63.5	0.6	66.9	5.2	94.9	−4.3
This	Apr	66.7	3.9	64.6	0.3	103.3	3.6
This	May	65.2	2.0	60.5	−1.9	107.8	4.1
This	June	67.5	−0.1	63.8	−3.5	105.8	3.5
This	July	70.2	1.9	64.1	0.9	109.5	0.9

FIGURE 7.4   STAR Report: Occupancy Trend Segment

divided by competitive set performance. Thus, for example, last year, in February, your hotel's (Occupancy) Index was 102.6 percent.

$$\frac{\text{Last February Property Occupancy}}{\text{Last February Competitive Set Occupancy}} = \text{Last February Occupancy Index}$$

$$\frac{59.7\%}{58.2\%} = 102.6$$

Stated another way, your hotel was able to achieve an occupancy rate 2.6 percent higher than that of your competitors. When the index is less than 100, your property is not achieving an occupancy rate equal to or higher than its competitors (see, e.g., March, Last Year in Figure 7.4). As a GM, in all but the most unusual of circumstances, you will want to achieve an occupancy rate higher than that of your competitors and an occupancy index higher than 100.

The % Change column represents the performance change from the previous year's same time period. For example, the occupancy change for your property this January versus last January was 4.2 percent.

$$\frac{\text{Occupancy \% This Year} - \text{Occupancy \% Last Year}}{\text{Occupancy \% Last Year}} = \% \text{ Change}$$

$$\frac{57.5 - 55.2}{55.2} = 4.2$$

Therefore, your property increased its occupancy 4.2 percent from the prior January. Note that the competitive set, in the same time period, actually showed a decrease (21.7) in their occupancy percentage during this period. Note also that your property's index does not always exceed 100. In fact, in March, April, September, October, and November of last year, your property was outperformed by its competitors.

It is important to remember that occupancy rate is of course related to ADR. Thus, a complete analysis of the STAR Report for this property would need to include, at the minimum, a review of its ADR and RevPar indices. Occupancy reviews, however, can be helpful. For example, several things can be learned from an analysis of this segment of the STAR Report, including:

- In most months, the property outperforms its competitive set.
- This year, the occupancy trend for the property, as well as its competitors, is an upward one.
- The property's occupancy performance last year was weakest in September, October, and November and strongest in August.
- While occupancy rate for the property was down in June of this year, compared with June of last year, the hotel's competitors experienced an even greater decline.
- The hotel may want to consider yield managing ADR more aggressively in August this year based on its strong occupancy performance in August last year.

To accurately gauge the effectiveness of a hotel's management, a property's STAR Report must be viewed in its entirety. It is always the case, however, that achieving performance indices of less than 100 percent means the hotel is performing at a rate below its competition, while obtaining performance indices above 100 percent means the hotel is outperforming its competitive set.

STAR performance goals can be established for any operating criteria, including occupancy rate, ADR, RevPar, market penetration, or growth. When STAR performance does not reach the goals set by the hotel's owners or managers, there can be a variety of problems, not all of which can be solved solely through the efforts of the GM or the sales and marketing department.

STAR Reports, properly interpreted, are indeed a valuable tool for assessing the performance of a sales and marketing department, as well as the entire property. The GM and DOSM should learn to understand their terms (see Figure 7.5), analyze them, and to then review them on a monthly or more frequent, basis.

To understand Smith Travel Research reports, it is important for GMs to understand this excellent company's terminology. The following are 12 key terms used by STR.

1. **ADR (Rate) Index:** An ADR index is designed to measure a property's fair share of average daily rate (ADR).
2. **Census:** The total number of properties and rooms in a segment.
3. **Chain Scale:** The chain scale segments are based primarily on the actual systemwide average room rates of the major chains. They are divided as:
   - Luxury
   - Upper Upscale Chains
   - Upscale Chains
   - Midscale Chains with Food and Beverage
   - Midscale Chains without Food and Beverage
   - Economy Chains
4. **Competitive Set:** A competitive set consists of a group of four or more properties selected by a hotel for purposes of comparison. A single hotel or brand can comprise a maximum of 35 percent of the reporting rooms of any competitive set in order to protect proprietary data.
5. **Index:** An index measures a property's performance in one of three key areas of Occupancy, ADR, or RevPAR. An index of "100" indicates that the property has captured its fair share of the market. Anything greater than 100 indicates a property is capturing more than its fair share, while anything below 100 indicates the property is capturing less than its fair share.
6. **Market:** A geographic area composed of a Metropolitan Statistical Area, a group of Metropolitan Statistical Areas, or a group of counties. There are currently over 150 U.S. STR markets.
7. **Market Price Segments:** The five categories of a STR market that are defined by actual or estimated average room rate. The five price categories used are:
   Luxury—top 15% average room rates
   Upscale—next 15% average room rates
   Midprice—middle 30% average room rates
   Economy—next 20% average room rates
   Budget—lowest 20% average room rates
8. **Market Share:** Total room supply, room demand, or room revenue as a percent of a larger group.
9. **Occupancy (Penetration) Index:** An index designed to measure a property's share of rooms sold.
10. **Regions:** STR defines nine separate regions in the United States. These are:
    New England (Maine, New Hampshire, Vermont, Massachusetts, Connecticut, Rhode Island)
    Middle Atlantic (New York, Pennsylvania, New Jersey)
    South Atlantic (Maryland, Delaware, West Virginia, Virginia, North Carolina, South Carolina, Georgia, Florida)
    East North Central (Michigan, Wisconsin, Illinois, Indiana, Ohio)
    East South Central (Kentucky, Tennessee, Alabama, Mississippi)
    West North Central (Minnesota, North Dakota, South Dakota, Iowa, Nebraska, Missouri, Kansas)
    West South Central (Arkansas, Oklahoma, Texas, Louisiana)
    Mountain (Montana, Idaho, Wyoming, Colorado, Utah, Nevada, Arizona, New Mexico)
    Pacific (Alaska, Washington, Oregon, California, Hawaii)
11. **RevPAR (Yield) Index:** An index that blends both occupancy and ADR and is designed to measure a property's revenue productivity.
12. **Sample:** The number of properties and rooms in a segment from which data is received.

FIGURE 7.5   A Guide to STR Terminology

MANAGERS AT WORK

"Well, Michele, how does it look?" asked J.D. Ojisama, the hotel's GM.

"About like last month," replied Michele Austin, the hotel's DOSM, as she glanced up from the document she was intently studying. "This month's Pace Report for future group room sales is about four percent below last year's level."

This was not good news, as J.D. well knew. The drop-off in sales was now in its third consecutive month. The same was true, to a smaller degree, in the food and beverage department's catering bookings; although the hotel was not experiencing an occupancy decline or occupancy index decline evident in the monthly STAR Report, it was clear that future business bookings, which would be measured by future STAR Reports, were declining.

"Well," replied J.D. "What do you think is causing the drop-off?"

"I'm not positive," stated Michelle, "but it could be several things. Citywide bookings may be down, the new sales manager we hired for corporate groups may not be up-to-speed yet, or perhaps we are being too rate aggressive in our bidding. I know that unless things turn around quickly we will have real difficulty meeting our revenue goals next quarter. What would you like me to do?"

What are some additional possible reasons for the decline revealed by the PACE Report? If you were J.D., how would you go about assessing the sales difficulties experienced by the hotel and the DOSM? What tools would you use to help understand and solve the revenue problem? How responsible should the GM be held for the sales level of a hotel?

HOTEL TERMINOLOGY AT WORK GLOSSARY

The following terms were defined within this chapter. If you are not familiar with one of them, please review the segment of the chapter that contains the term.

DOSM
Booking
Group sale
Site tour
Chamber of commerce
Networking
Convention and visitors
   bureau (CVB)
Sales call
Travel agent
SMERF
Drop-in

Package
Consortia
Pickup
Sales and marketing committee
Rooms division manager
Bid
RFP
Group contract
Attrition
Block
Prospect
Trace system

Lead
Cold calling
Marketing plan
Headquarter hotel
Link
Demand generator
Opt out (e-mail)
Pace Report
YTD
STAR Report

ISSUES AT WORK

1. The distinctions between the terms *sales* and *marketing* are as many as there are authors writing about the topics. Find at least three books devoted to the sales and marketing area and compare the definitions of these two terms in each book. What similarities did you find? What differences? How would you define the difference between sales and marketing? Why do you think HSMAI is titled as it is, rather than as "HMSAI"?
2. Effectively networking in a room full of strangers is a crucial skill but one that is often lacking in younger, less experienced sales team members. As a GM, discuss five specific steps you (or your DOSM) could take to ensure that the least experienced of your sales team rapidly develops this important skill. How important is it

that the GM be good at networking? Why? How does this skill affect cold-calling ability?

3. Technology has impacted the sales and marketing departments of hotels more than any other department. Assume you were the GM for a very large (over 1,000 room) hotel. What technological advances do you see in the near future that you believe will most affect your hotel? What could you and your DOSM do to foresee these changes and prepare your hotel for them?

4. Departmental structure is important to the success of a sales and marketing department. Of the three approaches to departmental structure described in this chapter (product, market, and source), which do you believe would be most effective in the hotel you hope to manage? Why? What influence do you believe the GM should have on the DOSM's decision on this matter? How do you think the size of the sales and marketing department will influence the decisions made by the GM and the DOSM in regard to departmental structure?

5. Some in the hotel industry believe too heavy a reliance on the STAR Report to evaluate a hotel's sales effort has a negative effect. Others defend the STAR as the only independent way to evaluate a sales staff's effectiveness. Discuss three positive and three negative factors involved in an analysis of a hotel's STAR Report. What alternative performance indicators of a hotel would you choose to evaluate? Why?

8

The Front Office

This Chapter at Work

As a GM, you will depend on the performance of an outstanding front office to help you meet your guest service and profitability goals. The front office and its manager(s) assist in, or are responsible for, a variety of important hotel functions, each of which is analyzed in detail in this chapter.

Because the rooms sold by a hotel are extremely perishable (i.e., a guest room left unsold on a given night can never again be sold on that night), it is very important that hotels do the best job possible in matching guest room availability with guest room demand. Also, since it is not possible to change the number of rooms available to sell up or down on a daily basis (because the hotel was constructed with a fixed number of rooms), an important responsibility of the front office is the sale of rooms at a rate that management feels will maximize RevPar. An aggressively managed and talented front office will do this well.

The making of guest reservations is often the first thing that comes to mind when considering the major functions of a front office, and this is indeed an important and often complex aspect of the front office's role. In addition to reservations, however, it falls upon the front office to actually assign arriving guests to specific guest rooms and respond to their special needs during their stay. These needs can include anything from transportation and information to medical assistance. In all of these situations and more, the unwavering role of the front office is to make the guest's stay as comfortable and as welcoming as possible.

An essential aspect of the front office is its responsibility for collecting the revenue charged to guests for their rooms, restaurant meals, telephone calls, and a host of other hotel services. This means that the front-office manager, working with the GM and controller, must devise and administer revenue management systems that ensure guests are properly charged for the services they use and that the hotel fully collects all monies it has earned.

When forecasting room demand, accommodating guests, and collecting monies for services rendered, the front office generates a large quantity of data, much of which are critical for management decision making. It is the role of the front office to collect, sort, and present these data in a way that assists in management decision making. As a GM, your daily tasks can be made much easier by the support of an effective front office and a technologically savvy front-office manager. In this chapter, you will see why a well-supervised front office helps you do a better job of managing your entire hotel.

Chapter 8 Outline

OVERVIEW OF THE FRONT OFFICE

Even though the front office is sometimes referred to as the front desk, the front office controls much more than the activities occurring at the front desk. In a small, limited-service hotel, the **front office** may consist, physically, of only that area reserved for guest registration. In a larger property, the front office will consist of many staff members, each responsible for a portion of the office's management or operation.

Regardless of its size, the front office must be organized to manage its key tasks and areas of responsibility. In this chapter, you will first read an overview of the front-office area, and then examine each of the major functional areas within the front office in greater detail.

A property's size will often determine the scope of a front office's responsibilities. (Bellagio Hotel & Casino/MGM Mirage)

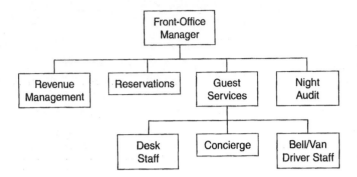

FIGURE 8.1   Front Office Functions

HOTEL TERMINOLOGY AT WORK

Front Office: The department within the hotel responsible for guest reservations, registration, service, and payment.

In a typical 350-room full-service hotel, the organization of front-office functions would be similar to that detailed in Figure 8.1.

In most cases, the **front-office manager (FOM)** reports directly to the GM.

HOTEL TERMINOLOGY AT WORK

FOM: Short for front-office manager.

Reporting to the FOM would be the individual(s) responsible for:

- Establishing and the daily monitoring of room rates (revenue manager).
- Managing the reservation process (reservations manager).
- Providing for guest services (guest service manager) including services related to guest registration (desk staff), guest information (**concierge**), and guest assistance (**bell staff**).
- Managing the front-office-related accounting and data collection process (night auditor).

In smaller properties these duties will overlap. In fact, in a small limited-service property, one person may perform all of these tasks and more. For the purpose of fully understanding these important responsibilities, however, it will be useful to take a brief look at each, followed by a more detailed examination of how these functions interrelate in a properly managed front office.

HOTEL TERMINOLOGY AT WORK

Concierge: The individual(s) within a full-service hotel responsible for providing guests with detailed information regarding local dining and attractions, as well as assisting with related guest needs.

Bell Staff: Those uniformed attendants responsible for guest services, including luggage handling, valet parking, airport transportation, and related guest services. The title originally arose because, in earlier years, the staff would come to the "front" (desk) to assist a guest when a bell was rung as a summons to them.

THE INTERNET AT WORK

Despite the industrywide use of the term, technically only members certified by the International Association of Concierges (Les Clefs d'Or) are permitted to use the title "concierge." Translated literally, Les Clefs d'Or is "The Order of the Keys," and its certified members proudly wear a golden crossed key lapel pin to signify their accomplishment. To view the requirements for certification and to learn more about this association, visit their Web site at

www.lesclefsdor.com

Responsibilities of the Front Office

Complete and detailed texts have been written on how to manage a hotel front office. Those interested in studying this area in detail are referred to *Professional Front Office Management*, (ISBN 0131700693), published by Prentice Hall. This four-part text includes up-to-date information on the following:

Part 1: Overview
- History of Lodging and Front-Office Operations
- Strategies To Manage Guest Service
- Overview of the Front Office
  - Responsibilities of Front-Office Department
  - Organization of Front-Office Department
- Human Resource Management
  - Recruitment
  - Training

Part 2: Front-Office Technology
- Data Collection
  - PMS Management
- Data Forecasting
  - Room Demand Forecasts
  - Reservation Forecasts
- Applying Forecast Data
- Revenue Management Data
  - Pricing
  - Yield Management
- Distribution Channel Management
- Systems Management
  - Interfaced Systems
  - Noninterfaced Systems

Part 3: Front-Office Responsibilities
- Guest Reservations
- Guest Reception
- Check-In Procedures
- Guest Services
  - Bell Services
  - Concierge Services

- Resolving Guest Complaints
- Guest Charges
  - Folio Posting
  - Payment
- Front-Office Accounting
  - Direct Bill Accounts
- Night Audit
  - Data Reporting
  - Data Management

Part 4: Additional Responsibilities
- Legal Aspects of Front-Office Management
  - The Guest Reservation Contract
  - Guest Privacy
- Intrahotel Interactions
  - Guest Services Departments
  - Building Services Departments

It is not the goal of this text to duplicate other, more comprehensive front-office management books. But as a GM, you must know what can be expected of an effectively managed front office, and just as important, how you can determine if the front office is, in fact, being well managed. This task is made especially difficult today because technology has developed so quickly in this area that GMs who have not kept up with these technological advances, especially those in the area of the property management system (PMS), can quickly find their knowledge base inadequate for the decision making required. Although it may vary somewhat based on the organizational structure of a specific size hotel, essentially the functional areas of the front office can be summarized as follows:

- The PMS and its management
- Revenue and reservations management
- Management of guest services
- Accounting for guests
- Data management

The PMS and Its Management

As described in Chapter 5, the PMS is the computerized system used by the hotel to manage its rooms revenue, room rates, reservations and room assignments, guest histories, and accounting information, as well as other selected guest service and management information functions. A simple PMS will have limited features; more extensive (and expensive) systems offer a wide range of management information features.

THE INTERNET AT WORK

Often, the specific PMS system used in a hotel is mandated by the franchisor. There are, however, many generic PMS systems on the market. To examine one such popular system's many features in detail, go to

www.innsystems.net/products/products_pms_features.html

Guest Tracker Features

Windows 95/98/2000/XP True 32-Bit Application
Multi Platform Servers and Databases
   (Access, SQL, Oracle)
All Inclusive Software Package Price
Unlimited Rooms, Rates, Users, and Workstations
Room Chart Reservations
Extensive Lookup Features
Call Accounting Interface Module

Internet Reservations
Club Membership Control
Travel Agent Accounting/Commissions
Group Master Billing
Revenue Forecast Reports/Graphs
View or Print All Reports
Mailing Labels Sorted and Filtered
Export to External Files

Reservation Features

Complete Reservation System
Unlimited Rooms, Room Types, and Rates
Book by Room Type and/or Room Number
Unlimited Guest Notes
Guest Lookup by Name or Stay
Room Chart Reservations
Room Chart Color Printout by Month
Automatic Room Selection
Automatic Rate Selection
Automatic Rate Calculation By Dates
Daily, Weekend, Monthly, and Package Rates
Monthly Leases

Extended-Stay Capabilities
Discount Reservations
Tax-Exempt Options
Deposits Setup on the Fly
Advanced Deposits Postings
Prepost Charges at Check in
Quick Check-In Procedures
Custom Confirmation Letters
Arrival/Departures in Detail
Arrival/Departures in Summary
Reservation History
Reservation Audit by Date/User

Group Features

Group Room Chart
Group Block Multiple Room Types
Group Master Billing

Group Confirmation Letters
Group Alpha Lookup
Group Check in
Group Check out

Guest Ledger—Folio Billing

Complete Folio Maintenance
Manual Folio Adjustments and Insertions
Group Master and Individual Folios
Automatic Posting of Room Charges/Taxes
Up to 3 Taxes Predefined
Rate Adjustments during Check in
Auto Calculate Balance Due
Split Folio Payment Options
Refund Button Full or Partial by Time

Complete Expense/Income Tracking
Payment Methods Tracking by Account
Deposits Due Aging Report
Advanced Deposits
Folio Details and Summary Reporting
Folio Detail by Room or Guest Name
Room Availability and Reserved Levels
POS Register Module/Interface
Complete A/R System Interface
Billing Statements And Inquiry Screens

City Ledger—Direct Billing

City Ledger Accounts Setup
Automatic Invoice Creation at Time of Check out
Assign Direct Bill Account at Time of Reservation
Receipts, Invoices, and Payments Module

Adjustments, Voids, and Partial Payments
Customer Aging Reports
A/R Statements
Fully Integrated Module

Night Audit Reporting

Automated Night Audit Procedures
Unlimited G/L Account Codes and Groupings
Folio Audit Report by User Shift

Occupancy Report by Guest
Housekeeping Maintenance Maids Lists
Room Status Updates

FIGURE 8.2 Guest Tracker PMS Hotel Management Features

Complete User Shift Reporting	Auto Update Room Status
Shift Reporting By User	Auto Update Status from In-Room Phone
	Out of Service

History Reporting

History Reports by Market Code	Folio History by Guest or G/L Account
History Reports by Guest Type	Reprint Folio Invoice History
Mailing Labels by Guest Criteria	Audit History of All Transactions by Date
All History Filtered by Date/Type	Message History by Guest Pop-Up Display
Guest History Detail by Room/Rate	Occupied History Statistics Reporting
Folio Billing Summary Reports by Date	History Graphs by Room Types
	Average Rate History

FIGURE 8.2   *(Continued)*

Figure 8.2 is an example of the features offered on a PMS system. This PMS, previously sold under the name "Guest Tracker," had features typical of those offered for sale today.

Essentially, the PMS records who is coming to the hotel, what they spend when they are there, and their form of payment upon departure. As a GM, it is critical that you know all of the features that exist on your PMS. Often the PMS includes features that should be used, but are not currently in use by the front office. Your role as a GM includes ensuring that the PMS used to operate your hotel is utilized to its maximum effectiveness.

It is important to remember that the PMS, like any other piece of equipment, requires its own care and maintenance. Imagine, for example, the difficulties that would ensue if, one hour before check-in time on a sold-out night, the PMS responsible for informing the front-desk staff about who was coming to the hotel, the room type these guests requested, and the room rates they were to pay for their room "crashed." It happens. In many cases it can be avoided.

A PMS consists essentially of a hardware component and a software component. Management of the hardware requires that the front-office staff keep the computer equipment clean and free of dust. Cables connecting PC workstations to the main computer should be examined periodically and replaced as needed. The source of power to the system should be managed and surge protected so that unanticipated power surges do not affect the continued operation of the system. Any installed **backup system** hardware related to the PMS should be inspected and tested on a regular basis.

HOTEL TERMINOLOGY AT WORK

Backup System: Redundant hardware and/or software operated in parallel to the system it serves. Used in times of failure or power outages, these are often operated by battery systems. For example, a backup system to the hotel's telephones would enable outside calling even if the main digital telephone system were to shut down.

∎

Although hardware problems can sometimes occur, most frequently it is a software-related problem that causes PMS difficulties. Often, because the PMS is connected by a modem to the PMS's software support organization, repair can be achieved simply by calling PMS software support. In fact, one of the primary features separating outstanding PMS systems from less effective ones is the system's level and availability of software support. Software support from the PMS vendor is not typically free; thus securing service on the system's software at an affordable price is an important consideration when selecting a PMS vendor.

In relation to the management of the PMS, it is reasonable to expect that an effective FOM will provide the GM with:

- Proof that the hotel uses all appropriate PMS features
- Evidence of a regularly scheduled hardware maintenance program
- Evidence of the ability to rapidly secure software support if needed

Truly, the PMS can be considered the heart of the hotel. As such, its care and maintenance are critical to the successful operation of the front desk, as well as the entire hotel.

Revenue and Reservations Management

The front office is one of the areas that directly affect the amount of revenue a hotel achieves. One of the most important roles played by the front office is that of maximizing the hotel's revenue per available room (RevPar). Recall that RevPar is computed as

$$\text{Occupancy\%} \times \text{Average Daily Rate} = \text{RevPar}$$

Thus, in a hotel with an annual occupancy of 70 percent and an ADR of \$105.00, RevPar would be

$$(70\%) \times (\$105.00) = \$73.50$$

Put another way, each of the hotel's rooms generate, on average, \$73.50 of revenue each day.

Obviously, to improve RevPar, the goal must be to either increase the occupancy percent and/or the ADR. It is the job of the FOM to help achieve one or both of these goals. To do so, the FOM must:

- Estimate (forecast) guest demand for rooms
- Practice yield management

Forecasting Guest Demand for Rooms

As we saw in Chapter 6 (Revenue Management), the daily demand for hotel rooms, even within the same geographic area, varies greatly. This is a reality and a challenge, faced by all hotel managers but especially FOMs. Imagine, for example, the difference in demand for hotel rooms in Indianapolis, Indiana, the day before the Indianapolis 500 is run (traditionally a **sell-out** period for the entire Indianapolis area), compared with the Wednesday night before Thanksgiving (traditionally a very slow day for business travel of all types) in that same city. The point to remember is that an FOM must know when there is strong demand for the hotel's rooms—that is, what special events, group activities, holidays, or other factors will impact room demand. Recall that to maximize RevPar, the hotel's management staff must attempt to drive (increase) ADR when demand for rooms is high and attempt to drive occupancy (by offering lower rates) when demand is low. Both strategies, if successfully implemented, will have the effect of increasing RevPar, and both strategies depend on the ability of the management team to forecast room demand.

HOTEL TERMINOLOGY AT WORK

Sell-Out: (1) A situation in which all rooms are sold or oversold. A hotel, area, or entire city may, if demand is strong enough, sell-out. (2) A period of time in which management attempts to maximize ADR.

■

To illustrate the importance of forecasting demand, consider a hotel in a large college town. Five times per year, the college's football team plays a home game. Traditionally, the games cause all area hotels to sell-out at a high ADR. The importance of knowing the dates of these games as far into the future as possible so that sales-related staff will not inadvertently sell rooms on those dates for a low rate is evident.

On a less obvious scale, many hotels find that the demand for their rooms varies on a weekly basis, regardless of special events that may be held in the area. Those hotels that service primarily business travelers, for example, will generally find that Tuesday or Wednesday are the days when demand for their rooms is greatest. Those hotels that service leisure travelers will likely find that weekends generate the most business. Forecasting demand effectively requires that the front office:

- Keep accurate historical records to understand past demand.
- Know about special events or circumstances that will impact future room demand.

In all cases, the front office must be able to forecast the demand for rooms well enough to allow the hotel to practice the concept of yield management described in Chapter 6.

Practicing Yield Management

Earlier in this text you learned that yield management is a set of techniques and procedures used to manipulate occupancy, ADR, or both for the purpose of maximizing the revenue "yield" achieved by a hotel. As a result, each reservation taken by the front-office staff reflects the yield management strategies put in place by the FOM. The methods employed by FOMs, revenue managers, and automated PMS systems to utilize demand forecasts and establish yield management strategies are many and are as varied as the individuals operating their respective hotels. GMs must understand and approve these strategies.

To illustrate the total impact of effective yield management, assume a hotel sells its rooms for $150 per night at rack rate. It is appropriate to sell at rack when the hotel is confident that the demand for hotel rooms will be greater than the supply. That is, when it is forecast that all or nearly all rooms will be sold, it is not necessary to discount the rooms to help ensure their sale. When demand for rooms is less than supply, discounts are typically offered.

Assume also that the hotel routinely offers discounts plans of 10, 20, and 30 percent off rack rate based on forecasted demand. That is, when demand is very light, discounts as high as 30 percent off rack are offered to maximize occupancy rates. When demand is stronger, the hotel offers only discounts of 20 percent, 10 percent, or as in the case where the demand for rooms will equal or exceed supply, no discounts are offered at all.

In a high demand period, guests requesting reservations with 30 percent discounts would be told that such discounts are not available, and the hotel would not accept their reservation request. On another, lower demand date, however, that same request for a reservation at the 30 percent discount rate would indeed be accepted. The opening and closing of discounted rates is the core activity of yield management

Forecasted Room Demand	Rate Strategy
90–100% occupancy	Offer no discounts
70–90% occupancy	Offer discounts up to 10%
50%–70% occupancy	Offer discounts up to 20%
Less than 50% occupancy	Offer discounts up to 30%

FIGURE 8.3   Yield Management Strategies Based on Room Demand

and a good revenue manager is effective in this task. Figure 8.3 is an example of a strategy that might be employed by the hotel used to "manage the yield" from the sale of rooms on a given night.

Sophisticated FOMs are likely to use highly advanced and often complex methods of managing yield. It is the function of the GM to approve such methods if they are in keeping with the long-term goals of the hotel.

Management of Guest Services

The front office is responsible for a variety of guest services. These include the welcome the guest receives at check in, as well as services related to the stay. Some of these are:

- Airport transportation
- Parking cars
- Handling luggage
- Providing directions to attractions within the local area
- Making restaurant reservations
- Taking guest messages
- Routing mail
- Newspaper delivery

MANAGERS AT WORK

J.D. Ojisama, GM of the Austin Plaza Hotel, must make a decision. It is noon on Wednesday, and the 400-room hotel managed by J.D. has 30 rooms left to sell because 170 guests currently have rooms in the hotel and another 200 guests have reservations for arrival that night.

Approximately one hour ago, Tech-Mar Holdings, one of the Plaza's largest customers, called Dani Pelley, the FOM, to reserve 35 rooms for that very evening. Ms. Pelley replied that she would get "right back" to the Tech-Mar representative.

Ms. Pelley, a talented but newer FOM, has asked J.D. how the situation should be handled. After being filled in on the details of the guest's request, J.D. asks that the FOM supply the past eight week's no-show history for the hotel. That data are presented below:

Austin Plaza No-Show History

Weekday	Weeks Ago	No-show % of Total Reservations
Wednesday	1	5%
Wednesday	2	0%
Wednesday	3	2%
Wednesday	4	4%
Wednesday	5	1%
Wednesday	6	4%
Wednesday	7	0%
Wednesday	8	3%

What do you think J.D. should tell Ms. Pelley? What is your rationale for the decision? Would you advise J.D. differently if you knew that each of the Tech- Mar reservations was for a ten-night stay at full rack rate?

Assume you accept the 35 room reservations. What would you tell a guest that must be walked despite arriving with a confirmed reservation? What ethical issues are involved in this situation?

- Management of safety deposit boxes
- Supplying directions for areas within the hotel
- Setting wake-up calls
- Providing for guest security via the careful dissemination of guest-related information
- Handling guest's concerns and disputes

Depending on the location of the hotel and the services it offers, the guest service function may be attended to simply by those individuals employed as front-desk agents. In a larger property with more activity, guest services may be a separate area within the front office employing a rather large staff.

Accounting for Guests

The front office is the department charged with the major responsibility of performing the accounting tasks related to the guest's stay. Although the billing of guests for their night's lodging would appear fairly straightforward, the intricacies of the financial transactions that must be recorded by the front office can be quite complex. For example, assume that four men traveling to a hotel to attend a softball tournament share a room for two nights. Upon departure, each wants to pay their share of the **folio's** balance. One man wishes to pay with cash, one with check, one with a credit card, and another with a debit card. As can be seen, even the simplest of transactions can get complex, but it is the job of the front office and its management staff to ensure that all guest folios are properly processed and recorded.

HOTEL TERMINOLOGY AT WORK

Folio: The detailed list of a hotel guest's room charges, as well as other charges authorized by the guest or legally imposed by the hotel.

Additional accounting-related tasks that must be completed by the front office include maintaining an accurate list, by room number, of guest room occupants, verifying accuracy in the room rates charged to guests, and the confirmation of checkout dates.

Data Management

An extremely important front-office function is that of data management. Some of these data relate to guests and some relates to the effective management of the hotel. The amount of data processed in a hotel is large and growing larger each year.

An effective FOM in a U.S. hotel in the precomputer 1930s would very likely have kept a record of a specific guest's preferences for rooms, food, and the like. This information would have been written down by hand and referred to when that specific guest reserved a room or checked into the hotel. Today's FOM would have such information and much more available through the features of the PMS. At the very least, the FOM would know:

- The date of the guest's last stay
- The guest's address, telephone number, and credit card information
- The room rate paid and **room type** occupied by the guest
- A history of the guest's prior folio charges
- The form of payment used by the guest to settle his or her account with the hotel
- The guest's membership in groups receiving a discount from the hotel
- Guest's company affiliation
- Guest's room type preferences

Depending on the sophistication of the PMS, even more data may be secured (by desk staff) and maintained on an individual guest.

HOTEL TERMINOLOGY AT WORK

Room Type: The term used to designate specific configurations of guest rooms. For example, smoking versus nonsmoking, king bed versus double beds, or suite versus regular sleeping room. Commonly abbreviated (i.e., K for King, NS for Nonsmoking, and so forth), the hotel's holding of the proper room type is often as important to guests as whether or not the hotel, in fact, has a room for them.

It is important to note, however, that most hotel chains guarantee only the availability of a guest's room, not room type, when a reservation is made.

In addition to maintaining data on individual guests, the front office collects and evaluates information related to the hotel's operation. Some guest-related examples include the tracking of guest telephone calls, including both those that are free-to-guest

Roll away beds are often provided for younger children at no (or a reduced) charge to the guest.

and those for which the hotel imposes a charge, the viewing of in-room movies, and the clean or dirty status of rooms (necessary to ensure that a guest checking into the hotel is checked into a room that has, in fact, been cleaned). Other data management tasks include monitoring the use of electronic keys, maintaining safety-related data (such as daily safety inspections for hotel-operated motor vehicles), and the recording of reservation-related information. As can be seen, the front office and its management staff's ability to provide good data are critical to the operation of the front office and to your success as a GM.

Each of the functional areas discussed in this overview of the front office deserve special attention that is beyond the scope of this text. It is possible, however, to evaluate each in terms of the GM's relationship to that functional area.

MANAGING GUEST RESERVATIONS

In most hotels, the front office is the department assigned the primary task of taking and recording guest reservations. The job is an important one and, properly performed, can provide GMs with data that is very helpful in making a variety of decisions. Guests will supply specific information when they contact a hotel for a reservation. FOMs use their PMS to manage this information. Depending upon the method used to make the reservation, the amount of data collected can range from extensive to minimal. Although each PMS is formatted somewhat differently, some basic information related to the guest, and his/her request must be collected. Figure 8.4 shows a data screen that appears on a typical PMS when a guest contacts a hotel directly to request a new reservation.

Calling the hotel directly is still the preferred way to make reservations for many guests.

1

Account: **139675** | Arr/Dep Info | Status: **Reserved** | Balance: **.00**

STAY INFORMATION:

Arrival:	**00/00/00**	**2**	Adults:	**A**	Rate Plan:	**7**	Room:	**10**
Nights:	**0**	**3**	Child:	**B**	Room Type:	**8**	Suppress Rate:	**11**
Departure:	**00/00/00**	**4**	No. of Rooms:	**6**	Room Rate:	**9**		
GTD/CXL:		**5**						

GUEST INFORMATION:

Frequent Travel ID: **C**

Last Name:	**D**	Company:	**H**
First Name:	**E**	Address:	**I**
Phone:	**F**	City St ZIP:	**J**
Caller:	**G**	E-Mail:	**K**

GUARANTEE INFORMATION: **12**

Gtd/Pant:

Deposit: Due Date:

Credit Card: /   **$.00**

Card Holder:

TRACKING: **13**

Source: Geo:

Track: Open:

ID:

Vehicle: **M**

OPTIONS: **14**

Confirm:

Exempt:

Vip:

No Post:

ASSOCIATED ACCOUNTS: **15**

Group:

A/R

T/A 1:   Comm:

T/A 2:   Comm:

NOTES   **L**

Reserve: **06/01/07**   Cxl: **00/00/00**

16   **17**

FIGURE 8.4 Reservation Screen

Note that the reservation screen in Figure 8.4 contains the following information (data) **fields** that relate directly to the guest. These are labeled by letter and include:

A. *Adults:* The number of adults staying in the room.

B. *Child:* The number of children staying in the room.

C. *Frequent Traveler ID:* Many hotels have "frequent traveler" programs that reward guests who frequently use a specific hotel or hotel brand. This field allows the hotel to credit the traveler's account for the stay.

D. *Last Name:* This field is very important, and proper spelling is critical.

E. *First Name.*

F. *Phone:* This provides a way to contact the guest before arrival if necessary and allows for creation of PMS reports that track the geographic (by telephone area code) source of reservations.

G. *Caller.* The name of the person making the reservation (frequently, this individual is not the person who will be staying in the hotel).

H. *Company:* The company the traveler works for (if a business traveler).

I. *Address.* The guest's home or business address.

J. *City St. Zip:* In addition to helping with guest contact, this information, like telephone area codes, is useful to generate reports about the origination of business.

K. *E-Mail:* An increasingly popular manner in which to communicate with guests.

L. *Notes:* This open field can be used for special guest requests or other guest-related information that would be helpful when the guest arrives. Examples might include requests for a specific floor or type of room, requests for late check out or early check in, or specific information regarding the guest's payment of charges.

M. *Vehicle:* Some hotels require guests with cars to register them at the time of check in (but not typically when the reservation is made).

HOTEL TERMINOLOGY AT WORK

Field: A data entry location in a PMS. For example, the reservation screen on a PMS will contain a "field" for the guest's name and another "field" for the guest's telephone number (along with many other fields). Data for these fields are typically entered at the time the reservation is made and may be modified at the time of guest registration. Fields are sometimes referred to as "data fields."

■

Guest Request Information

In addition to specific information about the guest, a room reservation typically includes an extensive amount of information about the guest's specific reservation requests. As can be seen in Figure 8.4, these fields include:

1. *Account:* This number is also known as a **confirmation number** and identifies this specific reservation within the PMS.

HOTEL TERMINOLOGY AT WORK

Confirmation Number: A number (or combination of numbers and letters) that identifies a specific guest reservation.

2. *Arrival:* The date the guest will arrive.

3. *Nights:* The number of nights the guest(s) will stay.

4. *Departure:* The date the guest will leave the hotel.

5. *GTD/CXL:* In this PMS, this field is activated when a reservation has been completed (GTD) or canceled (CXL).

6. *Number of Rooms:* Guests may reserve more than one room at a time.

7. *Rate Plan:* Hotels often negotiate or offer special rates to some guests, and these are identified by code numbers or letters. (For example, a rate plan of "AAA" may be used to identify the rate to be charged to members of the American Automobile Association [AAA]). As we will see in future chapters, the proper use of the PMS rate plan feature simplifies the reservation process and allows the tracking of activities of various groups.

8. *Room Type:* Most hotels offer several room types based upon bed size (for example, king size, queen size, and double) and other features including location, smoking/nonsmoking and in-room amenities.

9. *Room Rate:* The per night charge for the room. (This rate typically does not include applicable taxes.)

10. *Room:* The number (if known) of the specific room reserved.

11. *Suppress Rate:* This field is checked if the reservation agent making the reservation prefers that the room charge not show on the folio.

12. *Guarantee Information:* Reservations are typically guaranteed with some form of payment. This may be cash, credit card, or debit card. This section of the reservation screen allows the hotel to collect information required for the guest's payment.

13. *Tracking:* This section is used to record information about:
    - *Source:* Whether, for example, the reservation was made by telephone, fax, e-mail, letter, or other form of communication.
    - *Track:* The type of guest (business, leisure, or other designated type of traveler).
    - *ID:* Driver's license number (sometimes required of guests based upon hotel policy).
    - *Vehicle:* License tag information (sometimes required of guests based upon hotel policy).
    - *Geo:* State, County, or City.
    - *Open:* A field that may be used by the hotel to collect its own property-specific information of interest.

14. *Options:* This section notes information about:
    - *Confirm:* Checked if the guest wishes to receive written confirmation of the reservation. If so, the PMS automatically prints a confirmation letter addressed to the guest.

- *Exempt:* Used for those individuals who are exempt from specific hotel taxes.
- *VIP:* Used to identify Very Important Persons (VIPs—i.e., Guests).
- *No Post:* Used to waive specific guest charges.

15. *Associated Accounts:* This section is used to record information about:
   - *Group:* The name of the group (if any) with which the guest is associated.
   - *A/R:* Used to route charges to a specific accounts receivable (A/R) account.
   - *T/A1 and T/A2:* Used to record to whom the hotel will pay any TA commission that is due.
   - *Comm:* The percentage amount of the guest's charge to be paid as a TA commission. (Typical TA commissions range from 5 to 15 percent of the guest's total, pretax sleeping room charges.)

16. *Reserve:* The date the reservation was made.

17. *Cxl:* The date (if cancelled) on which the reservation cancellation was recorded.

Although the names of specific fields vary based upon the PMS in use, all systems collect important information about guests and their reservation requests. Given the extensive information collected in the reservations screen data fields, even a modestly priced PMS allows FOMs to create a large number of reports that they and their GMs can use to enhance their decision-making abilities.

In most hotels, guests can make a room reservation for almost any future date. Until that date, it may be modified, extended, or with some restrictions, cancelled as the guest wishes. The reservation changes to an "arriving" reservation or **arrival** on the date the guest is to begin occupying the reserved room(s). Guests may modify their reservation up until the time they arrive at the hotel and are actually assigned to a room. However, it can become more difficult to accommodate these reservation change requests as the arrival date draws nearer. In most hotels, FOMs and their staff manage future reservations, changes to reservations, and arrivals.

HOTEL TERMINOLOGY AT WORK

Arrival: An arriving guest. Arrivals are typically counted by the number of individuals as, for example, in "There will be 300 arrivals tonight including 150 children."

The effective management of guest reservations is, not surprisingly, one of the most complex tasks that must be achieved in a successful hotel. Because the hotel's revenue is dependent, in large measure, on the front office's ability to effectively forecast demand, establish rates, and manage occupancy, a GM needs a thorough understanding of the challenges faced in this area. For purposes of examining precisely how a hotel receives its guest reservations, those reservations may be segmented by type and by delivery method.

By Reservation Type

Perhaps the most important distinction that must be made in the area of reservations is that of **transient sales** versus group sales. Many people who do not understand the hotel industry believe the great majority of rooms sold in a hotel are sold to individual travelers. This is true in some hotels, but in others, such as convention site hotels, by far the greatest numbers of rooms are sold to those traveling as a group or attending a group function.

HOTEL TERMINOLOGY AT WORK

Transient Sales: Rooms and services sold primarily through the efforts of the front office and its staff.

Reservation types may be further subdivided into individual or group reservations.

Individual Reservations

Individual reservations comprise the vast majority of business for many properties, especially small, limited-service hotels without meeting space. In these as well as many other properties individual reservations are taken by a **reservations agent**.

HOTEL TERMINOLOGY AT WORK

Reservations Agent: A front-office employee whose job consists primarily of taking and entering individual and group reservations into the hotel's PMS.

Earlier you saw the information recorded in the PMS when a typical reservation is made. Now we will consider how different types of individual and group reservations are processed at the front desk when a guest arrives. When guests make a reservation, they may actually pay for the room by providing an advance deposit (**prepaid reservation**), guarantee the reservation with a payment card (guaranteed reservation), or request a reservation without providing payment to guarantee the reservation. Note: These **nonguaranteed** room reservations are typically honored until 4:00 P.M. or 6:00 P.M. on the day of the guest's arrival. To ensure consistency in the brand, some franchisors mandate the time of release after which the reserved room can be sold to another guest and the guest with the original reservation will not be charged for the room. GMs should ensure that their front-office procedures for releasing nonguaranteed reservations are consistent with their franchisor's recommended policies.

HOTEL TERMINOLOGY AT WORK

Prepaid (Reservation): A room reservation in which guests, prior to their arrival, provide payment for their rooms. Sometimes referred to as an "advanced deposit" reservation.

Nonguaranteed (Reservation): A room reservation for which guests do not provide payment at the time the reservation is made.

Depending on the size of the hotel, the minimum number of rooms to be sold before the reservation will be considered a group sale might be as few as five, or as many as twenty (or more).

Group Reservations

In Chapter 7 you learned that when a group reserves hotel rooms, the rooms are placed in a group "block," and the rooms are held for the exclusive use of the group that reserved them. When the contract terms between a hotel and a group are established, the **cut-off date** when the rooms will be released from the block should be promptly communicated to the FOM, who must then monitor those cut-off dates. If a group's pickup is less than anticipated, the FOM will return the nonreserved rooms to the rooms inventory. Alternatively, if the group's pickup is very strong (it exceeds original estimates), the group's representative may request that more rooms be added to the block as the cut-off date approaches. The FOM may (or may not) agree to do so. Group members selecting rooms from a block can do so either as individuals (by contacting the hotel directly) or by use of a single reservation (rooming) list with the name and arrival/departure dates of the group members. GMs must ensure that their hotels' specific procedures for recording each of these two reservation methods are understood and well managed by the front-office staff.

HOTEL TERMINOLOGY AT WORK

Cut-Off Date: The date on which any unreserved rooms remaining in a group's block are returned to a hotel's general rooms inventory and thus are available for sale to others.

■

Regardless of when a group room sale is large enough to be serviced by the hotel's designated sales department, it is important for the GM to remember that an extremely effective sales department may mask the efforts of an ineffective front-office sales effort. For example, assume that a hotel routinely sells 60 percent of its rooms via the front-desk staff and 40 percent through the group sales department. It may well be that the hotel should, with the proper front-office staff, sell even more rooms through the front desk, even though these individual sales currently make up the majority of the room nights sold. Put another way, that a hotel's revenue and occupancy levels are acceptable does not, by itself, indicate that the front office is effective at selling individual reservations or recording group reservations made. It is for that reason the GM must maintain standards levels for effectiveness through all the varied delivery methods affecting reservations sales at the front desk.

By Delivery Method

The number of ways a hotel actually receives its reservations are varied and often not well understood. Often called distribution channels (see Chapter 6) or simply channels, the number of ways a hotel's front desk may receive a room reservation are many and worth examining in detail. Despite explosive growth in the Internet as a means of delivering reservations to a hotel, the most common form of hotel reservation delivery today remains the use of the **Global Distribution System** or **GDS**.

HOTEL TERMINOLOGY AT WORK

Global Distribution System: Referred to as the GDS for short, this system connects those travel professionals worldwide who reserve rooms with hotels offering rooms for sale.

■

Global Distribution System

To truly understand today's GDS, a GM must first understand its conception. In the earliest days of the hotel industry, travelers' first contact with a hotel was after they had physically arrived at a property. With no dependable mail service or telephone and without even an assurance about when they would arrive at a destination, early travelers were truly on their own when securing overnight accommodations.

The advent of a government-operated mail service was an important milestone in the hospitality industry. For the first time, guests could use this new distribution channel (mail service) to communicate directly with hotels. Equally importantly, intermediaries such as TAs could contact hotels on behalf of their clients and maintain a written record about what the intermediary had requested for the traveler and in turn about what the hotel promised to provide.

Prior to the 1970s, the primary distribution channels used by hotels, travelers, and TAs were the telegraph, the mail system, and the telephone. In the mid-1970s, their relationship began a major transformation. Interestingly, the change was initiated not by hotels but by the airlines.

As the commercial airline business in the United States developed, it created the same traditional relationships with travel intermediaries as hotels, cruise lines, and trains had done earlier. In the early stages of the airline industry, TAs referred to printed flight schedules distributed by the airlines. They then contacted an airline to inquire about seat availability for clients on specific flights. By the end of the 1970s, however, airlines provided travel agencies with an electronic method for verifying availability and making airline reservations. The GDS provided the emerging airline industry with an electronic ticket booking system that was more efficient and cost-effective than the existing distribution channels of telephone, telegraph, or mail. Its continued development soon allowed travel agents to book car rentals and hotel room reservations on the same systems.

As travel agencies increasingly found electronic booking on the GDS less costly for their own businesses, they began to insist that all of the products they reserved or purchased be available for booking through this emerging distribution channel. In the late 1970s, GDS bookings made up less than 5 percent of all hotel reservations made. It now exceeds 20 percent despite fierce recent competition from the Internet (another distribution channel that would, when it emerged in the 1990s, radically change the way hotels sold rooms).

The GDS initially consisted of two main systems: Sabre (the American Airlines electronic booking system) and Apollo (used by United Airlines). Other airlines including Eastern, TWA, and Delta also created and named their own electronic reservation systems. Unfortunately (but not surprisingly), since each of these systems was initiated by airline competitors, they were developed independently of each other and not interfaced (electronically connected). As a result, a TA using, for example, the Sabre system to book a client's outbound American Airlines flight had to use a completely different electronic system (Apollo) to book the client's return flight on United Airlines. This created a problem when the ticket was booked and a significant amount of TA confusion. One airline, for example, might identify its flights by letters, while another used numbers or a combination of numbers and letters. Some systems abbreviated a city with four letters; others used three. In addition, each airline's system required its own directly connected, designated computer terminal within the travel agency.

The expansion and improvement of the GDS focused on the airline industry, and because it was developed for them, it evolved with that industry's needs foremost in mind. Some airline officials found the fact that travel agencies wanted to book both air travel and hotel rooms on the same system to be bothersome. As a result, hotel companies had to interface their own reservation systems with the airline systems in the GDS. Travel agencies soon discovered that they could not compete effectively within their own industry unless their agents knew and could use the numerous GDSs available. To entice travel agents to book flights with them, airlines worked hard to constantly improve and enhance their own reservation segment of the GDS. The result was constant change within the GDS and increased confusion as hotels struggled to keep up with it.

Not surprisingly, the airlines did not allow hotels access to their GDS without paying for it. Large chain hotels had the financial ability to develop room reservation systems that interfaced directly with the GDS. Smaller hotels had to employ specialized companies to create interfaced reservations systems.

Financially, the use of the GDS altered a hotelier's traditional view of room rate. In the past, a hotel guest that walked into a hotel and rented a room for $99.00 actually gave the hotel $99.00. Today, if that same guest's travel agent booked a reservation through the GDS, however, the hotel would be required to pay:

- A commission to the travel agent (usually 10 percent)
- A fee set by the airlines for the use of the GDS
- A reasonable amount to the hotel chain or brand's centralized reservations department to help offset the cost of developing the chain's reservation interface system

The higher costs associated with securing a GDS reservation meant that hotel chains did not want to use it heavily. However, travel agents rapidly embraced it. To understand why, consider the case of a TA in St. Louis, Missouri, whose client wants to reserve a room in New York City for a weekend day two days from now. The agent's mailed inquires to New York City hotels requesting rates and availability would not be received until after the guest's requested arrival date. In addition, it was not realistic to assume that the agent would:

- Manually identify New York hotels
- Place several long-distance toll calls to hotels to verify room availability
- Compare quoted room rates
- Place a second call to the selected hotel and make the client's room reservation

All of those labor-intensive, time-consuming, and expensive tasks could be accomplished in seconds and at little cost to the travel agency when the GDS was used. Centralized reservation systems developed by the hotel chains helped reduce TAs' telephone costs by providing "Travel Agent only" toll-free numbers. However, the reality was still that a TA calling, for example, Hilton Hotel's toll-free number could not make a reservation at a Marriott property.

Faced with the reality of increased GDS use, several of the largest hotel chains banded together to share the costs of developing their own reservation interface systems and then negotiate a lower per-reservation GDS usage fee with the airlines. The organization developed to design and maintain the hotel chains' reservation interface systems was called THISCO, short for "The Hotel Industry Switch Company." Developed by Best Western, CHOICE, Day's Inns, Hilton, Holiday Inns, Hyatt, La Quinta, Marriott, Ramada, Sheraton, and Forte, THISCO was founded in 1989. Its goal was to develop a "switch," which would act as a GDS systems translator to interface information from all hotel and airline systems. The result

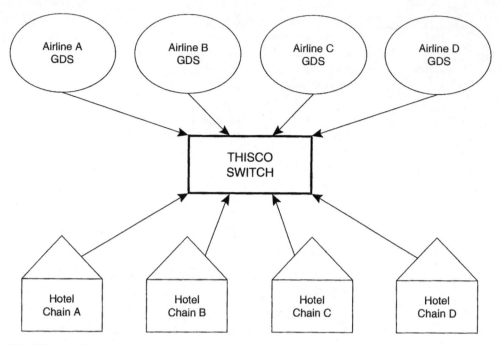

FIGURE 8.5   THISCO

(see Figure 8.5) was to be a seamless system in which TAs could simultaneously look at the availability and rates of a variety of hotels and select the one best fitting their clients' needs.

THISCO met with such great success that, in the years to follow, other entities developed additional hotel, car rental and other industry switches. THISCO (now called Pegasus Solutions) remains the largest switching provider in the hospitality industry. However, Cendant, a very large hotel franchisor, also maintains a switch. In some cases, large hotel chains have found it cost-effective to build and maintain their own switches to Sabre, Galileo, Amadeus, and Worldspan (the four remaining but much advanced components of the original GDS).

Today, the basic communications structure of the GDS can be visualized as seen in Figure 8.6. Information flows from travel agent to hotel and back depending on the communication being delivered. Essentially, the communication process begins when the hotel delivers its room rates and availability to one of the switches. The switches then deliver rate and availability to all four GDS sites. Travel agents as well as others with access use the GDS sites to review room rates and availability and to make their

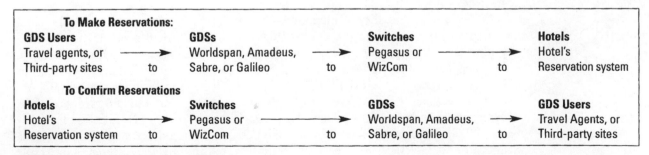

FIGURE 8.6   Information Flow of the GDS

reservation selections. The GDS sites deliver reservation requests to the hotel's central reservation systems through the switches, and in turn, the hotel uses the system to confirm the reservation to the travel agent.

Clearly it is an important role of the FOM to make sure that all hotel information used by the GDS sites is current and accurate. On at least a quarterly basis, the GM should review the hotel's GDS information for accuracy.

Franchise Toll-Free Numbers

Typically, another significant source of transient room reservations is the toll-free number operated by the hotel's franchisor. In most cases, the franchisor distributes a print and/or e-directory of affiliated hotels, and then staffs one or more reservation centers with individuals who answer calls and act as reservation agents for the individual hotels within the franchisee network. Potential guests simply dial the toll-free number, make their reservation request known to the individual answering the telephone, receive information on the desired hotel(s) rates and availability, and finish the call having completed the reservation process with a confirmation number, or if they are canceling a reservation, their **cancellation number**. In some cases, group rooms are also sold via the toll-free number, but these sales usually account for a fairly small amount of the total room nights sold.

HOTEL TERMINOLOGY AT WORK

Cancellation Number: A series of numbers and/or letters that serve to identify the cancellation of a specific hotel reservation.

■

An effective franchise toll-free number will deliver between 5 and 40 percent of a hotel's total transient room nights sold, depending on the location of the hotel. A transient hotel near a city may receive only 10 to 20 percent of its volume from the franchisor, but a resort location will be much higher. Generally, the better known the franchisor, the larger the contribution of room nights sold by its toll-free number. Just as important, the better known franchisors typically deliver reservations sold at rates higher than those achieved by the hotel's own front-office reservationists.

Because the reservation agent accepting telephone calls in a national reservation toll-free call center is not likely to be familiar with each specific hotel in the franchise system, it is critical that the information available to the agent about the hotel is 100 percent accurate. In general, a toll-free number call center will request that the hotel supply as much information as possible on a variety of topics, including:

- Room availability
- Blackout dates
- Room rates
- Seasonality of rates
- Room types
- Distances to local attractions
- Hotel amenities and services offered
- Directions to the property
- Ratings and ranking information

Technically, a toll-free number call center is part of the GDS, and just as the information in all GDS components must be accurate, the information reported to the toll-free number must also be accurate.

It is a good idea for GMs to occasionally make **test calls** to their franchisor-operated call center to verify the accuracy of the information used by the center. If the information about the hotel is not accurate, the GM, working with the FOM, must see that it is corrected.

HOTEL TERMINOLOGY AT WORK

Test Calls: Calls made to a toll-free number or other reservation system to verify the accuracy of information about a specific hotel and/or about the quality of selling done by the reservation center's staff.

Internet

The Internet is fast becoming the single most popular way for individual travelers to serve as their own travel agents and book rooms with hotels without having to call the hotels directly. Hotel companies like individual consumers to use the Internet for making reservations because, unlike travel agents, these individual travelers do not charge the hotel a fee for making the reservation. Some of the sites on which consumers book rooms, however, may charge hotels very large fees. GMs should be aware of the fees charged by each type of Internet site (see Chapter 6) on which their hotel is listed. As more consumers use the Internet, and as more hotel companies see the Internet as a significant marketing tool, this source of transient reservations is likely to continue to grow.

THE INTERNET AT WORK

Navigating a hotel's Internet site to make reservations has become increasingly easy for consumers. To see what the traveler sees, select either of the following hotel sites

www.choicehotels.com
www.marriott.com

Find the rates and availability of rooms for your next birthday at the hotel nearest your own hometown or school.

In addition to Web sites operated by hotel franchise companies, many independent hotels, as well as those hotels affiliated with chains, have developed their own Web sites. Often these technologically savvy hotels link their sites with those of local area attractions, businesses, nonprofit organizations, and others who are likely to need transient guest rooms on a regular basis.

THE INTERNET AT WORK

Some hotels are very creative in developing their own special Web sites. To view one such site, go to

www.mandalaybay.com

Note how the hotel has used the site to advertise in-house activities and encourage online booking.

Increasingly, special Internet sites are developed by third parties (operated by neither the hotel itself nor its brand) simply to make the reservation process easier for potential guests. For example, a couple wishing to visit New York City in November for a holiday shopping trip may not know the name of a specific hotel they wish to use. Thus, they are not likely to access the site of a specific hotel company or individual hotel. By accessing a designated travel site, such as Travelocity.com, the travelers can enter the dates a room is needed and then view pricing and amenity alternatives, as well as make reservations on that Web site. While the use by hotels of such systems is primarily a marketing decision (which is explored in Chapter 7, Sales and Marketing), the accuracy of the information contained on any Web site is a matter generally monitored by the front office. This is true because the rates and availability of rooms posted on the Web must coordinate with the data in the PMS. As with the toll-free number reservation center information, it is important that any information on a hotel's Web site be accurate, and the GM should periodically check to ensure that it is.

Telephone

The many guests who still prefer to call a hotel directly for their reservations expect to have their calls handled quickly and accurately. FOMs can improve the quality of their staff skills by training extensively in the areas of:

- Telephone etiquette
- Qualifying the guest
- Describing the property
- Presenting the rate
- Overcoming price resistance
- Closing the sale
- Recapping the sale

The GM should know whether the individuals answering the telephone and selling rooms via telephone are effective in that task. If they are not, sales will suffer until staff training improves. A periodic review of front-office telephone skills and training methods, by the GM, is imperative if this important area is to get the attention it deserves.

Walk-In

In nearly all hotels, **walk-ins** occur on a regular basis.

HOTEL TERMINOLOGY AT WORK

Walk-In: A guest seeking a room who arrives at the hotel without an advance reservation.

There are many travelers who, for one reason or another, find themselves in need of a hotel room but without an advance reservation. Some travelers whose plans are variable may not in fact know where they will be at the end of the day. Other travelers find their plans change during the day and still others simply prefer not to make advanced reservations. Regardless of the reason, walk-ins can very positively affect the overall profitability of a hotel. In some hotels, particularly those in highway locations, walk-ins account for as much as 30 percent or more of total room nights sold. Excellent **curb appeal**, as well as a friendly initial greeting from the front-office staff, helps ensure that walk-ins are converted to guests.

HOTEL TERMINOLOGY AT WORK

Curb Appeal: The term used to indicate the initial visual impression the hotel's parking areas, grounds, and external building aesthetics create for an arriving guest.

As we have seen, the sources from which a guest reservation is generated vary greatly. However, in all cases the FOM, working with the GM, marketing, and sales personnel must ultimately ensure the hotel secures those reservations in a manner that maximizes guest satisfaction and minimizes any potential misunderstanding that may exist when the guest actually arrives at the hotel. As a GM, you can help make sure this is the case by periodically monitoring and assisting the FOM in improving the management of all reservation sources.

MANAGING GUEST SERVICES

Although the front office is not, by itself, responsible for the entire hotel guest's experience, it is an area that is especially visible to guests, and because of its responsibility for providing a large number of guest services, it is important that the front office be properly staffed and managed.

Modern property management systems speed the processing of guest reservations and free desk agents to focus on improving guest services.

Front Desk: Arrival

When a guest arrives at a hotel, it the responsibility of the front office staff to greet the guest and complete the registration process as quickly and efficiently as possible. This process is, however, more complex than it may seem. Each time a guest interacts with a member of the hotel staff, the hotel makes an impression on that guest, be it a positive or a negative one. To illustrate how the front-office management staff must influence the entire guest service encounter, we will examine the hypothetical experience of Mr. and Mrs. Shingi, two guests with an advanced reservation, as they arrive, register, stay, and then depart from their chosen hotel.

Prearrival

Guest services at the front desk actually begin at the time the guest makes an advance registration. This is true because, on the night before a guest's arrival date, the front-desk staff will request, as part of their nightly work, that the PMS print (or hold in memory) a **registration (reg) card** for all guests scheduled to arrive the next day.

HOTEL TERMINOLOGY AT WORK

Registration (reg) Card: A document that provides details such as guest's name, arrival date, rate to be paid, departure date, and other information related to the guest's stay.

In conversation, most often shortened to "reg" card, as in "Who filed the reg card for room 417?"

The reg card is important because it forms the basis for the legal contract that exists between the hotel and the guest. In this contract, the hotel agrees to supply a room, and the guest agrees to pay for that room. The procedures of the hotel and the features of the hotel's PMS dictate some of the information contained on a reg card, but all such cards should accurately contain the following:

- Guest name
- Guest address
- Guest telephone number
- E-mail address (if expressly allowed by the guest)
- Arrival date
- Departure date
- Number of adults in the room
- Rate to be paid
- Room type requested
- Form of payment used to reserve the room

When a guest arrives at the hotel, an accurate reg card should await. If it does not, the hotel's front-desk staff is most likely not securing complete information at the time of reservation, or if the reservation was made by a third party, at the time the reservation was entered in the PMS. In either case, an effective FOM will ensure that the front desk has generated appropriate reg cards for all known arriving guests. In older PMS systems, the reg cards may be preprinted and held for the guest's arrival, with any changes to the reg card initialed by the guest at check in. In modern systems, the PMS simply holds the reg card information in memory. It is revised as needed upon guest check in, and a corrected copy is printed (if requested) for the guest.

Returning to our hypothetical guests, when the Shingis arrive, the hotel, first and foremost, should know that they are arriving! When they present themselves at the front desk and announce that they have a reservation and would like to check in, the desk agent should be able to quickly retrieve a hard copy of their reg card. Travelers arriving at a hotel to find that their reservation has been "lost" are likely to be very upset, especially if the hotel is sold out and has no alternative available for the guest. In a similar manner, a reg card that contains a misspelled name, erroneous room rates, or incorrect room types will create negative first impressions for the guest.

Effective GMs will periodically observe the guest registration process directly. From the first greeting a guest receives upon entering the hotel to the accuracy of reg cards, the prearrival/arrival activities of the front desk make a tremendous impression on the guest. GMs who put themselves in a position to observe these initial impressions are in an excellent position to work with the FOM to improve the experience.

Bell Station

Depending on the size and service levels of the hotel, the Shingis may, upon arrival, have been greeted and offered assistance by a member of the bell station staff. Bell staff, originally prevalent in nearly all hotels but now limited primarily to upper-market, full-service hotels, assist guests in getting baggage into the hotel and their rooms, as well as sometimes explaining hotel services and guest room features to guests. These staff members should be friendly, knowledgeable, well groomed, and always properly in uniform.

Valet

If the Shingis arrived by car and if the hotel they have chosen is upscale or located in the downtown area of a larger city, it is likely that they will take advantage of **valet** parking, provided by the hotel either free or for a charge. This service, if offered, may be contracted to an outside company. If the hotel controls it, however, the FOM typically manages it. As with bell staff, if valets are employed, they should be friendly, well groomed, properly uniformed, and respectful of the guest property entrusted to them.

HOTEL TERMINOLOGY AT WORK

Valet: Originally a term used to identify an individual who cared for the clothes of wealthy travelers; its most common use now is in reference to those individuals responsible for parking guest vehicles.

Registration

Perhaps the most important guest service function that can be provided by a front-desk agent is that of properly registering guests. This is a five-step process that consists of the following:

1. *Greeting the Guest.* When the Shingis arrive at the front desk, a professionally dressed, well-trained staff member should greet them in a friendly way. Because most hotel guests arrive in the evening and check-in time can be very busy, it may not always be possible to avoid guests having to wait in line for registration. Proper staffing, however, should minimize the wait. When it is their turn to be registered, guests above all else should be made to feel welcome!

2. *Confirming the Information on the Reg Card.* It is imperative that all the information on a reg card be accurate. This includes the spelling of the guest's name, arrival date, departure date, room rate (both of which should be initialed by the guest), and any other information related to that specific guest. Since the reg card will serve as the record of the guest's stay, it must be complete and precise. In addition, misunderstandings regarding room rate (one of the most frequent causes of guest dissatisfaction) can be minimized if the room rate is clearly communicated and understood by both the hotel and the guest prior to room assignment. It is critical that all information on the registration card be accurate and complete.

3. *Securing a Form of Payment.* In most hotels, guests must either pay for their room in advance or provide a valid alternative source of credit at registration. Although many hotels accept checks, the most prevalent source of credit provided by guests is that of a credit or debit card. These cards must be legitimate, however, before they represent an acceptable form of payment. To establish the card's legitimacy, the desk agent should **authorize** the card at the time of guest registration.

HOTEL TERMINOLOGY AT WORK

Authorize: To validate.

When used in reference to credit cards offered by guests at the time of check in, this term refers to the desk agent's validation of the card. Validation means:

- The card is being used legally.
- The card has sufficient credit (or debit) remaining to pay for the guest's estimated charges.
- A "hold" for a dollar amount determined by front-office policy has been placed on the card to ensure the hotel's payment.

As in "Lisa, please authorize Mr. Shingi's MasterCard for $1,000."

To authorize credit cards, hotels use a verification service. Typically, by telephone modem and keypad or magnetic swipe, a desk agent enters the information from the card (account number and expiration date), as well as the dollar amount to be authorized. If the card is not stolen and is valid, the verification service issues an authorization code number that lets the hotel know it can accept the card for payment.

Effective front-desk staffs always authorize the credit cards they accept as a promise of guest payment. In fact, one objective measure of how well a front office is managed is the desk's consistency in securing and authorizing valid cards.

4. *Room Assignment.* Once a guest's registration information has been confirmed and an acceptable form of payment has been offered, the guest should be assigned to a specific guest room. In some hotels, all guest rooms are identical and room assignment is of little consequence. In other hotels, the room types may vary greatly in perceived quality and/or rate based primarily on the room's:

- Location
- View
- Bed type
- Amenities

Whenever possible, of course, guest's preferences should be accommodated. Thus, for example, if Mr. and Mrs. Shingi prefer a nonsmoking room with a king-size bed, on a lower floor, facing the hotel's courtyard, that is precisely the room they should be assigned, if at all possible.

5. *Issuance of Keys.* The final step in the Shingis registration process is the issuance of their room keys. The actual number of keys to be issued is a matter of hotel policy and guest preference. It is important, however, that the issuance of guest room keys be tightly controlled because the theft, loss, or unauthorized duplication of keys could seriously threaten guest safety.

Upon receiving room keys, the Shingis would be taken or directed to their room. If bell staff were needed to provide assistance with luggage, this staff member would likely escort the Shingi's to their room. In most midsize hotels, however, the front-desk agent would simply direct the guests to their room.

Concierge

The concierge is an extremely important position to hotel guests. If the Shingis find that they need assistance beyond the services typically found in their hotel, they would go to the concierge. Traditionally, the concierge in a full-service hotel is responsible for assisting guests in:

- Making dining reservations
- Securing tickets for theater and sporting events
- Arranging transportation
- Providing information on local attractions
- Language translation
- Providing hotel specific information

In hotels without a concierge staff, it is vital to remember that guests still desire many of these services. Those hotels that can provide all or most of them are in a stronger position to gain guest loyalty and repeat business. For that reason, the GM should be aware (as should all guests!) of the services provided by the front-office staff.

Front Desk: Guest Privacy

Once a guest has been registered for a room, the courts have ruled that these guests enjoy many of the same constitutional rights in the room as they would in their own home. It is not simply the legal thing to do, but it is the moral thing as well, to protect the rights of guests to privacy.

Guest Information

A professionally managed front office is one in which guests are confident that their privacy is maintained by all staff members. This includes maintaining a guest's anonymity. To that end, front-desk agents should:

- Never confirm or deny that a guest is in fact registered in the hotel without the guest's express permission.
- Never give out information related to a guest's stay (arrival, departure, rate, room number, and so on) to any third party without that guest's express permission.
- Always be vigilant in informing the guest of any unusual third-party information requests regarding their stay.

Room Information

Just as guests expect their own privacy to be maintained, they should also feel confident that information regarding their actual room is kept confidential. This is both a safety and a privacy issue. To that end, front-desk agents should:

- Never give out a guest's room number to any third party without that guest's express permission.
- Never perform registration tasks in such a way as to allow guest room information to be overheard by others in the front-office area.
- Never mark room numbers directly onto keys.
- Never issue a duplicate room key to anyone without confirming the positive identification of that person as the room's properly registered guest.

The Shingis, and all guests, upon check in, should be confident that personal details of their stay will remain confidential; that information the hotel may have about them, including their address, telephone number, and credit card is secure; and that no unauthorized person can gain access to their room. An effective front office can perform no more important task than ensuring guest privacy, and it is the FOM's job to make certain this is the case.

Front Desk: Stay and Departure

During their stay, including the point at which they check out, guests will constantly interact with the front office. Its staff may be called upon to supply a variety of services or information at any time during the guest's stay.

Guest Satisfaction Issues

One of the most challenging aspects of providing guest service at the front desk relates to ensuring that guests are satisfied during their stay. When guests experience difficulties in the hotel, they will most likely turn to the front desk and its staff for assistance. As noted in the previous chapter, there are a variety of reasons guests may have special needs or experience dissatisfaction during their stay. During their stay and at time of check out, guests are likely to bring up any issues they find that detracted from their experience. Routine items such as requesting room repairs, additional in-room amenities, or information, if handled professionally, can actually enhance the guest's experience. As a GM, it is a good idea to monitor the efforts of the front-desk staff to ensure that guests, especially those who have legitimate complaints, are treated courteously and with empathy.

The Walked Guest

One of the most difficult situations that can be confronted by a front-desk agent is that of walking a guest. Recall that a guest who must be walked is one who has a confirmed reservation but cannot be accommodated by the hotel. When this occurs, it is imperative that the front-desk agent carefully follows the hotel's established policies for walking a guest. As a GM, it is your responsibility to work with the FOM to establish those policies and see that they are implemented when needed. In all cases, when confronted with the task of walking a guest, the front-office staff should be observed to:

- Apologize to the guest for the inconvenience.
- Clearly explain the hotel's walk policy to the guest.
- Offer any reasonable assistance possible to the guest to minimize the difficulties of the situation.

ACCOUNTING FOR GUESTS

Accounting for guests, while less visible than providing guest services, is another critical responsibility of the front office. During their stay, the Shingis are likely to have purchased a variety of hotel goods and services in addition to having rented their room. Accounting for guests simply means that all charges incurred by a guest's use of the hotel are charged for properly. Depending on the services and amenities offered by the hotel, the source of guest charges can be numerous. The following product and services list is not inclusive, but does represent some of the many possible guest charges that must be accurately collected and **posted** to the guest's folio.

- Guest room charges including appropriate taxes
- In-room minibar purchases
- In-room safe charges
- Pay-per-view movies/games
- Internet access charges
- Restaurant charges
- Bar charges
- Room service charges
- Telephone tolls
- Gift shop purchases
- Laundry charges
- Valet parking charges
- Meeting room charges
- Audiovisual equipment rental
- Banquet charges
- Service charges

HOTEL TERMINOLOGY AT WORK

Post: To enter a guest's charges into the PMS, thus creating a permanent record of the sale, as in "Please post this meeting room charge to Mr. Walker's folio."

Rooms Management/Assignment

Perhaps no job performed by the front office is more important than the seemingly straightforward task of assigning guests to the right room, at the right room rate, with the right required form of payment. In reality, this process, despite the use of a sophisticated PMS, can be quite complex. Essentially, there are two methods employed for the registration of guests. These are front-desk check-in and self check-in.

Front-Desk Check In

Guests arriving at a hotel to check in want to be quickly assigned to a room. In the typical case, guests present themselves at a front-desk area to begin the registration process. Depending on the level of service provided and priority of the guest, special

It is important for the front-office agent and the guest to be in agreement about charges posted to the guest's folio. (Rob Brimson/Taxi/Getty Images)

check-in areas may be established within the hotel. Regardless, however, of where the check-in area is, it is important that the front-desk agent confirm the status of the selected room prior to room assignment. Clearly a guest should not be assigned to a room that has not been cleaned or that is occupied by another guest. Although each hotel may use its own abbreviations, typically a vacant room is identified in the PMS with a "V" (for vacant) or an "O" (for occupied). Further, the room must be designated as "C" (for cleaned) and ready to rent. As can be seen, it is important that those individuals responsible for cleaning and inspecting rooms are in close contact with the front desk so the status of guest rooms can be updated continuously throughout the day.

Self Check In

Automated self check out systems are currently in greater use than self check in systems, but the technology exists to create a kiosk that allows guests to enter personal information such as that found on their credit card or smart card, choose from a display of available rooms, and receive a key to the selected room. There are, perhaps, two reasons why this self check-in option has not been as widely adopted as it's advocates would like, despite the obvious advantage of speeding up the check-in process. The first is the lack of personal contact. The second is the obvious legal liability that could exist for the hotel should a malfunction of the self-operated system allow a guest to check in to an already occupied room. As guests become more accustomed to the self-check-in process and its security is ensured, its use in the hotel industry will surely increase.

In either check-in situation, it is important that the FOM has systems in place that allow the front-desk staff to:

- Verify and document personal information positively identifying the guest to whom the room is rented.
- Assign guests, whenever possible, to the room type they have requested.
- Assure the status of the room assigned to the guest is "Clean and Vacant".
- Confirm the rate to be paid by the guest prior to the issuance of room keys.
- Confirm the guest's departure date prior to the issuance of room keys.
- Secure an acceptable form of payment from the guest.

The GM wishing to minimize accounting difficulties resulting from guest misunderstandings and billing errors will work with the controller and FOM to confirm that systems are in place to achieve the above objectives.

Bucket Check

Errors in recording the information related to a guest's stay make the hotel's accounting records inaccurate. In addition, room rate adjustments made at checkout are both annoying and time-consuming to guests. To help eliminate these problems, professional FOMs develop and implement an effective **bucket check** program for all front-desk shifts. The "bucket" is the industry term for the location of the actual registration cards signed by guests at check in. The bucket check is simply a manual procedure for assuring the accuracy of information related to the guest's actual room assignment, rate to be paid, departure date, form of payment, and any other accounting-related information deemed important by the FOM.

HOTEL TERMINOLOGY AT WORK

Bucket Check: A procedure used to verify, for each guest, the accuracy of that guest's registration information.

When performing the bucket check, the desk agent physically verifies that the information on the guest's registration card is complete and matches that in the PMS. And if an appropriate bucket check is performed at each shift, the number of errors related to billing guests' folios is greatly reduced. As a GM, if you detect excessive room rate adjustments, numerous guest complaints due to erroneous billing, or uncollectable guest charges due to insufficient documentation of form of payment, the FOM is likely not enforcing bucket check procedures.

Billing the Folio

Busy hotels process hundreds or even thousands of guest-related billing transactions daily. Depending on the type of PMS in use, some of these charges will be posted automatically by the PMS while others must be posted manually. In all cases, the controller's office will want to verify the accuracy of the charge and to have a transactional trail for each charge. That is, the front desk should be able to produce independent supporting documentation for each charge posted to a guest's folio. For example, assume that a guest has ordered a bottle of wine from the hotel's room service department. The guest has asked that the cost of the bottle of wine and an appropriate gratuity for the room service waitperson bringing the wine to the room be added to the guest's folio. Upon check out, the guest may wish to review these charges. The front-desk agent responsible for checking the guest out may need to produce some documentation of the charge. In this case, the documentation would likely be the actual room service ticket signed by the guest when the wine was delivered. It is the responsibility of each shift of the front desk to ensure that all appropriate guest charges incurred are posted to the appropriate guest's folio and that the documentation supporting such charges has been thoroughly reviewed prior to posting. The **night auditor** depends on appropriate documentation provided by each shift of the front desk to support the charges that will be finalized and posted to the guest's folio during the night audit.

HOTEL TERMINOLOGY AT WORK

Night Auditor: The individual who performs the daily review of guest transactions recorded by the front office.

Night Audit

Because hotels are open seven days a week, twenty-four hours a day, an interesting accounting issue arises: When does one day's hotel sales end and another's begin?

To illustrate the issue, assume that, on a winter night, due to inclement weather, a hotel on an interstate highway checks different guests into the hotel at the following times: 11:00 P.M., midnight, 1:00 A.M., 2:00 A.M., 3:00 A.M., 4:00 A.M., 5:00 A.M., and so on.

At what point are these guests considered Monday night guests, and at what point should they be considered Tuesday guests?

Traditionally, the "end" of the day (and therefore the beginning of the next day) is not a fixed time period at all, but rather is designated as the time at which the night auditor concludes (closes) the **night audit**. Even though the night audit could theoretically be performed at any time during the day or night, traditionally it has been performed in the late evening/early morning hours when the hotel's overall activity is at its slowest because most guests have, at that point, checked in for the night.

HOTEL TERMINOLOGY AT WORK

Night Audit: The process of reviewing for accuracy and completeness the accounting transactions from one day to conclude or "close" that day's sales information in preparation for posting the transactions of the next day.

The night audit function is important for many departments in the hotel. Essentially, completing it consists of the following eight key items:

1. Posting the appropriate room and tax rates to folios of the guests currently in the hotel

2. Verification of an accurate room status (in the PMS) of all rooms

3. Posting any necessary adjustments or allowances to guest folios

4. Verification that all legitimate nonroom charges have been posted throughout the day to the proper guest folio

5. Monitoring guest account balances to determine whether any are over the guest's credit limit

6. Balancing and reconciling the front desk's cash bank

7. Updating and backing up the electronic data maintained by the front office

8. Producing, duplicating, and distributing all management mandated reports, such as those related to ADR, occupancy percentage, source of business, in-house guest lists, and the like

With a computerized PMS, some of the above tasks may be completed automatically. In most hotels, the night auditor completes the audit between 1:00 A.M. and 4:00 A.M. It is important that this task is completed correctly and on time because some guests will begin to check out of the hotel very early in the morning and their folios must be as up-to-date as possible at that time.

Check Out

Increasingly, hotels provide guests the option of using express or self check out systems when they conclude their stay. These are popular and appropriate for some guests. In the normal case, however, when guests check out, the front desk should perform two important tasks.

The first, of course, is the settlement of the guest's bill. This consists of a several step process, including:

- Confirmation of the guest's identity
- Checking for and giving to the guest any mail, late faxes, or guest messages that may not have been delivered
- Inquiring about and returning any guest belongings held in the hotel's safety deposit boxes
- Posting of any final charges
- Producing a copy of the folio for the guest's inspection
- Processing the guest's payment
- Revising the room's status in the PMS to designate the room as vacant

In most cases, guest check-out is a relatively straightforward process. This is especially true if the guest's form of payment has been confirmed at check in and if bucket checks have been performed throughout the guest's stay to verify that the appropriate room rate has been charged.

In some cases, guests will have experienced a difficulty with their stay and an adjustment of their bill may be in order. It is important that the FOM and each desk agent know the limits to their authority to make adjustments. That is, the desk agent may be authorized by the FOM to make folio adjustments up to a predetermined dollar amount, but only a supervisor or manager could authorize adjustments exceeding that amount. In a like manner, the FOM may be authorized to make adjustments subject to the level of authority delegated by the hotel's GM.

The second essential task that can be accomplished by the desk agent when a guest checks out is the rebooking of the guest for a future stay. If the guest's stay has been a positive one, it is proper, as well as good front-office management, to ask the guest if future reservations can be made for them at the hotel or, if appropriate, at another hotel within the chain. This is an often overlooked selling opportunity. In addition, a GM can frequently determine the selling focus of an FOM by the presence or absence of this front-office activity.

DATA MANAGEMENT

The front office is the center for the hotel's data management systems. At the front office, the PMS, as well as other accounting systems, maintain the financial and operational records of the hotel. In most cases, these systems are extensive as well as complex. Their management requires a talented and technologically savvy FOM because an increasing number of important data-generating systems are, or should be, **interfaced** with the hotel's PMS.

HOTEL TERMINOLOGY AT WORK

Interfaced: The term used to describe the process in which one data-generating system shares its data electronically with another system.

■

The process of interfacing two data management systems can be challenging because, in most cases, different companies manufacture the systems. For example, the company that produces the hotel's PMS will not be the same as the company providing the hotel with its electronic guest room door lock system. Clearly, however, it is ideal that a guest, who is checked in to room 101 by the PMS, automatically is issued a key for room 101 (not room 102!) by the electronic locking system. When the PMS and lock system are interfaced, this happens immediately. When they are not, the key maker must produce the key separately, which introduces the possibility of an error.

To complicate matters further, in many cases multiple system interfaces are required, not all of which are completely under the control of the hotel. For example, a hotel that wishes to upgrade its **call accounting** system will find that the new system must be interfaced with the existing telephone system, the local telephone call provider's system, the long-distance call provider's system, and the hotel's PMS. The challenges of implementing such an integrated system are many and fall primarily to the FOM.

HOTEL TERMINOLOGY AT WORK

Call Accounting: The system within the hotel used to document and charge guests for their use of the telephone.

■

Payment Cards

Since the 1960s, **credit cards** and **T&E cards** have been a common form of guest payment at most hotels. Today, **debit cards** are increasingly used by guests to pay bills.

HOTEL TERMINOLOGY AT WORK

Credit (Bank) Card: Also known as bank cards, a system by which banks loan money with interest to consumers as purchases are made. Merchants accepting the cards for payment are charged a fee by the banks for the charges made by their customers with the credit card. Examples of credit cards are Visa and MasterCard.

T&E Card: Short for "Travel and Entertainment card." A payment system by which the card issuer collects full payment from the card users each month. The card companies do not typically assess interest charges to consumers. Instead, they rely on fees collected from merchants accepting the cards. Examples of T&E cards are American Express (Amex) and Diners Club.

Debit Card: A payment system in which money collected by a merchant (hotel) are automatically (electronically) deposited into the merchant's local bank account. As with bank and T&E cards, merchants accepting the cards are assessed a fee for the right to do so.

■

For the FOM, payment cards of these types (as well as in the near future, **smart cards**) are helpful because, when interfaced with the PMS, they can speed guest payment and check out.

HOTEL TERMINOLOGY AT WORK

Smart Card: Payment cards in which user information such as demographics, purchase history, and product preferences are contained within a computerized "chip" imbedded in the card.

■

In many hotels, payment cards rather than currency are typically used by guests to settle accounts. Credit cards remain the most common form of payment card used in most hotels. Properly processing charges to credit (and, increasingly, debit) cards is an important responsibility of the front office. Accuracy and a commitment to security when processing guest payment card charges are two characteristics every GM should seek from the FOM. Increasingly, payment cards are issued with three-dimensional designs, magnetic strips, encoded numbers, smart chips, and other features to reduce consumer fraud. In addition, electronic payment card verification systems are fast, accurate, and designed to reduce loss. Although these verification systems, which are currently in use in most hotels, cut down on the number of processing errors, security and fraud prevention remain significant considerations. Federal laws prohibit the fraudulent use of payment cards, yet many times hotels are the victims of such fraud. An effective FOM implements systems to minimize payment card fraud while, at the same time, protecting the security of the guest's payment card number and the integrity of the hotel's payment card database.

In some cases, hotels face the challenge of payment card holders who pay their full bill with their card but later protest all or part of that bill. Unless the dispute can be settled between the hotel and guest, the FOM may have to defend the hotel's card-processing procedures. Each major card issuer has its own preferred procedures, and FOMs should be familiar with those required by the cards their hotels accept.

Payment card issuers have a responsibility to both the hotel and the cardholder. To be fair, the card issuer will require the hotel to have followed the issuer's procedures for accepting cards and billing for products and services. Then, if guests have a legitimate complaint, these guests will be treated fairly, while at the same time, the hotel is protected from fraud. As a GM, you should monitor the payment card procedures used at the front desk. Payment card acceptance and processing guidelines that should exist in written form for ease in training front-desk agents include:

- Confirmation procedures ensure that the name on the card is the same as that of the individual presenting the card for payment. (Driver's license or other acceptable forms of identification can be used.)
- Examination of the card for obvious signs of alteration.
- Confirmation that the card has not expired.
- Comparison of the signature on the card with the one made by the guest paying with the card.
- Documentation (usually by initialing) of the employee who processed the charge.
- The balancing and reconciling of payment card charges at the conclusion of each front-office shift.

Locking/Security Systems

An extensive discussion of hotel key and locking systems and their role in guest safety and security is included in this book (Chapter 12, Safety and Property Security). However, because the front office is responsible for issuing guest room keys, it is appropriate to examine the FOM's role in maintaining the data and the security systems related to the issuing of room keys.

Modern hotels use a **recodable locking system** to ensure guest safety. The typical installed cost of such a system is approximately $500–$1000 per guest room. Whether keys are lost, stolen, or accidentally thrown away, the challenge for you as a GM becomes how to cost-effectively protect your guests, your property, and your bottom line. Recodable locking systems help you do just that.

HOTEL TERMINOLOGY AT WORK

Recodable Locking System: A hotel guest room locking system designed such that when a guest inserts the "key" (typically an electromagnetic card) into the guest room lock for the first time, the lock is immediately recoded, canceling entry authorization for the previous guest's key and thus enhancing guest safety.

■

Most recodable locking systems in use today are independent and stand-alone. That is, no wiring back to a central computer or PMS is required. Except in life-threatening emergencies, only standard magnetic strip cards issued to hotel staff as well as guests open the lock. This means that the hotel's entire room security system is controlled by software programmed into the individual locks, activated by cards coded on a card-issuing computer. **Keycards** are time sensitive and can be issued up to twelve months in advance, meaning that individuals or groups can be sent room keys prior to their arrival when reservations are confirmed; to speed registration.

HOTEL TERMINOLOGY AT WORK

Keycards: The electromagnetic card used in a recodable locking system.

■

The advantages of recodable locks are so great that no hotelier would seriously consider building a hotel today without including such a system.

The data management challenge for the FOM managing a recodable lock system is to ensure that front-desk agents do not issue keys to individuals not properly registered in the guest room. For example, assume the (very common) situation where a guest approaches the front desk and states, "I have misplaced my room key." Clearly the staff member must:

1. Be trained to issue duplicate keys only to confirmed registered guests
2. Maintain an accurate data system that actually identifies registered guests and their assigned room numbers

The advantages of an interfaced recodable locking system and PMS are clear in this case. As a GM, you must ensure that the required security training is in place to handle the above situation. As well, data systems must be maintained well enough to avoid issuing guest room keys to unauthorized individuals.

Telephones

One of the most complex data and equipment management areas within the hotel is that of telephones and telephone-related services. Even the smallest of hotels is large enough to have its own private branch exchange, or **PBX.**

HOTEL TERMINOLOGY AT WORK

PBX: The system within the hotel used to process incoming, internal, and outgoing telephone calls.

Today's hotel PBX is highly automated, as it must be because of the tremendous use made of telephones within the typical hotel. The PBX is typically maintained by the front office. Therefore the FOM is responsible for the proper operation of the following areas.

Call Accounting

When guests make telephone calls to outside the hotel, it is in the best interest of the hotel to route those calls in a way that minimizes the hotel's cost. For example, if a registered guest directly dials someone in another state from his or her hotel room, it is the hotel that will actually be billed for the call. Of course, the hotel would want its cost of providing the call to be as low as possible while still assuring that guests have quality long-distance service. The hotel will, depending on the distance and length of the long-distance call, add a charge to the guest's folio to offset the cost of the call. For those hotels providing in-room fax machines, these calls, like all others, can be charged to the guest's folio when the call accounting system is interfaced with the PMS.

The call accounting system records the time, length, and number called of each telephone call made within each guest room (as well as those made from administrative phones). These call records must be accurate if guests are to be expected to pay for the calls they have initiated. The hotel's management determines which of these made calls will be billed to guests and which will not. Some hotels use the call accounting system to charge guests for local calls as well as long distance, whereas other hotels routinely allow guests to make free local calls. The call accounting system, when interfaced with the PMS, posts these charges directly to the guest's folio. It is important to remember that even local calls are not "free" to the hotel. Proper operation of the call accounting system is important because telephone calls, for many hotels, are a significant source of revenue. Telephone revenue, as a percentage of total hotel revenue, has been declining in recent years due to the increased use of cell phones and pagers; however, a properly managed call accounting system is still a vital part of any effective front-office operation because telephone revenue that goes uncollected due to an improperly managed system is damaging to the hotel's bottom line.

Wake-Up Calls

Traditionally, guests who wish to wake up at a given time have called the front desk to request a "wake-up" call. A member of the front-office staff would then call the guest at the requested time. Today's telephone systems automate these calls, and they can be programmed into the PBX either by guests in their own rooms or by staff at the front desk.

Voice Mail

Voice mail is a feature that may be interfaced with the PBX but is, in fact, a separate telephone component. A properly operating voice mail system is nearly mandatory for those hotels seeking to attract business travelers, and hotels increasingly provide this service to guests. In a modern PBX system interfaced with voice mail, the voice mailbox for the guest is activated by the PMS at check in and then deactivated by the PMS when the guest checks out. Voice mail is also critical for administrative staff that must have telephone contact with guests or potential guests. This is especially true of the sales and marketing department.

Message on Hold

This telephone feature allows the hotel to play a "message" on the line when a caller is placed on hold. For example, a caller attempting to make a room reservation may be placed on hold for a short period of time until the next reservationist is available. During this time, the hotel may play a recorded message that can include features of the hotel, unique services offered, and a general "apology" for placing the caller on hold, while, at the same time, assuring the call will be answered shortly. Typically a message on hold apparatus interfaces the PBX with a combination of pleasant music and well-written marketing script.

Additional use of hotel telephones includes those calls made by guests to other guests within the hotel (room-to-room); calls made to the front desk from **house phones**; emergency phones such as those located in elevators, at the pool, or fitness areas; and the hotel staff's own interoffice calls.

HOTEL TERMINOLOGY AT WORK

House Phone: A publicly located telephone within the hotel used to call the front desk, or, in some cases, the front desk and guest rooms.

■

The telephone system in a hotel is a critical service to guests, as well as an effective management tool. Its uninterrupted operation is important, and it is the FOM in conjunction with affected departments that must ensure its smooth operation.

THE INTERNET AT WORK

For an overview of the many features and capabilities provided by today's telephone systems, review the site of one of the industry's leading providers of telephone systems for smaller properties. You can do so at

www.nortel.com

For larger property telephone systems, check out

www.mitel.com

When you arrive at the Mitel site, click on "Solutions", and then "Hospitality."

Point of Sale (POS)

In most cases the hotel's PMS will be interfaced with one or more **point of sale** systems. Any sales recording system not located at the front desk is technically considered to be a POS system. In a larger hotel, there are multiple POS systems in operation. Some examples include:

- Restaurants
- Room service
- Lounges
- Laundry
- Valet
- Shops
- Fitness centers
- Business centers

It is the role of the front office to ensure that all legitimate purchases made at a POS and charged to an account are posted to the proper guest or nonguest folio.

HOTEL TERMINOLOGY AT WORK

Point of Sale (POS): A location, excluding the front desk, at which hotel goods and services are purchased. In many hotels, the POS(s) is interfaced with the PMS.

In-Room Services

Increasingly, guests can use the televisions, telephones, and/or hotel-provided keyboards in their rooms to access products and services provided by the hotel. As the traveling public becomes even more computer sophisticated, look for this trend to continue and expand. Currently some of the most popular products and services guests can access from their rooms include movies, games, minibars, safes, and Internet connections.

In-room movies are one type of service many hotels provide their guests.

Movies

Pay-per-view movie systems have long been a popular feature offered to hotel guests. Essentially, these systems offer guests the opportunity to view movies that are currently, or that have just recently finished, showing in movie theaters. In addition, most pay-per-view providers offer a variety of adult-oriented movies as well. The demand for these current and popular movies can be quite strong. Guests pay the hotel for viewing the movies. Then, at month's end, the movie provider charges the hotel based on the number of movies viewed, as well as for any equipment charges included in the hotel's pay-per-view contract. If a movie shown on the system is defective (e.g., poor audio or color quality), the provider typically allows the hotel to not bill the guest, and in turn does not bill the hotel. Some guests, often those who view the adult movies offered by the pay-per-view system, dispute that they have watched the movies. A good FOM has systems in place that distinguish between those guests who truly have had problems with their movie quality while at the same time minimizing the number of guests who might attempt to defraud the hotel. As a GM, it is important to monitor the number of movies viewed per month versus the number of movies actually billed to guests. If the difference between these two numbers is excessive, a review of front-office policy in this area is needed.

Originally devised as videotape-based systems, today's in-room movie services are more likely to be delivered by satellite and to include enhanced features that allow guests to review their folios on their television screens, and even to check out of the hotel using a PMS interfaced pay-per-view system.

THE INTERNET AT WORK

For a sample of the type of movies shown to guests on a pay-per-view system, review the offerings of Lodgenet, one of the largest pay-per-view movie and services providers. You can do so at

www.lodgenet.com/guests/index.html

Games

Guests are increasingly offered the chance to play "video" games on the television screens in their rooms. The games are typically accessed in the same manner as pay-per-view movies. While these game services are very similar to pay-per-view movies (they are pay-per-play), the significant difference is the requirement for an in-room joystick, mouse, or keyboard to actually play the game. This means that the hotel must provide these electronic devices and keep them secure in the rooms. The logistics and difficulty of doing so has made some GMs reluctant to actively offer games as an in-room amenity. The FOM is not responsible for the security of the in-room devices, but is responsible for maintaining an effective interface so that all games played are, in fact, charged to the proper guest folio.

In-Room Minibars

Hotels have long provided in-room **minibars** that allowed guests the convenience of selecting alcoholic beverages, soft drinks, and snacks from in-room storage units (minibars). Only recently, however, have advances in bar-coding technology created a situation in which in-room minibars can be interfaced with the PMS so that, as a guest removes an item from the minibar, the time of the transaction as well as the selling price of the item removed is automatically posted to the guest's folio.

HOTEL TERMINOLOGY AT WORK

Minibars: Small, in-room refrigerated or unrefrigerated cabinets used to store beverages, snacks, and other items the hotel wishes to offer for sale to guests.

Safes

Recently more hotels have begun offering in-room safes for guests' use. These safes are electronic and can be opened only by the guest and the hotel's own staff. Charges, if any, for the use of the safe are typically posted to the guest's folio.

Beginning in the mid-1800s and continuing today, each state has developed its own view of how liable hotels should be for the possessions of their guests. The laws in each state vary considerably, however, so it is extremely important that hotel managers familiarize themselves with applicable laws before implementing an in-room safe service. In most states, if a hotel wishes to take advantage of its state's laws limiting liability for the theft or loss of a guest's possessions, the guest must be made aware of the existence and content of that law. Also in most states, if the hotel is to provide in-room safes under the control of the guest, the hotel must also offer, and publicize the fact that it offers, a safety deposit box at "no-charge" where guests can keep their valuables during their stay.

A hotel is not required to accept for safekeeping an unlimited amount of personal property. A hotel is not a bank, and it is not reasonable to assume that it would be as secure as a bank. However, guest demand for in-room safes is increasing, and in nearly all states, a hotel is fully responsible for theft by its employees. Just as important, the hotel becomes liable for the full amount of any property loss resulting from the actions of the hotel's staff. For that reason and others, many hotels have been slower to implement this guest service. GMs interested in providing in-room safes for a fee are well advised to consult their property's attorney or security expert prior to implementation of the service.

Internet Connections

In the late 1990s, some hotels began to aggressively market in-room Internet services. The intent was to capitalize on the increasing use of the Internet by travelers of all types. Some of these efforts met with success, while others, the victim of the famous "dot.com" bust of 2001, were canceled or delayed when companies offering the services failed to deliver because of defective business models.

Certainly, the use of the Internet has exploded. In many ways (e.g., the marketing of hotel properties and the ability of guests to make reservations directly using the Internet), the impact of the Internet on hotels has been very positive. The ability of hotels to profitably harness the Internet on a pay-to-connect basis in a guest's room, however, is still undetermined. This is especially the case when the guest's own personal computer is used to make the connection. Nevertheless, some hotels do profitably charge for Internet usage; for those that do, their interface to the PMS must be maintained and controlled by the FOM. Increasingly, hotels are turning away from hardwired Internet connections that limit guest mobility when using the Internet. As a result, **wi-fi** and **hot spots** have become familiar terms for FOMs and GMs.

HOTEL TERMINOLOGY AT WORK

Wi-Fi: Short for <u>Wi</u>reless <u>Fi</u>delity. A data delivery system that does not rely on wiring to provide users with an Internet connection.

Hot Spot: A wi-fi area that allows for high-speed wireless Internet access or other data transmission (analogy: a reception zone for a cell phone).

■

Back-Office Accounting Systems

As we saw in the previous chapter, the financial data from the PMS must ultimately be transferred to the controller's office. The **back-office system** used by the controller to prepare the hotel's financial documents will get a large portion of its data from the PMS; therefore, it is important that the data in the PMS be accurate.

HOTEL TERMINOLOGY AT WORK

Back-Office System: The accounting system used by the controller to prepare the hotel's financial documents such as the balance sheet, income statement, and so on.

■

It is somewhat surprising that few makers of PMSs develop their products with the capability of interfacing directly with the most popular back-office systems on the market today. As a result, the data collected and maintained by the FOM are sometimes inconsistent with that needed by the controller. The advantages of a seamless integration are many, and when the software required for such integration is fully developed and functional, will be anxiously awaited by GMs as well as controllers and FOMs.

Although it is not mandatory that the back-office system used by a hotel is computerized, few hotels today would attempt to operate a back-office system that does not rely on the most advanced accounting software available. There are hundreds of accounting software packages available in the marketplace today. Nearly all of these packages offer unique features and capabilities that are to be commended, admired, and sometimes applauded. However, the majority of these products also suffer from glaring weaknesses and shortcomings. Assuming that the back-office system is not interfaced directly to the PMS or manufactured by the PMS maker, GMs will find that the FOM and controller will coexist best when the back-office accounting system selected for use in the hotel offers:

- A good underlying technology
- A strong company behind the product, including good leadership
- Compatibility with popular hardware products
- A sizable customer base
- Good customization capabilities
- Expandability
- Ease of use by nontechnology-based employees
- Excellent support via telephone
- Excellent on-line support
- The potential for PMS interface

In the future, more PMS developers will likely include back office accounting systems as part of their package. It is also probable that call accounting and POS systems will soon make their way to become part of the standard PMSs from which GMs can choose.

THE INTERNET AT WORK

For an example of an excellent back-office system that could be even better were it interfaced with the most popular property management systems in use, review the latest "Great Plains" accounting software version. This Microsoft-owned entry into hospitality back-office systems software can be found by searching the Microsoft Web site. To do so, go to

www.microsoft.com/

The FOM is often the hotel's guest service expert and, increasingly, the hotel's technological leader. Few other hotel departments have been, nor likely will be, as impacted by the changing capabilities of equipment and of guest expectations. As a GM, the need for a talented front-office staff that can maximize revenue, provide outstanding guest service, and record the data needed for the smooth operation of the property is unquestionable.

MANAGERS AT WORK

J.D. Ojisama, the hotel GM, has been approached by a salesperson from Lucid Technologies. Essentially, Lucid is proposing, for a fee, to install the Wi-Fi Hot spots required to provide rapid Internet access to each guest room in J.D.'s hotel. The Lucid representative maintains that the cost of the installation will be recouped via the fees the hotel can charge Internet users for the high-speed service. Guests can use their own computers or, for a higher fee, Lucid will provide the hotel keyboards so that guests can use the in-room TV for their monitor.

The clientele the hotel serves is 80 percent business traveler and 20 percent leisure traveler through the week, with the reverse true on the weekends. The Internet service is touted by Lucid as a critical need of the business traveler.

In addition to the financial cost/benefits of the service, what specific front-office interface issues must J.D. consider before committing to the purchase? Which other areas of the hotel would be affected by the decision to implement or not implement the service? How can J.D. obtain the technology-related information needed to make a wise decision? Identify at least three specific sources of such information.

HOTEL TERMINOLOGY AT WORK GLOSSARY

The following terms were defined within this chapter. If you are not familiar with one of them, please review the segment of the chapter that contains the term.

Front office	Cut-off date	Credit (bank) card
FOM	Global Distribution System	T&E card
Concierge	Cancellation number	Debit card
Bell staff	Test calls	Smart card
Backup system	Walk-in	Recodable locking system
Sell-out	Curb appeal	Keycards
Folio	Registration (reg) card	PBX
Room type	Valet	House phone
Field	Authorize	Point of sale (POS)
Confirmation number	Post	Minibars
Arrival	Bucket check	Wi-fi
Transient sales	Night auditor	Hot spot
Reservation agent	Night audit	Back-office system
Prepaid (reservation)	Interfaced	
Nonguaranteed (reservation)	Call accounting	

ISSUES AT WORK

1. In some hotels, the position of revenue manager reports to a sales and marketing director, whereas in others it reports to the FOM. Why do you think this is so? As a GM, how would these two alternative arrangements affect the way you would manage the property?
2. Rapid advances in technology create a situation where, often, the FOM has greater technical expertise in using the PMS than does the GM. What difficulties do you see in such a situation? As a GM, what techniques and resources can you use to overcome these difficulties?
3. Brand-operated Internet sites have moved aggressively to promote themselves as "lowest cost." What drawbacks are such sites likely to face as they promote "low cost" as the primary reason for shopping their sites? How can FOMs help their hotels benefit from this?

4. As advances in technology make the self-registration of guests more easily achievable, some hotel companies have moved aggressively to implement such technologies. Those who have not cite the diminished role personal service plays in the process and the potential long-term negative affects to consumer loyalty that may result. Do you think the average business traveler prefers the speed of self-check in or the human interaction of a front-desk agent? How about the average leisure traveler? Please explain your positions in detail.

5. The increased use of personal cell phones and the consumer's perception that hotel telephone charges are excessive have led to industrywide reduced revenue derived from telephone services supplied by the hotel. Telephone costs, however, have increased as features such as voice mail and other automated options have been added to even the most basic PBX systems. List three specific methods you would employ to encourage in-room telephone use (and thus revenue) in a hotel you would manage. Describe how you would use the front-office staff to help implement each of these plans.

9

Housekeeping

This Chapter at Work

GMs are sometimes asked by those outside the hotel business to identify the "most important" department in their hotels. It is not really possible for a GM to answer that question because all departments are important, but from the point of view of the hotel's guests the answer would be simple. It is the housekeeping department. Hotel industry surveys consistently confirm this fact. Guests want, first and foremost, a clean room. It is the role of the housekeeping department to provide that clean room, as well as to clean most other areas within the hotel.

There are three primary areas within the hotel that are the responsibility of the housekeeping department: (1) public spaces such as restrooms, exercise areas, pools, lobbies, and corridors, (2) guest rooms, and (3) the hotel's laundry area. To manage the care and cleaning of the hotel, a GM will employ the services of an excellent executive housekeeper. This individual will direct the inspectors (those who review the work of the housekeeping staff), the public area cleaners, the room attendants who actually clean guest rooms, and the laundry attendants who wash, dry, and fold towels and linen.

The job of the executive housekeeper is complex and growing more so every day. Properly cleaning a hotel requires knowledge of the available tools and chemicals that make cleaning jobs easier. Just as important as the selection of the best cleaning aids is the training of staff in the safe and proper use of these aids. This can be especially challenging if, as is often the case, the staff of the department is multinational and thus multilingual. Increasingly, hotel managers are aware that training housekeeping staff to work safely and to perform their work in a way that ensures the safety of guests is just as important as making sure the hotel is clean.

As a GM you will count on the expertise and professional standards of an excellent executive housekeeper to select employees who understand the importance of cleaning, to train those employees to meet the standards for cleanliness you have established, and to manage the inventories of cleaning supplies and guest service products needed to efficiently operate the housekeeping department.

In this chapter you will see how the work of the housekeeping department affects the work of other departments in the hotel and learn about the specific tasks involved in cleaning public spaces and guest rooms. It is critical that guests as well as hotel staff feel the housekeeping department does an excellent job. As a GM, it is an important part of your job to ensure that they do.

Chapter 9 Outline

Finishing/Folding
Storing
Delivering

HOTEL TERMINOLOGY AT WORK
GLOSSARY
ISSUES AT WORK

THE ROLE OF THE HOUSEKEEPING DEPARTMENT

The housekeeping department in a hotel is responsible for the hotel's cleanliness. Because that is true, every guest or visitor to the hotel will be able to readily see the results of the housekeeper's work. When a hotel's housekeeping staff is effective, guest satisfaction is high, employee morale is good, and ultimately the hotel is profitable. When the housekeeping staff's work is below par, guest complaints soar, employees at the front desk and in other areas of the hotel become disillusioned about management's commitment to quality service, and profits suffer due to increased allowances and adjustments made at the front desk to compensate guests for poor experiences. In addition, guests who feel the hotel was not clean simply do not return.

The number of areas within a hotel that must be kept clean are so many that the housekeeping department will nearly always be the hotel's largest department in terms of the number of employees. Depending on the type and size of hotel, the housekeeping department will generally be responsible for cleaning and maintaining all of the following:

Public Spaces
Lobby areas
Public restrooms
Exercise areas
Pool and spa areas
Employee break rooms
    and locker rooms
Selected meeting and food
    service areas
Front-desk areas
Management offices
Game rooms

Guest Room Areas
Elevators
Corridors
Stairwells
Guest rooms

Laundry
Laundry preparation areas
Laundry supply closets
Guest linen and supplies storage areas

Public Space

The **public space** in a hotel is among the first seen by the guests. In a larger hotel, these areas require the efforts of one or more full-time **house persons** to maintain proper cleanliness levels.

HOTEL TERMINOLOGY AT WORK

Public Space: Those areas within the hotel that can be freely accessed by guests and visitors. Examples include lobby areas, public restrooms, corridors, and stairwells.

House Person: The individual responsible for the cleaning of public spaces (the house). Also sometimes referred to as a PA (public area) cleaner or porter.

The decisions made about the number of employees required to clean these areas, as well as the frequency of cleaning, are the responsibility of the **executive housekeeper**.

HOTEL TERMINOLOGY AT WORK

Executive Housekeeper: The individual responsible for the management and operation of the housekeeping department.

It can sometimes be unclear whether a space in a hotel is public and thus the responsibility of the housekeeping department or if the space is specific to another department. A good example is the dining area in a full-service hotel. In some hotels, it may be the decision of the GM that housekeeping staff clean the dining room, whereas in other hotels the GM may decide it would be the responsibility of the food and beverage department to do the cleaning. The important rule is that every department knows its cleaning responsibilities and completes them.

MANAGERS AT WORK

"It isn't fair," Jenna Walbert, the executive housekeeper, said to J.D. Ojisama, the hotel GM. "My staff cleans the men's employee locker room every day, but just look at this!"

J.D. carefully inspected the area. Ashtrays overflowed, food was left on benches, dirty uniforms littered the ground, and newspapers were strewn about the floor. It was a mess.

"The guys in food and beverage and maintenance do this every day," continued Jenna angrily. "Our house person is too busy trying to keep the lobby carpets sharp to spend an hour a day down here cleaning up after our own staff. I think you should make the food and beverage and maintenance departments keep this clean. They are the ones who are messing it up."

Assume that housekeeping has been charged with the responsibility of cleaning employee locker rooms. What should J.D. tell Jenna Walbert? What should be done to solve her problem? What should be communicated to the other departments involved in the problem?

There will always be areas within a hotel where management judgments must be made about who should clean them. The GM, in conjunction with the executive housekeeper, must make these decisions so that the cleaning of every area within the hotel is the responsibility of a specific department. To facilitate this process, many hotels use a color-coded map of the entire property. Areas of cleaning responsibility are then assigned to each department by color code. Each department is responsible for cleaning and maintaining the areas that match its assigned color code. The responsibility for the cleaning of every area within the hotel is then known by the department head assigned to the area, and accountability can be ensured.

Guest Rooms

Providing perfectly cleaned guest rooms is a top priority for any well-run hotel. The cleaning of guest rooms is always the responsibility of the housekeeping department and must be executed flawlessly. The specifics of guest room cleaning are examined later in this chapter; however, what is less well known, but of utmost importance, is the communication role the housekeeping department must play in relaying **room status** information to the front-desk staff and room maintenance issues to the engineering and maintenance department.

Providing exceptionally well-cleaned rooms helps the front office sell a hotel's rooms at the highest possible rate.

HOTEL TERMINOLOGY AT WORK

Room Status: The up-to-date (actual) condition (occupied, vacant, dirty, etc.) of the hotel's individual guest rooms.

In most hotels, it is a strict policy that staff does not assign a guest to a room unless that room has been:

1. Properly cleaned by the housekeeping department
2. Verified as clean by a second member of housekeeping
3. The room's status has been reported to the front desk

At first glance this might appear to be a simple process, but it is quite complex and contains the potential for a variety of miscommunications if the process is not managed properly.

To examine the importance of maintaining accurate guest room status, let's examine the hypothetical stay of Mr. and Mrs. Flood. This couple checks into a room at the Waldo Hotel at 4:00 P.M. on Monday afternoon and are assigned to a room that the housekeeping staff has reported to the front desk is "Clean and Vacant." That is, housekeeping has communicated that the room has been cleaned and inspected for cleanliness and that no other guest is occupying the room. If, in fact, the room is clean and no other guest is assigned to it, the Floods, upon arriving at the room, should have no housekeeping-related complaints about it.

Consider, however, the problems that could occur if the room, instead of being clean, was scheduled for cleaning but the cleaning had not yet occurred. In this case,

Housekeeping Term	Meaning
Clean and Vacant	The room is vacant, has been cleaned, and can be assigned to a guest.
Occupied	The room is registered to a current guest.
On-Change	The room is vacant but not yet cleaned.
Do Not Disturb	The room is occupied but has not been cleaned due to the guest's request not to be disturbed.
Sleep-out (Sleeper)	The room is reported as occupied, but the room was not used (bed not used, no personal belongings in room) and the guest is not present.
Stay-over	The guest will stay in the room at least one more night.
Due Out	The guest(s) have indicated this is the last day they will use the room.
Check Out	The guest(s) have departed.
Out of Order	The room is unrentable and thus unassignable at this time.
Lock Out	The guest has left personal items in the room, but will be denied access until approved to reenter by management.
Late Check Out	The guests have requested and been given an extension of the regular check-out time.

FIGURE 9.1   Room Status Terminology

the couple would have been checked into a dirty room and, of course, would return to the front-desk area unhappy and concerned about the overall quality of their stay. In a similar manner, if the room is cleaned but the Floods discover someone's possessions (or someone!) in the room upon their arrival, they will again be upset and return to the front-desk area unhappy and concerned about the quality of the hotel's management staff.

As a GM, it is critical that your housekeeping staff continuously and accurately maintain the room status of all guest rooms in the hotel that are subject to rental. Figure 9.1 lists the room status definitions commonly used in U.S. hotels. Specific companies or areas of the country may vary the terms (and the abbreviations used to designate them) somewhat; however, these terms or their equivalents must be used in the hotel if housekeeping is to accurately represent room status to the front desk.

It is easy to see that the housekeeping department must carefully report the status of rooms. The process of communicating room status between housekeeping and the front desk begins each morning when the housekeeping department receives, from the front desk, an occupancy report produced as part of the night audit. This occupancy report will detail, for each room, the room status the PMS is displaying for front-desk agents. If there are no discrepancies, the report will accurately show those rooms that are stay-overs, occupied, clean and vacant, on-change (dirty), out of order, and so forth. It is up to the housekeeping department to take this report and, as room status changes are made, report those changes to the front desk, just as the front desk should communicate its known room status changes to housekeeping.

If both departments perform their jobs well, an accurate, up-to-date room status is maintained in the PMS throughout the day. Generally, the front desk notifies the housekeeping department of room status changes, such as check outs, throughout the day by calling the executive housekeeper or a housekeeping supervisor, updating the PMS (when the housekeeping department has easy access to it), or using another communication device such as a two-way radio. Changes in room status made by housekeeping can be communicated to the front desk in a variety of ways also, including having a housekeeping supervisor contact the front desk by telephone (from each room as that room's status changes), via radio or handheld computer, or by using the telephone's interface with the PMS to make the changes via codes entered into the telephone in the affected room.

At the end of the housekeeping shift, the housekeeping department will prepare a final room status report based on a physical check of each room. This report is then compared with the updated PMS occupancy report to identify any discrepancies. If any exist, the front-office manager would then investigate these discrepancies. As a GM, it is important that you ensure this cross-checking is completed daily. If, for example, a front-desk agent is fraudulently selling rooms to guests (assigning the guests to a room but not posting the income to the hotel's PMS), the discrepancy report would uncover this activity because the guest room, reported as "vacant" in the PMS, would show as "occupied" on the housekeeping room status report.

An additional and absolutely critical communication line must exist between housekeeping and the engineering and maintenance departments. As guests use guest rooms, repair and replacement issues occur. For example, when lightbulbs burn out in a guest room, they must be replaced. This simple task may be assigned to housekeeping. If, however, a guest accidentally breaks the leg off of a chair in the room, or if a toilet is running constantly, a repair must be requested by housekeeping. It will always be the case that the ability of the housekeeping department to aggressively identify and then quickly report needed room repairs makes a significant difference in the satisfaction level of guests subsequently using the rooms. The actual method used by housekeeping to report room issues to the engineering and maintenance department is detailed in Chapter 11 (Facility Engineering and Maintenance). The important point to remember is that the housekeeping department, because its staff members are in the rooms most frequently, plays a critical role in maintaining room quality by reporting room defects quickly and accurately to those individuals responsible for eliminating those defects. Engineering and maintenance makes the repairs, cleans up their work, or if appropriate, contacts housekeeping to retidy the room prior to renting it to a guest.

Laundry

Hotels generate a tremendous amount of laundry. Some hotels, especially smaller ones, may not actually do their laundry on site. Most hotels, however, do their own laundry. When you consider the time, equipment, and expertise required to properly wash, dry, and fold the large amount of **linen** and **terry** generated by a hotel, as well as employee uniforms and other laundry items, it is not surprising that laundry represents one of the hotel's largest expenses and that an **OPL** must be properly managed if the hotel is to control this important cost.

HOTEL TERMINOLOGY AT WORK

Linen: A generic term for the guest room sheets, pillowcases, tablecloths, and napkins washed and dried in the laundry area.

Terry: A generic term for the bath towels, hand towels, and washcloths washed and dried in the laundry area.

OPL: Short for "on premise laundry."

A hotel's laundry needs will vary with its size and product offerings. A smaller (less than 100 rooms) extended-stay or limited-service property may find that it does less than 500,000 pounds of laundry per year. At this volume level, the hotel may use linens that are wrinkle free, and thus the OPL may consist simply of washers and dryers. Larger, full-service hotels with extensive food and beverage volume will find their OPL needs expanded due to the tablecloths and napkins processed in the laundry, as well as the increased linen and terry needs when there are more guest rooms. In hotels of this type, additional laundry equipment required to press and fold the laundered items may be required. In very large hotels, the OPL may process well over 1 million pounds of laundry per year and will likely employ dozens of staff, as well as maintain a substantial number of high-volume laundry-related pieces of equipment. For some selected hotels, it makes the most sense to enter into a contract with a company that specializes in laundry operations and then allow that company to operate the laundry or provide all of its linen and terry on a daily delivery basis. Thus, just as a hotel might enter into a contract with a lawn service to cut and trim the hotel's grounds, or with a window washing company to keep its windows clean, contracted laundry services can be beneficial, especially when the hotel's laundry needs are particularly complicated or unique. Regardless of its size, or who operates it, however, the laundry is a major responsibility of the housekeeping department and the executive housekeeper.

THE INTERNET AT WORK

Large-volume OPLs require large-volume equipment. One of the hotel industry's leading suppliers of large-volume laundry equipment is the Pellerin Milnor Corporation. To review some features of their "tunnel washer" designed specifically for OPLs that process laundry for hotels of 500 rooms or more, go to

www.milnor.com

When you arrive, review the information about their tunnel washers.

STAFFING THE DEPARTMENT

Traditionally the housekeeping department has been one of the most difficult to staff in the entire hotel. This is because of the large number of housekeeping staff needed, the difficulty of the work, and, unfortunately in some cases, a wage structure that does not ensure that the best potential employees seek careers in this department of the hotel. Properly approached and fairly treated, however, this department can be well staffed with stable, highly professional employees who add tremendously to the success of the hotel.

Executive Housekeeper

Those GMs whose staff includes a highly trained, motivated, professional executive housekeeper have a tremendous advantage over those who do not. An effective executive housekeeper is not only a valuable member of the EOC, he or she is also an effective administrator, department motivator, and team player.

At many hotels, the executive housekeeper is an individual that worked his or her way up from an entry-level housekeeping position. In other hotels, the executive housekeeper may not have held any entry-level housekeeping positions. In either case, the skills required to be an effective executive housekeeper, like the skills needed by all managers, include those related to planning, organizing, directing, and controlling

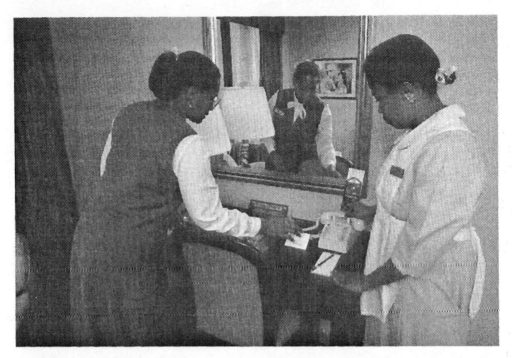

Professional executive housekeepers will motivate their staffs without appearing overly critical.

the activities of the department. Executive housekeepers' commitment to cleanliness must be unquestioned, their standards must be impeccable, their dedication to their area unflinching, and their human resources skills well above average for managers. It is only with these characteristics that the hotel's executive housekeeper will provide the departmental leadership required in today's competitive hotel environment.

THE INTERNET AT WORK

Those GMs who want to stay abreast of the rapidly changing health, safety, and technology issues involved in housekeeping would do well to join, or encourage the hotel's executive housekeeper to join, the International Executive Housekeeper's Association (IEHA). With over 6,000 members, the IEHA offers educational programs and certification and publishes a monthly magazine. To view their Web site, go to

www.ieha.org

Room Inspectors

In most hotels, one or more individuals hold the position of **inspector** in the housekeeping department. These individuals report directly to the executive housekeeper.

HOTEL TERMINOLOGY AT WORK

Inspector: The individual(s) responsible for physically checking the room status of guest rooms, as well as other tasks as assigned by the executive housekeeper.

Regardless of a hotel's size, it is important that someone verify the actual readiness of guest rooms before they are listed in the PMS as clean, vacant, and available to sell. This job falls to the inspectors. An inspector is the individual who physically enters and checks a guest room after it has been cleaned to determine whether any areas that should have been cleaned have been missed or if there are other defects in the room that require further attention.

In a large hotel, there may be several inspectors working at the same time. The primary responsibility of the inspector is to assess the quality of room cleanliness, but more importantly, it is to point out deficiencies to **room attendants**, get those deficiencies corrected, and report revisions to room status to the executive housekeeper or the front desk.

HOTEL TERMINOLOGY AT WORK

Room Attendants: The individual(s) responsible for cleaning guest rooms. Sometimes referred to as "housekeepers." Also sometimes called "maids," by a hotel's guests, but this term is not used by members of any enlightened hotel management team.

An effective inspector is one with high standards of cleanliness and the ability to point out deficiencies in rooms reportedly cleaned by room attendants in a way that motivates those attendants to do their very best work without appearing overly critical of sincere efforts to do a good job. Inspectors are truly a hotel guest's best friend because it is this sharp-eyed individual who will enforce the standards of cleanliness established by the executive housekeeper and the GM.

Each executive housekeeper creates an appropriate inspection checklist for guest rooms based upon the contents and the physical layout of the room. As a GM, you should review this checklist on a regular basis with the executive housekeeper and compare it with your own checklist (presented later in this chapter). The executive housekeeper's checklist should be revised as needed to ensure appropriate attention is paid to potential problem areas that may be frequently overlooked by room attendants (who may have their own room checklists), as well as to institute additional staff training when consistent deficiencies become apparent.

Room Attendants

Highly skilled and motivated room attendants are incredibly vital to a hotel's success. Yet in many hotels recruiting, selecting, and retaining a sufficient number of room attendants to adequately clean the number of rooms sold is a difficult process. Hotels operate shorthanded in the room attendant area and room cleanliness suffers, managers end up cleaning rooms, and inspectors sometimes are not able to inspect because they are too busy helping clean rooms to do their jobs properly. When GMs inquire about the difficulty of retaining quality room attendants and the problems that result, they are often told things like:

- We don't pay enough to attract the right people.
- The work is too hard.
- There is a labor shortage.

- Today's workers simply won't work.
- Workers don't care about doing a good job anymore.

As a GM, it is sometimes tempting to accept statements such as these as truth. You should not because they are simply not true. The best executive housekeepers and GMs not only have adequate numbers of room attendants on staff, but they also have a waiting list of room attendants from other area hotels hoping to join their staff. Strategies designed to properly recruit and retain room attendants must be put in place if your hotel is to be perceived as the employer of choice for your area's best room attendants.

Properly cleaning guest rooms can be hard and physically demanding work. It is also true that entry-level room attendant wages are often among the lowest in the hotel. It is possible, and critical, however, to build a highly motivated, dedicated staff of room attendants. The approaches to doing so are many but, at minimum, include:

- Treating room attendants with the respect they deserve at all times.
- Ensuring that room attendants are supervised only by excellent supervisors.
- Maintaining room cleaning assignment policies that are perceived as fair by the room attendants.
- Providing excellent, ongoing training.
- Providing a realistic career ladder for room attendants.
- Enforcing housekeeping department policies that affect room attendants consistently and without favoritism.
- Ensuring room attendant safety through training and appropriate hotel policies.
- Providing benefit packages competitive for the area.
- Paying fair wages.

Many hotel GMs disagree about what it means to pay "fair wages" to room attendants. Some hotels simply pay room attendants an hourly wage. Others add incentives for extra effort to the hourly wage such as meeting established quality levels. Still others pay room attendants a designated dollar amount for each room cleaned. Regardless of the payment approach used, it is important that room attendants are treated fairly. Some hoteliers treat room attendants as if they are not important. Hotels that do this will inevitably lose their best room attendants to those hotels that demonstrate real concern for these crucial staff members.

THE INTERNET AT WORK

It is often hard to recruit and retain highly qualified workers. In addition, getting new people off on the right foot and training people to become good trainers are major housekeeping issues today. The following two books provide tips that are just that: handy and quick ideas to help address the hourly employee shortages sometimes found in housekeeping (and other) departments:

50 One-Minute Tips for Recruiting Employees
50 One-Minute Tips for Retaining Employees

You can find these books at www.courseilt.com

Additional Housekeeping Staff

In addition to the executive housekeeper, inspectors, and room attendants required, the housekeeping department will employ, depending on its size, one or more house persons for the cleaning of public spaces as well as records or payroll clerks who serve as administrative assistants to the executive housekeeper and OPL workers.

The OPL in a hotel is often a hot and physically demanding place to work. Employees needed in this area include those actually moving linen and terry from the guest rooms to the laundry area, those loading and unloading washers and dryers, and those responsible for folding and storing the cleaned items, as well as transporting them back to carts or storage areas located near guest rooms. In some special cases, seamstresses are even employed to care for uniforms and guest clothes.

Some GMs believe these OPL jobs are easily filled. In fact, maintaining quality workers in the OPL is as difficult as any other area of the hotel. The same employee approaches previously identified as assisting in the recruitment and retention of room attendants, however, will be extremely helpful in maintaining a quality OPL staff. A hotel's financial investment in linen, terry, and the machines used to clean and maintain them is significant. Without a quality OPL workforce, and proper supervision, the value of these investments can quickly be reduced.

MANAGING HOUSEKEEPING

The executive housekeeper in a hotel must be a very knowledgeable individual. He or she must know about personnel administration, budgeting, laundry sanitation, fabrics and uniforms, and room-cleaning chemicals and routines; of course, he or she should be guest-service oriented. Only the GM has more responsibility for the cleanliness of the facility. Because of this, the partnership between the executive housekeeper and the GM must be a strong one, based upon mutual respect for the ability of each.

MANAGERS AT WORK

"The problem, I'm afraid, is just age," Jenna Walbert, the executive housekeeper, said to J.D. Ojisama, the hotel GM.

"What do you mean?" asked J.D.

"Well, Penny Cooper has worked as a housekeeper in this hotel for over twenty-five years and has always done an excellent job. But recently she has had more trouble doing her share of the rooms in the time allowed. Some of the other room attendants are complaining because, after they finish their own rooms, they are assigned to help Penny finish hers."

"She tries," continued Jenna, "but as you know, room cleaning is a tough, physically demanding job. Lots of the younger room attendants are challenged until they get the hang of things. In Penny's case, she knows what to do—it's just that she can't do it as fast as she used to. The room inspectors are finding the quality of her work acceptable; it's the quantity that is the problem. I wonder how long we can keep her?"

Assume you are J.D. What would you advise Jenna to do about Penny's situation? What would you advise her to say to the other room attendants? What human resources–related issues and laws might come into play in this situation?

Managers in the housekeeping department must be among a hotel's most talented. The challenges of keeping a hotel clean are many, and the special issues faced by the executive housekeeper and the housekeeping staff requires that, as a GM, you are especially encouraging and supportive of this area. Some of the unique issues faced by the department include those related to safety, employee scheduling, and inventory management.

SPECIALIZED CLEANING KNOWLEDGE FOR HOUSEKEEPERS

Just as those managers in the controller's office, food and beverage or hotel sales will have specialized knowledge, so too must those in housekeeping management. Knowing the best way to instruct employees in the removal of different stains from various surfaces is just one example. Professional cleaners use:

Acid-Based Cleaners. For mineral deposits such as iron stains, lime buildup, rust, scale, and water spots. Works best when used on china, metal, glass, cement, quarry tile, and plastic.

Alkali-Based Cleaners. For normal soil, grime, dirt, food stains, scuff marks, crayons, and ink. Works best when used on vinyl, metal, china, linoleum, glass, carpets, fabrics, wood, Formica, and cement.

Solvent-Based Cleaners. For grease, motor oil, paint, varnish, and human fingerprints. Works best when used on glass, engines, metal machine parts, quarry tile, and concrete.

Safety

Employee accident rates in the housekeeping department are generally among the highest in the hotel. There are two reasons for this. First is simply that the housekeeping department is usually one of the hotel's largest in terms of the number of workers it employs. The second reason, however, relates to the physical nature of the job. Housekeepers often work with equipment and supplies that must be very carefully handled if accidents are to be avoided. Proper housekeeping equipment and supplies help improve productivity and safety as well as reduce accidents; therefore, these items should be provided to each housekeeper and placed appropriately on every **room attendant cart**. If they are not, unnecessary on-the-job injuries will result and medical-related costs for the hotel will increase.

HOTEL TERMINOLOGY AT WORK

Room Attendant Cart: A wheeled cart that contains all of the items needed to properly and safely clean and restock a guest room.

■

Training the housekeeping staff properly is just as important as providing them with the tools to do their jobs. Employee training is always a crucial aspect of the executive housekeeper's job, and safety training is the most essential type that can be provided. As the hotel's GM, it is part of your job to ensure that this department has the necessary equipment, supplies, and training programs in place to minimize threats to worker safety. In nearly all cases, a hotel's franchisor will be a significant source of assistance in providing training aids. This is especially true in housekeeping. Although the proprietary nature and length of such training materials (usually in the form of video or audio training and often in several languages) prevents their publication in this text, generic materials for safety training in housekeeping, like many other areas of a hotel, can be readily examined at the EI-AH&LA's Web site (www.ei-ahla.org).

Equipment and Supplies

Housekeepers' jobs often require the use of machines such as vacuum cleaners, washers, dryers, high-capacity linen ironing and folding apparatus, and other equipment.

Workers should never be allowed to operate these until they are fully trained. Supplies used by housekeepers in the completion of their daily tasks include powerful cleaners and chemicals that, properly used, make these worker's jobs easier. Improperly used, the same chemicals and cleaners can cause nausea, skin rashes, vomiting, blindness, and even death. A good rule to follow is that all housekeeping employees handle only those pieces of machinery and supplies that they have been properly and thoroughly trained to handle. Specific information on how to safely handle special chemicals and cleaners can be found on the mandatory material safety data sheets (MSDSs) that must be secured and made readily available for employee inspection for each chemical or cleaning product used by the hotel (see specific MSDS information in Chapter 12, Safety and Property Security).

Training

All hotel employees require both general and department-specific training, and the housekeeping department is no exception. In housekeeping, particular areas of training concern include:

- Chemical handling
- Cleaning procedures
- Correct lifting techniques
- Properly entering guest rooms
- Contending with guest rooms containing:
  - Firearms
  - Uncaged pets/animals
  - Individuals perceived to be threatening
  - Guests who are ill/unconscious
  - Drugs and drug paraphenalia
  - Blood and potential **blood-borne pathogens**
- Guest service
- Guest room security
- Lost and found procedures

HOTEL TERMINOLOGY AT WORK

Blood-Borne Pathogen: Any microorganism or virus, carried by blood, that can cause a disease.

Chemical warning labels should include information related to a product's health, flammability, reactivity, and personal protection.

Of the special training required by housekeeping staff, blood-borne pathogens and lost and found training deserve the special attention of the GM. Blood-borne pathogen training is especially important for room attendants because they can readily come into contact with body fluids and/or bloody sheets, towels, or tissues as they clean guest rooms. If employees are not trained in the proper procedures for such situations, they could become infected. In addition, needles from intravenous drug users or those with medical conditions requiring the use of hypodermic needles can result in threats to the safety of room attendants. Human immunodeficiency virus (HIV) is a serious disease spread by blood-borne pathogens. This and other health threats must be addressed through proper training, and it is the responsibility of the executive housekeeper and GM to see that such training takes place. Of particular concern to executive housekeepers should be the minimization of hepatitis threats.

Hepatitis is a general term used to describe inflammation (swelling) of the liver. Hepatitis B is an infection of the liver caused by the hepatitis B virus (HBV). Workers who are exposed to human blood can be at risk of acquiring hepatitis B at the workplace. Most people infected with HBV develop antibodies (produced by the body's immune system) against the disease and will totally clear the virus from the body without ever getting seriously ill. The 5 percent–10 percent of those persons who do not produce antibodies will develop chronic hepatitis B.

Hepatitis B is a very resilient virus. Although HIV, the virus that causes AIDS, can only live for 24 hours in dried blood, the hepatitis B virus can survive for at least a week in dried blood at room temperature on floors and other surfaces. The hepatitis B virus can be detected through a blood test about six weeks after exposure to HBV, and a safe and effective vaccine exists to prevent hepatitis B infection. The vaccine is a series of three shots taken at specific intervals typically within six months. It offers full protection against the virus and is one of the safest vaccines available, having virtually no side effects. The Occupational Safety and Health

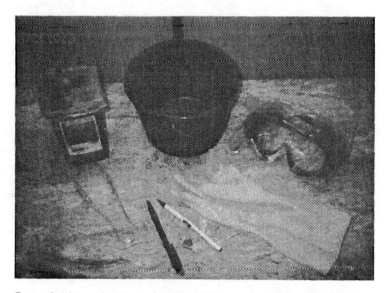

Executive housekeepers should provide room attendants with required safety equipment, including those related to blood-borne pathogens.

Administration's (OSHA's) Blood-Borne Pathogens Standard requires employers to offer the hepatitis B vaccine to workers such as housekeepers, laundry workers, and others who may be exposed to blood and other infectious materials before they begin their jobs.

THE INTERNET AT WORK

The federal government is very involved in the development of standards, education, and training materials for workers who could be exposed to blood-borne pathogens. To view a Web site devoted exclusively to this topic, go to

www.osha-slc.gov/SLTC/bloodbornepathogens/index.html

THE INTERNET AT WORK

Because housekeepers often come from a variety of backgrounds, language barriers in the housekeeping department can make training difficult. To view an innovative, dialogue-free video training program for room attendants developed for the EI-AH&LA, with the vision and support of then Executive Director E. Ray Swan, and now marketed extensively by them, go to

www.ei-ahla.org

When you arrive, select "Products and Resources," then select "Product by Classification: Department/Position," then select "Housekeeping," then select "World Trainer: Guestroom and Bathroom Cleaning."

Employee Scheduling

Properly scheduling employees in the housekeeping department requires skill on the part of the manager creating the schedule and often flexibility on the part of the staff. Depending on the size and occupancy rate of the hotel, it is not unusual to find housekeeping staff working at any time of the day or night. Public-space cleaners may find that late night or early morning hours are best for completing their work, and laundry workers, to complete the number of loads needed to support the hotel's occupancy levels, may also work very late or early.

Room attendants' work schedules are generally less flexible with regard to when they can work. That is, guests in stay-over rooms will expect their rooms to be cleaned between the time they leave and the time they are reasonably likely to return to their room after their day's activities. Therefore, unless the guest requests alternative times, stay-over rooms in the typical hotel should be cleaned between 8:00 A.M. and 3:00 P.M. In addition, the housekeeping staff must have cleaned enough rooms to allow front-desk staff to check guests in at the check-in time established by the hotel. Thus, if check in is at 3:00 P.M., sufficient rooms must be ready to allow guests to be assigned a room promptly upon their 3:00 P.M. arrival. If this is not done and arriving guests are told by front-desk staff, "Your room is not ready yet, housekeeping is working on cleaning rooms now!" guest dissatisfaction will likely result.

The number of room attendants that should be scheduled on any given day depends on several factors, including the size of the guest rooms, amenities in the rooms, the number of rooms to be cleaned, and the amount, if any, of **deep cleaning**, taking place.

HOTEL TERMINOLOGY AT WORK

Deep Cleaning: The intensive cleaning of a guest room, typically including the thorough cleaning of items such as drapes, lamp shades, carpets, furniture, walls, and the like.

Regularly scheduled deep cleaning of guest rooms is one mark of an effective housekeeping department.

∎

Larger guest rooms take more time to properly clean than smaller ones, and rooms with special amenities such as refrigerators, microwaves, stoves, and dining areas require more attendant time than those without these features.

The actual number of rooms to be cleaned is the variable most critical to effective scheduling, and it is important to realize that this number is subject to normal, but rapid, fluctuation. Assume, for example, that an executive housekeeper wishes to inform employees one week ahead of time about that week's work schedule. That is, if Monday were the first day of the month, the executive housekeeper would like to post, on that day, the room attendant work schedule for the week of the 8th through the 15th. Based upon the room sales forecast provided by the GM or front-office manager, the executive housekeeper determines the proper number of room attendants needed and then posts the schedule. If, however, on the 5th of that same month the sales department makes a large (75 rooms per night) but last-minute sale to guests arriving on the 7th and staying through the 10th, the number of room attendants needed will vary greatly from the original schedule. Alternatively, if significant numbers of guest reservation cancellations occur, the number of room attendants originally scheduled may be too great. This can be the case when inclement weather, airport closings, or other unusual events cause major disruptions in typical travel patterns.

Some inexperienced executive housekeepers, in an attempt to firmly quantify the number of workers needed on a given day, rely exclusively on a **minutes per room** target to establish the room attendants' schedule.

HOTEL TERMINOLOGY AT WORK

Minutes per Room: The average number of minutes required to clean a guest room. Determined by the following computation:

$$\frac{\text{Total number of minutes worked by room attendants}}{\text{Total number of guest rooms cleaned}} = \text{Minutes per room}$$

∎

For example, if the number of minutes typically required per room in a hotel is 30, and if it is estimated that 200 rooms are to be sold, the two-step formula used to compute the number of room attendant hours that should be scheduled would be:

30 minutes per room × 200 rooms = 6,000 minutes

$$\frac{6{,}000 \text{ minutes}}{60 \text{ minutes per hour}} = 100 \text{ hours of room attendant time}$$

The actual number of room attendants scheduled would depend on the number of full- and part-time housekeepers placed on the schedule. In some hotels, the housekeeping staff may, on occasion, be augmented by one or more externally contracted workers who work for companies that provide cleaning services. These companies contract with hotels to provide additional housekeepers during busy times. This can be beneficial for hotels that for rather short periods of time may sell more hotel rooms than their regular housekeeping cleaning can adequately clean. These contract workers, however, typically are quite expensive and may not know the specific cleaning procedures used in an individual hotel as well as that hotel's regular housekeeping staff. They nevertheless can sometimes be a valuable addition to a hotel's regular cleaning staffs' and provide a valuable service when needed.

Experienced housekeepers rely both on rooms per minute computations and knowledge of the guests themselves to determine the actual number of room attendant hours that should be scheduled on a given day. For example, executive housekeepers know it takes more minutes to clean a room in which the guest has checked out than one in which the guest is a stay-over. As a result, when the percentage of guest rooms that are stay-overs increases, the number of room attendant minutes (and therefore total hours) required to clean those rooms declines. Likewise, when a room has multiple occupants, it is more likely to require additional cleaning time than does a room housing only a single guest. With experience, executive housekeepers and GMs can agree upon a formula that uses both minutes per room and the unique characteristics of the hotel's guests and sales patterns to determine achievable productivity levels and thus scheduling levels for room attendants.

Inventory Management

The housekeeping department maintains a large number of products used in the cleaning and servicing of rooms. The following partial list gives some indication of the number of inventory items that must be maintained by the executive housekeeper:

Sheets (all sizes)	Glass cleaners
Pillowcases	Furniture polish
Bedspreads	Acid-based cleaners
Bath towels	Glassware
Hand towels	Cups
Washcloths	Coffee/coffee filters
Soaps	In-room literature
Shampoos	Telephone books
Conditioners	Pens
Sewing kits	Paper pads

If too many units of any item are kept in storage, the hotel may have committed money to housekeeping inventory levels that could be better put to use elsewhere in the hotel. Alternatively, if too few items are kept on hand, housekeepers may not have the products they need to properly clean and service rooms. Therefore, the executive housekeeper must know how much of each item is in use, in storage, and/or on order. Purchasing and receiving replacements for some items such as custom bedspreads, drapes, or logo items may take weeks or even months. Because that is true, an actual monthly count of all significant housekeeping supplies is strongly recommended. As a GM, these counts should be submitted to you to ensure that they have in fact been taken.

A second value of monthly inventories is that they allow the executive house-keeper to compute monthly **product usage reports**.

HOTEL TERMINOLOGY AT WORK

Product Usage Report: A report detailing the amount of an inventoried item used by a hotel in a specified time period (i.e., week, month, quarter, year).

■

Figure 9.2 is an example of a monthly product usage report for king-size bedsheets. It is completed using actual product counts taken at the beginning of each month by the housekeeping staff. Note that this format can be used to compute product usage in any department and for any product in the hotel, as well as for any housekeeping product.

When determining the count of products in housekeeping, it is important to remember to count the entire product on hand, whether it is in use, in storage, or in reserve. In the example of king-size bedsheets, to accurately determine the total number of these actually on hand, physical counts would need to be taken in:

- Guest rooms
- Room attendant carts
- Soiled linen areas (including washers and dryers)
- Clean linen storage areas
- New product (unopened) product storage areas

Note that in Figure 9.2, 117 bedsheets were "used" in the month. This may mean the sheets were taken out of service because they were too badly stained to continue using, that the sheets had become torn or frayed beyond use, or that they were stolen. Regardless of the reason, if the physical count of the king-size bedsheets is accurate, management knows the number and can easily compute the cost of king-size sheets taken out of service in January. The executive housekeeper, assisted by the housekeeping staff, should compute monthly usage rates on all significant housekeeping items.

Department: Housekeeping	Item: King-size Sheets
Prepared By:	Date:
For Period:	to

Count on: January 1		850 units
	Plus	
Purchased in month		144 units
Total in service		994 units
	Less	
Count on: February 1		877 units
Total Monthly Usage		**117**

FIGURE 9.2 Waldo Hotel Product Usage Report

Lost and Found

Often, guests either intentionally or accidentally leave valuable items in their rooms when they check out. As a result, the housekeeping department must have specific written lost and found procedures in place.

Sometimes it is hard to know what to do with property whose ownership is unknown. In most states, the law makes a distinction between three types of property whose ownership is in doubt. Each of the three types of unclaimed property requires that your housekeeping staff respond differently. The three property types are:

- *Mislaid Property.* The owner has unintentionally left the item(s) behind.
- *Lost Property.* The owner has unintentionally left the item(s) behind, then forgotten them.
- *Abandoned Property.* The owner has intentionally left the item(s) behind.

The law requires that hotels safeguard mislaid property until the rightful owner returns. For example, a laptop computer left in a guest room is to be protected by the hotel until its owner returns. To throw or give the computer away on the same day it was discovered in the room would be illegal. In fact, if the hotel were to give it away to someone other than its rightful owner, the hotel itself would be responsible to the actual owner for the value of the computer. As the GM, you should make sure a policy is in place requiring that employees discovering mislaid property turn it over to their supervisor.

In the case of a laptop computer, it is highly likely that the guest, upon discovering that the computer has been mislaid, will contact the hotel to arrange for the computer's return. If that does not happen in a reasonable amount of time (in most states 60 to 90 days) the mislaid property would now, from a legal perspective, be considered lost property (property that the owner has forgotten).

A hotel must hold unclaimed property until the rightful owner returns to claim it. Also, in many states, the item's finder must make a good-faith effort to return the lost item to its owner. For example, if a leather jacket is left in a guest room, the hotel, upon discovering the owner's name and telephone number sewn into the jacket's lining, must attempt to reach the jacket's owner. As with mislaid property, employees who find lost property in the course of their work should be required to give the property to their employer.

The length of time a hotel must hold lost property depends on the value of the property. The greater the value, the more reasonable it is to hold it for an extended period of time. The GM should establish, in conjunction with the executive housekeeper, the length of time mislaid and lost property should be held before the hotel disposes of it. In most cases, 90 days is a reasonable time to hold items found in a hotel.

In the case of abandoned property, the owner has no intention of returning to retrieve the item(s). Interestingly, the law does not require a hotel to attempt to find an abandoned property's owner. It is also true that the majority of guest items left in hotel rooms fall into this category. Magazines, worn-out clothing, personal toiletry items such as combs and razors, and a variety of grocery items are often abandoned.

It can be difficult for a hotel manager to know when an item has been abandoned rather than misplaced or lost. Therefore, when in doubt, property left behind in a room or found in a lobby area should be treated as either mislaid or lost. After it is held for a reasonable period of time, the hotel should dispose of the property. Some hotels give such items to local charities; others give the items to the hotel employee that found them.

Regardless of the hotel's abandoned property policy, it is the job of the executive housekeeper to have a written lost and found procedure in place that protects guest property until it is in fact declared abandoned. In those hotels with designated safety and security departments, the head of that department may develop this policy and may even be responsible for the security of any misplaced, lost, or abandoned items.

In all cases, preprinted forms for keeping information related to lost and found items are readily available from a variety of business forms sources and can be useful. Regardless of the form(s) used, the executive housekeeper, to protect the hotel, should have a written record of:

- The date the item was found
- A description of the item
- Location where the item was found (room number, if applicable)
- Name of the finder
- Supervisor who received the item

When returned to the rightful owner, or disposed of, the written record should include:

- The date the item was returned to the owner
- Owner's name/address/telephone number
- Housekeeping manager returning the item
- Method of return (mail, in person, and so forth)
- Date the property was declared to be abandoned
- Name of hotel employee receiving the abandoned property

THE INTERNET AT WORK

There are a variety of companies that sell complete "lost and found" documentation packages that include forms and log books.

The American Hotel Registry company is a full-service hotel products supplier. To view this innovative company's lost and found (and other) product offerings, go to

www.americanhotel.com

FACILITY CARE AND CLEANING

Although it is beyond the scope of this book to detail the specific how-to's of public-space cleaning, guest room cleaning, and laundry operations, it is important that GMs know what to look for when inspecting these areas. GMs often see and work in the public spaces of the hotel in the course of their daily activities, and therefore it is common for GMs to identify public space areas that need further attention from housekeeping to maintain desired cleanliness standards.

What is less common is for the GM, working with the executive housekeeper, to participate in consistent, physical guest room and laundry room inspections. GMs simply must inspect these areas on a regular (weekly) basis. It is only through this process that executive housekeepers and inspectors will have a good idea about the cleanliness standards that the GM expects to be in place. Also, it is often the GM who knows, because of interaction with the front desk, those cleanliness deficiencies within guest rooms that have generated the most guest complaints.

Inspection sheets developed to identify areas to be evaluated during routine inspections of public spaces, guest bathroom and sleeping room areas, and the laundry are a good idea. They focus attention on every area affecting guest satisfaction. Of course, the actual property inspection sheets used by a hotel must be built upon the specific needs and characteristics of that hotel. Inspection checklists, however, can provide an excellent starting point for the inspection process and are presented next in this chapter.

Public-Space Cleaning

A consistent theme in this chapter is the importance of guest room cleanliness because it is very critical to the long-term success of the hotel. Public spaces, however, are equally important because they form the basis for a guest's initial impression of the property. It is therefore essential that goals for all public-space areas include excellent appearance and impeccable cleanliness. Each hotel will have its own requirements for public-space cleaning based on its size and product offerings. Figure 9.3 is an inspection checklist designed to help the GM (and managers on duty) examine some public spaces common to many hotels. It should be modified to reflect the needs of the hotel using it.

Guest Room Cleaning

Effective guest room cleaning is the heart of the housekeeping department, as well as the entire hotel. In most hotels, this activity, more than any other, will determine the long-term success or failure of the property. It must be done extremely well. A motivated executive housekeeper and well-trained staff are required, but so, too, is the interest of the GM. Routine inspections that identify areas for improvement and reinforce good practices are a tremendous help in keeping the housekeeping department operating at its best. Too often, GMs seek to evaluate the effectiveness of their housekeeping departments only through the computation of labor, cleaning, or guest supplies **costs per occupied room**.

HOTEL TERMINOLOGY AT WORK

Cost per Occupied Room: Total costs incurred for an item or area, divided by the number of rooms occupied in the hotel for the time period examined.

For example, in a hotel that spent $7,000 on room attendant wages in a week that the hotel sold 1,000 rooms, the cost per occupied room for room attendants would be computed as

$$\frac{\$7,000 \text{ room attendant cost}}{1,000 \text{ rooms sold}} = \$7 \text{ room attendant cost per occupied room}$$

∎

It is wrong to think that lower costs per occupied room or fewer minutes spent cleaning each room is always "better." In fact, spending too few dollars or too few minutes cleaning each guest room is as bad, or worse, than spending too many dollars or minutes. The proper approach for a GM is to inspect guest rooms and then determine whether the hotel is maximizing the effectiveness of the housekeeping department. If it is not, additional staff training in procedures or staff additions or replacements may be required, and the GM or executive housekeeper should implement these changes.

GM's Public Space Inspection				
Date: _____	Inspection assisted by: _____			
Item/Area	**Outstanding**	**Acceptable**	**Unacceptable**	**Comments**
Lobby/Front Desk				
Entrance door/glass clean				
Ashtrays clean				
Front-desk counter area clean				
Drapes/window treatments clean				
Decorative pieces dust free				
Carpets, floors clean				
Furniture straight/clean				
Pictures straight/dusted				
Lobby telephones clean				
Ceiling/wall vents clean				
Pool/Spa/ Exercise Areas				
Wet terry collected				
Terry supplies adequate/ properly placed				
Carpet unspotted/clean				
Floors clean				
Windows/ledges clean				
Exercise equipment clean				
Wall coverings clean				
Public restrooms clean				
Air vents dusted				
Safety equipment clean/in place				
Administrative Areas				
Lightbulbs/lamps clean and functioning				
Telephones clean				
Carpet unspotted				
Windows clean				
Upholstered furniture clean				
Furniture/desks dusted				
Waste containers clean/ in place				
Pictures, wall hangings straight/dusted				
Air vents dusted				
Wall coverings clean				

FIGURE 9.3 Sample Public Space Inspection Sheet

Sleeping Area

The sleeping area of a guest room is typically the first part seen by the guest when entering the room. It must be absolutely clean. Figure 9.4 is an example of an inspection sheet a GM could use to inspect the sleeping area of a guest room. The actual inspection sheet used would be tailored specifically for the hotel inspected.

GM's Guest Room Sleeping Area Inspection

Date: _____   Inspection assisted by: _____

Room Number: _____

Item/Area	Outstanding	Acceptable	Unacceptable	Comments
All lightbulbs functioning				
Lamps clean/functioning				
Carpet unspotted				
Drapes/cords/hooks in place				
Outside windows/ledges clean				
Bedspread clean				
Pillows in good condition				
Pictures straight/dusted				
Air vents dusted				
Mirrors clean				
TV clean/dusted				
Counters/furniture dusted				
Guest amenities (iron/boards, etc.) in place				
Guest literature in place				
Telephone clean				
Telephone handset clean				
Night stand clean				
Furniture dusted				
Closet doors clean				
Closet shelf clean				
Proper number/type hangers				
Laundry bags in place				
Extra pillows/blankets in place				
Refrigerators/microwaves clean				
Dresser top clean				
Dresser drawers clean				
Area under bed or bed box clean				
Coffeepot clean				
Coffee items stocked				
Waste basket in place				
Logo items in place				
Inside of corridor door clean				
Print material posted on door				
Evacuation sign in place				
Do Not Disturb sign in place				
Other				
Other				
Other				
Other				
Other				

FIGURE 9.4   Sample Guest Room Sleeping Area Inspection Sheet

Bathroom Area

The bathroom area of a guest room is one that is very closely inspected by guests for cleanliness. Inadequate cleaning of this area by the housekeeping staff will inevitably result in guest dissatisfaction and complaints. Like the sleeping area of the guest room, the bathroom area must be absolutely clean. Figure 9.5 is an example of an

---

GM's Guest Room Bath Area Inspection

Date: _____   Inspection assisted by: _____

Room Number: _____

Item/Area	Outstanding	Acceptable	Unacceptable	Comments
Lights working				
Light fixtures clean				
Fans working				
Air vents clean				
Telephone clean/functioning				
Shower head clean				
Bathtub fixtures clean				
Tile and tub clean				
Safety handles clean				
Shower rod clean/all hooks in place				
Shower curtain clean				
Toilet free of water stains inside				
Toilet exterior and back clean				
Sink fixtures clean				
Sink and stopper clean				
Mirror(s) clean				
Countertops clean				
Hair dryers/other amenities clean				
Floor tiles clean				
Soaps/amenities in place				
Electrical switches/outlets clean				
Towel bars clean				
Proper terry in place				
Tissues in place				
Toilet paper holder clean				
Toilet paper in place				
Wall coverings clean				
Inside door clean				
Locks polished/working				
Exterior of bath door clean				
Other				
Other				
Other				
Other				
Other				

FIGURE 9.5   Sample Guest Room Bath Area Inspection Sheet

inspection sheet a GM would use to inspect the bathroom area of a guest room. The actual inspection sheet used would be tailored specifically for the hotel inspected.

LAUNDRY

When most people think of a laundry, they think of clothes washers and dryers. In an OPL, the process is more complex, involves more equipment, and actually begins not in the laundry area but in the guest rooms, pool area, dining rooms, and meeting spaces. It is in these areas that room attendants will collect the dirty linen and terry that must be cleaned by the OPL. Operating an effective OPL is a multistep process that includes:

- Collecting
- Sorting/repairing
- Washing
- Drying
- Finishing/folding
- Storing
- Delivering

Collecting

Room attendants collect dirty linen from guest room sleeping areas, and dirty terry products from guest room bath areas, spa areas, and pools. In the guest rooms, room attendants strip beds and place dirty linens directly into laundry bags attached to their

Proper laundry methods help ensure the quality and long life of terry products. (www.comstock.com)

cleaning carts. When full, these laundry bags are either hand carried or carted to the OPL. Dirty linen and terry should never be used as rags to actually clean a guest room because doing so could damage these items. In some cases, laundry is presorted in the guest room before it ever reaches the OPL. This is the case when linen or terry is blood-stained and must be placed separately into a **biohazard waste bag** to help OPL workers avoid unneeded exposure to blood-borne pathogens. Bags of this type should be placed on every housekeeping cart, and room attendants should be required to use them.

HOTEL TERMINOLOGY AT WORK

Biohazard Waste Bag: A specially marked plastic bag used in hotels. Laundry items that are blood- or bodily-fluid-stained and thus need special handling in the OPL are placed into these bags for transporting to the OPL.

■

The food service department will generate tablecloths and napkins that must be cleaned; in larger hotels, employee uniforms may be processed in the OPL. As a result, the executive housekeeper must have efficient methods in place to collect these items from their various locations and deliver them to the OPL.

Sorting/Repairing

Once in the OPL, laundry is sorted both in terms of its fabric type and degree of staining. Different fibers and colors require different cleaning chemicals in the wash and, in many cases, different water temperatures or length of washing. Linens made of 100 percent cotton, for example, are washed in a different manner than an employee uniform that has a high polyester content. In a similar manner, a white terry washcloth used by a guest to polish black shoes would not be washed in the same load as the regular terry collected in the hotel because the heavily soiled cloth would need special prewash stain removal treatment to come completely clean, or in some hotels, it may be laundered in a special washer designated only for heavily stained laundry. In some cases, a tear or rip in a cloth item can be repaired. When this is the case, these repairs are typically made prior to washing.

Washing

Washing is the most complex part of the laundering process. Despite the fact that today's laundry items are made from very durable fabrics and that washers can be pre-set to dispense cleaning products into the water at the right time and in the right amounts, the executive housekeeper must still teach laundry workers to monitor washing times, wash temperatures, chemicals, and **agitation** when actually washing laundry.

HOTEL TERMINOLOGY AT WORK

Agitation: Movement created by the washing machine resulting in friction as fabrics rub against each other.
■

Length of washing time is a key factor because heavily stained items will need to be washed longer than lightly soiled items. Too long a washing cycle may waste time, water, energy, and chemicals. If the washing cycle selected is too short, the laundry may not come clean. Wash water temperature is important because some fabrics can handle exposure to very hot water while others cannot. Generally, hot water cleans better than cold, but fabrics washed in overly hot water for their fiber type can be damaged.

The chemicals used to wash items are determined by the type of fabric to be cleaned. Typically, chemicals used in the laundry area include detergents, bleaches, heavy stain removers, and fabric softeners. The amount of each that should be used is important both to maximize the cleanliness of the fabric washed and to control the cost of chemical usage. Lastly, agitation length and strength must be determined for each fabric type. Agitation is the friction of the laundry against itself during the wash cycle. With too little agitation (caused when the washer is packed too full), the items washed will not be cleaned properly. With excessive agitation, the fabrics washed will wear out too rapidly because of the damage done to the fibers in them.

The next step in the wash cycle is water extraction. By removing the most water possible, washed laundry is lighter and easier for laundry workers to handle. In addition, those items that require drying will dry more quickly. When the water has been extracted from the cleaned fabrics, the wash cycle is complete.

In today's modern washing machines, the time, temperature, chemical, and agitation levels can be preset. These must first be determined, however, by a knowledgeable executive housekeeper in consultation with the washing equipment manufacturer and the chemical supplier if wash results are to be maximized and if OPL costs are to be controlled to the greatest degree possible.

THE INTERNET AT WORK

The number of possible setting combinations on a commercial washer/water extractor is extremely large. To review one manufacturer's options using microchip technology to preselect settings, go to

www. speedqueen.com

and review the features of the Micro Master Laundry System found in the "On-Premise" section.

Drying

Some fabrics are not dried after they are washed. This is the case with some linens that are removed from the washer and then immediately ironed. Terry, however, as well as most other fabrics, must be properly dried before folding or ironing. Drying is simply a process of moving hot air (140–145° F) through the fabrics to vaporize and remove moisture. Fabrics that are dried must go through a cool-down period in the dryer before they are removed from it. This minimizes any damage done to the fabric and helps prevent wrinkling. Once removed from the dryer, however, these items should be immediately finished.

Finishing/Folding

The finishing of fabrics is important because washers and dryers should not produce more clean laundry than workers can readily process by ironing and/or folding it. Since more and more hotels use wrinkle-free fabrics, more finishing work today involves folding than it does ironing. Regardless of how much ironing is done, the space required for finishing laundry must be adequate. In larger hotels, the folding of linens and terry may be done by machine, while in smaller properties it is generally done by hand. The finishing area must be very clean so that the finishing process itself does not soil the laundry. Once the laundry has been finished, it moves to the storage area(s) of the housekeeping department.

Storing

The storage of linens is important because many fabrics must "rest" after washing and drying if the damage to them is to be minimized. Most laundry experts suggest a rest time of 24 hours for cleaned laundry. Therefore, the housekeeping department should strive to maintain **laundry par levels** of three times normal use. For example, in a 350-room hotel, the GM should provide the laundry area with enough linen and terry to have:

- One set in the rooms
- One set in the laundry (being washed and dried)
- One set in storage

In this manner, the hotel will have adequate products for guests and enough reserve to permit the laundry to rest before being placed back into rooms.

HOTEL TERMINOLOGY AT WORK

Laundry Par Levels: The amount of laundry in use, in process, and in storage.

If laundry par levels are too high, storage may be difficult, and excessive dollars will have been committed to laundry inventories. If laundry par levels are too low, guests may not get the items they need, and room attendants may not be able to complete their work in a timely manner because they must wait for cleaned laundry products to finish cleaning rooms. In addition, fabrics may not be allowed to rest properly if they are needed immediately to make up rooms that must be sold.

Delivering

In smaller hotels, room attendants may go to laundry storage areas in the OPL to pick up linen and terry items. In larger properties, these items may be delivered to housekeeping storage areas located in various parts of the hotel. Because these linens and terry are frequent targets of theft by hotel guests and staff, the storage areas containing these items should be kept locked and the housekeeping staff should inventory them on a regular basis.

Although GMs will not generally need to inspect laundry areas as often as guest rooms, a periodic inspection of these areas is a good idea both for the safety and morale of laundry workers. Figure 9.6 is an example of an inspection sheet that can be modified and used.

GM's Laundry Area Inspection				
Date: _____ Inspection assisted by: _____				
Item/Area	**Outstanding**	**Acceptable**	**Unacceptable**	**Comments**
Bags and carts used to collect laundry are clean and in good condition				
Area used to sort laundry is clean/uncluttered				
Washers clean inside and out				
Washing instruction signs easily read				
Area around washers clean/free of clutter				
Chemicals properly labeled and stored				
Material Safety Data Sheets available				
Dryer temperatures controlled, posted				
Folding area adequate, clean of all debris				
Storage areas clean, labeled				
Other				
Other				
Other				
Other				
Other				

FIGURE 9.6   Sample Laundry Area Inspection Sheet

HOTEL TERMINOLOGY AT WORK GLOSSARY

The following terms were defined within this chapter. If you are not familiar with one of them, please review the segment of the chapter that contains the term.

Public space	OPL	Minutes per room
House person	Inspector	Product usage report
Executive housekeeper	Room attendants	Cost per occupied room
Room status	Room attendant cart	Biohazard waste bag
Linen	Blood-borne pathogen	Agitation
Terry	Deep cleaning	Laundry par levels

ISSUES AT WORK

1. Some executive housekeepers prefer to allow room attendants to work independently, with only one attendant assigned to each room to be cleaned. Others prefer a system that teams two or more attendants together for each room assigned to be

cleaned. Those preferring the single attendant system cite the tendency of the team system members to "talk" too much to each other and thus not complete their tasks in a timely manner. Those favoring teams point to the increased security provided by having two attendants work together, as well as the advantages of "two sets of eyes" on each room. Discuss at least three additional advantages and disadvantages of each approach. Which do you believe is the best for guests? For the hotel? For the hotel's room attendants? Which would you use in your hotel? Why?

2. Housekeeping is one of the departments in the hotel that must work every holiday because the hotel is open and often very busy. Assume you have a housekeeping department with 24 employees and your hotel recognizes New Year's Day, Memorial Day, Fourth of July, Labor Day, Thanksgiving, and Christmas as paid holidays. Also assume that at least one-quarter (6) of your housekeeping employees need to work each holiday to clean the stay-over rooms. Design a scheduling system that fairly assigns these holidays to the employees. What factors would you take into consideration in developing the system?

3. Some GMs feel room attendants must be able to fluently speak the language of the majority of the hotel's guests to do their jobs effectively. Essentially, these GMs feel guest contact is an important role of the room attendant's job and to converse with the guests they must have strong language skills. Other GMs feel a command of the principal language used by guests is not required. How important is it that room attendants and public space cleaners can speak fluently to guests? List three challenges you may encounter if you make a command of the guests' language a job requirement for housekeepers and three challenges you may face if you do not. How would you encourage your executive housekeeper to overcome these challenges?

4. Nearly all hotels experience "peak" and "slow" occupancy times. For those hotels catering to the business traveler, the Christmas holidays often represent slow periods. In some hotels, the result is a temporary layoff or reduction in work hours of some hourly housekeeping employees. What specific strategies can you and your executive housekeeper employ to reduce the chances of negatively impacting the income of your lower paid housekeeping employees during these times? How important is it for you to do so? Why?

5. In some hotels, the GM allows, and even encourages, tipping of room attendants. This is typically done through the placement of a "tip envelope" in the room. Should there be tip envelopes in guest rooms? Defend your position in a memo that you, as a GM, will direct to your housekeeping staff.

10

Food and Beverage

This Chapter at Work

A hotel is considered "full service" when it provides guests with extensive food and beverage products and services. GMs at full-service hotels are routinely paid better than their limited-service GM counterparts. This is because, in nearly every situation, operating a full-service hotel is more complex and requires higher levels of knowledge and skill than does managing a limited-service hotel. If you want to manage a full-service hotel, you will find the supervision of the F&B department to be both challenging and rewarding. You will also find that operating a hotel's F&B department is vastly more complex than simply operating a restaurant.

In this chapter you will explore some of the features that make hotel F&B so complex. This chapter is not designed to teach you how to operate an F&B department. Rather, its focus is on features of F&B unique to hotel management including room service, banquets and catering, and some aspects of serving alcoholic beverages. GMs must be actively involved in these aspects of the department even though they probably have a manager/director with immediate responsibility for it.

Full-service hotels can offer guests a variety of F&B options. A large, 1000+ room property may operate several restaurants, each with its own theme or style of cuisine, as well as several lounges or bars. A smaller, 150-room hotel may operate a single dining room and lounge. However, both hotels will likely provide room service, a unique style of F&B that you, as a GM, must understand well, and that is explained in detail in this chapter.

In addition to restaurants and room service, the F&B department is responsible for the hotel's banquet and catering efforts. In many full-service hotels, the revenue from these sources will exceed that of its restaurants. Profits, too, are higher in the banquet and catering area. As a result, it is important for you to fully understand this major responsibility of the F&B department.

In the majority of full-service hotels, the sale of food is accompanied by the sale of alcoholic beverages. Hoteliers, like restaurateurs, have a professional responsibility, as well as a legal obligation, to serve alcohol responsibly. This special concern of full-service hotel GMs is important, and concludes the chapter's discussion of the F&B department.

In recent years, full-service hotels have lost market share in many areas to newer and smaller limited-service properties. There will continue to be, however, a need for full-service hotels. As a result, there will be a need for hotel GMs who understand F&B. This chapter begins a serious student's study of this essential and intricate area.

Chapter 10 Outline

OVERVIEW OF HOTEL FOOD AND
BEVERAGE OPERATIONS
    Similarities: Hotel and Restaurant Food Services
        Operational Similarities
        Personnel Requirement Similarities
    Differences: Hotel and Restaurant Food Services
        Profitability Differences
        Marketing-Related Differences
        Other Differences
ROOM SERVICE OPERATIONS
    Profitability Concerns
    Menu Planning Factors
    Operating Issues
    Within Guest Room Service

BANQUET OPERATIONS
    Profit Opportunities
    Menu Planning
    Service Styles
    Beverage Functions
    Labor and Other Charges
    Banquet Room Setup
    Banquet Contracts and Billing Policies
ALCOHOLIC BEVERAGE SERVICE
IN HOTELS
HOTEL TERMINOLOGY AT
WORK GLOSSARY
ISSUES AT WORK

OVERVIEW OF HOTEL FOOD AND BEVERAGE OPERATIONS

Some hotel managers believe managing a hotel with a food and beverage **(F&B)** department means that they are in the restaurant business. They are not. Operating a profitable hotel F&B department is much more complex than operating a profitable restaurant. In fact, some hotel F&B departments lose money for their hotels. As a result, it requires a GM who understands how hotel F&B is similar, and dissimilar, to managing a traditional restaurant if the hotel is to maximize the effectiveness and profitability of this important department.

HOTEL TERMINOLOGY AT WORK

F&B: Shortened term for "food and beverage." Used, for example as in the following: "Please let the F&B director know about the changes the guest has requested."

Hotel F&B is complicated for many reasons, one of which is the variety of offerings. A typical restaurant generally offers one type of cuisine and serves that offering for one or two meal periods per day (for example, lunch and dinner). Consider popular-priced or fine-dining restaurants with which you are familiar. Do these offer breakfast and are they open seven days per week? In most cases, the answer to these two questions is likely to be "no." Although many quick-service restaurants serve breakfast, lunch, and dinner and are open seven days a week, these restaurants also serve their food on self-serve trays and/or "deliver" their food in paper bags to the driver's side window of the customer's car. A hotel restaurant, however, must offer at least breakfast, lunch, and dinner on a daily basis, and it must offer these meals in a manner in keeping with the quality of the hotel's other products and services.

In addition, an effective F&B department in a hotel may offer multiple, additional restaurant operations, 24-hour room service, banquet operations, and a wide range of other F&B alternatives. These include snack bar, coffee break, and meal services as part of convention/meeting operations, take-out and off-site catering, vending and alcoholic beverage outlets in lounges, show bars, and lobby areas. The individual responsible for the effective operation of the F&B department is the **food and beverage director**. He/she is critical to the effective management of the F&B department in the hotel and, as a result, normally reports directly to the GM.

HOTEL TERMINOLOGY AT WORK

Food and Beverage Director: The individual responsible for the operation of a hotel's F&B program(s).

Experienced GMs know that the F&B department will generate less revenue, more complaints, and fewer profits than will the rental of the hotel's guest rooms. In general, full-service hotels generate 60 percent to 75 percent or more of their revenue from the sale of guest rooms. The F&B department generates 20 percent to 35 percent, and the balance of hotel revenue is generated from telephone and other sources. The F&B department, however, will not often, if ever, generate this same proportion of a hotel's profit. In fact, even when they are operated extremely well, some hotel F&B departments have a difficult time contributing any significant profits.

It is critical for full-service GMs to remember, however, that in many cases it is only because of the F&B department that guests come to the hotel. To fully understand this concept, consider a hotel's swimming pool. Swimming pools attract guests. A GM would not expect the swimming pool to make a "profit," yet the appearance of the pool, the temperature and clarity of the water, and the cleanliness of the pool area are all important to the hotel's profitability. In a similar manner, F&B products are important, regardless of their contribution to profitability. This is true because, first, some guests (especially those planning conventions, conferences, and other group meetings) select a hotel, in part, by considering the quality and value of the F&B services that are offered. Second, other travelers and those within the community choose to spend discretionary dining dollars in hotels with a reputation for providing quality dining services at fair prices. Third, while hotels may generate profits from F&B services, F&B will always support the sale of other, more profitable hotel features such as meetings and convention services.

Similarities: Hotel and Restaurant Food Services

There are many similarities between hotel and restaurant food services. Basic principles for planning, for managing financial resources, for sanitation and food preparation, and for controlling costs, among many other factors, are the same. GMs will find that they do not need to be experts in the culinary arts to understand how these concepts relate to food quality and departmental efficiency. Unfortunately, some GMs tend to avoid the F&B area because of its complexity. This is a mistake because, improperly managed, the F&B department can be a tremendous drain on a hotel's financial resources. This area of the hotel deserves the very best of management attention, and it is up to the GM and F&B director to provide it.

Some aspects of managing F&B operations in hotels are identical to those needed to manage these services in other venues. In fact, the basics of managing a **commercial food service operation**, including those in hotels and restaurants, are almost identical to those used to successfully operate an **institutional (noncommercial) food service operation**. Commercial businesses such as hotels, which desire to make a profit from F&B operations and from the sale of guest rooms, must address financial, human resources, product control, and marketing issues.

HOTEL TERMINOLOGY AT WORK

Commercial Food Service Operations: Food services offered in hotels and restaurants and other organizations whose primary purpose for existence involves generation of profits from the sale of food and beverage products.

Institutional (Noncommercial) Food Service Operations: Those food services provided by health care, educational, military, religious, and numerous other organizations whose primary reason for existence is not to generate a profit from the sale of food/beverage products but rather is to support another organizational purpose.

■

These same general concerns confront their institutional counterparts such as hospitals and schools that must offer food services to support their primary purpose (for example, health care for hospitals and education for schools). In fact, for those GMs who believe the primary function of an F&B department is to promote hotel guest room and **function room** sales, the operation of this department is, philosophically, very much like that of an institutional (support) food service.

HOTEL TERMINOLOGY AT WORK

Function Room: Public space such as meeting rooms, conference areas, and ballrooms that can frequently be subdivided into smaller spaces and that are available in the hotel for banquet, meeting, or other group rental purposes.

Operational Similarities

Hotel food service operations are similar to other food service operations in numerous ways, including:

- *Planning Issues.* The need to begin planning by considering a menu driven by the wants, needs, and/or preferences of those who will be served is critical. The menu, in turn, impacts the design, facility layout, and equipment needs of the operation, as well as the labor required to produce and serve the menu items.

- *Financial Concerns.* Economic issues are important regardless of whether the food service operation desires to generate profit (commercial operations) or to minimize expenses (noncommercial facilities). Operating budgets are required to estimate revenues and plan for expenses.

- *Emphasis on the Guest (Consumer).* When an F&B department is well managed, guests return (in a hotel's operation) and its personnel enhance the reputation of the organization (in commercial and noncommercial food services). The **repeat business** generated by a properly managed F&B department is important to the hotel's overall financial success.

HOTEL TERMINOLOGY AT WORK

Repeat Business: Revenues generated from guests returning to a commercial operation such as a hotel as a result of their positive experiences on previous visits.

Consider, for example, the full-service hotel that successfully books a city's annual chamber of commerce holiday party. Attendees will represent significant business leaders in the community. If the event is a success, the guests will experience the ten components of a successful F&B event. These are:

1. An attractive parking and reception area when they arrive
2. An event that began at the scheduled time
3. A clean, well-lit, and attractive function room
4. Properly attired staff
5. The proper number of attentive and well-trained service staff
6. Quality food served at the proper temperature

7. Clean restroom facilities

8. A visibly present F&B manager or other "contact person"

9. Fair pricing

10. Accurate and timely billing

If these components are experienced, the local business leaders will likely come back to the hotel for future events, and purchase or recommend the purchase of more profitable guest rooms to serve their business needs. If one or more of the above components are not in place, not only will the chamber of commerce staff be less likely to rebook their event at the hotel, the attendees are less likely to use it as well. GMs should regularly use the above ten components as a checklist to help ensure the quality of the F&B events they provide and should work with the F&B director to take corrective action, if needed.

Cost Control Procedures.   Food service operations of all types provide numerous cost control challenges when managing all available **resources.**

HOTEL TERMINOLOGY AT WORK

Resources: Something of value to the organization. Typical resources include money, labor, time, equipment, food and beverage products, supplies, energy, and methodologies (procedures).

Consider, for example, the food and beverage products used in the hotel's F&B department. Standard operating procedures are needed to manage these products during each step in the control cycle, and as a GM, you should ensure that procedures such as these are visibly in place. Figure 10.1 details examples of procedures that can be used to control food and beverage products.

The examples of applicable control concerns at each step noted in Figure 10.1 represent just a few of the hundreds (or more!) of procedures that must be carefully thought out and, where appropriate, incorporated into operating procedures designed to effectively manage product costs. Each of these, as well as management concerns related to all other resources used in the F&B department, should be addressed in every type of food service operation, including hotels.

Personnel Requirement Similarities

The number of staff needed in a F&B department is dependent in large measure on the size of the hotel and the complexity of its F&B offerings. As a result, an F&B department can require relatively few employees in less complicated operations (one dining room and limited function space) to hundreds (or more) of staff members in properties with multiple restaurants, bars, lounges, extensive function space, and associated F&B outlets.

THE INTERNET AT WORK

One of the largest and most extensive F&B programs in a United States hotel is operated at the Opryland Hotel in Nashville, Tennessee. To view their F&B choices, go to

www.gaylordopryland.com

Control Step	Examples of Applicable Control Concerns
Purchasing	• Development of purchase specifications indicating quality requirements for all products to be purchased. (Beverages are often purchased by brand, and guest preferences must be known.) • Supplier selection, which assures that product prices and vendor service/information are optimized. • Purchasing correct quantities ranging from just-in-time (JIT; daily or more frequent) purchases to those required for longer-term needs. • Use of practices to help reduce the possibilities of collusion between property and supplier staff. • Evaluation of manual and computerized aspects of the purchasing process.
Receiving	• Development of receiving procedures, including incoming product inspections, weighing and counting, and other tactics to ensure that the hotel "gets what it pays for." • Completion of necessary receiving reports, which address financial and security concerns.
Storing	• Effective use of an appropriate inventory system. • Control of product quality during storage. • Tactics to reduce theft while products are in storage. • Predetermined location of products within storage areas.
Issuing	• Product rotation concerns to assure that products in storage the longest are issued and used first. • Matching quantities of products issued with quantities of products needed/used. • Procedures to trigger purchase procedures as issuing depletes product inventories.
Prepreparation	• Mise-en-place (a French word meaning everything in its place), which results from accurate production planning to determine quantities of items to be prepared. • Careful prepreparation of food products to minimize food waste and to assure maximum nutrient retention.
Preparation	• Use of standardized recipes to control ingredient costs and preparation times and to better assure that the quality of food and beverage products produced meet the hotel's standards. • Use of portion control (for example, scoops, scales, and ladles) to help assure that product costs and guest goals about value (price relative to quality) are attained. • Requirements for food safety (sanitation) and employee safety standards to reduce burns, slips, falls, and numerous other injuries that can occur from working in fast-paced, hot, and potentially dangerous conditions.
Serving	*Note: Serving involves moving food and beverage products from production personnel (cooks and bartenders) to service personnel (food and beverage servers).* • Timing of food delivery. • Portion control. • Revenue management concerns relating to items that servers must order from production personnel versus soups, salads, beverages, and desserts, that servers may obtain for themselves.
Service	*Note: Service involves moving food and beverage products from service personnel (food and beverage servers) to the guests.* • Revenue control concerns. • Serving alcoholic beverages responsibly in beverage operations. • Sanitation and cleanliness. • Food and beverage server attentiveness.

FIGURE 10.1   Steps in Food and Beverage Product Control

HOTEL TERMINOLOGY AT WORK

Serving: The process of moving food and beverage products from production personnel (cooks and bartenders) to food and beverage servers who will serve them to guests.

Service: The process of moving food and beverage products from service staff to the guests.

■

Just as quality restaurants depend on selecting and retaining trained F&B professionals, so, too, do those hotels with excellent F&B departments. In addition to the F&B director, the F&B department is likely to employ staff in numerous positions:

- *Culinarians.* These individuals are highly trained in food preparation and kitchen management responsibilities and activities.

THE INTERNET AT WORK

Some of the very same best culinarians are members of the American Culinary Federation (ACF). Its emphasis on training is very strong, and the ACF promotes professionalism among its members. To view their Web site, go to

www.acfchefs.org

- *Restaurant and Dining Room Managers.* These individuals operate the "open to the public" restaurant facilities within the hotel.
- *Catering Managers.* These individuals supervise the banquets, meetings, catering, and special events held at the hotel.

THE INTERNET AT WORK

The National Association of Catering Executives (NACE) is the professional association for those managers who specialize in catering. To view the NACE Web site, go to

www.nace.net

- *Beverage Managers and Bartenders.* These individuals manage and operate the hotel's alcoholic beverage outlets.

THE INTERNET AT WORK

Skilled bartenders are extremely valuable to a hotel. To view the Web site of a professional bartenders' association, go to:

www.americanbartenders.org

- *Kitchen Stewarding Staff.* These maintain the kitchen spaces, wash dishes, and assist the hotel's food production personnel.
- *Service Staff.* These individuals serve the guests in the restaurants, bars, lounge, room service, and banquet areas of the hotel.

Is this dining room in a hotel or a restaurant? There may be few operating differences but a significant difference in profit level.

Hotel F&B managers recruit, to a great degree, the same type of individuals as do their restaurant counterparts. As you can see, then, depending on its business volume, the F&B department can be very large and, as a result, it can be costly to operate. In addition, it is one in which guest difficulties often arise.

Many observers believe the vast majority of all problems in any hotel operation including the F&B department are actually caused by managers! Often this is true. A GM must help the F&B and other department heads to perform at their very best. From a staffing perspective, operating an effective F&B department consists of at least three mandatory steps. First, F&B staff must receive the necessary training to learn the knowledge and skills required to work according to standardized procedures. Second, managers must provide direction to employees by telling them about the wants, needs, and expectations of the guests being served. Third, managers must provide the necessary resources required to perform the work properly. As a GM, if you experience repeated F&B-related difficulties, a review of the existence, or absence of, these three steps can help you to pinpoint operating difficulties so they can be resolved quickly.

Differences: Hotel and Restaurant Food Services

The above section has suggested many similarities between F&B operations in lodging and restaurant properties. There are, however, also significant differences between the F&B operation within the hotel and a restaurant. A restaurant manager wants to financially support the *restaurant* itself through sales. In a properly managed hotel F&B, the department head wants to financially support the *hotel* through sales. The philosophic and practical differences between these two approaches are immense.

The service of food and beverages in the guest rooms provides an example of one way that hotel food service operations differ from their restaurant counterparts. Many full-service hotels offer room service: the delivery of food to the guest's room. Significant planning by room service managers is required to determine how quality goals can be attained when food must be transported over long distances involving relatively long time periods between plating and guest service. Imagine, for example, the challenges faced by a 500-room hotel oriented to the corporate traveler if 100 guests have requested room service breakfast to be served to their rooms between 7:00 A.M. and 7:30 A.M.! There are, sometimes, guest complaints about room service. Typically these involve cold and/or low-quality food—both of which usually result from timing problems as food moves from the kitchen to the guest room. Most restaurant managers do not face these same issues.

Of course, room service menus can be planned to address these quality concerns. As well, careful communication between the guest placing and the employee taking the order, the production person(s) producing the order, and the room server delivering the order is required. If communication is not effective, the guest will be dissatisfied, and the hotel will suffer from guest perceptions that room service standards are low.

The extent of banquet operations is another way that hotel F&B operations differ from most restaurants. Many hotels generate significant revenue from the sale of food and beverages at group functions. In fact, in many full-service hotels, the main focus of the F&B department is on banquets and in-house catered events, and not on its open-to-the-public restaurants and bars. In banquets, as in room service, attention to detail is absolutely critical. There is a need for coordination between departments as marketing/sales personnel interact with the guests and communicate their needs to F&B production staff and as service personnel within the F&B department setup and service the group function. In large hotels with staff members designated to service conventions and large meetings, another communication and coordination challenge occurs: representatives from this area must interact with the guests and staff members within the hotel to make the group function successful.

Well-planned and executed banquets are very profitable. Therefore, the GM should frequently evaluate the quality of these events. This can be done by careful planning and coordinating of events with the F&B director before events begin, reviewing guest comments about the functions, and discussing problems and solutions with the F&B director and his or her staff of professionals.

Banquets, apart from their profitability, are important because they allow guests and potential guests to experience what the hotel can offer. This provides opportunities for repeat business in the sale of guest rooms, public dining alternatives, and future banquet events. There is much that hoteliers can do to set their banquet events apart from their competitors. Utilizing a variety of service styles, serving food that is of the proper quality, and paying attention to the many details that address guest preferences and needs are among them.

Unlike most restaurants, a hotel's F&B department is responsible for fulfilling guest requests for **audiovisual (AV) equipment**. Increasingly, the AV equipment requested is sophisticated and these items must be kept in good working order.

HOTEL TERMINOLOGY AT WORK

Audiovisual (AV) Equipment: Those items including DVD players, laptops, LCD projectors, microphones, sound systems, flip charts, overhead projectors, slide projectors, monitors, and VCRs that are used to communicate information to meeting attendees during their sessions.

In addition to room service, an emphasis on banquets, and the management of AV equipment, there are other fundamental differences between hotel F&B and restaurants about which hotel GMs should be aware. One of the most important relates to profitability.

Profitability Differences

Profitability relates to the extent to which the revenues generated by an F&B operation exceed assigned expenses.

HOTEL TERMINOLOGY AT WORK

Profitability: Revenue (−) Expenses = Profit.

How a GM assigns (allocates) revenues and expenses to a department can, in great measure, dictate profit levels in that department.

The amount of profit generated by a traditional restaurant is relatively easy to calculate. All revenue is generated from the sale of food and/or beverage products in the restaurant. As well, all **expenses** normally will be clearly identified in the accounting records of the establishment.

HOTEL TERMINOLOGY AT WORK

Expenses: The amount of money spent to generate revenues.

By contrast, the process of assigning revenues and expenses applicable to the F&B department in a hotel is more difficult. Consider, for example, a holiday weekend package plan that includes a one-night's stay, dinner, and breakfast and is sold to guests for one price. How should the revenue generated from the guests be split between room revenue and the F&B department? Consider applicable expenses also. How much (if any) of the salary paid to the hotel's GM, controller, and other staff specialists along with other expenses including utilities, landscaping, and marketing, be allocated between departments (including F&B) within the hotel?

It can, then, be difficult to compare the profitability of a restaurant with that of its F&B counterpart in a lodging property. With this as a caution, let's review Figure 10.2. Although the financial data provided are from the most current and reputable sources, the issue of assigning expenses noted earlier does make generalization about the data more difficult.

Upon initial review, it appears that F&B operations in hotels are much more profitable than their restaurant counterparts (28.5 percent departmental income [profit] in hotels versus only 3.9 percent in restaurants). Note, first, however, that hotels generate approximately 26 percent of their revenue from two sources (room rental and other income) not available to restaurants. "Other income" includes charges for audio/video rental, and **service charges** initially collected for subsequent distribution to employees as additional compensation.

HOTEL TERMINOLOGY AT WORK

Service Charges: A mandatory amount added to a guest's bill for services performed by a hotel staff member(s).

	Hotel F&B		Restaurant F&B	
Net Revenue	100.0%		100.0%	
Cost of F&B Sales	(26.7%)		(31.2%)	
Gross Profit (from combined sales)		73.4%		68.8%
Room Rentals	7.3%		—	
Other Income	18.5%		—	
Gross Profit/Other Income		99.2%		68.8%
Departmental Expenses				
Salaries/Wages	44.0%		30.4%	
Payroll Taxes/Benefits	14.5%		2.9%	
	58.5%		33.3%	
Other Allocated Expenses	12.2%		31.6%[1]	
Total Expenses		(70.7%)		(64.9%)
Departmental Income (Profit)		28.5%		3.9%[2]

Lodging data calculated from information in *Trends in the Hotel Industry*, USA edition—2005. PKF Consulting, (Data is from 2004.) Restaurant data calculated from information in *Restaurant Industry Operations Report*. National Restaurant Association and Deloitte & Touche, 2003. (All data are from 2002 and are for full-service restaurants with an average check per person of $15.00–$24.99.)
[1] Includes occupancy costs of 6%.
[2] Before income taxes.

FIGURE 10.2   Profitability of Food and Beverage Operations in Hotels and Restaurants

Without these revenue sources, the hotel's departmental income (profit) from F&B operations would be 2.7 percent (28.5 percent − 28.8 percent). Additionally, there are a wide range of expenses directly incurred by the restaurant that are not allocated to the F&B operation in the hotel. For example, restaurant occupancy costs are 6 percent of revenue; these expenses include leasehold payments, interest on leasehold improvements, real estate taxes, and others that are not allocated (assigned) to the F&B department in the typical hotel. If all costs were accurately allocated between the F&B and other hotel departments, it is likely that the hotel's "bottom-line" profit from food and beverage sales would likely be much less than that generated by a restaurant.

In an effort to contrast the profit levels of hotel food and beverage departments and restaurants, it is also possible to study just the two highest costs: those for products and labor. These two costs (costs of food and beverage sales and payroll [salaries/wages and payroll taxes/benefits]) are relatively easy to identify and are likely to be (relatively) carefully allocated to the F&B department within the hotel. Note, in Figure 10.2, for example, that the cost of food and beverage sales in a restaurant is 4.5 percent higher in the restaurant than in the hotel (31.2 percent − 26.7 percent). This may be because a hotel can more effectively control food and beverage costs; however, it may also be because many hotels charge more for their meals. (Many hotels position their F&B operations to be "special-occasion" dining outlets for the local community and therefore do not compete with lower guest check average full-service restaurant properties in the marketplace.)

Payroll costs (salaries, wages, payroll taxes, and benefits) are much higher in the hotel F&B department than in the restaurant (58.5 percent of revenue versus 33.3 percent of revenue). Wages for a specific position within a community are likely to be similar, so salary/wage rates are not likely to account for this significant difference. There are several factors that likely influence the higher payroll costs in hotel F&B operations. Restaurants are open at the times when the majority of guests want to be served. (For example, a dinner steak house restaurant is not likely to be open for breakfast; a breakfast diner will not be open for an evening meal.) By contrast, a hotel restaurant will most likely remain open for three meal periods daily to serve hotel guests. In extreme cases, for example, a hotel restaurant may remain open for several hours after the "normal" dinner business subsides to provide food services for guests arriving on late night airline flights. As a second example, restaurants may close for a day or more during weather emergencies; hotel restaurants will likely remain open to provide food services to its guests. **Fixed labor costs** (the labor hours and dollars associated with keeping a food service operation open for minimum business) therefore can be excessive as business slows in a hotel F&B operation, and yet it remains open.

HOTEL TERMINOLOGY AT WORK

Fixed Labor Costs: The minimum number of labor hours and associated labor costs required to operate the food service operation whenever it is open regardless of the number (if any) of guests that are served.

Marketing-Related Differences

As already noted, the rental of guest rooms in a hotel generates higher levels of income (profit) than does the sale of food and beverage products. For this reason, many hotels emphasize guest room rentals—not restaurant operations—in their marketing efforts. There are, of course, some lodging properties in some communities that compete with freestanding restaurants and aggressively advertise in local news media to retain and, hopefully, to increase their market share. Other hotels recognize that their guests select a hotel, in part, because of the dining alternatives within it. With these exceptions, it is generally true that many restaurants more effectively market their food and beverage products and services than do hotel F&B operations.

Several other marketing-related differences between F&B operations in hotels and restaurants can be noted:

- *Location Within the Community.* Successful restaurant operators know that location is a very significant factor in operating success. They want to place their restaurants in locations that are easily accessible to potential guests. By contrast, hotels are placed in locations that are most accessible to those guests desiring lodging accommodations. These sites may differ from those convenient to guests desiring food and beverage services. Historically, F&B operations in large urban hotels were often seen as the preferred dining location in the community. Holiday and special occasion events were held at these facilities. Over time, in part because of an increase in upscale restaurant alternatives, the position of hotel restaurants in the dining hierarchy of many communities was reduced. In addition, as popular national chains spread across the country, hotels were seen as less attractive purveyors of "quality" dining experiences.

  To pursue local banquet and catering business, hotels routinely advertise, participate in local community service organizations, and otherwise promote their F&B alternatives to the community. The property's location is, however, still a factor in guest preference decisions. Consider, for example, a hotel in a downtown location attracting weekday business travelers. On weekends, when this business is absent, it may be hard to attract diners from the distant suburbs who are a potential market for the hotel's restaurant.

- *Location Within a Hotel.* Ideally, hotels catering to local ("walk-in") guests have outdoor signage and outdoor entrances to attract local diners. Sometimes, however, this is not possible. Immediate parking, building access, and the remote location of a restaurant within a hotel can be major obstacles to overcome and hinder the popularity of a hotel's restaurant operation.

- *Menu.* Often a hotel restaurant is designed to cater to the traveling guests it desires to attract. It may need to offer, for example, an upscale menu or, perhaps, one in concert with a local theme, which may be of less interest to potential guests in the community.

- *Marketing to Hotel Guests.* Guests in restaurants are there to enjoy the food, beverage, service, and environment. They do not need to be "sold" on dining at the property. By contrast, hotel guests may or may not be interested in or even know about dining opportunities at the hotel, and it is the job of hotel staff members to encourage the use of the food and beverage facilities.

Imagine an all-too-familiar scenario in which a guest is checking into a property and asks, "Where's a good place to eat in this town?" Do staff members refer them to a restaurant outside of the property or respond by saying, "We have an excellent restaurant here. The chef prepares daily specials in addition to a great regular menu. If you wish, I'll ask someone from the restaurant to call your room after you've had time to check in and let you know about today's specials. They can also answer any other questions that you may have about the menu."

Signage around the property, a coupon or other discount for hotel guest diners, in-room advertising (such as in the room "guest directory"), features on the hotel's television channel, and an attractive display including the menu and other food/wine-related items outside the restaurant's lobby entrance are examples of ways to alert and encourage guests to dine within the hotel. Another suggestion: **cross-selling.** A menu for one meal can encourage guests to visit at other convenient times. For example, the dining room's dinner menu can suggest, "Our spectacular Sunday Buffet is very popular with our guests and is also a tradition within our community. If you will be here this weekend, we invite you to enjoy this great event. The server or receptionist will be pleased to help you with reservations."

HOTEL TERMINOLOGY AT WORK

Cross-Selling: Using messages designed to advertise the availability of other hotel services; for example, a dinner menu may provide information about the hotel's Sunday brunch.
■

Many of the differences between hotel and restaurant food services relate primarily to the fact that offering F&B services is not the primary business purpose of a hotel. (The sale of guest rooms is, of course, its primary objective.) Instead, food service is viewed as an amenity to attract guests and to provide food and beverage alternatives to increase the hotel's revenues from the guest base established by guest room rentals. To some extent, then, the role of the F&B department is, appropriately, secondary to that of those departments that sell and service guest rooms. Experienced

GMs understand this and resist the temptation (often advocated by managers in the F&B department) to aggressively (and expensively) market the F&B operation to nonhotel guests in the local area.

Other Differences

In this section, we'll consider two other differences between food and beverage operations in hotels and in restaurants: the option of contracting the food service operation to outside suppliers and the opportunity to package food services with guest room sales.

The "Contract-Out" Option.   Commercial restaurants exist to generate profits from the sale of food and beverage products. By contrast, hoteliers want to sell guest rooms. Many see additional profit opportunities in their food and beverage operations; however, others do not and retain the services of a second party to do so. Alternatives range from restaurant chain organizations with known brand names to independent entrepreneurs well known in their local communities to very large organizations that operate restaurants and hotels under varying names.

THE INTERNET AT WORK

To view the Web site of Landry's Restaurants, Inc., that operate several types of restaurants under numerous names including restaurants in resorts and hotels, go to

www.landryrestaurants.com

Another restaurant organization, TS Restaurants, has several hotel restaurant outlets in Hawaii and California. To view its Web site, go to

www.hulapie.com

Why might a hotel owner choose to secure the services of an outside party to operate food and beverage services? Several reasons include:

- A history of past unprofitable experiences.
- Concern that the hotel should focus on its main revenue source (guest rooms) and leave food and beverage operations to an organization that specializes in that business.
- Belief that the "operational headaches" from F&B operation and the resulting relatively low levels of profit represent time and effort that could be better spent in maximizing the sale/profitability of guest room rentals.
- New franchisors/owners may have had previous management/operating experience in lodging but little or no experience in food and beverage operations, are aware of the financial risks involved in the operation of the latter and decide to subcontract services initially.

There are numerous other factors important to consider as the outsource decision is made that are specific to a property. Consider, for example, the hotel with a significant convention and group business that generates high-volume coffee break, hospitality suite, and banquet business. These food service venues can be profitable and provide a disadvantage to contracting with an external operator. By contrast, another hotel located in a **"restaurant row"** with numerous dining alternatives and with no (little) convention/group facilities may find that most guests are only interested in the breakfast (generally a low-profit **day-part**). This therefore suggests an advantage to outsourcing food services.

HOTEL TERMINOLOGY AT WORK

Restaurant Row: A term used to describe an area with numerous competing restaurants in a very short (often walking) distance from each other. In some locations, especially tourist destinations, municipal parking lots accommodate the vehicles of persons who visit these areas for dining and entertainment.

Day-part: A segment of the day that represents a change in menu and customer response patterns (for example, time during which breakfast or another menu is offered).

■

Some limited-service hotels are built on a site that also has a family-service or other restaurant and can market the availability of an "on-site" restaurant. Other limited-service properties are built in a location close to an existing restaurant for the same reason. Large hotels and resorts may operate some outlets and feature other contract-operated food services on-site to increase the variety of dining alternatives available to their guests. A popular contractual arrangement includes monthly fees and/or a profit-sharing arrangement paid to the lodging property. Contracts must be carefully developed to assure that all costs to be borne by both parties are clearly identified.

Hoteliers that offer contracted restaurant outlets should be aware that, from their guest's perspective, the facility is being operated by the hotel. This is understandable because, in many instances, guests are not made aware of the split operational management responsibilities (nor do they care!). Even if they did know, the hotelier still made the decision to outsource food services and has made the decision about the operator to be used. Therefore, guest complaints about issues related to food services will likely be brought to the hoteliers' attention, and guests' attitudes about their total hotel experience will likely include their experiences with the food and beverage operations. Wise hoteliers understand, therefore, that food service outsourcing decisions must be made in consideration of guest experiences as well as potential profitability.

Package Pricing Possibilities.   Most restaurants have one thing to offer their guests: food and beverage products. By contrast, hotels can package a guest room and food and beverage product sales to guests, and they frequently do so, for example, on occasions such as Valentine's Day, New Year's Eve, and Weekend "Getaway" promotions. Special concerns are important when packages are planned, as will be shown in the following Sleep Way Plaza Hotel's Valentine's Day Promotion advertised for those in the local community. Assume the Sleep Way is a full-service hotel that operates as part of a franchise and sells its rooms at an average ADR of $85.00 per night.

The proposed package will include a regular guest room, dinner and cocktails for two, champagne, chocolates and roses in the guest room, and breakfast for two the following morning. The Sleep Way, in keeping with its franchise agreement, pays an 8 percent franchise fee on all of its guest room revenues. It also must collect from the guest a local sales tax (5%) as well as an occupancy tax (11%) on the guest's room charges. The hotel manager, after meeting with the property's director of sales and marketing, believes the entire holiday package can be effectively advertised and sold at $199 per night before taxes are assessed. Here is how the costing for the package might be planned:

Package Charge		
Guest room	$89.00	Excludes taxes
Champagne	$5.00	In room
Chocolate	$3.00	In room
Roses	$5.00	Two long stem flowers in room
Dinner	$60.00	$30/meal for 2 persons
Cocktails/wine	$16.00	2 cocktails/person for 2 persons @ $4.00 each
Service charge	$10.00	For dinner and cocktails (13.2%)
Breakfast	$10.00	$5.00/person for 2 persons
Service charge	$1.00	For breakfast (10%)
	$199.00	

Recall that the hotel must collect occupancy taxes on guest room revenues and will also be required to collect any applicable local sales tax that applies to the entire package.

The hotel's management team for this project (general manager, director of sales and marketing, and food and beverage manager) decides to allow guests to select from three "Valentine's Day Dinner Specials," and the package charge for the dinner ($60.00) is established with a markup based upon the average cost of the three meals. They also recognize that the guests will likely order premium cocktails/ wines, and so beverages are priced accordingly in the package. Although the guest's folio would show only one "Valentine's Special Charge," the PMS would be programmed to assign rooms revenue to that department and F&B related revenue to that department. Appropriate tax levels would also be programmed to comply with local tax ordinances.

The package price just discussed is for the hotel's standard rooms, but this property also has in-room whirlpool rooms. The planning team decides to offer a second package that includes this room type for $239.00 per night. How should the $40.00 in additional revenue ($239.00 [−] $199.00 = $40.00) be incorporated into the package prices? A simple response would be: "Calculate the guest room charge to be $129.00 ($89.00 [+] $40.00 = $129.00) and consider, for revenue purposes, that all $40.00 should be collected as incremental room sales. However, this rate may not be equitable to the hotel (because a higher franchise fee would need to be paid) nor to the guest (because a larger amount of occupancy taxes would be owed). An alternative decision would be to increase the price of the room by $10.00 (now computed at $99.00) and to add $15.00 per meal ($30.00 total) for dinner. This plan allows the food and beverage manager to generate additional revenues, provides an additional $10.00 to compensate for any additional guest room housekeeping/related costs, but still provides additional funds for the franchisor and taxing authority. Some franchisors might complain that the pricing structure suggested above represents an effort by the hotel to escape paying higher franchise fees. From the hotel management's view, however, it may not be perceived that way because the base room charge ($89.00) and the upgraded room charge ($99.00) both represent significantly higher rates than the ADR upon which the hotel's franchise fees would normally be based ($85.00). GMs who review and approve pricing decisions and their tax impact should understand well the local ordinances affecting tax collection and the franchise fee requirements of their own franchisors (see Chapter 13).

There are two major ways in which the hotel's F&B operations differ from those in restaurants. These two major areas of difference, which must be understood by the GM, involve the availability of room service and the significant amount of business generated by banquet and convention services. These special dining services provide unique challenges to managers in a hotel's F&B departments and deserve additional attention.[1]

ROOM SERVICE OPERATIONS

Luxury and first-class hotels typically offer room service; many provide this amenity to guests 24/7 (24 hours per day, 7 days per week). Smaller full-service hotels generally offer room service as well, but on a more limited basis. Guests of all types use room service, ranging from the business traveler wanting a quick breakfast to small groups desiring a lunch while meeting in guest room suites, to couples desiring a romantic meal alone in the evening.

In large hotels, a room service manager with total responsibility for this service will be employed. In these operations, there may even be a separate food preparation area staffed by one or more cooks whose primary responsibilities involve preparation of room service orders. Likewise, room service orders from guests will be taken and delivered by, respectively, order takers and room service attendants whose primary responsibilities involve these tasks. In smaller properties, the F&B director may plan

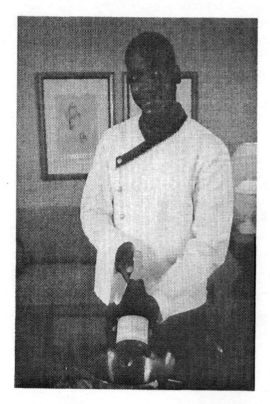

Champagne served in the guest room—a nice touch!

[1]Many books have been written about the field of quantity food production management and food service operations in a la carte dining operations. See, for example, Jack Ninemeier and David Hayes, *Restaurant Operations Management: Principles and Practices*. ISBN 0131100904. Upper Saddle River, NJ. Pearson Prentice Hall. 2006.

the room service menu, which is prepared by the same cook who produces restaurant meals. The meal would then be delivered to the guest room by a restaurant server according to the order written up by a server, dining room receptionist, or even front-desk agent who serves as the order taker.

Profitability Concerns

Guests and others who look at room service menus may think, "With these high prices, hotels must make a lot of profit on room service." In fact, relatively few properties generate profits from room service.[2]

If room service is not profitable for the hotel, why then is it offered? First, it is a service to guests. Some may select properties on the basis of room service availability. Examples include those arriving on late airline flights, guests wanting food and beverage services for small business meetings in their guest rooms, or simply individuals who wish to enjoy the luxury of "breakfast in bed." Also, hotel rating services such as the AAA and Mobil assign their highest ratings to properties that offer room service, as well as numerous other amenities.

Why does room service frequently lose money? One reason is that labor costs are very high. It can take a significant amount of time to transport food from the kitchen to guest room areas. Vertical (elevator) transportation required in high-rise hotels, and travel to remote locations when rooms are located in cottages or condominium units in resort properties require time and experienced delivery staff who know the fastest way to guest room locations.

Expenses incurred for capital costs such as delivery carts and warming devices can also be significant. Likewise, if costs were assigned to the F&B department for elevators needed to transport room service items and for "staging" areas needed to store room service carts and to prepare them for deliveries and other associated room service costs, true F&B expenses would even be greater. Finally, items such as glasses, cups, flatware, and serviceware increase room service costs still further. The need to return soiled room service items to kitchen areas often creates operating, as well as financial, problems. Even when quality food products are delivered quickly and guest satisfaction is high, dirty trays and dishes placed outside the room in hallways must be picked up and returned to the F&B department.

Housekeeping personnel, maintenance and security staff, and even managers who encounter these items often notice but do not pick up and return these to the F&B area, and this necessitates even more F&B labor to do so.

Some hotels use the room service department to provide F&B service in **hospitality suites** and for other group functions within a guest room.

HOTEL TERMINOLOGY AT WORK

Hospitality Suite: A guest room usually rented by an entity during conventions/conferences to provide complimentary food and/or beverages to invited guests.

---

[2]Recall difficulties with allocating expenses between departments and within the F&B department noted earlier. Without careful allocation, the financial status of one F&B activity—restaurant, bar, room service, or banquets—will be difficult to accurately assess. It is unlikely that many hotels allocate costs other than direct food and labor costs to the room service profit center, although costs for equipment, supplies, menus, utilities, and other costs may be significant.

For example, in convention properties, vendors and other exhibitors may invite current and prospective customers to visit hotel rooms for **hosted events** that include complimentary food and beverage items.

HOTEL TERMINOLOGY AT WORK

Hosted Events: Functions served by a hotel, which are complimentary to invited guests because costs are borne by the event's sponsor.

For example, a hosted bar may offer free beverages to guests of a wedding party, or a corporate sponsor may pay for a hosted reception with appetizers in a banquet room.

■

In hotels where this service is provided by room service rather than by banquet service, the likelihood that room service is profitable on those specific events does increase. GMs must understand the challenges of room service offerings and allocate the proper resources to this essential, but often less profitable, area of F&B.

Menu Planning Factors

Special concerns must be addressed when planning room service menus. First, as with any other food service alternative, quality is an important concern. Therefore, room service menus should offer only those products that can be transported relatively long distances from food preparation areas without decreases in quality. As distance increases, so does the time required to transport items. We have already noted that many guests perceive room service prices to be excessively high. They will certainly demand that food quality be maintained to help justify the perceived high prices. Unfortunately, some popular items such as omelets and french fries are not ideal room service menu items because of the quality deterioration that occurs when these products are held at serving temperature for long periods of time as they are transported to guest rooms. It is relatively easy for a GM to check food quality in a hotel restaurant or even in a banquet setting. Food and beverage items in these areas can (and should) be sampled. However, GMs have less access to the products served in room service. A proactive effort to solicit feedback from guests is critical to help assure that quality requirements are consistently attained.

Cross-selling on room service menus is one possible way to help improve profitability of the F&B department. For example, an invitation on the room service breakfast menu to call about daily dinner specials available through room service or in the dining room can be of interest to guests "thinking ahead" about evening plans.

Hotels in airports, urban, and other locations housing international guests may experience another room service challenge: language barriers. A guest who does not speak English and who is alone in a guest room with a menu written in English may have great difficulty in ordering. Alternatives such as pictures and menu item descriptions written in the languages most used by international guests visiting the specific hotel may be among the solutions. If there are minimum order charges, mandatory tipping policies, and/or other requirements for guest room orders, these should be clearly indicated on the menu and perhaps should also be stated by the order taker, if applicable. Increasingly, hotels are using in-room movie services to display room service menus in a variety of languages. This tactic also provides an opportunity for guests to evaluate the hotel (including F&B) from their own television screens using the TV's remote control.

THE INTERNET AT WORK

Pay-per-view (in-room) movie companies offer a variety of services to hotels, including those related to F&B. To view one such company's Web site, go to

www.oncommand.com

and review their F&B, and other product offerings.

Operating Issues

GMs must be assured that numerous room service operating issues are satisfactorily addressed within their property. For example, it is important that highly trained order takers be available regardless of whether this is a full-time position or only part of their responsibility. "Communication" problems occur all too frequently in room service. If complete orders are not taken, guest dissatisfaction is likely. The same types of questions asked in an à la carte restaurant must be asked by the room service order taker:

- How would you like your steak prepared?
- Would you like sour cream with your baked potato?
- Would you like tartar sauce with your fish fillet?
- Would you like a glass of wine to complete your dinner? ("Tonight's special wines would go well with your entrée, and they are a great value.")

It is often difficult to correct errors in any food service operation. However, an inaccurate order in the dining room can sometimes be quickly corrected. For example, ketchup for French fries can be immediately retrieved from the kitchen or servers' station for guest service in the dining room. However, the ketchup or other condiment omitted from the room service tray will require a relatively long and time-consuming trip back to the kitchen. Should the guest wait with lowered food quality as a result? Alternatively, should the guest consume the meal without the desired condiments? Either way, guest dissatisfaction will occur, and the negative impressions that arise may carry over to other experiences within the hotel. At the same time, room service attendants who must spend additional time on this re-work task will be unavailable to serve other guests. These guests, in turn, may become dissatisfied as the wait for their own room service order increases. A "minor" problem, then, can create a ripple effect that significantly impacts the guests' perceptions about their entire lodging experience.

Opportunities for upselling are also very useful for room service but, unfortunately, are often overlooked. The room service **guest check average** can be increased if guests are informed about items such as appetizers, cocktails, desserts, and à la carte entrée accompaniments that they may not have initially ordered because they did not know or think about them.

HOTEL TERMINOLOGY AT WORK

Guest Check Average: The average amount spent by a guest in a room service or dining room order. The guest check average typically includes the food and alcoholic beverage sales. Guest check average = total revenue ÷ total number of guests served.

If effective communication is very important between the guest ordering room service and the order taker who receives the order (and it is!), then communication between the room service food production staff and service staff is likewise critical. Room service orders may be handwritten or, increasingly, may be entered into a point-of-sale (POS) terminal. Orders can then be printed on hard-copy tickets that are given to the room service cook(s). In this case, a copy is also given to the server when the order is transported to the guest room. Alternatively, the POS system can be used to transmit orders to the cook(s) via a **remote printer**. Either way, it is important that any abbreviations (does "sp" stand for shrimp plate or seafood platter?) be clearly understood by both the order taker and food production personnel. It is also important for the room service attendant to carefully note that the items ordered are, in fact, the exact items that have been plated and placed on the cart for delivery.

HOTEL TERMINOLOGY AT WORK

Remote Printer: A unit in the kitchen preparation area that receives and prints orders entered through a point-of-sale terminal located in the dining room, room service order taker's workstation, or other area.

■

Technology has improved the accuracy of room service orders. For example, today's systems typically indicate the room number and the name of the guest registered in the room from which the order is placed. Using the guest's name is an effective selling and communication tactic, and it then becomes easy for the order taker to do so. Also, when the order is placed, information about the ability of the guest to charge a room service meal becomes available. For example, guests who pay cash for a room at time of check in are not usually permitted to charge room service or other product/services purchases to their room. Likewise, as guests using a credit card near a preestablished credit limit, this information is also readily available when the room service area is interfaced with the property management system (PMS). It is important, however, that GMs enforce security precautions by not allowing food and beverage personnel to print an unsecured document that could threaten guest safety with the guest's room number and name on the same printed ticket.

Within Guest Room Service

From the perspective of guests, room service does not "end" when the order reaches the guest room. In fact, that is only the beginning. Room service attendants must be adequately trained in service procedures, including:

- Asking guests where the room service meal should be set up
- Explaining procedures for retrieval of room service items
- Presenting the guest check and securing payment
- Opening bottles of wine, if applicable
- Providing an attitude of genuine hospitality (as opposed to being rushed to return to the kitchen for another room service delivery)

GMs must be aware of how room service in their hotel can be maintained and improved. In some properties, a section relating to room service is included in a general guest rating form used to evaluate the entire property that is left by housekeeping staff in all guest rooms. Alternately, a specific evaluation form provided when room service is delivered is used by other properties. The results of all guest feedback should be randomly requested from the F&B director and should be personally reviewed by the GM. When results are favorable, affected personnel should be complimented. If challenges arise, the GM should work with affected staff to resolve identified issues.

MANAGERS AT WORK

"Ya see, J.D., your problem is you have no 'Wow' factor," said Robert Fooley. "That's why you aren't packin' em in like me and the Outback Steakhouse."

J.D. Ojisama, the hotel GM, and David Berger, the hotel's F&B director, were having lunch with Robert Fooley, the manager of a successful Italian restaurant located near the hotel.

David had met Robert at a chamber of commerce meeting, invited him to lunch at Seville's, the hotel's main dining area, and asked the GM to join them because David knew Fooley's restaurant was one of J.D.'s favorites.

"If this were my place," continued Robert, "I'd put in an Italian menu, because that's popular with everyone. You could call it Gardino's or something Italian. Create some specialty items that are really good. Then advertise it all over the city. That's how you get business. And I'd close at breakfast. There's too little volume then anyway because everybody wants fast food in the morning. Drive-ups are too popular . . . ya know? Let me tell you, I know from experience, focus on what you do best and eliminate the rest. That's my motto, and it saves on labor costs!"

J.D. listened politely. "Interesting ideas, Bob," said J.D. "I'll discuss them with David after lunch."

If you were J.D., how would you react to Mr. Fooley's ideas? Why? What are some things that the average restaurateur may not understand about hotel food service? If you were J.D., and David left his employment at your hotel, would you hire Mr. Fooley as a replacement? Why or why not?

BANQUET OPERATIONS

The ability to plan and deliver a wide variety of types and sizes of **banquet** events sold by a **catering** salesperson is an important factor that separates F&B departments in hotels from many of their counterparts in other segments of the hospitality industry.

HOTEL TERMINOLOGY AT WORK

Banquet: A food and/or beverage event held in a function room.

Catering: The process of selling and carrying out the details of a banquet event.

In a large hotel, there may be a separate catering department, or it may be a unit within the marketing and sales department. Often catering responsibilities are shared between the F&B and the sales and marketing departments.

■

The volume of banquet business helps determine whether banquet operations are the responsibility of food production and service staff or, alternatively, whether persons with specialized banquet duties are utilized. The hotel's sales and marketing staff will normally be responsible for generating banquet business by negotiating contracts and arranging details for specific banquet events. However, there is an old saying in the hotel business: "You are only as good as your last banquet." Repeat business generated from guests who have enjoyed previous banquets can be very helpful in "selling" future ones. By contrast, the negative **"word-of-mouth" advertising** created by dissatisfied banquet guests can significantly increase (and undo) the work of the sales and marketing staff. It is just as important to satisfy banquet guests as it is to please guests being served in the hotel's restaurants, bars, lounges, and in-room service.

Hotel banquets may offer a lavish buffet to guests who are willing to pay for it.

HOTEL TERMINOLOGY AT WORK

"Word-of-Mouth" Advertising: Informal conversations between persons as they discuss their positive or negative experiences at a hotel.

■

Hotels that attract extensive convention and meeting business will have additional banquet needs. Large properties will likely have a separate convention services department whose personnel plan and coordinate all activities (including those that are F&B related) for the groups visiting the hotel. Planning a banquet for a group staying at the hotel is similar to planning a function for someone who is hosting an event for guests who are not staying at the hotel. There are, however, some differences, including:

- The need for numerous coffee and refreshment breaks for attendees during intermissions in business meetings
- The provision of hospitality suites and other functions within guest rooms

- The potential setup of receptions, breaks, and even dinner/buffet food services in public spaces within the hotel that may not normally be used for these purposes

GMs of smaller hotels in which the F&B director administers the banquet function and their counterparts in larger properties with specialized banquet managers reporting to the F&B director have something in common: they must both know and understand how banquet functions "work," how they can be evaluated, and how the banquets provided can better meet the hotel's profitability and guest-related goals.

Profit Opportunities

Banquet events are generally more profitable than restaurant (dining room) operations in hotels for several reasons:

- Banquets are frequently used to celebrate special events. This provides the opportunity for menu items that are more expensive and therefore higher in **contribution margin**.

HOTEL TERMINOLOGY AT WORK

Contribution Margin: The amount that remains after the product (food) cost of a menu item is subtracted from its selling price.

- The number of meals to be served at a banquet is known in advance; in fact, there is a formal **guarantee**. It is thus easier to schedule food production staff to reduce the "peaks and valleys" in labor that often occur during, respectively, busy and slow periods in dining room operations. Often some parts of a banquet's food production can be done one or more days prior to the event. There is also less likelihood of overproduction of food with subsequent waste because guest counts are known.

HOTEL TERMINOLOGY AT WORK

Guarantee: A contractual agreement about the number of meals to be provided at a banquet event. Typically, a guarantee must be made several days in advance of the event. At that time, the entity contracting with the hotel for the event agrees to pay for the larger of the actual number of guests served or the number of guests guaranteed.

- Banquet planners are frequently able to sell **hosted bars** or **cash bars**, which enable increased sales of alcoholic beverages to guests desiring them.

HOTEL TERMINOLOGY AT WORK

Hosted Bar: A beverage service alternative in which the host of a function pays for beverages during all or part of the banquet event; also called an "open" bar.

Cash Bars: A beverage service alternative where guests desiring beverages during a banquet function pay for them personally.

- Banquet service is performed within a relatively short time frame with known starting and ending times that make it easier to plan service labor. In addition, servers find working these events attractive because, in most cases, mandatory service charges result in significant increases in their income.
- Often charges for the actual function space in which the banquet is held represent significant additions to food and beverage product sales. For example, a hotel's ballroom, on a Saturday night in December, may command a significant rental fee in addition to the meal(s) and beverages purchased, because of the increased demand for such space around the December holidays.

For these reasons, banquet business is very desirable, and GMs should assure that their property is receiving its reasonable portion of the market's available banquet business. It is a good idea to collect data about, review, and evaluate banquet revenue separately from other sources of revenue within F&B.

Menu Planning

Most of the factors involved in planning a menu for the hotel's restaurant(s) and other dining outlets are important when planning banquet menus. These include concerns about:

- Guest preferences
- The ability to consistently produce items of the desired quality
- The availability of ingredients required to produce the menu items
- Production/service staff with appropriate skills
- Equipment/layout/facility design issues
- Nutritional issues
- Sanitation concerns
- Peak volume production and operating concerns
- The ability to generate required profit levels at the selling prices charged

There are additional special concerns applicable to planning banquet menus. For example, the menu planner must be confident that the items offered can be produced in the appropriate quantity at the appropriate level of quality and within the required time schedule. The old saying, "The guest (host) is always right," must be tempered when banquet menus are planned. "Cooked-to-order" steaks, for example, are not typically practical when 500 guests must be served in 30 minutes. The menu planner must recognize that the hotel, not the host, will likely be criticized if there is a failure to deliver according to anticipated standards.

For example, consider an overzealous host desiring a flambéed entrée, table-side Caesar salad, and handmade pastries for hundreds of guests. These items are very labor-intensive and a large amount of specialized service/equipment is needed. Personnel in the sales and marketing department are setting up a "no-win" situation for the hotel if they book this event when hotel employees are not able to adequately execute it. If the hotel accepts the business and is unable to effectively deliver the promised banquet event, all or many of the guests will likely be upset. If the host cannot be "sold" on a more practical menu at the time the event is planned, future business may be lost because the hotel will not perform well. As a result, it is certainly in the hotel's best long-term interests to refuse banquet business that cannot be delivered according to quality standards.

Because of the potential complexity of banquet menus, many hotels offering banquets have developed preestablished banquet menus. Carefully planned to consider the hotel's production limitations and to incorporate the property's desired contribution margin, these menus are an excellent starting point for negotiations with prospective clients. Often these menus can be used without change, or relatively minor changes such as a substitution of a specific dessert or vegetable item can be made.

On other occasions a menu designed specifically for the host and his/her special event is needed or desired. A talented banquet planner working in close conjunction with the property's culinarians can develop a menu that meets the guests' expectations and the hotel's financial requirements. By contrast, when there is not close cooperation between the sales and marketing department and food preparation personnel, concerns to generate short-term business (for example, to meet revenue goals) may overshadow longer-term goals of consistently pleasing guests to generate repeat business. Alternatively, if F&B departments put excessive restrictions on sales personnel (for example, by overly restricting what food items can be produced), sales revenue will suffer. GMs must continually monitor this relationship to assure that neither the sales and marketing nor F&B personnel are operating in ways that are detrimental to the hotel's success.

Successful catering is a matter of paying attention to numerous details. To help in the planning process, most hotels utilize a customized **banquet event order (BEO)**. A sample BEO is shown in Figure 10.3. Properties doing extensive business in certain events, for example, weddings or bar mitzvahs, may have specialized BEOs for these occasions. Figure 10.4 shows a Sample Wedding Banquet Event Order Checklist. Banquet event orders can be very simple (all details might be included on a single BEO); alternatively, they can be much more extensive.

HOTEL TERMINOLOGY AT WORK

Banquet Event Order (BEO): A form used by the sales, catering, and food production areas to detail all requirements for a banquet. Information provided by the banquet client is summarized on the form, and it becomes the basis for the formal contract between the client and the hotel.

Service Styles

Banquet events can involve numerous ways to serve food and beverage products to guests. In fact, frequently more than one service style is used in a single event. Examples include:

- *Butler Service.* Appetizers and prepoured champagne, for example, can be passed by service personnel as they circulate among guests standing at a reception.

- *Buffet Service.* Quantities of food are prearranged on a self-service line; guests pass through the line and help themselves. Sometimes items such as roast beef or ham are carved or omelets are prepared at the guests' request by production staff.

- *Family Style.* Also called "English" style, platters and bowls of food are filled in the kitchen and are brought to the guests' tables. Guests help themselves to the food and pass platters to each other just as they might do at home.

EVENT DATE:
Organization:
Billing Address:

Contact Name:
Account Executive:
Guaranteed: (   ) persons

BEVERAGES

• Full	• Limited
• Hosted bar	• Non-hosted bar

• With bartender	( ) bars
• Cash bar	( ) cashiers

• Premium	• Call	• House

(   ) per drink   (   ) bar package
(   ) hours of operation

Time: **Room:**

Bar Opening/Closing Instructions:
Bar to close at: _____ A.M. / P.M.
Bar to reopen at: _____ A.M. / P.M.

Wine with Lunch / Dinner
_____ with entrée,
servers

Time: Location:

Additional Instructions:

FOOD MENU

_____ baseplates
_____ waterglasses
_____ butter rosettes on lemon leaves

• Introduction	• Invocation
• Nothing before meal	

First Course Served at: _____ A.M. / P.M.
Meal Served at: _____ A.M. / P.M.

BEVERAGE MENU

BANQUET EVENT ORDER (BEO) #:

Business Phone #:
Business Fax #:
Business E-Mail:
Room Rental: $

ROOM SET UP

• Classroom	• Theater
• Other: _____	

• Diagram below
Need:

• Registration table / chairs:
• Wastebasket
• Easels
• Podium: • standing   • tabletop
• Pads / pencils / pens / mints
• Water / glasses

Diagram:

Linen:
• White   • Other:

Skirting:

Napkin:
• White   • Other:

Music:

AUDIO/VISUAL

• Microphone: _____
• Slide Projector — package: _____
• Overhead Projector — package: _____
• VHS / monitor / package: _____
• Mixer _____ channel   • AV—cart
• White board / markers   • Screen
• Flipchart/pads/tape/pens
• LCD projector

COAT CHECK

• Hosted   • Cash: _____
(   ) Attendant(s)   (   ) Coat Racks

PARKING

• Hosted   • Cash: $ _____
• Fee per car: $ _____

BILLING (METHOD OF PAYMENT)

• Deposit received: $ _____

FIGURE 10.3   Sample Banquet Event Order (BEO)

REHEARSAL   Time: _____   Room: _____
- Skirted Table: _____
- Theater Style facing: _____
- Water Station: _____
- Coat Rack
- Juice—Charge to: • Client   • A&P
- Soft Drinks—Charge to: • Client   • A&P
- Coffee/Tea—Charge to: • Client   • A&P

PICTURES   Time: _____   Room: _____
- Finger Sandwiches: _____
- Assorted Juices: _____
- Assorted Soft Drinks: _____
- Cabaret Style Seating: _____
- Water Station: _____

PRE-CEREMONY RECEPTION   Time: _____   Room: _____
- Beverage:
- Food:
- Placecard Table
- Other Information:

CEREMONY   Time: _____   Room: _____
Doors Open: _____
Invitation Time: _____
Wedding Ceremony: _____
- Theater Style facing: _____
- Skirted Table: _____
- Placecard Table
- Linen:
- Skirt: _____
- Musicians   • Piano
- Florist   • Coat Check
- A/V—1 standing mike

RECEPTION   Time: _____   Room: _____
- Postceremony Beverage Service: _____
- Hosted Bar: _____
- Closing Instructions: _____
- Champagne Toast: _____
- Wine Toast with Dinner: _____
- After Dinner Beverage Service: _____

HORS D'OEUVRES
- Butler Style
- Buffet Style
- Station Style

FIGURE 10.4   Sample Wedding Banquet Event Order Checklist

RECEPTION INSTRUCTIONS
- Set _____   Bars: _____
- Seating: _____
- Votives: _____
- Hurricanes: _____
- Receiving line on _____ wall
- Piano on _____ wall
- See diagram for buffet station location(s):
Smoking: • Allowed   • Not-Allowed

DINNER/DANCE   Time: _____   Room: _____

ANNOUNCE/TOAST/DANCE INSTRUCTIONS
- Bride & Groom to be announced   • Bridal Dance
- Blessing Before the Meal
- Wedding Toast: _____
- Dance Sets: _____
- Cake Cutting: _____

WEDDING SPECIAL INSTRUCTIONS
- Base Plates
- Water Glasses

MENU
- Entrée
- Meal Substitutions

CAKE/SWEET/TABLE/COFFEE
- Wedding Cake   • Client's Own
- Sweet Table   • Client's Own
- Sweet Table Server(s): _____
- Wedding Coffee Service: _____ gallons

DINNER/DANCE INSTRUCTIONS
- Rounds per floor plan to be numbered: _____
- Table numbers provided by: • Client   • Hotel
- Dance Floor: _____
- Cake Table set per diagram
- Sweet Table set per diagram
- Extra Cabaret Tables set: _____
Smoking: • Allowed   • Not Allowed
- Linen: _____
- Skirting: _____
- Napkin Fold: _____
- Entertainment   • Florist
- Photographer   • Videographer
- Parking Valet: $_____ /car
- Hosted   • Guests to handle own charges
- Consultant: _____

Hors D'oeuvres

FIGURE 10.4   *(Continued)*

Dinner	
Wedding Cake	
Coffee Service	
Sweets Table	
Other Information	

FIGURE 10.4   *(Continued)*

- *French Service.* This most elegant of service involves table-side preparation or finishing of food items such as tossing a Caesar salad or flambéing an entrée, beverage, or a sauce for dessert.
- *Platter Service.* Also called "Russian" service, this style involves the plating of food in the kitchen onto large serving trays. These trays are then brought to the table where the server places individual portions on guest plates that have been preset.
- *Plated Service.* Also called "American" service, this style involves the proportioning of food on plates that are then brought to the table for service to the guests.

Service styles can be a way to differentiate an elegant and often higher-priced banquet from their less-elegant and lower-priced counterparts. For example, a Caesar salad might be prepared as a "demonstration" for those seated at a **head table**, and then preportioned servings of the Caesar salad could then be brought to the remaining guest tables for service.

HOTEL TERMINOLOGY AT WORK

Head Table: Special seating at a banquet reserved for guests of honor.

■

Alternatively, vegetables for a soup course could be brought to the guest table in a bowl (American service); service staff could pour broth from a sterling pitcher into each guest's bowl (modified Russian service). These are examples of simple ways to make a banquet appear more elegant.

Contrast these examples with a more traditional banquet service style where salads are preset when guests arrive and the entrée with accompanying vegetables is served American-style after salad plates are removed. GMs should be aware of the impact that elegance can have on banquet events and should encourage catering and banquet staff to sell, produce, and deliver high-quality and creative banquet services that are within their capabilities. Guests will think, "Wow; what a great surprise," and the first steps toward repeat banquet business will have been taken.

Beverage Functions

Banquets often feature the service of alcoholic beverages. This can involve receptions before an event and wine service during the function, as well as continuing service of beverages during and after the meal service has concluded.

Keeping in mind that banquets often celebrate special occasions, there may be increased opportunities to offer **"call brand"** or **"premium brand" beverages** in addition to or in place of the property's **"house brand" beverages**.

HOTEL TERMINOLOGY AT WORK

"Call Brand" Beverages: High-priced and higher-quality alcoholic beverages that are sold by name (such as Johnny Walker Red Scotch or Bombay Gin) rather than sold by type of liquor (scotch or gin) only.

"Premium Brand" Beverages: The highest-priced and highest-quality beverages generally available. Examples include Johnny Walker Black Scotch and Bombay Sapphire Gin; these brands are sometimes referred to as "Super Call" brands.

"House Brand" Beverages: Alcoholic beverages that are sold by type (scotch and gin, for example) rather than by brand name and that are served when a call brand beverage is not requested. Sometimes referred to as "Well" brands.

■

There are several common ways that beverages sold at banquet events can be charged for and priced. For example, beverages can be sold at a cash bar where guests desiring beverages pay for them personally. By contrast, some events may offer a "Host" (open) bar in which beverages are paid for by the host. Still other events have a combination cash and host bar where, for example, drink tickets are issued for complimentary drinks and the guest can then purchase additional beverages. Another variation of this arrangement occurs when drinks are complimentary for a specified time period (for example, before dinner) and are then paid for on a cash basis by guests desiring them after that time (such as during and after dinner).

There are several ways that charges for beverages can be assessed:

- *Individual Drink Price.* With this method, cash or a ticket sold for cash is collected when each drink is sold. Alternatively, with a host bar, a tally is made of the number of each type of drink sold, and the host is charged an agreed-upon price per drink basis at the end of the banquet event.

- *Bottle Charge.* With this method, commonly used with a host bar, beverages are charged for on a by-bottle basis for each bottle consumed and/or opened. Normally, any bottle opened is charged at a full, agreed-upon rate. Guests are not generally allowed to take open bottles away from the hotel.
- *Per-Person Charge.* This method involves charging a specific price for beverages based upon attendance at the event. For example, the same number of guests used for the meal guarantee discussed earlier may be used as the basis for the per-person charge for alcoholic beverages. A deduction from the guarantee is made for minors attending the event who will not be permitted to consume alcoholic beverages.
- *Hourly Charge.* This method involves charging the host a specific price for each hour of beverage service provided. Properties using this pricing method must first determine the number of guests to be present (the food guarantee can be used with adjustment for guests who will not consume alcoholic beverages) along with the estimated number of drinks to be consumed per hour to arrive at a proper price.

Labor and Other Charges

Costs for labor required to produce and serve banquet food is normally included in the price charged for the banquet. However, sometimes, especially when the estimated number of guests is small and the variety of services requested is large, additional charges for the following types of labor are assessed:

- Bartenders and barbacks (bartender assistants)
- Beverage servers
- Beverage cashiers
- Security personnel
- Valet (parking) staff
- Coat room employees

Some hotels charge a **corkage fee** for alcoholic beverages brought into the property for use during the event.

HOTEL TERMINOLOGY AT WORK

Corkage Fee: A charge levied by a hotel when a guest brings a bottle (for example, of a special wine) to the hotel for consumption at a banquet function or in the hotel's dining room.

Often misunderstood by banquet guests, hotels do incur fees when guests bring in prepurchased beverages. For example, the beverages must be served (a labor cost is incurred), and the bar and dining areas must be clean; glasses are subject to breakage and must be used and washed; stir sticks, cocktail napkins along with appropriate garnishes, if applicable, and perhaps other supplies will also still be necessary.

Hotels charge for meeting space and function room space. Most frequently, this occurs when the number of guests to be served, and therefore the amount of revenue to be generated, is small. These charges may be waived or reduced when a specified minimum amount of revenue will be generated by a banquet event.

Banquet Room Setup

In large hotels, banquet rooms may be set up by housekeeping (public-space) staff. In other facilities, especially properties such as those discussed in this text, this activity may be the responsibility of staff members within the F&B department. Regardless of the department responsible, the required activities are the same.

The function space assigned for a banquet is normally determined when the banquet event is booked and will be specified on the banquet event order. Unfortunately, hoteliers are sometimes confronted with ethical, financial, and/or legal issues when, for example, space originally committed to one event is reallocated for the retention of another event. This often occurs when larger (and more profitable) events are brought to the attention of the personnel in the sales and marketing department after commitments with groups hosting smaller events have been made.

Numerous details are involved in setting up a banquet room. Size is obviously determined by the number of guests expected, although local fire safety codes and ordinances may also impact this decision. In addition to the number of guests, the type of dining room tables (round or rectangular, for example) along with their size and the number of seats per table and required space for aisles, dance floors, bandstands, other entertainment, head tables, and reception/buffet tables, if applicable, will impact requirements. Timing also becomes critical as when, for example, the same space is to be used for different functions throughout the same day or when a very large evening event precedes a very large breakfast event in the same space on the following day.

Banquet Contracts and Billing Policies

GMs must confirm that plans, procedures, and policies are in effect to help assure that there are "no surprises" as banquets are being planned and served. A banquet contract is an excellent tool in this effort. It is wise to have the hotel's standard banquet contract reviewed by an experienced attorney to assure that the best interests of the hotel are legally protected. Topics to be addressed by banquet contracts typically include:

- Guest contact information.
- Agreed-upon charges and prices.
- Specific function room assignment.
- Last date that function space will be held without a signed contract.
- Time by when a guarantee of attendance must be received.
- Cancellation policies, including an explanation of fees to be assessed if the banquet contract is canceled. For example, if the contract date is 180 or more days in advance of the event, the fee for canceling may be 50 percent of the anticipated billing; if the contract is voided from 61 to 179 days before the event, there may be a cancellation fee of 75 percent; a 100 percent fee may apply if a cancellation occurs 60 days or less from the date of the event.
- Guarantee reduction policy. If, for example, the final guarantee is less than a specified percentage of the initial guarantee, an additional charge (often equal to the meeting room charge) may be assessed.
- Billing. Information about the amount and schedule for guest payment is frequently included. Typically, the full remaining payment is due at the beginning or end of the event.

○ Information about the service of alcoholic beverages (if applicable).

○ Other information applicable to the specific event.

A sample copy of a banquet contract is shown in Figure 10.5.

Date _____

Address

Dear, _____

It was a great pleasure speaking with you today, and I would like to thank you for selecting the new Waldo Hotel & Conference Center for your meeting location. We are extremely pleased to do business with you and your group. Based on our discussion the following arrangements have been made.

Schedule of Events:

Room Rental:
Your events will be held in our _____ room at a rate of $_____/day plus applicable tax. Meeting rooms are reserved on the basis of anticipated attendance. Setup style and times are required. The hotel reserves the right to change the room accommodations to best suit your needs and actual final guest count guarantee. A request to change the contracted setup of a meeting room (once the room has been set) will result in a $___ reset fee.

Audiovisual:
Should you require any audiovisual equipment, please let me know as soon as possible as I may need to order the equipment in advance.

Food and Beverage:
The hotel must supply all food and beverage. Menu arrangements should be concluded at least 14 days prior to each function and a guarantee of the number of guests is needed 7 business days in advance, with final adjustment of guarantee at least 72 hours prior to your scheduled function date. The Waldo Hotel will allow for a variance of 5 percent over the number of guests guaranteed in preparation of food and table settings.

Billing:
All meeting room and food charges will be the responsibility of _____.

Form of Payment:
A deposit in full, valid credit card number, or completed direct bill application must be returned with this signed contract for guarantee purposes.

General Liability:
The Waldo Hotel reserves the right to inspect and control all functions. The Waldo Hotel is not responsible for loss or damages no matter how caused, to any samples, displays, properties, or personal effects, brought into the hotel.

Cancellation Policy:
This agreement may be canceled by either party, without penalty, or liability, in the event of Acts of Nature, government regulations, disaster, strikes, labor strife, civil disorder, construction activities, fire, flood, earthquake, or other emergency or event making it inadvisable, illegal, or impossible to provide facilities or to hold the function upon written notice to the other party specifying such cause.

FIGURE 10.5   Sample Copy of a Banquet Contract

Should it be necessary to cancel your function less than 14 business days prior to your arrival a cancellation fee of $ _____ will be billed to _____.

No-Show Policy:
In the event of a no-show on your behalf, we will bill your company for the cancellation fee and any food, audiovisual, or setup fees that your group would have accrued.

The above outlined arrangements are currently being held on:

A tentative first-option basis for _____ days

To confirm these arrangements, please sign and return one copy of this Letter of Agreement by _____. After this date, we reserve the right to release the space you have requested.

Our entire hotel is looking forward to working with you and your group. If you have any questions, please feel free to call me on my direct line at (xxx) xxx-xxxx.

Sincerely;

Signature

Agreed To:

By the Hotel   _____   By the Client   _____

Title   _____   Title   _____

Date   _____   Date   _____

FIGURE 10.5   *(Continued)*

Accurate and timely billing of banquets at their conclusion is critical. It is the final step in the catering process and must be handled well. As a hotel GM, it is important to remember that a banquet properly executed will still become a negative experience for the client if the billing is not appropriately handled. It will also be a negative experience for the hotel if the billings are not accurately made, and if monies are not collected in a timely manner. Working with the F&B department and the controller, the GM must assure that proper procedures are in place to achieve these goals.

MANAGERS AT WORK

The DOSM was very excited and couldn't wait to tell J.D. Ojisama, the hotel's GM.

"You won't believe who I just talked to, J.D." said Michele Austin. "I just got off the phone with the meeting planner for the Accidental Insurance group. They want to book us for four days of meetings here. Basically, they want all the function space we have available, plus a large block of overnight rooms."

"That's great," replied J.D. "Nice job, Michele. You rock! I know your sales team has worked hard to get them to give us a try. This could be really big for us. I would estimate they buy 2,000 to 3,000 room nights per year, every year, in this city."

"That's not all," continued Michele. "The big news for us now is that they want to have a gala reception and banquet at the end of their meeting to honor their new incoming president . . . who's best friend happens to be the governor! So the governor will be attending! I might be overstating it a little bit, J.D., but, basically, my contact said that for this event, money is no problem. They want it nice, and they understand the costs."

"How many people at the gala?" asked J.D.

"They want to hold a function for about 450 people with predinner cocktails, ice carvings, live entertainment, a four-course meal, and just about anything else we want to suggest for them," replied Michele.

"Well," said J.D., "this is great, but it will also be a challenge! Everyone will really have to be on top of things that night. Let's go see the F&B director and give him the news."

"You have got to be kidding!" exclaimed the F&B director when he heard about the sale. "I requested that weekend off three months ago for an Alaskan cruise, and I already bought nonrefundable tickets for my wife and myself. You approved my request, J.D. Remember? Now what do we do?"

If you were J.D., would you ask the F&B director to cancel his vacation? What types of F&B-related concerns might you have about the event as it has been described? How much of a role should J.D. play as this event is being planned? In which departments? How important is it that this event makes a profit for the hotel? What level of food production skills must J.D. have to be able to lead the department heads in the successful execution of this event? Why?

ALCOHOLIC BEVERAGE SERVICE IN HOTELS

Those hotels that serve alcoholic beverages face even greater responsibilities in the operation of their F&B department than do hotels that do not have a license to serve these products. The consumption of alcoholic beverages is, of course, common with meal service, at premeal receptions, and in a hotel's bars and lounges. For centuries, alcohol has been enjoyed, in moderation, before, during, and after meals. Today, moderate (not excessive) consumption of alcohol is obligatory for those who serve and those who consume alcohol because, in part, of the expansion of **third-party liability (Dram shop)** legislation.

HOTEL TERMINOLOGY AT WORK

Third-Party Liability (Dram shop): A legal concept that holds the second party (the hotel serving alcohol) responsible for acts caused by the first party (the drinker), if the drinker subsequently causes harm to a third party (the victim of an accident).

This is often referred to as Dram shop liability.

Like restaurants, all hotels selling alcoholic beverages must comply with numerous state and local laws and regulations as a condition to do so. As a result, the need to develop procedures and to provide employee training designed to help assure the responsible service and consumption of alcoholic beverages is an integral part of the responsibility of the F&B director's job. This is an area that the GM must personally

Hotel managers have legal and societal concerns to assure that their guests consume alcoholic beverages responsibly.

monitor for compliance. It is important to assure that every individual who will serve alcoholic beverages has been trained in proper service procedures and that this training is well documented. You owe this duty to your hotel owners, your franchise affiliation, your guests, your own staff, and of course the community in which you live.

The effects of a highly publicized case in which your hotel illegally served alcohol to a guest that results in injury to another is reason enough for you to absolutely ensure that training in alcohol service is mandatory in your hotel. Fortunately, materials to conduct such training are readily available.

THE INTERNET AT WORK

One of the most popular alcohol server programs is TIPS (Training for Intervention ProcedureS). To view the Web site for this program, go to

www.gettips.com

In fact, many GMs require that every employee (even those not in F&B) be trained in some aspect of alcohol awareness. Such training is important for many reasons. Some examples include:

- Hotel personnel in non-F&B positions can be trained to recognize and respond to obvious and visible signs of guests' and nonguests' intoxication and report these to management.
- Any employee may observe guests consuming alcohol within the hotel but in locations where such consumption is not allowed.

- Front-desk, housekeeping, maintenance, and/or security staff may observe guests appearing to be underage bringing alcoholic beverages on to the property and into guest rooms.
- Employees of any department may observe guests who are legally able to consume alcohol supplying that alcohol to underage guests.

Controlling the sale of alcoholic beverages is difficult enough in dining rooms, bars, and lounges, but is even more difficult in banquet rooms where guests do not have a designated server but instead go to a portable bar area and then return to their tables. In cases such as this, it can be difficult to monitor the number of drinks consumed by each guest. The service of alcoholic beverages during banquets is just another example of why managing a hotel's F&B department is more difficult than managing a traditional restaurant or bar.

Recognizing the seriousness of the alcoholic beverage service issue, the EI-AH&LA has developed an extensive array of hotel-specific training materials designed to assist F&B directors and GMs in providing the proper alcohol-related training for all hotel staff members. As the hotel's GM, you must assure that this training occurs as part of your property's efforts to protect guests, the public, and the hotel itself from tragedies and lawsuits that can arise when this training is not provided.

THE INTERNET AT WORK

The Educational Institute of AH&LA continually improves "C.A.R.E." its alcohol-related training program. To download clips from their most recent C.A.R.E. training videos, go to

www.ei-ahla.org

Under "Products" select, "Product Showcase." Scroll down to "C.A.R.E."

Food and beverage service is the defining characteristic of full-service hotels. This department may be large or small, but it is always a complex and fascinating area of hotel administration. The serious GM is advised to become as knowledgeable as possible in the intricacies of F&B management to ensure that this important department contributes to, rather than detracts from, the hotel's guest service and financial performance goals.

HOTEL TERMINOLOGY AT WORK GLOSSARY

The following terms were defined within this chapter. If you are not familiar with one of them, please review the segment of the chapter that contains the term.

F&B	Repeat business	Service charges
Food and beverage director	Resources	Fixed labor costs
Commercial food service operations	Serving	Cross-selling
	Service	Restaurant row
Institutional (noncommercial) food service operations	Audiovisual (AV) equipment	Day-part
	Profitability	Hospitality suite
Function room	Expenses	Hosted events

Guest check average
Remote printer
Banquet
Catering
"Word-of-mouth" advertising
Contribution margin

Guarantee
Hosted bars
Cash bars
Banquet event order (BEO)
Head table
Call brand beverages

Premium brand beverages
House brand beverages
Corkage fee
Third-party liability (Dram shop)

ISSUES AT WORK

1. This chapter has identified some similarities and differences between F&B operations in hotels and restaurants. If you were interested in an F&B management position, how would you decide the segment in which you would initially seek employment? What are some advantages and disadvantages to an F&B career in hotels versus restaurants?

2. How does the extent to which revenues and expenses are assigned (allocated) between hotel departments impact the ability of an F&B department to show a profit? As a GM, what guidelines could you establish to help assure that all F&B expense allocation procedures are practical and fair?

3. One ongoing source of potential hotel conflict involves the F&B department and the sales and marketing department. As a future GM, do you feel that catering event coordination management should be a part of the sales and marketing department or the F&B department? Identify at least three advantages and disadvantages of each organizational placement.

4. Some hotels use dining room servers and room service attendants interchangeably. What kind of special training would a room service attendant need to become an efficient dining room server? What types of additional training would a dining room server require to be an effective room service attendant? What are the advantages and disadvantages to utilizing the same persons to work in both of these positions during the same shift?

5. This chapter has stated that all personnel in the hotel require training in the responsible service of alcoholic beverages. How would you explain the need for this training to a new room service attendant, front-desk clerk, and maintenance department employee? How would you incorporate this training into the new employee orientation of each?

Facility Engineering
and Maintenance

This Chapter at Work

GMs know that their guests have expectations about the hotel that must consistently be met. These include such basic items as ample hot water for baths and showers, operating guest room lights, and comfortable temperatures in the hotel's public spaces and guest rooms. In addition, the hotel's owners have expectations. These include ensuring that the routine building repair and maintenance required to protect the value of their asset is diligently performed. The expectations of both of these constituencies will best be met if GMs create and support a dynamic engineering and maintenance (E&M) department within their property.

The hotel's E&M department head is called the chief engineer. This individual, along with the department's staff, ensures that the hotel's grounds and physical plant are well maintained. A well-run department assists the hotel's sales effort because the appearance and maintenance of the building's exterior and interior affects the ability of sales staff to sell rooms and events.

It is easy to see why, for example, it is critical to change a burned-out lightbulb in the hotel's parking lot. Guests need to be able to see in the parking lot at night, guest safety is affected, and the entire hotel's appearance will improve if the lightbulb is promptly replaced. In a similar manner, a guest room television that does not work properly should be promptly identified, repaired, or replaced so guest satisfaction will not be adversely affected. It is less easy to see, yet just as important, for someone to be responsible for maintaining all of the hotel's equipment and facilities in the public areas, guest rooms, and food

service and laundry areas. If this is not done, guest complaints and a reduction in the hotel's financial value are inevitable.

The general condition of public spaces, including exterior grounds, lobbies, and corridors, make a big impression on guests who stay in your hotel. In this chapter the maintenance needs of these visible spaces, as well as important areas within guest rooms and the hotel's food service and laundry facilities, are examined in detail. This will help you gain the knowledge needed to implement procedures designed to ensure that guests enjoy their stay at your hotel.

In addition to affecting guests, the way a hotel's physical plant is maintained has a tremendous impact on the hotel's profitability. When utilities such as water, gas, and electricity are not well managed, and the equipment that utilizes these resources is not well maintained, the hotel's operating costs will be higher than necessary. Just as importantly, valuable natural resources will be wasted, and the environment will be negatively affected. In this chapter, you will learn how to effectively oversee this important area of your hotel.

Finally, GMs must know how modern technology can assist with the hotel's engineering and maintenance functions. As well, they must know how to assess which maintenance and other services should be performed by staff members and alternatively, which, if any, should be outsourced. In addition, they must work with the chief engineer to manage and evaluate any service contracts in effect. These issues are addressed in a final section of the chapter.

Chapter 11 Outline

Every hotel has a variety of assets including its staff, cash in the bank, guest base, and reputation. The hotel's grounds, buildings, and equipment comprise its most visible and, usually, its most expensive asset. These assets directly affect the value of all other assets. How guests perceive the hotel's facilities makes a tremendous impact on its profitability. It is therefore important that the hotel's owners, GM, and other managers protect and maintain them.

ROLE OF THE ENGINEERING AND MAINTENANCE DEPARTMENT

When a hotel's building, equipment, and grounds are properly maintained, guests will be more likely to enjoy a positive experience during their stay and the hotel's ability to increase revenues is enhanced. This is the primary job of the engineering and maintenance (E&M) department. When guests experience poor facilities such as potholes in parking areas, leaking faucets, burned-out lightbulbs, poor heating/cooling capacities, or insufficient hot water, guest dissatisfaction increases, and the hotel's sales potential is diminished. In addition to guest satisfaction, however, an effective E&M department achieves other important goals, including:

- Protecting and enhancing the financial value of the building and grounds for the hotel's owners
- Supporting the efforts of all other hotel departments through the timely attention to their E&M needs
- Controlling maintenance and repair costs
- Controlling energy usage
- Increasing the pride and morale of the hotel's staff
- Ensuring the safety of those working in and visiting the hotel

These goals will be achieved if the E&M department, using outside consultants and/or contractors if necessary, meets its responsibilities for designing and constructing the building (engineering), maintaining the building (maintenance), and periodically renovating and modernizing it (design and renovation).

Hotel managers rely on their chief engineers to maintain and repair today's complex building systems.

Engineering

Many hotel managers use the terms **engineering** and **maintenance** interchangeably. Hoteliers are just as likely to refer to the department responsible for the care of the hotel as "engineering," as they are to call it "maintenance," or some combination of both terms.

HOTEL TERMINOLOGY AT WORK

Engineering: Designing and operating a building to ensure a safe and comfortable atmosphere.

Maintenance: The activities required to keep a building and its contents in good repair.

■

Engineering, as a building specialty, however, is distinct from maintenance. The engineering of a building refers to the application of physics, chemistry, and mathematics to design and operate buildings that provide a comfortable atmosphere for guests and employees. For example, since a hotel lobby must usually be air-conditioned, an engineer must calculate the amount of air-conditioned air required to properly cool it. Factors to be considered include the temperature and humidity of the outside air, the desired lobby temperature, the temperature at which air-conditioned air enters the lobby, and the movement of the air once inside the lobby. Based on these calculations, the size of the air-conditioning unit required to cool the lobby is determined, as is the optimum number and location of air vents to deliver the cold air to the area.

The knowledge required to balance each of these features and to make the proper decisions is significant. GMs do not usually have the engineering background required to make unassisted decisions about the engineered systems within a hotel and must therefore look to the chief engineer for help. Many large properties employ persons with the knowledge needed to make these calculations. Most small hotels do not, and engineering consultants must be retained when these and related issues are of concern.

Improperly engineered facilities can result in under- or overpowered equipment, increased building deterioration, excessive energy use, and higher-than-necessary operating costs. Typically, the chief engineer in a hotel will not have designed the **HVAC** systems within the building; however, he or she must be knowledgeable about them, as well as the engineering of the electrical, water, and waste systems within the building. If the chief engineer is not, even routine maintenance will be difficult to perform (or even worse, will be performed improperly).

HOTEL TERMINOLOGY AT WORK

HVAC: Shorthand for "heating, ventilating, and air-conditioning."

THE INTERNET AT WORK

Engineering a building's heating, refrigeration, ventilation, and air-conditioning systems is quite complex, and special knowledge is required to manage it. To familiarize yourself with an organization whose members specialize in this field, go to the Web site of the American Society of Heating, Refrigerating, and Air-Conditioning Engineers, Inc., at

www.ashrae.com

Maintenance

As the term implies, *maintenance* refers simply to "maintaining" the hotel's physical property. It has been said that maintenance costs are like taxes; if they are not paid one year, they will be paid in the next year—and with a penalty!

The maintenance-related costs of a hotel vary with its age. Older buildings generally incur increased maintenance costs. Even new hotels, however, require **POM**-related expenditures for staff wages and benefits, replacement parts, contract services, and energy costs listed separately on the property's income statement.

HOTEL TERMINOLOGY AT WORK

POM: Short for "property operation and maintenance." The term is taken from the Uniform System of Accounts for Hotels and refers to the segment of the income statement that details the costs of operating the E&M department.

A GM should expect E&M staff to maintain the property in the most effective manner possible given its budget. To do so, hotel maintenance must be:

- *Planned.* From routinely changing air filters in heating and cooling units to awarding a contract for tree trimming, the E&M department performs too many tasks to leave these activities to chance. An effective chief engineer is a careful administrator who reviews every piece of equipment and required activity in the hotel and then plans what should be done, when it should be done, and who should do it.

- *Implemented.* Some chief engineers know what should be done in their properties and have good intentions of completing all the required tasks, yet do not do so. Shortages of budget or properly trained staff, lack of supervisory skills, insufficient tools, and/or underestimation of the time required to perform a given task can impact the ability of an E&M department to achieve it goals.

   There are many excellent checklists and suggested activities developed for E&M departments. Virtually every franchisor offers these checklists free of charge to its franchisees because it is in the best interest of the franchisor if all hotels in the system properly represent the brand. Note: a later section of this chapter will discuss computerized maintenance systems that help identify the "when" and "what" of maintenance requirements for a specific property.

   Checklists and suggested activities, however, that are not properly implemented, will not yield an acceptable maintenance program. When a GM evaluates the E&M department, the important factor is not whether an acceptable maintenance program has been planned, but rather the degree to which the planned programs have been effectively implemented.

- *Recorded.* Recordkeeping is an immensely important maintenance function. Routine, scheduled maintenance tasks cannot be properly planned unless E&M personnel know when these tasks were last performed. For example, if the plan is to lubricate hot water pumps every six months, a written record must be kept of the last time the pumps were lubricated. Similarly, if a faucet in a guest room is replaced, a record should be kept of when the replacement was made. Then, the E&M department can evaluate the quality (life) of faucets used and take advantage of any warranty programs that apply to the replacement parts and to new equipment purchased by the hotel.

   In many cases such as fire suppression systems and elevators, local ordinances or laws may require that records documenting the performance of system maintenance be kept on file or displayed publicly. Even when it is not mandated by local ordinance, however, excellent recordkeeping in all areas of the E&M department is a good indicator of overall departmental effectiveness.

Design and Renovation

The cost of maintaining a building is closely related to its original design and size and the facilities it includes. Those hotels with, for example, food service and banquet facilities, swimming pools, and exercise rooms will incur greater maintenance costs than limited-service hotels without these facilities. High-rise facilities will require elevator systems that must be maintained; one-story hotels will not. Resort facilities spread over multiple acres will require greater landscape care costs than those located on smaller plots of ground.

   The quality of construction used in building the hotel will also affect POM costs. A hotel with an exterior that must be painted will incur painting costs while a hotel made of masonry will not. Energy costs will also be affected by construction. Properties built with good insulation and well-made windows will generally experience lower energy costs than those not built this way.

   The finishes and equipment specified for installation by the hotel's builders have a tremendous impact on the E&M department. Durable finishes and high-quality, long-life equipment may have higher purchase prices, but will often save money in the longer term with reduced operating and maintenance costs.

   Despite the very best of maintenance programs, however, hotel buildings do wear out with use and must be renovated to compete against newer hotel properties and

Building Age	Building Characteristics and Requirements
1–3 years	Low maintenance costs incurred
3–6 years	Maintenance costs increase
6–8 years	Refurbishment required; average maintenance costs incurred
8–15 years	Minor renovation and refurbishment required
15–22 years	Major renovation as well as refurbishment required
22+ years	Restoration required; high-maintenance costs incurred

FIGURE 11.1   Hotel Life Span Costs

others that have recently been renovated. Hotel buildings have a predictable life span that directly affects their maintenance and renovation needs. Figure 11.1 details the typical life span of a hotel. You can see that, as a building ages, the challenges of maintaining it increase as do the costs.

Because **renovation** and **refurbishment** will, at some point, be needed, GMs must take steps to reserve funds for the time when this is necessary. This is done by establishing an **FF&E reserve**.

HOTEL TERMINOLOGY AT WORK

Renovation: The process of making repairs that brings a building into good condition.

Refurbishment: A process that involves the major cleaning and redecoration of hotel areas.

FF&E Reserve: Funds set aside today for the future furniture, fixture, and equipment replacement needs of a hotel.

■

Generally, FF&E reserves should average 2 percent to 4 percent of a hotel's gross revenue. If designated funds are not reserved, minor or major renovation or restoration cannot be done when needed. Figure 11.2 lists specific items that must be considered when planning a hotel's short- and long-term renovation program.

	Minor Renovation	Major Renovation
Guest Rooms	Drapes, bedspreads	Bed frames, mattresses
	Lamps, shades	Wall lights
	Carpets	Wall vinyl
	Upholstered furniture	Case goods
	Faucets	Sinks, countertops
	Mattresses	Televisions
Food and Beverage	Carpets, chairs, reupholster booths	Decorative lighting
	Table top décor	Tables
	Dishes, flatware	Serving equipment
		Wall coverings
Public Space	Table lamps, lobby furniture	Overhead lighting
	Lobby carpet	Corridor carpet
	Lobby wall coverings	Corridor vinyl
	Meeting rooms	Restrooms

FIGURE 11.2   Selected Hotel Renovation and Replacement Considerations

Refurbishment and minor renovation is actually an ongoing process in most hotels. Major renovation typically takes place every six to ten years and involves high cost. Extra cleaning costs are likely to be incurred during construction. It is almost inevitable that guest services will be disrupted, and this results in unhappy guests who must be soothed and in lost revenue from out-of-service areas that normally generate revenue.

Restoration occurs when a hotel undergoes renovation that is so complete that walls are relocated, rooms and public spaces are totally reconfigured, and mechanical systems are replaced to modernize the hotel.

HOTEL TERMINOLOGY AT WORK

Restoration: Returning a hotel to its original (or better than original) condition.

The typical hotel undergoes a restoration every 25–50 years, and this is a challenging time for management, the E&M department, and guests. If restoration is not undertaken when needed, however, the revenue-producing potential of the hotel will decline.

STAFFING THE DEPARTMENT

You have learned that a guest's (or a potential guest's) impression of the quality of a hotel depends on the work of the E&M department. When maintenance work is performed poorly or not at all, it shows. The solution to this potential problem lies in the selection of an excellent E&M department head and appropriate assistants.

The hotel GM of a smaller property will most often directly supervise the work of maintenance staff.

Chief Engineer

In the hotel industry, the head of E&M is referred to as the chief engineer or maintenance chief. This person has a significant role to play on the EOC and as the leader of one of the hotel's most important departments.

In smaller hotels, the chief engineer may take a very hands-on role in the maintenance effort. This could actually involve performing maintenance and repair tasks. In larger hotels with larger staffs, the chief engineer serves a more administrative role that consists of planning work, organizing staff, directing employee efforts, and controlling the POM budget. Regardless of a hotel's size, however, the chief engineer must be well organized, pay great attention to detail, and be a cooperative member of the management team.

Maintenance Assistants

In addition to the chief engineer, the E&M department will employ one or more individuals with varying degrees of skill in the areas of

- Engineering
- Mechanics
- Plumbing
- Electricity
- Carpentry
- Water treatment (for pools and spas)
- Landscaping
- Grounds maintenance

The needs of a specific hotel will dictate the actual skill, makeup, and number of E&M staff required. It is difficult to find one person skilled in all of the technical E&M areas encountered in a hotel. When the skills or manpower needs of an E&M department exceed the capabilities of the in-house staff, the chief engineer and the GM must decide to outsource work. The ability to effectively determine what tasks are best performed by in-house E&M staff versus contracted outside experts is the real mark of an excellent chief engineer. Note: contracted maintenance and repairs will be discussed in a later section of this chapter.

Even entry-level staff members in the E&M department must perform relatively sophisticated tasks. Consider, for example, in-guest room entertainment and communication equipment and the need to operate and maintain sophisticated building systems equipment.

Modern hotel rooms increasingly offer Internet access, electronic games, high-definition televisions, sophisticated alarm clocks, and AV recreational units that many guests do not know how to operate. Maintenance personnel may be called to assist guests with their operation, and they must also know when defective equipment must be repaired or replaced.

The purchase cost of major equipment often includes training sessions for E&M personnel who will operate the equipment. Training time can be extensive, and the chief engineer must be assured that there is continuity in on-site knowledge when there is staff turnover within the department. GMs must assure that training clauses are included in contracts and lease agreements, and that E&M staff are properly trained to assist guests in operation of in-room equipment amenities. As well, the GM should assure that the property has at least a minimal number of guest room equipment items such as clock radios, DVD players, and telephones to replace items found to be in need of repair.

MANAGING MAINTENANCE

The maintenance of a hotel occurs after it has been designed, engineered, and built. It can be examined in a variety of ways, but one helpful way to view its management is to consider maintenance as routine, preventive, or emergency.

Routine Maintenance

When managing a hotel's routine maintenance, the chief engineer is directing the customary care of the facility. For example, in hotels with lawns and plant beds around entrances or parking areas, it is routine to periodically cut and edge the grass and to maintain the visual integrity of the plant bed by pulling weeds and replacing foliage as needed. If this work is not done, the hotel's curb appeal suffers. Cleaning interior windows, picking up trash in the parking lot, and shoveling snow in those climates that require it are additional examples of routine maintenance. Often only limited employee training is required to adequately complete routine maintenance tasks.

Generally, the chief engineer, with input from the GM, decides whether to perform routine maintenance work in-house or to contract with an outside vendor to perform it. Regardless of the decision, an effective chief engineer must be concerned with routine maintenance of the hotel's exterior and interior.

The exterior of this hotel on a Greek island features freshly painted walls and attractive landscaping: the result of ongoing attention from the maintenance department.

Exterior Maintenance

Outside the hotel, lawn care, landscaping, and leaf and snow removal are important issues. Also important is the attention to actual building details. This includes items such as routine roof inspection and repair, window cleaning and seal inspection, and the care and painting, if required, of the building's exterior finishes. The hotel's location will dictate, to a large degree, what must be considered for routine exterior maintenance. A resort hotel in Florida will have different needs from those of a downtown high-rise hotel in the upper Midwest. Regardless of the setting, however, maintaining the outside of the hotel impacts curb appeal, operational costs, and ultimately the building's value. The GM, working with the chief engineer, must ensure that routine exterior maintenance is being performed effectively and in a timely and cost-effective manner.

Interior Maintenance

Inside the hotel, E&M staff also perform routine maintenance. Some areas include the care of indoor plants, the washing of interior windows (if not assigned to housekeeping), and in some cases, the care and cleaning of floors and carpets.

One significant task nearly always assigned to the E&M department is the changing of lightbulbs. Lightbulbs, regardless of their type, burn out and then must be replaced. In some instances, individual lightbulbs are immediately replaced when they burn out. That is, the E&M department implements a **replace as needed** program for bulbs.

HOTEL TERMINOLOGY AT WORK

Replace as Needed (Maintenance Program): A parts or equipment replacement plan that delays installing a new, substitute part until the original part fails or is in near failure. For example, most chief engineers would use a "replace as needed" plan for the maintenance of refrigeration compressors.

The cost to a hotel of replacing a lightbulb consists of two components: the price of the bulb itself and the labor dollars required to change it. Therefore, in special cases, such as the lightbulbs in a multistory hotel with high ceilings that require special lifts or ladders for access, the hotel may implement a **total replacement** program that involves changing all bulbs, including those that have not burned out, on a regularly predetermined schedule.

HOTEL TERMINOLOGY AT WORK

Total Replacement (Maintenance Program): A parts or equipment replacement plan that involves installing new or substitute parts based on a predetermined schedule. For example, most chief engineers would use a "total replacement" approach to the maintenance of lightbulbs in high-rise exterior highway signs.

This approach, while it involves the discarding of some bulbs or lamps with life remaining, significantly reduces bulb replacement labor costs and makes the hotel's total bulb replacement costs lower.

Another form of routine maintenance involves guest room and public space items that must be attended to on a regular basis when they malfunction, wear out, or break

---

Waldo Hotel Work Order

Work Order Number: _____ *(Preassigned)* _____   Initiated By: _____

Date: _____   Time: _____   Room or Location: _____

Problem Observed: _____

_____

_____

Received On: _____   Assigned To: _____

Date Corrected: _____   Time Spent: _____

E&M Employee Comments: _____

_____

_____

_____

_____

_____

Chief Engineer Comments: _____

_____

_____

_____

_____

FIGURE 11.3   Work Order

and need repair or replacement. For example, a room attendant may notice that a guest room chair leg is broken, or that the tub drains slowly. A front-desk agent may report that a guest has complained about poor television reception or a toilet that does not flush properly. When events such as these occur, the E&M department is given a **work order,** or maintenance request. Figure 11.3 shows a sample work order.

HOTEL TERMINOLOGY AT WORK

Work Order: A hard-copy or electronic form used to initiate and document a request for maintenance. Sometimes referred to as a "maintenance request."

In a well-managed hotel, any staff member who sees an area of concern can initiate a work order. Hard-copy work orders are prenumbered, multicopy forms that, depending on the number of copies preferred by the GM, are used to notify E&M, the front desk, housekeeping, the GM, and others who may need to know when a maintenance request is initiated or completed. In some hotels, blank work order forms are actually placed in the guest room for guests to initiate. Increasingly, work orders are generated electronically.

Regardless of their original source, the work orders, once received by E&M, are reviewed and prioritized. For example, a work order indicating an inoperable guest room lock would receive a higher priority than one addressing a picture hanging crooked in another guest room. After an E&M employee completes the task(s) called for on the work order, he/she informs the proper personnel of task completion, and the information related to the work performed is carefully retained. In a well-run department, the chief engineer keeps a guest room-by-guest room record of replacements or repairs made. Then, necessary decisions about repairing or replacing in-room items can be more easily made because a history of the room and its contents has been preserved.

In many hotels, housekeeping staff work with the maintenance department to reduce the work orders needed for minor guest room problems. For example, the chief engineer and the executive housekeeper may jointly determine that housekeepers can, among other tasks, replace lightbulbs in lamps, change batteries in television remote control devices, and tighten dresser drawer pulls/knobs if they note these problems during their room inspections. After these responsibilities are agreed upon, housekeepers can be trained, and their carts can be stocked with the minimal supplies and necessary hand tools. GMs can be involved in these decisions and monitor the effectiveness of the procedures after they are implemented. This can be an effective way to minimize the number of work orders. However, the GM should be aware that workloads will increase for housekeepers at the same time that the productivity of engineering personnel will decrease, and changes in the scheduling patterns of both departments may be in order.

Some GMs evaluate the effectiveness of their entire E&M department based on the rapidity with which work orders are completed. Although the timely completion of maintenance requests should not be the only factor for judging the successfulness of the department, it is a key indicator of effectiveness and efficiency. When work orders are not completed promptly (or at all), the E&M department loses credibility in the eyes of the hotel's staff and with guests. An effective GM monitors the speed at which work orders are prioritized and completed and then takes corrective action, if needed.

Preventive Maintenance

Even when they are not performing routine maintenance or responding to work orders, E&M department staff have a large number of maintenance-related tasks to perform. In fact, in the eyes of many GMs, the most important type of maintenance performed in a hotel is the **PM**, or a **preventive maintenance program**.

HOTEL TERMINOLOGY AT WORK

PM (Preventive Maintenance) Program: A specific inspection and activities schedule designed to minimize maintenance-related costs and to prolong the life of equipment by preventing small problems before they become larger ones.

An effective PM program will save your hotel money by reducing:

- Long-term repair costs by prolonging equipment life
- Replacement part costs because purchases of these parts can be planned

- Labor costs by allowing PM to be performed in otherwise slow periods
- Revenue losses from refunds and charge backs due to guest dissatisfaction
- The costs of emergency repairs by minimizing their occurrence

In addition to saving money, a good PM program reduces guest complaints, eases the job of the sales staff, improves the eye appeal and functionality of the hotel, and improves employee morale.

Schedules for PM programs can come from a variety of sources. Equipment suppliers often suggest maintenance activities; franchisors may mandate PM schedules; local ordinances may require specific PM activities; and most importantly, the skill and experience of the chief engineer, combined with his or her knowledge of the hotel's needs, dictate PM schedules. Most PM activities involve basic inspection, replacement, cleaning, and lubrication. PM is not generally considered to be a repair program nor should it be viewed as one. Repairs must be completed as they are needed, while PM activities should be performed as scheduled.

Some chief engineers design PM programs segmented by activities to be performed daily, weekly, monthly, semiannually, and annually. Others prefer a system that segments the hotel into major areas (for example, food service and laundry) and then develop area-specific PM schedules. In both cases, the PM program should identify what is to be done, when it is to be done, how it is to be done, and should provide an easy method to document the completion of the activity.

Figure 11.4 is a sample daily, monthly, and annual PM task list for a dryer in the hotel's laundry. The chief engineer should have a written and complete PM program in place. All equipment such as furnaces, air-conditioners, water-heating equipment, and elevators must have PM programs. In addition, the E&M department should create a specific PM program for the following areas:

- Public space
- Guest rooms

PM Activity: LAUNDRY AREA DRYER

DAILY

- Clean lint trap
- Wipe down inside chamber with mild detergent
- Clean and wipe dry the outside dryer shell

MONTHLY

- Vacuum the inside of dryer (upper and lower chambers)
- Tighten, if needed, the bolts holding dryer to floor
- Check all electrical connections
- Check fan belt for wear; replace if needed
- Lubricate moving parts

ANNUALLY

- Check pulley alignment
- Adjust rotating basket if needed
- Lubricate motor bearings
- Lubricate drum bearings if needed

FIGURE 11.4   Sample PM Task List for Laundry Area Dryer

- Food service
- Laundry
- Other equipment

Public Space

Public space PM programs are vitally important but relatively simple to develop. In public spaces such as lobbies, corridors, and meeting areas, PM programs should include items such as windows, HVAC units, furniture, lights, elevators, and carpets. Carpet care is one of the most challenging PM areas for an E&M department. These duties are often shared between housekeeping and the E&M department, with housekeeping taking responsibility for minor (spot) cleaning needs, and the E&M department responsible for long-term carpet PM.

THE INTERNET AT WORK

Carpet and area rug care can be complex, but a variety of resources are available to help you determine how to best care for these items. To view one such resource, go to the Web site of The Carpet and Rug Institute at

www.carpet-health.org

Obviously, it is important that the appearance of public space is well maintained, as it significantly influences guests' opinions about the entire hotel. GMs know that a good first impression goes a long way toward ensuring a satisfactory guest stay.

Guest Rooms

Perhaps the most important, and certainly the most extensive, areas for PM are the hotel's guest rooms. Unfortunately, some GMs are not fully aware of the quality of the guest room PM program in place at their hotels. This is a huge mistake. The guest room PM program is critical to the sales effort, to the hotel's ability to retain guests, and to the maintenance of the asset's monetary value. In fact, there are few things a GM should pay more attention to than the PM program used for guest rooms.

An effective PM program requires a quarterly, or more frequent, inspection of guest rooms with a careful examination of each item on the guest room **PM checklist**.

HOTEL TERMINOLOGY AT WORK

PM Checklist: A tool developed to list all of the critical areas that should be inspected during a PM review of a room, area, or piece of equipment.

The checklist for any PM area should be developed to help maintenance staff with their inspections. Figure 11.5 is a sample PM checklist used for guest rooms.

Note that the checklist in Figure 11.5 is extensive and must be tailored for each property. Hotels, for example, that have in-room microwaves and refrigerators must add these items to the guest room PM checklist. If some guest rooms contain

Hotel Waldo Guestroom PM Checklist

Place an "x" by any item not meeting hotel standards

Year _____   Room Number _____

Area Inspected	Item Inspected	1	2	3	4	Area Inspected	Item Inspected	1	2	3	4
Entrance Door	Number sign					Bathroom continued	Floor tile/grouting				
	Exterior Finish						Telephone				
	Interior Finish						Blow Dryer				
	Peep hole						GFI plug operational				
	Door closer					Drapes	Drape Hooks				
	Deadbolt						Drape wand				
	Lock/lock plate						Valance				
	Evacuation/fire safety plan						Drape rods and brackets				
	Innkeeper's laws frame					Bedroom	Entrance ceiling				
	Hinges						Room ceiling				
Closet	Shelf Stable						Night stand				
	Clothes Hooks						Night stand drawers				
	Clothes Rod						Dresser				
	Carpet/Covebase						Dresser drawers				
	Luggage Rack						Headboard				
	Vinyl/Walls						Desk				
	Closet door finish						Desk chair				
	Closet door operation						Upholstered chairs				
	Closet door mirror						Bed frames				
Fixtures, lights and bulbs	Entry light						Mattress (condition)				
	Closet light						Mattress (turned)				
	Swing lamps						Mirrors				
	Dresser lamps						Art work				
	Desk lamp						Wall vinyl				
	Pole lamp						Electrical switches				
	Bathroom					HVAC	Filters changed				
	Smoke Detector						Fan				
	Sprinkler head						Motor				
Bathroom	Door finish						Controls				
	Door lock						Condensate pan				
	Ceiling condition						Wiring				
	Overhead Fan					TV/Radio	Picture quality				
	Toilet operation						Swivel				
	Toilet caulking						Lock down				
	Tub driver spout						Volume				
	Tub tile/grouting						Remote control				
	Tub stopper						Cabinet condition				
	Shower head						Connections				
	Curtain rod secure						Video game controls				
	Safety bar secure					Telephone	Line 1				
	Nonskid surface						Line 2				
	Sink Faucet						Jacks secure				
	Sink stopper					Connecting Door	Interior Finish				
	Piping						Exterior Finish				
	Aerator						Frame				
	Toilet Paper holder						Door stop				
	Towel rack						Lock(s) operation				
	Mirrors						Doorknob				
	Vinyl/Walls						Hinges				
Inspector Initials						Other					

Waldo Hotel, 20XX

FIGURE 11.5   Guest Room PM Checklist

whirlpool-type tubs, they should be included. It is the responsibility of the GM and the chief engineer to develop a custom PM checklist and inspection schedule for guest rooms. Then it is the responsibility of the chief engineer and/or his/her designated representative(s) to perform the inspections on the agreed-upon schedule. When this is done, guest room quality complaints will be minimized and long-term repair costs will be reduced because small problems will be uncovered and attended to before they become big ones.

Food Service

In the food service area, there are three major PM concerns. The first is back of the house (kitchen) equipment. The ovens, ranges, griddles, fryers, and other production equipment in the kitchen are heavily used and must be maintained. Specialty equipment such as dishwashers, fryers, and convection ovens may require the PM expertise of specifically trained technicians. If so, these vendors should be selected and their work scheduled by the chief engineer or the F&B director. In all cases, every piece of kitchen as well as mechanical bar equipment should be included in the PM program.

The second area of PM concern within the food services area is the dining space used by guests. Included in this program should be tabletops and bases. An especially annoying PM issue for guests involves table leveling; there is simply no excuse for wobbly tables or for foreign objects placed under tables to make them level. In addition, PM must include chairs and booths, self-serve salad or buffet areas, lighting fixtures, and guest check processing equipment.

A third area of PM concern within F&B, and one often overlooked, is that required for meeting and conference rooms and equipment. Included in this PM program are light fixtures, tables, chairs, and wall coverings within the hotel's meeting rooms, as well as food service equipment. In addition, the PM program must include transport carts and the audiovisual-related items owned by the hotel. These may include flip chart stands, TVs, overhead projectors, computer projection units, speaker telephones, and the like.

Laundry

In the laundry, the washers, dryers, folding equipment, water supply lines, drains, lighting fixtures, and temperature control units require PM programs. An especially important concern is the clothes dryer because of the potential for fire. Dryer drum temperatures can be very high, and the lint buildup that occurs during the natural drying process requires vigilance on the part of E&M and housekeeping personnel. Lint traps should be cleaned at least once per day, and they should be thoroughly inspected monthly.

In many cases, the company supplying laundry chemicals to the hotel maintains the equipment used to dispense chemicals into the washers. This does not mean that the E&M department need not concern itself with this area. In fact, if chemical use is too high, the chemical supplier may have adjusted equipment to overdispense chemicals in an effort to sell more product. As well, improperly maintained chemical dispensing units may result in substandard laundry quality. Therefore, E&M staff should make chemical dispenser maintenance part of the laundry PM program, even if it is performed in conjunction with the dispensing equipment supplier.

Other Equipment

Additional areas of concern when developing a PM program include those related to pools and spas, front-desk equipment, electronic locks (if not included in the guest room maintenance program), exterior door locks, motor vehicles, and in-hotel transportation equipment (for example, housekeepers' and luggage carts), to name but a few. As can be seen, the number of pieces of equipment and the number of areas involved in a quality PM maintenance program is large. As a GM, you will count on your chief engineer to develop, maintain, and document an effective and comprehensive PM program that both reduces repair costs and preserves the image of the hotel.

Emergency Maintenance

The strongest rationale for implementing well-designed and aggressive routine and preventive maintenance programs is the ability to manage repair costs; however, despite the very best routine and preventive maintenance efforts of the chief engineer and the E&M staff, your hotel will sometimes experience the need for emergency maintenance. Emergency maintenance items are generally defined as those that:

- Are unexpected
- Threaten to negatively impact hotel revenue
- Require immediate attention to minimize damage
- Require labor and parts that may need to be purchased at a premium cost

For example, assume that, in the middle of the night, a water pipe bursts in one of the hotel's unoccupied guest rooms. A short time later, the guests in the room one floor below the room with the broken pipe call the front desk to complain about water coming into their room from the ceiling. Clearly, this situation requires emergency maintenance. If not attended to immediately, extensive repair work to the pipe as well as the ceilings and walls around the leak will likely be required.

As a GM, you certainly want to be notified about any significant emergency maintenance required in the hotel so you can help plan or evaluate the hotel's response. Also, emergency maintenance repairs may require the authorization of overtime for E&M staff or outside repair personnel. In addition, repair parts that might normally be purchased through customary sources may need to be secured quickly (and often at a premium price) from noncustomary sources.

An effective chief engineer keeps the GM informed of significant emergency maintenance concerns and seeks his/her advice about the best course of action for responding to them. In addition, maintaining accurate records about the cost of emergency repairs will help when budgeting for routine and preventive maintenance costs. Generally, the stronger the routine and PM programs, the fewer the dollars spent on emergency repairs.

Technology and Maintenance

The basic procedures used to manage routine, preventive, and emergency maintenance in a hotel are important and should be consistently done in all properties of all sizes. Unfortunately, however, traditional manual systems can make the process cumbersome, and details can be misplaced as copy forms are routed between departments in the hotel and as they are filed in the engineer's office. An alternative: automated property maintenance systems.

Bar codes can be used to tag equipment included in a property's preventive maintenance program. Once scanned at the time of PM, a series of questions are prompted on a handheld device that must be answered by the E&M employee directly into the mobile equipment. If the response suggests that a work order is needed, it will automatically be generated and routed to the appropriate E&M staff member who will complete and record the job. By contrast, if the maintenance person observes that something requires attention, this can be noted and an open work order will be generated. Details about preventive maintenance inspection tasks, equipment warranty data, and other required information can be added to the system and viewed on the handheld device while the engineer is at the equipment.

Maintenance scheduling and tracking is typically a part of automated PM systems. Maintenance information for the property can be managed at an on-site personal computer. It is also possible for the person responsible for several properties to view data applicable to each property. Alerts can even be generated to inform this multiunit engineer when maintenance is not being properly performed on specific equipment at a specific property. Statistics, problems, and other information identified by the computerized system can be distributed to the applicable person by e-mail and/or pager.

Automated equipment maintenance systems can be used for fixed assets such as building systems equipment and for all components in a guest room preventive maintenance program. In addition to quickly generating work orders, activities such as scheduling lightbulbs for replacement can be included in a PM schedule and the inventory of affected supplies such as lightbulbs can be tracked.

THE INTERNET AT WORK

For information about one computerized preventive maintenance system that includes online demos, go to

www.mintek.com

As with technology adoptions in other departments throughout the hotel, the GM must work with the chief engineer to assure the system most appropriate for a specific property is in use; both managers must keep alert to potential changes that can improve guest services and/or reduce operating costs.

MANAGERS AT WORK

"The telephone is ringing off the hook!" Dani Pelley, the front-office manager, told J.D. Ojisama, the hotel's GM. "I called maintenance, and they said they were looking into it."

"It" was a complete outage of the satellite system used to deliver television reception to the hotel. The pay-per-view features of the hotel that were satellite based still worked, but the free-to-guests channels were completely down, and guests were calling the front desk to complain or to request a repair on their television sets.

J.D. picked up the telephone, called the chief engineer, and got the bad news.

Satellite reception was down. It was not an equipment failure on the hotel's part, but rather, the satellite service provider was experiencing equipment difficulty. The chief engineer had just gotten off the telephone with the provider to report the problem, and their representative estimated a repair time of between 2 and 24 hours. Until the problem was fixed, there would be no free-to-guests channel reception. J.D. hung up the telephone and went to talk with Dani Pelley about what to do next.

Given that the televisions may be out for a significant amount of time, what steps would you take to inform guests?

Employees? Why is it important for all employees to be aware of the repair status of the televisions?

What should the front desk say to a guest who calls requesting a television repair?

What would you do if, the next day, after the televisions were working again, a guest demanded a full refund for the prior night's stay because he/she had missed a favorite weekly television show and your hotel features a "100% guest satisfaction guarantee?" What factors would influence your decision?

MANAGING UTILITIES

Utility management is an important part of a hotel's overall operation. Utility costs in hotels include expenses for water and sewage bills, gas, electricity, or fossil fuel for heating and cooling the building, fuel for heating water, and in some cases, the purchase of steam or chilled water.

Energy-related expenses that had been taken for granted by most hoteliers became very important and costly during the energy crisis of 1973. Since that time, these costs have moderated somewhat. When the cost of utilities is relatively low, few Americans, including those in the hotel industry, take strong measures to conserve resources and to implement **energy management** programs. Alternatively, when energy costs are high, managers have a heightened sense of awareness about these costs. Good GMs require that the E&M department, as well as each member of the hotel's staff, always use energy-effective management tactics.

HOTEL TERMINOLOGY AT WORK

Energy Management: Specific policies and engineering, maintenance, and facility design activities intended to control and reduce energy use.

It is important to remember that most of the utility cost involved in lighting, heating, and operating the equipment required to run a hotel will be incurred regardless of occupancy levels. Higher hotel occupancy will result in some incremental increase in utility costs, but as much as 80 percent of total utility costs are actually fixed. A hotel's original design and construction and the age of the building affect its energy use. It is most influenced, however, by the regular maintenance and calibration of the energy-consuming equipment.

Depending on the location of the hotel, energy costs can represent as much as 3 percent to 10 percent of total operating costs. In addition, energy is a valuable resource and, as responsible members of the hotel industry and the community within which the property is located, it is important that GMs attempt to conserve it. Therefore, it is easy to see why an effective E&M department should be very concerned with conserving energy and controlling utility costs.

Electricity

Electricity is the most common and usually the most expensive form of energy used in hotels. To be effective, the hotel's electrical source must be dependable, and the E&M department must maintain the hotel's electrical systems in a safe manner. Although some hotels generate their own electricity in an emergency outage situation through the use of a **backup generator**, most hotels rely on one or more local power providers to deliver electricity.

HOTEL TERMINOLOGY AT WORK

Backup Generator: Equipment used to make limited amounts of electricity on-site. Used in times of power failure or when the hotel experiences low supply from the usual provider of electricity.

Should the chief engineer require that the bulbs in these lobby chandeliers be changed as they burn out or should a total replacement be implemented?

In some locations, electric bills account for well over 50 percent (and sometimes as much as 80 percent) of a hotel's total utility costs. Controlling electrical consumption, then, can really pay off for a GM interested in lowering hotel utility bills.

Electricity is used everywhere in a hotel. It powers the hotel's administrative computers, operates fire safety systems, keeps food at proper storage temperature in freezers and refrigerators, and provides power for security systems, to name but a few uses of this important resource. When considering the total electrical consumption of hotels, however, the two most important uses of electricity and therefore those that the chief engineer must manage most carefully, are related to lighting and HVAC systems.

Lighting

The lighting in a hotel is tremendously important to curb appeal, guest comfort, worker efficiency, and property security. Lighting is sometimes referred to as illumination, and light levels are measured in **foot-candles**. Generally, the greater the number of foot-candles present, the greater the illumination. Hotels require varying degrees of illumination in different locations, and the type of light fixtures and bulbs used play a large role in producing the most appropriate light for each hotel setting.

HOTEL TERMINOLOGY AT WORK

Foot-Candle: A measure of illumination. One foot-candle equals one lumen per square foot. (The European counterpart of the foot-candle is the Lux, a light intensity of one lumen per square meter.)

Artificial light is produced to supplement natural (sun)light. Natural light is, of course, very cost-effective and when used properly can have a very positive impact on utility costs by limiting the amount of artificial light that must be produced. When lighting must be supplemented, the hotel can choose from two basic lighting options. The first is **incandescent lamps**.

HOTEL TERMINOLOGY AT WORK

Incandescent Lamp: A lamp in which a filament inside the lamp's bulb is heated by electrical current to produce light.

∎

Incandescent lights are the type most people think of when they think of the lightbulbs used in their homes. Incandescent bulbs have relatively short life spans (2,000 hours or less) and therefore must be frequently changed. They are fairly inefficient because they produce only 15–20 lumens per watt used. For example, a 100-watt bulb produces 1,500–2,000 lumens when it is turned on. Incandescent lights are popular, however, because they are easy to install, are easy to move, are inexpensive to purchase, and have the characteristic of starting and restarting instantly. Incandescent lamp bulbs such as spot or floodlights can be made in such a way as to concentrate light in one area.

In cases where a conventional incandescent light is not best suited for a specific lighting need, hotels can select an **electric discharge lamp** as a lighting option.

HOTEL TERMINOLOGY AT WORK

Electric Discharge Lamp: A lamp in which light is generated by passing electrical current through a space filled with a special combination of gases. Examples include fluorescent, mercury vapor, metal halide, and sodium.

∎

Electric discharge lamps do not operate directly from electricity. They must be assisted in the process by the use of a **ballast**.

HOTEL TERMINOLOGY AT WORK

Ballast: The device in an electric discharge lamp that starts, stops, and controls the current to the light.

∎

Electric discharge lamps are characterized by longer lives (5,000–25,000 hours) and higher efficiency (40–80 lumens per watt). The most common of this lamp type is the fluorescent, and it is frequently used where high light levels and low operating costs are a consideration. If an electric discharge lamp stops working, either the bulb or the ballast may need replacing.

Other types of electric discharge lamps used include those for parking areas or security lighting. In these cases, sodium lamps are a good choice as they can generate 200 lumens per watt used and have extremely long lives. However, the cost to purchase and install these lights is also greater.

In the late 1980s, compact versions of fluorescent lights became popular in many hotels. These lights were designed to combine the energy efficiency and long life of a traditional fluorescent light with the convenience and ballast-free operation of an incandescent light. For many applications, they provide an excellent blend between operational savings and convenience.

THE INTERNET AT WORK

Compact fluorescent lights are increasingly popular and cost-effective, but they do have limitations. To read an in-depth discussion of these lights, their uses, and their special disposal requirements, go to

www.energystar.gov/index.cfm?c=cfls.pr_cfls

A hotel can select from a wide choice of lights, bulbs, and fixtures. The proper type, color of light, and operational costs must all be considered when selecting lighting fixtures and lamps. In all cases, lighting maintenance, including lamp repair, bulb changing, and fixture cleaning, must be an integral part of the hotel's PM program.

HVAC

Another significant consumer of electrical power is the hotel's HVAC system. Heating, ventilation, and air-conditioning are considered together within the hotel's maintenance program because they all use the hotel's air treatment, thermostats, **duct**, and **air handler systems**.

HOTEL TERMINOLOGY AT WORK

Duct: A passageway, usually built of sheet metal, that allows fresh, cold, or warm air to be directed to various parts of a building.

Air Handler Systems: The fans and mechanical systems required to move air through ducts and to vents.

A properly operating HVAC system delivers air to rooms at a desired temperature. The efficiency at which a hotel's HVAC system operates and therefore the comfort of the building is affected by numerous factors, including:

- The original temperature of the room
- The temperature of the air delivered to the room
- The relative humidity of the air delivered to the room
- The air movement in the room
- The temperature-absorbing surfaces in the room

HVAC systems can be fairly straightforward or very complex, but all consist of components responsible for heating and cooling the hotel.

Heating Components.   It is possible that all of a hotel's heating components are run by electricity, but this is not normally the case. Heating by electricity, especially in cold climates, is not generally cost-effective. Therefore, hoteliers generally heat at least some parts of their buildings using natural gas, liquefied petroleum gas (LPG), steam, or fuel oil, although electricity can be used to heat small areas.

In most hotels, the heating of hot water is second in cost only to the heating of air. A hotel requires an effective furnace (or heat pump system) for heating air and a properly sized boiler for heating water. Regardless of the heat source, electricity is used by fans or pumps to move warm air produced by the furnace, or hot water produced by the hot water heater, to the appropriate parts of the building. The maintenance of these two heating components can be complex, but an effective chief engineer maintains them in a safe and cost-effective manner, performing **calibration** and maintenance tasks in accordance with manufacturer's recommendations and local building code requirements.

HOTEL TERMINOLOGY AT WORK

Calibration: The adjustment of equipment to maximize its effectiveness and operational efficiency.

■

Cooling Components.   Just as a hotel must heat air and water, it must frequently cool them as well. The major cost of operating air-cooling or conditioning systems relates to electricity usage.

Essentially, an air-conditioning system uses electrically operated equipment to extract heat from either air or water; it then uses the remaining cooled air or water to absorb and remove more heat from the building. The effectiveness of a cooling system is dependent on several factors, including:

- The original air temperature and humidity of the room to be cooled
- The temperature and humidity of the chilled air entering the room from the HVAC system
- The quantity of chilled air entering the room
- The operational efficiency of the air-conditioning equipment

Some cooling systems are designed to produce small quantities of very cold air that are then pumped or blown into a room to reduce its temperature; other systems supply larger quantities of air that is not as cold, but because the quantity supplied is greater, has the same room cooling effect.

The ability of a cooling system to deliver cold air or water of a specified temperature and in the quantity required determines its effectiveness. Many times, especially in hot and humid weather, the demands placed upon a hotel's cooling system are intense. The ability of the E&M department to maintain cooling equipment in a manner that minimizes guests' discomfort and the resulting complaints is critical. Effective seasonal and PM maintenance on cooling equipment is a crucial part of the chief engineer's job in climates where air-conditioning is used.

Reducing Electricity Consumption

It makes good economic and environmental sense to reduce electricity consumption in ways that do not impact on quality guest service. Wise GMs include this responsibility in the work tasks assigned to their chief engineer. In addition, they encourage E&M personnel to be creative as they plan and implement tactics to reduce energy consumption. We have already noted, for example, the use of energy-efficient lightbulbs to replace incandescent bulbs. There are numerous other examples that range from no-cost (turn off lights in areas where they are not needed) to relatively expensive options such as installing thermopane windows or building insulation that must be preceded by **payback analysis** or other objective methods to assess feasibility.

HOTEL TERMINOLOGY AT WORK

Payback Analysis: A financial analysis model that involves comparing annual cash flow savings of alternatives to determine whether the payback period is equal to or less than that allowed for project approval.

■

No cost
- Instruct housekeeping personnel to use natural light when cleaning guest rooms.
- Close drapes, turn off lights and heating/air-conditioning systems when rooms are not occupied. When possible during periods of low occupancy, keep a guest room floor empty and turn off air-conditioning in these rooms.
- Reduce hot water temperatures.
- Use covers on pools and hot tubs.

Minimal cost
- Develop incentive programs to encourage staff to participate in and suggest energy conservation tactics.
- Seal heating and cooling duct work.
- Insulate supply pipes and hot water tanks.
- Perform routine maintenance on refrigeration equipment and replace worn door caskets.

Longer-term investment
- Repaint building exteriors using light colors to deflect sunlight and heat.
- Install motion sensors to turn lights on when needed.
- Install programmable thermostats in guest rooms.
- Retrofit incandescent or florescent exit signs with low-energy LED exit signs.

Adapted from: The California Travel and Tourism Commission Provides Powerful Energy Saving Tips for Hoteliers and Inn Keepers. To see this reference, go to

www.hotel-online.com

Scroll to the top of the home page to the search box. Type in "Powerful Energy Savings Tips" and click on "Find It Fast."

FIGURE 11.6   Energy Conservation Techniques

Figure 11.6 illustrates examples of energy conservation techniques.

Technology can help with energy conservation. For example, computerized energy control systems can manage energy use in public spaces such as lobbies and restaurant dining rooms. These systems can monitor and control energy use automatically. Another example: guest room energy management systems can be used to monitor and control energy use for heating and air-conditioning without compromising guest satisfaction. Programmable digital thermostats are available to do this as are other types that, in addition, control guest room lighting systems.

Natural Gas

In some areas, natural gas, because it is plentiful and cost-effective, is used to heat water for guest rooms and to power clothes dryers in the laundry area. In addition, natural gas is used in many hotel power plants to directly or indirectly provide heat to guest rooms and public spaces. Interestingly, the overwhelming majority of chefs and cooks also prefer natural gas for cooking because of its rapid heat production and the degree of temperature control that it allows.

Managed properly, natural gas is an extremely safe source of energy. If a hotel is using natural gas equipment of any type, each gas hot water heater, furnace, or other piece of equipment should have a PM program designed specifically to minimize operating costs, ensure safety, and maximize the efficiency of the unit. This is especially important because the combustible nature of natural gas requires that gas leaks be avoided at all times. In addition, the calibration of the oxygen and fuel mixture required to maximize the efficiency of the combustion process must be continually and carefully monitored. GMs should recognize that there are few areas of PM more important to evaluate and review regularly than those related to natural gas equipment.

THE INTERNET AT WORK

Gas equipment manufacturers are understandably proud of their products. For more information on gas-operated food service equipment, as well as managerial tips and restaurant operations information, go to

www.cookingforprofit.com

Water

Aggressively managing a hotel's water consumption is very cost-effective because to do so:

- Reduces the number of gallons of water purchased
- Reduces the amount the hotel will pay for sewage (water disposal)
- Reduces, in the case of hot water, water-heating costs because less hot water must be produced

Water costs can be dramatically reduced if E&M department personnel conscientiously monitor water usage in all areas of the hotel. Figure 11.7 lists, for several areas, just a few of the activities that E&M and/or other hotel staff can undertake to help reduce water-related costs. Working together, the GM and the chief engineer should implement those water-saving activities that impact the hotel's bottom line but do not negatively affect guest satisfaction levels.

The hotel's laundry system is a big water user. Some properties are converting to an ozone laundry system that eliminates the need for hot water and the use of chlorine when bed linens are washed. In addition to reducing hot water and chemical cost, linen expenses are reduced because they are not subjected to harmful chemicals during the laundry process. Other advantages: the capacity and productivity of laundry operations can be improved because cycle times are reduced, rebates from local utilities can sometimes offset part of the initial capital equipment costs, and sewer usage fees are also reduced.

THE INTERNET AT WORK

To learn general information about energy and water conservation efforts in general and ozone laundry systems more specifically, go to

www.greensuites.com

Solid Waste

Hotels generate a tremendous amount of solid waste or trash. Sources of waste include packaging materials such as cardboard boxes, crates, and bags used to ship hotel supplies, kitchen garbage, guest room trash, and even yard waste generated from landscaping efforts. Increasingly, the hotel industry has come to realize that excessive waste and poorly conceived waste disposal methods are detrimental to the

---

Guest Rooms
- Include inspection of all guest room faucets on the PM checklist
- Inspect toilet flush valves monthly; replace as needed
- Consider installing "water-saver" showerheads
- Investigate "Earth Friendly" procedures designed to enlist the aid of guests in the water conservation process

Public Space
- Include inspection of all public restroom faucets on the PM checklist
- Install automatic flush valves in men's room urinals
- Where practical, reduce hot water temperatures in public restrooms
- Check pool and spa fill levels and water pump operation daily

Laundry
- Include, as part of the PM program, the monthly inspection of water fittings on all washers
- Presoak stained terry and linen rather than double washing
- Use the lowest hot water wash setting possible while still ensuring clean terry and linen

Food Service
- Serve water to diners only on request
- Operate dishwashers only as needed
- Use sprayers, not faucets, to prerinse dishes and flatware intended to be machine washed
- Use chemical sanitizers, rather than excessively hot water to sanitize pots and pans
- Use sprayers, not faucets, to rinse/wash produce prior to cooking or storage

Outdoors
- Inspect sprinkler systems for leaking and misdirected spraying daily
- Utilize the sprinkler system only when critically needed. Do not overwater
- Minimize the use of sprayed water for cleaning (driveway and parking areas for example). Sweep and spot clean these areas instead

---

FIGURE 11.7   Sample Water Conservation Techniques

environment and represent a poor use of natural resources. In addition, as landfills become scarce, the cost of solid waste disposal has risen. Wise hoteliers encourage manufacturers who ship products to them to practice **source reduction**, and they aggressively implement creative programs to reduce the generation of their own solid waste.

HOTEL TERMINOLOGY AT WORK

Source Reduction: The effort by product manufacturers to design and ship products to minimize waste resulting from the product's shipping and delivery to a hotel.

Recycling, minimizing waste generation, and wise purchasing can all reduce waste disposal costs. They should be implemented wherever possible.

Effective waste management also involves keeping inside and outside trash removal areas clean and, to the greatest degree possible, attractive. This can be achieved by proper sanitation procedures and by enclosing the trash removal areas with fencing or other eye-appealing materials.

Poorly maintained trash removal areas are unsightly and can attract insects, rodents, and other scavenging animals. The chief engineer should regularly inspect these areas for preventive maintenance of fencing or other surroundings and for the cleanliness of the trash removal areas.

MANAGING "GREEN" HOTELS

In the previous section you learned about important concerns that GMs should have as they work with the chief engineer to manage utility consumption without sacrificing the quality of guest service. These issues are part of an increasing emphasis on "green" hotels.

HOTEL TERMINOLOGY AT WORK

Green Hotels: Lodging properties that use programs to conserve water and energy and reduce solid waste in efforts to preserve the environment and conserve its resources.

An increasing number of hotels participate in environmental conservation efforts. These range from those using just a few tactics that do not require basic changes in operating procedures to others that may require extensive planning, significant capital investments, and changes in operating procedures to make extensive contributions to environmental management efforts. Hoteliers recognize that concerns about the environment can positively affect natural resources and reduce operating expenses. They also provide marketing and sales opportunities to the growing number of travelers who share these concerns and who would opt to frequent properties that share their environmental conservation views. This is a natural reaction to the global concern that efforts to increase travel often has a detrimental impact on the destination area including its environment.

GMs should work with their chief engineer and others to objectively evaluate the benefits, costs, societal pressures, and marketing impacts on environmental management issues such as:

- Recycling wastewater for landscaping purposes
- Implementing basic recycling programs
- Purchasing energy-efficient appliances
- Utilizing thermopane windows and energy-efficient building insulation materials at times of renovation and new construction

Many environmentally conscious practices are in common use, and many properties belong to groups such as the Green Hotels Association, which promotes activities and provides educational and training resources to further assist hoteliers including chief engineers.

MAINTENANCE AND OTHER SERVICE CONTRACTS

Equipment that is part of major building systems such as HVAC, electrical, and plumbing can be very expensive and very complicated; this is increasingly so as sophisticated "high-tech" systems are used to operate them. As well, specialized knowledge experience and even tools/equipment are often required to service some systems. Examples include fire suppression systems in kitchen ventilation areas and the application of landscaping chemicals.

The chief engineer working with the GM and the property's controller may negotiate service **contracts** for specialized tasks. Increasingly, maintenance contracts are used for telephone, computer, and security systems and for AV and in-guest room equipment. Although chief engineers and GMs cannot be trained and experienced attorneys, they must know something about contracts as they attend to their responsibilities.

HOTEL TERMINOLOGY AT WORK

Contract: An agreement between two or more parties that will be enforceable in a court of law.

Many contractual topics are important in any type of agreement between an outside supplier and a hotel manager. These include issues that address **indemnification** for damages, insurance, contracting/subcontracting, licenses, payment amounts/terms, performance (quantity and quality) standards, and starting/completion dates.[1]

HOTEL TERMINOLOGY AT WORK

Indemnification: To reimburse someone for a loss that has been incurred.

Standard hotel maintenance contracts are used to identify the responsibilities of an external service organization to assist with a hotel's equipment and/or system service needs. Consider, for example, kitchen production equipment. The knowledge and experience to properly service this equipment may be beyond the expertise of E&M personnel, especially in small properties.

The chief engineer can develop a preventive maintenance schedule using information from the equipment manufacturer to develop a specialized request for proposal (RFP) and may then solicit proposal responses and negotiate the contract with suppliers judged able to provide required services.

Many observers suggest that service contracts should have an ending date and that they then be renegotiated, for example, annually. This will allow the chief engineer to more formally evaluate the supplier's service and work quality.

Another alternative to equipment maintenance contracts also exists: maintenance and repair insurance with work orders dispatched through a toll-free telephone number. With this plan, covered equipment items are identified and stored in an equipment history database. When covered equipment requires repair, a toll-free number is called and, since the insurance company knows the vendor(s) responsible for that equipment, work orders are dispatched. After the service is completed, the vendor sends the invoice to the insurance company rather than to the hotel. Follow-up management reports, repairs made regardless of the cause, in-house repair reimbursement, and reduced hotel administrative costs for PM contract negotiation, payment, and other administrative tasks are among the potential advantages. Proponents of the

---

[1]Readers interested in basic information about hospitality contracts are referred to Stephen Barth. *Hospitality Law: Managing Legal Issues in the Hospitality Industry.* Second Edition. New York, John Wiley & Sons, Inc. 2005.

program indicate that, in addition to savings over costs incurred from a traditional maintenance program, additional benefits include ease of administration, outsourced vendor dispatch, and direct pay.

THE INTERNET AT WORK

For more information about equipment maintenance and repair insurance, go to

www.aon.com

The impact of an improperly developed agreement for contracted services can cause significant negative consequences for the hotel. The chief engineer, working with the GM, the hotel's attorney, controller, and/or other persons with the required expertise, should assure that all agreements provide the best possible services at a reasonable cost.

HOTEL TERMINOLOGY AT WORK GLOSSARY

The following terms were defined within this chapter. If you are not familiar with one of them, please review the segment of the chapter that contains the term.

Engineering	Work order	Duct
Maintenance	PM (preventive maintenance)	Air handler systems
HVAC	program	Calibration
POM	PM checklist	Payback analysis
Renovation	Energy management	Source reduction
Refurbishment	Backup generator	Green hotels
FF&E reserve	Foot-candle	Contract
Restoration	Incandescent lamp	Indemnification
Replace as needed	Electric discharge lamp	
Total replacement	Ballast	

ISSUES AT WORK

1. For many routine maintenance replacement items, the GM has a choice between doing all of the maintenance at once (such as changing air filters in guest rooms quarterly) or doing it as needed (such as replacing hot water heater pumps as they go out). In still other cases, such as parking lot lightbulb replacement or fan belts on motors, the GM has a choice between systematic total replacement and a "replace as needed" approach. Assume you were required to make the replacement-type decision for exterior parking lot lights in a hotel with parking for 500 cars. What factors would influence your decision? Discuss at least three of these in addition to replacement cost.

2. Lawn care is a good example of the many maintenance tasks that can be done in-house or contracted to an outside vendor. Assume you operate a 350-room hotel with three acres of total lawn and landscape area. Prepare a list of questions you

would ask a potential provider of lawn and landscape services. What factors would most influence your decision to select an outside vendor for your lawn and landscape work?

3. Often repair and maintenance costs are highest when occupancy rates are lowest. This is true because much repair and maintenance work (damaged ceiling repair, for example) can only be done when guest rooms are empty for extended periods. This makes POM costs highest when hotel revenues are lowest. What are some steps management can take to minimize this effect?

4. Many hotels have implemented aggressive recycling programs. Assume an employee group within the hotel approached you about starting a comprehensive recycling program. What factors would influence the time and financial resources you would be willing to commit to such an effort?

5. For major hotel repairs that cannot be done in-house, some chief engineers prefer to establish a relationship with one major contractor in each area (for example, plumbing, heating, and electrical), and then employ that contractor for all the needed repairs. Other chief engineers prefer to solicit competitive bids for each major project and then select the best bidder. What are the advantages and disadvantages of each approach? Which approach would you suggest to your own chief engineer? Why?

12

Safety and Property Security

This Chapter at Work

Your guests depend on you as the GM to provide an atmosphere that assures their safety to the greatest degree possible. Your guests, however, are not the only individuals concerned with your safety efforts. Your employees also count upon you to provide a working environment that allows them to do their jobs free from the concern of unnecessary risks.

Hotel owners depend on the GM to develop practices and procedures that will safeguard the hotel's assets and to minimize their legal liability. In addition, there are agencies at all governmental levels charged with monitoring the safety-related efforts of hotels. One of the most important is OSHA, the federal agency responsible for ensuring a safe workplace for employees. In this chapter, you will learn about the important role that OSHA plays in the hospitality industry and how documenting your safety efforts will help you stay in compliance with its requirements.

A primary focus in this chapter is the issue of legal liability. You will learn about safety- and security-related legal responsibilities to your guests, employees, and owners. You will also discover the importance of security as a department within the hotel and as a shared responsibility of each of its employees.

The hotel industry is committed to safety. Concerned GMs have a variety of security-oriented tools, including recodable locks, alarm systems, surveillance systems, and emergency plans that can be used to reduce safety and security risks. In this chapter, you will learn about them.

Depending on their location and the services offered, some hotels are confronted with unique safety and security issues. These include protecting guests in swimming pool areas, spas and in nearly all cases, parking lots. Although hoteliers are not the insurers of guest safety, they do have a responsibility to exercise reasonable care in protecting their guests. In this chapter, you will learn how to meet the reasonable care standard.

Threats to the security of hotel assets can come from both internal and external sources. To protect assets adequately, programs must be in place to guard against these threats. In this chapter, you will learn how to develop programs that reduce the chances of incurring losses due to dishonest guests and employees. In some cases, safety and security threats are unique to specific hotel departments. For example, in the front office, cash is routinely kept on hand and must be safeguarded. In this chapter, the important department-specific security concerns of the front office, housekeeping, food and beverage, sales and marketing, and maintenance and engineering departments are examined in detail.

Hotel emergency planning must also address guest disturbances, medical emergencies, hotel fires, and bomb threats as well as the procedures to notify and protect guests in the event of these and other emergencies. These ever-present concerns are reviewed in the chapter.

Hotels, like all other organizations in these modern times, are subject to terrorism threats; hotels in some areas of the world, including the United States, have been victims of actual terrorist attacks. Some of the basic safeguards to address these "front-page" concerns are addressed in this chapter; the role of the recently organized Department of Homeland Security is also examined.

Chapter 12 Outline

PERSONAL SAFETY
  Legal Liability and Guest/Employee Safety
  Staffing for Security
    Employee Safety Training
    Local Law Enforcement Agencies

Safety Resources
  Recodable Locks
  Alarm Systems
  Surveillance Systems
  Emergency Plans

PERSONAL SAFETY

Regardless of the hotel's size, all GMs have **safety** concerns for their guests and employees and for the **security** of their possessions. This is not merely good business; it is also a legal responsibility of the hotel's ownership. Safety and security becomes an important responsibility of each staff member because guests, employees, and nonguests all have a legal right to expect that management is interested in protecting, to the greatest degree possible, their health and well-being.

HOTEL TERMINOLOGY AT WORK

Safety: Protection of an individual's physical well-being and health.

Security: Protection of an individual or business's property or assets.
■

Legal Liability and Guest/Employee Safety

Since the earliest days of travel, guests have been rightfully concerned about their safety when they sleep. Innkeepers and hoteliers have responded to these concerns by striving to provide a safe haven for travelers. In addition to the good intentions of hotel managers, however, there are laws that require those who operate hotels to provide the traveling public with an environment that is safe and secure. These laws do not, however, hold hotels responsible for everything that could happen to guests during their stay because guest safety cannot be ensured. For example, a guest may slip and fall in a bathtub. The hotel will not be held responsible for any resulting injuries if it is determined that the hotel has exercised **reasonable care** in the manner in which it provides and maintains its bathtubs.

HOTEL TERMINOLOGY AT WORK

Reasonable Care: A legal concept identifying the amount of care a reasonably prudent person would exercise in a specific situation.
■

GMs must remember that the legal standard of reasonable care means that they must operate their hotels with the degree of care equal to that of other reasonable persons (general managers). For example, if there is **foreseeable** harm, you will know, or should know, about a threat to the safety of your guests and/or employees. Then it is reasonable to assume that you would either immediately eliminate the threat or clearly inform your guests and employees about it. Not to do so would likely indicate that you exhibited an absence of reasonable care for their safety. If there is a threat to safety that results in loss or injury, and if it is determined that the hotel did not exercise reasonable care in regard to that threat, it is possible that the hotel will be held wholly or partially **liable** for the resulting loss or injury.

HOTEL TERMINOLOGY AT WORK

Foreseeable (Legal Concept): The concept that the liability of a party should be limited to acts that a reasonable person would be able to predict or expect from the results of his/her actions.

Liable: Legally bound to compensate for loss or injury.

If a hotel is found liable for injuries to a guest or employee, the hotel will likely bear the cost of that liability. For example, assume that a hotel manager knew about a defective lock on a guest room door yet did not authorize its immediate repair. Subsequently, Ms. Stevens rented the room with the defective lock and was robbed and assaulted by an assailant who obtained unlawful entry to the room through the door with the defective lock. In this case, it is highly likely that an attorney hired by her to seek **damages** against the hotel would be successful. The **judgment** would likely include **compensatory damages** and possibly even **punitive damages** that the hotel would be required to pay Ms. Stevens.

These costs could have been avoided by the hotel had the guest room lock been repaired, as it should have been, in a timely manner.

HOTEL TERMINOLOGY AT WORK

Damages: The actual amount of losses or costs incurred due to the wrongful act of a liable party.

Judgment: A court's decision about a matter that has been presented to it.

Compensatory Damages: Also known as actual damages, this monetary amount is intended to compensate injured parties for actual losses or damage they have incurred. This typically includes items such as medical bills and lost wages.

Punitive Damages: This monetary amount is assessed to punish liable parties and to serve as an example to the liable party as well as others not to commit the wrongful act in the future.

Effective managers do not manage well simply to avoid paying damages. A demonstrated concern for guest and employee safety is not merely a good business practice, it is also the right thing to do. Safety is an important part of every manager's job. Indeed, the emphasis placed upon safety by a GM and his or her management team is a good indication of the true professionalism of the GM and that team.

Staffing for Security

Even when management is truly committed to safety, it takes the effort of every hotel employee to eliminate, to the greatest degree possible, threats to the safety and security of guests, employees, and the hotel. In larger hotels, there may be a full-time director of safety and security as well as departmental staff that routinely patrol the hotel's grounds, make safety and security checks, and direct the hotel's safety programs. In other cases, the hotel may contract with a private security firm to provide some security services. In still other cases, off-duty police may be hired to assist the hotel's security efforts. In smaller properties, safety and security would not likely be a completely separate department, but rather safety and security programs would be administered within each hotel department and overseen by the GM or a designated **safety and security committee**.

HOTEL TERMINOLOGY AT WORK

Safety and Security Committee: An interdepartmental task force consisting of the GM, other hotel managers, supervisors, and hourly employees charged with the responsibility of monitoring and refining a hotel's safety and security efforts.

■

Many GMs find that maintaining an effectively operating safety and security committee is actually preferable to a separate safety and security department. Its operation reinforces the fact that guest/employee safety and hotel security is the responsibility of every hotel manager, supervisor, and employee. Regardless of the organizational structure of the hotel's safety and security efforts, the training of hotel staff is a key component of any effective program. In addition, local law enforcement officials can be of great assistance in your efforts to help ensure safety. The combined activities of your own well-trained staff along with those of your local police will go a long way toward demonstrating reasonable care on the part of your management team should the need ever arise.

Employee Safety Training

Training employees to help ensure guest safety, to work safely, and to assist the hotel's security efforts is an ongoing process. One way to view the safety training needs of employees is in terms of training that is required by all employees and other training that is essential only to members of a specific department. For example, teaching all employees to promptly report any unauthorized or suspicious person found lurking in the hotel's parking lot would be appropriate. However, providing training about the safe handling of food would likely be appropriate only for those employees involved in the food and beverage department.

Many individual hotels and hotel companies develop and implement many fine safety-training programs. In addition, excellent safety- and security-related training materials are developed and continually updated by applicable professional associations and for-profit organizations.

Local Law Enforcement Agencies

Your employees can and should be well trained, but their safety and security efforts will be helped tremendously when you establish and maintain an excellent relationship with your own local law enforcement professionals. Effective GMs personally know the individuals responsible for law enforcement in the area in which their hotel is located. Local law enforcement officials can advise and assist you and, in many cases, provide no-cost safety and security training for your employees. For example, you can request a property safety and security review from your local police department. This will likely result in the identification of specific steps your hotel can take

Hotel managers and their security staff should interact closely with personnel from local law enforcement and fire agencies.

to reduce safety and security threats, as well as actions you can take to make improvements. Good GMs make it a point to meet frequently with local police because they are an important source of information and assistance.

Safety Resources

In addition to the training resources that can assist in your guest and employee safety efforts, other hotel resources are available from industry manufacturers and suppliers to help you achieve your safety and security goals. The appropriate selection and use of these tools depends on the safety and security needs of each hotel.

Recodable Locks

At one time, a hotel's purchase and use of a recodable locking system was such a significant event that the hotel could actually market its use of such locks to its potential guests. Today, recodable locks are the industry standard and, simply put, no hotel should operate without them.

Recodable lock systems are sold by a variety of companies. Essentially, however, a quality system, regardless of manufacturer, consists of electronic door locks that "stand-alone." That is, there's no need to wire the locks to a central computer. Except in life-threatening emergencies, only a standard magnetic stripe card issued by the front desk or management will open the door lock. Therefore, the hotel's entire guest room security system is controlled by software contained in the locks themselves and activated by cards coded on a keycard-issuing computer.

Each lock contains a card reader and electronic lock control module connected to a motor-actuated lock mechanism. Standard AA alkaline batteries power the entire lock. A warning light visible only to staff warns when the batteries are within three months of needing replacing. When a guest inserts the keycard into the lock for the first time, the lock is immediately recoded to cancel entry authorization for the previous guest. In a quality system, multiple keycards can be issued to the same guest. In addition to guest rooms and exterior doors, recodable locks can be used to limit guest access to designated hotel areas including special elevator floors, such as those offering upgraded concierge or business-class amenities, swimming pools, spas, exercise rooms, and reserved breakfast or bar areas. They can also limit employee access to specified storage, office, or other areas within the hotel.

Since guest rooms must be regularly cleaned and maintained, hotel managers should issue master keycards to those hotel staff that need them. With today's recodable lock systems, an electronic record is kept of all keycards used in the lock for a specific period of time. As a result, should the need arise, it is easy to determine whose keycard was used to open a lock and at what day and time the key was used.

Unlike nonrecodable locks, the use of recodable locks severely reduces the chance for guests to be victimized in their room by someone who had rented the same room on a prior night. In addition, recodable locks help reduce the incident of employee theft from rooms.

THE INTERNET AT WORK

To view the operational features of one of the most popular recodable locking systems, go to

www.tesalocks.com

and click on "Hotels and Resorts."

Alarm Systems

Alarms of many types are used within the hotel industry. They can be either audible or silent. Audible alarms typically consist of high-pitched buzzers, bells, or alternative noises. Alarm devices, whether audible or silent, normally consist of electrical connections, photoelectric light beams, seismic detectors, infrared beams, magnetic contacts, or radio frequency (RF) fields that create, when activated, the alarm.

Alarms many be classified as either **internal alarms** or **contact alarms**.

HOTEL TERMINOLOGY AT WORK

Internal Alarm: A warning system that notifies an area within the hotel if the alarm is activated.

Contact Alarm: A warning system that notifies (contacts) an external entity such as the fire or police department if the alarm is activated.

Internal alarms are generally designed to serve as a deterrent to criminal or mischief activity. For example, a warning buzzer on a hotel's fire exit door would typically be wired only to notify hotel personnel if the door was used. In a like manner, an alarm on a liquor storeroom door might notify a manager or the food and beverage director. Conversely, an alarm activated by a front-desk agent during or after an armed robbery would most likely be wired directly to the local police department for the purpose of contacting them immediately.

Some important spaces that may be protected by internal alarms include:

- Storage locations
- Hotel facilities such as pools, spa, and exercise areas
- Hotel grounds and perimeter

Some important areas that are more likely to be protected by contact alarms include:

- Front desk
- Food and beverage cashier stations
- Controller's office

Hotel fire alarms are so important that federal law, as well as local building codes, mandate them. Good hotels will have these devices wired as both internal and contact alarms. Remember that, in case of a fire, hotel staff, guests, and the fire department all must be made aware of the danger. Therefore, heat or smoke detectors in a guest room may set off an internal alarm that would be heard by the guest in the room, and should be checked immediately by the appropriate hotel staff. By contrast, a fire alarm activated in a public area may result in an automatic contact and summons of firefighters because the alarm was wired directly to the local fire department.

First and foremost, effective GMs have reviewed their alarm system requirements to determine these areas of the hotel that must be part of the overall alarm program. Second, they are responsible for ensuring that, periodically and frequently, all alarms are checked for proper operation. A GM whose hotel has a nonfunctioning alarm system will have great difficulty demonstrating that it exercised reasonable care toward employee and guest safety should the need arise. An effective and comprehensive alarm system is an invaluable tool in every hotel's complete safety and security effort.

Surveillance Systems

Properly implemented, electronic surveillance can play a big role in a hotel's safety and security programs. This surveillance generally is one of two types. The first involves use of a VCR to record activities within an area of the hotel. For example, a VCR could be set up to record the activity outside a liquor storeroom. Then if the storeroom was broken into, a videotaped record of the break-in could be useful in identifying the thieves. Recording activity at the front desk, in parking areas, and near cashiers are among the most frequent use of a VCR surveillance system.

Some hotels use **closed-circuit television (CCTV)** as a tool in their safety and security programs.

HOTEL TERMINOLOGY AT WORK

Closed-Circuit Television (CCTV): A camera and monitor system that displays, in real time, the activity within a camera's field of vision. A CCTV consisting of several cameras and screens showing the camera's field of vision may be monitored in a single hotel location.

There are many potential uses of CCTV within a hotel. It can be used, for example, in a multiple-entry property where management desires to monitor activity outside each entrance. It is important to remember that, to be most effective, a CCTV system must be monitored. Viewing monitors are typically placed in a central location and viewed by an assigned employee trained to respond appropriately to activities seen on the monitor. For example, if an outside entrance is being monitored and the monitor shows that a break-in is being attempted, the employee may have been trained to summon the local police. Some hotels add an intercom to the area being monitored to extend the effectiveness of the individual monitoring the system. Within casino hotels, states typically mandate the use of CCTV to improve security.

Some hotel managers attempt to give the illusion of having a CCTV system in place, when in fact the "cameras" are not truly cameras—either that, or the monitors are not constantly monitored. This is typically done in an effort to save money on the cost of operating the CCTV system. The rationale for this has been that the mere presence of the cameras would be sufficient to deter criminals, who would not know that the CCTV system was not operational. The courts and juries have found, however, that this approach may not establish reasonable security care. For instance, victims may think that help is on the way because they believe their situation is being monitored, and thus may base their behavior on that belief. In fact, since the monitors are not being viewed, no such help is likely to arrive. Hotel managers wishing to operate a CCTV that is not monitored should consult with both their insurers and their legal counsel before implementing such an approach.

When considering the use of either the VCR or CCTV system, the issues for management involve balancing guest and employee privacy with safety and assessing whether visible cameras increase or detract from a guest's sense of security in the hotel.

Emergency Plans

Despite your best efforts, safety and security emergencies will occur in your hotel. When they do, the hotel must be ready to respond appropriately. Preplanning is perhaps the very best tool available to managers concerned with safety and security. In cases of unforeseen emergencies, it may not be possible to determine the proper response until the actual event occurs. In the case of crises that are foreseeable such as severe weather storms or power outages, some of the things your hotel must be prepared to do will be quite similar, if not routine, in each crisis.

To prepare the hotel for a crisis, the GM should develop and implement an **emergency plan**.

HOTEL TERMINOLOGY AT WORK

Emergency Plan: A document describing a hotel's predetermined, intended response to a safety/security threat that it may encounter.

▮

An emergency plan identifies a threat to the safety and/or security of the hotel, as well as the hotel's planned response to it. For example, an emergency plan for a hotel near a heavily wooded area might include an evacuation plan that should be implemented in case of a forest fire. Alternatively, a hotel on a Florida coast should include in its emergency plan a method of evacuating the hotel in the event of an impending hurricane.

Responses to events such as the following are included in most hotels' emergency plans:

- Fire
- Power outages
- Severely inclement weather

- Robbery
- Death of or injury to a guest or employee
- Bomb threat
- Intense negative publicity by the media

In all of these cases, the hotel's managers and employees may be called upon to react quickly. The emergency plan helps to prepare them to do so. This can be accomplished because many crises share similar characteristics that can be controlled to some degree by preplanning: These characteristics include:

- Extreme importance
- Disruption of normal business
- Potential for human suffering or death
- Financial loss
- Potential scrutiny by the media
- Threat to the reputation or financial health of the business

An emergency plan must be a written document. This is important because you must identify precisely what is expected of management and employees in times of crisis. In addition, if the hotel becomes subject to a lawsuit as a result of the crisis, a written emergency plan can help show that your hotel exercised reasonable care in preparing for the crisis.

An emergency plan should be kept simple because it will likely be implemented only in a time of heightened stress. For each crisis identified, a clearly developed emergency plan would include:

- Type of crisis
- Who should be told when the crisis occurs (include telephone or pager numbers)
- What should be done and who should do it in the event the crisis occurs
- Who should be informed of the results or impact of the crisis when it is over

The actual plan should be reviewed frequently by management and shared with employees so they know what to do during the emergency. Where practical, hotels should practice the implementation of their plan. By doing so, they demonstrate strongly their commitment to ensuring the safety and security of the hotel and all who are in it.

Hotel Emergency and Security Tactics[1]

After security and safety plans are developed, staff must be trained. You have learned that GMs who make sure this training occurs will be certain that emergency situations will be properly managed if they arise. The close interaction between all hotel employees is important; however, since front-office personnel communicate with guests more frequently than do most employees in other departments, their contact with guests and security staff is critical. In this section, we will look at several potential problems and review basic tactics to address them. They suggest fundamental procedures that GMs should consider for their properties.

[1]This section is adapted from: Robert Woods, et al. *Professional Front-Office Management*. Upper Saddle River, New Jersey. Pearson Education, Inc. (See Chapter 14.)

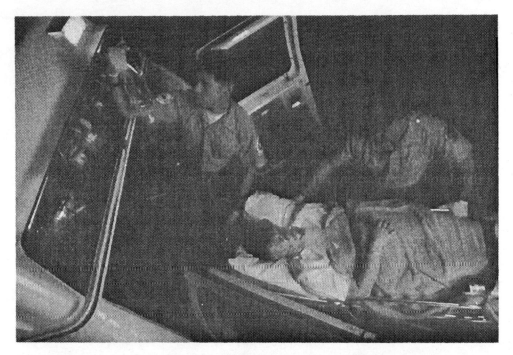

Plans must be in place to quickly bring aid to guests with medical emergencies.

Disturbances

Guests experiencing noise or other disturbances from adjoining or nearby guest rooms or hallways, parking lots, or other locations often initially notify the front desk. If the disturbance is from a guest room, a front-office employee typically calls the guest room to request that the disturbance be ended. If there is a subsequent complaint, in some hotels a second call from the front desk is made; in other properties, someone from the security department is sent to the room.

If there are complaints about noise or other disturbances occurring in public areas including hallways and parking lots, a security department employee typically visits the location.

Medical Emergencies

Front-desk personnel may receive calls from guest rooms about medical emergencies. The telephone systems in many hotels route emergency (911) calls to the front desk. In these potentially life-threatening situations, there is an obvious need to quickly and carefully follow the hotel's procedures for immediately alerting the 911 operator, designated physician, or other emergency service provider. Increasingly, hotels require that every security staff member be trained in cardiopulmonary resuscitation (CPR), first aid, and the use of an on-site **defibrillator**.

HOTEL TERMINOLOGY AT WORK

Defibrillator: A machine used to deliver an electrical shock to the heart in case of cardiac arrest (heart attack) in efforts to reestablish a normal heartbeat.

MANAGING MEDICAL EMERGENCIES

When notified about a medical emergency, front-office staff should obtain the following information:

- The person's name
- The person's location
- The nature of the emergency

They should notify the proper emergency responder and provide the following information:

- The hotel's name
- Address
- Nearest cross street
- The nature of the emergency
- The person's general condition and location
- The hotel entrance nearest the site of the person's location (if not the main entrance)
- The hotel's call-back number

If appropriate, security personnel should secure the largest elevator in the lobby or other applicable area for use by the emergency personnel. As well, someone should go to the person's floor to assist.

- When emergency personnel arrive, they should be met at the appropriate hotel entrance, given all relevant information, and escorted to the person's location.
- Cooperate fully with emergency personnel.
- In the event of a death, secure the area around the body until police arrive. Do not allow others in the area. Seek assistance from other employees, if necessary.
- Never refuse to call emergency personnel for anyone who requests it. Call emergency personnel even if the person requesting emergency attention does not seem like a responsible person, if he/she appears to be in good health, or does not appear to need emergency assistance. Never, under any circumstances, make the decision that someone does not need emergency assistance after they have requested it.

Guest Notification

It may be necessary to alert persons in guest rooms about the presence of a fire or a potentially life-threatening storm or other natural disaster. Instructions about precautions necessary when there is a power blackout, a bomb threat, or other need for an emergency evacuation may also be necessary.

Specific evacuation procedures must be developed for each property; however, several general procedures are integral to the plans used by many hotels. Front-office staff:

- Call 911 and state the nature of the emergency—be specific. Set off the fire alarm.
- Update and print, if time permits, a list of all occupied rooms; attach a room layout to the evacuation plan.
- If an emergency such as a fire pertains to a specific area of the hotel, first call the rooms occupied next to the emergency area on both sides and any rooms above or below that area. For instance, as seen in Figure 12.1, assume a two-story hotel has rooms numbered in a normal pattern. If room 246 is on fire, call rooms 244, 248, 144, 146, and 148 because rooms immediately below and

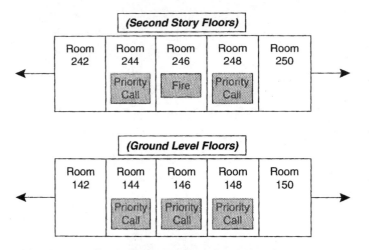

FIGURE 12.1 Fire in Room 246 (Two-Story Hotel)

above the fire area should be evacuated as quickly as possible. Rooms on either side of the room on fire (same floor) and the rooms immediately below the room on fire (bottom floor) should be called first in a fire emergency.

- Note rooms of guests who could not be contacted. Do not panic guests; remain calm and direct guests outside the building.
- If practical, security and other employees can begin knocking on doors to evacuate these rooms. Note: if there is a fire, do not attempt to fight it unless someone's life is in danger, or the fire is very small, and staff are trained to do so.
- If they are not already present, call the GM and chief engineer and advise them to go to the hotel immediately.
- Front-desk staff should not leave the front-desk area unless that location is affected by the emergency because they will need to handle calls from guests. In multibuilding properties, if guests call from the affected building, ask them to evacuate rooms until they are instructed to return.
- After all guests have been called, rooms should be called a second time to ensure that everyone has evacuated.
- In the case of a tornado, call guests and instruct them to go into the guest room bathroom. Hotel employees should go into an office bathroom or storage room closest to their work areas.

Other important tactics applicable to persons evacuating the hotel include:

- Do not evacuate unless told to do so because danger is imminent.
- Follow instructions given by emergency personnel.
- Walk and keep noise to a minimum.
- Do not use elevators.
- Do not push or crowd. Use handrails in stairwells and move to the right if emergency personnel are evacuated.
- Remove high heels to avoid tripping.
- Move to the designated evacuation area unless otherwise instructed. Check doors for heat before opening.

Assist any nonambulatory and visually or hearing-impaired persons.

The following supplies should be readily available and inspected weekly to assure an adequate supply and/or proper working condition:

- Well-stocked first-aid kit
- Flashlights and spare batteries
- Weather band radio and transistor radio with spare batteries
- Camera/film
- Chalk (to mark doors of evacuated rooms)
- Scissors and/or sharp knives
- **Incident reports** and security log

HOTEL TERMINOLOGY AT WORK

Incident Report: A document prepared to record the details of an accident, injury, or disturbance, and the hotel's response to it.

Hotel Fires

Unfortunately, hotel fires are more common than many people think. They are frequently started by cigarettes or other smoking material in guest rooms. However, they can also begin in storage areas, kitchens, and laundries with electrical or even suspicious origins. Most hotel fires are small and involve little property damage and few, if any, injuries. However, a small fire can become out of control quickly if there is the right combination of heat, ventilation, and combustible materials. Then a fire can spread rapidly from room-to-room, down corridors, and/or through ventilation shafts until an entire section or wing of the hotel is involved.

Hotel fires can threaten hundreds of guests who are in unfamiliar surroundings, often tired or asleep, with widely varying physical capabilities. They may be housed multiple stories above the street and well out of reach of fire department ladders.

A hotel fire need not be a major disaster to have a significant effect on the hotel and its employees. Any fire will cause disruption and property damage and can lead to injuries and lawsuits. A fire of any proportion will generate adverse publicity (sometimes nationwide) and can result in a loss of business and a loss of jobs.

The GM, director of security, and other managers and employees are the best fire protection available to the hotel. Managers can provide the appropriate fire safety equipment and can develop exemplary disaster response procedures. As well, they can implement a continuous training program with prevention and appropriate response goals. Employees are the first line of protection because they are working throughout the hotel and can discover hazards, alert appropriate supervisors, and if trained (for example, in the use of fire extinguishers) can even deal with a fire in its very early stages.

All reports of a fire should be considered real, should be responded to, and need to be investigated immediately. After a possible fire is reported, the following should be done:

- The **manager on duty (MOD)** and security officer should immediately visit the area to determine if the fire is real.

HOTEL TERMINOLOGY AT WORK

Manager on Duty (MOD): The individual on the hotel property responsible for making any management decisions required during the period he or she is the ranking management at the property.

■

- If the fire is real, the fire department should be contacted immediately.

- If evacuation is necessary, the MOD should contact the front-desk staff and tell them to implement the hotel's emergency evacuation procedures. Note: Evacuate the fire floor first, room-by-room. Initiate a system to keep track of every guest including those who do not respond to a room call. Assist handicapped guests. Members of the hotel's emergency response team should go to the designated areas. After rooms on the fire floor are evacuated, the floor above the fire floor and then below the fire floor should be evacuated.

- Guests should be called and told to evacuate. They should be informed about the need to first feel the door before opening it (and to do so only if it is cool). They should take their room keys with them, should not use the elevator, and if they encounter smoke, should return to their room and call the front desk.

- If the room door is hot or if guests cannot leave the area, they should remain in their rooms. Then they should seal all cracks (particularly at the bottom of the door), turn off the air-conditioner and fan, hang a sheet from the window (to alert the fire department), and fill the tub with water if needed later to fight the fire.

A security department or other employee should be stationed in the parking lot to direct the fire department to the fire's location. According to the property's crisis plan, employees should assemble at a predetermined place or begin emergency duties such as assisting guests. If it is safe to do so, staff members should be assigned to verify that all guest rooms are vacant. After rooms are checked, an "X" should be marked on the door to alert fire department personnel that room is vacant. (Chalk supplies should be available at the front desk or another easily accessible and well-known location[s]).

Bomb Threats

Bomb threats are typically received by the hotel's switchboard or at the front desk. Procedures to manage bomb threats typically require that, first, the GM, MOD, and/or director of security be alerted. That individual would then determine whether local law enforcement or emergency service authorities should be contacted.

The bomb threat caller may provide information to assist authorities in their subsequent investigation of the call and in their search for the caller. The staff member taking the call can help in this effort by remaining calm and asking the caller questions such as "When will the bomb explode?" "Where is the bomb located?" "What kind of bomb is it?" "Where are you calling from?" "What is the reason for the bomb threat?"

Listening for unique background noises may help to determine where the call was made—for example, if there is traffic noise, music, or the sound of machinery. In addition, the caller's gender, approximate age, race, voice, accent, or whether the voice appeared disguised might be noted. All possible details about the call should be recorded to begin tracking the communication and activities undertaken during the threat response.

Contact all department heads immediately. Tell them that all employees should report to a predetermined location and remain available until they are released by an applicable manager.

One employee, typically from the security department, should be assigned to guide police upon their arrival; if the situation dictates, other staff members should be used to keep stairwells, public restrooms, and other public areas under surveillance for unauthorized persons. They should not touch, handle, or move any suspicious objects. Examples of areas where bombs may be hidden include restrooms, large ash trays, cabinets, equipment rooms, electrical panels, water fountains, and air ducts.

If a suspicious package or bomb is found, it should not be moved, touched, or disturbed, and the area should be evacuated. Block off a 300-foot area in all directions and assure that all doors and windows are open. Assign a staff member to meet the bomb squad members outside the building to lead them to the location. Hotel employees throughout the property will need to follow instructions provided by law enforcement officials to help assure their safety.

Other Emergencies

GMs and their hotels will be confronted with the same types of emergencies as any other business. These include:

- *Severe Winds.* Hurricanes and tornadoes occur frequently in many parts of the country. Frequently National Weather Service personnel can provide warnings (the possibility of severe weather) and information about watches (alerts that severe weather may occur within a specified general area). Evacuation plans should be predetermined and whenever possible followed. If there is no time for evacuation, everyone within the building should seek protection next to an inside wall but away from windows or, preferably, in basements or cellars. After the storm has passed, it is important to check the exterior of the building and grounds for anything that could pose a safety hazard. Those hoteliers who worked in New Orleans and other portions of the U.S. Gulf coast and experienced the devastation of Hurricane Katrina (2005) know only too well the power of strong winds as well as the consequences of inadequate planning for catastrophic events. In that storm, over 150 hotels were damaged, closed, or completely destroyed. Nearly 1,000 persons were killed. Followed 30 days later by the strong impact of Hurricane Rita, hoteliers in the entire United States (as well as those around the world who observed Katrina's impact on the local area) learned very well the importance of proper planning for the results of exceedingly strong winds and, in the case of hurricanes, massive amounts of water.

- *Floods.* Many hotels are located in areas where flooding from melting snow, heavy rains, water surges (water pushed ahead of high winds), or other causes can occur. Frequently, there is little notice about these emergencies. Hopefully, there will be no employees or guests in hotel buildings after flood alerts have been sounded. However, fire is a serious threat from live electrical circuits and electrical equipment that become exposed to water. As well, floating flammable liquids and debris can cause fires and/or other structural problems that will need to be dealt with before the building can be reoccupied.

- *Earthquakes.* Earthquakes cannot be predicted with any accuracy, and there is little that can be done to protect the structural soundness of a building after it is constructed. Ideally, building codes in earthquake-prone areas governing new construction should consider the implications of building occupants and others close to buildings if earthquakes occur. Building inspections by qualified personnel will likely be required before buildings can be reoccupied after an earthquake.

- *Winter Weather.* GMs, their staff, and everyone else in areas with severe winters must learn how to cope with the problems winter storms can bring. For example, roofs can collapse from the weight of heavy snow and ice, and icicles formed on building overhangs can fall and injure anyone who may happen to be underneath them. Slippery parking lots and sidewalks create obvious problems, heavy storms can disrupt power, and dangerous roads may prevent some guests and employees from being able to safely leave the building.

Ironically, many people seek hotels when there are (or have been) emergencies in the area. Consider, for example, those who must evacuate as hurricanes approach, travelers who must find shelter when roads and airports are closed, and others in the community whose houses are damaged or destroyed by fires or natural disasters. There are untold stories of hoteliers and their staff who work hard during shifts of many hours to accommodate those who require shelter in these emergencies. Many, of course, do so even though their own families need them and their own properties need attention. In these instances, it is often necessary to be very creative as guests are given a safe place (often complimentary) to stay in hotel lobbies, offices, and other public areas, and as they are provided with food services in volumes that the property was never designed to produce (and sometimes without the availability of electric or gas utilities).

Special Safety Issues

Hotels are unique places of business with unique guest safety concerns. GMs wishing to reduce their legal liability would do well to monitor the staff's efforts in all areas where extra caution or efforts are required. For many hotels, three of the most important of these special areas of concern are swimming pools, spas, and parking lots.

Swimming Pools

Hotel swimming pools are exceptionally popular even though they are typically used by only a small percentage of hotel guests. Consistently, in opinion polls regarding desirable services, travelers rank the mere presence of a swimming pool near the top of hotel amenities that influence their hotel selection. The potential legal liabilities that result from accidental slipping, diving, or even drowning, however, requires that the individuals responsible for managing and maintaining the pool area, as well as the GM, be extraordinarily vigilant in enforcing pool safety procedures.

It is not possible to avoid all potential accidents in a pool area. It is possible, however, to minimize the chances for such an accident. Figure 12.2 lists ten key practices that affect swimming pool safety and legal liability. The GM should review them on a monthly basis with affected employees to ensure consistent compliance.

1. Post the pool's operational hours and open the pool only during those hours.
2. Clearly mark the depths of pools accurately and in both metric measure and in feet/inches.
3. Make sure the pool and pool area is properly illuminated and that any electrical components are regularly inspected and maintained to meet local electrical codes.
4. Install self-closing and self-latching and/or locking gates to prevent unauthorized access to the pool area. If possible, lock the entrance to the pool with a recodable lock.
5. Have appropriate lifesaving equipment on hand and easily accessible, as well as at least one cardiopulmonary resuscitation (CPR) certified employee on duty at all times the pool is opened.
6. Allow pool use only by registered guests and specifically authorized others.
7. Contact the hotel's insurer to determine the number, placement, and content of necessary pool warning signs.
8. Post all pool policy and information signs in the language(s) of guests. Enforce the policies at all times.
9. Provide an emergency telephone in the pool area that rings directly either to the front desk or to 911 depending on the preference of the hotel's insurer.
10. Carefully document all activities related to pool maintenance, local ordinance compliance, and operational policy enforcement.

FIGURE 12.2   Swimming Pool Safety

Spas

Hotels that have common-area spas or hot tubs face special safety and liability concerns. Although the spas are popular, they can be dangerous to young children, the elderly, intoxicated individuals, and those on special medications. Like pools, it may be impossible to prevent all possible accidents; however, the practices listed in Figure 12.3 can go a long way toward improving guest safety and minimizing a hotel's legal liability. As with pools, the GM should review these practices with affected staff on a monthly basis to ensure compliance. In addition, pool and spa practices can be observed whenever he/she is in these areas.

1. Inspect and document the inspection of spa drain covers on a daily basis.
2. Post all spa policy signs in the language(s) of guests.
3. Install a thermometer and check the spa temperature frequently; record your readings. (A range not to exceed 102°F–105°F [39°C–41°C] is recommended.)
4. Display spa temperatures in a manner that is easily readable by guests.
5. Clearly mark the depths of the spa in both metric measures and feet/inches.
6. Do not allow the consumption of alcohol while using the spa.
7. Install nonslip flooring surfaces around the spa and provide stairs/ladders for entry.
8. Prohibit spa use by young children and nonguests.
9. Provide an emergency telephone in the spa area that rings directly either to the front desk or to 911 depending on the preference of the hotel's insurer.
10. Carefully document all activities related to spa maintenance, local ordinance compliance, and operational policy enforcement.

FIGURE 12.3   Spa Safety

The parking lot at this large convention hotel could be a potential safety risk to guests and employees. The hotel manager must work with the security staff to assure that it remains safe.

Parking Lots

Most hotels have parking areas for guest vehicles. Even though they are not the insurers of vehicles parked in their lots, the hotels are responsible for providing reasonable care in the protection of vehicles and guests using the lots. Figure 12.4 lists ten key practices that affect the safety of parking areas. Again, the GM should review them with affected personnel on an ongoing basis to ensure compliance.

1. Inspect parking lot lighting on a daily basis. Arrange for replacement of burned-out lights immediately.
2. Inspect parking lot surfaces daily and arrange for pavement patches immediately if they threaten guest safety. Keep surfaces free of ice and snow in inclement weather.
3. Ensure parking lot stripes and directional signs are easily seen to avoid pedestrian/vehicle accidents.
4. Post easily readable signs in the parking lot reminding guests not to leave valuables in their vehicles.
5. If valet parking is provided, document the training of all drivers.
6. Require guests to identify their vehicles by license number or make/color upon check in.
7. Keep landscaping around parking lots well trimmed to avoid dangerous areas that may provide hiding places for individuals that could threaten guest safety or property security.
8. If possible, arrange for regular and frequent parking lot "drive-through" patrols by local law enforcement officials.
9. Arrange for daily daytime and nighttime "walk-through" patrols by hotel staff.
10. Use a manager's daily log to document your parking lot maintenance procedures.

FIGURE 12.4   Parking Lot Safety

MANAGERS AT WORK

Bill Frisbee, the director of security for the hotel, walked quickly to the hotel's pool area.

"There are an awful lot of kids . . . and only one adult . . . down at the pool" was the statement made a few minutes earlier to the front-office manager by a housekeeper who had gone to the pool area to replenish the towel supply. All housekeepers had been trained to report any activity that could possibly be con-

sidered dangerous, and this housekeeper had performed well.

Because she could not leave the front-desk area unattended, the front-office manager had called Bill to ask for assistance.

"What's the problem?" asked the guest when Bill arrived in the pool area. "I rented a room at this hotel to hold my son's eleventh birthday party. These are his friends. Are you saying we are not

allowed to invite guests to visit us when we are registered in your hotel?"

Bill quickly counted over 20 young people attending the "party."

If you were the hotel's GM, would you impose limits on the number of "guests of guests" allowed to use hotel facilities? Who do you believe is responsible for the safety of the young people attending the party? Why? What should Bill say to the guest to whom he is now speaking?

Documenting Safety Efforts

All hotels should carefully document their safety- and security-related efforts. If it were ever needed, this documentation could be powerful evidence that the GM took his/her safety and security responsibilities very seriously. For example, if the duties of the evening MOD include a "walk around" the property as part of the safety and security program, these checklists or documents should be maintained.

MOD checklists that demonstrate a consistent effort on the part of the hotel to maintain safety and security standards are excellent. Each hotel must determine the frequency, content, and number of checklists that are appropriate. These should be prepared and completed for each area of the hotel. Figure 12.5 is an example of an MOD checklist related to parking areas in a hotel.

Accidents can and will happen. When **incident reports** are prepared that list the "who, what, where, how," and the hotel's response to an accident or injury, these should also be filed and maintained.

HOTEL TERMINOLOGY AT WORK

Incident Report: A document prepared to record the details of an accident, injury, or disturbance, and the hotel's response to it.

THE INTERNET AT WORK

For an excellent example of a hotel incident report, go to

www.hospitalitylawyer.com

Then use the Search field and enter the words "Incident Report."
This site charges no fee and is an exceptional source of up-to-date safety and security-related information.

Other examples of documentation that the GM should assure is maintained by the hotel include minutes from safety and security committee meetings, general staff meeting notes relevant to safety issues, and records of employee training related to safety and security including safety seminars attended or certifications acquired by employees.

Waldo Hotel
MOD Checklist for Parking Areas

Performed by: _____

Date of Inspection:_____

Time of Inspection:_____

To ensure the integrity of your walk-through, this checklist should be completed in sequence as it appears.

As appropriate, a check must be placed in the "yes" or "no" column. If "no," please indicate the problem in the "Comments" section. If a work order is submitted, note the work order number in the "Comments" section.

Item	Yes	No	Comments
Outdoor parking lot is well lit.			
Outdoor parking lot is free of trash and debris.			
Painted stripes are in good condition, i.e., yellow, white, and red stripes.			
Directional signs are posted in conspicuous locations.			
Lot patrolled at irregular intervals.			
All entrance gates locked after 8:00 P.M. with the exception of the main entrance.			
Emergency call boxes are located throughout the parking lot and are functioning properly.			
Closed-circuit cameras function properly and send clear images to security.			
Gangs or vagrants are noticed.			
Cars are checked for length of stay (cars covered with tarp, excessive dirt, and so on).			
Security is aware of long-term stay automobiles.			
Correct percentage of ADA parking is available and well marked.			
Grass areas and bushes are well maintained.			
Bushes and plants are trimmed and away from entrance doors.			
Walkways are well lit.			
Closed-circuit cameras function properly and send clear images to security.			
Outside entrances are free of trash and debris.			
All external doors leading to the inside are closed, locked, and card accessible.			
Keycard readers work properly at each entrance.			
All entrances are well lit.			
All entrances are secured.			
Directional signage at each entrance is compatible with ADA requirements.			
Outdoor ADA requirements are met regarding wheelchair ramps.			
Other: _____			
Other: _____			
Other: _____			

FIGURE 12.5   MOD Checklist for Parking Areas

In summary, any and all efforts of the hotel related to the safety and security needs of guests should be documented. Reasonable care can sometimes be a difficult concept to prove, and any documentation the hotel has that can help establish its presence will be useful.

The Occupational Safety and Health Administration (OSHA)

Guest safety is important, but the safety of employees when they work is equally important. The federal government passed the Occupational Safety and Health Act that created, within the Department of Labor, the Occupational Safety and Health Administration **(OSHA)** in 1970.

HOTEL TERMINOLOGY AT WORK

OSHA: The Occupational Safety and Health Administration. A federal agency established in 1970 that is responsible for developing and enforcing regulations related to assuring safe and healthful working conditions.

The purpose of the Occupational Safety and Health Act is to help assure safe and healthful working conditions. OSHA is very aggressive in enforcing the rights of workers. Your hotel is legally required to comply with the extensive safety practices, equipment specifications, and employee communication procedures mandated by OSHA. As the hotel's GM, your interaction with OSHA can be an adversarial one or, preferably, one in which this agency is viewed as a partner in your safety efforts. In either case, OSHA will perform its main tasks related to worker safety. These include ensuring that businesses:

- Provide a safe workplace for employees by complying with OSHA safety and health standards.
- Provide workers only with tools and equipment to do their jobs that meet OSHA specifications for health and safety.
- Establish training programs for employees who operate dangerous equipment.
- Report to OSHA within 48 hours any work site accident that results in a fatality or requires the hospitalization of five or more employees.
- Maintain the "OSHA Log 200" (an on-site record of work-related injuries or illnesses) and submit it to OSHA once per year.
- Display OSHA notices regarding employee rights and safety in prominent places within the hotel.
- Provide all employees access to the **Material Safety Data Sheets (MSDSs)** that provide information about the dangerous chemicals they may be handling during work.
- Offer no-cost hepatitis B vaccinations for employees who may have come into contact with blood or body fluids.

HOTEL TERMINOLOGY AT WORK

Material Safety Data Sheet (MSDS): A written statement describing the potential hazards of, and best ways to handle, a chemical or toxic substance. An MSDS is provided by the manufacturer of the chemical or toxic substance to the buyer of the product and must be posted and/or made available in a place where it is easily accessible to those who will actually use the product.

OSHA has inspectors that monitor the safety-related efforts of businesses. These inspectors can visit your hotel to ensure your compliance with their regulations. When initially developed, some businesses did not view OSHA as a partner in their worker safety efforts. Today, astute GMs recognize that compliance with OSHA standards results in fewer accidents, lower insurance costs, and a healthier workforce.

THE INTERNET AT WORK

OSHA maintains an active Web site with valuable information that can be easily accessed. To stay current on OSHA regulations and enforcement programs visit and bookmark

www.osha.gov

PROPERTY SECURITY

As stated earlier in this chapter, safety-related hotel programs are designed to keep people safe from harm, while security-related efforts are directed toward protecting property from theft or damage. The safety of people is always more important than the security of property, but good GMs know that they must use sound judgment and establish effective programs to protect the personal assets of guests while they travel, as well as the assets of the hotel itself. Not to do so would be a disservice to the traveler and the hotel's owners.

Threats to Asset Security

Threats to the security of assets can come from individuals inside the hotel itself or from people outside the hotel. In both cases, these individuals seek to steal or damage property that rightfully belongs to the hotel's guests, employees, or owners. Effective GMs and department heads design, implement, and monitor security programs that reduce, to the greatest extent possible, these internal and external threats to asset security.

Internal Threats

Sometimes employees steal assets owned by guests or the hotel. When it is clear that an employee is involved in such activity, the response of the GM should be appropriate and, above all else, consistent. Some hotels include in their employee handbook a phrase that indicates theft will be considered grounds for dismissal. When the theft or loss of property involves significant amounts of money, the GM may elect to file charges against the individual employee. Regardless of the approach used, it should be applied equally to all employees at all levels.

Consider, for example, a supervisor or manager involved in criminal activity that is caught, but then allowed to resign, while in the same hotel an hourly employee caught in the same activity is fired and/or prosecuted. If this occurred, the hotel leaves itself open to charges of discrimination or unfair labor practices against which it may be difficult to defend. It also sends a mixed message to others still employed at the hotel about management's view of theft.

If the GM wishes to communicate to employees that theft of all types will be dealt with swiftly and severely, it must pursue internal threats to security just as aggressively as threats posed by nonemployees.

Cash. In many cases, when hotel managers think of employee theft, they think of employees stealing money. **Embezzlement** is a potential problem in hotels, but using procedures and policies designed to prevent it can minimize its likelihood.

HOTEL TERMINOLOGY AT WORK

Embezzlement: The theft of a company's financial assets by an employee.

■

Some hotels are so concerned about employee theft that they **bond** those employees who are in a position to embezzle funds.

HOTEL TERMINOLOGY AT WORK

Bond(ing): Purchasing an insurance policy against the possibility that an employee will steal.

■

The methods used by employees to defraud their employers of cash are numerous, and a good GM will stay current in the areas of cost and revenue control systems. Good financial controls, based on solid accountability principles, will go a long way toward reducing employee theft. Of particular importance are controls related to cashiering positions because cashiers can defraud the hotel and/or to steal cash from guests in a variety of ways. Typical methods of fraud related to cashiering include:

- Charging guests for items not purchased, then keeping the overcharge.
- Misadding legitimate charges to create a higher-than-appropriate total with the intent of keeping the overcharge.
- Purposely shortchanging guests when giving back change, then removing the extra change from the cash drawer.
- Voiding legitimate sales as "mistakes" and keeping the cash amount of the legitimate sale.
- Charging higher-than-appropriate prices for hotel goods or services, recording the proper price, then keeping the overcharge.

In addition to cashier theft that can affect the hotel and/or hotel guests, the theft of cash by employees can occur in the accounts payable area by paying the hotel's bills in a way that funnels money to the embezzling employee or the accounts receivable area by fraudulently diverting funds intended for the hotel. The responsibility for preventing the theft of hotel funds falls to the controller and each hotel department head involved in the handling of cash. Effective GMs oversee these efforts with diligence.

THE INTERNET AT WORK

Many police departments provide Web-based suggestions about tactics to control internal cash theft. For example, go to

www.sonoma-county.org/crimecrushers/internaltheft.htm

Additionally, you can type, "Internal Cash Theft" into your favorite search engine.

Other Assets.   Cash is not the only hotel asset that can be stolen by dishonest employees. In fact, the number and type of assets that can be unlawfully taken by employees is large. As a GM, you must be aware of all the threats to your assets and implement programs to reduce or eliminate employee theft. Many GMs find it helpful to create programs designed to protect the three noncash assets most subject to employee theft. These three loss areas involve the stealing of time, company property, or services.

It may seem strange to consider time a hotel asset, yet it is the resource most easily taken by employees. In nearly all cases, employees are paid for their work by the hour or, as in the case of salaried individuals, by the week or month. In effect, the hotel is exchanging one asset (cash) for another (employee time). When an employee takes a hotel's cash but does not give back the time agreed upon, the hotel loses. The theft of time can be caused by **fraud**: employees can fill out time sheets or punch time cards for times they do not work. In some large hotels, particularly those with weak supervision programs, theft of time may result from employees simply "disappearing" for hours at a time with the result that work they should have performed is not completed.

HOTEL TERMINOLOGY AT WORK

Fraud: Purposeful deception (deceit) that results in legal injury to a person.

■

The best way to prevent theft of time by employees is to have strong time control systems in place. To help in this area, more and more hotels are issuing individual employee identification cards to reduce the chances of one employee fraudulently punching another employee in or out.

When considering plans to reduce employee theft that involves lack of productivity, managers must be vigilant. This can be challenging, especially in large properties. Good supervision, however, and a realistic workload for each employee on a schedule reviewed daily will go a long way toward improving the hotel's ability to detect such theft.

Company property can disappear through the actions of employees as easily as through those of guests. In fact, employees usually know best which assets management has neglected to protect as well as they could. From apples in the food and beverage department to zippered laundry bags in housekeeping, employees often find that the physical assets of a hotel are the type they could use at home. That makes these items very susceptible to employee theft. The best approaches to preventing the theft of company property include to:

- Carefully screen employees before hiring
- Reduce the chances for theft through the use of effective recodeable locks, inventory systems, and other security measures
- Ensure that managers, as well as employees, are aware of the penalty for theft
- Treat all proven cases of similar theft in a similar manner

It is unlikely, even with the best controls, that all employee theft can be eliminated. There are too many opportunities for dishonest employees to take advantage of their access to the hotel's physical resources. Effective employee screening, however, and the creation of an environment that discourages stealing and that consistently disciplines, terminates, or prosecutes employees for known cases of theft, will go a long way toward reducing employee-related **pilferage**.

HOTEL TERMINOLOGY AT WORK

Pilferage: Petty theft of small, less than full package (case) amounts from inventory.

Some employees steal company property while others steal hotel services. In many ways, this type of theft is even harder to detect than is the theft of company property. For example, assume that a front-office supervisor, working late at night, spends an hour or more per day making a long-distance call to his girlfriend who lives several states away. That inappropriate use of hotel assets will result in the hotel incurring a larger than necessary long-distance telephone bill for the month as well as experiencing the theft of time discussed earlier. This theft of services may go undetected unless someone at the property is effectively monitoring long-distance telephone bills generated by each administrative telephone extension number. In-room movies and games, telephone tolls, copy and faxing services, and the like are all susceptible to employee theft. It is critical that proper management controls be in place to minimize, to the greatest degree possible, the chances for loss of hotel services.

External Threats

Hotels are open around the clock and are susceptible to asset threats any time of day or night. Guests or nonguests can pose these threats. As is the case of protecting assets from threats posed by employees, managers protecting hotel assets from the illegal activities of nonemployees must guard both cash and noncash assets.

Cash.   Nearly all hotels keep some money on the property at all times. As well, many hotels offer thieves the chance to make rapid getaways by automobile. They are open late at night (or all night) and they typically have only one or a few employees working on these late/early morning shifts. Therefore, hotel staff may be confronted by armed or unarmed robbers. Preventing robberies is best achieved by the GM and other managers working with the hotel staff and local law enforcement officials to identify and eliminate opportunities thieves may have to rob the hotel.

It is important to understand that a robbery is not an occasion to attempt the protection of cash assets. A robbery is a time to protect staff! In the event of a robbery, the hotel staff member(s) involved should obey the robber's demands and make no movements that might be perceived by the robber to be an attempt to stop the crime. Employees should do nothing to risk or jeopardize their lives. Employees can be trained to observe the robber carefully to later recall physical characteristics including height, weight, color and length of hair, color of eyes, mustaches or beards, tattoos, and accents. During a robbery, complying with the robber's demands and observation of the robber should be the employee's only concern.

To help apprehend robbers, many GMs install a contact alarm system in their cashier's cash drawers. This alarm is activated when a predetermined bill or packet of bills is removed. The alarm is wired to summons local law enforcement officers trained to deal with robbery-in-progress situations. If no such alarm is in place, an employee who is robbed should contact local law enforcement officials at the earliest safe opportunity, as well as others indicated in the hotel's applicable emergency plan.

Other Assets.   Robbers steal from hotels, but so do guests. In fact, guests are generally much greater threats to the noncash assets of hotels than are robbers. Most often, the targets of guests are not cash but rather the products and services hotels offer for sale. Every experienced hotel manager has a story about a guest who illegally removed (or tried to remove!) a significant asset from a hotel. From furniture and artwork to minor items such as towels, robes, and ashtrays, guest theft costs hotels millions of dollars annually in lost assets.

The reality of most guest theft, however, is that it is simply recognized as a cost of doing business. It makes little sense, for example, to accuse a guest of stealing a wooden clothes hanger even if the hanger was, in fact, taken by the guest and then attempt to charge the guest for the item. Some hotel managers place small signs in guest rooms offering to "sell" guests those items that frequently disappear. Other managers, in an effort to deter theft, word guest room signs in such a way as to imply that a housekeeper will be held responsible for loss of guest room items. Whether GMs use these in-room sign approaches (neither of which is necessarily recommended by the authors) or other less obtrusive ones, guests and visitors to a hotel represent a significant threat to asset security. Therefore, it is good business practice to take precautions to reduce theft. To that end, security-conscious managers:

- Hang all artwork in lobbies and guest rooms with lock-down style hangers.
- Avoid placing valuable decorations and décor pieces in areas where they can be easily taken by guests.
- Train room attendants to alert management if excessive amounts of terry cloth products or in-room items are missing from stay-over rooms.
- Bolt televisions securely to guest room furniture.
- Train all employees to be alert regarding the loss of hotel property and to report any suspicious activity they encounter.

It is important to remember that theft of services by guests can happen just as easily as the theft of physical assets, and proper controls must be in place to prevent these occurrences.

Just as retail stores endure losses due to shoplifters, hotels will lose items to guest pilferage. However, both retail stores and their hotel counterparts must be diligent to limit losses caused by shoplifters through the implementation of policies and procedures designed to reduce such losses.

Departmental-Specific Threats to Asset Security

Threats to a hotel's assets can occur at any time and in any department. Some departments, however, by the nature of their operation, are subject to specific security threats of which the GM should be aware.

Front Office. In addition to the threats to cash posed by employee theft or robbery, the largest area of concern within the front desk is that of fraudulently selling rooms. Consider, for example, the night auditor who checks a guest into the hotel very late at night. The late-arriving guest states the room is only needed for a few hours. The auditor collects the guest's payment in cash at the time of check in, but later reduces the day's room revenue by that same amount, stating that the guest was unhappy with the room and left early, and that the guest's cash was refunded. Obviously, this could have happened. On the other hand, it is also possible that the guest stayed as indicated upon check in and the auditor has defrauded the hotel of one night's room revenue.

Alternatively, assume that a member of the front-office staff simply gives the key to a vacant guest room to a friend or relative and collects no room revenue from that individual. The room, as in the previous example, must be cleaned the next day by the housekeeping staff. Again, the hotel has been defrauded of its rightful room revenue and has incurred direct expenses as well.

GMs and front-office managers must have systems in place that minimize the chances for employee fraud. In regard to room revenue fraud, one significant detection tool that managers can use is the housekeeping **discrepancy report**. This report compares the room status of rooms as listed by the PMS with the room status the housekeeping department determines during their daily inspection of all rooms.

HOTEL TERMINOLOGY AT WORK

Discrepancy Report: A daily comparison between the status of rooms as listed by the PMS at the front office and the status of rooms as listed by the housekeeping department.

Each discrepancy should be investigated. Assume, for example, the PMS lists room 417 as "clean and vacant." However, upon physical inspection housekeeping staff report the status of the same room as "on-change." It is the joint responsibility of front-office and housekeeping department personnel to determine the cause of the discrepancy. If discrepancy reports are not generated with findings resolved on a daily basis, there will be many opportunities for employees to commit fraud by the inappropriate selling of rooms.

Housekeeping. In the housekeeping department, GMs must be aware of two distinctly different security issues. The first is the theft of the housekeeping supplies including in-room amenities, towels, and bed linens. Thefts such as these can be committed either by guests or employees. Although it is virtually impossible to stop the theft of all minor amenities and in-room items, proper controls and systems should be in place to detect and respond to significant thefts of this type.

The second, and much more sensitive housekeeping issue, involves theft of guest items from guest rooms by room attendants or other employees. When guests travel, they often keep valuables in their rooms. This is true despite the recommended use of safety deposit boxes for such items. When a guest claims that there has been a guest room theft, there are at least four possible scenarios:

1. The guest actually is mistaken, and the item(s) reported stolen has/have been misplaced.
2. The guest is attempting to defraud the hotel.
3. The theft was committed but by another guest.
4. A hotel employee, in fact, committed the theft.

Obviously, the GM must be very careful in a situation such as this. If, upon inquiry, the GM believes a theft by anyone has in fact occurred, it is the best policy to report the incident to local law enforcement officials who are trained to investigate the actual existence of a crime.

Food and Beverage. Food and beverage items can be consumed by virtually everyone, and they are a common target for theft. Guests may take silverware and glassware as mementos of their stay, and employees may pilfer the same items for their own homes. More significantly, however, employees who purchase products for the F&B department may defraud the hotel by accepting kickbacks from vendors or by purchasing, then stealing, F&B items intended for the hotel. The GM and controller must continually assess the need to develop systems and procedures to reduce the threat of these types of fraud.

MANAGERS AT WORK

J.D. Ojisama, the GM, asked Ms. Cooper, the guest in room 117, to carefully explain what had happened.

"What happened," stated the guest, "is that I found your employees are thieves!"

The guest then related to J.D. that she had left her room in the hotel that day at 7:00 A.M. and at that time placed a valuable gold necklace, given to her by her grandmother, in her room on the night-stand near the bed. When she returned at 6:00 P.M. that same day, stated Ms. Cooper, the necklace was gone.

"What I want to know now," said the guest, "is what are you going to do about this!"

Assume that J.D. performs an electronic lock audit and finds that only one housekeeper (9:00 A.M.) and the inspectress (2:00 P.M.) were in the room between 7:00 A.M. and 5:00 P.M. that day. Assume further that neither individual had ever previously been identified as having been inside a room where a guest reported a theft. What would you advise J.D. to do?

Would you change your advice to J.D. if it were discovered that the specific room attendant who cleaned Ms. Cooper's room had, on three previous occasions over a six-month period, been revealed by lock audit to have cleaned a room where a guest reported a theft? What would you then do?

Sales and Marketing.   Sales and marketing staff are responsible for preventing fraudulent behavior directed at the hotel by unscrupulous individuals. Often this takes the form of outside parties billing the hotel for services not rendered or not requested. For example, this scam can occur when an official-looking invoice arrives in the sales and marketing department by mail or fax. It states that the hotel owes money for its listing in a published directory of hotels targeted toward a specific group such as government employees. The invoice further states that the hotel must pay promptly to avoid being dropped from the directory. In fact, however, the directory does not even exist. Those responsible for sending the invoice hope that the hotel will pay the invoice without investigation. This scam and others of a similar nature are common, and GMs that do not have sufficient control of their accounts payable system may fall prey to it.

It may seem unusual to consider sales and marketing employees themselves as a source of fraud; however, due to the nature of their interactions with clients, potential threats to asset security do exist. Some of these threats take the form of irregularities with expense accounts. Misstating mileage traveled, clients entertained, and/or sales trips taken can cause the expense accounts of sales staff to be overstated and, as a result, their reimbursements to be too high. To combat such potential problems, GMs must have a good check and balance system that requires documentation of sales expenses and routine audits of reimbursements.

Maintenance and Engineering.   A unique problem in the maintenance and engineering department relates to the loss of small, but sometimes expensive, hand tools and supplies. GMs must remember that the types of items typically used in a hotel's repair shop are the same items employees and guests would use for repairs in their own homes. Therefore, portable hand drills, electric saws, wrenches, and similar items can be stolen if they are not carefully controlled.

It might seem as if this would be an easy problem to alleviate. However, taking a monthly inventory of small hand tools like a set of pliers or screwdrivers is time-consuming and is often not done. Then dishonest employees know that they can take small items without detection. In addition, tools left at the work site within the hotel during lunch or other breaks can, if unsecured, be stolen by guests or others. To prevent either of these sources of fraud, small hand tools should always be inventoried monthly to determine losses, if any. In addition, hand tools should never be left unattended in a public area within the hotel. The temptation for theft and potential for loss is too great. Although it may inconvenience the department, if regular inventories indicate that theft is a problem, the GM may require implementation of a **sign-in/sign-out program** for all tools.

HOTEL TERMINOLOGY AT WORK

Sign-in/sign-out program: An arrangement in which individuals taking responsibility for hotel assets such as hand tools, power equipment, or keys to secured areas must document their responsibility by placing their signature as well as the date and time on a form developed to identify responsibility for possession.

Hotels and Terrorism

GMs in strategic city, airport, and other locations along with those providing facilities for a large number of guests and/or for large group meetings must be increasingly concerned about terrorism. In fact, global uncertainty, of which terror attacks are an important (but not only) example, was recently identified as an issue and challenge that was very likely to have a great impact on the lodging industry.

The tragedies of September 11, 2001, and the August 2003 truck bombing at the Jakarta (Indonesia) JW Marriott are among those dictating that hotel security procedures must be updated to address terrorism-related concerns. A recurring challenge: to protect the safety of guests while discouraging the expansion of terrorism.

Developing the proper response to a terror threat or an actual act of terrorism will require concentrated study and changes to the emergency plans and safety procedures

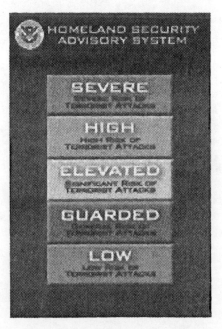

FIGURE 12.6   Homeland Security Advisory System

for many hotels. Individuals and businesses including hotels have some assistance with this task through the Homeland Security Advisory System established by the U.S. Department of Homeland Security. Figure 12.6 illustrates the alert system.

THE INTERNET AT WORK

To learn more about the U.S. Department of Homeland Security, go to

www.dhs.gov

Hoteliers can undertake some actions at each alert level. For example:

Alert Level	Possible Actions[1]
Low (Green)	Develop emergency and business continuity plans.
Guarded (Blue)	Interact with community officials and government agencies about disaster preparedness.
Elevated (Yellow)	Contact private security firm for risk assessment.
High (Orange)	Determine if any restrictions of access to the hotel should be implemented.
Severe (Red)	Listen to news media for current information and instructions.

[1]These actions are among those suggested by the American Red Cross (www.redcross.org). Click on the Homeland Security Threat Advisory graphic and then click on PDF files for "Businesses."

THE INTERNET AT WORK

The American Red Cross has developed recommended actions for businesses in general. To review these, go to

www.redcross.org

Hoteliers can consider lodging-specific tactics that can be implemented as the risk of terror attacks increase. Some of these are outlined in Figure 12.7. GMs should be aware of these proactive terrorism precautions and work with their director of security and other members of the property's management team to implement the necessary precautions at the appropriate time.

When reviewing Figure 12.7 note that, as the risk of terror attack threats increase, more stringent requirements are needed. These, unfortunately, have a negative impact upon guest service but, hopefully, a positive effect on guest safety. The tactics suggested for times of the highest risk of attack were in use at the time of the bombing at the Jakarta JW Marriott. Note: the vehicle containing the bomb was stopped as it entered the hotel's driveway about 40 yards from the lobby entrance. The bomb exploded and killed 12 persons. Only one victim was inside the hotel, and it is believed this tactic saved lives.

Will hotel security, door attendants and/or other personnel need training to screen luggage and to assist persons entering the hotel through metal detectors? This may be a rhetorical question. However, it suggests that the GM, the director of security, and others on the hotel's safety committee must reconsider how they can protect the safety of guests and employees. The "answer" may involve ways that were not even imaginable only a few years ago!

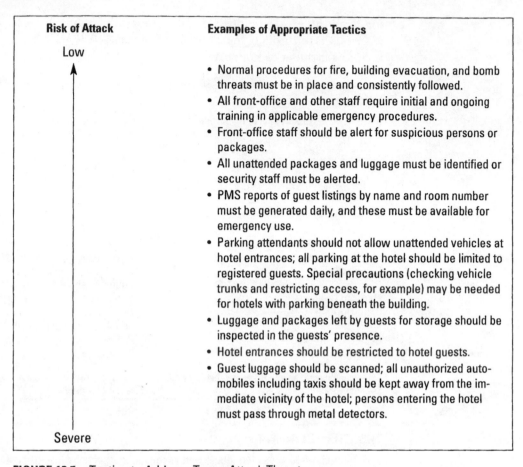

FIGURE 12.7   Tactics to Address Terror Attack Threats

HOTEL TERMINOLOGY AT WORK GLOSSARY

The following terms were defined within this chapter. If you are not familiar with one of them, please review the segment of the chapter that contains the term.

Safety
Security
Reasonable care
Foreseeable (Legal concept)
Liable
Damages
Judgment
Compensatory damages
Punitive damages

Safety and security committee
Internal alarms
Contact alarms
Closed-circuit television (CCTV)
Emergency plan
Defibrillator
Incident Report
Manager on duty (MOD)
OSHA

Material Safety Data Sheet (MSDS)
Embezzlement
Bond(ing)
Fraud
Pilferage
Discrepancy report
Sign-in/Sign-out program

ISSUES AT WORK

1. Some hotel managers believe uniformed security personnel within the hotel increase the comfort level of guests in the same manner as do uniformed police officers. Other managers feel uniformed security personnel increase a guest's concern about security and safety and have a net negative effect. Assume you as the GM were required to make a decision about the issue at your hotel. Would you put your security force in "police-style" uniforms or uniforms that "blend" with your clientele. What factors would influence your decision?

2. Guest safety is a primary concern of all effective hotel managers. What specific steps can you take to ensure that all of the hotel's employees share your concern for guest safety? Identify at least three general and three departmental-specific activities. Who at the property should be responsible for ensuring that these types of steps and activities are implemented? Consider a larger property with a designated security department and a smaller property without one.

3. Every hotel location faces unique threats to the safety of its guests and the security of its assets. Hotels near the ocean may face threats related to storms and water damage and properties in cold climates face threats related to winter storms. Regardless of the threats, GMs must be prepared to deal with emergency situations. Outline a plan for creating a program you would implement to prepare your hotel for the potential outbreak of a serious fire. What hotel departments should be involved in the plan's development? What external entities should be involved? Where would you go for resources that could help your efforts? Would your plan include "fire drills" that involve clearing the hotel of all guests as a way of practicing the final plan's implementation? Why or why not?

4. MSDSs are a valuable source of safety-related information to workers. In most cases, however, these documents are provided only in English and Spanish. Increasingly, the hotel industry employs individuals whose native language is neither. What obligation do you believe a hotel has to provide an MSDS in the language of every employee? Assume that your hotel employs 25 such individuals speaking five different languages. How would you help ensure the safety of these workers with regard to handling chemicals and other toxic materials?

5. Assume that your hotel's F&B department is experiencing periodic losses of products that you believe are due to employee theft. What specific steps would you, as the GM, want your food and beverage director to use to address this issue? How would you monitor the success of his/her efforts? How would you ensure that the director himself/herself was not involved in the thefts?

13

Franchise Agreements and Management Contracts

This Chapter at Work

From the perspective of the traveling public, perhaps one of the most misunderstood aspects of hotels is the question of who owns them and who manages them. This is because in most cases hotels are owned by a business entity that elects, for the good of that business, to affiliate with a group of similar hotels and to operate under the name of that hotel group. These hotel groups are called brands, flags, or chains. The company administering and directing the brand itself is not usually an owner of hotels, but rather, as a franchise company, it is responsible for the growth of the brand.

Hotel operations can be further complicated because the business entity owning the hotel and choosing brand affiliation may also elect to hire a management company that will actually select a GM and operate the hotel. Thus, a typical traveler is likely to be staying at a hotel owned by one business entity that has elected to affiliate the hotel with a brand (a second entity) and entrust the management of the hotel to a management company (a third entity), who actually hires the GM.

Good GMs are operational professionals who may at various times find themselves working directly for those who own the hotel and at other times for a management company selected by the owners to operate the hotel. In most cases, a franchise company will be involved as well. Because of this, it is important for GMs to know about both the relationship that exists between a hotel's owners (the franchisee) and the hotel brand (the franchisor) when both parties sign a franchise agreement and the special relationship that exists between owners and a management company when a management contract is in place.

In this chapter you will learn about major franchise companies and the brands they operate. The owners of hotels often ask experienced GMs their opinions about the best brand to be selected for a specific hotel. Therefore, you will also learn how to evaluate alternative brand options with the goal of choosing the best brand for a specific hotel. Managing a franchised hotel presents special challenges to the GM. This chapter reviews the advantages of brand affiliation from the perspectives of both the owners of a hotel and the franchisor with an emphasis on how the franchise agreement, which is the legal document governing the relationship between the hotel and the managers of the selected brand, affects the work of the GM.

Just as brand affiliation influences the activities of the GM, so, too, does the special situation in which the GM is employed not directly by the hotel but rather by the management company selected to operate the hotel. In this chapter you will learn about how some of the major hotel management companies operate. In addition, you will review how the management contract, which is the legal document governing the relationship between the owners of a hotel and the company selected to operate the hotel, affects the day-to-day responsibilities of the GM.

Chapter 13 Outline

THE HOTEL FRANCHISE RELATIONSHIP
  Hotel Franchising
    Origin and Structure
    Governmental Regulations Related to Franchises
  The Franchise Agreement
    Major Elements
    Advantages to the Franchisee
    Advantages to the Franchisor
  Selecting a Franchisor
    Basic Considerations
    The Franchisor Questionnaire

    The Product Improvement Plan (PIP)
    Negotiating the Franchise Agreement
THE HOTEL MANAGEMENT COMPANY RELATIONSHIP
  Management Companies
    Origin and Purpose
    Hotel Management Company Structures
  The Management Operating Agreement
    Major Elements
    Advantages to the Hotel Owner
    Disadvantages to the Hotel Owner

Issues Affecting the GM
  Managing the Franchise Relationship
  Managing for a Management Company

HOTEL TERMINOLOGY AT WORK
GLOSSARY
ISSUES AT WORK

THE HOTEL FRANCHISE RELATIONSHIP

Franchising is a business strategy that allows one business entity to use the logo, trademarks, and operating systems of another business entity for the benefit of both. As a result, franchising is a network of interdependent business relationships that allows a number of people to share a brand identification, a successful method of doing business, and hopefully, a strong marketing and distribution system.

For the franchisee, franchising helps reduce risk. Proven operational methods, developed by the franchisor, are used to manage the business. The franchisee gives up the freedom of being completely independent to become part of a group committed to building a brand and increasing their group's market share. A franchise system can (but may not) also provide group-buying power to reduce the franchisee's operating expenses. The trade-offs for the franchisee are the fees paid to the franchisor for the operating license and the restrictions imposed by the franchisor. For the franchisor, franchisees and their financial capital expand the brand faster than it would ever be possible for the franchisor to do so alone.

Hotel Franchising

One of the biggest challenges faced by those who would buy or build a hotel is that of which **flag**, if any, the property should "fly." The question is an important one both to the owners of the property and to the GM who operates it.

HOTEL TERMINOLOGY AT WORK

Flag: A term used to refer to the specific brand with which a hotel may affiliate. Examples of currently popular flags include brands such as Comfort Inns, Holiday Inn Express, Ramada Inns, Hampton Inns, Residence Inns, Best Western, and Hawthorn Suites. The hotels affiliated with a specific flag are sometimes referred to as a chain. Used, for example, in "Which flags are you considering for your new hotel project?"

A hotel **franchise** relationship exists when the owners of a hotel choose a flag and enter into a **franchise agreement** with the managers of that specific brand.

HOTEL TERMINOLOGY AT WORK

Franchise: An arrangement whereby one party (the brand) allows another (the hotel owners) to use its logo, name, systems, and resources in exchange for a fee.

Franchise Agreement: The legal contract between the hotel's owners (the franchisee) and the brand managers (the franchisor), which describes the duties and responsibilities of each in the franchise relationship.

It is important to note that, unlike some other franchise industries, the majority of hotel brand managers (franchisors) do not operate hotels. They own and operate franchise companies. Hotel owners (the franchisees) and their GMs are the operating entities in most hotel franchise relationships.

Origin and Structure

Franchising has long been a part of American business. The history of hotel franchising, however, is relatively short. Many in the hotel industry believe the first significant hotel franchising arrangements began in the 1950s with Kemmons Wilson and his Holiday Inn chain.

In a combination of what may well be part historical fact and part hotel lore, the story is told of how, in 1951, Wilson, a resident of Memphis, Tennessee, loaded his wife and five children into the family car and drove to Washington, DC, for a vacation. He was quite unhappy with the motel accommodations he found along the way. The rooms he encountered were, he believed, too small, too expensive, and in many cases not clean. Wilson returned to Tennessee convinced that he could build a chain of hotels across the country that would operate under the same name and provide the traveling public with a lodging experience they could count on to be clean, comfortable, and moderately priced. He hired an architect to draw up the plans for a prototype hotel. The architect, according to legend, was watching an old Bing Crosby movie titled *Holiday Inn* while he was working and sketched that name on the top of the plans he was drawing. Wilson, upon seeing the plans, liked them and the name at the top as well. As a result, the Holiday Inn was born. The first Holiday Inn opened in Tennessee in 1952 and the 400th Holiday Inn franchise began operation in December 1962. Today, Holiday Inn franchises its name as part of the InterContinental hotel group that consists of over 3,500 properties (and more than 530,000 guest rooms!) worldwide, including the brands InterContinental Hotels, Holiday Inn, Holiday Inn

It is believed by many hoteliers that Holiday Inn was the first hotel franchise company.

Select, Holiday Inn Express, Holiday Inn Crowne Plaza, Candlewood Suites, Hotel Indigo, and Staybridge Suites.

Today's hotel owners increasingly elect to affiliate their hotels with other hotels under a common brand name. In fact, as we saw in Chapter 1 (Figure 1.6), the great majority of hotels in the United States currently operate as part of a regional or national brand. Many of these brands are grouped under a common brand ownership group. For example, Choice Hotels International owns and manages the Cambria Suites, Clarion, Quality, Comfort Inn, Comfort Suites, Sleep Inn, MainStay Suites, Roadway Inn, and Econolodge brands. Cendant, as of the time of this writing, owns and manages the Amerihost, Day's Inn, Howard Johnson, Knights Inn, Ramada, Super Eight, Travelodge, Wyndham, and Wingate Inn brands, as well as other franchised names including Avis (car rental) and Century 21 (real estate sales). Hilton Hotel brands include Hilton, Conrad, Doubletree, Embassy Suites, Hampton, Hilton Garden Inn, and Homewood Suites.

As you learned in Chapter 1, while the actual brands managed by any single franchisor change as these brands are bought and sold, the ten largest individual brands (as compiled by Hotel Business) at the time of this writing are included as Figure 13.1.

Each brand, depending on the parent company's structure, will have a brand manager or president responsible for growing the number of hotels in the brand and maintaining the quality standards that have been established for that brand. It is important to recall that in the overwhelming majority of cases franchise companies do not actually own the hotels operating under their brand names. Companies such as these own, instead, the right to sell the brand name and determine the standards that will be followed by those hotel owners who voluntarily elect to affiliate with their brands.

With the ownership of a hotel vested in one business entity and the responsibility for brand standards resting with another business entity, it is not surprising that conflict can arise between the hotel's owners and the brand managers. For example, assume the managers of a given brand decide that the logo for their brand, and thus the exterior building signage identifying the brand to the traveling public, has become dated and is in need of modernization. The brand managers may have the authority, because of the franchise agreement, to require affiliated hotel owners to update their hotel signage. The owners, however, facing significant purchase and installation costs for replacing signs that are in perfectly good working order but that have

	Brand	Properties	Rooms
1.	Best Western International	4,107	309,385
2.	Holiday Inn	1,519	286,520
3.	Marriott Hotels & Resorts	487	178,331
4.	Days Inns Worldwide	1,898	157,025
5.	Comfort Inn	2,021	150,570
6.	Sheraton Hotels & Resorts	391	134,442
7.	Hampton Inn/Hampton Inn and Suites	1,283	129,636
8.	Super 8 Motels	2,079	125,754
9.	Holiday Inn Express	1,497	124,523
10.	Radisson Hotels and Resorts	436	102,574

Copyright HOTEL BUSINESS ® *The Green Book 2005*. May not be reprinted without express written permission.

FIGURE 13.1   Ten Largest Brands

been declared "dated" by the brand managers, may well attempt to resist the purchase of the new signs. In fact, these hotel owners may disagree with the brand managers about numerous operating issues.

As a GM, it is important for you to understand that if you are operating a branded hotel, you have a responsibility to your employer; however, you also have a responsibility to abide by the franchise agreement signed by your hotel's owners. That agreement will always include a section that requires your best efforts in maintaining the established standards of the brand. Conflicts can and do arise between hotel owners and brand managers. As a GM, it falls to you to balance the legitimate interests of your hotel and the brand in a manner that reflects positively on your own professionalism.

Unlike the history of some other industries, the history of hotel franchising does not include widespread cases of franchisor fraud or deception. Despite that fact, hotel franchise relationships are subject to the same federal and state laws that have been enacted to protect franchisees from unscrupulous franchisors in all industries.

Governmental Regulations Related to Franchises

In the past, some companies offering franchises to individual business owners did so in ways that were unscrupulous and often illegal. In an effort to level the playing field between those who sell and those who would buy franchises, the **Federal Trade Commission (FTC)** in 1979, issued regulations with the full force of federal law. This set of laws are titled "Disclosure Requirements and Prohibitions Concerning Franchising and Business Opportunity Ventures." Commonly referred to as the "Franchise Rule," the rules spell out the obligations of franchisors when they attempt to sell their franchises to potential franchisees.

HOTEL TERMINOLOGY AT WORK

Federal Trade Commission (FTC): The FTC enforces federal antitrust and consumer protection laws. It also seeks to ensure that the nation's business markets function competitively and are free of undue restrictions caused by acts or practices that are unfair or deceptive.

■

THE INTERNET AT WORK

To read the entire "Franchise Rule" developed by the FTC and to familiarize yourself with the requirements placed upon those who sell franchises, go to

www.ftc.gov/bcp/franchise/16cfr436.htm

Essentially, the Franchise Rule requires that franchisors:

- Supply potential franchisees with a disclosure document at the earlier of the first face-to-face meeting or ten business days before any money is paid by the franchisee to the franchisor.
- Provide evidence, in writing, of any earnings claims or profit forecasts made by the franchisor.
- Disclose the number and percentage of franchisees achieving the earnings rates advertised in any promotional ads that include earnings claims.
- Provide potential franchisees with copies of the basic franchise agreement used by the franchisor.

- Refund promptly any deposit monies legally due to potential franchisees that elected not to sign a franchise agreement with the franchisor.
- Not make claims orally or in writing that conflict with the written disclosure documents provided to the franchisee.

In addition to federal laws and regulations, most states also have franchise investment laws that require franchisors to provide a presale disclosure document known as a **franchise offering circular (FOC)** to potential franchisees.

HOTEL TERMINOLOGY AT WORK

Franchise Offering Circular (FOC): A franchise disclosure document that is prepared by a franchisor and then registered and filed with the state governmental agency responsible for administering franchise relationships in that state.

These states prohibit the sale of a franchise inside their borders until a franchisor's FOC has been filed with the proper state authorities. Although these states, like the FTC, impose disclosure requirements on franchisors, none verify the accuracy of the information in the disclosure documents. Verification of a franchisor's claims is the responsibility of the buyer (franchisee). For example, a hotel franchise company can make a claim that its 800 number provides the average franchisee with fifty sold guest rooms per night. This claim will not be verified as accurate by either the FTC or the state in which the franchisor files an FOC. The potential franchisee should seek verification of any item in the FOC that is questionable prior to signing a franchise agreement.

FOCs are typically designed to comply with both the laws of the state in which they are filed and the FTC's Franchise Rule and will generally include information about:

- The name of the franchisor and the type of franchise it offers for sale
- The business experience of the franchise company's officers
- Fees and royalties that must be paid
- Initial investment requirements
- Rights and obligations of the franchisor and franchisee
- Territorial protection offered by the franchisor
- Required operating policies
- Renewal, transfer, and termination procedures
- Earnings claims
- Current franchisees
- A sample franchise agreement
- Specific information required by each state in which the FOC is to be filed
- The name and address of the legal representative of the franchisor

It is important to remember that hotel franchise FOCs must be prepared to meet the same requirements as those in any other industry. Companies issuing FOCs should be honest, but those who read them should be prepared to verify every important claim made in the document.

THE INTERNET AT WORK

Potential franchisees can learn a great deal about buying and operating a franchise by joining the International Franchise Association (IFA). To review the type of information they provide to their members, go to

www.franchise.org

The Franchise Agreement

When a hotel's owners elect to affiliate their hotel with a brand, they will sign a franchise agreement with the franchisor's brand managers. The franchise agreement will spell out, in great detail, the responsibilities of both the brand managers (franchisor) and the hotel owners (franchisee). In the past, many owners within the hotel community felt brand managers had too much power to control the terms and conditions contained in the franchise agreements. More recently, vocal groups of owners, led chiefly by the **Asian American Hotel Owners Association (AAHOA),** have proposed, and actively campaigned for, fundamental changes in the basic franchise agreements that have long been in use. These proposed changes seek to give hotel owners more control over the content of franchise agreements and a more equal say in the operation of their hotels.

HOTEL TERMINOLOGY AT WORK

Asian American Hotel Owners Association (AAHOA): An association of hotel owners who, through an exchange of ideas, seek to promote professionalism and excellence in hotel ownership.
■

THE INTERNET AT WORK

The AAHOA has been at the forefront of promoting fairness in hotel franchising. Their associate members interact with many brand management companies. To learn more about AAHOA and to review their 12 Points of Fair Franchising, go to

www.aahoa.com

Major Elements

A franchise agreement is simply a written contract between a franchisor (the brand managers) and a franchisee (the hotel owner). Each brand will develop its own franchise agreement, but the following information is typically included:

- *Names of the Parties Signing the Agreement.* In this section, the name of the legal entity representing the brand as well as the corporation, partnership, or sole proprietor owning the hotel is listed.

- *Detailed Definitions.* In this section, any definitions used in the agreement that could be subject to misinterpretation by the parties to the agreement are defined. For example, many franchisee agreements base the fees to be paid by owners on the gross room revenue achieved by the hotel. In this section of the agreement, the franchisor would detail exactly what gross room revenue means. The following is an example of a definition that describes the term in great detail and is of the type found in this section of the document:

"Gross rooms revenue" means the revenue from the rental of sleeping rooms and meeting rooms at the hotel. It does not include revenue from Internet access fees, telephone calls, in-room safes or minibars, vending machines, food and beverage sales, or room service.

- *License Grant.* Here the franchisor will describe the manner in which the hotel owner is allowed to use the brand's logos, signage, and name in the operation of the hotel.
- *Term (Length of Agreement).* The beginning and ending date of the agreement will be spelled out in detail. The most common franchise agreements are written for a length of twenty years. Most, however, also contain a **window** at the fifth, tenth, and fifteenth, years. More recently some agreements have been written with **early outs** as franchisors aggressively seek to entice hotel owners to choose their brands.

HOTEL TERMINOLOGY AT WORK

Window: A clause in a franchise agreement that grants both the franchisor and the franchisee the right, with proper notification, to terminate the agreement after it has been in effect for a relatively short period of time.

Early Out: A clause in a franchise agreement that grants both the franchisor and the franchisee the right, with proper notification, to terminate the agreement after it has been in effect for a relatively short period of time. When this clause exists, a window may be granted after only one, two, or three years.

■

- *Fees.* This section details the fees the franchisee must pay to the franchisor. Although each brand is free to set its fees as it wishes, the typical fees in a hotel franchise agreement will include:
  - *Affiliation Fees.* These are flat fees, paid up front (upon signing the agreement), to affiliate with the brand.
  - *Royalty Fees.* These fees are paid based upon an agreed upon formula and are typically tied to the level of revenue generated by the hotel.
  - *Marketing Fees.* These fees are also determined by the hotel's revenue levels and are to be used exclusively to advertise the brand name. Such marketing efforts may include ads placed on national or regional radio, magazines, newspapers, or television.
  - *Reservation Fees.* These are collected to operate the brand's reservation system (toll–free reservations number and Web site).
- *Reports.* This section lists any monthly or annual reports that must be provided by the hotel owner to the franchisor and when such reports are due. Examples may include reports related to room revenue generated, occupancy levels, and **occupancy taxes** paid and ADR.

HOTEL TERMINOLOGY AT WORK

Occupancy Tax: Money paid by a hotel to a local taxing authority. The room revenue generated by the hotel determines the amount paid. This tax is also known, in some areas, as the "bed" tax. For example, "In our city, the occupancy tax is four percent."

■

- *Responsibilities of the Franchisor.* This section details the obligations of the franchisor under the agreement and lists what the hotel owner will receive in exchange for paying fees and royalties. It will include items such as inspection schedules, marketing efforts, and brand standards enforcement.

- *Responsibilities of the Franchisee.* This section details what the hotel owner will do in exchange for the right to use the name of the franchisor's brand. It will include items such as signage requirements, operational standards that must be implemented, and payment schedules that must be met.

- *Assignment of Agreement.* Here the ownership transfer and its effect upon the agreement are detailed. In most cases, the hotel owner must have the approval of the franchisor to transfer (assign) its rights in the agreement to another; however, the franchisors are typically free to assign the agreement to any business entity they choose without the approval of the franchisee.

- *Termination or Default.* The events that permit a termination, or define a default, by either party are detailed in this section. In most cases, a default on the part of the franchisee will result in penalties that must be paid by the franchisee to the franchisor.

- *Insurance Requirements.* To protect both parties, the hotel owner will be required to provide insurance. In this section the types and amounts of required insurance will be listed. Typical requirements include proof of general indemnification policies, automobile insurance, and mandatory workers' compensation (injury) insurance.

- *Requirements for Alteration.* This section details the rights of the franchisor to change the agreement.

- *Arbitration and Legal Fees.* In this section, the responsibilities of each party related to legal disputes are detailed. Also included in this section is information about the geographic location of the court where such disputes are to be resolved. In most franchise agreements, disputes are to be resolved in the state in which the franchisor is incorporated.

- *Signature Pages.* The authorized representatives of the brand, as well as the owners of the hotel, will sign the franchise agreement.

Advantages to the Franchisee

The primary advantages to a hotel of buying a franchise are that doing so allows the hotel's owners to acquire a brand name with regional or national recognition and to connect the hotel to the GDS. As seen earlier, connectivity to the GDS is still a necessity in today's hotel market. An independent hotel can, in fact, purchase this connectivity; however, it is costly.

Affiliation with a strong brand increases the hotel's sales and thus its profitability. The total fees paid by the hotel owner to the brand managers are related to the strength of the brand name and the revenue that the name will bring to the hotel. Although the fees related to a franchise agreement are sometimes negotiable, they will, on average, equal from 3 to 15 percent of a hotel's gross room revenue.

In addition to increased sales levels, affiliation with a brand affects the ability of a hotel's owner to secure financing. When owners seek financing from banks or other lending institutions, they find that these lenders will, almost without exception, require an affiliation with an established brand prior to considering the hotel for a loan.

Additional advantages, depending on the franchisor selected, may include assistance with financing and on-site training, advice on purchasing furnishings and fixtures, reduced operating costs resulting from vendors who give brand operators preferred pricing, and free interior design assistance.

Advantages to the Franchisor

The greatest advantage to a franchisor of entering into a franchise agreement with a hotel owner is the increase in fee payments to the brand that will result from the agreement. Like all businesses, franchise companies desire growth. The greater the number of hotels that operate under a single brand name the greater, in general, the value of the name and thus the fees that can be charged for using that name. In addition, each additional hotel that affiliates with a hotel brand helps to pay for the fixed overhead of operating that brand. Therefore, additional hotel properties operating under the same brand name usually result in greater profits for the franchise company. Also, the greater the number of individual brands operated by the same franchise company, the lower the per unit operating overhead for the franchisor. As a result, franchisors are aggressive in soliciting agreements with hotel owners even if these owners are affiliated with another brand. Franchisors, as well, actively pursue those owners developing new hotels who have not yet selected a franchise brand. Franchisors seek to expand both the number of hotels operating under the brand(s) they manage as well as the number of brands they offer.

Selecting a Franchisor

Perhaps one of the most useful services a hotel GM can provide to an owner is that of assistance in the selection of a hotel brand when such assistance is requested. It is simply true that an experienced GM, more so than an inexperienced owner or the franchisor

GMs and their owners should learn as much as they can about a franchise company before branding their hotels. (Reprinted by permission of Meristar Hotels & Resorts, Inc.)

(who has a vested interest in the sale), is in the best position to provide advice about how well a given brand name will "fit" a specific hotel property. It is also true that many hotel brands go through a life cycle that includes early buildup, in which nearly every property entering the system is newly built. Later in the development of the brand, and in an effort to promote unit growth, brand managers may allow **conversions**.

HOTEL TERMINOLOGY AT WORK

Conversion: As a verb: The process of changing a hotel's flag from one franchisor to another. Also known as "reflagging." For example, "We need a GM experienced in managing a hotel conversion."

As a noun: The term used to describe a hotel that has changed its flag from one franchisor to another. For example, "Has this hotel always been a (brand name), or is it a conversion?"

Conversions can be beneficial to a brand because they allow the brand to grow more quickly. They can be a detriment to the brand, however, if the converted properties do not have the features and quality levels of the hotels already in the brand.

For a hotel's owners, purchasing a hotel franchise is actually very much like purchasing the long-term services of other professionals, such as attorneys or accountants, who help the owner maximize the value of his or her asset. For example, when selecting a franchise, there will be a number of companies (franchisors) offering the service. These service providers offer a variety of experience, skills, and knowledge. In addition, the prices charged for their services will vary. Last, as is true in many relationships, the franchisor is likely to have a unique "style" of doing business that attracts (or repels!) potential franchisees.

Basic Considerations

As a GM advising an owner about franchise selections available, it is important to know as much about a potential franchisor as possible so that your advice will be as accurate as it can be. As we have seen, franchisors are required, by law, to disclose a great deal of information. This information should be reviewed carefully by potential franchisees. Even more information can be obtained through a diligent process of investigation and interview. For the purpose of illustrating the procedure of selecting a franchise brand, assume that you are approached by an investment group that has decided to build a new 150-room limited service hotel. They want to hire you to advise them on selecting the best possible brand for the hotel. You will have much to investigate, but some of the factors that you would certainly want to consider before making a recommendation would be:

- *The quality and experience of the brand managers.* Brand management, like hotel management, is complex. Those brand managers experienced in their work will operate the brand better than those who are not. In addition, when brand managers are experienced, it is possible for the hotel's owners to see a track record of success (or failure) on the part of the managers. The relationship between a franchisor and a franchisee is not, despite the claims of the franchisor, a true partnership because, in the case of losses incurred by the hotel, the brand and its managers are not financially responsible. In fact, no brand available today bases the fees it collects on the achieved profits, rather than the achieved revenue, of its branded hotels. As a result, it is the hotel owners, not the brand managers, who bear the financial risk of poor brand management. Because that is true, it is critical that the brand managers be experienced and talented and that they demonstrate great integrity in dealings with their franchisees.

- *Perceived quality/service level of the brand.* Travelers associate some brands with higher-quality service levels and cost than other brands. A Holiday Inn Crown Plaza, for example, will likely be perceived by most travelers as having more services (and thus a higher ADR) than a Holiday Inn Express. In most cases, franchisors, in an attempt to offer a franchise product that appeals to hotel owners at a variety of desired investment levels, will offer brands at a range of quality and guest services provided. Those hotel owners who elect to operate the highest-quality brand offered by a franchisor will spend, on average, more to build or renovate each of their hotel rooms than if they selected a lower quality level. In addition, total operating costs are likely to be higher with brands that offer guests more services, although ADRs are also likely to be higher in these cases. Of course, a well-managed, lower-cost, limited-service brand can be more profitable for an owner than a poorly managed, limited-service brand property with a higher **systemwide** ADR. Hotel owners that seek to maximize their return on investment must select a brand that is both well managed and that is appropriate (meets quality/service expectations) for the travelers to which the hotel will be marketed.

HOTEL TERMINOLOGY AT WORK

Systemwide: The term used to describe all hotels within a given brand. Used for example, in "Last year, the systemwide ADR for the brand was $115.20, with an occupancy rate of 63.7%."

- *The amount of fees paid to the franchisor.* Far too many hotel owners, when evaluating alternative franchisors, focus only on the fees the hotel will pay to the brand. Although the fees paid to a franchisor are certainly one factor to be considered, it is not the only factor, nor is it even the most important. Nearly all hotel owners feel the franchise fees they pay are too high; conversely, nearly all franchisors feel what their franchisees receive in exchange for their fee payments is a great value to the hotel. In fact, the fees paid to a franchisor are a negotiable part of the franchise agreement and should be considered seriously only after the hotel owner has narrowed down the list of potential franchisors to those that meet other criteria the owner has established for selecting the brand.

Earlier in this chapter you learned that a franchisor's FOC must include a description of the fees to be paid to the franchisor. In the majority of cases, the most obvious and hotly negotiated of these are reservations fees (fees paid based upon the number and/or dollar value of reservations delivered by the brand's central reservations system) and royalty fees (based upon a hotel's total rooms sales volume). In addition to these fees, however, there are others that are less readily obvious but that vary greatly by brand and can be very significant. GDS, Internet connection, accounting, regional advertising, e-mail programs, and satisfaction survey fees are all items that, if charged to the franchisee, must be disclosed in the FOC. Additionally, hoteliers should pay close attention to variation in the following type fees:

1. *Liquidated Damage Fees.* Most franchise agreements are written for a term of ten to twenty years. Sometimes, due to the sale of a hotel or its owner's desire to reposition it, the franchisee may wish to end the contract before its agreed-upon expiration date. If the franchisee wishes to terminate the agreement prior to its expiration date, both parties will have agreed, at the time the original agreement was signed, on exactly how the amount of damages to the franchisor will be calculated. Doing so saves needless litigation on either party's part. The dollar amount of liquidated damages to be paid by a franchisee who seeks early agreement cancellation, however, will vary greatly from brand to brand; these damages should be well understood before signing a franchise agreement.

HOTEL TERMINOLOGY AT WORK

Liquidated Damage Fees: Money charged to a franchisee that elects to terminate their franchise agreement prior to its contractual expiration date.

2. *Hardware and Software Fees.* In most cases, a franchisee will be required to purchase or lease their hotel's PMS from the franchisor. If a hotel converts from one brand to another, ensuring PMS compatibility will likely require new and continually upgraded hardware, brand-specific software, and perhaps other software licensing and/or maintenance costs. Again, the amount of money required to install the brand's mandated hardware and software will vary significantly from chain to chain.

3. *Training, Meetings and Conventions.* Nearly all brands hold annual conventions or meetings. In addition, the best of brands will offer regional training classes to continually upgrade the skills of their franchisees. In some cases, attendance at these events is voluntary, but in most cases, the franchisor will charge franchisees to attend, even if the franchisee elects not to do so. The annual total of these type fees can range from several hundred to several thousand dollars per year.

• *Direction of the Brand.* By far the most important factor in the long-term success of the franchisor/franchisee relationship is the future direction of the brand. Obviously, it is impossible to predict the future, yet knowing how a brand will be perceived by the public in five, ten, or twenty years is important when signing a franchise agreement for that same number of years. Clues to the future success of the brand can be detected by asking the franchisor about:
  • The number of hotels currently operating under the brand name.
  • The percentage of hotels, on an annual basis, that have elected to leave the brand in the past five years.
  • The number of new properties currently being built under the brand's name.
  • The number of existing hotels converting to the brand (if conversions are allowed).
  • The ADR trend for the last five years in comparison to the ADR trend for the industry segment in which the brand competes.
  • The occupancy rate trend for the last five years in comparison to the occupancy rate trend for the industry segment in which the brand competes.

- The percentage of total hotel room revenue contributed by the brand's reservation system and the percentage of hotels within the brand that achieve that average rate of contribution.

THE INTERNET AT WORK

There are a variety of tools developed to help potential hotel franchsiees compare alternative franchisor fee arrangements. To view one such tool, go to

www.hvs.hotelmotel.com

The Franchisor Questionnaire

One way for a potential franchisee to begin the process of narrowing down the number of prospective franchisors to be selected is through the use of a structured series of questions to which all franchisors under consideration must respond. Lists of and addresses for hotel franchise companies can be easily obtained on the Internet.

THE INTERNET AT WORK

Lists of hotel franchisors, their mailing addresses, and the individual(s) responsible for each brand they manage can be quickly obtained on the Internet. For one such source of hotel franchisor contact information, go to

www.franchisehelp.com

Once a list of potential franchisors has been obtained, it is possible to begin the selection process. Figure 13.2 shows a survey that could be used to search for a franchisor.

The questions that are important to any specific hotel owner will determine the information requested on the franchisor survey, but by using the results of the information gathered in a survey such as that presented in Figure 13.2, owners of the prospective hotel would contact, and then interview in person, the franchisor finalists.

The Product Improvement Plan (PIP)

While a large number of hotels are built each year, an even larger number of brand conversions are undertaken each year. A brand conversion may occur for a variety of reasons, including a franchisor/franchisee dispute, because the owners of the hotel decide the future prospects for the brand they are currently affiliated with are not good, or because a new brand appears to offer a better financial return on the owner's investment.

Selecting a new franchisor when converting a hotel from one brand to another is complicated by the fact that the new brand managers are likely to impose renovation, repair, or upgrade conditions on the hotel's owners. For example, a new franchisor may agree to enter into a franchise agreement only if a hotel's owners are willing to replace older carpets and furniture in the hotel's guest rooms with new carpets and furniture. Brand managers want to make sure that each hotel converting into the system will meet the **brand standards** established for the brand they manage.

HOTEL TERMINOLOGY AT WORK

Brand Standard: A hotel service or feature that must be adopted by any property entering a specific hotel brand's system. Used, for example, in "The franchisor has determined that 'free local telephone calls' will become a new brand standard effective January 1."

■

MEMO

To: POTENTIAL FRANCHISORS
From: J. D. Ojisama
Subject: Attached Franchisor Questionnaire
Date   1/1/20XX

I represent an ownership group that will be building a 150-room, limited-service hotel in our city. The investors have asked me to assist them in evaluating options for flagging the property. In an effort to fairly compare the offerings of alternative potential franchisors, please respond, in writing, to the following questions if your brand has an interest in being considered as a potential franchise partner. Please e-mail your responses to J. D. Ojisama at the following e-mail address: JDOJISAMA@ournewhotel.com.

In addition, our group would like to receive any print materials available regarding your brand. Thank you in advance for your interest in our project.

1. **Application Fees:**
   - What (if any) franchise fees are required as an up-front affiliation (nonoperating revenue) fee to join the brand?
   - Can the above fee be waived or reduced?
   - If so, what is the name and address of the individual in your organization authorized to waive such fees?
   - Who in your organization will determine the exact date that the property may be promoted, signed as, and advertised as your brand?

2. **Area of Protection:**
   - What is the **area of protection (AOP)** proposed by your organization?
   - Does your AOP restrict any other brands you operate (or will operate in the future) from this AOP? If so, name those brands.
   - Does your AOP give our organization the right of first refusal for any brand(s) you currently operate? If so, name those brands.

3. **Reoccurring Fees**
   - Please identify your proposed fee structure for EACH of the first five years of this agreement. Include all fees, that is,
     - Royalty
     - Marketing
     - Reservation
     - All other (including required purchases)
   - Is there flexibility in regard to these fees? If so, who in your organization is authorized to negotiate these fees?

4. **Standards**
   - Please identify the scoring range used in your brand inspection program, as well as the number of times the property will be inspected each year.
   - Please identify the average score (past three years) of all properties in this brand that are within 150 miles of our city.
   - Are inspection scores published? If so where?
   - What is the current number of properties operating under this brand? How many of those properties are operating as three diamond (or higher) properties (under AAA inspection standards)?

5. **Mandatory Service Programs**
   - Please describe any mandatory food and beverage programs required by the brand, that is, room service, breakfasts, manager receptions, and so forth.

(continued)

FIGURE 13.2   Franchisor Survey

6. **Operating Performance**
   - Please identify for the previous two years, the brandwide statistics related to
     - ADR
     - Occupancy percent
     - RevPar
     - Reservation system room night contribution
   - Location of all branded (your proposed brand) hotels in our state that are now open or will open next year
   - List of any hotels in our state converting out of your brand last year
   - Address of Web site listing all current properties
7. **FOC**
   - Please send an up-to-date FOC to our address.
8. **Fair Franchising**
   - Do you subscribe to AAHOA's published 12 Points of Fair Franchising? If not, with which points do you disagree?
9. **Financing Assistance**
   - Please describe the assistance your organization can supply us in the area of securing funding for our hotel project.
   - Please identify the individual within your organization who would supply such assistance.
10. **Termination**
    - What is the length of your proposed agreement?
    - Please describe the penalties incurred and the procedures used should the franchisee elect to take advantage of early termination.

FIGURE 13.2   *(Continued)*

HOTEL TERMINOLOGY AT WORK

Area of Protection (AOP): The geographic area, which is designated by a franchisor and granted to a franchisee, in which no directly competing franchisees will be sold. Used, for example, in "The AOP the franchisor is proposing consists of a five-mile radius around the hotel and lasts for five years."

In some cases, the renovation and replacement requirements imposed upon a hotel will be extensive. Major construction, room additions, and far-reaching facility upgrades may be required. In all cases, installation of new outdoor signage, the purchase of new logo items, and removal of the old items required by the previous franchisor would also need to be done. In general, a conversion will always require some facility modification. These can be quite costly in some cases.

Some hotels are reflagged because the hotel's owners have determined it is not in their best interest to continue to meet the brand standards enforced by the brand managers in charge of their current flag. These owners will take advantage of the windows or early outs available to them to end their relationship with their current franchisor and switch to a new brand. In cases such as these, the owners will often seek a franchise that has lower brand standards. These lowered standards may include everything from a reduced weight of the towels that must be used in the guest bathrooms to the quality of carpet used in corridors. Lower standards generally mean the owners are unlikely to incur large expenses for improving the property prior to joining the new franchise. In fact, reflags such as this can happen in a matter of only several weeks or months because the main changes involve replacement of some interior signage and the logos on guest room items. Even in these cases, however, the hotel's owners will typically be required to complete some physical modifications of the property (e.g., new exterior signage) prior to being accepted into the new franchise system.

Since all conversions will require at least some property change and improvement (such as, for example, changing signage and logoed in-room amenity items), owners contemplating a brand conversion will want to know the extent of the changes they must implement prior to being accepted by the new brand. When a potential franchisor inspects a hotel property whose owners are interested in a conversion, a **product improvement plan (PIP)** will be prepared.

HOTEL TERMINOLOGY AT WORK

Product Improvement Plan (PIP): A document detailing the property upgrades and replacements required if a hotel is to be accepted as one of a specific brand's franchised properties. Used, for example, in "We estimate the PIP on the property to be $4,000,000 if we decide to go with that brand."

■

While hotel franchisors will not estimate, as a rule, the actual cost of the changes required for implementing the PIPs they prepare, the hotel's owners must do so to obtain a true total cost of the improvements necessary for converting to the new flag. An aggressive PIP can increase an owner's conversion costs by many thousands of dollars; therefore, a thorough review of the required PIP is crucial prior to beginning the franchise agreement negotiation process.

Negotiating the Franchise Agreement

The franchise agreement is, in the final analysis, simply a contract between the brand's managers and the hotel's owners. As such, it is negotiable. The stronger the position of each side, the more power each will bring to the negotiating process. It is always in the best interest of the hotel's owners, as well as the GM advising them, to be represented by an attorney during the franchise agreement finalization period because these agreements are detailed and complex. In the opinion of many in the hotel industry, franchise agreements, which are drafted by the franchisor, tend to be written in favor of the franchisor. Because this is true, owners should carefully read every line of the franchise agreement to determine exactly what the hotel must do to stay in compliance with the agreement, as well as the penalties incurred if the hotel does not stay in compliance.

Owners should certainly evaluate all components of their proposed franchise agreements; however, one area of special concern, especially to those managing and investing in a hotel, is the matter of the **impact study**, that is, when these studies should be undertaken and who should pay for them.

HOTEL TERMINOLOGY AT WORK

Impact Study: An in-depth evaluation of the effect on occupancy percent and ADR that a new hotel in a given market will have on an existing hotel(s) in that same market.

▮▮

To illustrate, assume that, in our example, J.D. Ojisama and the hotel's owners, after a thorough investigation, select the "Sleep Well" brand as the franchise affiliation for their proposed 150-room, limited-service hotel. Assume also that the Sleep Well brand is managed by the same corporation (Excalibur Hotels) that manages the "Sleep Better" brand. The Sleep Better brand is also a limited-service hotel; however, unlike a Sleep Well hotel, franchisees selecting this brand must offer an indoor swimming pool, as well as provide guests a complimentary hot breakfast each morning. Neither of these requirements exists for a Sleep Well.

If the AOP granted J.D.'s group excludes only the building of additional Sleep Well properties within the protected area, it may be the opinion of Excalibur Hotels, after seeing how well the original hotel performed in the market (recall that franchisors have an undisputed right to review the revenue records of their franchisees), that it is in the best interest of Excalibur Hotels to franchise a Sleep Better hotel directly across the street from J.D.'s hotel. Of course, the question then arises as to the potential "impact" such a decision will have on the hotel franchised by J.D.'s group. The issue of negative impact has become increasingly important as brand consolidation places more and more hotel brands in the hands of fewer and fewer franchisors. Increasingly, hotel owners have demanded that impact studies, prepared by an independent party, be undertaken and paid for, when appropriate, by the franchisor. Impact studies are most likely to be needed when a franchisor that manages two similar hotel brands seeks to grant franchise rights to one brand within the AOP granted to another of their own brand's franchisee. If the impact study indicates that the granting of a competitive franchise could damage the value of the original franchisee's hotel, compensation for that damage should, in the opinion of many hotel owners, become a negotiable part of the franchise agreement.

Franchise agreements are complex and are increasingly important. They should be entered into only after a great deal of consideration and with expert assistance. The fact is, however, that only a few hotels can survive without a nationally recognized brand affiliation. As a result, GMs must become adept at operating hotels in the best interest of their owners as well as in compliance with their owner's franchise agreement.

MANAGERS AT WORK

"We wanted to get your input, J.D., because you are closest to the operation," said Daniel Flood. Daniel, known to J.D. Ojisama as "Dan," was the head of the investment group that owned the 350-room full-service hotel at which J.D. was the GM.

"As you know," continued Dan, "we have a window coming up on our franchise agreement with Premier Hotels. If we are going to switch flags, we need to make a decision within the next sixty days."

J.D. was aware that meetings had been held between the owners of his hotel and an alternative franchise company. In their efforts to secure a franchise agreement with Flood's group, the new franchisor was offering very attractive reductions in royalty and reservation fees for the first three years of the agreement.

"What we need to understand better," said Dan, "is exactly what the impact would be of changing flags. We are especially concerned about conversion

costs in their PIP and the new franchise company's short-term ability to drive revenues through their 800 number and Web site."

What are some of the factors J.D. should discuss with the hotel's owners? How do you think a name change would affect the hotel's management staff? How would it affect guests? How could it affect the hotel's standing within the community?

THE HOTEL MANAGEMENT COMPANY RELATIONSHIP

If you are a GM in the hotel industry for very long, you will likely work for a hotel management company—or at least have the opportunity to do so. As discussed in Chapter 1, a management company is an organization formed for the express purpose of managing one or more hotels. Hotel owners sign **management contracts** that clearly establish the fees, operating responsibilities, and length of time for which the management company will operate their hotel. When a management company secures a contract to operate a hotel, it must provide a GM. In such a situation, the management company itself, rather than the hotel's owners, employs the GM. As a result of the popularity of management companies, most GMs will spend at least a portion of their careers working not directly with a hotel's owners but rather directly for a management company.

HOTEL TERMINOLOGY AT WORK

Management Contract: An agreement between a hotel's owners and a hotel management company under which the management company operates the hotel for a fee. Also sometimes known as a management agreement.

■

Management Companies

In many cases, those who invest in hotels are not the same individuals as those who want to manage the hotels. These nonoperating hotel owners can either hire individual GMs to direct their hotels or they can hire a management company to do so. In some cases, the owners of a hotel have absolutely no interest in managing or even in the continued ownership of the hotel. For example, assume that a bank has loaned money to a hotel owner to develop a property. The owner opens the hotel but, over time, fails to make the required loan repayments. As a result, the bank is forced to repossess the hotel. In a case such as this, the bank, which is now the owner, will likely seek a management company that specializes in distressed properties to manage the hotel until it is put up for sale and purchased by a new owner.

The hospitality industry, because it is cyclical, sometimes experiences falling occupancy rates and ADRs. Sometimes these cycles result in properties that fall into receivership and lenders who face the consequence of becoming involuntary owners. In cases such as these, effectively managing a hotel may simply mean optimizing the property's value while offering it for sale. Management companies that specialize in helping lenders maintain repossessed properties until they can be resold will:

- Secure, and if it has closed, reopen the hotel.
- Implement sales and marketing plans to maximize the hotel's short- and long-term profitability.
- Generate timely and reliable financial statements.
- Establish suitable staffing to maximize customer and employee satisfaction.
- Show the hotel to prospective buyers.
- Report regularly to the owners about the hotel's financial and physical condition.

Company	Properties	Gross Annual Revenues[1]
1. Interstate Hotels and Resorts	293	2,100.0
2. Tishman Hotel Corp.	22	584.1
3. Ocean Hospitalities	133	580.0
4. Destination Hotels & Resorts	27	515.7
5. Sunstone Hotel Investors	57	476.9
6. John Q. Hammons	59	431.2
7. Outrigger Enterprises	47	403.0
8. Lodgian	96	373.0
9. White Lodging Services Corp.	88	326.0
10. Rosewood Hotels and Resorts	12	269.1

[1]In millions of dollars.

FIGURE 13.3   Ten Largest Hotel Management Companies

Clearly, in the previous situation, a management company provides a vital service to the hotel's lender(s). An individual GM might be able to provide similar services (and usually at a lower initial cost), but many hotel investors and owners prefer to hire management companies.

While the actual number of hotels managed by any single management company varies from year to year, the ten largest management companies based on annual revenue and the number of properties they manage at the time of this writing are included as Figure 13.3.

Origin and Purpose

The financial success of any lodging facility is dependent, in large measure, on the quality and skill of its on-site management. Before the mid-1950s, the owners of a hotel hired the best GM they could find to operate the hotel(s) they owned. If they needed a manager with a specific level of skill or experience, they would try to find one. Even talented GMs, however, may not have had experience in specific tasks that owners needed to be undertaken. When that was the case, the result was often less than satisfactory for both the owner and the hotel's GM.

In the 1950s and later, as more hotels became franchised and as hotel owner groups purchased ever larger numbers of hotels, these owner's inability to actively recruit, train, and supervise the many GMs they required to manage their properties resulted in the growth of companies formed simply to manage hotels under ordinary as well as out-of-the-ordinary circumstances. In addition, the increasingly common practice of operating hotels under the same brand name enlarged the demand for GMs who were familiar with a specific brand's standards. Thus, for example, an investment group interested in building a full-service Marriott or Hilton hotel would most likely seek a property GM with experience operating one or more hotels affiliated with those brands.

Today, with the advent of large (and small) management companies, owners often find that, because a hotel management company employs many managers, one or more of those managers has the exact experience that the owner is looking for. In many cases, owners face special circumstances in the operation of their hotels. Some of these special situations can include:

- Reflagging a hotel from a lower quality brand to a higher one
- Reflagging a hotel from a higher quality brand to a lower one
- Managing/directing a major (complete) renovation of a hotel
- Operating a hotel in a severely **depressed market**
- Bankruptcy/repossession of the hotel
- Managing a hotel slated for permanent closing
- Managing a hotel as a result of the unexpected resignation of the hotel's GM
- Managing a hotel for an extended period of time for owners who elect not to become directly involved in the day-to-day operation of the property

---

HOTEL TERMINOLOGY AT WORK

Depressed Market: The term used to describe a hotel market area where occupancy rates and/or ADRs are far below their historic levels. Used, for example, in "The permanent closing of the military base in that town resulted in depressed market conditions in the entire county."

■

As a GM, it is important for you to fully understand the relationship that exists when a hotel owner signs a management contract with a hotel management company. One way to better understand the relationship is to contrast the restaurant business with the hotel business. In the restaurant business, the owner of a restaurant who elects not to operate it but wishes to continue ownership will often lease the space to another restaurateur. In that situation, the person(s) owning the new business entity that leases the restaurant pays the restaurant's owner an agreed-upon amount and assumes responsibility for all the expenses associated with operating the business. If the restaurant makes money, the benefit goes to the person(s) who leased the space. If the restaurant loses money, the same person(s) is responsible for the loss.

Unlike the restaurant business, in most cases hotel owners find they cannot lease their properties to management companies. Rather it is the management company that receives a predetermined monthly fee from the hotel's owners in exchange for operating the property, and it is the owners who assume a passive position regarding operating decisions while at the same time assuming responsibility for all working capital, operating expenses, and debt service. The fees charged by management companies to operate a hotel vary, but commonly range between 1 percent and 5 percent of the hotel's monthly revenue. Thus, regardless of the hotel's operating performance, the management company is paid the fee for its services and the hotel's owners receive the profits (if any) after all expenses are paid.

In some cases, hotel owners do negotiate contracts that tie management company compensation to the hotel's actual operating performance, at least to some degree. In some cases, this is acceptable, especially with hotels that are proven profitable. In other cases, however, it can take months or even years to turn an unprofitable hotel into a profitable one. Often, it is the owners of unprofitable or distressed market hotels that seek the assistance of management companies. Understandably, however, few hotel management companies are willing to enter into risky management contracts that may result in them financially subsidizing investors who own a hotel that either has been poorly managed in the past or that is not likely to be a profitable hotel in its current condition.

Hilton is an example of a first-tier management company.

Hotel Management Company Structures

Hotel management companies can be examined from a variety of different viewpoints. One way to view management companies is to consider whether they are **first tier** or **second tier**. The term *tier* refers simply to whose name is on the hotel the management company is operating. Tiering does not refer to the quality of the management operating, or GMs working for, the management company.

HOTEL TERMINOLOGY AT WORK

First Tier: Management companies that operate hotels for owners using the management company's trade name as the hotel brand. Hyatt, Hilton, and Sheraton are examples.

Second Tier: Management companies that operate hotels for owners who have entered into an agreement to use one of a franchisor's flags as the hotel brand. American General Hospitality, Summit Hotel Management, and Winegardner and Hammons, Inc., are examples.

■

Another way to examine management companies is by the number of hotels they operate. Because a hotel management company that operates one resort hotel with 750 rooms is likely to employ more managers and have responsibility for higher revenue than another hotel management company that operates three limited-service hotels, each of which consists of 100 rooms, historically hotel management companies have been ranked (in size) by the number of "rooms" they manage rather than the number of hotels they manage. The hospitality trade press publishes rankings of the largest hotel management companies periodically.

The size of a hotel management company may indeed say something about the successfulness of the company, but it is often more useful to segment hotel management companies by the manner in which they participate, or do not participate, in the actual risk and ownership of the hotels they manage. As a result, these companies can be examined based upon their participation in one (or more than one) of the following arrangements:

- *The management company is neither a partner in nor an owner of the hotels it manages.* In this situation, the hotel's owners hire the management company. This is common, for example, when lenders involuntarily take possession of a hotel. In other cases, the management company may, for its own philosophical reasons, elect to concentrate only on managing properties and will not participate in hotel investing (ownership).

- *The management company is a partner in the ownership of the hotels it manages.* A common arrangement within the hotel community is that of a management company, partnering with an investor(s) to jointly own and manage hotels. Frequently, in this situation, the management company either buys or is given a portion of hotel ownership (usually 1 percent–20 percent), and then assumes the management of the hotel. Those hotel owners who prefer this arrangement feel the partial ownership enjoyed by the management company will result in better performance by them. On the other hand, if the hotel experiences losses, the management company may share these losses, and this fact can also help serve as a motivator for the management company!

- *The management company only manages hotels it owns.* Some management companies are formed simply to manage the hotels they themselves own. These companies want to participate in the hotel industry as both investors and managers. Clearly an advantage of this situation is that the management company will benefit from its own success if the hotels it manages are profitable. If the company is not successful, however, it will be responsible for any operating loses incurred by its hotels.

- *The management company owns, by itself, some of the hotels it manages, and owns a part, or none at all, of others it manages.* Some management companies will vary their ownership participation depending on the hotel involved. Thus, a given management company may:
  - Own all of a specific hotel as well as manage it
  - Manage and be an owning partner in another hotel
  - Manage, but not own any part of, yet another hotel property

Each of the above structure types has advantages and disadvantages to both the management company and those with whom it partners. If a management company employs you as a GM, it is important for you to know your company's ownership participation level in the specific hotel you are managing so that you can better understand the company's operating philosophy, as well as advise your staff about the ownership of the hotel.

THE INTERNET AT WORK

Management companies concentrate on a variety of specialty areas. Swan, Inc. (Richfield Hospitality), is one of the most technologically advanced. To view its site and services, go to

www.swanhost.com

There can be many benefits enjoyed by a hotel that chooses to employ a management company.

The Management Operating Agreement

There are as many different contracts between those who own hotels and the management companies they employ to manage them, as there are hotels under management contract. Depending on the management company selected, every hotel owner will have a unique management contract, or operating agreement, for each hotel owned. In some cases, these contracts may include preopening services that are provided even before the hotel is officially open. Preopening activities may include hiring and training staff, purchasing inventories, and other operational activities that must be done before the first guest can be housed. Because you now understand the business relationship that can exist between an owner of a hotel and a management company, it is important that you, as a GM, know about the basic elements found in a management company's operating agreement.

Major Elements

In his 1980 book, *Administration of Hotel and Restaurant Management Contracts*, James Eyster detailed many of the components typically included in a management agreement. Considered a classic work in the field of hotel management contracts, it is an excellent addition to the serious GM's personal library.

Although times have changed, and certainly each specific management contract is different, many of the negotiable issues identified in Eyster's book must still be addressed by owners and prospective management companies when they are discussing a potential management agreement.

THE INTERNET AT WORK

Copies of James Eyster's 1980 book titled, *Administration of Hotel and Restaurant Management Contracts* are rare and quite difficult to locate. You can, however, still find articles written by him and published by the *Cornell Hotel and Restaurant Administration Quarterly* (The Quarterly). To do so, go to

www.amazon.com

When you arrive, select books and then enter the author name: "James Eyster." In the meantime, keep your eyes open for a copy of the original book! It's worth the extra effort to secure this valuable addition to your own management library.

Today, major elements of management agreements would include:

- The length of the agreement
- Procedures for early contract termination by either party
- Procedures for extending the contract
- Contract terms in the event of the hotel's sale
- Base fees to be charged
- Incentive fees earned or penalties assessed related to operating performance
- Management company investment required or ownership attained
- Exclusivity conditions (Is the management contract company allowed to operate other hotels that may directly compete with the hotel under contract?)
- Reporting relationships and requirements (How much detail is required and how frequently will these reports be produced?)
- Insurance requirements of the management company (Who must carry insurance and how much?)
- Status of employees (Are the hotel's employees employed by the hotel owner or the management company?)
- The control, if any, that the owner has in the selection or removal of the GM and other managers employed by the management company and working at the owner's hotel

Advantages to the Hotel Owner

A variety of benefits can accrue to hotel owners who select a qualified management company to operate their hotels. Among these are:

- *Improved management quality.* In some cases, a management company is able to offer talented GMs a better employment situation than that afforded by an individual hotel owner. A GM's opportunities for advancement, increased training prospects, and employment security are frequently enhanced by working for a management company. As a result, owners benefit from the efforts of GMs who are more highly skilled. In addition, a management company may have specialists on staff that can assist the property GM in areas such as hospitality law, accounting, and F&B management. In many cases, the hotel's owners could not supply these additional resources.

- *Targeted expertise can be obtained.* Some hotels have special needs. Reflagging, renovation, and repositioning skills are not equally possessed by all GMs. A management company may well have managers on its staff who are experts in these areas, and this expertise can be used to the hotel owners' advantage.

- *Documented managerial effectiveness is available.* Banks, mortgage companies, and others who are asked to supply investment capital to owners want to know that the hotel the owners are purchasing or for which loans are sought in fact, will be operated with professional hotel managers. The selection of an experienced management company with documented evidence of past success in running hotels similar to the one for which investment is requested adds credibility to loan applications submitted by hotel owners.

- *Payment for services can be tied to performance.* Most management companies charge a revenue-based fee to operate a hotel, but owners can negotiate additional payment incentives that help assure the very best management company performance possible. In this way, all of the resources of the company can be applied in ways that benefit both the company and the hotel. Good management companies welcome such arrangements because they allow for above-average fees to be earned in exchange for above-average management performance.

- *Partnership opportunities are enhanced.* Many hotel owners are involved in multiple properties. When that is the case, an established management company and an ownership entity can work together in a variety of hotels. The management company will become knowledgeable about the owner(s) and the goals the owner has for its hotels. The owner will become familiar with the abilities as well as the limitations of the management company. In cases such as these a long-term partnership can be synergistic.

Disadvantages to the Hotel Owner

Despite many advantages, hotel owners face some disadvantages inherent in the selection of a management company. These include:

- *The owner cannot control selection of the on-site GM and other high-level managers.* Throughout this book we have sought to demonstrate the importance of the GM to the success of a hotel property. When using a management company, the hotel's owner (who may be allowed some input) will not typically choose the hotel's GM. As a result, the quality of GM employed may be related more to the choice of GMs available (currently employed by) the management company than to the quality needed by the hotel. Experienced owners know the importance of quality on-site management and should insist upon the best GM (as well as other managers) that the management company can provide.

- *Talented managers leave frequently.* Assume you were the owner of a hotel management company. You have contracts to operate large hotels (that pay you large fees) and smaller hotels (where the fees you earn are less). One of your GMs shows considerable talent operating a smaller hotel. The owner of that property is very happy with her. An opening for a GM arises at one of your larger hotels. Do you move the GM? In many cases, the answer is probably "yes." In those cases, hotel owners may experience frequent turnover of GMs, especially if the hotel owned is smaller, is in a less popular geographic location, or for some other reason is not viewed as desirable by GMs within the management company that has the contract for operating it.

- *The interests of hotel owners and the management companies they employ sometimes conflict.* On the surface, it would seem that the interests of a hotel owner and the management company selected to operate the hotel would always coincide. Both are interested in operating a profitable hotel. In fact, disputes arise because hotel owners typically seek to minimize the fees they pay to management companies (because reduced fees yield greater profits), while management companies seek to maximize their fees. As a result, hotel owners who hire management companies often have serious disagreements with those companies over whether the hotels are indeed operated in the best interest of the owners.

- *The costs of management company errors are borne by the owner.* Unlike a lease arrangement, in a management contract it is the owner, not the management company, that is responsible for all costs associated with operating the hotel. As a result, the unnecessary costs incurred by any errors in marketing or operating the hotel are borne not by the management company making the errors but rather by the hotel's owner.

- *Transfer of ownership may be complicated.* The term (length) of a management contract, especially if the hotel is large, can be several years. As a result, if the owners decide to put the hotel up for sale during the life of the contract, those potential buyers who either operate their own hotels or use a different management company may not be interested in buying. If the contract is written in such a way as to have a **buyout** of the contract, the cost of the buyout may be so high that the owner can only sell to those potential buyers willing to pay the very highest price for the property, which limits the number of potential buyers.

HOTEL TERMINOLOGY AT WORK

Buyout: An arrangement in which both parties to a contract agree to end the contract early as a result of one party paying the other an agreed-upon financial compensation.

■

Issues Affecting the GM

As a professional GM, you are likely to find yourself, at one time or another during your career, managing a hotel in one of the following situations related to franchisors and management companies:

- The hotel is operating as a franchise.
- The hotel is operating under a management contract.
- The hotel is a franchise operating under a management contract.

MANAGERS AT WORK

"I wanted you to know up-front, J.D.," said William Zollars to J. D. Ojisama, the manager of a 350-room full-service hotel.

J.D. was meeting for breakfast at William's request, and the purpose of the meeting had become clear almost immediately.

As the regional vice president for sales, it was William's job to secure new management contracts for Richerland Hospitality, one of the largest management contract companies in the United States.

"Thanks for letting me know Bill," said J.D., "but I had already heard from our hotel owners that you were going to present a proposal." In fact, the owners of the hotel had let J.D. know that Richerland had approached them with the idea of assuming the management of the hotel. Because the hotel J.D. operated had high visibility in the city, and because it was very profitable, it was not unusual that a management company would attempt to secure a management contract for it. It happened almost every year.

"Don't be concerned, J.D.," continued William. "Our proposal will recommend that we keep most of your management team in place, including you . . . of course."

What factors would cause hotel owners to think about selecting a management company to operate their hotel rather than hiring J.D. directly? What types of owners' groups do you believe are best served hiring management companies? Do you believe J.D. should inform the others on his management team that a proposal for a management contract is being submitted to the hotel's ownership? Why or why not?

When franchise agreements and/or management contracts exist, they will affect your role as a GM, as well as how you perform your job. In this section we examine how working in a branded property affects the GM and how working for a management company can impact the GM's daily efforts.

Managing the Franchise Relationship

Most hotels are affiliated with a franchise. This is especially true of hotels with more than 75 rooms. As a result, it is likely that you will manage a hotel where the owners and a brand's managers have signed a franchise agreement. As the GM, this agreement will affect your relationship with:

- *The Hotel's Owners.* It is a simple fact that hotel owners often find themselves in conflict with, or at the very least in disagreement with, brand managers about how to best operate the brand itself, as well as how to operate the individual hotels making up the brand. Unfortunately, when these disagreements occur, it can put the hotel's GM in the middle of the conflict.

  Assume, for example, that the brand managers for your hotel have established, as a brand standard, breakfast hours for the hotel's complimentary continental breakfast to be from 6:00 A.M. to 9:00 A.M. The hotel's owners, however, instruct you to begin the breakfast at 7:00 A.M., rather than 6:00 A.M. on the weekends, to reduce labor costs. If you follow the directive of the brand managers, you violate your owner's wishes; however, if you follow the instructions of your hotel's owner, you will be in violation of a brand standard.

  When owners instruct GMs to violate or ignore brand standards, the resulting influence on the hotel's relationship with the brand can be negative. Alternatively, when brand managers seek the GM's compliance with acts that may be in the best interest of the brand managers, but not the hotel's owners, difficulties may also arise. Issues regarding loyalty to owner/employers and ethical standards for functioning as a professional GM are always present, but these take on extra complexity when a hotel is operated as part of a franchised chain.

- *The Hotel's Franchise Service Director (FSD).* Each franchise company assigns an individual to monitor the franchisee's compliance with the franchise agreement. The title of the individual who performs this task is the **franchise services director (FSD).**

HOTEL TERMINOLOGY AT WORK

Franchise Services Director (FSD): The representative of a franchise hotel brand who interacts directly with the franchised hotel's GMs.

■

The title of this individual may vary somewhat, but the position is always responsible for the day-to-day relationship between the franchisor and the franchisee. In some cases, the FSD may perform the quality assurance inspections required by the franchisor. Other routine tasks include assisting the hotel's sales effort, monitoring and advising about the hotel's use of the franchise-provided reservation system, and advising the franchise on the availability and use of franchisor resources.

Legitimate differences of opinion and conflicts can arise between a hotel GM and the franchisor's representative. The personal relationship, however, that ultimately develops between the FSD and the GM is an important one. When the relationship is good, the FSD is viewed as a valuable resource. When it is not good, conflicts between the FSD and the GM could escalate to the point that they negatively impact the GM's ability to effectively operate the hotel.

- *The Brand.* Even when a hotel's owners do not initiate brand-related conflict with a GM and the GM's relationship with the FSD is good, personal conflict may still arise between a GM and the brand's managers. Assume, for example, that those brand managers responsible for selling franchises to owners were successful in convincing those who own your hotel to reflag the property to their brand. After one year of operation, the owners complain to the franchise company that the number of reservations received through the franchisor's national reservation center is not consistent with the amounts promised by the sales representatives. In fact, complain the owners, the volume of reservations received is only one-half of that promised. In cases such as these, it is not at all unusual, and in fact is most likely, that the brand managers will claim that it is the GM, the work of the EOC, and the operation of the hotel itself that is the cause of the shortfall. Not surprisingly, as the hotel's GM, you are highly unlikely to agree with this assessment. The potential for conflict is clear.

  The example above is simply one instance of possible brand conflict, but there are certainly many others. The important factor to remember in cases such as these is that the hotel industry is relatively small and GMs (as well as brand managers) can quickly develop reputations that will follow them throughout their careers. As a professional GM, it is always in your best interest to approach any potential conflict situation with brand managers in a way that is credible, principled, and straightforward.

- *Your Staff.* Your staff will also be influenced by the requirements of your franchisor. From standards related to the appearance and content of room attendants' carts, to emergency equipment that should be available in hotel shuttle vans, to the hours room service must be available, brand standards will affect every department in the hotel. In some cases, these standards may conflict with your instructions to your staff. When they do, you must manage that conflict.

Assume, for example, that a guest checks into your hotel. The guest is tired and irritable. The hotel is busy because a tour bus with many check ins arrived just before this guest and as a result it takes nearly 10 minutes to get the guest checked in. The guest complains to the FOM about the time it has taken to get registered. The FOM, realizing that the front-desk staff was working at their top speed, apologizes, explains that other guests had arrived first, but takes no other action. When the guest demands that his room be "comped," the FOM declines to do so. The guest, upon arriving in his room, calls the brand's national guest service telephone number to complain that check in took nearly "30 minutes," and demands, according to the brand's "satisfaction guaranteed" program, that his room be "comped." Depending on the brand manager's decision about this guest, as a GM you may well have to explain to your FOM that his or her decision must be overturned in order to comply with the brand standard of "satisfaction guaranteed."

This example is simply one of many in which the policies used and decisions made by staff may be influenced by the requirements of a brand. As the hotel's GM, it is part of your job to blend the operating policies that you and the hotel's owner prefer with those dictated by the brand and explain your actions to your staff if conflict between the two approaches should arise.

- *Your Guests.* Kemmons Wilson's vision for Holiday Inn was a chain of hotels where arriving guests knew exactly what to expect from their stay. This same vision exists in the minds of most brand managers today. However, hotels as well as those who operate them can and will vary. As a result, guest experiences can vary also. When the guest's expectations are exceeded, this variation can be good. Unfortunately, that same guest may expect the same experience at the next hotel affiliated with the brand, and he or she may, in fact, be disappointed.

  For example, assume a hotel brand allows hotel owners to charge guests for local telephone calls (some brands do not allow this). As the GM in a competitive market, you determine that many of your guests will expect free local calls because that is what your competitors offer. If you implement the free local call policy, your guests will be pleased, but these same guests may be unhappy if they later stay at one of the other hotels in your chain that does not offer complimentary local calls. These guests may be disappointed because they believed, and justifiably so, that all hotels affiliated with your brand offered free local calls. As a GM, when it is your own hotel that falls short of a feature offered by another hotel within your brand, you may be challenged to satisfy a guest whose expectations exceed that which your hotel is able to meet.

Managing for a Management Company

As we have seen, sometimes a management company owns the hotel it operates. When that is the case, the property GM is, of course, working directly for the hotel's owners. In many cases, however, the management company does not own the hotel it operates. When that is so, the GM, because he or she does not work directly for the hotel's owners, may be faced with special challenges. These can include:

- *Career Management Challenges.* When you work for a management company, advancement in your organization comes through satisfying the desires of the company, not necessarily the owners of the hotel you are managing. An example that involves positive conflict points to one of the challenges you may face in your own career working for a management company. Assume you are a talented GM operating a 350-room hotel. Your management company has just gained a 10-year contract to operate a 550-room hotel in your hometown. The hotel will require a GM and it is a position you would very much like to assume, yet the owners of your current hotel are adamant that they want you to remain and have even threatened the management company that they will not renew the management contract when it expires if you are allowed to transfer. This problem (and it is a good one!) as well as others like it can occur when long-term career advancement with your management company conflicts with the desires of the hotel owners for whom you are currently managing. In a situation such as this, your company will evaluate your long-term employment worth (just as you also must evaluate it), as well as the course of action best for the long-term growth of the management company. Clearly, however, it will not be possible to satisfy at the same time your desire for promotion with your current hotel owner's desire for GM stability.

- *Dual Loyalty Issues (Owners vs. Management Company).* As the GM of a hotel operated by a management company, there may be times that the business interests of the owners of the hotel you are managing conflict with the business interests of your employer. It is important to remember that in these cases you will most often be rewarded for loyalty to your management company. For example, assume that the contract for managing the hotel at which you are the GM is up for renewal. Most unbiased observers would maintain that it is in the best interest of the hotel's owners to negotiate as short a contract length as possible and one that holds the management company responsible for financial results that fall short of expectations. These same observers would likely state that it is in the best interest of the management company to negotiate as long a contract as possible and one that holds the hotel's owners, not the management company, financially responsible in the event that hotel operating performance does not meet anticipated levels. As a GM working for a management company, you may not be in a position at all times to advise the hotel owner of his or her best course of action because, in fact, that course of action works against the best interests of your own company.

- *Strained EOC Relationships.* An important part of a GM's job is to assure each member of the EOC that he or she is a valuable partner in the hotel's ultimate success. Certainly this partnership is easier to maintain when the management company is not threatened by the loss of the contract to manage the hotel. When the management company is in danger of losing the contract, the partnership the GM wishes to develop may be strained by the fact that some members of the EOC enjoy greater job security than others.

  Consider, for example, the hotel in which an owner is considering changing to a tier-two management company. If the change takes place, it is likely that the GM, the director of sales and marketing, the controller, and if it is a full-service hotel, the F&B director will be replaced. Other department heads, such as the FOM, the executive housekeeper, and the maintenance chief are much less likely to be replaced. This is true because a management company winning a new contract does not replace, as some believe, every employee at the hotel. In fact, to do so would disrupt the hotel tremendously. Thus, depending on the size of hotel and philosophy of the management company assuming the contract, the GM (almost always) as well as some managers (but generally not all) will be replaced.

The result is that, even though the same management company currently operating the hotel employs all EOC members, some may feel more loyalty to the hotel and its owners than to the company. As a GM, it is not hard to understand these managers' perspectives, yet as the leader of the hotel operating team, you must do your best to prevent this dichotomy of interests from influencing the experience that guests in your hotel receive.

- *Affected and Concerned Employees.* GMs working for management companies know to whom they directly report and generally will be familiar with the employment policies and procedure of the management company employing them. Hourly employees may not be as familiar with the management company, and this can be a real concern when an owner chooses to employ a new management company. When, for example, an owner decides to allow one management contract to expire and elects a different management company, the hotel's employees, under the terms of the contract, will likely be terminated by the first management company and "hired" by the new company, even though they may have been at the hotel for many years. A variety of employment-related issues may arise. For example, assume that Maria, a housekeeper, has been at the hotel for 15 years as an employee of Management Company 1. That company loses its management contract to Company 2. As a result, Maria's employment with the first company is terminated. As a 15-year employee of Management Company 1, Maria was entitled to three weeks' paid vacation per year. Management Company 2, however, views Maria as a new employee, and under its policies Maria will qualify for only two weeks' vacation per year. In fact, she must be employed by the new company for a minimum of six months before she is allowed any vacation at all! The impact on Maria is obvious, as are the resulting challenges a GM faces when a new management company must implement its benefit, pay, seniority, and related employment policies in place of those of a previous management company.

- *Conflicts with Brand Managers.* Some management companies have excellent relations with the brands they manage for owners but others do not. As a GM, you may find that some of the wishes or even the directives of the brand managers are in conflict with those of your management company. For example, a franchise company, in an effort to promote business, may send to the hotel large, exterior banners that advertise a special rate or hotel feature. Obviously, the brand would like these signs displayed on the property. The management company's sales philosophy, however, may not include hanging exterior banners because it believes such banners cheapen the image of the hotel. As a result, the banners are not displayed. It is likely that the FSD will complain to the GM who was, quite rightly, simply following the directive of the management company to whom he or she reports.

Conflicts with brand managers can range from the very minor to the very serious. As the owner's representative to the brand, virtually any conflict that could arise between a franchisor and an owner could arise between a franchisor and the owner's management company. As a professional GM, you must be aware of these potential conflicts and be ready to act in the long-term best interests of your employer.

HOTEL TERMINOLOGY AT WORK GLOSSARY

The following terms were defined within this chapter. If you are not familiar with one of them, please review the segment of the chapter that contains the term.

Flag
Franchise
Franchise agreement
Federal Trade Commission (FTC)
Franchise Offering Circular (FOC)
Asian American Hotel Owners Association (AAHOA)

Window
Early out
Occupancy tax
Conversion
Systemwide
Liquidated damage fees
Area of Protection (AOP)
Brand standard

Product Improvement Plan (PIP)
Impact study
Management contract
Depressed market
First tier
Second tier
Buyout
Franchise Services Director (FSD)

ISSUES AT WORK

1. Some GMs believe they can best further their careers by choosing to manage only hotels affiliated with a specific brand (i.e., Hyatt, Westin, Holiday Inn, and so on). Other GMs believe they are most marketable if they have experience managing several different hotel brands. Assume you were a hotel owner. Which type of GM do you think would be most valuable to your hotel? Would the brand with which you are affiliated affect your decision? Would your opinion be altered if you were considering changing the flag at your property? Why or why not?

2. Some hotel managers believe the "brand" name on a hotel is critical to its success whereas others feel profitable hotels can still be operated as independents or that the brand name on the hotel is actually less important than it once was. What do you believe are the major obstacles faced by independent hotels? How can an effective management team overcome these? Do you believe the trend toward an increased number of hotels affiliated with brands will continue? What is the likely impact on independent hotels?

3. Product segmentation in the hotel industry is typically good for franchise companies because it allows them to maximize the number of hotels they have in a given geographic area and thus maximize the fees they receive. Critics contend, however, that excessive product segmentation unfairly pits hotel owners against other owners operating virtually identical hotel products (albeit with different brand names) within the same franchise group and in the same geographic area. As fewer and fewer franchise companies own increasingly larger numbers of brands, this debate will likely intensify. As a GM concerned about guest satisfaction, how, if at all, does this issue affect guests? Consider both positive and negative impacts. Do the positives outweigh the negatives? Why or why not?

4. Traditionally, management companies have been paid a monthly fee (usually a percentage of gross rooms revenue) to manage a hotel. More recently, management fees are tied to actual hotel performance as measured by RevPar indexes generated by the STAR Report (see Chapter 7). Critics of this newer approach contend that, while the STAR Report measures the sales ability of the management team, it does not measure the team's ability to control costs and maximize

profitability. If you formed a management company, would you propose to manage hotels for a percentage of the gross rooms revenue, for a fee determined by your STAR Report results, or for a fee determined by the hotel's profitability? Why? Which do you believe would appeal most to hotel owners? As a professional GM, under which system would you most like to manage?

5. GMs sometimes face difficult decisions when they are employed by a management company and operate a branded hotel. In such a situation, the GM's loyalty can be tested because of the conflicting interests of staff, guests, the brand, the management company, and the hotel's owners. Consider a situation in which the financial interests of two (or more) of these groups directly conflict (e.g., management companies seek to maximize management fees while hotel owners seek to minimize them). What would be in the best interests of each party in your example? To whom do you believe GMs owe their greatest loyalty? Why?

14

Purchasing a Hotel

This Chapter at Work

Just as many restaurant managers desire to someday own their own restaurant, many GMs aspire to personal hotel ownership. Although it is true that large corporations own many hotels (especially very large hotels), it is also true that many hotels are owned and managed by an individual or family. In fact, some GMs manage their own hotels so well that they become the owners of multiple properties. This chapter identifies the process of buying and opening a smaller to midsize hotel. The process begins with the decision about whether to buy an existing property or to develop a new one. The second step in the process and one that is very important is that of establishing a purchase price that is reasonable. This chapter identifies several methods used to establish a hotel's fair market value.

Very few individuals purchase a hotel without obtaining a mortgage or seeking investors. To secure financing, however, is always a challenge for a hotel project, and this chapter identifies some sources of loans you may investigate as you seek funding for your hotel, as well as the information a lender will require you to provide. Typically, this will involve securing an appraisal of the hotel, preparing a detailed business plan, and projecting (forecasting) sales revenue to demonstrate that the hotel will be able to repay those who invest in it or who lend you the money you will need to buy it.

When a purchase price has been established and financing is secured, the real work of opening the hotel begins. This chapter concludes with a detailed listing of the many activities GMs must undertake prior to opening a new hotel—theirs or another's. These are presented in timeline fashion, beginning six months prior to opening and concluding with the activities a GM must undertake after the hotel's grand opening has been held.

It is the authors' real hope that this chapter inspires many enterprising, talented hotel GMs to "go for it" when considering buying or developing their own hotel property. This is our hope because we believe individuals with a thorough understanding of the hotel business own the best-managed hotels, and those who understand hotel management best, we believe, are the owners who have been lucky enough to be GMs.

Chapter 14 Outline

SELECTING A PROPERTY

If you are interested in buying a hotel, you can choose between buying an existing hotel and developing a new property. In either case, you are likely to be considering self-ownership for the same reasons any individual **entrepreneur** wants to own a business. These reasons may include financial rewards, a sense of accomplishment, freedom of operation, and long-term investment potential.

When purchasing a property, buyers generally decide to buy performance or potential performance.

HOTEL TERMINOLOGY AT WORK

Entrepreneur: A person who assumes the risk of owning and operating a business in exchange for the financial rewards the business may produce.

It is important to understand that, when you own a hotel, you own two distinctly different assets. The first asset is the real estate involved. This includes the land, building(s), furnishings, and fixtures that make up the hotel. In many cases, the value of these assets may increase annually. For example, the value of a hotel's property in a highly desirable downtown location in Las Vegas, New York, Chicago, or Atlanta, to name but a few such cities, may increase annually simply because of its choice location. Alternatively, a hotel located in an area of a city or town in which property values are quickly—or even slowly but steadily—declining may find that the value of the hotel's land and building is falling each year despite the best efforts of the hotel's owners to maintain its interior furniture and fixtures in excellent condition. In nearly all cases, it makes much more sense to purchase a hotel in a location where property values are improving each year than one in which the property value is expected to decline.

The second asset involved in owning a hotel is the operating business itself. For example, in a hotel that is currently operating, the value of the hotel consists of both its real estate value and the profits (if any) made by running the hotel. In a hotel that has yet to be built, the value of the real estate may be known and building costs can be estimated, but the value of the operating business must be projected. Because that is true, it is usually easier to establish the worth of a hotel that is operating than the worth of one that has yet to be built.

In a successful hotel with high ADRs and occupancy rates, the value of the operating business may be excellent and even increasing, even though the value of the property itself is not. Alternatively, a business may be only marginally successful operationally (or even lose money!), yet achieve very significant annual increases (appreciation) in the value of the hotel's land and buildings. When reviewing and appraising a hotel or other lodging facility for potential purchase, savvy investors ensure that they have considered the current and potential value of the property's physical assets as well as its operational efficiency.

Buying an Existing Property

Hotels are bought and sold on a regular basis. Buyers and sellers are typically brought together through the use of a hotel **broker**.

HOTEL TERMINOLOGY AT WORK

Broker: An entity that, for a fee, lists (offers) hotels for sale on behalf of the hotels' owners and solicits buyers for the hotels it lists. Used, for example, in "I know that hotel is listed with Vince Cheravelli, a broker with Clear Water Hotel Brokers."

■

THE INTERNET AT WORK

If you are interested in buying a hotel or selling a hotel you own, you are likely to use the services of one or more hotel brokers. These companies list hotels for sale and solicit bids for those hotels from interested buyers. To view the Web site of one such broker, go to

www.hotel-broker.com

Some hotel brokers specialize in listing and selling only larger properties while others may assist in the sale of properties of any size. Some brokers will work only within a limited geographic region while still others may be involved in assisting in hotel sales worldwide. To establish the value of a property's real estate holdings, furniture, and fixtures, a hotel buyer may enlist the aid of an **appraiser** to make an appraisal, or unbiased estimate, of a hotel's **fair market value**. Consultants knowledgeable in the operation of hotels may also be employed to provide their opinion about the quality and value of the hotel as an operating business.

HOTEL TERMINOLOGY AT WORK

Appraiser: An individual who, for a fee, will provide an unbiased estimate of the fair market value of a hotel property.

Fair Market Value: The price that a reasonable buyer would pay and that a reasonable seller would accept for a specific hotel property. Hotels may be sold at, above, or below their fair market value.

■

THE INTERNET AT WORK

Hotel operations consultants can be located in a variety of ways. One such way is by contacting the International Society of Hospitality Consultants (ISHC). You can search their list of experts by going to

www.ishc.com

Hotels are sold for a variety of reasons, including the retirement of the hotel's owner, the owner's desire for the cash that results from the sale, or the owner's desire to reap the rewards of fully developing a hotel property and selling it for a profit.

An owner of an existing hotel who wishes to sell it typically will contact a hotel broker and enter into a contractual agreement that authorizes the broker to solicit offers to buy the property. As a GM, you may be contacted by a broker to buy a hotel, or you may contact a broker yourself to determine if a hotel you are interested in purchasing has been listed for sale with the broker. If the hotel you are interested in buying in fact has been listed, the broker will send you information on the hotel, including the number of rooms it contains, a summary of its most recent financial performance, current STAR Reports (see Chapter 7), the listed (asking) purchase price, and additional information that the broker believes a potential buyer would find useful.

After reviewing the broker-supplied information for an operating hotel and probably visiting the property, you would be in a position to make a most important determination. That determination is whether the hotel is operating at reasonable levels of performance, or whether, for some known or unknown reason, it is not operating at a reasonable level of performance.

A hotel performing well will most likely have a sales price that reflects that performance. A hotel underperforming will generally be sold for less on a per-room basis because there is no guarantee that, even with the proper investment and management, it will be able to perform better than it does currently. As a result, there is a significant difference between buying "performance" and buying "potential performance." As a buyer, you must understand this difference very clearly.

Buying Performance

Assume you own a very profitable hotel. Assume also that the hotel outperforms its STAR Report competitive set in both occupancy percentage and ADR and that it is flagged with a very popular and widely known brand. Further assume that the hotel's location is excellent; its quality assurance scores are among the top 5 percent within its brand; its preventative maintenance program is strong and has been in place for many years; and its measured customer satisfaction levels were also among the highest in its brand. A hotel such as this is performing very well, and its sales price, should you decide to sell it, would likely reflect the excellent performance of the property. A buyer of this hotel would receive not only the real estate involved, but also an exceptionally solid operating business.

As a potential buyer of this hotel, you would likely pay more, per room, for a hotel of this type than for one not performing as well. Indeed, it would be worthwhile in many cases to pay more because, with continued proper management, the hotel is likely to continue to perform at its high level. In addition, those who would lend money to buy such a hotel could be confident that they are assisting in the purchase of a strong business that is most likely able to repay the money loaned.

Buying a strongly performing hotel is often a safer investment than buying one not performing as well. Of course, with that safety comes the probable case that the hotel will be, on a per-room basis, a higher priced property to buy than if it were not performing as well.

THE INTERNET AT WORK

Selecting a hotel to buy is an extremely important decision that can be made easier by using the services of a professional hotel broker. To view the Web site of an international hotel brokerage group, go to

www.hotelbrokersintl.com

Buying Potential Performance

When a hotel buyer considers purchasing a hotel that is not operating near its peak potential, that buyer is said to be considering the purchase for its **upside potential**.

HOTEL TERMINOLOGY AT WORK

Upside Potential: The possibility that, with the proper investment and management, a hotel will yield significant increases in real estate value and/or operational profitability. Used, for example, in "The broker says the hotel is priced right because, with its location and proper management, it has tremendous upside potential."

■

Nearly all sellers of an underperforming hotel will maintain that their property has strong upside potential. As a potential buyer, however, you must be assured that this is true because, even though an underperforming hotel will sell for less on a per-room basis than will one performing well, the risk involved in buying an underperforming hotel is in most cases greater than the risk of buying an established, more profitable property.

Hotels may be underachieving for a variety of reasons. Assume, for example, that a hotel's RevPar is not comparing favorably with its STAR Report competitive set. It may be that the hotel needs a renovation to effectively compete in its market. The hotel's current owners, for a variety of reasons, may not be able to fund the needed renovations. A new owner, with the proper renovation funds in place, may well be able to take advantage of the upside potential in such a property. Alternatively, assume that a hotel is not performing well because it is older, is in a poor location, and the city in which it is located has had many newer and more modern hotels built in recent years. In a situation such as this, it will likely be much harder for a buyer to develop upside potential. The selling price, however, of such a hotel will likely be lower to reflect the difficulty inherent in developing this hotel's upside potential.

Many hotel investors look exclusively for underperforming properties with strong upside potential, because if that potential truly exists and the cost of acquiring the hotel is low enough, the likelihood of making significant profits on the future operation or sale of the hotel also exists.

Buying a Property to Be Built

In some cases, the best hotel to purchase may be one that does not yet exist. Assume, for example, that you are a GM managing a hotel and that you are looking for an ownership opportunity. You learn that a large shopping complex is to be built on the north side of your city and you believe the demand for hotel rooms in that area will be significant because no hotels are located nearby. In a case such as this, it may make the most sense for you to pursue the ownership and development of a new hotel constructed in that area.

Building a new property is a complex task and not one to be undertaken without the assistance of hotel professionals, including architects, designers, builders, franchise professionals, and attorneys. Often those who seek to build a hotel will encounter multiple hurdles, including building codes, zoning requirements, restrictions on height or signage allowed, and mandates on the number of parking spaces that must be built to support the hotel. The building process can be challenging. Although each element in the process can be very complex, the steps required to build a new hotel are essentially the same for each property. These are:

Step 1: Secure the Site. Securing a site involves its purchase or lease, as well as the determination that local building codes will allow the construction of a hotel on the site.

Step 2: Select a Franchisor. In nearly every case, a new hotel will be affiliated with a franchise. Because each franchise company has differing requirements for their properties (e.g., number of rooms, room size, amenities, furnishings, and so forth), it makes sense to identify the franchise requirements you must meet prior to beginning construction of the hotel.

Step 3: Design the Building. Based upon the site, the requirements of the franchisor, and your own ideas, an architect will be selected to design the hotel building. An experienced GM can be of great assistance to an architect in this phase of the project because a properly designed hotel will be easier to manage, and more profitable, than one that is poorly designed.

Step 4: Coordinate the Building Process. This is done by consistently meeting with the architect, franchise representatives, and builder to ensure that all building, design, and construction plans meet local building code requirements, the requirements of the franchisor, and the desires of the hotel's owner.

Step 5: Build the Hotel. Constant monitoring and coordination is required as the actual building process is undertaken.

Step 6: Furnish the Hotel. In most cases, the franchisor will dictate the quality and type of furnishings to be installed. In some cases, the franchisor may also suggest vendors who can supply these furnishings, but the hotel's owners will make the final decisions about furnishing suppliers.

Step 7: Perform Preopening and Grand Opening Activities. Before a hotel can actually open, there are many activities that must be undertaken. Many of these are detailed later in this chapter. In all cases, it is important that when a hotel opens, it is able to immediately provide the excellent service and positive guest experiences that its owners intend to offer.

HOTEL TERMINOLOGY AT WORK

Grand Opening: An event held at a hotel that marks the "official" opening of that hotel. It can be held several days or even weeks after the hotel actually opens and is intended to market the hotel to its client base and the local community.

SECURING HOTEL FINANCING

Hotels are expensive. The purchase price of a small (65-room), limited-service hotel that is newly built will average from a low of $50,000 **per key** to a high of $150,000 or more per key, plus the cost of land. As a result, the purchase of a hotel is generally a multimillion dollar real estate transaction.

MANAGERS AT WORK

"J.D., you're the only one I'm going to talk to about this project," said Ray Schwan. "I think it's a great opportunity for you . . . and for me."

J.D. Ojisama listened carefully. Ray Schwan had been a friend for three years, since the time when Schwan had stayed for five months in the hotel J.D. managed. As Mr. Schwan was a long-term stay guest, J.D. had many opportunities to see him around the property, and they had chatted frequently about the hotel business and the new manufacturing plant Mr. Schwan had come to town to develop. Since that time they had seen each other often at chamber of commerce events as well as the charity fund-raisers they both frequently attended.

J.D. considered Schwan a professional colleague and a good friend.

"My business is booming," said Schwan, "and I know that the hotel adjacent to my plant could be a gold mine . . . for both of us! We have to buy it!" continued Mr. Schwan.

J.D. knew about the hotel Schwan was proposing that they buy. It was the Hardley Plaza hotel, located on the city's far west side. It was an older, full-service property, but one that enjoyed a great location, and it was near Schwan's new manufacturing plant. For the past two hours, Schwan had been carefully laying out to J.D. how the property could be purchased and renovated.

"You'll need to pick a franchisor for us, J.D.," said Schwan, "and operationally, it's all you. We'll be 50–50 partners. I'll front the down payment for us, you manage the hotel. The way I see it, with good management, in three or four years we stand to make 2–3 million dollars by improving the operation then refinancing or selling. Split two ways, that's not too bad! Are you in?"

If you were advising J.D., would you suggest involvement in the proposed venture with Mr. Schwan? What factors would influence your decision? What risks are involved in the new project? What are the potential benefits of J.D.'s involvement?

HOTEL TERMINOLOGY AT WORK

Per Key: A term used to describe the cost of a hotel acquisition based on the number of rooms (keys) purchased. Its value comes in allowing comparison between hotels of unequal size (number of rooms). It is computed as

$$\text{Total Hotel Cost/Number of Units (Rooms) in the Hotel} = \text{Cost Per Key}$$

Used, for example, in "The hotel has 220 rooms, and is selling at a cost of $78,000 per key."

With purchase prices of new and existing properties so high, most hotel transactions involve the use of borrowed money. The purchase of a hotel is complex, and one of the most difficult aspects is that of securing financing. Many lending institutions are wary of making hotel loans because of the complexity of the hotel business. If you are to succeed in obtaining a loan to buy a hotel, you must be prepared to demonstrate the true value of the property, as well as your ability to service (repay) the debt.

Although each purchase is different, it is important for the individual investor/owner to understand the basics of how a hotel's fair market value is established, the potential sources of funding that may be available, and the supporting documentation these funding sources are likely to require before lending money for a hotel purchase. In the final analysis, all lenders or investors will want to see a realistic estimate of their ROI. In the hotel business, fully understanding ROI requires a basic understanding of **capitalization (cap) rates**.

HOTEL TERMINOLOGY AT WORK

Capitalization (Cap) Rates: A measure of investor return on investment. The computation for a cap rate is

$$\text{Net Income/Property Sales Price} = \text{Cap Rate \%}$$

Capitalization rates, commonly referred to as "cap rates," generally indicate the rate of return investors expect to achieve on their investments. As well, the direct capitalization approach is a simplistic method of determining (estimating) the value of a hotel. To determine the value of a hotel using the direct capitalization method, the hotel's net income is divided by a cap rate to yield the hotel's estimated value:

$$\frac{\text{Net Income}}{\text{Cap Rate}} = \text{Hotel Value (Estimated)}$$

By the rules of algebra, the following is also true:

$$\frac{\text{Net Income}}{\text{Hotel Value}} = \text{Cap Rate}$$

To illustrate, assume a hotel was offered for sale for $8,000,000. The hotel's net operating income for the past annual accounting period was $1,000,000. The computation of the cap rate in this example would be

$$\frac{\$1,000,000}{\$8,000,000} = 12.5\%$$

If the same hotel generated only $600,000 in net income per year, the cap rate would be computed as

$$\frac{\$600,000}{\$8,000,000} = 7.5\%$$

Cap rates that are higher tend to indicate a hotel is creating very favorable net operating incomes relative to the hotel's value (selling price). Cap rates that are lower indicate that a hotel is generating a smaller level of operating income relative to the hotel's estimated value (selling price). Historically, hotel cap rates have averaged between 8 and 12 percent, reflecting differences in financial markets and investor's requirements when purchasing hotels.

There can be two areas of confusion when computing cap rates. The first is the definition of net income itself and the second is the accounting period on which the net income is based. To illustrate, assume that two hotels are offered for sale at the same price and each seller states that their hotel yields a net operating income of $2,000,000. If you were considering the purchase of either hotel, it would be important for you to know exactly what expenses were and were not included in each seller's computation of net operating income. For example, should a reserve for FF&E replacement, management fees, franchise fees, debt service, and depreciation be deducted as expense? The decision to include or not include any or all of these expenses will negatively or positively affect the overall net income achieved and, as a result, will affect the calculated cap rate. In most cases, the savvy buyer will require potential sellers to calculate net income prior to debt service or depreciation, but inclusive of a reserve for replacement, management fees, and franchise fees, with management fees and a reserve for FF&E replacement each typically equal to 3–5 percent of the hotel's total revenue.

The accounting period analyzed can also significantly impact the cap rate and is an important factor to understand. Net income for a single (good or bad) year may or may not be a true reflection of a hotel's ability to create a consistent flow of operating income. It is best to analyze several years net operating income when that is possible, with a particular focus on whether net operating income is increasing, staying the same, or declining each year. Thus, while cap rates are a critical element to understanding how the hotel investment market is functioning, it is also important to clearly define and understand the two major variables used to calculate them.

Establishing Property Market Values

Even for real estate experts, it has always been difficult to determine the true "value" of a hotel. For example, assume a hotel is in a good location and is in good physical condition, but is poorly managed and thus is not profitable. Should the selling price of such a hotel be based on its current net operating income and profitability or the profitability that it might achieve with better management? If you were the seller of the hotel, you would certainly take the position that the hotel is more valuable than it first appears because, with proper management, its worth would increase. As a buyer, you would seek to purchase the hotel at the lowest possible price and thus would likely take the position that improved management may indeed improve the hotel, but no guarantee exists that it would do so. Thus, significant price negotiation between buyer and seller is a common part of virtually every hotel sales transaction.

THE INTERNET AT WORK

There are a variety of tools managers can use to improve their negotiating skills. One of the best is *Getting to Yes: Negotiating Agreement Without Giving In*, a best-selling book written by Roger Fisher and William Ury. To purchase it go to

www.barnesandnoble.com

When you arrive, type in the name of the authors or of the book.

Current profitability is often one important factor in establishing the value of a hotel; other factors include annual revenues achieved, physical condition, location, brand, and the quality and experience of the hotel's staff. Additional factors often considered in establishing a hotel's value include the hotel's STAR Report results, its competition, the number of new hotels to be built in the area, and the growth (or lack of growth) in the market within which the hotel is located.

Traditionally, hotel values have been established through the use of one or more of the following:

- *Replacement Approach.* This approach assumes that a buyer would not be willing to pay more for a hotel than the amount required to build (replace) a similar hotel in a similar location. For example, if a buyer could build an equivalent hotel for $75,000 per key, that buyer would be unlikely to pay the owner of an existing hotel more than that amount. Although this approach is useful for many new hotel construction projects, it is less useful, for example, when attempting to estimate the value of a hotel when no replacement hotel has recently been or could be built in the area.

- *Revenue Stream Approach.* This approach views a hotel primarily as a producer of revenue. Thus, a hotel's value is established as a multiple of its annual room's revenue. Using the logic of this approach, the more revenue produced, the more valuable the hotel. Under this system, hotels in good condition will generally sell for between two and four times their most recent annual room revenue. For example, a hotel with room revenue of $5 million per year might be valued at between $10 million (2 times revenue) and $20 million (four times revenue), depending on other conditions affecting the hotel. Hotel brokers often use this approach when developing advertisements offering hotels for sale.

• *Sales Comparison Approach.* This evaluation system assumes that similar type hotels in a given area should sell for similar per key prices. For example, assume that five hotels are located adjacent to a large city's airport. Two of those hotels are of similar age, size, and quality level. If the first of these hotels sold on January 1 of a given year for $100,000 per key, that selling price would be used, during that year, to help establish the value of the second, similar hotel. Using the sale of comparable properties to help establish the value of a property offered for sale is common in the residential real estate market and is also popular in the commercial hotel real estate market. This system is, of course, less reliable to use in a market where no hotels have been recently sold, or where no hotels that are truly comparable to the one being offered for sale have recently been sold.

• *Income Capitalization Approach.* The income capitalization approach is most often used to establish a value for income-producing properties such as apartment complexes and hotels. Essentially, as we have seen, this system seeks to develop a mathematical relationship (capitalization rate) between a hotel's projected income, expenses, and its market value. The actual computations used can be very complex and an in-depth analysis of them is beyond the scope of this text, but the method essentially:

  • Estimates a hotel's potential gross revenue
  • Estimates the hotel's operating expenses
  • Estimates the hotel's net income
  • Performs a value analysis of the hotel based upon the real costs of acquiring the property

  This approach, while the most complex, is also currently the most widely used.

• *ROI Approach.* In this approach, a hotel's value is based upon the owner's anticipated ROI. For example, assume that a buyer has a choice of two similar hotels. In the case of the first hotel, the purchase would likely yield a ROI of 11 percent. The second hotel has a potential ROI of 15 percent. Using the ROI approach, the value of the second hotel would be higher than the first. In practicality, a potential owner would establish the desired rate of return first, and then use that rate to establish a hotel's market value.

Although each of the above approaches to hotel valuation has its advocates and detractors, as a GM interested in borrowing money to purchase a hotel, it is most critical that you understand the importance of not paying more for a hotel than it is truly worth.

THE INTERNET AT WORK

Some companies specialize in helping potential sellers and buyers establish the fair market value of hotels. To view the Web site of one of the largest and most well known of these, go to

www.hvsinternational.com

THE INTERNET AT WORK

Hotel GMs and others who are interested in learning more about hotel investment strategies will find solid information on the topic available.

Hotel Investments: Issues and Perspectives, second edition, is published by EI-AH&LA. It is an excellent addition to the library of the serious potential hotel owner. To purchase the book, go to

www.ei-ahla.org

Select: "Products" in the Search bar. Next, select: "Books." Finally, under "Financial Management," select "Hotel Investments: Issues and Perspectives."

Applying for the Loan

In most cases, potential hotel owners will find it is to their advantage to borrow money to help buy the hotels in which they are interested. It may be possible for a hotel buyer to pay 100 percent of the purchase price at the time of **closing**, but few hotel buyers elect to do so.

Instead, much as the case with personal home ownership, the buyer will elect to put a down payment on the property and seek a **mortgage** for the balance of the purchase price because the use of borrowed money helps buyers **leverage** their own funds.

Many hotel buyers purchase their hotels with a combination of their own money and a loan from financial institutions.

HOTEL TERMINOLOGY AT WORK

Closing: The legal process of transferring property ownership from a seller to a buyer. Used, for example, in "The closing for our new hotel is set for May 22 at the Trans American Title Company offices on Main Street."

Mortgage: A legal document that specifies an amount of money a lender will lend for the purchase of a real estate asset (hotel), as well as the terms for the loan's repayment.

Leverage: The use of borrowed funds to increase purchasing power.

■

For example, assume you are considering buying two different hotels, each of which makes a 35 percent gross operating profit (GOP). One has a purchase price of $4 million with annual sales of $2 million. The other has a purchase price of $8 million with annual sales of $4 million. Assume also that you have raised and/or saved $4 million of your own funds. Even though it is possible for you to buy the first hotel and own it "free and clear" (no debt), it may be to your advantage to use your own funds as a down payment on the larger hotel because that hotel may produce, even after debt service, a better ROI for you than the first hotel. Effectively leveraging funds can be a complex process, and the advice of a professional CPA experienced in hotel real estate transactions is extremely helpful in determining how much borrowed money it is best to seek for each hotel purchase you are considering.

THE INTERNET AT WORK

To find a CPA in your own area who is experienced in real estate transactions, look for one on the home page of the American Institute of Certified Public Accountants at

www.aicpa.org

Of course, seeking a loan is not the same thing as actually getting a loan. Many borrowers seek loans because it is in their own best interests to do so. Those borrowers who actually receive loans get them because the lender feels the loan is in the best interests of both the entity seeking the loan and the institution providing the funds. To demonstrate that your own proposed hotel purchase or project is worthy of a loan, you must be able to show, at the time you apply for the loan, your ability to comply with the loan repayment schedule established by the lender.

Liability for Repayment

When an individual applies for and receives a loan, the lending institution will, of course, hold that same individual responsible for repayment of the loan. When it is a business that receives the loan, the same principle holds true, and the lender will look to the business that borrowed the money to repay the loan. If the loan is not repaid, the lender has **recourse**. Funds lent to individuals or businesses are classified as either full recourse, limited recourse, or nonrecourse loans, and the assets that are used to secure the loan vary for each type.

HOTEL TERMINOLOGY AT WORK

Recourse: The right to demand assets as payment for a loan. Loans can be full recourse, limited recourse, or nonrecourse.

■■

A *full recourse loan* refers to the right of the lender to take any (and all) assets of the borrower if repayment is not made. A *limited recourse loan* only allows the lender to take assets specifically named in the loan agreement. A *nonrecourse loan* limits the lender's rights to the specific asset being financed. The nonrecourse loan is common, for example, in most home mortgages, as well as for many hotel loans.

A lender's rational for preferring to make full and limited recourse loans becomes more clear when you realize that lenders typically do not want to own or operate the hotel upon which they have **foreclosed**.

HOTEL TERMINOLOGY AT WORK

Foreclose: The process in which a lender terminates the borrower's interest in a property after a loan is defaulted.

In a foreclosure, the lender will typically sell the property in an effort to recover the defaulted loan amount. The process can be long and cumbersome with no guarantee to the lender that all funds loaned will actually be recovered. In addition, operating the hotel until the time of its sale can be difficult because lenders are in the lending business, not the hotel business. As a result, a lender will generally feel more comfortable lending to a hotel borrower if the hotel for which the funds are sought, as well as additional borrower assets, are pledged as security for the loan. Borrowers, understandably seeking to protect their personal and company assets from repossession if the hotel encounters financial difficulty and thus cannot repay funds loaned, prefer to seek and secure noncourse funding whenever possible.

Funding Sources

The funds required to purchase a hotel can come from a variety of sources. In most cases a traditional local bank will not be the source of a hotel loan because of the high-risk factor. In nearly all cases, however, if you seek funding to buy or develop a hotel

Hotel Type	Funding Source	Loan Amounts
Luxury Hotels	Life insurance companies Pension funds	$15,000,000 or more
First-Class Hotels	Life insurance companies Credit companies International banks National banks	$3,000,000–$30,000,000
Midmarket Hotels	Credit companies International banks National banks Regional banks Community banks	$1,000,000–$15,000,000
Economy/Budget Hotels	Regional banks Community banks **SBA** loan providers	$5,000,000 or less

FIGURE 14.1 Funding Sources for Hotels

property, you must be willing to face initial rejection of your loan application because all lenders are very cautious about making loans to hotels. To acquire a hotel loan, you must be committed, aggressive, and willing to compromise on key aspects of the loan. Figure 14.1 identifies the type of lender and the range of funding they typically supply for a hotel's purchase or development project.

HOTEL TERMINOLOGY AT WORK

SBA: Short for the United States Small Business Administration. Established in 1953, the SBA provides financial, technical, and management assistance to help Americans start, run, and expand their businesses. The SBA is the nation's largest single financial backer of small businesses.

■

Different lenders have different goals for the loans they make. Some lenders prefer low-risk loans on which they make less money whereas other lenders are willing to assume more risk in exchange for greater profit on the loans they make.

THE INTERNET AT WORK

The SBA is an excellent potential source of funds for those individuals seeking to buy properties with purchase prices in the $1,000,000–$5,000,000 range. To view their Web site and learn about the many services they offer to small business owners, go to

www.sba.gov

An owner must secure the required funds before the construction of a hotel can begin.

As the average size of hotels built in the United States continues to decline (due to increased construction of smaller, limited-service properties), the SBA has become an increasingly significant source of hotel funding. Through a variety of programs, the SBA assists those small business entrepreneurs whose planned hotel purchase meets the following general criteria:

- The potential buyer must invest some portion of his or her own money in the project. This actual amount required may vary from as little as 15 percent to as much as 30 percent of the total cost of a new project.
- The borrower must be actively involved in the management and operation of the project.
- The borrower and any partners that person includes in the project must have a satisfactory credit history.
- The borrower must be able to demonstrate that his or her project will provide an amount of net operating income adequate to repay the loans underwritten by the SBA.

Regardless of the lending source utilized, and how conservative or aggressive the lender may be, borrowers must typically be able to demonstrate the following to successfully secure a loan:

- *A Strong Market.* Lenders prefer to lend money to purchase or develop hotels in markets that are strong and that are likely to stay strong. As a result, hotels in the largest 25–30 urban markets tend to attract the greatest lender interest. In addition, hotels in smaller cities located close to proven demand generators such as airports, colleges, universities, tourist attractions, and highways also are preferred. Hotels located in undeveloped or underdeveloped areas (particularly properties yet to be built) are often very difficult to finance because lenders are wary of funding hotels in unproven locations and markets.
- *Appropriate Equity.* Lenders will not lend a buyer 100 percent of the money required to buy a hotel. In fact, lenders may require borrowers to have as much as 50 percent **equity** in the property they wish to purchase.

HOTEL TERMINOLOGY AT WORK

Equity: The value of an asset beyond the total amount owed on it for mortgages and other loans.

For example, assume you are interested in building a hotel that will cost $10 million. A lender might require that you have 50 percent equity ($5 million) as a down payment to secure the loan. This equity rate can also be expressed as the relationship between a property's value and the amount that a lender will lend on the property. This relationship, known as the loan to value ratio, is computed as:

$$\frac{\text{Amount of loan requested}}{\text{Property value}} = \text{Loan to value ratio}$$

Many lenders require loan to value ratios of up to 50 percent; however, the average for non-SBA loans is generally in the 20–60 percent loan to value range. SBA loans can approach 85 percent or more loan to value. The variance in loan to value requirements is typically determined by the size and risk involved in the project under consideration.

- *Strong Franchise Affiliation.* Few lenders will lend money to a nonbranded property. Those potential hotel buyers who seek to save money by not paying franchise-related fees quickly discover that funding for their project is nearly impossible to obtain. The best franchise names, such as Marriott, Hyatt, Hilton, and Sheraton, yield the greatest lender interest. Lesser-known brands, or those with lower perceived quality, often attract less lender interest. As a result, brand managers who sell lesser known or less desirable franchise names must often identify specific lenders who look favorably upon their brands and who will lend money to develop hotels under these franchises.

- *Proven Operational and/or Development Experience.* Lenders do not want to lend money to hoteliers who learn the hotel business at the lender's expense. As a result, it is always important to clearly demonstrate to a lender that the property for which you are seeking funds will have experienced and talented management on-site. In addition, when a new hotel is proposed, the lender must be confident that those who will develop the hotel have experience in the site selection, construction, and hotel opening skills required for a successful venture.

- *Defensible Appraisal, Business Plan, and Revenue Forecasts.* As a buyer, it is important that you do not pay more for a hotel than it is worth. Lenders also know that it is important that they not lend more money to a hotel owner than that owner's hotel would be worth if the loan repayments were not made and the lender had to assume possession of the hotel. The best way to fairly estimate the fair market value of a hotel is to conduct a professional **appraisal**. Nearly all lenders will require that an independent appraisal be done prior to funding a loan for an existing hotel.

HOTEL TERMINOLOGY AT WORK

Appraisal: The establishment of (real estate) value.

■

In addition to an appraisal, nearly all hotel lenders will require that a **business plan** be submitted as part of any application for a loan.

HOTEL TERMINOLOGY AT WORK

Business Plan: A written document that details an owner/manager's strategy for operating a hotel.

■

The business plan is an important document and is discussed in detail later in this chapter. A critical part of the business plan and one that all lenders will require is a realistic forecast (prediction) of the hotel's future revenue and expense.

The Hotel Appraisal. Before lenders will lend money for the purchase of an existing hotel, they will want to review the appraisal for the property. When a hotel does not exist, a lender will likely request that a **feasibility study** be substituted for the appraisal and submitted in support of the loan request.

HOTEL TERMINOLOGY AT WORK

Feasibility Study: A determination that a proposed (hotel) development will (or will not) meet the expectations of its investors. The study should include the estimated market demand for the property, as well as its economic viability.

■

For example, assume you want to build a new hotel on the beach in a popular area of Florida. The value of that hotel cannot be established by an appraisal because it does not yet exist. In such a case, the feasibility study would serve as a substitute for the appraisal.

The hotel appraisal submitted in support of a loan request is much more than an estimate of a hotel's market value. As we saw earlier in this chapter, there are a variety of methods that can be used to establish a hotel's estimated market value. When a funding source requests that an appraisal be supplied in support of a loan application, the potential lender wants to know:

- The legal description of the property and the land upon which it is located
- The physical condition of the property
- An assessment of market conditions affecting the geographic area in which the hotel is located
- An assessment of market conditions affecting the hotel
- Current valuation of property for tax purposes
- The valuation method(s) used to estimate the property's market value
- The qualifications/certifications of the individual or company conducting the appraisal
- Assumptions used in developing the appraisal
- The date the appraisal was conducted
- The estimated market value of the property

It is important to realize that an appraisal is performed to benefit both the individual seeking to purchase a hotel and the lender who is asked to help fund the purchase. A hotel purchase (or new construction) consists of three essential components. These are the land, the building, and the furnishings. It is imperative that these components be in balance if the hotel is to be financially successful.

For example, it is not surprising that new budget or economy hotels are rarely built on New York's Manhattan Island, or in the most densely populated areas of Paris or Tokyo. The land costs in these areas are so high that an economy hotel is generally not economically feasible. For a full-service hotel, land costs should generally comprise between 10 and 20 percent of the total project's cost. In a limited-service hotel, land costs may rise as high as 25 percent of the total project cost. Land costs above these levels could seriously jeopardize a hotel's economic viability.

Similarly, a hotel buyer/developer who buys or leases land at a good price, but who then builds too expensive a building, or furnishes the hotel with excessively expensive artwork, furniture, and fixtures, will also find it difficult to be financially successful.

True market value is an elusive concept. In a free market society, the value of an item is, ultimately, a reflection of what a willing buyer will pay. Sometimes, however, hotel buyers are willing to pay too much to acquire a property. This is especially true with inexperienced buyers or those who ignore professional appraisals. Lenders generally will not ignore a professional appraiser's estimate of market value. That is the reason an appraisal is a requirement of the loan application process.

The Hotel Business Plan.   Once the market value for a hotel has been established by a professional appraiser, a lender will want to know your specific plans for making the hotel you want to buy a successful one. If the hotel is to be newly built, the lender will want to know when the building project will be completed, how operating losses that will be incurred in the initial opening months will be funded, and how long it is likely to be before the hotel will show profits.

If the hotel is an older property to be renovated, the lender will want to know when the renovations will begin, how much they will cost, and the likely impact of the renovations on future sales. If the property is an existing one that does not require extensive renovation, the lender will still want to know your plans for improving (or maintaining) sales and for operating the hotel. Additional information the lender will require may also be included in the business plan.

A business plan should always begin with a cover letter that explains why the plan has been sent to the reader. Traditionally, the business plan begins with a title page, followed by a table of contents. The plan's actual content should start with an overview statement summarizing the plan's content. It should also include a specific request for the amount of money you wish to borrow as well as a brief description of your plan for paying the money back. While the order of information may vary, the business plan should always address:

- A physical description of the hotel
- The plan to market the hotel
- The hotel's financial management plan
- The hotel's operating (management) plan.

In addition, the business plan should include, as addendums or appendices, any data required to support the assumptions or statements made in it. The specific contents of a business plan may be somewhat different based upon lender requirements; however, Figure 14.2 is an example of a business plan outline that would meet the general information requirements of most lenders.

A well-written business plan can play an important part in securing financing for a hotel. For those potential hotel buyers who need help in preparing a business plan, there are many hospitality consultants and specialized companies offering this specific assistance. It is important to remember, however, that the best business plans secure funding because they demonstrate to the lender that the hotel

1. Cover letter to lender
2. Table of contents page
3. Plan summary/overview
4. Description of hotel
   a. Location description
      i. Property size, features, and physical condition
      ii. Construction/renovation plan (if applicable)
      iii. Appraisal summary
5. Marketing plan
   a. Description of hotel's primary market
      i. Competition
      ii. Current marketing efforts and results
      iii. Proposed marketing efforts
      iv. Anticipated future results
6. Financial plan
   a. Statement of equity available/funding requested
      i. Revenue forecast
      ii. Forecasted revenue and expense
      iii. Forecast assumptions
      iv. Hotel breakeven analysis
      v. Balance sheet of individual/business seeking funds
7. Management plan
   a. Description of current management team
      i. Description of proposed management team
      ii. Operational philosophy/strategy
      iii. Resumes of proposed owners and managers
8. Supporting documentation
   a. Appraisal
   b. Copy of proposed purchase agreement (price)
   c. Franchise agreement (if a franchised property)
   d. Management contract (if a management company is involved)
   e. Other supporting documentation

FIGURE 14.2   Sample Business Plan Outline

project being proposed is sound, the risk to the lender is reduced to the greatest degree possible, and the individuals involved in the project have both experience and integrity.

THE INTERNET AT WORK

Regardless of the type of business, a well-developed business plan is essential for anyone seeking to borrow money to start or buy a business. Some software companies have developed programs to assist in developing professionally written business plans. To view the site of one of the most popular of these companies, go to

www.bplans.com

The Hotel Revenue Forecast.   Regardless of whether the hotel for which you seek a loan is an existing property or requires new construction, your lender will want to know the sales revenue that you expect the hotel to produce. The lender may want to see your revenue forecast for one **quarter**, one year, five years, or even longer.

HOTEL TERMINOLOGY AT WORK

Quarter: A three-month period. Often used to summarize accounting data. Used, for example, in "What is our sales forecast for the first quarter of next year?"

■

It is important that this sales forecast be as accurate as possible. If your forecast is too conservative, you may not show enough revenue to convince the lender that you can make the required loan repayments. If, however, your forecast is unrealistically high, knowledgeable lenders may deny the loan because they lack confidence in your forecast ability and business plan. Also, if the forecast is unrealistically high, you may be successful in securing the loan; however, because you will not likely achieve your forecasted revenue amounts, you may lack the ability to repay the property's debt as promised.

The best sales forecasts include estimates of hotel revenue and expenses. An accurate revenue and expense forecast can be developed if you use realistic assumptions regarding:

- The hotel's opening date
- Achievable occupancy rates
- Achievable ADR
- Required operating expenses

In an existing hotel, these assumptions may be easy to make because you know the hotel's current revenue and expense levels. In a hotel that will be built or that requires extensive renovation, the income and expense levels may be harder to predict. Franchisors can be helpful in providing information about average operating costs, as can a number of industry sources that publish such data on an annual basis. Additional sources of information regarding probable revenues may be obtained through the local visitor's and convention bureau or your state's hotel and lodging association. There are also hospitality industry consultants that can be employed to help you develop a revenue and expense forecast that is realistic and that will help maximize your chances of securing a loan.

Figure 14.3 is an example of a revenue and expense forecast that might be required by a lending institution. Note that it projects:

- Revenues (sales) for a four-year period
- Expenses for the same period
- An increasing occupancy percentage
- An increasing ADR

It is highly likely that a lender will ask for backup information about how these assumptions were made and perhaps independent verification that they are realistic.

New Hotel Forecast For Fiscal Years One thru Four
Financial Summary Detail

Description	Year 1	Pct	Year 2	Pct	Year 3	Pct	Year 4	Pct
Revenue (Sales)								
Rooms	4,835,520	67.44%	5,555,186	69.18%	6,317,078	70.96%	6,944,695	71.27%
Food	1,750,000	24.41%	1,850,000	23.04%	1,925,000	21.62%	2,100,000	21.55%
Beverage	350,000	4.88%	385,000	4.79%	410,000	4.61%	450,000	4.62%
Telephone	135,000	1.88%	130,000	1.62%	125,000	1.40%	120,000	1.23%
Other Income	100,000	1.39%	110,000	1.37%	125,000	1.40%	130,000	1.33%
Total of Departmental Sales	7,170,520	100.00%	8,030,186	100.00%	8,902,078	100.00%	9,744,695	100.00%
Direct Operating Expenses								
Rooms	1,250,000	17.43%	1,350,000	16.81%	1,425,000	16.01%	1,450,000	14.88%
Food	1,575,000	21.96%	1,665,000	20.73%	1,732,500	19.46%	1,890,000	19.40%
Beverage	175,000	2.44%	192,500	2.40%	205,000	2.30%	225,000	2.31%
Telephone	150,000	2.09%	175,000	2.18%	195,000	2.19%	225,000	2.31%
Other Expenses	100,000	1.39%	110,000	1.37%	120,000	1.35%	130,000	1.33%
Total of Direct Operating Expenses	3,250,000	45.32%	3,492,500	43.49%	3,677,500	41.31%	3,920,000	40.23%
Gross Operating Income	3,920,520	54.68%	4,537,686	56.51%	5,224,578	58.69%	5,824,695	59.77%
Undistributed Expenses								
Admin & Gen.	650,000	9.06%	675,000	8.41%	690,000	7.75%	700,000	7.18%
Sales & Marketing	450,000	6.28%	475,000	5.92%	500,000	5.62%	525,000	5.39%
Franchise Fees (5% room rev.)	241,776	3.37%	277,759	3.46%	315,854	3.55%	347,235	3.56%
Utility Costs	300,000	4.18%	325,000	4.05%	350,000	3.93%	375,000	3.85%
Property Operations and Maintenance	375,000	5.23%	400,000	4.98%	425,000	4.77%	450,000	4.62%
Total of Undistributed Expenses	2,016,776	28.13%	2,152,759	26.81%	2,280,854	25.62%	2,397,235	24.60%
Gross Operating Profit	1,903,744	26.55%	2,384,927	29.70%	2,943,724	33.07%	3,427,461	35.17%
Fixed Charges								
Management Fees (3%)	215,116	3.00%	240,906	3.00%	267,062	3.00%	292,341	3.00%
Taxes	225,000	3.14%	250,000	3.11%	250,000	2.81%	275,000	2.82%
Insurance	45,000	0.63%	50,000	0.62%	55,000	0.62%	60,000	0.62%
Depreciation	450,000	6.28%	450,000	5.60%	450,000	5.05%	450,000	4.62%
Mortgage Loan Payment	1,200,000	16.74%	1,200,000	14.94%	1,200,000	13.48%	1,200,000	12.31%
FF&E Reserve (3%)	215,116	3.00%	240,906	3.00%	267,062	3.00%	292,341	3.00%
Total of Fixed Charges	2,350,231	32.78%	2,431,811	30.28%	2,489,125	27.96%	2,569,682	26.37%
Net Profit or (Loss)	−446,487	−6.23%	−46,885	−0.58%	454,599	5.11%	857,779	8.80%
Hotel Room Count	250		250		250		250	
Annual Rooms Sold	46,720		51,556		57,168		61,594	
Annual Rooms Available (250 × 365)	91250		91250		91250		91250	
Occupancy %	51.20%		56.50%		62.65%		67.50%	
ADR	$103.50		$107.75		$110.50		$112.75	
RevPar	$52.99		$60.88		$69.23		$76.11	

FIGURE 14.3   Example of Revenue and Expense Forecast

HOTEL START-UP

When you have selected a hotel to buy, secured financing, and arranged to build (or take possession) of your hotel, the real work has just begun. There are essentially three scenarios involved in starting up a new hotel. These are:

- A new hotel is built
- An existing hotel is purchased and operated under the same flag
- An existing hotel is purchased and **reflagged**

HOTEL TERMINOLOGY AT WORK

Reflag: To change a hotel from one franchise brand to another (see Conversion in Chapter 13). Used, for example, in "We can buy the property, reflag it, and reposition it in the upper-scale transient market."

■

Regardless of the scenario you have undertaken, as the new owner/GM there are a variety of tasks for which you will be responsible. Most of these should be accomplished before the hotel officially opens, but some, as you will see, require on-going attention. Although it is not possible to detail every required management task to be accomplished before and after a hotel is opened, the following pre- and postopening responsibilities suggest some of the many activities you will undertake or supervise.

There are many tasks to accomplish before a hotel's doors are open to the public.

Selected Preopening Responsibilities of the GM/Owner

Opening a new hotel is a daunting task. In fact, some management companies have developed special opening teams specifically trained to accomplish the preopening, opening day, and postopening tasks required. In other cases, the opening "team" may consist only of the GM/owner. Regardless of the size of the opening team, however, there are many tasks to be completed. The following list, though not exhaustive, provides a sense of the scope and variety of preopening responsibilities for which you, as the GM/owner, will be responsible. In keeping with the majority of hotel development projects today, the activities list assumes the hotel will be operated as a franchise. In addition, some of these tasks are unique to a hotel reflag (conversion) project, and these are italicized.

Six Months Prior to Opening

- GM arrives on-site (the office is in an on-site trailer when the project involves new construction)
- Office supplies, business cards, stationary, and envelopes ordered
- Office telephone, answering machine, and fax lines installed
- Begin search for EOC members (especially DOSM and chief engineer)
- Secure all required franchisor operating manuals
- Order hotel Internet as well as telephone systems and in-room telephones, and determine information to be listed on the telephone faceplates
- Install "Coming Soon" sign with hotel name on the site
- Join local chamber of commerce; subscribe to local and state business magazines
- *Inform GDS contact(s) of new property affiliation and projected opening date*
- Establish hotel depository account(s) with local bank
- Establish petty cash account
- Order hotel courtesy van (if one is to be used)
- Order property walkie-talkies or wireless communication system
- *Coordinate, with telephone vendor, all PMS requirements and cabling needs*
- Assure interface capability of PMS and all required interfaces
- Enter contract with landscaper
- *Order all needed exterior signs*
- *Order all necessary interior signs*
- Plan direct mail campaign and begin implementation of sales plan
- Order needed laundry and maintenance equipment
- Set up accounts payable system
- Open needed vendor accounts, including:
  - Overnight shipper
  - Office supply store
  - Florist
  - Printer
  - Trash removal
  - Hardware store

- • Building supply store
- • Gas station
- • File for all necessary licenses (liquor) and operating permits
- Order vending machines
- Place Yellow Pages ad
- Create area information guide with location of restaurants and attractions
- Obtain federal tax I.D. number
- Prepare job descriptions
- Order cable channels/movie services

Three Months Prior to Opening

- DOSM selected and begins work
- Chief engineer selected and begins work
- *Order business cards for known EOC members*
- Food and beverage suppliers selected
- Undertake wage survey in area to determine prevailing local wages
- Contact newspaper to begin employee solicitation/advertising process
- Begin FOM and executive housekeeper search
- Determine policies necessary for processing reservations, including:
  - • Pets
  - • Check in, check out times
  - • Cancellations
  - • Credit card requirements
- *Order customized folio paper, keycard holders, and assorted front-office forms*
- Purchase exterior trash receptacles
- Confirm orders for:
  - • Fitness equipment
  - • Kitchen supplies
  - • Housekeeping supplies (terry, linen, and so on)
  - • *In-room directories*
  - • Guest in-room amenities
- Executive housekeeper arrives on property
- FOM arrives on property
- Secure credit card accounts and assure that authorization system is in place
- Select pest control vendor
- Order employee time clock
- Place order for in-room Bibles (Gideon)
- Order phone books
- Order audiovisual equipment/meeting room furniture
- *Select local laundry dry cleaner; order laundry tags from printer*

- Order insurance liability cards for guest room doors
- Order roll-away beds, cribs, and high chairs
- Order ADA compliance items
- Secure/install emergency master key box for fire department
- Conclude supervisory hiring
- Plan grand opening party

THE INTERNET AT WORK

Historically, hotels have been able to request and receive, from the Gideons, Bibles for in-room distribution and guests use. Today, most hotels and motels still provide their guests with access to a copy of the Bible distributed by the Gideons. To learn more about this organization and its goals, as well as how to order Bibles for hotel use, go to

www.gideons.org

One Month Prior to Opening
- Review all insurance policies/coverage with insurance carrier
- Install guest safety deposit boxes
- *Install decals (logos) on courtesy van*
- Select fire extinguisher service company
- Begin hiring hourly employees
- Establish partnerships with local restaurants to encourage referrals
- Mail grand opening invitations
- Order employee uniforms
- *Order franchise directories*
- Designate smoking/nonsmoking rooms, install signage
- Contact health department for F&B facility inspections
- Purchase first-aid and biohazard kits
- Install cellular telephone/citizen's band radio (CB) in van
- Begin training of hourly employees
- Purchase laundry chemicals and dispensing equipment
- Prepare MSDS binders for affected areas
- Test fire alarm system
- *Inform vendors of name change*
- *Inform current direct-bill guests of name change*
- *Do mass fax to travel agents announcing change of hotel name*
- Secure all remaining in-room amenities and supplies
- Plan rooms preventative maintenance program
- Purchase tools, jumper cables, and other maintenance supplies

One Week Prior to Opening

- Test all systems
  - Electronic locks
  - Credit card processing
  - Safety systems
  - Televisions/remotes
  - Water
  - HVAC
  - Cable/in-room movies
  - Room telephones/voice mail
- Send grand opening party press release to local news media
- Conduct practice meals in the room service, breakfast, lunch, and dinner areas
- Host grand opening party
- "Keep smiling"

Selected Postopening Responsibilities of the GM/Owner

After the grand opening party has been held, the real work of operating the hotel continues. As a GM, you will find that there are many postopening tasks that must be completed, and although neither you nor the GM is responsible for each of these, you are responsible for ensuring that they are undertaken and completed.

Postgrand Opening Activities

- Mail thank-you cards to grand opening attendees
- Follow-up on all leads made during the grand opening party
- Thank the media for attending
- Thank all hotel employees for their assistance during the opening

Ongoing Activities

- Train staff, train staff, train staff!
- Improve constantly through continued study of the hospitality field
- Spend time daily with:
  - Each department head
  - Your hourly staff
  - Your guests
  - Your family
- Assist the hotel sales effort whenever possible (because by doing so you will continue to better understand your client's wishes and needs)
- Manage your hotel (because only you know how to do it best)

Serving as GM of a hotel is, without a doubt, one of the best, most rewarding jobs in the world. Owning the hotel you manage can be even better.

MANAGERS AT WORK

"Well, Leroy, October seems strong, but what is the forecast for room sales in November and December?" asked J.D. Ojisama, the hotel's new owner, at one of the first weekly EOC meetings since J.D. assumed ownership of the property. It was late August and final planning was well underway for the year's fourth quarter.

"November starts well, then softens in the last week, because business travelers stay home for Thanksgiving. Then we get a bump up in occupancy in the first two weeks of December, but then nothing much until January. Nobody wants to travel for business around the holidays," replied Leroy Gates, the DOSM.

The controller spoke up. "The way I see it, if we don't cut expenses, and I mean significantly cut expenses, we could actually show a loss in the fourth quarter. As a property that targets business travelers, I know this hotel has traditionally been slow in the fourth quarter and does great in the second and third quarters, but I think we need to plan our fourth quarter budget cuts now."

"But my housekeepers are always the first to be cut," protested Maggie Pennycuff, "and the holidays are a poor time to ask them to reduce their hours and their take-home pay. J.D., I hope we can avoid that this year!"

Assume that you are J.D. and that you have forecasted a decline in occupancy percentage of 10–15 points for a given quarter of the year. What specific steps could you take to increase sales and/or reduce expenses in that quarter? What are additional steps that could be taken through the year to prepare for such a quarter? Given the choice, do you think a hotel should reduce room rates, cut expenses, or increase spending on sales efforts in anticipation of a down period? Who should make such decisions? Do you believe J.D.'s experience as a GM will help in this decision making? Why or why not?

HOTEL TERMINOLOGY AT WORK GLOSSARY

The following terms were defined within this chapter. If you are not familiar with one of them, please review the segment of the chapter that contains the term.

Entrepreneur	Capitalization (cap) rate	Equity
Broker	Closing	Appraisal
Appraiser	Mortgage	Business plan
Fair market value	Leverage	Feasibility study
Upside potential	Recourse	Quarter
Grand opening	Foreclose	Reflag
Per key	SBA	

ISSUES AT WORK

1. With some notable exceptions, the concept of the owner/on-site manager is not as common in the hotel business as it is in the restaurant business. Why do you think that has been the case? List five factors that would lead you to want to own your own hotel(s). Are there factors that would make you seek an alternative investment for your time and money? What are they?

2. Some hotel buyers are interested only in properties with strong upside potential (a distressed property), while others prefer to purchase hotels with known levels of profitability. If you were buying a hotel, which would you choose? Why? How do you think your ability to secure investor support would be influenced by your decision?

3. One of the most difficult (but also most important aspects involved in buying a hotel) is the determination of the appropriate price to pay. This chapter presented several approaches to establishing a hotel's market value. Some valuation systems

place great emphasis on the hotel's real estate value, while others place a greater emphasis on the hotel's ability to generate operating profits. Which do you think is more important? List three factors that support your point of view.

4. Financing sources usually feel most comfortable lending funds to experienced hotel operators. If you were a bank loan officer who was evaluated, in part, by the quality of loans you approved, how many years experience would you want a GM to possess before approaching your lending institution for funding to buy a hotel? What type(s) of experience would you want that GM to have? How would you determine the quality of the GM?

5. The time (number of hours worked per week) involved in the preopening of a hotel is extensive. What are some specific nonwork activities you could do to keep balance in your life while managing the preopening of your own hotel? What could you suggest for your top management staff to keep the same balance in their lives? Do you think most GMs buy their own hotel for its financial rewards or for the freedom of managing their own hotel? Which would appeal most to you?

15

Managing in the Global Hotel Industry

This Chapter at Work

Are you interested in an "international assignment"? First, we need to define terms because an international assignment can be of several types. It can be a position that involves frequent business trips to a specific country or region of the world if, for example, one is an executive in a global hotel organization. Alternatively, a person with an international assignment can live in a foreign location for several weeks or even longer but on a relatively short-term visit such as when assisting in the opening of a new property. As a third example (and the topic of this chapter), an international assignment can involve living and working in another country for a contractual term of one or two years (or even longer!).

There are many factors to consider if you are offered an assignment to work for an extensive period of time in another country. Examples are issues related to the political environment, economics, and the culture you will encounter in the host country. The time to evaluate these concerns is before a relocation decision is made and, hopefully, the hotel organization that employs you will provide significant assistance in this task.

Other potential concerns include personal factors such as your own interest (and perhaps those of your family members) in the relocation required for an international assignment. Hoteliers accepting an international assignment should receive special training before they begin working in the new position and should be coached about work-related experiences that should be expected while they are living in another country. Numerous examples of these are presented in this chapter.

Upon arrival in the new country, many on-the-job management and supervisory tactics will be required for success. Some of these tactics may not have been used in the manager's previous domestic assignments. These include recognizing the cultural impacts of your own management style on the hotel's staff, paying attention to (seemingly) innumerable new details, and becoming a more effective communicator.

All of the above and additional related topics discussed in this chapter suggest that a career in international hotel management can be very rewarding if you are prepared for it. If, however, a general manager accepts an international assignment without proper preparation, the results could be disastrous for the hotel organization, its employees, guests, family members of the manager, and for the unprepared GM as well!

Chapter 15 Outline

MANAGING IN THE GLOBAL HOTEL INDUSTRY

Living and working in paradise! Warm weather and close to the ocean. Palm trees, beautiful scenery, and the lifestyle that will be the envy of all your friends and family! Are these your thoughts when you think about living and working on an island in the Pacific Ocean? How about working and living in a Southeast Asian, South American, or European city? Each of these locations likely also offer professional and personal experiences that are vastly different from what you would likely experience at home.[1]

Since people travel literally everywhere, hotel organizations must be everywhere to provide travelers with the lodging services and products that they require. Working at a hotel and living in a location outside of one's own country can be especially rewarding and personally enjoyable. However, these experiences can also create significant professional and personal challenges. A decision to seek an assignment in the global hotel marketplace is important and must be carefully considered before it is made.

Executives in a U.S. hotel group or a hotel group from another country with a property not located in their home country have three options for selecting a manager for the property. They can choose to:

- Select and relocate a hotel manager from the United States who is a U.S. citizen and is currently managing a property in the United States.
- Select a citizen from the country where the hotel is located. In some cases, this individual could already be employed by the U.S. company.
- Select a person who neither a U.S. citizen nor a citizen of the country in which the hotel to be managed is located.

Each of the above alternatives is frequently used in efforts to find the very best manager for a property. In this chapter, we will be focusing on the first alternative listed above because many domestic GMs would like an international assignment and it is important that they understand critical details about it.

Why might hoteliers working in the United States be given international assignments by their employers? There are numerous reasons why hotel professionals may be asked to live and work in another country including:

- No local staff is currently qualified for the position to be assigned.
- Local staff must be trained for a long period of time.
- Local persons are being trained for positions that will replace the need for an international manager but they are not yet qualified for these positions.
- Technical expertise may need to be transferred to the foreign location.
- The employer desires to instill global perspectives in selected management employees.
- There is interest in improving the cultural understanding between persons in a company's international components.
- An international assignment is considered an integral part of a staff member's professional development process.

---

[1]Except where noted, the first two sections of this chapter are adapted from: Jack Ninemeier and Joe Perdue. *Introduction to Hospitality: Careers in the World's Greatest Industry.* Upper Saddle River, New Jersey. Pearson Prentice Hall. 2005.

- There is an interest in obtaining tighter administrative control over a foreign division.
- There are property start-up, operating, or other issues that require long-term (more than a year) on-site management direction to properly resolve the concerns.

Persons selected for international assignments most typically assume top management positions in hotels. Sometimes, especially in **developing countries**, citizens of the host country can be trained to assume middle- and lower-level management positions relatively quickly. However, as noted above, it still becomes the task of the international manager to train these persons to assume more responsible positions. By contrast, in **developed countries**, citizens of the country in which the property is located are often likely to be qualified for almost all management-level positions or require less training time to do so. When that is the case, there may be less need for making international assignments.

HOTEL TERMINOLOGY AT WORK

Developing Country: A low- or middle-income country in which most people have a low standard of living and access to fewer goods and services than do persons in countries with higher income levels.

Developed Country: A country whose income per person is high by world standards and that enjoys the higher standard of living that the wealth makes possible.

■

Governments of most countries want hotel groups to use local citizens in management positions. One big reason: more of the hotel revenues (that are used for the managers' compensation) is likely to remain in the country and to increase the **multiplier effect**.

HOTEL TERMINOLOGY AT WORK

Multiplier Effect: The resulting financial ripple that occurs within in a local economy when money is spent and respent and creates income for additional persons who, in turn, spend the money in the local economy.

■

For example, significantly more hotel revenues are used to pay the compensation of upper-level managers than lower-level managers and employees. If top wages are paid to persons who then save much of the money and return to their country of residency with it when they depart, these funds cannot benefit the local economy. Contrast that with compensation paid to local persons who spend it in the community and as they do, transfer it to other persons who, in turn, also spend it locally.

Multinational hotel groups often prefer local citizens in top management positions for several reasons, including:

- A local citizen is more likely to be familiar with the country's and local business environments and cultures and therefore can be more effective in managing the operation.

- There will be lower payroll and related relocation costs involved in the position because, at the least, transportation and subsistence costs will not likely be necessary.

- There may be improved relationships between the hotel group and the host country because the former is helping the foreign government to improve its labor force.

- There may be longer management continuity and greater employee morale because local citizens recognize that they have opportunities for promotion to the highest levels of management within the hotel.

MANAGERS AT WORK

Jae Min was an excellent student at the University in the South Korean city where she had grown up. She had majored in business, moved to the United States, and received a graduate degree in hospitality management. As part of her graduate studies, she had completed an internship in a hotel in the United States and had worked at another hotel while she was completing her education.

With this experience and education background, Jae Min returned to South Korea and began work in the hotel industry as a front-desk clerk. After a year, she was transferred to the hotel's dining room, where she spent another year as an assistant food server. After completing several other assignments, she marked her fourth year with the property with a promotion to special events coordinator for the hotel's public dining rooms. This position basically involved coordinating small functions that did not require a larger public function room.

Jae Min was well aware that, historically, women rarely if ever received department-level or higher leadership responsibilities in hotels or other businesses in her native country. Instead, these positions were most often reserved for men as the result of promotional considerations that sometimes emphasized gender over knowledge and ability.

Assume that you are an executive in a United States hotel group that has partial financial interest in and a management contract for a property in which Jae Min works. What would be your perception of the situation that confronts Jae Min and other women employees of the hotel? What, if anything, might you be able to do about it? What, if anything, could you do to reduce its impact on the hotel's recruitment efforts?

The Hotel Industry Is Global

You have learned that the hotel industry is more sophisticated and complex than many **laypersons** believe. Large U.S. hotel organizations own and/or operate properties in the United States and throughout the world. As well, large hotel organizations owned by Asians, Europeans, and persons of other nationalities own and/or operate hospitality properties in the United States and throughout the world. It is therefore increasingly possible that promotions within an organization may involve relocating around the country and to other parts of the world. Many hotel professionals desire international positions and seek employment with global companies. There are, however, many important items to be considered when a decision to become an **expatriate** hotel manager is made.

HOTEL TERMINOLOGY AT WORK

Laypersons: Persons who are not professional in or very knowledgeable about a specific subject such as hotel management.

Expatriate: A citizen of one country who is employed in another country. Example: A U.S. citizen working in Asia would be considered an expatriate by his/her Asian counterparts.

Managing and Living in Another Country

Persons considering work in a foreign country must take into account a variety of factors, including that country's political environment, economic issues and cultural factors.[2]

Political Environment

The United States enjoys long-standing and stable legal and political systems. Political changes are relatively slow, and processes leading to them are democratic and well-established. This is not, however, the case everywhere. Governmental structures are much less stable in some countries. This can result in societal turmoil, fast-paced changes in leadership, legal and travel restrictions, and the potential for personal harm during coups and wide-ranging wars. The idea of managing a business while protecting oneself and family in these environments creates an immediate "Don't go!" decision for some persons. Fortunately, despite legal and political environments in other countries that are very different from those it in the United States, opportunities for professional success and personal enjoyment do exist and can be very rewarding.

Economic Issues

The cost of doing business and living in other countries is often of concern to expatriate managers. Diverse tax laws can affect individuals and businesses. In addition, currency **exchange rates** and **inflation** impact both business and personal decisions. Expatriate hotel managers have an advantage when, for example, they are paid a competitive salary in U.S. dollars and work and live in a country where that dollar (or its equivalent) purchases significantly more than it would in the United States. As well, living in countries with very high inflation rates (which can sometimes be 2000 or more percent annually!) presents special challenges when purchasing goods and services for business or personal use.

HOTEL TERMINOLOGY AT WORK

Exchange Rate: The rate at which money of one country is traded (exchanged) for the money of another country.

Inflation: The economic condition that exists when selling prices increase throughout the economy of a country.

■

Cultural Factors

Persons living in a country often share a **national culture** of values and attitudes that influence their behavior and shape their beliefs about what is important. National culture can have a significant impact on how employees view their work and each other. Differences between people from different countries relating to how they treat each other, behave, compete, and value punctuality (being on time for meetings and appointments), for example, are issues that can significantly affect one's attitudes about and ability to work and live in another country.

[2]Stephen P. Robbins and Mary Coulter. Management: 2003 Update. 7th Edition. © 2003. Adapted by permission of Pearson Education, Inc., Upper Saddle River, NJ.

Commuting to work in foreign cities may require an understanding of alternative cultures. (Demetrio Carrasco © Dorling Kindersley)

HOTEL TERMINOLOGY AT WORK

National Culture: The values and attitudes shared by citizens of a specific country that impact behavior and shape beliefs about what is important.

■

Expatriates choosing to work in a country with a similar natural culture are less likely to suffer from **culture shock** than will their counterparts relocating to a country with a more dissimilar natural culture. For example, those from the United States working and living in Western Europe (where the cultures are not identical but are quite similar) will likely feel more at home than will those same persons working in Southeast Asia or in West Africa.

HOTEL TERMINOLOGY AT WORK

Culture Shock: The feeling of disorientation, confusion, and changes in emotions created when one visits or lives in a different culture.

■

PERSONAL FACTORS IN EXPATRIATE MANAGER'S SUCCESS

Figure 15.1 provides a checklist that can help you determine whether an international hotel management assignment might be appropriate for you. It identifies several personal influences likely to influence the success of an international position. Some of these factors are really quite easy to assess and to understand why they would likely impact an international assignment. Others are more complex. In most cases:

Check (√) one box for each factor noted below.

PERSONAL INFLUENCE FACTOR	NO	MAYBE (A LITTLE)	YES
You are able to adapt to change.	❑	❑	❑
You want to live in another country.	❑	❑	❑
You understand the country's national culture.	❑	❑	❑
You know the country's language.	❑	❑	❑
You have the knowledge/skill needed for successful job performance.	❑	❑	❑
You have the necessary human relations abilities to manage persons whose backgrounds may be significantly different than yours.	❑	❑	❑
You have previous experience(s) working/living in another country.	❑	❑	❑
Your family will support the decision to accept a global assignment and to adapt to life in another country.	❑	❑	❑
You have positive reasons (motivations) that influence your interest in a global assignment.	❑	❑	❑
You have reasonable expectations about the experiences you will have.	❑	❑	❑
You are willing to listen to and try to understand the perspectives of others.	❑	❑	❑

FIGURE 15.1   Checklist of Personal Influences That Impact Expatriate Success

- A person who does not adapt well to change is more likely to have difficulty adjusting to work and living in another culture.
- Persons desiring an expatriate position because of the international experience it brings will likely be happier than their counterparts who take the position only for reasons of, for example, career advancement.
- Expatriates with an understanding of the host country's national culture and language will know what they might expect; as a result, fewer surprises are likely that may detract from their continued interest in living and working in the country.
- Persons with the knowledge and skills required for successful job performance will have less stress on the job and greater levels of job security than will others who do not.
- Interactions with people on and off the job are likely to be significant factors that influence whether an expatriate position is successful. Hospitality professionals typically think of themselves as people persons; however, they must be effective when interacting both with persons in their organizations and within their professional community as well as in the neighborhood where they live while not at work.
- Managers with previous experience in another country are likely to better know what to expect and both their positive attitude and previous professional and personal experiences will be helpful to them.
- The interest that family members have in relocating and their general support of and input into the decision to accept the international assignment are very significant concerns that will dramatically affect the success of the global assignment.

- One's motivation to accept an international assignment is important. Consider, for example, the manager who volunteers for reasons of personal and professional growth and adventure versus another manager who is told that it will be good for his/her career.
- Expectations about a global assignment must be reasonable. Effective transitional training is discussed in the next section. You will learn that this tactic can help to assure that a candidate for a position in another country realizes what is and what is not likely to happen.
- The ability to listen and attempt to understand the beliefs of others is important. Expatriate managers are likely to encounter ideas expressed by coworkers, employees, and others in the host country that are profoundly different than theirs.

OTHER FACTORS IN EXPATRIATE MANAGER'S SUCCESS

Let's assume you have answered "yes" to all or most of the factors noted in Figure 15.1 and that you are interested in a global assignment. What else is likely to influence your decision about whether or not such an assignment is right for you? Seldom, if ever, is a global hotel management assignment successful by chance alone. More specifically, many factors must be in place for an assignment to become ideal. When these factors work against the international assignment, they can cause strain and stress at best and at worse can yield disastrous professional and/or personal experiences.

Figure 15.2 reviews some factors that influence the success of global assignments. Note that Figure 15.2 first addresses the candidate. The types of personal concerns and other factors noted in Figure 15.1 and that we just examined are very important considerations. These are summarized in Figure 15.2 as job skills and abilities, family support, experience, expectations, and motivations for the assignment.

Figure 15.2 also notes that the selection process, transitional training, and the experiences of the expatriate GM in the new culture also impact the success of the international assignment. Theses are the topics of the next section of this chapter.

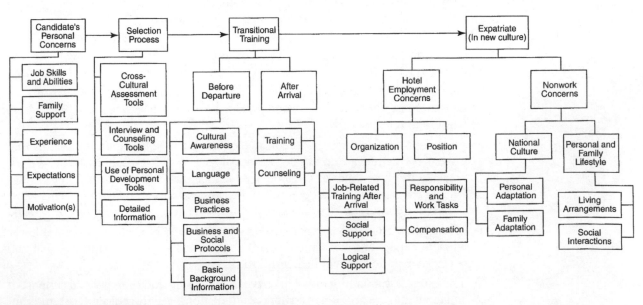

FIGURE 15.2 Factors Influencing Success of Global Assignments

The Selection Process

Figure 15.2 notes that the selection process is an important event in the success of a global assignment. Until recently, some hotel organizations made international assignments by doing little more than asking the question, "Who wants to go?" or by making the statement, "You really should go!" Today, however, a more focused and formalized selection process is generally used.

The success of an international hotel operation will be influenced by the selection and placement decisions made by the hotel group's executives about the professionals who will manage it. Also, the personal success of an expatriate assignment is more likely to be influenced by the ability of the manager and his/her family to make cultural adjustments than by the expatriate's lack of management or technical knowledge and skills. As well, significant financial costs are incurred as expatriate managers are trained, relocated, and compensated or subsidized in the host country. Problems with past global assignments point to the need for a more objective selection process.

Since expatriate assignments often fail because the employee and/or his or her family cannot adjust, the **cross-cultural adaptability** of the employee and spouse/family becomes important to assess as part of the selection process. As seen in Figure 15.2, the extent to which one can adapt to a new culture can be evaluated by:

- Administering cross-cultural assessment tools to the employee and spouse and family, if applicable. These assessment devices attempt to assess the attitudes and attributes judged important for adjustment to a culture that is different from one's own.

- Interviewing and counseling sessions with the employee and spouse, if applicable, that further explore the potential for cultural adjustment.

- Considering specialized ways that the employee should plan and implement personal cross-cultural development tools.

Deciding to live and work in another country should be a family decision.

- Providing detailed information to help the staff member understand the new international assignment and to adapt to daily life within the host country. (This topic is explored in greater detail in the next section of the chapter.)

HOTEL TERMINOLOGY AT WORK

Cross-Cultural Adaptability: The extent to which one can adjust (adapt to) another culture.

Transitional Training Programs

Figure 15.2 indicates that, after personal issues applicable to the candidate are addressed and after the selection process is completed, transitional training becomes important. Transitional training should occur before and after arrival in the host country.

Before-Arrival Training

Persons selected for international assignments will, ideally, receive training before they depart and are relocated. On what topics should training be provided? Examples of subject matter in an ideal curriculum for an international assignment suggested in Figure 15.2 include:

- *Cultural Awareness:* To allow persons accepted for international assignments to learn how the national culture affects work relations and how teamwork and productivity can be enhanced when working with staff members from that culture.
- *Language Training:* Many Americans think that English is (or should be) the world's universal language. In fact, English is widely spoken (at least in the world of business) in many countries. However, expatriates must also live in the community and will likely need to acquire basic language fluency to go about their lives off the job.
- *Business Practices:* Knowledge about changes in basic business practices that will be necessary in the new country including information about applicable laws, tax issues, and the availability of required resources will be important.
- *Business and Social Protocols:* Specific "do's" and "don'ts" of business/social practices must be learned.
- *Basic Background Information:* Figure 15.3 reviews examples of basic background information about a country that would be important for expatriate managers to know as they live and work in the country. It suggests the type of detailed information that candidates for an international position should be informed about because it should be an integral part of their interest in being considered for the assignment.

Examples of transitional training topics and anecdotes will be presented in the remainder of this chapter.

After-Arrival Training

Figure 15.2 also indicates that after-arrival transitional training is very useful. This training can be provided several weeks after the expatriate managers and their families arrive in the host country. By this time, they will have had an opportunity to experience the new environment and to interact with local citizens, and they may be seeking answers to numerous questions. Some may be homesick. Their beginning efforts at becoming culturally aware can form the foundation for training and counseling that can make their foreign assignment more enjoyable and rewarding.

A central theme of transitional training is the need to help the manager and his/her family, if applicable, recognize that old methods and ideas will need to be unlearned (or at least be put aside during the assignment). In their place, new methods and ideas based upon the employees and workplace within the new culture will often be necessary.

THE INTERNET AT WORK

Grove Well, LLC, is a company that specializes in preparing persons for and improving the management and leadership skills of persons in international assignments. You can learn about the company and review basic information about tactics that promote successful global on-the-job performance at

www.grovewell.com

There are many things that you absolutely must know about a country when considering an assignment to it and certainly before relocating to it. These can be very basic and include:

- What is the form of government? Who is the national head of the government? What does the country flag look like?
- What role does the government play in business? What taxes do residents pay? Expatriates? Businesses?
- What is the prevalent religion? What are its basic tenants? What influence does it have on daily life?
- What are the most important social standards? Cultural standards?
- What are prevalent attitudes about marriage? Divorce?
- What words, gestures, and body language are viewed as respectful? Profane?
- What language(s) are spoken? (Singapore, for example, has four official languages with different dialects of each.)
- What are attitudes and laws applicable towards alcoholic beverages?
- What kind of literature can be admitted into the country?
- What are some laws that one could violate because of ignorance if proper pre-departure and post-arrival training is not provided?
- What are the country's major industries, products, exports, and imports?
- What is the size and population of the country?
- What is its history?
- What are the most important holidays? When and how are they celebrated?
- What are favorite recreational activities of the citizens?
- What medical facilities are available? When? Where? To what extent can an expatriate use them? Where *exactly* does one go for serious medical problems? How does one get there? How, if at all, does medical insurance work in the country? Is air transport to another country generally necessary for serious (or even not-so-serious) ailments?
- What medicinal drugs are available?
- What visas are needed to enter or leave the country?
- How are drivers' licenses obtained? Who can drive?
- What is the normal dress of the country's men? Women?
- What are local costs for housing? Food? Utilities? Telephone service and other necessities? Does one's compensation include (or consider) these costs?
- What is the availability and quality of schools for expatriate children?
- What English-language newspapers and magazines, if any, are readily available?
- What is the local currency? The dollar exchange rate? The trend in exchange rates?
- When shopping, to what extent should one bargain about the proposed selling prices?
- How do people greet each other? (Shake hands? Embrace? Other?)
- What are local-language expressions for "Good morning," "Hello," "No," and "Yes," and other common terms?
- Is it appropriate to tip service employees?
- What foods are generally safe to eat? Unsafe to consume?
- Are there personal safety and security concerns? (If so, how should they be addressed?)
- What is the accepted standard for punctuality?
- How are expatriates generally viewed by applicable business persons? By society in general?

FIGURE 15.3 Examples of Country–Specific Background Facts

The Expatriate in the New Culture

Our review of Figure 15.2 continues as we note factors that can influence the success of a global assignment after the expatriate general manager has arrived in the country. These are classified into two categories: hotel employment concerns and nonwork concerns.

Hotel Employment Concerns

On-the-job factors that impact the success of expatriates in their assignments include the extent that their organization provides job-related training after arrival, social support on- and off-the-job, and logistical advice (for example, Where are the best schools? The best medical facilities?). Further, the position itself (responsibility and work tasks, for example) and compensation is important. In many cases, compensation for expatriate managers typically includes a salary as well as benefits normally paid to those working in their own country. However, they can also include other benefits such as extended annual leave, travel costs to and from the host country, educational expense reimbursements for family members, costs of moving household belongings to and from the host country, and insurance or reimbursement for emergency travel costs.

Nonwork Factors

Expatriates and their families must be able to adapt to the host country's culture. As well, the personal and family lifestyles that they experience will dramatically influence the success of their assignments. For example, an expatriate's living arrangements

---

CASE STUDY: ADVICE FROM AN EXPERIENCED EXPATRIATE MANAGER

Chef Stephen Marquard completed a four-year degree in hospitality management and began his professional culinary career at the Breakers Hotel in Palm Beach, Florida. He then joined the staff of the AAA five-star Maisonette Restaurant in Cincinnati, Ohio. His next position was as Executive Chef of the Outrigger Marshall Islands Resort on Majuro, the capitol of the Republic of the Marshall Islands. After a three-year assignment there, he joined the Outrigger Fiji Resort as executive chef. As part of the opening team, Chef Stephen was responsible for hiring, purchasing, and establishing systems and procedures for the new 254-room property on the Coral Coast of Viti Levu (Fiji's main island). Upon completion of his contract, Chef Stephen transferred to the Ohana Keauhou Beach Resort (an Outrigger property) on the Big Island of Hawaii where he currently serves as executive chef.

Here are some questions and Chef Stephen's insightful responses that provide an inside look at expatriates' assignments and living experiences.

What are the advantages to working and living in another country? The disadvantages?

Depending upon your career goals, there can be lots of potential professional advantages. Since I was willing to transfer or relocate to a remote island, my opportunities to assume the responsibilities of executive chef were increased. The position in the Marshall Islands was offered to me, and I took it! Another professional advantage to working overseas is that it teaches you new ways to solve problems. Even working within a large organization such as Outrigger, there is much autonomy in a remote location and therefore opportunities to experiment. It is important to know that what works in one location or country does not always work in another. A manager can take many approaches.

There are other professional rewards as well. It was a wonderful experience to work with people who have such a rich culture and traditions. I came from America with a degree in hospitality to train the staff at the hotel. They did learn, but in the process, I learned a lot about genuine hospitality. This exchange of knowledge and experiences is perhaps the most rewarding aspect of working on an international level. I was able to learn different languages and was able to work with different types of people, and I learned an important lesson: to appreciate and utilize diversity wherever you work.

There are also financial advantages to working internationally. First of all, there are tax advantages. The foreign earned income exemption provides that the first $80,000 dollars of foreign earned income is tax deductible. Typically, there are numerous benefits with international assignments, including free lodging, meals, telephone and other utilities, and in effect, full maintenance. Finally, if you are paid in U.S. dollars and live in a country where the exchange rate is beneficial, you can live very inexpensively and bank (save) the rest.

There are some potential disadvantages to international assignments. Although it did not affect me, some people have a culture shock and get homesick. Access to high-quality health care can also be a concern. Even with the Internet, it is still possible to lose touch with the real world. Technology allows one to keep up with current events around the world, but it is still more difficult (time-consuming) to keep current. It is also possible to feel isolated, especially when you are off the job.

What are examples of positive and negative things that can happen in an international assignment that would be totally unexpected?

This is an easy question for me. The most positive thing is that I met the woman who would become my wife! On an incredibly trivial scale, you will never know all that one can do with a coconut!

When I moved to the Marshall Islands, I erroneously thought that most of the people with whom I would interact would speak English. This was not correct. Therefore, to be effective on the job I learned the Marshallese language. My efforts to do so earned me respect in the kitchen and the community as well.

Chefs in many parts of the world have much less access to convenience foods than we do in the United States. This was good for me because I was able to learn and practice my culinary skills in a way that would probably not have been possible in a domestic position.

There are some negative things that I recall. With any job there are trade-offs, and one of the benefits that I missed out on was not being able to stay on the cutting edge of the culinary profession as I might have if I was working in New York, San Francisco, or Miami.

Also, while I was working in Fiji, there was an attempted coup. Citizens had to comply with a curfew at night, there were military checkpoints manned by soldiers with guns during the day, and the international airport was shut down for a while. My employer (Outrigger Hotels) couldn't have been more helpful during this time. Employees were offered the opportunity to go to an outer island (that would be safer) or to fly home at any time and at any cost. In retrospect, this experience was more of an inconvenience than a serious problem. It was short-lived, I kept in touch with the U.S. embassy, and the impact upon me personally and professionally was minimal at the most!

What are the most important things to consider as you decide whether an international assignment is right for you?

Many factors are common sense, such as these:

- Get as much information about the location as you can.
- Have an offer in writing from your employer before you leave.
- Talk with others who have "been there and done that."
- Negotiate a trip to the location to look around.
- Remember that a standard contract is two years; you are making a significant professional commitment.

Personal factors are also important. It was an easy decision for me because I always liked to travel and experience new cultures. Living in a country for an extended time is much different than visiting 20 countries in six months. You are not just a tourist passing through but, rather, you are a resident working with the locals and indigenous people who can teach you a lot about their country and its society. This is a significant dimension to international assignments; one does not just go for the money and the adventure. You must want to do it for the right reasons.

including transportation to and from work, and the numerous nonwork social interactions will also influence his or her interest in continuing the assignment.

AND NOW THE INTERNATIONAL ASSIGNMENT BEGINS!

Assume you have decided to accept an international assignment to live and work in another country for an extended time period. You are doing so for the "right" reasons, you have been selected for the position, you and your family have received the appropriate transitional training, and you are an expatriate in a new culture. Hotel employment and nonwork concerns such as those identified in Figure 15.2 and discussed in the above sections of the chapter have been addressed. In this section, we will review some of the types of issues that you as a hotel manager are likely to experience as you work with many staff members of a workforce from a different culture than your own.

Managing on the Job

Contemporary books addressing supervisory topics in the domestic hospitality industry typically indicate that different approaches should be used to manage different types of employees. For example, teenagers, "twenty-something" employees, baby boomers, those who are much older, and even "**empty nesters**" have different perceptions about work and respond differently to a specific leadership style. The United States does have a workforce that is increasingly culturally diverse, and factors unique to sub groups within a hotel should be considered as managers and supervisors interact with their subordinates.

When working in Asia, the culture of Asian employees and guests must be understood by those expatriate managers who interact with them.

HOTEL TERMINOLOGY AT WORK

Empty Nesters: Middle-aged persons whose children are grown and have left their home.

■

In much the same way that the GMs in the United States must consider the use of different leadership tactics with different employee groups and employees within these groups, no "one size fits all" approach can be used when expatriates manage employees in another country. Instead, unique approaches must be used when leading staff members in different countries and when facilitating the work of individual employees within a country. It becomes difficult, therefore, to generalize about "how to manage" employees in an international hotel setting.

Many factors such as language, culture, legal concerns, and business practices impact what expatriate managers can and should not do. Once known, these should influence, for example, the way that work-related instructions are given and received, the way that new employees are selected, orientated, and trained, the process by which change is introduced into the hotel organization, and even the role of and relationship between general managers and their staff members.

Let's see how culture can impact the hotel, its organization and its employees. Imagine that you are a GM from the United States managing a hotel in China or Japan and that your "**direct reports**" are department heads. Figure 15.4 identifies examples of attributes in one's personal philosophy that are likely to be significantly different between these staff members and their North American or European counterparts.

HOTEL EMPLOYEE BACKGROUNDS CAN BE VERY DIFFERENT FROM WESTERN CULTURES

The background experiences of and living environments within which subordinate employees in international hotels come to the workplace can be very similar to or very different from that of their peers in the domestic lodging industry. Contrast, for example, employees in North America and Western European nations with those in developing and/or less affluent countries. Hoteliers from the United States will likely need to make some adjustments as they begin assignments in, for example, England or Canada. However, many more significant issues are likely to arise when they begin employment in less developed cultures.

One of the authors has conducted training programs for hospitality employees in rural areas of Nigeria. Many of the newly hired restaurant staff in hotels had never eaten with flatware (knives, forks, and spoons). Instead, they primarily ate foods with their fingers. Initial dining room service training had to include the purposes of the utensils as well as their placement on dining room tables. In addition, it was interesting to note that the cost of a breakfast in the hotel's dining room was more than one week's wage that was paid to a member of the dining services staff.

One of the authors has also conducted extensive hotel employee training in Fiji. This country is developed and is the predominant trade and business center in its part of the world. However, Fiji has only a limited compulsory education program, and there is no government subsidy beyond the first several years of schooling. Consequently, hotel training is perceived to be as important as formal education and many training sessions conclude with religious ceremonies. As well, Kava (a nonalcoholic beverage made from the Kava plant root) is prepared and served on numerous occasions according to and with the use of very ceremonial preparation and consumption procedures.

In both of the examples cited above and, in almost every other international work situation, many factors initially unfamiliar to domestic hoteliers have an obvious impact on employee perceptions that influence work practices.

HOTEL TERMINOLOGY AT WORK

Direct Reports: Those staff members for whom one has immediate supervisory responsibility; also called subordinates.

∎

Of course, Figure 15.4 presents generalizations. Recall our earlier discussion about the inability to categorize all employees of any culture into any specific stereo-

Attribute	Western Culture	Eastern Culture
(Personal "Philosophy")	Example of Attribute	Example of Attribute
Power Distance	All persons are equal	Supervisors should be obeyed
Professional Development Goals	Problem-solving/creative thinking tactics that can be applied in diverse situations	Basic knowledge and skills
Planning Horizon	Short-term (3–5 years)	Long-term (10 years or longer)
Work Approach (goal)	Focus on results	Focus on process
Uncertainty Avoidance (Attitude Toward Risk)	Risk taking	Risk avoiding
Motivation	Self-starter	Passive
Emphasis on Persons	Individuals	Work Groups
Context (Amount of Knowledge Before Effective Communication Occurs)	Low context: nonverbal cues must be "double-checked" verbally	High content: nonverbal cues such as organizational position convey messages just as effectively as do written words
Rituals	The definition of correct social behavior is inconsistent	Human interaction follows a pattern
Business Relationships	Can be formed quickly (sometimes with a handshake in a single meeting)	Are formed very slowly and only after a long-term relationship is established
Role of Subordinates	Subordinates are frequently empowered and encouraged to make suggestions	Senior officials are not questioned about their decisions
Role of Operating Procedures	Operating procedures are designed to yield specified quantitative and qualitative outputs	Procedures at best are a sequence of tactics in a process that focuses on quality
Interest in Change	New approaches are emphasized because "there is always a better way" to do something	Emphasis tends to be on the "status quo"
Employee Recognition	Employees may be given incentives to "do better"	Employees do not want to do something that will make them "stand out" from their peers
Use of Body Language	Body language does not replace verbal (oral or written) communication	Body language is an integral aspect of the communication process

FIGURE 15.4 Differences in Western and Eastern Cultures Impact On-the-Job Behavior

type. With that understood, however, you can begin to see the management challenges that occur when many employees with whom you as the GM must interact are influenced by attitudes and beliefs that are vastly different from your own.

Hopefully, you will have participated in a transitional training program such as that discussed earlier in this chapter before you accepted the international assignment. If so, you would first have known that the culturally driven differences such as those noted in Figure 15.4 were likely to be encountered. Second, you would have received some training that provided suggestions about the most appropriate way to manage department heads and others in this environment. However, to actually experience these differences on the job, to begin to apply what you have learned about the best ways to manage in this new assignment and to actually use this information to make the best management decisions is still likely to require time and significant effort.

WHAT TIME IS IT ANYWAY?

Americans typically value punctuality. For example, if they have an appointment at 11:00 A.M., most persons make every effort to be where they need to be at 11:00 A.M. By contrast, the concept of "11:00 in the morning" can mean something entirely different to persons in other countries. For example, in some South Pacific Islands, "11:00 in the morning" means anytime during the hour of 11:00 in the morning. Therefore, if a person arrives at an 11:00 meeting at 11:50 A.M. or even 11:59 A.M., attendees will be "on time" for the 11:00 A.M. meeting. (Equally frustrating for the expatriate U.S. manager, the meeting set to convene at 11:00 A.M. may not actually begin until 11:30 A.M., 11:45 A.M., or later!)

If transitional training has been effective, a hotel manager with only domestic experience may be able to avoid and will be less likely to blame subordinates for personnel-related problems that might otherwise be incurred because of the manager's lack of understanding about the employees' culture and its influence on behavior.

Here are some examples of work situations that initially appear to involve a "problem" employee when, in fact, the situation involves a cultural issue that hotel managers could address if they were aware of it:

- A front-office manager in Taiwan is very autocratic, and it is difficult for subordinates to get along with him. (In fact: His Asian culture encourages the use of this type of supervisory style.)

- A female front-desk agent in the Philippines is not "friendly" with guests. (In fact: Overly friendly behavior by women in this culture is considered inappropriate.)

- A male maintenance person becomes very aloof and even irritated after a "friendly" conversation with a male expatriate manager is concluded by the latter patting him on the shoulder. (In fact: Casual body contact is generally unacceptable in many Asian cultures.)

- Housekeepers do not like their new (and expensive!) black uniforms, and supervision problems begin soon after they are issued. (In fact: The color black is avoided in many Asian countries because it is associated with death.)

- A new expatriate manager in Japan likes to be friendly and calls staff members by their first name. He also likes to have a "face-to-face" conversation with staff members. The result, however, is increasingly unfriendly employees who seem to resent the GM's attempts to be friendly. (In fact: Many Japanese do not like to be referred to by their first name and regard constant eye-to-eye contact during conversations as impolite.)

- The department head meeting called for a specific time in Fiji never begins at the appropriate time, and this irritates the Western expatriate manager. (In fact: The concept of time and punctuality is very different to many Fijians.)

- An Asian restaurant manager in the hotel's dining room does not seem interested in resolving some relatively new problem that has arisen. (In fact: Many Asian managers often accept problems as a significant component of the management process. As well, they often look within their background of experience rather than to seek out "new ideas" for problem resolution.)

- The hotel's "employee of the month" program is meant to recognize outstanding achievement. Instead it is not accepted, and the employees resent it. (In fact: Systems that reward an Asian staff member who is "different" than the group often will not be effective.)

THE INTERNET AT WORK

For detailed information about country profiles that provides basic demographic data along with cultural, personal etiquette, and basic business practices, go to

www.kwintessential.co.uk

Click on "Country Profile" in the "Resources" section of the home page.

Details Make a Difference!

The above section presented examples of how cultural backgrounds can significantly impact the effectiveness of hotel expatriate managers. Without effective transitional training and/or extensive experience, managers can perceive that they are dealing with "problem" employees when, in fact, cultural differences are influencing the work situation. To compound the problem, almost every aspect of conducting business and interacting with employees and guests can be impacted by the cultural background of those in the situation.

Figure 15.5 shows just a few differences in the ways that the negotiation process and business meetings are conducted in several countries. As well, to emphasize the point that small details can make a big difference, the gesture of exchanging business cards (certainly not a "big deal" in the United States) is also reviewed because the act can be almost a ceremony in some countries.

Communication Is Critical

Many of the most significant problems encountered by expatriate hotel managers involve communication. In addition to knowing what one should and should not do in a host country, there are some general tactics that help to minimize communication-based cultural improprieties. These include:

- *Manage within a work environment that anticipates and tolerates errors.* Although errors will occur, wise expatriate managers can learn from them and minimize their replication. Employees everywhere dislike making decisions if mistakes stemming from them yield punishment.

- *Use written communication.* This allows employees to read and reread documents to assure a better understanding. As well, a written history also helps provide for continuity when employees move on to another location.

Country	Negotiation Process	Business Meetings	Business Cards
Singapore	There may be a pause of up to 15 seconds before a question is answered. A Singaporean is not likely to say "no;" a "yes" response may not mean agreement.	Punctuality is important. Do not disagree with or criticize a person who is in a senior position to you.	Your business card should be in perfect condition. Exchange cards using both hands. Read cards carefully before putting them in a business card case.
Turkey	A Turkish negotiator is likely to start at the extreme to assess the other party's response. When a concession is made, it is done so as a favor out of respect for the other person.	First meetings are more social than business in focus. Printed materials should be available in Turkish and English.	No formal exchange ritual is used. Many Turks will not present a business card unless they know that they want to have a business relationship.
Egypt	Business moves slowly. Several meetings may be needed for a simple decision. If there is no response to an offer, this typically means "no."	Most business meetings are not considered private. There may be frequent interruptions. Meetings typically are preceded by lengthy social discussion.	No formal exchange ritual is used. The card should be given in a way that the recipient can read it.
Japan	Phrase questions so they can be answered "yes" (Example, "Does this create difficulty for you?"). Contracts are not seen as final agreements; they can be negotiated.	The most senior Japanese official sits furthest from the door. Long-term relationships are desired; do not refuse an early request even if it is difficult or not profitable to do so. Present a small gift to the most senior official at the end of the meeting.	There is significant ceremony involved in the exchange of business cards. They are given and received with both hands and a bow. During a meeting, cards should be placed in front of you in the same sequence as persons are seated.
France	Sit where you are told to sit; use direct eye contact when speaking. Discussions may be intense. Good debating skills and a grasp of details are appreciated.	Meetings are used to discuss issues rather than to make decisions. Do not make unsubstantiated claims.	No formal ritual is used for the exchange. Business cards are often larger than those used in other countries.

FIGURE 15.5   Some Business Etiquette Basics

- *Use the simplest language whenever possible.* Don't use slang and **jargon**. Recognize that, even though some employees can read and speak English, in many countries, this may not be their first (native) language. For those who have not grown up speaking English at home, a rudimentary understanding of a very complex language such as English may not include the nuances of words used by those with a better understanding of the language.

HOTEL TERMINOLOGY AT WORK

Jargon: Special terms or phrases used by persons in a profession.

Example: A hospitality industry phrase, "The soup is 86," means that soup is no longer available.

The concept of effective communication usually involves much more than just "talking" to someone from a different cultural background.

- *Use pictures/graphics whenever possible.* Hotel restaurant managers do this, for example, when they use drawings to identify where dining room service items should be placed on a dining room table as part of their training programs and use pictures to show how items on preportioned banquet plates should appear.
- *Be aware of information sent internationally.* Expatriate managers should review information if it is also intended to be circulated to employees in their hotel. It is helpful to "translate" common messages to help local staff members better understand them. As well, managers who are unfamiliar with the local language should become more familiar with it. Hopefully, efforts to do so began during the transitional training and continue during the GM's tenure with the property.
- *Be respectful of one's culture and the impact that it has on business customs and the language of business that is used.*
- *Be aware of potential cultural "hot spots."* Consider, for example, a Fijian tribe that supplies the vast majority of all entry-level employees for a nearby resort. It is the tribal custom for young persons to respect their elders. What happens, then, when a young person is promoted to a supervisory level in the resort and, in this position, must manage the work of an older uncle or aunt at the property?
- *Go out of the way to assure that employees understand.* This tactic is not acceptable by asking a closed-ended question such as "Do you understand?" Rather, it is implemented by asking subordinates to explain exactly what they believe a written or spoken message requests them to do. This approach works well in a situation that is founded on mutual respect and where the cultural diversity of employees is seen as a "plus" for the hotel.

REQUIREMENTS FOR EXPATRIATE MANAGEMENT SUCCESS

Successful expatriate hospitality managers have:

Empathy. They try to place themselves in the role of those with whom they interact in their host country.

Respect. They are considerate of and courteous to their employees and neighbors and learn the appropriate ways that respect and courtesy are shown in their new culture.

Interest. They desire to learn about the local cultures that they experience.

Flexibility. They make adjustments for the new culture in which they live.

Tolerance. They make every effort to understand differences between cultures.

Initiative. They have the interest in and recognize the need to reach out to persons within their new country.

Self-Esteem. They recognize the contributions that they can make to their employer while, at the same time, they understand that they will also learn much in their expatriate management experience.

MANAGERS AT WORK

Chermo was the new GM at a world-class resort that was part of a multiunit hotel group that had just opened on an island in the South Pacific. His organization had purchased an existing property at a beautiful beach location and had spent 18 months and millions of U.S. dollars to renovate the property. In efforts to appease the community and because it needed experienced staff members, it had employed many of the previous hotel's employees during the remodeling process and had offered them positions in the new property when it opened.

One of these staff members was Bula Ben (not his real name but that which he preferred) who was responsible for the property's landscape maintenance.

During the first three weeks after the property opened, he was responsible for three problems: he had purchased and directed his grounds persons to spray toxic chemicals around the pool and outdoor dining areas to control insects and ground lizards; he had, without permission, begun building a storage shed to house equipment used to protect windows during cyclone emergencies; and he unilaterally determined which of his staff should be available to interact with guests during their arrival and departure ceremonies.

If you were the expatriate GM, what would you do about "Bula Ben"? What might cause him to act without approval? What, if any, critical concerns might these "problem" examples suggest about the property's management and leadership procedures?

IN CONCLUSION

In this book of 15 chapters, you have taken a journey that had the goal of providing you with an overview of what successful hotel GMs must know and do to be successful. It has been in fact a brief journey because our discussion has been limited to their most basic roles and responsibilities. Those who manage full-service properties of all types and in all locations must typically take many "detours" as they confront out-of-the-ordinary challenges throughout almost every working day.

You have learned about some of the standard protocols that GMs can effectively use to interact with the functional experts that they employ and who comprise the property's EOC. The authors have provided generalizations about what top property-level managers should and should not do as they make decisions about how to best meet the needs of their constituencies, especially the hotel's guests, employees, and owners/investors. This information will be a helpful addition to the other knowledge that you bring to your future job.

This textbook journey, however, cannot replace the invaluable experience that you will gain while on the job. Many persons find the world of hotel management to be exciting, and the position of GM will become easier as you begin to apply what has and has not been effective for you in similar past instances. The key tactic, for you, is to determine whether and how the present situation is similar to others so you can apply your experience.

When hotel managers do experience job performance problems, it is not typically because they do not know how to do their job. Rather, it is because of issues related to their ability to lead and motivate others to do their respective jobs well. Only you will know whether you have the passion for quality, the appropriate guest service attitude, and the interest in working with your property's team of staff members necessary for success. How you address these and related issues will have a significant influence on your professional development.

The authors wish you the very best in your hotel management career. We hope that the journey you have now completed has been an interesting one, and that it has prompted you to learn even more about the fascinating hospitality industry.

HOTEL TERMINOLOGY AT WORK GLOSSARY

The following terms were defined within this chapter. If you are not familiar with one of them, please review the segment of the chapter that contains the term.

Developing country	Exchange rate	Empty nesters
Developed country	Inflation	Direct reports
Multiplier effect	National culture	Jargon
Laypersons	Culture shock	
Expatriate	Cross-cultural adaptability	

ISSUES AT WORK

1. What differences, if any, do you think exist in the way that one would manage an American-owned hotel in the United States or a European- or Asian-owned hotel in the United States?
2. What are examples of how the predominate culture in the United States affects the way its hotels are managed and operated? How do you think the national culture of another country affects the management of hotels in that country?
3. What are examples of ways that the government in the United States affects the management and operation of U.S. hotels? What are differences in the way governments in other countries affect the management and operation of hotels in those countries?
4. What would be some of the biggest challenges in your professional and work life if you were an expatriate managing a hotel in a country where you were fluent in the country's language? If you were not fluent in that country's predominant language?
5. Would you like to manage a hotel in another country? Why or why not?

Glossary

AAHOA (Asian American Hotel Owners Association)   An association of hotel owners that, through an exchange of ideas, seeks to promote professionalism and excellence in hotel ownership.—Chapter 13

Accountability   An obligation created when a person is delegated duties/responsibilities from higher levels of management.—Chapter 3

Accounting   The process of summarizing and reporting financial transactions.—Chapter 5

Accounts Payable   The sum total of all invoices owed by the hotel to its vendors for credit purchases made by the hotel. Also called AP.—Chapter 5

Accounts Receivable   Money owed to the hotel because of sales made on credit. Sometimes referred to as AR.—Chapter 5

Accounts Receivable Aging   A process by which the average length of time money is owed to the hotel because of sales made on credit is determined.—Chapter 5

ADR   Short for "average daily rate," the average selling price of all guest rooms for a given time period. The formula for ADR is Total Room Revenue ÷ Total Number of Rooms Sold = ADR.—Chapter 4

ADR Index   A ratio measure computed as: ADR of a selected hotel ÷ ADR of that hotel's competitive set = ADR Index.—Chapter 6

Agitation   Movement of the washing machine resulting in friction as fabrics rub against each other.—Chapter 9

Ala Carte   A food service operation in which the menu items that are offered are individually priced.—Chapter 1

Air Handler System   The fans and mechanical systems required to move air through ducts and to vents.—Chapter 11

All-Inclusive Plan (Rate)   A special rate that typically includes all guest meals and unlimited beverages as well as the use of other specifically identified hotel amenities and services.—Chapter 6

Allowances and Adjustments   Reductions in revenue credited to guests because of errors from not properly recording sales or to appease a guest for property shortcomings.—Chapter 5

Amenities   Hotel products and services designed to attract guests.—Chapter 1

American Plan   A special rate that includes specifically identified guest meals (typically breakfast, lunch, and dinner).—Chapter 6

Appraisal   The establishment of real estate value.—Chapter 14

Appraiser An individual who, for a fee, will provide an unbiased estimate of the fair market value of a hotel property.—Chapter 14

Area of Protection (AOP) The geographic area that is designated by a franchisor, and granted to a franchisee, in which no directly competing franchises will be sold.—Chapter 13

Arrival An arriving guest.—Chapter 8

Attrition The difference between the original request and the actual room purchases of a group. For example, a group might reserve 100 rooms, but actually use only 50. The hotel's standard group contract may stipulate in such a case that the group pay a penalty for "overreserving."—Chapter 7

At-Will Employment The employment relationship that exists when employers can hire any employee as they choose and dismiss that employee with or without cause at any time. The employee can also elect to work for the employer or terminate the work relationship any time that he or she chooses.—Chapter 4

Audiovisual (AV) Equipment Those items including DVD players, laptops, LCD projectors, microphones, sound systems, flip charts, overhead projectors, slide projectors, TVs, and VCRs that are used to communicate information to meeting attendees during their sessions.—Chapter 10

Audit An independent verification of financial records.—Chapter 5

Auditor The individual(s) who conducts an independent verification of financial records.—Chapter 5

Authority The power to tell others to do or not to do something in efforts to attain the hotel's objectives.—Chapter 3

Authorize To validate.—Chapter 8

Back-Office Accounting The process of summarizing and documenting the financial activity and standing of the entire hotel.—Chapter 5

Back-Office System The accounting system used by the controller to prepare the hotel's financial documents such as the balance sheet and income statement.—Chapter 8

Backup Generator Equipment used to make limited amounts of electricity on-site. Utilized in times of power failure or when the hotel experiences low supply from the usual provider of electricity.—Chapter 11

Backup System Redundant hardware and/or software operated in parallel to the system it serves. Used in times of failure or power outages, these are often operated by battery systems. For example, a backup system to the hotel's telephones would enable outside calling even if the main digital telephone system were to shut down.—Chapter 8

Ballast The device in an electric discharge lamp that starts, stops, and controls the current to the light.—Chapter 11

Banquet A food and/or beverage event held in a function room.—Chapter 10

Banquet Event Order (BEO) A form used by the sales, catering, and food production areas to detail all requirements for a banquet. Information provided by the banquet client is summarized on the form, and it becomes the basis for the formal contract between the client and the hotel.—Chapter 10

Bell Staff Those uniformed attendants responsible for guest services, including luggage handling, valet parking, airport transportation, and related guest services. The title originally arose because, in earlier years, the staff would come to the "front" (desk) to assist a guest when a bell was rung as a summons to them.—Chapter 8

Benchmark The search for best practices and an understanding about how they are achieved in efforts to determine how well the hotel is doing.—Chapter 3

Benefits Indirect financial compensation consisting of employer-provided rewards and services other than wages or salaries.—Chapter 4

Bid An offer by the hotel to supply sleeping rooms, meeting space, food and beverages, or other services to a potential client at a stated price. If the bid is accepted, the hotel will issue the client a contract detailing the agreement made between the hotel and the client.—Chapter 7

Biohazard Waste Bag A specially marked plastic bag used in hotels. Laundry items that are blood or bodily fluid stained and thus need special handling in the on-premise laundry are placed into these bags for transporting to the laundry. Chapter 9

Blackout Date Any day on which the hotel will not honor a negotiated rate. Blackout dates should be identified at the same time the hotel and the client agree on a negotiated rate. Common blackout dates include New Year's Eve and other times the hotel believes its best interests are served by disallowing acceptance of the negotiated rate.—Chapter 6

Block Rooms reserved exclusively for members of a specific group. As in "We need to create a block of fifty rooms for May 10 and 11 for the Society of Antique Furniture Appraisers."—Chapter 7

Blood-Borne Pathogen Any microorganism or virus, carried by blood, that can cause a disease.—Chapter 9

Bond(ing) Purchasing an insurance policy against the possibility that an employee will steal.—Chapter 12

Bonified Occupational Qualifications (BOQs) Qualifications to perform a job that are judged reasonably necessary to safely or adequately perform all tasks within the job.—Chapter 4

Booking Hotel jargon for making a confirmed sale. As in "What is the current booking volume for the month in the food and beverage department?" or "How many out-of-state tour buses were booked into the hotel last month?"—Chapter 7

Bottom-up Selling A tactic to first sell the hotel's least expensive rooms.—Chapter 6

Brand The name of a hotel chain. Sometimes referred to as a "flag."—Chapter 1

Brand Standard A hotel service or feature that must be adopted by any property joining a specific hotel brand's system. Used, for example, in "The franchisor has determined that 'free local telephone calls' will become a new brand standard effective January 1."—Chapter 13

Broker An entity that, for a fee, lists (offers) hotels for sale on behalf of the hotels' owners and solicits buyers for the hotels it lists. Used, for example, in "I know that hotel is listed with Joe Johnson, a broker with Mid-State Hotel Brokers."—Chapter 14

Bucket Check A procedure used to verify, for each guest, the accuracy of that guest's registration information.—Chapter 8

Business Plan A written document that details an owner/manager's strategy for operating a hotel.—Chapter 14

Buyout An arrangement in which both parties to a contract agree to end the contract early as a result of one party paying the other an agreed-upon financial compensation.—Chapter 13

Calibration The adjustment of equipment to maximize its effectiveness and operational efficiency.—Chapter 11

Call Accounting The system within the hotel used to document and charge guests for their use of the telephone.—Chapter 8

Call-Around A telephone "shopping" technique in which a hotel staff member calls competitive hotels to inquire about room rates and availability. The information is used by calling the hotel to help determine room rates.—Chapter 6

Call Brand Beverages   High-priced and higher-quality alcoholic beverages that are sold by name (such as Johnny Walker Red Scotch or Bombay Gin) rather than sold by type of liquor (scotch or gin) only.—Chapter 10

Cancellation Number   A series of numbers and/or letters that serve to identify the cancellation of a specific hotel reservation.—Chapter 8

Capital Expenditure   The purchase of equipment, land, buildings, or other fixed assets necessary for the operation of the hotel.—Chapter 5

Capitalization (Cap) Rate   A measure of investor return on investment. The computation for a cap rate is: Net Income ÷ Property Sales Price = Cap Rate %.—Chapter 14

Career Ladder   A plan that projects successively more responsible professional positions within an organization/industry. Career ladders also allow one to plan developmental activities judged necessary to assume more responsible positions.—Chapter 1

Cash Bars   A beverage service alternative where guests desiring beverages during a banquet function pay for them personally.—Chapter 10

Catering   The process of selling and carrying out the details of a banquet event.—Chapter 10

Centralized Accounting   A financial management system that collects accounting data from an individual hotel(s), then combines and analyzes the data at a different (central) site.—Chapter 5

Central Reservation System (CRS)   An entity operated by a franchisor, that offers potential guests the opportunity to make reservations at its affiliated (branded) hotels by telephone, fax and/or the Internet.—Chapter 6

Certified Public Accountant (CPA)   An individual designated by the American Institute of Certified Public Accountants as competent in the field of accounting.—Chapter 5

Chamber of Commerce   An organization whose goal is the advancement of business interests within a community or larger business region.—Chapter 7

Closed-Circuit Television (CCTV)   A camera and monitor system that displays, in real time, the activity within the camera's field of vision. A CCTV consisting of several cameras and screens showing the camera's fields of vision may be monitored in a single hotel location.—Chapter 12

Closing   The legal process of transferring property ownership from a seller to a buyer. Used, for example, in "The closing for our new hotel is set for May 22 at the Trans American Title Company offices on Main Street."—Chapter 14

Coaching   A process whose goal is helping staff members and the hotel team to reach their highest possible levels of performance.—Chapter 3

Coding   The process of assigning incurred costs to predetermined cost centers or categories.—Chapter 5

Cold Calling   Making a sales presentation to a potential client without having previously set an appointment to do so.—Chapter 7

Collusion   Secret cooperation between two or more hotel employees for the purpose of committing fraud.—Chapter 5

Commercial Food Service Operation   Food services offered in hotels and restaurants and other organizations whose primary purpose for existence involves generation of profits from the sale of food and beverage products.—Chapter 10

Comp (Complimentary)   Short for "complimentary" or "no-charge" for products or services.—Chapter 2

Compensation   All financial and nonfinancial rewards given to management and nonmanagement employees in return for the work they do for the hotel.—Chapter 4

Compensatory Damages   Also known as actual damages, this monetary amount is intended to compensate injured parties for actual losses or damage they have incurred. This typically includes items such as medical bills and lost wages.—Chapter 12

Competitive Set   The group of competing hotels to which an individual hotel's operating performance is compared.—Chapter 6

Concierge   The individual(s) within a full-service hotel responsible for providing guests with detailed information regarding local dining and attractions, as well as assisting with related guest needs.—Chapter 8

Concierge Level   A section of a hotel (usually with restricted access) reserved for special guests paying higher room rates and receiving special amenities.—Chapter 6

Confirmation Number   A series of numbers and/or letters that serve to identify a specific guest reservation.—Chapter 8

Consortia   Groups of hotel service buyers organized for the purpose of reducing their client's travel-related costs. A single such group is a consortium.—Chapter 7

Contact Alarm   A warning system that notifies (contacts) an external entity such as the fire or police department if the alarm is activated.—Chapter 12

Continuous Quality Improvement (CQI)   Ongoing efforts within the hotel to better meet (or exceed) guest expectations and to define ways to perform work with better, less costly, and faster methods.—Chapter 4

Contract   An agreement between two or more parties that will be enforceable in a court of law.—Chapter 11

Contribution Margin   The amount that remains after the product (food) cost of a menu item is subtracted from its selling price.—Chapter 10

Controller   The individual (or department) responsible for maintaining the book office accounting system. In some hotels, this position is referred to as the comptroller.—Chapter 5

Convention and Visitors Bureau (CVB)   An organization, generally funded by taxes levied on overnight hotel guests, that seeks to increase the number of visitors to the area it represents. Also called the "CVB" for short.—Chapter 7

Conversion (Verb)   The process of changing a hotel's flag from one franchisor to another. Also known as "reflagging." For example, "We need a GM experienced in managing a hotel conversion."—Chapter 13

Conversion (Noun)   The term used to describe a hotel that has changed its flag from one franchisor to another. For example, "Has this hotel always been a [brand name] or is it a conversion?"—Chapter 13

Corkage Fee   A charge levied by a hotel when a guest brings a bottle (for example, of a special wine) to the hotel for consumption at a banquet function or in the hotel's dining room.—Chapter 10

Corporate Culture   The generally accepted values and shared meanings that determine how employees within an organization will act.—Chapter 3

Cost Center   A hotel department that incurs costs in support of a revenue center. Two examples are the housekeeping and maintenance departments.—Chapter 1

Cost Per Key   The average purchase price of a hotel's guestroom expressed in thousands of dollars. For example, a 200-room hotel offered for $12,000,000 is selling at a cost of $60,000 per key ($12,000,000/200 rooms = $60,000). Sometimes called "cost per room."—Chapter 6

Cost per Occupied Room   Total costs incurred for an item or area, divided by the number of rooms occupied in the hotel for the time period examined.—Chapter 9

Credit (Bank) Card   Also known as bank cards, a system by which banks loan money with interest to consumers as purchases are made. Merchants accepting the cards for payment are charged a fee by the banks for the charges made by their customers with the credit card. Examples of credit cards are Visa and MasterCard.—Chapter 8

Cross-Cultural Adaptability   The extent to which one can adjust to (adapt to) another culture.—Chapter 15

Cross-Functional Team   A group of employees from different departments within the hotel that works together to resolve operating problems.—Chapter 3

Cross-Selling   Messages designed to advertise the availability of other hotel services.—Chapter 10

CTA   "Closed to arrival." In this situation, the hotel declines reservations for guests attempting to arrive on this specific date.—Chapter 6

Culture Shock   The feeling of disorientation, confusion, and changes in emotions created when one visits or lives in a different culture.—Chapter 15

Curb Appeal   The term used to indicate the initial visual impression the hotel's parking areas, grounds, and external building aesthetics create for an arriving guest.—Chapter 8

Cut-off Date   The date on which any unreserved rooms remaining in a group's block are returned to a hotel's general room inventory and therefore are available for sale to others.—Chapter 8

Damages   The actual amount of losses or costs incurred due to the wrongful act of a liable party.—Chapter 12

Data Mining   Using technology to analyze guest (and other) related data to make better marketing decisions.—Chapter 1

Day Of   Short for "Day of Arrival." Used as, for example, "Let's hold the rates at $100.00 per night for the 22nd; but reexamine the decision on the day of."—Chapter 6

Day-Part   A segment of the day that represents a change in menu and customer response patterns (for example, time during which breakfast or another menu is offered).—Chapter 10

Day Rate   A special rate that typically includes 8–12 hours (but not overnight) use of a room.—Chapter 6

Debit Card   A payment system in which money collected by a merchant (hotel) is automatically (electronically) deposited into the merchant's local bank account. As with bank and T&E cards, merchants accepting the cards are assessed a fee for the right to do so.—Chapter 8

Decentralized Accounting   A financial management system that collects accounting data from an individual hotel site and combines and analyzes that data at the same site.—Chapter 5

Deep Cleaning   The intensive cleaning of a guestroom, typically including the thorough cleaning of items such as drapes, lamp shades, carpets, furniture, walls, and the like.—Chapter 9

Defibrillator   A machine used to deliver an electrical shock to the heart in case of cardiac arrest (heart attack) in efforts to reestablish a normal heartbeat.—Chapter 12

Delegation   The process of assigning authority (power) to others to enable subordinates to do work that a manager at a higher organizational level would otherwise do.—Chapter 3

Demand   The total amount of a good or service consumers want to buy at a specific price.—Chapter 6

Demand Generator   An organization, entity, or location that creates a significant need for hotel services. Examples in a community include large businesses, tourist sites, sports teams, educational facilities, and manufacturing plants.—Chapter 7

Depreciation The process used to learn the value of a fixed asset during a specific accounting period that is assumed to have been "used up" during that period.—Chapter 5

Depressed Market The term used to describe a hotel market area where occupancy rates and/or ADRs are far below their historic levels. Used, for example, in "The permanent closing of the military base in that town resulted in depressed market conditions in the entire county."—Chapter 13

Developing Country A low- or middle-income country in which most people have a low standard of living and access to fewer goods and services than do persons in countries with higher income levels.—Chapter 15

Direct Bill An arrangement that allows a guest to purchase hotel services and products on credit terms.—Chapter 5

Direct Reports Those staff members for whom one has immediate supervisory responsibility; also called subordinates.—Chapter 15

Developed Country A country whose income per person is high by world standards and that enjoys the higher standard of living that wealth makes possible.—Chapter 15

Discipline Activities designed to reinforce desired performance (positive discipline) or to correct undesired performance (negative discipline).—Chapter 3

Discrepancy Report A daily comparison between the status of rooms as listed by the PMS at the front office, and the status of rooms as listed by the housekeeping department.—Chapter 12

Displace (Revenue) To substitute one source of revenue for another.—Chapter 6

Distribution Channel A distinct and definable source of hotel rooms or services sales. For example, the Internet is one distribution channel, and meeting planners are another.—Chapter 6

DOSM Short for "director of sales and marketing." Variations include DOS (director of sales) and DOM (director of marketing).—Chapter 7

Downsizing Reducing the number of employees and/or labor hours for cost-containment purposes.—Chapter 1

Drop-In A potential buyer (guest) who arrives at the hotel without an appointment.—Chapter 7

Duct A passageway, usually built of sheet metal, that allows fresh, cold, or warm air to be directed to various parts of a building.—Chapter 11

Early Out A clause in a franchise agreement that grants both the franchisor and the franchise the right, with proper notification, to terminate the agreement after it has been in effect for a relatively short period of time. When this clause exists, a window may be granted after only one, two, or three years.—Chapter 13

Economics The social science associated with the making, marketing, and consumption of goods and services and how the forces of supply and demand allocate scarce resources.—Chapter 6

E-distribution Channel Technically, any source of reservation delivered to the hotel electronically. Most commonly, however, the term is used to identify those distribution channels that utilize the Internet when communicating with the hotel.—Chapter 6

EI (Educational Institute of the AH&LA) The shortened version of the name given to the Educational Institute of the American Hotel and Lodging Association (AH&LA). Located in Orlando, Florida, and Lansing, Michigan, EI is the professional development and certification subsidiary of the AH&LA.—Chapter 2

Electric Discharge Lamp A lamp in which light is generated by passing electrical current through a space filled with a special combination of gases. Examples include fluorescent, mercury vapor, metal halide, and sodium.—Chapter 11

Embezzlement The theft of a company's financial assets by an employee.—Chapter 12

Emergency Plan A document describing a hotel's predetermined, intended response to a safety/security threat encountered by the hotel.—Chapter 12

Employee Handbook Written policies and procedures related to employment at a hotel. Sometimes called an employee "manual."—Chapter 4

Employment Agreement A document specifying the terms of the work relationship between the employer and employee that indicates the rights and obligations of both parties.—Chapter 4

Empowerment The act of granting authority to employees to make key decisions within the employees' areas of responsibility.—Chapter 3

Empty Nesters Middle-aged persons whose children are grown and have left the home.—Chapter 15

Energy Management Specific policies and engineering, maintenance, and facility design activities intended to control and reduce energy usage.—Chapter 11

Engineering Designing and operating a building to ensure a safe and comfortable atmosphere.—Chapter 11

Entrepreneur A person who assumes the risk of owning and operating a business in exchange for the financial rewards the business may produce.—Chapter 14

Equity The value of an asset beyond the total amount owed on it for mortgages and other loans.—Chapter 14

Ethics Standards used to judge the "right" and "wrong" (or fairness) of one's actions when dealing with others.—Chapter 3

European Plan (EP) A room rate that does not include guest meals.—Chapter 6

E-Wholesaler A room reseller that obtains reduced (wholesale) room prices and inventory commitments directly from a hotel or through an agreement with the hotel's corporate brand managers and then publishes "retail rate" on its Web sites, usually at a markup of 20–40%. Examples include Travelocity, Hotels.com, Travel-Web and Expedia.—Chapter 6

Exchange Rate The rate at which money of one country is traded (exchanged) for money of another country.—Chapter 15

Executive Housekeeper The individual responsible for the management and operation of the housekeeping department.—Chapter 9

Executive Operating Committee (EOC) Those members of the hotel's management team (generally department heads) responsible for departmental leadership and overall property administration.—Chapter 2

Expatriate A citizen of one country who is employed in another country.—Chapter 15

Expenses The amount of money spent to generate revenues.—Chapter 10

External Audit An independent verification of financial records performed by accountants who are not employed by the organization operating the hotel.—Chapter 5

External Recruiting Tactics designed to attract persons who are not current hotel employees for vacant positions.—Chapter 4

F&B Shortened term for "food and beverage." Used, for example, as in the following "Please let the F&B director know about the changes the guest has requested."—Chapter 10

Fade (Rate) A reduced rate authorized for use when a guest seeking a reservation exhibits price (rate) resistance. Sometimes called "flex" rate.—Chapter 6

Fair Market Value   The price that a reasonable buyer would pay and a reasonable seller would accept, for a specific hotel property. Hotels may be sold at, above, or below their fair market value.—Chapter 14

Feasibility Study   A determination that a proposed hotel development will (or will not) meet the expectations of its investors. The study should include the estimated market demand for the property, as well as its economic viability.—Chapter 14

Federal Trade Commission (FTC)   The FTC enforces federal antitrust and consumer protection laws. It also seeks to ensure that the nation's business markets function competitively and are free of undue restrictions caused by acts or practices that are unfair or deceptive.—Chapter 13

FF&E   The term used to refer to the furniture, fixtures, and equipment used by a hotel to service its guests.—Chapter 2

FF&E Reserve   Funds set aside today for the future furniture, fixture, and equipment replacement needs of a hotel.—Chapter 11

Field   A data entry location in a PMS. For example, the reservation screen on a PMS will contain a "field" for the guest's name and another "field" for the guest's telephone number (along with many other fields). Data for these fields are typically entered at the time the reservation is made and may be modified at the time of guest registration. Fields are sometimes referred to as "Data Fields."—Chapter 8

Fiduciary   A relationship built upon trust and the responsibility to act in the best interest of another when performing tasks.—Chapter 6

First Tier   Management companies that operate hotels for owners using the management company's trade name as the hotel brand. Hyatt, Hilton, and Sheraton are examples.—Chapter 13

Fixed Charges   Those expenses incurred in the purchase and occupation of the hotel itself. These include rent, property taxes, insurance, interest, and depreciation and amortization.—Chapter 5

Fixed Labor Costs   The minimum number of labor hours and associated labor costs that are required to operate the food service operation whenever it is open regardless of the number, if any, of guests who are served.—Chapter 10

Flag   A term used to refer to the specific brand with which a hotel may affiliate. Examples of currently popular flags include brands such as Comfort Inns, Holiday Inn Express, Ramada Inns, Hampton Inns, Residence Inns, Best Western, and Hawthorn Suites. The hotels affiliated with a specific flag are sometimes referred to as a chain.—Chapter 13

FOC (Franchise Offering Circular)   A franchise disclosure document that is prepared by a franchisor and then is registered and filed with the state governmental agency responsible for administering franchise relationships in that state.—Chapter 13

Folio   The detailed list of a hotel guest's room charges, as well as other charges authorized by the guest or legally imposed by the hotel.—Chapter 8

FOM   Short for front-office manager.—Chapter 8

Food and Beverage Director   The individual responsible for the operation of a hotel's F&B program(s).—Chapter 10

Foot-Candle   A measure of illumination. One foot-candle equals one lumen per square foot. (The European counterpart of the foot-candle is the Lux, a light intensity of one lumen per square meter.)—Chapter 11

Foreclose   The process in which a lender terminates the borrower's interest in a property after a loan is defaulted.—Chapter 14

Foreseeable (Legal Concept)   The concept that the liability of a party should be limited to acts that a reasonable person would be able to predict or expect as the results of his or her actions.—Chapter 12

Franchise   An arrangement whereby one party (the brand) allows another (the hotel owners) to use its logo, name, systems, and resources in exchange for a fee.—Chapter 13

Franchise Agreement   The legal contract between the hotel's owners (the franchisee) and the brand managers (the franchisor) that describes the duties and responsibilities of each in the franchise relationship.—Chapter 13

Franchisee   Those who own the hotel and buy the right to use the brand name for a fixed period of time and at an agreed-upon price.—Chapter 1

Franchisor   Those who manage the brand and sell the right to use the brand name.—Chapter 1

Fraud   Purposeful deception (deceit) that results in legal injury to a person.—Chapter 12

Free-to-Guests   A service provided at no additional charge (beyond normal room rental charges) to the hotel guest. Examples could include making local telephone calls, access to premium cable television channels such as HBO or Showtime, and use of the hotel's pool or workout facilities. [Ultimately, the hotel must absorb the cost(s) of providing these services to guests, but guests are not charged on a per-usage basis. Therefore, the term does not mean that the services provided are free to the hotel.]—Chapter 2

Frequent Guest Program   A promotional effort administered by a hotel brand that rewards travelers each time they choose to stay at the spicfic brand's affiliated hotels. Typical rewards include free night stays, room upgrades, and complimentary hotel services.—Chapter 6

Front Desk   The area within the hotel used for guest registration and payment.—Chapter 1

Front Office   The department within the hotel responsible for guest reservations, registration, service, and payment.—Chapter 8

Front-Office Accounting   The process of summarizing and reporting financial transactions at the front desk.—Chapter 5

FSD (Franchise Services Director)   The representative of a franchise hotel brand who interacts directly with the franchised hotels' GMs.—Chapter 13

Full-Service Hotel   A lodging property that offers complete food and beverage products and services.—Chapter 1

Function Room   Public space such as meeting rooms, conference areas, and ballrooms that can frequently be subdivided into smaller spaces and that are available in the hotel for banquet, meeting, or other group rental purposes.—Chapter 10

Generally Accepted Accounting Principles (GAAPs)   Standards and procedures that have been adopted by those responsible for preparing business financial statements for the purpose of ensuing uniformity.—Chapter 5

General Manager (GM)   The traditional title used to identify the individual at a hotel property who is responsible for final decision making regarding property-specific operating policies and procedures. Also the leader of the hotel's management team.—Chapter 2

Global Distribution System (GDS)   Referred to as the GDS for short, this system connects those travel professionals worldwide who reserve rooms with hotels offering rooms for sale.—Chapter 8

Globalization   The condition in which countries and communities within them throughout the world are becoming increasingly interrelated.—Chapter 1

GOP   Short for gross operating profit. This popular term is taken from a pre-1990 version of the Uniform System of Accounts for Hotels (USAH) published by the New York Hotel Association. It refers to hotel revenue less those expenses typically controlled at the property level. It is generally expressed on the income statement and in the industry as both a dollar figure and percent of total revenue.—Chapter 5

GoPar   Short for "gross operating profit per available room." Using the Uniform System of Accounts for Hotels, it is computed as: Total Revenue − (Direct Operating Expense + Indirect Operating Expense) ÷ Total Rooms Available to Be Sold. GoPar considers the "cost" of selling rooms (not simply the total revenue achieved) when evaluating sales effectiveness.—Chapter 6

Grand Opening   An event held at a hotel that marks the "official" opening of that hotel. It can be held several days or even weeks after the hotel actually opens and is intended to market the hotel to its client base and the local community.—Chapter 14

Green Hotels   Lodging properties that use programs to conserve water and energy and to reduce solid waste in efforts to preserve the environment and conserve its resources.—Chapter 11

Group Contract   A legal document used to summarize the agreement between a hotel and its group client.—Chapter 7

Group Sale   A large sale (in number of rooms or dollar volume) of the hotel's rooms or services. The sales and marketing department, not the front desk, books sales of this type.—Chapter 7

Guarantee   A contractual agreement about the number of meals to be provided at a banquet event. Typically, a guarantee must be made several days in advance of the event. At that time, the entity contracting with the hotel for the event agrees to pay for the larger of the actual number of guests served or the number of guests guaranteed.—Chapter 10

Guest   A hotel visitor. Most guests rent rooms and/or purchase food or beverages in a hotel outlet or a banquet function.—Chapter 1

Guest Check Average   The average amount spent by a guest in a room service or dining room order. The guest check average typically includes the food and alcoholic beverage sales. Guest Check Average = Total Revenue ÷ Total Number of Guests Served.—Chapter 10

Guest Service Agent   An employee working in the front-desk area of the hotel. Also referred to by some in the industry as a "desk clerk."—Chapter 2

Half-Day Rate   A special rate that typically includes 1–4 hours (but not overnight) use of a room.—Chapter 6

HR   Short for human resources.—Chapter 4

Head Table   Special seating at a banquet reserved for guests of honor.—Chapter 10

Headquarters Hotel   The hotel that hosts the main group of attendees during an event in which there are multiple host hotels.—Chapter 7

Horizontal Communication   Communication between individuals at the same organizational level.—Chapter 3

Hospitality Suite   A guest room usually rented by a vendor during conventions/conferences to provide complimentary food and/or beverages to invited guests.—Chapter 10

Hosted Bar   A beverage service alternative in which the host of a function pays for beverages during all or part of the banquet event; also called an "open" bar.—Chapter 10

Hosted Events   Functions served by a hotel, which are complimentary to invited guests because costs are borne by the event's sponsor.—Chapter 10

Hostel   Inexpensive accommodations, typically dormitory style with shared bathroom facilities, that are popular with young travelers.—Chapter 1

Hotel Brand   The name of a hotel chain; sometimes referred to as a "flag."—Chapter 1

Hotel Chain   A group of hotels with the same brand name.—Chapter 1

Hotel Group   An organization that owns or franchises groups of hotels that are of different brands.—Chapter 1

Hoteliers   Those who work in the hotel business.—Chapter 1

Hot Spot   A Wi-Fi area that allows for high-speed wireless Internet access or other data transmission.—Chapter 8

House Brand Beverages   Alcoholic beverages that are sold by type (scotch, gin, and so forth) rather than by brand name and that are served when a call brand beverage is not requested. Sometimes referred to as "Well" brands.—Chapter 10

House Count   An estimate of the number of guests staying in a hotel on a given day.—Chapter 5

House Person   The individual responsible for the cleaning of public spaces (the house). Sometimes referred to as a PA (public area) cleaner or porter.—Chapter 9

House Phone   A publicly located telephone within the hotel used to call the front desk, or in some cases, the front desk and guest rooms.—Chapter 8

HR   Short for human resources; for example, "When is HR going to distribute the results of the turnover study?"—Chapter 4

Human Relations   Skills needed to understand and effectively interact with other people.—Chapter 3

HVAC   A shorthand term for "heating, ventilating, and air conditioning."—Chapter 11

Impact Study   An in-depth evaluation of the effect on occupancy percent and ADR that a new hotel in a given market will have on an existing hotel(s) in that same market.—Chapter 13

Incandescent Lamp   A lamp in which a filament inside the lamp's bulb is heated by electrical current to produce light.—Chapter 11

Incident Report   A document prepared to record the details of an accident, injury, or disturbance, and the hotel's response to it.—Chapter 12

Indemnification   To reimburse someone for a loss that has been incurred.—Chapter 11

Induction   The process of providing specific information about a department that must be known by all employees in the department.—Chapter 4

Inspector   The individual(s) responsible for physically checking the room status of guest rooms, as well as other tasks as assigned by the executive housekeeper.—Chapter 9

Inflation   The economic condition that exists when selling prices increase throughout the economy of a country.—Chapter 15

Institutional (Noncommercial) Food Service Operation   Those food services provided by health care, educational, military, religious, and numerous other organizations whose primary reason for existence is not to generate a profit from the sale of food/beverage products but rather to support another organizational purpose.—Chapter 10

Interfaced   The term used to describe the process in which one data-generating system shares its data electronically with another system.—Chapter 8

Internal Alarms   A warning system that notifies an area within the hotel if the alarm is activated.—Chapter 12

Internal Audit   An independent verification of financial records performed by members of the organization operating the hotel.—Chapter 5

Internal Recruiting   Tactics to identify and attract currently employed staff members for job vacancies that represent promotions or lateral transfers to similar positions.—Chapter 4

Interstate Commerce   The commercial trading or transportation of people or property that occurs between and/or among states.—Chapter 4

Inventory (Rooms)   Rooms of all types that are available to be sold by the hotel.—Chapter 6

Jargon   Special terms or phrases used by persons in a profession.—Chapter 15

Job Description   A list of tasks that an employee working in a specific position must be able to effectively perform.—Chapter 4

Job Specification   A list of the personal qualities judged necessary for successful performance of the tasks required by the job description.—Chapter 4

Judgment   A court's decision about a matter that has been presented to it.—Chapter 12

Keycards   The electromagnetic cards used in a recodable locking system.—Chapter 8

Laundry Par Levels   The amount of laundry in use, in process, and in storage.—Chapter 9

Law of Demand   The concept of ecomonics that recognizes, when supply is held constant, an increase in demand results in an increase in selling price. Conversely, with supply held constant, a decrease in demand leads to a decreased selling price.—Chapter 6

Law of Supply   The concept of economics that recognizes, when demand is held constant, an increase in supply leads to a decreased selling price. Conversely, with demand held constant, a decrease in supply leads to an increased selling price.—Chapter 6

Laypersons   Persons who are professionals in or very knowledgeable about a specific subject such as hotel management.—Chapter 15

Lead   Information about a prospect who is likely to buy from the hotel.—Chapter 7

Length of Stay (LOS)   The number of nights a hotel's individual guests use their rooms. LOS is computed on a per-stay basis. For example, in a hotel that sold 300 group room nights to 100 guests, the LOS would be 3: Room nights sold ÷ Rooms sold to guests = LOS.—Chapter 6

Leverage   The use of borrowed funds to increase purchasing power.—Chapter 14

Liable   Legally bound to compensate for loss or injury.—Chapter 12

Limited-Service Hotel   A lodging property that offers no or very limited food services; sometimes a complimentary breakfast is served, but there is no table service restaurant.—Chapter 1

Line Departments   Hotel divisions that are in the "chain of command" and are directly responsible for revenues (such as front office and food and beverage) or for property operations (such as housekeeping and the engineering and maintenance departments).—Chapter 1

Line-Level   Those employees whose jobs are considered entry level or nonsupervisory. These are typically positions where the employee is paid an hourly (rather than salary) compensation. Examples include positions such as guest service agents, room attendants, and food and beverage servers.—Chapter 2

Linen   A generic term for the guest room sheets and pillowcases and tablecloths and napkins washed and dried in the laundry area.—Chapter 9

Link   A relationship between two Web sites. When Web site users select a link at one site, they are taken to another Web site address. An external link leads to a Web page other than the current one; an internal link leads elsewhere on the current page.—Chapter 7

Liquidated Damage Fees   Money charged to a franchisee that elects to terminate the franchise agreement prior to its contractual expiration date.—Chapter 13

Lowest Rate Guarantee   A program that assures travelers the lowest rate for a specific room type on a specific date will be found on the guarantor's Web site.—Chapter 6

Maintenance   The activities required to keep a building and its contents in good repair.—Chapter 11

Management   The process of planning, organizing, staffing, directing, controlling, and evaluating human, financial, and physical resources for the purpose of achieving organizational goals.—Chapter 2

Management Company   An organization that operates a hotel(s) for a fee; sometimes called a "contract company."—Chapter 1

Management Contract   An agreement between a hotel's owners and a hotel management company under which, for a fee, the management company operates the hotel. Sometimes known as a management agreement.—Chapter 13

Marketing Plan   A calendar of specific activities designed to meet the hotel's sales goals.—Chapter 7

Market Segmentation   Efforts to focus on a highly defined (smaller) group of travelers.—Chapter 1

Market Share   The percentage of the total market (typically in dollars spent) captured by a property.—Chapter 1

Market Value   The estimated worth of a hotel. Hotels may be purchased below, at, or above market value.—Chapter 14

Material Safety Data Sheet (MSDS)   A written statement describing the potential hazards of, and best ways to handle, a chemical or toxic substance. An MSDS is provided by the manufacturer of the chemical or toxic substance to the buyer of the product and must be posted and made available in a place where it is easily accessible to those who will actually use the product.—Chapter 12

Mentor   A senior employee of a hotel who provides advice and counsel to less experienced staff members about matters relating to the job, organization, and profession.—Chapter 1

Merchant Model   An Internet sales method in which hotels sell rooms to Internet site operators. These sites, in turn, allow consumers to enter requested location and arrival dates and are presented with a choice of specific hotels and associated rates available for immediate purchase on the site.—Chapter 6

Minibars   Small, in-guest room refrigerated or unrefrigerated cabinets used to store beverages, snacks, and other items the hotel wishes to offer for sale to guests.—Chapter 8

Minimum Wage   The lowest amount of compensation that an employer may pay to an employee covered by the FLSA or applicable state law. Minimum wage provisions cover most hotel employees; however, exceptions can include youthful employees being paid a training wage for the first 90 days of employment and some tipped employees.—Chapter 4

Minutes per Room   The average number of minutes required to clean a guest room determined by the following computation: total number of minutes worked by room attendants ÷ total number of guest rooms cleaned = minutes per room.—Chapter 9

MLOS "Minimum length of stay." In this situation, the hotel declines reservations for guests seeking to stay for fewer days than the minimum established by the hotel.—Chapter 6

MOD Manager on duty. The individual on the hotel property responsible for making any management decisions required during the period he or she is the ranking manager at the property.—Chapter 12

Modified American Plan (MAP) A special rate that includes a specifically identified guest meal (typically one per day, often breakfast).—Chapter 6

Moments of Truth Any time that a guest has an opportunity to form an impression about the hotel. Moments of truth can be positive or negative.—Chapter 1

Mortgage A legal document that specifies an amount of money a lender will lend for the purchase of a real estate asset (hotel), as well as the terms for the loan's repayment.—Chapter 14

Motivation An inner drive that a person has to attain a goal.—Chapter 3

Multiplier Effort The resulting financial ripple that occurs within a local economy when money is spent and respent and creates income for additional persons who, in turn, spend the money in the local economy.—Chapter 15

National Culture The values/attitudes shared by citizens of a specific country that impact behavior and shape beliefs about what is important.—Chapter 15

Negotiated Rate A special room rate offered for a fixed period of time to a specific hotel client.—Chapter 6

Negotiated Rate Agreement A document that details the specific contractual obligations of a hotel and client when the hotel has offered, and the client has agreed to, a negotiated rate. Typical agreement content includes start date, room rate to be charged, agreement duration, and blackout dates (if any). The agreement should be signed by a representative of the hotel and the client.—Chapter 6

Net ADR Yield The rate (ADR) actually received by a hotel after subtracting the cost of the fees and assessments associated with a room sale. The formula for Net ADR Yield is: Room Rate − Reservation Generation Fees ÷ Room Rate Paid = Net ADR Yield. Typical reservation related fees include those charged by travel agents, the GDS, a hotel's CRS, and the operators of Internet booking sites.—Chapter 6

Networking The development of personal relationships for a business-related purpose. For example, a chamber of commerce–sponsored breakfast open to all community business leaders interested in improving local traffic conditions would be an excellent example of a networking opportunity for a member of a hotel's sales team.—Chapter 7

Night Audit The process of reviewing for accuracy and completeness the accounting transactions from one day to conclude or "close" that day's sales information in preparation for posting the transactions of the next day.—Chapter 8

Night Auditor The individual who performs the daily review of guest transactions recorded by the front office.—Chapter 8

Nonguaranteed Reservation A room reservation for which guests do not provide payment at the time the reservation is made.—Chapter 8

Nonprogrammed Decisions Decisions that occur infrequently and require creative and unique decision-making abilities.—Chapter 3

No-Show A guest who makes a confirmed room reservation but fails to cancel the reservation or arrive at the hotel on the date of the confirmed reservation.—Chapter 5

Occupancy Index A ratio measure computed as: Occupancy Rate of a selected hotel ÷ Occupancy rate of that hotel's competitive set = Occupancy Index.—Chapter 6

Occupancy Rate   The ratio of guest rooms sold (including comps) to guest rooms available for sale in a given time period. Always expressed as a percentage, the formula for occupancy rate is: Total Rooms Sold ÷ Total Rooms Available = Occupancy Percent (%).—Chapter 1

Occupancy Tax   Money paid by a hotel to a local taxing authority. The room revenue generated by the hotel determines the amount paid. This tax is also known in some areas as the "bed" tax. For example, "In our city, the occupancy tax is 2 percent."—Chapter 13

On-the-Job Training (OJT)   Learning activities designed to enhance the skills of current employees. OJT programs are typically offered by management with the intent of improving guest service and employee performance at the hotel. There is generally no charge to the employee for the training.—Chapter 2

Opaque Model   An Internet sales method in which consumers "bid" an amount they are willing to pay for a room on a specific arrival date and the third party Web-site operator matches that bid with a hotel willing to sell a room(s) at that rate.—Chapter 6

OPL   Short for "on premise laundry."—Chapter 9

Opt Out (E-Mail)   To make e-mails stop by expressing the desire that unsolicited e-mails are unwelcome e-mails.—Chapter 7

Orientation   The process of providing basic information about the hotel that must be known by all of its employees.—Chapter 4

OSHA   Occupational Safety and Health Administration. A federal agency established in 1970 that is responsible for developing and enforcing regulations related to assuring safe and healthful working conditions.—Chapter 12

Other Revenue   Revenue derived from the sale of hotel products and services that are not classified as rooms, food, or beverages.—Chapter 6

Over   A situation in which cashiers have more money in their cash drawer than the official sales records indicate. Thus, a cashier with $10 more in the cash drawer than the sales record indicates is said to be $10 "over."—Chapter 5

Overbooking   A situation in which the hotel has more guest reservations for rooms than it has rooms available to lodge those guests. Sometimes referred to as "oversold."—Chapter 6

Overbuilt   The condition that exists when there are too many hotel guest rooms available for the number of travelers wanting to rent them.—Chapter 1

Overtime   The number of hours of work after which an employee must receive a premium pay rate. This premium rate is generally one and one-half times the basic hourly rate.—Chapter 4

Pace Report   A document summarizing confirmed (group) sales made by the sales and marketing department.—Chapter 7

P&L   Short for the profit and loss statement; also a synonym for the income and expense statement. The P&L records total hotel revenues and expenses for a specific time period.—Chapter 5

Package   A group of hospitality services (such as hotel rooms, meals, and airfare) sold for one price. For example, a Valentine's Day getaway package to Las Vegas offered by a travel agent might include airfare, lodging, meals, and show tickets for two people at one inclusive price.—Chapter 7

Payback Analysis   A financial analysis model that involves comparing annual cash flow savings of alternatives to determine whether the payback period is equal to or less than that allowed for project approval.—Chapter 11

PBX   The system within the hotel used to process incoming, internal, and outgoing telephone calls.—Chapter 8

Per Key   A term used to describe the cost of a hotel acquisition based on the number of rooms (keys) purchased. Its value comes in allowing comparison between hotels of unequal size (number of rooms). It is computed as: Total Hotel Cost ÷ Number of Units (rooms) in the hotel = Cost Per Key.—Chapter 14

Pickup   The actual number of rooms used by a client in a defined time period. As in "What was Travelsavers' pickup last year?"—Chapter 7

Pilferage   Petty theft of small, less than full package (case) amounts from inventory.—Chapter 12

PIP (Product Improvement Plan)   A document detailing the property upgrades and replacements that will be required if a hotel is to be accepted as one of a specific brand's franchised properties. Used, for example, in "We estimate the PIP on the property to be $4,000,000 if we decide to go with that brand."—Chapter 13

PM (Preventive Maintenance) Program   A specific inspection and activities schedule designed to minimize maintenance-related costs and to prolong the life of equipment by preventing small problems before they become larger ones.—Chapter 11

PM Checklist   A tool developed to list all of the critical areas that should be inspected during a PM review of a room, area, or piece of equipment.—Chapter 11

PMS   Short for "property management system." This term refers to the computerized system used by the hotel to manage its rooms revenue, room rates, room assignments, and reservations, as well as other selected guest service functions.—Chapter 5

Point of Sale (POS)   A location, including the front desk, at which hotel goods and services are purchased. In many hotels, the POS is interfaced with the PMS.—Chapter 8

Point of Sale (POS) Terminal   A computer system that contains its own input and output components and, perhaps, some memory capacity but without a central processing unit.—Chapter 10

POM   Short for "property operation and maintenance." The term is taken from the Uniform System of Accounts for Hotels and refers to the segment of the income statement that details the costs of operating the engineering and maintenance department.—Chapter 11

Post   To enter a guest's charges into the PMS, thus creating a permanent record of the sale; as in "Please post this meeting room charge to Mr. Walker's folio."—Chapter 8

Premium Brand Beverages   The highest-priced and highest-quality beverages generally available. Examples include Johnny Walker Black Scotch and Bombay Sapphire Gin; these brands are sometimes referred to as "Super Call" brands.—Chapter 10

Prepaid Expenses   Expenditures made for items prior to the accounting period in which the item's actual expense is incurred.—Chapter 5

Prepaid Reservation   A room reservation for which guests, prior to their arrival, provide payment for their rooms. Sometimes referred to as an "advanced depart" reservation.—Chapter 8

Product Usage Report   A report detailing the amount of an inventoried item used by a hotel in a specified time period (for example, week, month, quarter, year).—Chapter 9

Profitability   Revenue - Expenses = Profit. How a GM assigns (allocates) revenues and expenses to a department will dictate, in great measure, profit levels in that department.—Chapter 10

Programmed Decisions   Routine or repetitive decisions that can be made after considering policies, procedures, or rules.—Chapter 3

Progressive Discipline   A process of negative discipline in which repeated infractions result in an increasingly severe penalty.—Chapter 3

Prospect   An individual or group who, while not currently using the hotel, are considered potential clients with a good likelihood of using the hotel in the future.—Chapter 7

Public Space   Those areas within the hotel that can be freely accessed by guests and visitors. Examples include lobby areas, public restrooms, corridors, and stairwells.—Chapter 9

Punitive Damages   This monetary amount is assessed to punish liable parties and to serve as an example to the liable party as well as others not to commit the wrongful act in the future.—Chapter 12

Quality   The consistent delivery of products and services according to expected standards.—Chapter 3

Quality Inspection Scores   Sometimes called quality assurance (QA) scores, these scores are the result of annual (or more frequent) inspections conducted by a franchise company to ensure that franchisor-mandated standards are being met by the franchisee. In some cases, management companies or the property itself may establish internal inspection systems as well. In general, however, it is the franchise company's quality inspection score that is used as a measure of the effectiveness of the GM, the hotel's management team, and the owner's financial commitment to the property.—Chapter 2

Quarter   A three-month period. Often used to summarize accounting data. Used, for example, in "What is our sales forecast for the first quarter of next year?"—Chapter 14

Rack Rate   The price at which a hotel sells its rooms when no discounts of any kind are offered to the guest. Often shortened to "rack."—Chapter 5

Rate (Corporate)   A special rate offered to individual business travelers.—Chapter 6

Rate (Government)   A special rate offered to the employees of local, state, or federal governments.—Chapter 6

Rate (Group)   A special rate offered to a hotel's large-volume guest room purchasers.—Chapter 6

Rate (Package)   A special rate that allows a guest to pay one price for all of the features and amenities included in the package.—Chapter 6

Rate (Seasonal)   An increase (or decrease) in rack rate based upon the dates when the room is rented. For example, a beach front hotel may have a seasonal rate offered in the summer with a lower "winter" rate offered in the off-season.—Chapter 6

Rate (Special Event)   A temporary increase in rack rate based upon a specific event such as a concert, sporting event, or holiday. Also sometimes known as "super" or "premium" rack. Examples include rates for rooms during Mardi Gras (New Orleans hoteliers) and on New Year's Eve (Manhattan and other hoteliers).—Chapter 6

Rate Resistance   Refusal to make a reservation because the quoted rate is perceived to be too high.—Chapter 6

Rate Type   A single (unique) rate for a specific type of room. Rate types are typically pre-programmed into a hotel's PMS.—Chapter 6

Reasonable Care   A legal concept identifying the amount of care a reasonably prudent person would exercise in a specific situation.—Chapter 12

Recodable Locking System   A hotel guest room locking system designed such that when guests insert their "key" (typically an electromagnetic card) into the guest room lock for the first time, the lock is immediately recoded, canceling entry authorization for the previous guest's key and therefore enhancing guest safety.—Chapter 8

Recourse The right to demand assets as payment for a loan. Loans can be full recourse, limited recourse, or nonrecourse.—Chapter 14

Reengineering Reorganizing hotel departments or work sections within departments.—Chapter 3

Reflag To change a hotel from one franchise brand to another (see Conversion). Used, for example, in "We can buy the property, reflag it, and reposition it in the upper-scale transient market."—Chapter 14

Refurbishment A process that involves the major cleaning and redecoration of hotel areas.—Chapter 11

Registration (reg) Card A document that provides details such as guest's name, arrival date, rate to be paid, departure date, and other information related to the guest's stay.—Chapter 8

Remote Printer A unit in the kitchen preparation area that receives and prints orders entered through a point-of-sale terminal located in the dining room, room service order taker's workstation, or other area.—Chapter 10

Renovation The process of making repairs that brings a building to a good condition.—Chapter 11

Repeat Business Revenues generated from guests returning to a commercial operation such as a hotel as a result of positive experiences on previous visits.—Chapter 10

Replace as Needed (Maintenance Program) A parts' or equipment replacement plan that delays installing a new, substitute part until the original part fails or is in near failure. For example, most chief engineers would use a "replace as needed" plan for the maintenance of refrigeration compressors.—Chapter 11

Request for Proposal (RFP) A document sent to a vendor requesting that a price be submitted to provide applicable products/services. The document typically lists specifications and conditions/agreement terms proposed for the purchase; often abbreviated "RFP."—Chapter 7

Reservations Agent A front-office employee whose job consists primarily of taking and entering individual and group reservations into the hotel's property management system (PMS).—Chapter 8

Resident Manager The manager in a large hotel who is directly responsible to the GM for the property's operating departments that include food and beverage, purchasing, engineering and maintenance, front office, and security.—Chapter 1

Resources Something of value to the organization. Typical resources include money, labor, time, equipment, food and beverage products, supplies, energy, and methodologies (procedures).—Chapter 10

Restaurant Row A term used to describe an area with numerous competing restaurants in a very short (often walking) distance from each other. In some locations, especially tourist destinations, municipal parking lots accommodate the vehicles of persons who visit these areas for dining and entertainment.—Chapter 10

Restoration Returning a hotel to its original (or better than original) condition.—Chapter 11

Retention (Employee) The use of organizational and supervisory policies and procedures designed to encourage employees to remain with the property rather than to leave it.—Chapter 4

Revenue Money the hotel collects from guests for the use of rooms or from the purchase of hotel goods and services.—Chapter 1

Revenue Center   A hotel department that generates revenue. Two examples are the front-office and food and beverage departments.—Chapter 1

RevPar   Short for "revenue per available room," the average sales revenue generated by each guest room during a given time period. The formula for RevPar is: Occupancy % (×) ADR = RevPar.—Chapter 6

RevPar Index   A ratio measure computed as: RevPar of a selected hotel ÷ RevPar of that hotel's competitive set = RevPar Index.—Chapter 6

RFP   Short for "request for proposal."—Chapter 7

ROI   Short for "return on investment." The percentage rate of return achieved on the money invested in a hotel property.—Chapter 3

Role-Play   A training activity that allows trainees to practice a skill by interacting with each other in simulated roles such as pretending that one trainee is a guest and the other is an employee interacting with the guest.—Chapter 4

Room Attendant's Cart   A wheeled cart that contains all of the items needed to properly and safely clean and restock a guest room.—Chapter 9

Room Attendants   The individual(s) responsible for cleaning guest rooms. Sometimes referred to as "housekeepers."—Chapter 9

Room Mix   The ratio of room types contained in a hotel. For example, the number of double-bedded rooms compared with king-bedded rooms, the number of smoking permitted rooms to no smoking permitted rooms, and the number of suites compared with standard rooms.—Chapter 6

Room Service   Food and beverage services served to guests in their sleeping rooms.—Chapter 1

Room Status   The up-to-date (actual) condition (occupied, vacant, dirty, and so on) of the hotel's individual guest rooms.—Chapter 9

Room Type   The term used to designate specific configurations of guest rooms. For example, smoking versus nonsmoking, king bed versus double beds, or suite versus regular sleeping room. Commonly abbreviated (for example, K for King, NS for Nonsmoking, and so forth), the hotel's holding of the proper room type is often as important to guests as whether the hotel, in fact, has a room for them.—Chapter 8

Rooms Division Manager   An individual in a hotel responsible for the management of both the front-office and the housekeeping departments. (This position does not exist in every hotel.)—Chapter 7

Room Rate Economics   The processes by which revenue managers price rooms while considering how consumers may react to the pricing strategies that are used.—Chapter 6

Safety   Protection of an individual's physical well-being and health.—Chapter 12

Safety and Security Committee   An interdepartmental task force consisting of the GM, other hotel managers, supervisors and hourly employees charged with the responsibility of monitoring and refining a hotel's safety and security efforts.—Chapter 12

Salary   Pay calculated on a weekly, monthly, or annual basis rather than at an hourly rate.—Chapter 4

Sales and Marketing Committee   The group of individuals responsible for coordinating the hotel's sales and marketing effort.—Chapter 7

Sales Call   A meeting arranged for the purpose of selling the hotel's products and services.—Chapter 7

Sarbanes-Oxley Act   Technically known as the Public Company Accounting Reform and Investor Protection Act, this law provides criminal penalties for those found to have committed accounting fraud. In addition, this law covers a wide range of corporate governance issues including the regulation of auditors.—Chapter 5

SBA Short for the United States Small Business Administration. Established in 1953, the SBA provides financial, technical, and management assistance to help Americans start, run, and expand their businesses. The SBA is the nation's largest single financial backer of small businesses.—Chapter 14

Search Engine A Web site specifically designed for the purpose of directing its visitors to other Web sites.—Chapter 6

Seasonal Hotel A hotel whose revenue and expenditures vary greatly depending on the time (season) of the year the hotel is operating. Examples include hotels near ski resorts, beaches, theme parks, some tourist areas, sporting venues, and the like.—Chapter 5

Second Tier Management companies that operate hotels for owners who have entered into an agreement to use one of a franchisor's flags as the hotel brand. American General Hospitality, Summit Hotel Management, and Winegardner and Hammons, Inc., are examples.—Chapter 13

Security Protection of an individual or business's property or assets.—Chapter 12

Selection The process of evaluating job applicants to determine those more qualified (or potentially qualified) for vacant positions.—Chapter 4

Sell-Out (1) A situation in which all rooms are sold or oversold. A hotel, area, or entire city may, if demand is strong enough, sell-out. (2) A period of time in which management attempts to maximize ADR.—Chapter 8

Service (Food and Beverage) The process of moving food and beverage products from service staff to the guests.—Chapter 10

Service (Quality) The process of helping guests by addressing their wants and needs with respect and dignity in a timely manner.—Chapter 3

Service Charges A mandatory amount added to a guest's bill for services performed by a hotel staff member(s).—Chapter 10

Serving The process of moving food and beverage products from production personnel (cooks and bartenders) to food and beverage servers who will serve them to guests.—Chapter 10

Short A situation in which cashiers have less money in their cash drawer than the official sales records indicate. Thus, a cashier with $10 less in the cash drawer than the sales record indicates is said to be $10 "short."—Chapter 5

Sign-In/Sign-Out Program An arrangement in which individuals taking responsibility for hotel assets (such as hand tools, power equipment, or keys to secured areas) must document their responsibility by placing their signature as well as the date and time on a form developed to identify responsibility for lost possession.—Chapter 12

Site Tour A physical trip (tour) around the hotel, usually hosted by a sales and marketing staff member, for the purpose of introducing potential clients and other interested parties to the hotel's features.—Chapter 7

Smart Card Payment cards in which user information such as demographics, purchase history, and product preferences are contained within a computerized "chip" imbedded in the card.—Chapter 8

SMERF Short for social, military, educational, religious, or fraternal organizations as in "We should assign Vernon to work the SMERF market next year because he has extensive contacts with these groups."—Chapter 7

Solvency The ability of a hotel to pay its debts as they come due.—Chapter 5

Source Reduction The effort by product manufacturers to design and ship products so as to minimize waste resulting from the product's shipping and delivery to a hotel.—Chapter 11

Span of Control The number of people one supervisor can effectively manage.—Chapter 3

Staff Departments Hotel divisions that provide technical, supportive assistance to line departments. Examples include the purchasing, human resources, and accounting departments.—Chapter 1

STAR Report Short for the Smith Travel Accommodations Report. Produced by Smith Travel Research, this report is used to compare a hotel's sales results to those of its selected competitors.—Chapter 7

Stay-Over A guest who is not scheduled to check out of the hotel on the day his or her room status is assessed. That is, the guest will be staying at least one more day.—Chapter 6

Strategy A method or a plan developed to achieve a long-range goal.—Chapter 3

Suite This term generally refers to a guest room consisting of at least two physically separated rooms or, at the very least, a hotel room that is extra large when compared with the hotel's standard guest room.—Chapter 1

Supply The total amount of a good or service available for sale.—Chapter 6

Systemwide The term used to describe all hotels within a given brand. Used for example, in "Last year, the systemwide ADR for the brand was $115.20, with an occupancy rate of 63.7%."—Chapter 13

Tactic An action or method used to attain a short-term objective.—Chapter 3

Team A group of individuals who place the goals of the group above the individual goals of each team member.—Chapter 3

T&E Card Short for Travel and Entertainment card. A payment system by which the card issuer collects full payment from the card users each month. The card companies do not typically assess interest charges to consumers. Instead, they rely on fees collected from merchants accepting the cards. Examples of T&E cards are American Express (Amex) and Diners Club.—Chapter 8

Terry A generic term for the bath towels, hand towels, and washcloths washed and dried in the laundry area.—Chapter 9

Test Calls Calls made to a toll-free number or other reservation system to verify the accuracy of information about a specific hotel and/or about the quality of selling done by the reservation center's staff.—Chapter 8

Third-Party Liability A legal concept that holds the second party (the hotel serving alcohol) responsible for acts caused by the first party (the drinker), if the drinker subsequently causes harm to a third party (the victim of an accident).—Chapter 10

Third-Party Web Sites A Web site that is operated by an entity other than a hotel or a hotel's franchisor.—Chapter 6

Top-Down Selling A tactic to first sell the hotel's most expensive rooms.—Chapter 6

Total Replacement (Maintenance Program) A parts or equipment replacement plan that involves installing new or substitute parts based on a predetermined schedule. For example, most chief engineers would use a "total replacement" approach to the maintenance of lightbulbs in high-rise exterior highway signs.—Chapter 11

Tourism Industry All businesses that cater to the needs of the traveling public.—Chapter 1

Turnover Rate A measure of the proportion of a workforce that is replaced during a designated time period (for example, month, quarter, year). Computed as: Number of employees separated ÷ Number of employees in the workforce = Employee turnover rate.—Chapter 4

Trace System A methodical process used to record what has been done in the past and what must be done in the future to maximize sales effectiveness. An effective trace system includes a "contact management" component that allows records to be kept for each individual client (contact).—Chapter 7

Tracking Codes Guest types differentiated by traveler demographics. Typical tracking codes include those related to the travelers membership in a group (AAA or AARP), the purpose of the traveler's trip (such as business [corporate] versus leisure) and those related to length of stay (transient versus long-term). A tracking code can be created for any traveler demographic determined important enough to create and monitor a (reservation) field in the PMS.—Chapter 6

Transient Guests that are neither part of a group booking or tour group. Transient guests can be further subdivided by traveler demographic to gain more detailed information about the type of guest staying in the property.—Chapter 5

Transient Sales Rooms and services sold primarily through the efforts of the front office and its staff.—Chapter 8

Travel Agent A hospitality professional that assists clients in planning travel. Also known as TA.—Chapter 7

Travel Wholesaler An entity that purchases large numbers (blocks) of hotel rooms and, in turn, sells them to travel agents.—Chapter 6

Tricolumned Statement An income statement that lists (1) actual hotel operating results from a specific time period, as well as (2) budgeted operating estimates for the same time period, and finally (3) the actual operating results from the prior year's same time period.—Chapter 5

Unemployment Claim A claim made by an unemployed worker to the appropriate state agency asserting that the worker is eligible for unemployment benefits.—Chapter 4

Unemployment Insurance Funds provided by employers to make available temporary financial benefits to employees who have lost their jobs.—Chapter 4

Unemployment Rate The number, usually expressed as a percentage, of employable persons who are out of work and looking for jobs.—Chapter 4

Uniform System of Accounts for the Lodging Industry (USALI) A standard of accounting procedures used to record a hotel's financial transactions and condition.—Chapter 5

Unity of Command Each employee should report to/be accountable to only one boss for a specific activity.—Chapter 3

Upselling Tactics used to increase the hotel's average daily rate (ADR) by encouraging guests to rent higher-priced rooms with better or more amenities (view, complimentary breakfast and newspaper, and/or increased square footage) than those provided with lower-priced rooms.—Chapter 4

Upside Potential The possibility that, with the proper investment and management, a hotel will yield significant increases in real estate value and/or operational profitability.—Chapter 4

Valet Originally a term used to identify an individual who cared for the clothes of wealthy travelers; its most common usage now is in reference to those individuals responsible for parking guest vehicles.—Chapter 8

Vertical Communication Communication between individuals that flows up and down throughout the organization.—Chapter 3

Wage Pay calculated on an hourly basis.—Chapter 4

Walked A situation in which a guest with a reservation is relocated from the reserved hotel to another hotel because no room was available at the reserved hotel.—Chapter 6

Walk-In A guest seeking a room who arrives at the hotel without an advance reservation.—Chapter 8

"Warm Body Syndrome" (Employee Selection) The concept that proper employee selection procedures are deemphasized and, instead, the first applicant ("warm body") who applies is hired.—Chapter 4

Wi-Fi Slang for *Wi*reless *Fi*delity. A data delivery system that does not rely on wiring to provide users with a connection.—Chapter 8

Window A clause in a franchisee agreement that grants both the franchisor and the franchisee the right, with proper notification, to terminate the agreement after it has been in effect for a relatively short period of time.—Chapter 13

Word-of-Mouth Advertising Informal conversations between persons as they "discuss" their positive or negative experiences at a hotel.—Chapter 10

Work Order A form used to initiate and document a request for maintenance.—Chapter 11

Yield Management Demand forecasting systems designed to maximize revenue by holding rates high during times of high guest room demand and by decreasing room rates during times of lower guest room demand.—Chapter 6

YTD Short for "year to date." Used when comparing performance from the beginning of the year up through and including the present period.—Chapter 7

Zero Defects A goal of no guest-related complaints that is established when guest service processes are implemented.—Chapter 3

Zero Tolerance The total absence of behavior that is objectionable from the perspectives of discrimination or harassment. This is achieved by issuing appropriate policies, the conduct of applicable workshops, the development of procedures for employees alleging discrimination or harassment to obtain relief, and written protocols for reporting, investigating, and resolving incidences and grievances.—Chapter 4

Photo Credits

p. 1: Hawthorn Suites Las Vegas Strip. Courtesy of U.S. Franchise Systems, Inc.; p. 6: Kansas Industrial Development Commission; p. 10: AGE Fotostock America, Inc.; p. 13: Rough Guides Dorling Kindersley; p. 21: Getty Images Inc.—Stone Allstock; p. 27: Dorling Kindersley Media Library; p. 30: The Stock Connection; p. 37: Westin St. John, United States Virgin Islands, copyright Starwood Hotels & Resorts Worldwide, Inc. 2003; p. 41: Omni-Photo Communications, Inc.; p. 44: Dorling Kindersley Media Library; p. 49: Getty Images, Inc.—PhotoDisc; p. 53: PhotoEdit; p. 60: Sheraton Laguna Nusa Dua, Bali, Indonesia, copyright Starwood Hotels & Resorts Worldwide, Inc. 2003; p. 63: Michal Heron Photography; p. 67: Zaruba Photography; p. 79: PhotoEdit; p. 80: PhotoEdit; p. 83: PhotoEdit; p. 92: Radisson Lexington Hotel New York, East Side. Courtesy of Carlson Hospitality Worldwide; p. 102: PictureQuest; p. 107: PhotoEdit; p. 112: Mark Richards; p. 121: PhotoEdit; p. 124: Hyatt Regency Lake Tahoe Resort & Casino. Courtesy of Hyatt Hotels Corporation; p. 126: Pearson Education/PH College; p. 130: PhotoEdit; p. 131: Corbis/Bettmann; p. 137: Index Stock Imagery, Inc.; p. 143: PhotoEdit; p. 164: The Burj Al Arab or The Arabian Tower of the Jumeirah Beach Resort, Dubai, Dubai, United Arab Emirates, Middle East. Courtesy of Getty Images, Inc.—Lonely Planet Images; p. 167: The Image Works; p. 178: Photolibrary.com; p. 183: Getty Images, Inc.—Taxi; p. 191: Photo Researchers, Inc.; p. 201: Prentice Hall School Division. p. 221: The Best Western Laguna Brisas Spa Hotel, Laguna Beach, California. Courtesy of Best Western International, Inc.; Phoenix, Arizona; p. 223: PhotoEdit; p. 228: Getty Images, Inc.—Image Bank; p. 244: Corbis/Bettmann; p. 248: Stockbyte; p. 253: Getty Images, Inc.—PhotoDisc; p. 262: Ramada Plaza Hotel, San Diego, California. Courtesy of Cendant Corporation; p. 264: MGM Mirage; p. 274: Joshua D. Hayes; p. 275: PhotoEdit; p. 288: Getty Images, Inc.—PhotoDisc; p. 295: Getty Images, Inc.—Taxi; p. 305: The Stock Connection; p. 311: The Greenbrier Resort. Courtesy of The Greenbrier; p. 315: Getty Images, Inc.—PhotoDisc; p. 319: Stock Boston; p. 325: Joshua D. Hayes; p. 336: Comstock Royalty Free Division; p. 342: Radisson Resort Hill Country, San Antonio, TX, "Chazz." Courtesy of Carlson Hospitality Worldwide; p. 350: Getty Images, Inc.—Taxi; p. 359: Getty Images, Inc.—Image Bank; p. 365: Pearson Education Corporate Digital Archive; p. 379: Robert Harding World Imagery; p. 382: Clarion Hotel and Conference Center, Lansing, Michigan; p. 385: Getty Images, Inc.—PhotoDisc; p. 389: PhotoEdit; p. 391: Robert Harding World Imagery; p. 402: The Stock Connection; p. 413: Hyatt Regency Grand Cypress Resort. Courtesy of Hyatt Hotels Corporation; p. 418: Michal Heron Photography; p. 423: The Stock Connection; p. 431: The Image Works; p. 446: Holiday Inn Select, Chantilly, Virginia. Courtesy of Six Continents Hotels, Inc.; p. 449: PhotoEdit; p. 456: Meristar Hotels & Resorts Inc.; p. 468: Index Stock Imagery, Inc.; p. 470: Stockbyte; p. 481: Clarion Suites Southern Cross Towers Hotel of Sydney, Australia; p. 483: AP Wide World Photos; p. 492: Getty Images—Digital Vision; p. 495: Getty Images, Inc.—PhotoDisc; p. 503: Getty Images Inc.—Image Bank; p. 510: Burswood Hotel & Casino, Perth, Australia. Courtesy of Photolibrary.com; p. 516: Dorling Kindersley Media Library; p. 519: PhotoEdit; p. 524: David Bartruff Inc.; p. 530: Corbis/Stock Market.

Index